THE USE AND ABUSE
OF
SOCIAL SCIENCE

THE USE AND ABUSE
OF
SOCIAL SCIENCE

*Behavioral Research
and
Policy Making*

Edited by
Irving Louis Horowitz

Second Edition

ta

Transaction Books
New Brunswick, New Jersey

*tran*saction *books*
Rutgers University, New Brunswick, N.J. 08904

Contents

Preface to the Second Edition

The observation I made in the first edition of *The Use and Abuse of Social Science* that the term "policy" would be to the 1970s what the word "development" was to the 1960s, as an organizational paradigm, has held up remarkably well. We have seen a proliferation of policy research centers, periodicals and a deeper and ever-increasing connection between the policy apparatus as buyer and the social scientist as vendor. In strictly quantitative terms, the relationship between social science and public policy in the United States can only be described as a booming success. However, profitable results are not necessarily a consequence of large investments. Even novices in the area of policy making will attest to the fact that proliferation of periodicals and personnel does not add up to the kind of output in qualitative terms one might have hoped for given the huge volume of input. Of course, optimal conditions for conducting policy-oriented research never really exist. Thus, what one must deal with is a situation of considerable expansiveness at the fiscal and personnel levels and a sense of pessimism, even skepticism, at the qualitative level of the work performed.

Almost as an afterthought, social scientists have come to appreciate that there is many a slip between the cup of knowledge and the lip of policy making. Getting from the cup to the lip is where things get spilled. For the most part, social scientists are involved in the production of information involving a postresearch utilization (or nonutilization) that they hardly can appreciate, much less cope with. Social scientists are often involved in bookkeeping functions of evaluating the cost of projects in qualitative terms, much as the general accounting office evaluates in monetary terms. If they can get beyond that stage, the engagement with policymaking is still elusive, for there is the matter of reporting findings to committees, subcommittees, agencies and a hundred other ways in which results can be pidgeonholed, pocket vetoed or simply ignored. Only the fortunate few in social science are really involved in the conduct and actual context of policy making. If this collection of studies tends to emphasize this special segment of the social science community it is only because that is where the action is, not necessarily because all are engaged in this high-level input.

This second edition of *The Use and Abuse of Social Science* appears after my work on *Social Science and Public Policy in the United States*. In that volume, prepared first as an Organization for Economic Cooperation and Development (OECD) report to the International Intergovernmental Group on Social Science Policy, I found that as a general rule social science works best within a national context and works worst, or not at all, within an overseas context. Hence, in addition to the theory and practice of social policy, we must offer another dimension: the theory and practice of social policy within a context that provides a reasonable chance of success and against a nearly certain context of failure. The uses of social science are increasingly within a national context in which the parameters of decision making and decision taking are capable of being controlled; the abuses of social science are in the forced implementation of social information and data translated into action within situations that do not exist, which permit either a reasonable chance of success or a reasonable chance of review and readjustment.

The second edition of *The Use and Abuse of Social Science* thus carries as its subtitle *Behavioral Research and Policy Making*, instead of the first edition's *Behavioral Science and National Policy Making*, because whether successful or otherwise, whether useful or abusive, so much policy making by the social science community is wrapped up in a foreign policy context that one can scarcely ignore this level of operation. Having the splendid springboard of a special section of *Studies in Comparative International Development* for critical as well as constructive studies in the policy making end of foreign policy, I availed myself of the opportunity to draw upon these materials for the second edition. In this way, the second edition is enriched not only in the number of new studies but also in its sharp focus on the pragmatics of social science in its policy-making guise.

The work in this edition is divided into four parts: (1) the theory of social policy; (2) the practice of social policy; (3) the theory of foreign policy; and (4) the practice of foreign policy. This four-part paradigm better describes the context within which social scientists communicate their efforts to the policy-making sector. It also permits a much wider utilization of the researches that have been conducted in the past five years, both in domestic and foreign spheres.

The second edition has retained 13 of the original 17 papers. Those that were eliminated were in the main either peripheral to the main themes of the new volume as a whole or simply empirically obsolete in terms of their data bases. For the most part the first edition is intact, which itself bespeaks my own estimate of this anthology. In addition to a change in the organizational composition of the book, we have added 11 new papers, many drawn from *Studies in Comparative International Development,* some previously unpublished and others from sources like *The American Psychologist* yet nonetheless representing such significant work in the area that they could not possibly be overlooked for publication in this form. The papers have been selected for contemporary significance, for practicality in terms of insight into the policy process and in appreciation of the political context in which policy is produced by the social scientist, and even the specific politics of social science as such.

It would be conceit to question the possibility that one could assemble another volume of 24 papers (other than these) of equal merit, touching upon the same themes. However, I sincerely believe that no collection could be better or more representative of the current situation, and more sympathetic in approach that the one before you. To be sure, the considerable success of the first edition of *The Use and Abuse of Social Science* indicates that the book filled a real void in the professional literature on this subject. The ever-growing course offerings in this area also convinced me of the utility of preparing a new edition at this time.

From my own point of view, this volume, together with *The Rise and Fall of Project Camelot* and *Social Science and Public Policy in the United States,* completes a trilogy of volumes that offers a basic analytic framework for the study of social science and how it operates in a public policy context. Hopefully it is, at the same time, a compendium of collected wisdom with only a minimum amount of the collected folly of this area of investigation.

As the twentieth century wears on and it becomes clear that a political base of society determines the processes of allocation and diffusion of wealth and power, and that resources so allocated are finite and limited, to that extent has the role of policy making been acknowledged as central. Beyond that point, as politics itself becomes increasingly dependent on interest groups rather than upon mass politics, the role of the policy sector has likewise increased tenfold even in the short time spanning the two editions of this book. I am not prepared to say that this expansion has been for the better, or that the Platonic Paradise is upon us. It might turn out to be after all only a Comtean cookbook, filled with recipes that in time will become indigestable. But whatever my private judgment of the worth of the rise of the policy process, the fact that social science has become a crucial input into this process at decision-making levels of government and beyond cannot be denied. Hence the opportunities for the use of social science have magnified beyond the dreams of our more far-seeing intellectual ancestors. But one must sadly say that the possibility for the abuse of social science has also increased by similar percentages. Thus, this volume is submitted as an ongoing illustration of the human effort to cope with existential problems, with the social science effort to cope with social problems. That such an effort may yield new foibles as well as new facts does not alter the need to make the effort or to set the record straight.

Rutgers University
New Brunswick, N.J.
May 8, 1975

Preface to the First Edition

The history of social science, like most other history, tends to be carved up into decades, with each decade tidily labelled according to its dominant principle. In the 1950s we had functionalism; and developmentalism in the 1960s. For the 1970s the dominant organizing principle seems to be policy making. In the last year alone, eleven books on policy making by distinguished social scientists have crossed my desk, and there are doubtless others.[1] Even basic economic documents are being phrased in policy terms rather than strictly fiscal terms. It was once the case that economic issues were posed in terms of past performance; now they are presented in terms of "setting national priorities."[2]

There are many indications that the next few years will see a growing institutionalization of social science research and expertise as part of the policy-making process. The recent application of the program planning budget system (PPBS) to all federal government activities, the interest stimulated by work in the area of social indicators and future planning, and the ramifications of these interests throughout the executive and legislative branches of the federal government—all point to a growing use of social science in formulating and executing public policy. It can be surmised that the demand for policy-related activity on the part of social scientists will increase sharply over the next decade—regardless of differences in political party "styles." In a sense, then, we are at a turning point: The question in an age of social science affluence is not the *scientific status* of the social sciences, but the *social and political uses* of these "soft" sciences.

Four areas subsume most of the specific issues that might be raised about the social science/public policy relationship. These areas are over and above the particular substantive issues of exactly what social science has to say about particular public policy issues, and whether particular public policies are or are not desirable or effective. (These substantive issues, I believe, are most appropriately dealt with in conferences devoted to particular public policy problems, such as poverty, race relations, economic policy and so forth.) The key issues that crosscut all of these substantive problems seem to be the following ones.

First, there is the issue of the autonomy of social science versus its utility, relevance, and the commitment of social scientists to do policy-relevant work. Many social scientists are concerned, both in their own work and in their evaluation of what is done by others in the field, with the problem of preserving the autonomy of social science while at the same time performing socially constructive and useful work in connection with the public policy issues that confront the nation. One discovers in the recent literature a healthy amount of polemic, but little in the way of considered, systematic analysis of this issue. (There is also, of course, a wide range in the degree to which these issues have been historically relevant to the different social sciences; economists have lived with it longer than sociologists, for example.)

Second, there is the question of the availability of social science to all parties in the formulation of public policy. The appetite of the federal government for social science consultation and research increased rapidly during the 1960s, and many social scientists are concerned about the possible weakening of pluralistic policy debate and formulation due to the competitive disadvantage of private and local governmental groups vis-a-vis federal government-al agencies because of their relative lack of access to social science knowledge, research and expertise. Recently, individual social scientists and some foundations have taken a few steps to redress the balance between the "knowledge resources" of government and those of private organizations involved in policy formulation.

Third, there is the question of the relationship between the design of social systems and the analysis of such systems. Increasingly, the social sciences have come to perform a role in the technological change of forms traditional to modern ways of living. This design of the future has raised a host of new issues: What is the relationship between social design and personal autonomy and choice? How does designing reflect utopian as well as ideological elements in the present state of social science information? What is the relationship between long-range planning based on generic design and short-range planning based on continuance of the status quo?

These questions have thus far not been raised in any concerted way and deserve a wide consideration in any examination of the present state of the relationship between social science and public policy.

Finally, there is the question of the readiness of the social sciences to meet the growing demand for policy-relevant knowledge and research. The traditional training of social scientists within the separate disciplines seems to set up many barriers to policy-relevant work (of course there is a range here; economics and political science have been more concerned to provide such training than have sociology, anthropology and psychology). It seems clear that policy problems do not come in neat, discipline-defined packages, but rather require the simultaneous consideration of issues that traditionally have been regarded as the province of several social science disciplines. Therefore, it seems likely that training social scientists to do policy-relevant work requires a much higher level of disciplinary pluralism than has been traditional. At the same time, however, the historical experience in training interdisciplinary applied specialists (in urban planning, housing, social welfare, international relations and so forth) is generally considered not to have been very successful.

Ever since the collapse of the "policy-science" approach in the early fifties—a collapse made inevitable by the conflicting drives of professionalism within the social sciences on one hand and conceptual fuzziness within government on the other—there has been a constant undercurrent of concern and confusion over the secular status of the social sciences; that is, the worldly use of the social sciences. This problem finally becomes dominant with the flowering of formal social science disciplines. The great shock of such things as the so-called Moynihan Report on black family life in America and Project Camelot—among others—is due at least as much to the recognition that social science is indeed capable of rendering accurate predictions and judgments, as it is to any newfound moral revulsion for functionalism in the social sciences.

The fact is, too, that we have come to a much broader and deeper realization that social science does much more (or less, as the case may be) than study strictly human interaction. In part, decisions are made and actions taken on the scantiest warranties. Stated another way, social science may in part—a large part—serve as a legitimizing mechanism for enacting or originating policy at least as often as it serves empirically to explain the world.[3]

Thus the study of policy-making has become central as we come to realize the teleological, and not just the empirical aspects of our work. There is little point in bemoaning this condition, or in stating that causality is more scientific than teleology—God knows whether this is even so; and in any event God is not around to guide the advocates of policy-making roles for social scientists, or for that matter to bail them out lest they make fools of themselves.

Since policy making is concerned with many things—some pleasant, like setting up foreign and domestic policy; and some unpleasant, like the amount of coercion and deceit that may be necessary to implement such policy—the first need is for a social science of policy making: what is studied, how, and toward what ends.

The conference from which this volume emerged dealt with the natural history of social science products: how does a piece of research get commented upon; how does a piece of research get implemented; how does it get discarded; who makes use of any research? Then there are the institutional and informational factors involved: the biases of the investigators, the stipulated and real needs of the purchasers of information; the selective use of researchers in order to screen out undesirable elements, or overrepresent others.

There are two strategies for such a conference—design it in modest terms, reach the intended goals and have the whole business ignored; or design an immodest conference, have only a part of the aims realized and get taken seriously. Obviously the latter technique is infinitely to be preferred.

More than that we wanted to convert the moral propositions into empirical propositions: that is, change the current currency of younger social scientists in particular from problems about the value of social science into problems about social science values. How in fact have social science findings and personnel been used in the Vietnam War or in the War on Poverty? It may turn out that we have a pseudo-problem, that is, there may not be any real utilization of social science to begin with; only rationalization.

However, once the legitimizing services of policy-oriented social science research were fully exploited, the same problems which existed at the end of World War II reappeared a quarter of a century later—cutting a deeper swath in the American fabric and in a social milieu seemingly less subject to human control and planning. The problem of converting a wartime economy to a peacetime economy is amazingly still on the agenda. The problem of mass housing for the poor and slum clearance has become accentuated over the years by engineering concepts of crash housing for mass needs. The problem of overall planning itself seems more distant of solution than in the past. Thus the enormous increase in appropriations for such research agencies as the National Institute of Mental Health and the National Aeronautics Space Agency had the effect of creating a powerful inner group of social scientists, limited in number and restricted in intellectual horizons, but it failed to crack the hard crust of longstanding social ills that led to the veritable blank check federal appropriations to begin with. Under such circumstances, the necessity for some sort of non-cliche ridden "agonizing appraisal" became apparent. And this conference can be viewed as precisely one large-scale series of reevaluations, the consequence of which is a clearer idea of the scope and limits of social science intervention into the policy processes.

At first there was a concern for bringing in recent representative styles of policy making in foreign and domestic contexts, in public as well as private settings. While this original ambition is in part realized in the composition of the conference, it is far less important than the substantive issues we took up—for they have little to do with conventional barriers, boundaries or disciplinary affiliations.

This conference was designed without the usual panoply of panelists, moderators, discussants and so forth—the assumption being that it was to be a working conference in which each major participant not only delivered a paper, but also served to inform and enlighten the works of others. The conference was a success—in the sense that it helped to move both the social scientific and policy-making communities one step closer toward the truth of this relationship and toward the good for which such enormous expenditures of energy and funds have been made.

While these essays must each be considered individually, they do, interestingly enough, seem to fall into various and sundry categories. When the questions are raised from a microscopic viewpoint, a kind of "how to do it" level, what emerges are intensely autobiographical summaries. The role of personality and idiosyncracy looms extremely large in decision making—and this holds for organizing a task force for a federal presidential commission to setting up a national television system. When the questions of policy are raised from a macroscopic viewpoint, then autobiographical concerns tend to evaporate. Instead, functional and systemic considerations seem to predominate. And whether the concerns are these same commissions, or the effort to explain all of the paradigms and vectors that enter into policy-making activities, the world created is of order and reason. It might well be that the sort of decision-making theory and game theory ostensibly used to settle policy disputes come upon the irrationalities exposed by psychoanalytic and personality models. Just how rational and therapeutic models intersect, and with what effect, remains a task better raised than answered in these exploratory papers. But at least they have the merit of being acutely raised. And this will perhaps provide a more adequate social science for handling policy questions than the "game of chicken" approach that only elevates irrationality to the level of a system.

These essays also forcefully draw to our attention the different ways in which policy-related matters can be treated. Modestly, policy serves as a handmaiden for politics. Realistically, policy provides an independent input that can be estimated along with other considerations—such as evaluations in terms of constituencies and constitutionalities. Immodestly, policy lives independent of politics. The policy sector is a world of unlisted and unredeemed experts; while politics is a world of inexperts linked to electoral processes. It is the failure to resolve these sorts of conceptual problems that made the birth of the policy sciences abortive 20 years ago when it was first announced. Where does one go to find the policy scientist? No single branch of the behavioral sciences has been willing to house the policy sciences, yet none have been quite willing to discard the possibilities in this approach. Here too, the essays reveal an acute sensitivity as to the current status of policy making *as* a science, no less than the relationship between policy making and social science.

The conference provided an opportunity for renewed attention to the problem of disciplinary excellence versus disciplinary pluralism. (The inevitability of disciplinary pluralism in the application of social science perspectives to policy is apparent in the staffing of many government agencies. It has been common for high-level government executives who are concerned with program planning budget systems, social indicators and the like, to be economists, yet the variables by which they assess policy goals are very often "sociological" ones. Similarly, in private policy-oriented organizations the responsible executives are often trained in law, yet the variables they must assess in coming to policy positions may be economic or sociological or psychological.)

Finally, a question that gets raised with a unique urgency in these essays is the relationship between the actual conduct of policy and the indirect as well as direct social science inputs. For example, Lord Keynes' economics provide the underpinning for all economic decisions made by both Democratic and Republican administrations—yet the work of John Maynard Keynes was certainly not devised with the future of American society in mind. And while there is little comparable to the impact of Keynes on economics, there have in fact been many social science researchers that are hostile to, much less uninvolved with, the efforts of federal policy making. The Millsian notion of "military-industrial complex" and the Galbraithian notion of "techno-structure" both are firmly fixed in the parlance, if not the behavior of federal political officials, yet they were not done in connection with direct policy goals. Other levels of analysis, such as studies of national development, have served as basic policy briefings for State Department and Defense Department officials; yet these too, were unsponsored and unconnected to government. Finally, there are the works that are produced in connection with policy inputs per se. But this volume raises the interesting possibility that we are spending a much larger amount for direct policy research bearing a lower payoff than is warranted. That in fact, indirect support and greater cultivation of the policy-making sector may actually be a wiser course of action than the expenditure of greater amounts of money. In short, policy making may prove to be less dependent upon policy makers than upon the general intellectual productions of a given epoch.

It is important simply to note that these essays should be judged for their individual merits. It should surprise no one that in my opinion any conglomeration of 20 brilliant minds will produce a major intellectual event. And it can be demonstrated that the problems of the seventies for the social sciences will be different, but not any less demanding than those issues that came before.

Although I have purposely exchewed any mention of the moral dimension of policy making, an avoidance made necessary by how little we know about the ways in which things work, and how much we presume to know about the ways in which things ought to work, when push turns to shove, the ethical issue of detachment or involvement—an issue that can be and has been framed in many ways and in many social science languages—remains central to our concerns. And although it may be an example of my ex cathedra ministerial commitment, I nonetheless must believe that what brought these writers all together was not so much the struggle between detachment and involvement, as the agonies of involvement as such. In this connection, it is well to listen to the words of that fine good mind of the world of Canadian letters and politics, James Eayrs. "It is the intellect of commitment which in spite of all my cautionary tales I must finally commend to you. Not just because it is in short supply. But rather because it alone enables the intellectual to do his job. A detached mind may keep watch upon itself, but it watches over wasteland. Only a mind ethically anaesthetized, morally lobotomized, remains detached from what statesmen are doing to our world."[4] If anything, the problems that link social science to public policy have grown more severe during the past few years.

The essays contained in *The Use and Abuse of Social Science* are drawn from papers originally presented at a conference on the theme of social science and national policy, held in November 1969 at Rutgers University. Basically, I wanted to gather a group of people who not only write about how social science and public policy relate to each other; but more important, how social scientists working in public policy agencies perceive that relationship. In my introduction, this aspect of the conference is detailed. Suffice to say that, while every participant did not live up to the charge of the conference, most did; and even those that did not contributed new perspectives of the problem of policy-making. This they did by a mutually shared confidence in the moral nature of the process of policy-making.

The volume therefore is the rational synthesis of what transpired at the conference. And if as many problems are raised by the volume as are resolved by it, that too, is an accurate reflection of the conference proceedings. This is not said either as apologia or in resignation. Rather, the novelty of the conference, and the excitement involved, was in the general discovery that volition and choice are so much of the social world, and that therefore so much is determined by people. This shift from a deterministic to a stochastic model in appraising human events itself makes for a certain open ended quality to many of these studies.

My indebtedness is on two functional levels, separated in time by nearly a year: my appreciation for the people who funded and supported the conference and my equal sense of obligation to the people who helped me assemble this volume as a permanent record. What connects the conference to the volume is, of course, each contributor. And it is to them that I offer my sincerest thanks. I know how difficult I can be to work with at times, and their perseverance in producing these papers is at least as much a tribute to the partipant-authors, as to this participant-editor.

Heading the list of folks to whom I am obligated is S. Michael Miller of New York University. At the time, Mike was working with the Ford Foundation, and with his guidance and support, I managed to prepare a proposal that was found meaningful and meritorious enough to earn support from the National Affairs division of the Ford Foundation, in its special programs on the research and training of people working in public policy. In this connection, I must also express my appreciation to Lee Rainwater of Harvard University, who while unable to participate in the conference itself, did a tremendous amount to make sure that the initial proposal was intellectually sound and operationally feasible. David J. Pittman, head of the Social Science Institute at

Washington University also gave of his time and energy to make sure that my proposal for a policy conference would not falter prematurely. Thus to Mike, Lee and Dave go my deepest thanks.

The actual details of the conference were beautifully handled by a number of people, including J. Dudley Hill, director of the Center for Continuing Education at Rutgers—which undoubtedly has some of the finest conference facilities I have ever seen. Margaret May, who was in charge of details, handled them with the mastery of an aristocratic grande dame (which she is not) and with the ebullience of a teen-ager (which she is). The staff at *trans*action, particularly Mary S. Strong, Nelson W. Aldrich, Joshua Feigenbaum, and Mary E. Curtis, saw to it that every detail from transporting the participants to recording their commentaries was taken care of. With such excellent groundwork, the preparation of the book became a matter of routine. Mary Curtis did the sort of editing that made my own work move along without trial or tribulation; and in this effort, she was greatly helped by the sensitive support of Nelson Aldrich.

In short, the organizational cooperation of the Ford Foundation, Rutgers University, and Transaction Inc. worked in concert to make this conference possible; while the human cooperation of people at each of these institutions made this conference and this volume a notable experience. But when all is written in appreciation and acknowledgement, the book remains—and it is the final product, not the pleasure and pain that went into its manufacture—that remains decisive. As a book it is for its readers to determine its worth.

NOTES

[1] Raymond A. Bauer, and Kenneth J. Gergen (editors) *The Study of Policy Formation*. New York: The Free Press—Macmillan Co., 1968; Ralph L. Beals, *Politics of Social Research: An Inquiry into the Ethics and Responsibilities of Social Scientists*. Chicago: Aldine Publishing Co., 1969; Gunnar Boalt, *The Sociology of Research*. Carbondale and Edwardsville: Southern Illinois University Press, 1969; Lars Dencik, (editor) *Scientific Research and Politics*. Lund, Sweden: Student Literature, 1969; Yehezkel Dror, *Public Policy-making Reexamined*. San Francisco: Chandler Publishing Co., 1968; Howard E. Freeman, (General Editor) *Social Research and Social Policy*. Englewood Cliffs, N.J.: Prentice-Hall, Inc., 1969; Charles E. Lindblom, *The Policy-Making Process* Englewood Cliffs, N.J.: Prentice-Hall, Inc., 1968; Gene M. Lyons, *The Uneasy Partnership: Social Science and the Federal Government in the Twentieth Century*. New York: Russell-Sage Foundation, 1969; S.M. Miller, and Frank Reissman *Social Class and Social Policy?* New York and

London: Basic Books, Inc., 1968; Michael D. Reagan, *Social Science and the Federal Patron*. New York: Oxford University Press, 1969; Richard Rose, (editor) *Policy-Making in Britain*. New York: The Free Press, 1969.

[2] Charles Schultze, (with Edward K. Hamilton and Allen Schick) *Setting National Priorities: The 1971 Budget*. Washington, D.C.: The Brookings Institution, 1970.

[3] Irving Louis Horowitz, (editor) *The Rise and Fall of Project Camelot: Studies in the Relationship Between Social Sciences and Practical Politics*. Cambridge, Mass.: M.I.T. Press, 1967.

[4] James Eayrs, *Right and Wrong in Foreign Policy*. Toronto, Canada: University of Toronto Press, 1966.

Acknowledgments

Nathan Caplan and Stephen D. Nelson, "On Being Useful: The Nature and Consequences of Psychological Research on Social Problems," *American Psychologist* 28 (March 1973): 199-211.

Yale H. Ferguson, "United States Policy and Political Development in Latin America," *Studies in Comparative International Development* 7 (Summer 1973): 156-80.

Oliver D. Finnigan III and Dionisio Parulan, "Policy Guidelines for Collective Bargaining and Family Planning," *Studies in Comparative International Development* 8 (Fall 1973): 324-33

Bertram M. Gross, "The Administration of Economic Development Planning: Principles and Fallacies," *Studies in Comparative International Development* (no. 5, 1967-68): 89-108.

Irving Louis Horowitz, "Conflict and Consensus Between Social Scientists and Policy-Makers," *Journal of Applied Behavioral Science*, vol. 5, no. 3, pp. 309-35.

James Everett Katz, "Science, Social Science and Presidentialism," previously unpublished.

Arthur D. Martinez, "The Politics of Territorial Waters," *Studies in Comparative International Development* 8 (Summer 1973): 213-23.

Amos Perlmutter, "The Political Center and Foreign Policy," *Studies in Comparative International Development* 9 (Fall 1974): 90-102.

Raymond B. Pratt, "The Underdeveloped Political Science of Development," *Studies in Comparative International Development* 8 (Spring 1973): 88-108.

Ray C. Rist, "Race, Policy and Schooling," *Society* 12 (November/December 1974): 59-63.

J. David Singer, "Individual Values, National Interests and Political Development in the International System," *Studies in Comparative International Development* (no. 9, 1970-71): 197-210.

Editor's Note; selections other than those listed above appeared in the first edition of *The Use and Abuse of Social Science*.

Contributors

KENNETH E. BOULDING, University of Colorado (Economics)

NATHAN CAPLAN, University of Michigan (Psychology)

BENJAMIN CHINITZ, Brown University (Economics)

YEHEZKEL DROR, Hebrew University of Jerusalem (Political Science)

YALE H. FERGUSON, Rutgers University (Political Science)

OLIVER D. FINNIGAN III (United States Agency for International Development)

HERBERT J. GANS, Columbia University (Sociology)

BERTRAM M. GROSS, Syracuse University (School of Citizenship and Public Affairs)

IRVING LOUIS HOROWITZ, Rutgers University (Sociology and Political Science)

JOHN HOWARD, State University of New York at Purchase (Sociology)

JAMES EVERETT KATZ, Rutgers University (Education)

KURT LANG, State University of New York at Stony Brook (Sociology)

ROY E. LICKLIDER, Rutgers University (Political Science)

GENE M. LYONS, Dartmouth College (Government)

ARTHUR D. MARTINEZ, University of California at Riverside (Political Science)

STEPHEN D. NELSON, University of Michigan (Psychology)

DIONISIO PARULAN (United States Agency for International Development)

AMOS PERLMUTTER, The American University (Political Science)

NELSON W. POLSBY, University of California at Berkeley (Political Science)

RAYMOND B. PRATT, Montana State University (Political Science)

RAY C. RIST, Department of Health, Education and Welfare (Sociology

ALVIN L. SCHORR, Community Service Society (Sociology)

J. DAVID SINGER, University of Michigan (Political Science)

JEROME H. SKOLNICK, University of California at Berkeley (Criminology)

PIO D. ULIASSI (United States Department of State)

ADAM YARMOLINSKY, University of Massachusetts (Law)

Part I
THE THEORY OF SOCIAL POLICY

1

Social Science
for Social Policy

HERBERT J. GANS

In recent years, planners, systems analysts, policy specialists and others at work on the formulation or design of public policy have begun to develop a niche for themselves in government, particularly in Washington and in the larger American cities. At the same time, social scientists have become interested again in policy research, partly to train the policy designers but also to conduct studies that support, broaden and criticize government policies. Much of this research has itself originated or taken place in government agencies, but it is now also emerging in the universities, so much so that institutes of policy studies may soon complement or even replace institutes of urban studies on the campus.

Intellectually speaking, policy research is still in its infancy, deriving its theory and concepts largely from the existing academic social sciences. However, since policy researchers are concerned with changing society rather than understanding it, they must have—and create—a policy-oriented social science, independent of but related to and not estranged from the academic disciplines.

I want here to describe some of the characteristics of a policy-oriented social science. My analysis begins by considering the nature of social policy and policy design, and then suggests some conceptual and theoretical requirements of a policy-oriented social science through a discussion of the shortcomings of academic social science for policy research. A final section lists these requirements in summary form. The analysis of both types of social science will draw largely on my own discipline of sociology.

THE NATURE OF SOCIAL POLICY AND POLICY DESIGN

By social policy, I mean any proposal for deliberate activity to affect the workings of society or any of its parts. Properly speaking, the prefix social is superfluous, because all policies that affect more than one person are social. However, the prefix is often used to distinguish some types of policy from others, for example, economic or environmental policy. I shall use the term social policy in its broadest meaning, to include economic, environmental and other policies, because they too are intrinsically social. Some semantic confusion might be alleviated by the term societal policy, except that it connotes deliberate activities to affect the society in toto, and I could use the term public policy, since most policy is designed for and by public agencies, except that I do not wish to exclude consideration of "private policy," designed by and for non-public agencies.

As I understand it, social policy differs from planning or social planning only in scale; a plan is nothing more than a set of interrelated social policies.[1] Similarly, social policy differs from politics largely in degree; politicians also engage in deliberate activities to affect society. They tend, however, to choose activities which can be implemented through the political institutions, whereas the designers of social policy are less limited in their choice of activities or institutions. (Of course, policy design cannot take place without attention to political considerations, and policy implementation must normally take place with the help of politicians.)

The distinctive quality of social policy is its aim for what might be called programmatic rationality; it seeks to achieve substantive goals through instrumental action programs that can be proven, logically or empirically, to achieve these goals. Political activity, on the other hand, must by its very nature emphasize the politically rational, which places greater priority on political goals such as keeping the party in office than on substantive ones, and is as likely to stress expressive programs as instrumental ones.[2] For example, politicians may well resort to symbolic appeals for "law and order" when faced with a public demand for crime reduction, even if these appeals do not achieve the substantive goal. The designer of social policy, however, will be concerned first and foremost with programs that actually lead to a reduction in crime. (Even so, he will also and inevitably pursue his own political goals, and work to expand his own agency's budget.)

A Model for Social Policy Design

Inherent in these observations is a model of social policy design, which not only describes the components of the social policy process but also spells out the kinds of social science data needed by the policy designer. As I conceive it, social policy design has three major components: goals, programs and consequences, and the policy-designer works toward the achievement of a (social) goal by the development of programs that can reasonably be predicted to achieve that goal, accompanied by an optimal set of consequences.[3] By programs, I mean simply the specific activities required for goal-achievement; by consequences, the by-products, effects or externalities of a given program. Consequences may also be understood as the benefits and costs of a program for the various sectors of society affected by it, and an optimal set of consequences is that array of maximal benefits and minimal costs which will be most effective in achieving the goal. (Obviously, there can be no single optimum here, for not only do different programs have different benefits and costs, but alternative programs which may achieve a given goal differ widely as to which sectors of society obtain benefits and which must endure costs. Indeed, the major value question the policy designer must answer is, as Harold Lasswell put it over a generation ago, who gets what.)

The determination of consequences is a vital part of social policy design, for all programs have costs and benefits, and these must be determined or at least estimated before the final draft of the policy design so that the program can be revised to eliminate costs which would prevent it from being carried out, or which would be less desirable than the goal being sought. For example, a program which is so costly that funds for it cannot be obtained obviously needs revision; similarly, a delinquency prevention program that helps to make delinquents into heroin users should be revised, for the individual and social costs of delinquency are undoubtedly less than the costs of drug addiction.

The policy designer is typically most active in three stages of the policy design process: goal-operationalizing, determining goal-program relationships and dealing with program-consequences relationships. Although he may play a role in deciding what goal is to be achieved in the first place, in most instances his employer or sponsor, whether a public agency or a ghetto protest group, will make the final decision about the goal for which policy is to be designed.[4] The designer's role, then, is to operationalize that goal, reformulating it so that he can design programs which will achieve it, estimate their consequences, and undertake the program revision to make sure that the array of consequences is optimal.[5] In this process, he must pay particular attention to assuring that the program and its consequences are beneficial to the intended clients.[6]

The Role of the Policy Researcher

So far, I have limited the discussion to policy design, as carried out by policy designers (and, of course, implementers). The policy researcher's role in this process is to provide conceptual and theoretical inputs, the necessary empirical data, the empirical "guesstimates" when data are unavailable, and a critical analysis of the policy design when it is completed.[7]

In the model I have presented, the policy researcher participates in the same three stages of the process as the designer. At the goal-operationalizing stage, the researcher may have to do some intensive interviewing in the sponsoring agency, for sponsors are often vague about the goals they seek, and when the sponsor is an agency, there is likely to be disagreement about goals as well. Without knowing how different parts of an agency feel, the policy designer may find that he has designed a program that will not engender the participation or allegiance of the total agency, for example, the lower bureaucracy of a public agency, or the less active members of a ghetto protest group. And if the goal requires participation or allegiance from clients outside the sponsoring agency, information will be required on how they feel about the goal. For example, if a sponsor seeks to improve the quality of housing among poor people, he ought to know what kind of housing these clients want and will accept: whether they will live in public housing or would prefer rent subsidies to help them compete in the private housing market. If more than one goal is being sought by the various participants in the policy design, as is often the case, the researcher can also help the designer in determining which goals are most important, if all cannot be incorporated into a single policy design.

The policy researcher must also make the designer aware of latent goals, particularly institutional maintenance or growth, for sponsoring agencies rarely pursue a policy which does not at least maintain its present level of resources or power.

The major need for policy research is, however, in the other two stages of the policy design process. First, the policy-designer needs information about which programs will achieve his goal, and wherever possible, empirical evidence to this effect. Ideally, the policy researcher should be able to provide what I have elsewhere called a policy-catalog, that is, a list of programs relevant to all possible conceivable goals from crime reduction to economic equality that have been proven, by empirical research, to achieve these goals.[8] Since both goals and programs are nearly infinite, putting together such a catalog would require an immense amount of action research, social experimentation and evaluation studies. The policy catalog would allow a policy researcher to supply a policy designer with generalized programmatic statements, based on as many cases and studies as possible, which the designer can then apply to the specific situation or community in which he is working. In this application, he may require some bridging research to move from the generalized statement to a specific program.

When the goal in question is the elimination of a social problem the policy researcher must provide findings on the major causes, those explaining most of the variance, and on the immediate causes, for the most rational programs are those that eliminate the major causes, while the most easily implemented programs are usually those that get at immediate causes.

Moreover, policy research ought to provide the policy designer with a model, as empirically based as possible, of all the components and stages of the social-political process by which a social problem is eliminated or a goal achieved. This model should include all of the *activities* involved in the process, the *agents* (institutional and other) whose normal social role is to bring these activities into being or who can be recruited to do so, and the *levers* (incentives and sanctions) needed to activate these agents. Needless to say, activities, agents and levers must all be spelled out in highly specific terms, the ideal being a step-by-step model of the process by which a present state is transformed into an end-state.

Finally,the policy researcher must provide information, or at least estimates, of the consequences of a given program, from first order to nth order effects, preferably in terms of benefits and costs of all participants, direct and indirect, in both the program and its implementation. (By indirect participants, I mean especially the bystanders of a process, who may not be directly involved but who always play a role in the political climate that can spell success or failure to a program.) Ideally, the previously described policy catalog should also provide information on the various consequences of each program, and here the research task is even more massive, for effects research is difficult to do, at best, and many of the important consequences of any program cannot be isolated empirically. Thus policy designers may have to be satisfied with informed guesses on the part of policy researchers.

The major types of research needed are about financial and political consequences. The policy designer must have data to help him determine the money costs of a program, but he must also have some estimate of indirect costs paid by various participants, as well as financial benefits that might accrue to others. Data are also needed to estimate political consequences for direct and indirect participants, that is, for whom will a given program result in increases or decreases of political power. Political must be defined broadly, however, for data are also needed on the status consequences of a policy, for any program which results in a loss of status to some indirect participants in the process will inevitably result in political opposition to the policy.

In addition, the policy researcher needs to trace all other possible consequences of a program. Ideally, he should know how the beneficiaries and all other participants will be affected by it, that is, to what extent their own behavior and important attitudes may change as a result, if only to assure the political survival of his policy. He must also have such data to make sure that programs do not cause unintended harm to intended clients or other participants in the social process being generated. For example, the policy researcher must know that a birth control program will not wreak havoc with other aspects of the conjugal relationship among the intended beneficiaries; that the cooling of interethnic or interracial conflicts among teenage gangs in a mixed neighborhood does not just transfer such conflicts to the adults; or that a racial integration program on the job or in the community does not result in a white exodus. Such data are needed, as noted before, to revise programs so that optimal consequences result, or to encourage the design of additional programs to deal with unintended but harmful consequences.

Needless to say, most of the policy research I have suggested here will never be done, and in most policy design situations, a policy researcher can draw only on his understanding of society, the social process, and the effects of deliberate intervention in the process to offer help to the designer. But even this modest role cannot be carried out properly until we begin to develop policy-oriented social science.

THE UNSUITABILITIES OF ACADEMIC SOCIAL SCIENCE

One way of thinking about the characteristics and requirements of policy-oriented social science is to look at the unsuitabilities of academic social science for policy research. That such unsuitabilities exist is obvious; academic social science seeks to understand society, not to intervene in it, resulting in many organizational, theoretical and methodological features that cannot be applied to policy research.[9] This is not a criticism of academic social science, for understanding society is a prerequisite to intervening as well as a useful task per se, and besides, policy-oriented social science needs its academic peer.

It is of course impossible to generalize about as large and variegated a phenomenon as academic social science, but it is possible to identify some prevailing theoretical and conceptual features that make it unsuitable for policy purposes. These are: its detachment, "impersonal universalism," high levels of generality and abstractness, and last but not least, its metaphysical perspectives. Moreover, as noted earlier, I will limit my analysis to one social science, sociology.

Detachment

Academic sociology, like most academic social science, views itself as detached from society. For example, academic sociologists rarely make studies to affect the workings of society; instead, they are more likely to study the people who do so. By detachment, I do not refer here to the illusory attempt at objective or value-free research, but rather to a general perspective: that of the outside observer who is examining a society in which he is not involved, at least as researcher.

The detached perspective is not helpful in policy-oriented research, for it generates theories and concepts more suitable for the bystander to the social process than the participant. Although participants must sometimes take the bystander role to be able to evaluate their participation, the policy researcher must provide dynamic theories of the social process to the policy designer so that he can find footholds from which to intervene. Parsonian theory may be useful in understanding how society as such is put together, but it does not, despite its concern with "action", supply concepts that help the policy-designer initiate action. Even Mills' study of the power elite, though hardly detached in terms of values, does not enable a policy designer to come up with policies to obtain more power for his sponsor.

Impersonal Universalism

One of the correlates of detachment is "impersonal universalism," by which I mean the concern with identifying the broad impersonal causal forces that underlie events. Academic sociology developed in reaction to older personalistic theories of human behavior, for example the Great Man theory, and sought to show that individuals cannot be understood apart from society. This mode of explanation was and still is highly useful in discouraging the overly facile application of moral opprobrium to socially caused actions, and it is useful for policy design in that it tends to focus on major causes, but policy designers also need a less universal and less impersonal approach. For example, although there can be no doubt that urbanization and industrialization are responsible for many structural changes in the family, policy designers in the area of family policy cannot do anything significant about these broad forces and require analyses that deal with more manageable causes.

Policy designers also need less impersonal theories for they must, after all, design policies to be implemented among persons. The policy designer works in a sociopolitical context in which moral judgments are made, praise and blame are dealt out, and hypotheses about the motivations of actors are all important. Consequently, he must be able to understand how impersonal causes are translated into — and affect — moral judgments and motives. Similarly, while it is useful for the policy designer to know that all human beings play a multiplicity of roles and that conflicts between roles can lead to social and individual strain, he must design policies for people as combinations of roles and must know how to judge the consequences of a policy for a person who is at once a worker, homeowner, landlord, father and deacon of his church.

High Levels of Generality

The universalism of academic sociology also produces levels of generality that are often too high for the needs of policy. Although many of the social problems with which the policy designer deals may well be the results of urbanization, he must have research which tells him what specific aspects of urbanization are at play and how they affect people. Urbanization can mean many things: for example, the actual move from country to city, living at higher density than in the country, having more heterogeneous neighbors, holding an industrial rather than a rural job, participating in a more complex division of labor, or encountering the life-styles and forms of social participation that are typically found in the city. A social problem resulting from rural in-migration will have to be treated quite differently than one resulting from living at high density, and what is the policy designer to do when confronted with a group which, though it holds industrial jobs and lives in tenements in a heterogenous neighborhood, still practices the peasant life-style it brought from Europe?

Similarly, the policy designer is absolutely lost when confronted with a concept like social change, for it lumps into one term all the various activities in which he is involved. Like the Eskimo who requires more than 20 different words for snow, the policy designer must have very specific concepts of social change, which spell out for individuals, groups and institutions who or what is changing from what original position to what subsequent one, in which aspects of a person's life or group's activities, and with what consequences for the rest of his life or their activities.

Conceptual Abstractness

The high levels of generality at which much of academic social science operates also breeds conceptual abstractness which results in concepts that cannot be applied to the real-life situations in which the policy designer works. Such concepts as social structure, culture and institution are helpful in the academician's task of generalizing about human behavior, but the policy designer can only work with specific human organizations that play roles in the policy he is designing. He cannot deal with political institutions; he must deal with city hall, political parties and citizen groups. He will often be helped by information about what such groups have in common as political institutions, and what roles they play in the structure of power, but his policy must eventually involve individual organizations, and he must know exactly where the power lies in a specific situation if he is to be able to act.

Perhaps one of the most important concepts in modern sociology is class, but this concept is also of little use to the policy designer. Since classes do not exist in America as concrete entities, he cannot design policy to act on them directly; he must have data which is analyzed in terms of the specific and concrete variables that he can affect. In effect, he must break down the concept into its major components: income, occupation, education, power and prestige; for he can only design policies that affect people's earnings, jobs, schooling, political position and status. Likewise, the policy designer finds little of relevance in the descriptions of the class structure and the class cultures that sociologists develop; he can do something about poverty and poor schools but not about lower-class culture, and the sociologist's careful qualification that class cultures and life styles overlap cannot help a policy designer who must know how a specific group of people will react to a policy. He wants to know what this reaction is, not whether it is lower class or working class. He needs to know how different types of poor people will feel about the choice between a poorly paying or dirty, dead-end job and being on welfare; whether these feelings are part of a larger lower- or working-class set of norms is only of parenthetical interest. Moreover, his interest in whether people can be classified as lower or working class is limited to the consequences of the hierarchical fact that working-class people are higher in the sociopolitical pecking order than lower-class people, and may express discontent if the distinctions between the strata are altered by an antipoverty program.

Another aspect of the policy designer's conceptual needs may be illustrated by the term "slum." Aside from the fact that it is a value-laden term with some questionable empirical assumptions, it is, like class, a concept that lumps many components into one often useless whole. The policy designer's problem is that until American housing policy makes some provision for low-cost housing or rent subsidies at a scale that would allow him to propose tearing down anything that is or might be a slum, he must allocate limited resources in the most beneficial manner. Thus, he must know, not whether and how an area is a slum, but the various physical and social components of the area in question and what impact they have on their residents. This will enable him to determine which of these components are harmful and not harmful, and which are more and less harmful, so that, given limited resources, he can design a policy that will get rid of the most harmful components first.

I do not want to suggest that abstract academic concepts are irrelevant to policy; often, they are crucial but not sufficiently developed for the policy designer's purposes. A good example is the sociologist's emphasis on the distinction between manifest and latent phenomena and formal and informal groups. A great deal of highly useful research has shown the impact of latent functions and informal group patterns on the goals, structure and activities of formal organizations, and the policy designer could not work effectively without knowing about the latent and informal arrangements in group life. By and large, however, he can deal only with formal groups and their manifest activities, and he must know therefore how to develop policies which affect their informal and latent components.

The final and perhaps most important drawback of conceptual abstractness is the inaccessability of the relevant data. Until there is a plethora of policy-oriented and academic research, the policy designer will have to work with the data that are available, and these are usually limited to basic and not very subtle types, for example, census statistics. Thus, the highly developed conceptual virtuosity of the academic sociologist who has studied a lower-class community or a delinquent subculture is of little relevance to the policy designer who may know no more about a poor neighborhood than is available in census tract statistics or a health and welfare council analysis, or about delinquents than he can dredge up from police records or case worker reports. This is not the fault of academic sociology, of course, but the policy designer needs to know what he can make of the data he has.

The Metaphysics of Academic Sociology

Last but hardly least, the metaphysical assumptions of much academic sociology also make it unsuitable for policy research and design. I am not concerned here with its often conservative political bias or with the fact that all kinds of political values and implications usually enter into manifestly value-free research in the selection of topics, hypotheses and concepts. These issues have received much discussion of late, and besides, policy design is not wedded to a particular political outlook. Although most social scientists currently interested in what they call policy research tend to be left-liberals, other social scientists doing a form of policy research they call systems analysis are more frequently conservative, if not in intention at least in their work.[10] Moreover, policy design can also be reactionary, radical or anarchist. It is even possible for policy designers or researchers to be politically neutral, acting as technicians who develop programs and consequences for goals determined by others. In this case, they are neutral only in intent, for they are actually adopting the political values of those who determine the goals. As Amitai Etzioni points out, "some policy research serves those in power, some—those in opposition, but it is never neutral."[11]

Whether the goals are conservative, liberal or radical, all policy designers and researchers must accept one political value, the desirability of intervention, and in so doing, they depart from the paths of academic research. Policy design and research must be concerned with *what can be* or should be, whereas academic researchers see their task as studying *what is,* or if they are predictive, what will be. This is only another way of saying that policy research must be normative, but this in turn demands a different perspective. For one thing, the policy researcher must have a thorough understanding of what is, but only for allowing him to see how the present can be changed and at what points he can help the policy designer intervene. He must develop conceptual bridges to enable the designer to make the transition from what is to what can be, from the present to some desired future.

Academic sociology's emphasis on what is also results in what might be called a perspective of adaptation; it is mainly interested in studying how people adapt to the situations they face, and whether they are satisfied or dissatisfied with these situations, but it is not much interested in considering how people would adapt to different circumstances, or what circumstances they want. To put it another way, academic sociology has largely studied behavior, and attitudes about that behavior (how people feel about what is),[12] it has not often studied aspiration, or what people feel they should be.[13] Ironically, despite the great influence of Talcott Parsons on American sociology, most of his colleagues have ignored one of his central themes, that individuals and groups are goal-seeking, striving to achieve their aspirations. The policy researcher must of course place great emphasis on aspirations, for here is one major bridging concept between what is and can be.

Academic sociology is also especially sensitive to obstacles to change, not because researchers are conservative, but because of its emphasis on what is. Of course, the policy designer must be aware of such obstacles, but he must also have research on the readiness for change, a subject about which academic sociology has been relatively silent, except in some recent studies of black militancy. Similarly, studies of cultural factors in behavior have often defined culture as a conservative influence, partly because it has been assumed that culture is naturally persistent and hard to change. As a result, there has been little research on the "intensity" with which cultural norms are held and except in ethnic acculturation studies, on how culture changes when opportunities improve. For example, there have been many studies of the culture of poverty or lower-class culture among the poor, but none that I know of which investigated changes in culture when poor people obtained higher incomes, or what happened to behavior when people escaped from poverty.[14] These are the kinds of studies policy designers must have; they need to know what forms of situational change bring about cultural change and vice versa, and they require measures of the intensity or nonintensity and persistence or nonpersistence of all of the components of culture, social structure and personality. Instead of academic sociology's passive stance, the policy researcher must take an active one toward the subject of his study.[15]

Another unsuitable metaphysical stance of academic sociology is the systemic bias, that is, concern with the social system rather than with its parts that prevails among more traditional sociologists. For example, most functionalists study the functions and dysfunctions of social phenomena for the society as a whole, paying less attention to the functions and dysfunctions these phenomena have for individuals and groups within the society. Similarly, traditional students of deviance and social control concern themselves with the effect of deviant behavior on society, without asking who defines deviance and society or for whose benefit social control is instituted.

Likewise, when sociologists say that society defines certain activities as criminal or that it encourages deviant behavior to reinforce conformity to its norms, they reify society as a social unit that acts for its members. This reification is based on the ideas of Emile Durkheim, who developed the concept of society from his studies of small independent tribes living in a clearly bounded territory with a distinctive social structure and often without a formal government, but such an approach is not applicable to large interdependent nations.

This is clear when one looks at American society and asks not what it is but what it actually does as a society, for an identifiable unit that acts as a society does not exist. Of course, the State, that is, government, sometimes acts as a body, occasionally on the basis of considerable consensus, but more often by shoehorning a set of political minorities into a temporary majority so that a decision can be reached by majority vote. However, that decision is made by the State, not by society, and when sociologists use the term society, they really mean the State—although even it is rarely a homogeneous monolith, but rather an array of agencies which do not always act in concert. Thus it is not American society which deprives the heroin addict of easy access to his fix, and not even the State, but certain governmental agencies, who may argue and feel that they are supported by the majority of the population, but actually only speak in the name of the State and those citizens who favor taking a hard line toward the addict. This becomes evident when one looks at governmental decisions for which consensus is clearly lacking, for example, the search for victory in Vietnam or the prohibition of marijuana. In these instances, agencies of the State are pursuing actions favored by only part of the nation, and no one would suggest that these actions are approved by society.

The systemic bias encourages findings that identify the activities and interests of dominant social groups with society as a whole, and tends to underestimate the amount of dissensus and conflict. Aside from its implicit or explicit political position, however, this bias produces data that are of little help to the policy designer. Unless he is working for the federal government or for city hall and is asked to design policies that enhance control over their territories, he needs research based on a more pluralistic perspective. Most of the time, the policies he is concerned with are intended for selected clients, and the consequences of almost any program will result in benefits for some groups and costs for others. He must therefore know more about specific populations, interest groups and institutions than about society.

A final drawback of academic sociology for the policy designer is its relative inattention to theories and concepts of power. Because of the emphasis on what is and the systemic bias, sociologists in the past have not dealt sufficiently with the role that power plays—in maintaining what is, in holding the social system together, and in the life of nonpolitical institutions generally. For example, family studies have only rarely dealt with the use of power by its various members against each other—or against other families.

The policy designer who usually works in a political institution is constantly aware of the role of power in any social group, and because he is concerned with implementing as well as designing policy, he needs research on the nature and use of power, for example, by groups who would oppose a specific program. He must also know how power can be used to implement policies— and when the power of sanctions or of incentives is called for. He particularly needs data on the extent to which the use of governmental power is effective in overcoming cultural obstacles to change. Often, cultural norms, for example, in support of racial or sexual discrimination, are weaker than they seem and can be overcome by the exercise of governmental power.

Some Positive Functions of Academic Social Science

I have dwelt at length on the ways in which academic social science is unsuitable for policy design and research, but its positive role in policy must also be acknowledged, if more briefly. Indeed, policy research could not exist without academic research.

From what little is known so far of the sociology of policy design, it is clear that both policy designer and researcher frequently become so involved in the bureaucratic and political contexts in which they operate that their own perspective extends only as far as their side of the political game. Also, both are forced to pay so much attention to minor details that they lose sight of the larger picture. And when the political battles are over and their policy is implemented, both can become so enchanted with their victory that they fail to see the faults of their policy. The war on poverty is a good example, for many thoughtful researchers and policy designers became wedded to the policies they were able to get passed by Congress and soon forgot how little relevance these policies had for eliminating poverty. Moreover, because of the bureaucratic and political contexts in which they work, policy designers and researchers often find it difficult to be innovative, to scrap bad policies or to come up with ideas for new ones.

Ideally, these faults would be best dealt with if policy researchers could look at their problems with the detachment, universalism, generality and abstractness of the academic, for they would then be able to see their policies from both sides of the political fence, evaluate them coolly for their ability to achieve the intended goal, and look for innovation when it is needed. Since it is unlikely that most policy researchers can be both policy-oriented and academic in their perspective at the same time, they need to rely on academic researchers to function as outside evaluators and critics, although these academics should obviously have a general interest in policy as well as theory.

But policy research needs its academic counterpart in at least three other ways. First, one cannot design policy for intervening in society without first understanding society, and generally speaking, the better the academic research, the better the resulting policy research and design. This is particularly true at present, when policy research is an infant industry which must build on what academics have produced before, but I suspect it will always be true, for most policy research will, by definition, be specific and concrete, and must therefore look elsewhere for more general and abstract theories and generalizations.

Second, one of the major contributions of academic research, at least potentially, is its serendipity; its ability to spawn fresh ideas, unexpected findings and productive new tangents. To put it more simply, academic research will probably always be more innovative than policy research, and as such may also be a major source of innovation in policy research. This is especially true because almost all academic studies have some implications for policy, even if they are unintended, and usually unrecognized by the academic researcher. A good policy researcher should be able to spot these implications—or the leads to implications—in even the most abstract academic study.

Third, academic research is and probably always will be the methodological model for policy research, since policy researchers are typically forced to come up with quick answers and can therefore do only quick or "dirty" research. It is quite possible that they will make some significant methodological innovations for policy research, but it is also true that when it comes to rigor, reliability, validity and the like, academic researchers will provide the technical models and will themselves be the role models for their colleagues in policy research. Moreover, once the policy researcher has made the value commitments inherent in policy research, he must follow the same norms of rigor and objectivity in data collection that obtain in the academic sphere.

SOME CONCEPTUAL AND THEORETICAL REQUIREMENTS FOR A POLICY-ORIENTED SOCIAL SCIENCE

Academic research may often be unsuitable for policy purposes, but clearly, policy research cannot develop without it.[16] If policy research ever becomes a viable institutional activity, and policy-oriented social science disciplines are able to become equal in size and competence to academic disciplines, policy researchers working in government and other action agencies will satisfy many of the academic needs I have described here from academically inclined and located policy-oriented social scientists. Until this state of affairs is reached, however, they will continue to place heavy reliance on existing academic social science.

My analysis of the unsuitability of academic social science for policy has already indicated or implied most of the major requirements of a policy-oriented social science, so that it is possible to list these here in brief and summary form.

First, the purpose of policy-oriented social science is to provide the policy designer (as well as the policy implementer) with "general" and "specific" research. The former would deal with such general issues as the nature of social policy, the role of the policy designer in its various institutional contexts, the relationship between policy and the ongoing social-political process, the nature and problems of intervention in that process. General research would presumably be the distinctive task of academic policy-oriented social scientists. Specific research, done both in the academy and in action agencies, would provide detailed data on specific substantive policy fields, such as health, housing, family life and so forth, cataloguing for each issue the programs which would achieve specific goals and the resulting consequences.

Second, specific research must be based on highly specified theories and concepts which can, wherever possible, analyze the concrete groups, organizations and institutions with which the policy designer must deal. Moreover, such theories and concepts must lend themselves to maximal operationalization, so that the findings which result from them can be easily applied to the policy process.

Third, a fundamental necessity of policy-oriented social science is a model of the social-political process that is tailored to the needs of the policy designer. Such a model must have the following features:

☐It must view the social-political process as composed of goal-seeking groups and individuals, and must therefore provide concepts about the nature of goal-formation; the relationship between goals and behavior on the one hand, and goals and underlying values on the other.

☐It must analyze the socio-political process in terms of the specific activities (rather than abstract behavior patterns) by which goal-seeking groups and individuals proceed, and the incentives and restraints that impinge on on them and their activities.

☐It must attempt to explain the process in terms of specific causes, particularly major and immediate ones, for the policy designer seeks to encourage or overcome these causes in the programs he proposes.

□It must be a normative and future-oriented theory of action, which analyzes both what is and what can be, developing concepts that allow the policy designer to develop programs that bridge the present and the desired future. In each case, the theory must spell out the obstacles to change, the agencies and norms behind these obstacles, the strength or intensity of these obstacles, and the kinds of rewards or sanctions by which they could be overcome. (The theory must also specify what cannot be, identifying those elements of the sociopolitical process which cannot be changed by policy design and political action.)

□One of the central concepts in the theory of the social process must be power, for the policy designer must understand how power functions in both political and nonpolitical institutions, and what kinds of power can be exerted to implement programs.

Fourth, policy-oriented social science must of course be concerned with values; it cannot delude itself that it is value free, for it must provide the policy designer with the means to achieve values stated as goals. However, the data-gathering process must follow scrupulously the dictates of rigor and objectivity prevailing in academic social science; otherwise, it is possible that the policy researcher will supply the policy designer with findings that underestimate the difficulties and the obstacles to implementing programs.

Fifth, policy-oriented research must also be particularly concerned with the values of all those participating in or affected by a specific policy, not only to discourage the policy designer from imposing his own or his sponsor's values on the beneficiaries of the policy, but also to make sure that the designed policy bears some relevance to the aspirations of those affected by it. This is not to say that policy design must honor all existing values, for policies which provide benefits to some will also create costs to others. The policy researcher must therefore collect data not only on what values are held by people affected by a specific policy, but also how intensely these are held, and what incentives or sanctions would change them if necessary.

Finally, one of the prime values underlying policy-oriented social science and its research methods must be democracy. The policy researcher, like the policy designer, must be responsive to the values and aspirations of the people for whom they are designing policy, but their relationships with people involved in both research and policy design phases must also eschew the elitism sometimes found in academic social science which treats the researched as "subjects." People who want to participate in the research itself must be allowed to do so whenever possible, and policy research and design must be predicated on the notion of planning with, not planning for people.

NOTES

I am indebted to Gary Marx for critical comments on an earlier draft of this essay.

[1] Herbert J. Gans, "From Urbanism to Policy Planning," *Journal of the American Institute of Planners*, Vol. 36, July 1970, pp. 223-225.

[2] For a more systematic analysis of the relationship between researchers and politicians, see Irving Louis Howoritz, "The Academy and the Polity: Interaction Between Social Scientists and Federal Administrators," *Journal of Applied Behavioral Science*, Vol. 5, No. 3, 1969, pp. 309-335.

[3] The model is described in more detail in my *People and Plans*, Basic Books, 1968, Chapters 6 and 7. For a more complex version of this model, see Yehezkel Dror, "A General Systems Approach to Uses of Behavioral Sciences for Better Policy-Making," Santa Monica: RAND Corporation, May 1969, paper P-4091, and his chapter in this volume.

[4] Professionals involved in designing policy have argued about the extent to which the designer should be involved in the choice of goals: some arguing that as a professional, he has the expertise to play a major role in goal choice; others arguing that in his professional role, he should serve as a technician who limits himself to program and consequence determination, taking the goal as given; while yet others have proposed various combinations of these two polar alternatives. Although this vital question is not central to the concerns of this essay, I would argue that the policy designer is justified in advocating his own goals during the political process within the sponsoring agency, and that he is equally justified in stepping out if the process is not democratic, or if working for the democratically determined goals violates the dictates of his conscience, but that he should not set himself up as an expert who has the right to impose his own goals on others.

[5] Some planners have also argued that the planner's role is to propose several alternative programs, allowing the sponsor to make the final choice. This question is also tangential here, although it may be noted that planners have been able to espouse this notion largely because they have usually paid little attention to programmatic rationality and even less to the determination of consequences. In the real world, it is likely that for most goals, there are precious few rational programs which also result in a set of optimal consequences.

[6] J. Reiner, E. Reimer and T. Reiner, "Client Analysis and the Planning of Public Programs," in Bernard Frieden and Robert Morris, eds., *Urban Planning and Social Policy*, Basic Books, 1968, pp. 377-395.

[7] I am here considering a role as a person the policy researcher could also take a part in policy design, and as Martin Rein has often suggested,

the researcher who is not part of a policy designing bureaucracy ought to use his independence to act as a policy critic.

[8] Herbert J. Gans, "From Urbanism to Policy-Planning," *op. cit.*

[9] Henry W. Riecken, "Social Sciences and Social Problems," *Social Science Information,* Vol. 8, February 1969, pp. 101-129.

[10] On the politics of the systems analysts, see Robert Boguslaw, *The New Utopians,* Prentice Hall, 1965, Chapter 8. The re-inventors of policy research of a generation ago were also conservatives, at least by today's standards. Thus, Harold Lasswell and his colleagues developed the concept of the policy sciences in the late 1940s in part as a weapon in the Cold War. Lasswell's introduction to a book on this subject begins by noting that "the continuing crisis of national security in which we live calls for the most efficient use of the manpower, facilities and resources of the American people," and in the second paragraph refers to "the problem of overcoming the divisive tendencies of modern life and of bringing into existence a more thorough integration of the goals and methods of public and private action." See Harold Lasswell, "The Policy Orientation," in D. Lerner and H. Lasswell, *et. al.,* eds., *The Policy Sciences,* Stanford University Press, 1951, p. 3.

[11] Amitai Etzioni, "Policy Research," *American Sociologist,* forthcoming.

[12] Sociologists have of course devoted much attention to values, but largely to values implicit in behavior, that is behavioral values rather than aspirational values.

[13] The behavioral perspective of academic sociology seems to be on the wane, at least in studies of the poor. Because of the large and obvious gap between their behavior and their aspirations, most sociologists of poverty, have, since Hyman Rodman's seminal paper on the "lower class value stretch," studied these aspirations.

[14] For a more detailed analysis of these points, see my "Culture, Class and the Study of Poverty," in *People and Plans, op. cit.* Chapter 22.

[15] Amitai Etzioni, *The Active Society,* Free Press, 1968.

[16] Conversely, if and when policy research becomes established, it will undoubtedly provide a fertile source for new theories and findings in basic research, for one can often understand human behavior best when it is encouraged or forced to change.

2

Public Policy
and Private Interest

ALVIN L. SCHORR

It was said of Samuel Johnson that he was a pessimistic man, but cheerfulness kept breaking through. This distinction should be set forth explicitly. I am a reformer by temperament, and by training disposed to believe that scientific method can show the way. This combination produces a powerful optimism that may flicker but does not die. Still, I have spent ten years observing the development of national welfare policy at close hand and must acknowledge that social science had rather little to do with it. So the optimism in this essay will be temperamental and the pessimism a reflection upon my experience—which is limited, after all. When optimism and pessimism are mixed in the open air, the result is anger; a little of that may be discerned too.

THEORY OF RANDOMNESS

My point of departure in this essay is a theory of randomness concerning the movement of social policy. This means that the nation does not move from trial and error to new trials, from experience to correcting errors, or from systematic evidence to programs based on that evidence. It means also that, although needs produce solutions, the correspondence is very far from point to point, and some needs are never noticed. I use randomness here in this narrow but, I dare say,.rational sense. Of course, social policy does not develop randomly from a political point of view, but responds to the desires of the electorate as these are expressed through the political process. In effect, this is to say that, so far as welfare policy is concerned, the electorate has not been attentive to systematic evidence or even to experience. Although governments are permitted considerable flexibility within the broad issues to which electorates pay attention, they have not used this latitude to be more systematic than the electorate.

Several illustrations of the point come to mind. In welfare policy, we have for at least 15 years been behaving as if dependency were a curable handicap. Therefore, we enact programs of social services for fatherless children and their mothers, and vocational rehabilitation for unemployed men and women. Congressmen vote for these programs, in part, because they believe that they promise a reduction in the cost of public assistance. None of these programs has produced such a result and so, from time to time, officials discover that few people receiving public assistance are curable of the need for it. One such Eureka speech was delivered by then Secretary Abraham Ribicoff and another by then White House Special Assistant Joseph Califano. Each was greeted with public surprise. Yet the in some ways excellent new welfare proposals of President Richard Nixon have been wrapped in the same promise. In three or four years, no doubt, some high government official will make a speech like those of Ribicoff and Califano, which will again be greeted with surprise.

Another illustration of the point is the community action program. Probably, its central function was to act as a collaboration of social services that would bring down barriers to opportunity. If that was the intent when it was enacted, it went against the evidence that was beginning to accumulate. The so-called juvenile delinquency projects of the early 1960s were intended specifically as tests of the effectiveness of such programs in opening opportunity. The evidence was only beginning to come in when the poverty program began, and it was cloudy, but one would have had to read the findings at that point as negative.[1]

The history of the search for comprehensive urban planning offers a final illustration. For 20 years, we have moved from urban

renewal, through comprehensive redevelopment, workable programs, community renewal plans and into model cities, not
troubling to alter the slogans with each new name. We have acted
each time as if the earlier conception was partial and, by directing
attention to the need for comprehensiveness, we were entering a
new era. Comprehension has been in shorter supply than comprehensiveness. It is dangerous to oversimplify—some changes were
introduced with the new programs—but comprehensiveness was
not new. And nothing was done about the central reason that
comprehensiveness never took hold, namely, that the planners
lacked responsibility for or control over events.[2]

(Presumably, it is not necessary to say that I support the
provision of social services, and think community action and
comprehensive planning good things. I simply object to justifying
them on grounds we know or ought to know are unsound, or to
distorting *other* programs by stuffing these good ideas down their
bellies.)

Obviously, we do from time to time develop good new
programs and reshape old programs in ways that evidence would
suggest is sound. Community action was fine because it moved
poor people toward participation—a good in itself—and because in
some small way it redistributes social services. The Elementary and
Secondary Education Act of 1965 has produced marginal improvements in the education of rural children and, perhaps, slowed the
deterioration of central city schools; and it has fed quite a lot of
children who would have gone hungry. Nixon's welfare proposals
will, if enacted in the shape he offered them, raise levels of
assistance in four or five states and considerably broaden eligibility
in most states.

If one reflects on these or other progressive moves, however, it
is evident how little they have to do with their ostensible objective
or with social science. The three programs listed probably owe
their genesis more to the desperate financial plight of cities and
states than to any other single factor. The poverty program and
the Education Act came in a time and manner dictated by more
powerful developments than the need for them: the guilt of a
decade of dividing affluence among the affluent (a guilt which has
now, apparently, dissipated); the death of John Kennedy and the
inauguration of Lyndon Johnson, with all the passion and
ambition that were aroused; and the turning in frustration of the

still powerful civil rights movement to goals it *could* achieve. A strong force behind the poverty program and the president's welfare proposals in middle-and working-class hatred of bureaucracy (entirely akin to the anger that leads our young people to protest). But since the real objective is war against bureaucracy, it is not necessary to test or discard ideas that are dear to us—that eating is a sign of merit, for example. And when these programs fail to wipe out poverty or hunger—because we set the programs firmly on the road to failure—it adds fuel to our anger at the bureaucrats who balked us once more, as it seems.

The point being illustrated may be clear: We get forward movement in social policy out of the resonance of developments that are quite unrelated to social science and may be unrelated to reason. Because such forward movement must satisfy its sources before anything else, the actual design of programs shows little fundamental influence of social science. Along with that, as has already been said, on some matters we get no movement at all.

If social policy moves randomly, one constructive question is why. Ideas about this will be discussed under two headings—first, public values and definitions and then, limitations in the practice of social science.

GREED

It must be self-evident that public values determine the direction of social policy. It would be difficult to argue that it should be otherwise. It is hardly novel to observe that the Protestant ethic is at the root of the problem in welfare policy. If failure and dependency are signs of God's displeasure, truly those who suffer from it need treatment more than money—and evidence to the contrary is frivolous. Quite possibly, we deal with a similar value problem in educational policy. We are generally conscious of and troubled by the fact that we do not know very much about how to improve the quality of education. But we seem to be untroubled by the fact that generally rising levels of education do not greatly affect poverty in the United States. A grade school education was once a pretty good thing. A high school education sufficed not so long ago. Very soon, a college degree will be required to assure a moderate level of income. With education as with income, apparently, the absolute level achieved matters less than one's position relative to the average.

The point has been made by an international comparison: The average duration of education in Great Britain is no more than the educational level our poor people achieve. The fact that our poor people would be quite adequately educated in Britain—a country widely regarded as industrial—does them no good here. In short, it is the distributional pattern in education that affects one's ability to compete for a job. Yet, with our stubborn faith in self-improvement, we provide Head Start and special funds for high schools in the ghettoes and ignore the fact that we are improving the education of the rest of the population at least as quickly. (We are running to stand still and, to be sure, few would argue that we should do less.)

One is tempted to shrug fatalistically, leaving the work ethic and Calvinist theology in undisputed possession of the field. However, when values are asserted again and again despite experience that should qualify them or where they are irrelevant, one must look for their roots. One comes to see the underlying values at play as more primitive and not so sweetly overlaid with religion. The values being asserted are greed for money and status and the right of the powerful to the spoils. Most people in the country appear to be unwilling to give up having more than someone else or feeling better than someone else, whatever peace or sense of community might be produced. (In everyday speech, this is expressed as: "Who helped us when we came!" and "I worked hard all my life and now they're giving it away!") Those are the values we are dealing with. They have made us great and powerful—I say that without irony—but we are paying a terrible price for them.

CIRCULAR DEFINITIONS

Closely (even circularly) related to public values is the public definition of issues. One understands in general that the way a problem is defined may determine the conclusions about it. For example, the fiscal problem of federal, state and local governments is in large part a result of the growing welfare burden, according to widespread public definition. Yet the figures demonstrate that in recent years welfare costs (including social security) have grown less rapidly than health costs or education costs, considered either as federal expenditures or as state and local expenditures. Indeed, federal expenditures on health have tripled and education quadrupled while welfare was growing by only half. State and local expenditures have also increased faster in health and education than in welfare.[3] An instinctive reaction, upon absorbing these figures, is to observe that the increases in health and education costs are not relevant; they are increases on a smaller base and, more important, the public is willing to bear them. Welfare increases are scandalous mainly because they are quite unwanted. That is the point, of course. Welfare costs are defined as the fiscal problem *because* welfare is disliked. So the definition of welfare as the cause of the fiscal problem is circular. Yet it fuels public resentment of the program.

Similarly, it is intriguing to observe which facts and research findings gain currency and which do not. For example, the steady, sharp increase in public assistance rates in New York City began leveling off in the fall of 1969. It was a gratifying development; the Mayor and other prominent officials took pains to speak about it in public. But the newspapers did not pick it up until it had been said quite a number of times in their presence. Again, most sociologists are aware how little research supports the view that interfaith marriage is inordinately risky. But article after article on the subject has appeared that failed to make this point, although at least some of the authors understood it. The boldest statement that is permitted—and when it came, the writer regarded it as a breakthrough—is that interfaith marriages can be successful, *if the partners are especially mature.* These examples are not cited to look for a devil in the newspapers, or to say once again that Madison Avenue can shape our minds. Rather, the newspapers are in the public grip quite as much as the other way around. If the public has seized upon rising welfare rates or the breakdown of religious barriers to account for its troubles, it is not news to cite findings to the contrary. The newspaper that insists will be thought dull and preachy.

PRAGMATISM

Apart from public definition, public values also find support or at least protection from challenge in the pragmatic nature of government. Pragmatism is not used here to mean that the government relies on no assumptions or generalizations at all. At the other extreme, one does not expect government to seek a complete set of generalizations accounting for all the behavior in some field. But even short of this, government is not hospitable to the development of plausible new generalizations, derived from social science, on which policy may or would be based. This probably is not true of economic theory, which seems to be well, if only recently, established.

It may help to illustrate the point. I have written elsewhere of the almost clinical depression, as it seemed to me, with which high government officials responded to the Detroit riots of 1967.[4] Detroit deflated the assumption on which the government was then operating, namely, that if competent men worked desperately to create visible programs for the disadvantaged, people would respond with satisfaction or at least patience. When that innocent formulation was swept away, the administration was left with nothing to put in its place. Officials might well have found themselves depressed. It would appear that the succeeding administration did not try to develop a theory, but rather shifted attention to other problems or client groups.

A few programs may seem to rest on theories—the juvenile delinquency program, the poverty program, Model Cities. On closer examination, it appears that some of the people involved in the formulation of these programs had theories, but one person's theory differed from another's. The programs that were put together compromised these differing views, and accommodated the views of others who had no theories at all but would describe themselves as pragmatists. When the programs were launched, administrators selected for application the theories or non-theory that they found congenial. That accounts, in some measure, for the difficulty in securing agreement about the theory of the poverty program. When an administration turns over, of course, there is a certain loss of interest in demonstrating the validity of a theory of the prior administration. And so the Model Cities program, which may have held a theory, was quickly converted from experimentation into a simple conduit of federal funds to cities.

In any event, the juvenile delinquency, poverty, and Model Cities program were exceptional in even dealing with theory. The bulk of federal programming in these fields—welfare, education, youth and alienation, mental health—involves very little theory at all. Why should that be so? Theories or, at any rate, theorists are resistant to compromise in an arena where compromise is an everyday necessity. Theories are natural targets for hostile Congressmen or special interest groups. For example, Secretary Robert F. Finch began his introduction of the Family Assistance Act of 1969 to the House Ways and Means Committee with the following language: "We sought, in designing the Family Assistance Plan, to identify and deal directly with the most pressing problems facing public welfare today. While it is a far-reaching and fundamental reform of public welfare, the Family Assistance Plan is a practical and pragmatic program . . . This problem solving approach, rather than a theoretical approach. . ." and so on.[5] It is a particularly interesting statement because the Family Assistance Plan was, in fact, based on a theory about the significance of work in public assistance and how it may best be maintained. But the Secretary solicited the support of Congress by opposing his pragmatism and theirs to theory.

Theories themselves can also be tools of one interest group or another, limiting the inclination of officials to deal with them academically. For example, any reasonable theory about the social impact of the distribution of income in the United States might make it difficult to justify the 1969 tax cut. At the same time, the dubious theory that inflation hurts poor people more than anyone else helped to justify a policy that created unemployment. To continue with reasons that the government may be hostile to theory, as has already been implied, the fact that the time perspective of each administration is three years or less is inimical to the testing of theories which, in these complicated days, requires a little time. A final reason for abjuring theory may be a governmental tendency to rely on incremental developments. Increments have the advantage of accommodating old interests even while attempting to develop new patterns. Yet, some theories simply cannot be tested by increments. That is the heart of the argument about the Coleman report, for example, that children who do not demonstrably respond to *somewhat* better classroom situations would respond to *much* better classroom situations. Or, as another example, it can be argued that we will not get desegregation with any program less powerful in the 1970s than FHA was in 1950s. No demonstration effort or small program can tell us what would happen in such a case, that is, if we arranged matters so that private enterprise profits on a large scale from desegregation.

To sum up so far: Social science has rather little relation to policy development because policies are determined by values that are often unrecognized. These values, in turn, determine the very definition of the issues, and so we get fed back to us the solution to the issues that our values demand. Then our resolutely pragmatic approach to government makes it hard from one decade to the next to know what theories, and therefore what programs, are serving us well or poorly. To be sure, pragmatism is said to keep the body politic at peace (is someone asking, "What peace?") and to help to contain a temperamentally violent people in a highly stable government. One must place considerable value on stable government. The point is merely that, despite considerable testimony to the contrary, in certain areas we have a relatively inflexible set of values. This set of values is embedded in a system that protects it from searching examination. That does not contribute to rational or social scientific policy development, which is to say that policy develops at random.

We now turn to the way social scientists operate in and in relation to government. Included in what follows are clinicians such as social workers and psychiatrists who, while working on policy development, seek guidance in systematic research. I will consider intellectual difficulties first and then self-interest.

INTELLECTUAL PROBLEMS

A worrisome intellectual problem is that social scientists take a narrow view of problems that require a broader view. That is, they approach problems by way of a single discipline. It is barely necessary to repeat what has been said so often, but it is perhaps useful to illustrate how this limitation affects policy development. For example, "culture of poverty" explanations of the behavior of poor people draw vitality from two sources that are peripheral to the evidence. One source of vitality that should bring no surprise is that this set of ideas defines the problem in a way that supports current values. The other source of vitality is that social scientists are expert in description of attitudes and status situations.[6] They are largely inexpert on such matters as nutrition and in understanding what makes social patterns change over time. So "culture of poverty" reflects the expertise of the researchers more than it explains the situation or prospects of poor people. Yet this notion is the major support for social service and educational strategies in dealing with poverty.

Economists, more than others, often offer a warning that they are about to take too narrow a view of a problem. Having come to a conclusion about some economic aspect of a question, they mutter *ceteris paribus* before making their policy recommendation. "All things being equal" ought to be treated as a proclamation of ignorance, but is more often a ritual defense against considerations that one understands not to be very important at all. An illustration of the hazards when an economist moves narrowly from his discipline occurred in the deliberations of a United Nations group concerned with social defense. They were interested in the cost-effectiveness of various approaches to crime and delinquency—that is, dollar for dollar, is prevention more effective than jails, and so forth? At one point, they found themselves discussing the most cost-effective approach to preventing juvenile delinquency in Vietnam. The war, as it did not lend itself to cost analysis in quite the same terms, was never mentioned, nor was its relationship to juvenile delinquency.[7]

Another intellectual problem in the applicability of social sciences is the value that is placed on elaboration. Our universities may be directly responsible for this. Students are taught to abandon unlearned common sense and, with it, simplicity. Somehow the necessary search for rigor in thinking is converted into overvaluing the complex and technical. Therefore, simple matters may be overlooked. For example, the significance to social behavior of nutrition and shelter were all but ignored in post-World War II research. When one seeks a policy recommendation from people so disposed, the result is either a retreat to the need for more research or a hopelessly involved recommendation. This is not to plead for reductionism but only to name the parallel error of elaborationism. People who have been trained in this manner teach or do highly technical work; they tend not to address themselves to policy development anyway. However, the pattern of thinking influences those who do set out to deal with policy matters.

A third intellectual problem lies in the relevance to policy of the research that is done. On one hand, many of the issues that trouble sociologists and psychologists have very little consequence in the social policy world. The fact is too well known to require elaboration. On the other hand, a good deal of research is dominated by the government's needs and definitions. It is not necessary to argue that actual slanting of findings occurs very often. But the choice of research subject and the terms in which it is pursued quite often determines the outcome. As an example, it is not an accident that the negative income tax is the only substantial departure in income maintenance that has been experimented with. Staff at the Office of Economic Opportunity, The Department of Health, Education and Welfare and the President's Commission on Income Maintenance Programs decided before President Nixon assumed office that that was the program the country should have. And so an administration that came into office encouraging experimentation in various forms of income maintenance was, in less than a year, instructed by the president himself to support only income maintenance projects that had been approved in the White House. That may not be unusual behavior in a government. But how does one account for the fact that, with interest in the subject high, not a single university developed a study that broke through the government's definition or predilection?

Another intellectual issue troubles those social scientists who get directly involved with high government officials on a policy issue. They are likely to be offered friendly advice on how to shape their recommendations for maximum political effect. They may be told that a recommendation is sound, but needs to be clothed in different rhetoric. Or they may be told how large a step or what sort of strategy is likely to be effective at the moment. It is a difficult problem. One does not want to be intransigent or ingenuous nor, however, to abandon solid professional or technical ground. I offer you only my own observation. Social scientists err much more often in accommodating themselves to political advice than in intransigence.

From social scientists who are barely concerned with social policy—the elaborationists—the discussion has moved to those who are so concerned that they have to decide how purely to deal with their discipline. It is necessary to make a final point about the intellectual problem of those social scientists who try to affect social policy most broadly. Social scientists and professional organizations carrying such a role find that evidence that leads directly to policy recommendations is comparatively rare. Rather, these spokesmen are usually bringing to bear the basic values of their discipline—humanism, rationality, a therapeutic rather than a penal approach. Either that, or more explicitly, they are arguing the merits of the disciplines they know—the economist urging econometrics, the sociologist urging the importance of institutions, the social worker promoting group work and casework. The public is not really faced with social science but with contending values and interests. Decisions are not made on evidence but on who happens to have acceptance, power or the most persuasive line. The intellectual problem for these social scientists is that research and analysis is not being conducted in a manner that is useful to them. They argue from their values or intuitions, or desist.

SELF-INTEREST

We have been cataloguing intellectual difficulties in bringing social science to bear upon social policy, and perhaps it is already obvious how closely involved with these difficulties is the self-interest of social scientists. If social scientists are trained in elaborationism, it is because their professors are most secure with that. It is the surest route to academic success for faculty and students as well. The National Academy of Sciences and Social Science Research Council put the point as follows: "Many academic scientists value the prestige that their contributions to basic research and theory give them in the eyes of their peers more than whatever rewards might be obtained from clients who would find their work useful. It . . . leads not only to scientific knowledge, but also to respect and status tendered by those whose judgments they value most."[8] If universities waste no time on research that the government will not fund anyway, more students will be taught and provided stipends and more status and resources accrue to the department. If social workers promote social services and social scientists promote research, higher salaries and richer perquisites will be available all around. An example of the exception that proves the rule was the testimony of the National Committee for the Day Care of Children concerning the 1967 amendments to the Social Security Act. The association testified against those amendments because they would be damaging to children and their families, even though day care programs in particular were to be greatly expanded. There are not so many examples of that sort; not all the testimony on the 1967 amendments was so disinterested.

More insidious than the narrow self-interest of each discipline and more difficult to explain without being misunderstood, is the coalition of self-interests that gather around social research. Daniel Bell has made the argument that the intellectual class is now maneuvering for political power,[9] a development that facilitates and is in turn supported by building up financially secure bases of operation for intellectuals. Noam Chomsky makes a finer charge, that experts or "scholar-technicians" are maneuvering to take power from "free-floating intellectuals" who tend to be more attentive to values than techniques.[10] The two observations are not incompatible, and one may think them both right. The scholar arguing the merits of research asserts a class interest quite as much as the miner arguing the merits of coal. Certainly, excessive claims have been made for research. The point is beginning to be acknowledged retrospectively,[11] but nothing prevents social scientists from asking that funds for research be written into each new piece of legislation. There are matters we know how to study and others we do not. There are studies for which personnel is available and others for which it is not. Some research ought to be initiated by government and other research not. How is it that social scientists all together support—by silence, if not affirmatively—requests for funds for social research of any sort?

I do not, more than anyone else, want to seem impolite. One can bring to mind very fine work by social scientists, and some examples of courage and self-sacrifice. Yet it is necessary to examine the possibility that they do not represent the generality. It appears that the nation is now structured on professions and occupations as the medieval world was structured on guilds. There is no yielding of self-interest on any side, not among social scientists and not among the professions. If they believe their own

dire prophecies—those social scientists who make dire prophecies—should they not on occasion find recommendations to make
to Congress and the country that are counter to their self-interest?

CONCLUSION

The simplest conclusion is a summary that will itself seem
simple: Public policy is dominated by public values—naturally.
These values are comparatively inflexible, and are protected from
critical examination by social forces and the tendencies of
government. That is convenient, as it permits greed to operate
unimpeded and even unnamed. Social science is a mirror image of
the larger situation, despite the fact that its traditions demand that
it be quite different. Social science, too, has impediments to
substantial critical examination of major policy issues, and
tends—so the record shows—to pursue its own self-interest.
Therefore, in relationship to reason or social science, one would
expect social policy to move at random—as indeed it appears to
do.

That is how it seems to me; do I see any hope? The intellectual
tradition of social scientists provides grounds for hope. Ideologies
tend to carry on even when they are not practiced, and young
social scientists continue to be taught integrity and scientific rigor.
When they mix those ideas with the ones they are developing for
themselves—rejection of materialism and self-interest and a demand for relevance, we may see a different social science with
different effects.

As for the older social scientists, perhaps we may rely on their
sense of irony. We have already noted the cost-effectiveness
approach to juvenile delinquency in Vietnam. I have in mind also a
federal program that provides food for pregnant and nursing
mothers if their doctors will prescribe it. Jonathan Swift could
have thought of nothing finer. We might run all of public
assistance on the basis of physicians' prescriptions. One day such
black humor will be too much for social scientists, and they will
take on social policy in earnest.

NOTES
[1] Peter Marris and Martin Rein, *Dilemmas of Reform: Poverty and
Community Action in the United States,* New York, Atherton Press, 1967.

[2] For an elaboration of this argument, see "Planned Development: Vision or Fancy?" in Alvin L. Schorr, *Explorations in Social Policy*, Basic Books.

[3] U.S. Department of Health, Education, and Welfare, "Health, Education and Welfare; Accomplishments, 1963-1968, Problems and Challenges, And a Look to the Future," December 1968.

[4] *Explorations in Social Policy*, op. cit., p. 260.

[5] Statement of Honorable Robert H. Finch to the Committee on Ways and Means, U.S. House of Representatives, October 15, 1969.

[6] For example, for an exploration of the failure of sociologists to foresee the sit-in movement, see Kurt W. Back, "Sociology Encounters the Southern Protest Movement for Desegregation," presented at the International Sociological Association (Washington, D.C., September 1962); and Everett C. Hughes, "Race Relations and the Sociological Imagination," presented at the American Sociological Association (Los Angeles, August 28, 1963).

[7] United Nations, Consultative Group on the Prevention of Crime and the Treatment of Offenders, "The Economics of Training in Social Defense," Wroking Paper Prepared by the Secretariat, 8 July 1968, and Draft Report Prepared by P. J. Woodfield, 13 August 1968, Geneva.

[8] National Academy of Sciences and Social Science Research Council, *The Behavioral and Social Sciences, Outlook and Needs*, Washington, D.C. 1969, p. 193.

[9] Daniel Bell, "Notes on the Post-Industrial Society (K)," *The Public Interest*, No. 6, Winter 1967.

[10] Noam Chomsky, *American Power and the New Mandarins*, Random House, 1967.

[11] See for example Walter Williams and John W. Evans, "The Politics of Evaluation: The Case of Head Start," *The Annals of the American Academy of Political and Social Science*, v. 385, September 1969; and Thomas E. Glennan, Jr., "Evaluating Federal Manpower Programs: Notes and Observations," The RAND Corporation, September 1969.

3

The Policy Researcher:
His Habitat, Care and Feeding

ADAM YARMOLINSKY

Scholars have long been concerned with the subject matter that concerns the policy researcher. In fact there is an established discipline that deals in large part with this subject matter, a quite respectable discipline, with a muse all its own, many generations of graduate students, and more than its quota of university presidents drawn from its ranks. The only difference between the historian and the policy researcher is that the historian concerns himself with past policy choices, while the policy researcher concerns himself with policy choices not yet made. But the difference is a profound one, for at least two reasons.

First, the great bulk of the policy decisions that historians analyze was not influenced by policy research, because there was substantially no research input to those decisions. Policy research had not been invented, and government staffs were occupied until very recently almost entirely with implementing decisions, not with examining alternatives or evaluating results. Outside advisers were primarily personal counselors or glorified speechwriters, not systematic analysts.

And conversely, the historian has very little sense that he is, or may be affecting policy outcomes. As the policy researcher would say, the historian's computer is not operating in real time. Historians are beginning to apply the methods of policy analysis to past events. The Strategic Bombing Survey, at the end of World War II, from which so much later work on alternative military strategies developed, was in effect an historical study, using methods that should have been employed in making the basic decisions about strategic bombing, and that might have saved an enormous number of lives on both sides and spared great cities from destruction. Historical research and policy research may some day become aspects of the same general study, but that day is probably a long way off.

Meanwhile, it may be worth examining the situation of the historian today, in order to note the differences between his situation and that of the policy researcher. To define these differences may be to define the principal problems—and the principal opportunities—that face the policy researcher.

The historian belongs to a discipline that provides him with a generally accepted definition of his field and of its subspecialties. These definitions are revised from time to time, by relatively orderly processes. His primary audience is his students, and the first and last judgment on his work is the judgment of his peers, with whom he is in easy communication, within his own university department, and through journals and conferences. The tools of his trade are to be found in major libraries, although he may have difficulty getting access to particular sets of records. He may be able to use some help in gathering materials—and he can usually find it in the dependable, low cost graduate student labor market—but basically he works by himself. As an historian, he is, to a degree, a generalist, and he does not ordinarily seek a specialist's competence in other disciplines, even when they are relevant to his professional interests. True, there are overlapping specialties—history of science, economic history, legal history—but they have made their treaties with their sister disciplines, assimilating themselves, to a greater or lesser degree, to the concerns of scholars dealing with the substantive subject matter of science or economics or law.

The policy researcher, however, has essentially none of these landmarks or navigational aids to rely on. Whatever discipline he had been brought up in, it is no longer the focus of his activities and interests. Indeed, for some of the most effective policy researchers, their original disciplines served only to sharpen their minds and acquaint them with research methods generally, and they have since chosen a whole new set of navigational reference marks.

We can define policy research by an exclusionary process, as research designed to assist in the formulation or reformulation of policy, which is stretched beyond the traditional boundaries of a single discipline or a set of related disciplines by the needs of the policy maker. We can test the definition by examining limiting cases. It excludes both research which is not differentiated in character from other academic research by its policy objectives, and academic research on the nature of the policy process itself (although that research has yet to find a happy home in an established discipline). Clearly neither government-supported basic research nor government-supported applied research in particular disciplines is designed to advance the state of the art of policy research. Most of the research that goes into designing a new weapons system, or a new urban mass transit system or even a new welfare system is not policy research, but where the separate pieces of disciplinary research must be selected to meet policy needs, where new research must be undertaken that may cut across disciplinary lines, and where the product is assembled and shaped to the needs of the policy maker, the policy researcher must chart the course. By the same token, testing a new airplane design, or a new curriculum design is not of itself policy research. But choosing the criteria against which the system is to be tested necessarily involves policy research.

To elucidate further what I mean by policy research, it may be worthwhile to break it down under five headings (for which I am largely indebted to Yehezkel Dror, although I have shifted his categories somewhat): trend measurement, policy choice, program development, troubleshooting and evaluation.

When policy makers want to follow the trends in the phenomenon of poverty in the United States (or in stream pollution, or in the strategic military balance), they require a continuing research effort that necessarily transcends disciplinary limits.

Trend measurement research is nevertheless closer to traditional academic research than the research that is called for in deciding what mixture of incomes strategy and services strategy to use on the poverty problem (or in designing a pollution control policy at the national, state or local level, or in shifting from massive retaliation to flexible response in strategic nuclear policy). Because a new policy is not explicitly so designated does not obviate the need for research support in developing it. Early in the Kennedy administration it was decided, after sharp debate, not to revise and reissue the bulky volume "Basic National Security Policy" promulgated by the Eisenhower Administration, but to instruct the bureaucracy to rely instead on speeches and other public statements of politically responsible officials as sources of policy guidance. This decision did not stem the flow of policy papers and government-supported research designed to elucidate general issues of national security policy.

Even more mission-oriented and less academic research is called for in developing specific programs for the various elements of an antipoverty program, welfare services, job training and placement, education, housing, health care, and so forth (or for corresponding programs in pollution control or strategic doctrine and weapons development).

When it comes to day-to-day trouble-shooting in the operations of existing programs, policy research tends to shade off into staff work, although it may be farmed out to policy researchers where the problem seems to call for more time, or concentration of resources, or imagination than the staff is able to supply.

Evaluation is a special kind of policy research, demanding a combination of hard disciplinary skills and clear focus on the policy goals of the program or project to be evaluated. It is in this area that the failures of policy research are perhaps most evident.

None of these categories is discrete from the others, and individual pieces of policy research may be difficult to classify, while individual policy researchers may be engaged in research in several of these categories simultaneously. Indeed one man may be and often is engaged in disciplinary and policy research at the same time. But here the researcher's background in his own discipline cannot by itself provide a framework for his policy research.

In the absence of a disciplinary framework, the policy researcher needs another set of limitations and directions to shape his inquiry. He finds these in the policy process itself, and, having chosen his subject matter, he must anticipate the locus of policy choices, and correct for errors as he goes along. This is not to say that the policy researcher becomes merely an instrument of the policy maker's will. As a scholar, he is free to pursue his own interests. As, one hopes, an original thinker, he does not simply take policy problems in the terms they are put to him by policy makers and policy advisers, and then attempt to work out solutions. If politics is the art of the possible, the true artist may be the man who can find new possibilities. There is a necessary tension in every field between its possibilities and its limitations. As F. Scott Fitzgerald said: "There is always some damn condition."

But here the broad lines of the policy researcher's useful inquiry are determined by the views of men who do not live in this world, while he does not live in theirs. His views must be communicated to these men, and are ultimately judged by their impact on policy, which is to say what the policy makers do with and about them. Since this impact is to a large extent accidental, depending on how much other advice clogs the channels of communication, and how events move in response to random influences, the policy researcher gets less feedback for his efforts than his other scholarly colleagues do, both in quantity and certainly in quality. Too many of his returns, necessarily, come from people who don't know what is good research, but do emphatically know what they like. And too often his research results never get beyond the desk of the branch chief or the section chief, so that the policy maker who could use them doesn't even know they exist. This situation contrasts sharply with the openness of channels of communication in the scholarly world.

Brilliant and profound policy research may be done by a man alone in a room with a blackboard or a scratch pad. But it is more likely to require the collection and analysis of data from a number of fields, employing techniques derived from several different disciplines. Policy problems do not turn up neatly packaged as "economics," "sociology" or even "international relations." The importance of the computer in policy research has been considerably overstated. In preparing an article on the role of the computer in Pentagon decision-making,[1] I had no difficulty finding policy decisions based on a systems analysis where a computer had been unnecessary, but some difficulty finding an important case where the computer had been essential.

Yet the importance of facts and of numbers is still not fully appreciated. These are facts and numbers that must generally be derived from a wide range of sources, and subjected to critical examination in the light of several kinds of specialized knowledge, bearing in mind that most of the information that comes to the policy researcher has been gathered in an arena where objectivity is more often the exception than the rule. The researcher then generally needs to be extraordinarily tough in order to avoid becoming a prisoner of the staff, particularly where it is made up of individuals who are primarily operators rather than researchers.

Policy research in connection with a decision whether or not to proceed with the development of a new weapons system requires the collection of facts, and opinions, about United States foreign policy, the military capabilities, and, so far as it is possible to ascertain them, the intentions of potential antagonists, the effectiveness of existing weapons systems, the state of the art in a number of areas of technology, the probable shape of learning curves for production of the system, and the budgetary picture both for the Defense Department and for the federal government generally.

Policy research on a proposed income maintenance plan would involve disputed facts and issues in welfare economics, sociology, demography, budgetary pressures and the state of mind of the Congress, to name only a selection.

Policy research on automobile pollution control involves three quite separate technologies: internal combustion, external combustion and electric storage batteries, as well as the economics of the auto industry, antitrust law and urban sociology—and this is far from an exhaustive catalogue of subjects for research, in each of which there are passionately held special-interest positions, and standards of objective scholarship leave something to be desired.

In none of these cases can a single researcher hope to master all the fields of knowledge that are relevant to a policy recommendation, nor can he verify for himself more than a small fraction of the data collected. The skills that he must display are not only analytical and synthetic, but evaluative and executive as well. He must make some intuitive judgments, more so than his discipline-oriented colleagues, and he must manage and oversee the work of other professionals (and nonprofessionals), more than in most disciplinary research.

These difficulties obtain, to a greater or lesser degree, across the spectrum of policy research activities from trend measurement to evaluation, although they tend to increase as one moves across the spectrum towards the least academic and discipline-oriented kinds of policy research.

Having identified the policy researcher as a man with a lot of problems, and having defined him, by exclusion, as the scholar who has denied himself most of the benefits of the scholarly life, we can go on to try to place him in time and space. The policy researcher is, as has been suggested, a quite recent phenomenon. The National Academy of Sciences, which was created during the Civil War to put the resources of the scientific community at the disposition of the government, was seldom called on during the first three generations of its existence. The National Research Council, created for a similar purpose in World War I, played a very limited role. The development of Agricultural Experiment stations in connection with the land grant colleges and the agricultural extension system could be described as a primitive form of policy research, applying the results of experimentation in fields like plant genetics to the problems of American agriculture. Henry Wallace is more likely to be remembered for his introduction of hybrid corn than for any of the accomplishments of his later life.

The domestic economic crisis of the thirties produced a spate of legislation, most of it having its origins in academic speculation, but there were no systematic links between the research community and the economic policy makers. Wars are prime sources of innovation, and World War II saw an enormous expansion in the use of research, not only on technical questions but on issues of military and politico-military policy as well. The war's end saw the enactment of the Employment Act of 1946 and the creation of the Council of Economic Advisers to bring systematic research to bear on problems of economic policy. During the decade of the fifties, the principal subject of policy research was national security, and particularly the apocalyptic dangers of nuclear war. A number of high-level commissions studied various aspects of the problem, using many of the same people as commission members or advisers, who were also called on as consultants by the Defense Establishment. These "weaponeers" came to constitute almost a distinct class, although they tended to have academic or industrial career commitments of a more traditional character.

At the same time there began to appear a number of "think-tanks"—the RAND Corporation, the Institute for Defense Analysis, the Research Analyses Corporation and other organizations, most of them established to serve the military departments. Perhaps the most important fact about the think-tanks is that their professional staff could properly be described as full-time policy researchers. Within RAND, for example, the staff was not organized along traditional disciplinary lines. There was a department of economics, but there was also a department of logistics, and a department of social science, while particular projects could cut across departmental lines, and the most senior people in the organization were freed from departmental affiliations as members of the so-called research council.

Towards the end of the fifties, policy research was launched on a broader scale, in the Rockefeller Brothers Special Studies program, and the Eisenhower National Goals Commission, which attempted to apply the techniques of policy research to public policy issues across the board. But again they did so without making use of professional staff that was permanently oriented towards policy research. The staffs of these studies consisted primarily of people with a background in traditional disciplinary research, or of lawyers with a general background in public service—precursors, in some ways, of the full-fledged policy researcher.

With the advent of the Kennedy administration, a number of alumni of the think-tanks found their way into government, particularly in the Department of Defense, where their sympathetic presence in turn encouraged the creation of new private entities, from the Hudson Institute to the Logistics Management Institute, to special divisions of major corporations, like General Electric's Tempo. During the sixties, their influence spread to the domestic agencies of government, as exemplified in the diffusion of the planning, programming budgeting system (PPBS) throughout the federal government and into some state and local government units and the creation of quasi-public research entities like the Urban Institute, under a federal statute, and the Poverty

Research Institute at the University of Wisconsin, under an OEO grant. And on the anti-establishment side, one finds such institutions as the Institute for Policy Studies in Washington, and the Center for the Study of Democratic Institutions in Santa Barbara.

Since the Nixon Administration has taken office, new entities for policy research have been formed in and out of government, including a unit within the International Studies Division of the Brookings Institution that is prepared to do analyses of the annual defense budget and the Secretary of Defense's military posture statement, to compare with the analyses prepared within the Department of Defense. The Brookings group does not of course have access to classified material, but it is staffed to do the same kind of analytical work that was performed during the McNamara regime in the office of the Assistant Secretary for Systems Analysis—and with fewer constraints on the underlying assumptions of the research.

Plans for more elaborate use of policy research within the government have been articulated in the executive branch with the creation of the National Goals Research staff within the executive office of the president, and proposals for an organization to serve the Congress as an independent source of evaluations of executive branch proposals, even suggested by Daniel Patrick Moynihan as a fourth branch of government.

In the face of all this activity, who are the policy researchers and where are they to be found? Despite the excitement that surrounds them, they are indeed a little band of brothers. There are some 15,000 economists in the United States, and about an equal number of political scientists, but there are probably only a few thousand people who could be properly identified as policy researchers. They include no more than a few hundred people on the staffs of government-supported research institutions (since most of the staffs of these organizations are technicians concerned with the details of weapons development), a few score individuals in privately supported institutions, both profit and nonprofit, and a few hundred more university-based scholars whose primary interest is in policy-oriented rather than discipline-oriented research. These people cannot be identified in any formal fashion in the academic world, any more than within the research institutions. They recognize each other when they meet, but they tend to play down their unconventional interests, lest their discipline-oriented colleagues accuse them of lack of devotion to the "science" of economics—or sociology, or government, or whatever. They have no official learned journals—although their writing is to be found particularly in the pages of *trans*action and *The Public Interest* and in the new *Policy Sciences* and they have no regular meeting places—other than ad hoc conferences like the one at which this essay was first presented.

Because they have almost no group identity, they have yet to engage in collective bargaining on behalf of their common interests, which have thus far gone largely unrecognized. In anticipation of future bargaining sessions, it may be worth an effort of prediction as to what these demands will be. It seems likely that, at least in the university context, they will focus on three points: common funding across disciplinary lines, research staff and more integration of field work into the life of the university. The interests of policy researchers are shaped by concerns that cut across traditional disciplinary lines, and the formation of new departments or even of permanent interdepartmental committees is not an adequate answer to the problem. A shifting structure of research commitments, in which individual scholars are free to follow their interests beyond the limits of established disciplines, is essential to full participation in policy research.

This kind of structure in turn raises two problems: the relationships among research, teaching and academic advancement, which would have to be looser, in the dependence on fixed ladders of progression, than it is today; and the availability of research assistance.

There is still a good deal of resistance in the university community to bringing in as research assistants people who are not candidates for permanent teaching appointments. Yet in order to do most policy research, it is essential, as I have suggested, to be able to draw on staff resources, including people who have neither the qualifications nor the ambition for a permanent teaching position. Introduction of these people into the academic community is regarded as destructive of the collegial atmosphere, as introducing a kind of second-class citizenship, into what has been up to now a unique example of direct democracy. That it need not be seen this way is no guarantee that academic attitudes will change, but until they change, the policy researcher can only operate in the academic setting under substantial handicaps.

The need for extensive field work is perhaps a less troublesome problem. The tradition of field work on an extended schedule is well-established in anthropology and archaeology. There is no reason a priori why it cannot be established in more contemporary fields, particularly when it coincides with the expressed desire of students in professional schools for more direct and immediate contact with the problems and the people with whom they will be dealing after graduation.

It may be that policy research cannot be carried on effectively in a university context. After all, the major scientific advances of the eighteenth century took place in the scientific societies, because the universities would not afford them house room. But if the universities were to abandon the policy researcher, both parties would be the loser. The policy researcher needs exposure to scholars whose concerns are with issues that will outlast the institutions and the issues that occupy him from day to day, and he also needs exposure to students for whom the entire structure that he takes almost as a given, is an object alternatively of contempt and of all-out attack.

At the same time the university needs the presence of the policy researcher. More than 30 years ago, Robert Lynd wrote of the tendency of every social science "to shrink away from the marginal area where insistent reality grinds against the central body of theory." It is this grinding exposure to the problems of insistent reality that makes policy problems an important part of university-based research.

Perhaps the ideal arrangement would be one in which policy researchers could move freely back and forth between universities and independent research institutions, with occasional tours of service in government as well. Not all policy researchers would choose to take advantage of this freedom of movement, but for those who did, it would provide an extraordinarily broad perspective, serving research in somewhat the same fashion that government is served by persons who come and go between decision-making or high-level advisory posts in government, and careers in private life. These "in-and-outers," as Richard Neustadt and I have called them, are responsible for many of the new initiatives in any administration. For the policy researcher, the principal obstacles to this kind of lateral movement are still primarily in the university, rather than in government or in the research institutions.

There is a clear implication in the foregoing that policy researchers will not find a home in government itself. By and large, this is true. The business of government is too pressing to permit anything but the most short-range research to be carried on within the walls, and when longer range work is attempted, those who undertake it are likely to find themselves isolated from the mainstream of policy-making, as in the case of the State Department Policy Planning Council under Presidents Kennedy and Johnson. There have indeed been exceptions to this general rule, notably in the work of the Policy Planning Council during the Truman administration that resulted in the powerful national security policy document known as NSC (National Security Council) 68, but as a generality, the rule still holds.

If policy researchers have difficulty working within government, they must still learn to work with government. There is a necessary symbiotic relationship between the policy researcher, the policy adviser and the policy maker. Each one depends on the other two, and his psychic income is very much a function of the input he receives from them.

But even this happy situation does not guarantee a happy relationship between policy researchers and policy makers. If this is indeed to be a marriage of true minds, both partners have to learn to respect each other's roles, and to accommodate themselves somewhat to the limiting conditions within which the other fellow works. The policy maker has to realize that he cannot demand and obtain instant scholarship; that objectivity and reflectiveness and depth of perception can only be had at the price of some loss in immediate relevance—that word—to the policy maker's current concerns; and that a good batting average for a successful scholar is a lot lower than it is for a major league ball player.

A classic problem that policy makers have with their own bureaucracies is that bureaucrats are so much problem-oriented and so anxious to keep the machinery of government moving by solving problems, that they will not infrequently come up with a solution to a different problem than the one posed to them by the policy maker; since they can't find a solution to the problem that is put to them, they have to change the problem in order to get to a solution. This is commonly referred to in Washington as the street light syndrome, in honor of the drunk who told the policeman, puzzled by his posture on hands and knees under a street light, that he was looking for his door key. The policeman asked where he had dropped it, and the drunk replied, in his doorway. The policeman asked why he was looking under the street light, and the drunk pointed out that the light was better there.

When a policy maker refers an administrative problem to his bureaucracy with the warning that it is politically impossible to solve it by amending the legislation, he may get back a report that the best way to solve it is by amending the legislation, and here is the language proposed for the amendment.

Scholars, on the other hand—and even policy-oriented researchers—are by and large a good deal less problem-oriented than the policy makers who seek their advice. When asked what can be done about insurgency in Northeast Thailand, the scholar may reply with a learned dissertation on customs and folkways of Northeast Thailand, with extensive references to the customs and folkways of Southeast Thailand, which were particularly appealing to the scholar's own interests. But if the scholar is oriented to the underlying policy problem, it may turn out in the end that the key to the situation is a better understanding of the differences in ethnic patterns between the Northeast and the rest of the country. So that, as policy makers learn to be understanding of the foibles of their bureaucracies, they need to learn to be understanding of the systematic biases of scholars, and even of those enlightened scholars who are policy researchers.

But my concern here is more with the accommodations that scholars need to make in order to perform a more useful role in the process of policy-making than with the accommodations that government needs to make to scholars. And here I have to inject two caveats. Many scholars have no interest in contributing to the policy-making process in foreign affairs or elsewhere, and there is no reason why they should do so. What distinguishes the scholar from lesser mortals is that he is free to pursue his own interests, and that freedom must be preserved. The other caveat is that if the scholar ever abandons his pursuit of the truth in order to be more involved in policy-making, he destroys his own usefulness as a scholar, and his usefulness to the policy maker as well. There is no reason, as I've suggested earlier, why he shouldn't serve a term as a policy maker between periods of scholarly endeavor; but it is a positive disservice to the policy maker for the scholar to shade his conclusions in order to please his client.

Given these two caveats, there is nothing dishonorable or even inappropriate in the examination by scholars of policy problems, foreign or domestic. They can provide at least as much intrinsic interest as problems of theory or methodology. But if the scholar is to make a contribution to policy problems, he must be willing to address himself to the problems of the policy maker. He must be willing to help answer the policy maker's question, "What do you want *me* to do about it?" He may, and indeed he should try to, stretch the limitations within which the policy maker works, but he cannot ignore them.

Another way to put this requirement is to say that, if he is to be really useful to the policy maker or the policy adviser, the policy researcher must have a programmatic sense. To begin with, he must distinguish between ideas and programs. The policy researcher need not participate in this process, but he must understand its imperatives, if he is to serve the policy maker.

One way to try to clarify the relationship between the policy researcher and his clients is to look at it in a single field, and here I propose to look at the very broad field of foreign relations, where policy researchers have been involved perhaps longer than in domestic affairs.

At the outset, there is a role for the policy researcher simply in asking his client to stop and think "What difference does all my activity really make?" So much of the activity of foreign policy professionals consists of efforts to change the behavior of foreign policy professionals representing other countries, where reflection would indicate that the behavior of their foreign opposite numbers is largely determined by internal domestic politics, and that the United States has remarkably little control over such matters, beyond the reach of its sovereignty.

But if the scholar's role in foreign policy were only to ask the embarrassing questions, that would make it too easy. There is work to be done as well. And it is precisely in the area of advising the busy foreign policy professional on the nature and content of other societies that the scholar can make his greatest substantive contribution. The professional diplomat is the man who knows where, in Paris or in Phnom Penh, in Bonn or in Bujumbura, to find the door to which diplomatic notes should be delivered. He has a pretty good idea of what will happen to the note after it is slipped through the mail slot in the door. But he cannot be expected to have a really deep understanding of the internal political and economic and social lines of force that converge on the men on the other side of the door. For that understanding he must turn to the scholar who has specialized in the politics and economics and social patterns of the area.

If foreign policy is really foreign politics, and if politics is the art of the possible, a major role for the policy researcher in foreign affairs may be to advise the policy maker on what is indeed possible within the limitations of domestic politics in other continents and in other cultures. This is perhaps a reversal of the usual roles of scholar and activist. The scholar is more often thought of as the proponent of far-out ideas that the activist must scale down to what can actually be accomplished. But if we think of the truth that scholars seek as only unfamiliar reality, we see even this negative function as part of the scholar's traditional role. He can often be most useful when he is being most skeptical, when he is pointing out that the Emperor's new foreign policy scheme—as in the case of, say, massive retaliation, or the abortive proposal for a multilateral nuclear force in Europe—really does not amount to any scheme at all.

But still the scholar has some obligation to the policy maker to relate his observations to the range of alternatives available to the person he is advising, and to suggest a positive course of action that can take off from wherever the policy maker finds himself at the moment of choice. Because no policy maker worth his salt is going to accept the advice, "You can't get there from here." He may be persuaded to take a different route, or allow more time for the journey; he may even be persuaded that he is going in the wrong direction, or that he should change his ultimate objective. But if he were to find himself without any goal, even temporarily, he would lose his momentum, and this he cannot afford to do, any more than the scholar can afford to lose his objectivity.

Policy-making, like scholarship, suffers from the tendency that I referred to earlier in the words of Robert Lynd "to shrink away from the marginal area where insistent reality grinds against the central body of theory." Perhaps the principal function of the policy researcher, in his relations with government as in his relations with the university, is to help keep his opposite numbers in touch with reality.

4

Policy Initiation
in the American Political System

NELSON W. POLSBY

Optimists, it is commonly reported, contemplate the doughnut; pessimists, the hole. Attractive and plausible as this formula seems at first blush, it does not accord with my experience. Persons who are to any degree curious or reflective about the "buzzing blooming confusion" of life around them develop expectations; it is the violation of these expectations, and the consequent creation of anomalies, that quite properly draws and holds attention. Thus, for an optimist, whose world is full of doughnuts, it is holes that need explaining; a pessimist, contrariwise, grapples to understand the appearance of life's occasional doughnuts.

A study of policies that are in some meaningful sense eventually enacted is about doughnuts, and thus will probably appeal more to pessimistic than optimistic readers. Optimists who study American government have more than enough material available with which to gratify their taste for anomaly. The daily disasters of the morning newspaper aside, the literature on obdurate Congressional committees, venal or helpless regulatory agencies, slack or officious bureaucrats, autocratic judges, selfish politicians and so forth is readily to hand for the benefit of those who wish to gorge themselves on reasons why good things are done so seldom and bad things are done so often. My own ever-subtler contributions to this burgeoning art form I leave to other occasions. In these pages I hope to pursue a different tack, asking how it happens that new sets of policies are initiated in the American political system.

For the sake of simplicity I have restricted rather drastically the domain within which I have searched for answers. All the policies I will consider here have a highly visible and discrete enactment phase engaging the president and Congress. This sampling procedure has weaknesses.

First, it overrepresents the products of "events" or "happenings". Analogous to the journalist's enslavement to "news pegs", there is a systematic underrepresentation of innovations that build slowly, that accrete, for example, within the common law of administrative agencies.

Second, it artificially restricts the consideration of innovations to those kinds characteristically processed within the arenas chosen as the vantage point. It neglects innovation by state and city governments, by courts, and in the private sector.

Third, it classes as policy initiations those things that actually happened rather than those dozens or hundreds of nonevents which might have happened but did not.

There are undoubtedly other unmentioned problems, equally serious, which undermine a priori the generality one may claim for conclusions reached by careful study of the population of cases to be mentioned here. This is a serious handicap, however, only to those who feel ready to pronounce with finality upon the problem at hand. This essay is exploratory in character, and the restriction of coverage serves the function of providing a few crude controls so as to assure some sort of comparability between cases. Thus while our method forbids the formulation of universals worthy of a high degree of confidence, it does facilitate the discovery of a few low and middle-range generalizations.

Are there, to begin with, any such things as policy innovations or initiations in the American political system? It is perfectly sensible to argue, as some do, that there is nothing new under the sun. So, in a sense, a search for the genesis of policy innovations is bound to prove fruitless. We can never settle definitively the exact point in time at which any particular innovation emerged from the primordial ooze. We can, however, by tracing policy some of the way back upstream, learn something about the workings of the systems in which innovations occur. My modest purpose here is to suggest what we can learn.

I should stipulate, to begin with, that policy innovation and policy initiation are the same thing. If it isn't an innovation, it isn't an initiation. In retrospect, at least, it is clear enough what constitutes an important mutation in policy, and in reconstructing how these come about we discover policy initiations. Such initiations, of course, are different from the day to day initiatives that serve to activate the routines of government.

There is, nevertheless, ambiguity about what counts as an innovation. I do not see any clear way through this method-ological, and ultimately, I suppose, theoretical thicket. There is, so far as I know, no standard that currently commands universal acceptance, by which policies can be distinguished from non-policies, or innovations from noninnovations. Nor is there an accepted method to gauge with precision the magnitude of a policy or an innovation. There is, therefore, no entirely fastidious way to circumscribe a population from which a meaningful sample of policy innovations can be drawn for inspection. I do not believe, however, that this melancholy situation should be permitted to balk empirical inquiry, or even to free theoretical rumination from empirical constraints. We can go a short way, I think, with the conventional wisdom, case evidence that comes readily to hand, and a few reasonable ground rules.

Innovation, for our purposes, will consist in the creation of a new governmental agency or mechanism which subsequently is seen to enlarge or materially affect the repertoire of responses the government makes to a given range of social problems. Alternative-ly, innovation consists in a policy or a set of policies that seem to have altered (or promise to alter) the lives of persons affected by them in substantial and fairly permanent ways. Thus, to begin with, I shall invite attention to summary statements describing a "sample" of policies having three characteristics in common: First, they are relatively large-scale phenomena highly visible to political actors and observers. Second, they embody from at least one point of view a break with preceding governmental responses to the range of problems to which they are addressed. Finally, unlike major "crises" with which they share the preceding traits, "innovations" have institutional or societal effects that are in a sense "lasting." No doubt the men who stood "eyeball to eyeball" with Khruschchev in the Cuban missile crisis received lasting lessons from the experience, but unless these lessons are in some way given institutional form, it is hard to see how even such a dramatic event could be classed as a policy innovation, however momentous its immediate consequences, and even though it occasioned a temporary break with past policies and past methods of making policy.

So much, at least preliminarily, for ground rules. Now for conventional wisdom. There is, I think, a fairly firm consensus on how a great deal of policy is initiated in the American political system, and this consensus will provide a final set of empirical constraints within which our own speculations may conveniently find a focus. It is, of course, commonplace to observe that a major portion of·the policies that ultimately are enacted by Congress are initiated by the president.

Recently, for example, in an unusually thoughtful and rigorous presentation, Charles E. Lindblom discussed how Congressmen "depend upon 'central' executive leadership, especially in the initiation of policies . . . e.g., in the degree to which the President has taken over the task of designing a legislative program for each succeeding Congress . . . Congressional committees themselves, the chairmen themselves, have turned to the President for leadership in policy-making . . . Perhaps 80 percent of bills enacted into law originate in the executive branch."

In much the same vein James Robinson says, "Congress' influence in foreign policy is primarily (and increasingly) to legitimate and/or amend recommendations initiated by the executive to deal with situations usually identified by the executive. . .Parliaments, Congresses and legislatures react to executive initiative rather than take initiative." This observation is supported by a chapter describing 22 foreign policy decisions from the 1930s to 1961, accompanied by a table listing the executive branch as the "initiator" in 19 cases.

David Truman says: "The twentieth century, it is often noted, has been hard on legislatures. Compelled in some fashion to deal with the complexities of increasingly urbanized, rapidly industrialized, and irrevocably interdependent societies, they have found themselves alternating in varying degrees between two equally dangerous and distasteful situations; yielding the initiative as well as the implementing responsibilities to bureaucrats whose actions might be imperfectly mediated by political officials, or attempting to retain one or both of these functions at the expense of delay, indecision and instability." Samuel P. Huntington echoes the theme: "The Congressional role in legislation has largely been reduced to delay and amendment." He quotes Senator Abraham Ribicoff: "Congress has surrendered its rightful place of leadership in the lawmaking process to the White House. No longer is Congress the source of major legislation. Now it merely filters legislative proposals from the President, straining out some and reluctantly letting others pass through. These days no one expects Congress to devise the important bills." Huntington quotes a report of a Congressional committee: "More and more the role of Congress has come to be that of a sometimes querulous but essentially kindly uncle who complains while furiously puffing on his pipe but who finally, as everyone expects, gives in and hands over the allowance, grants one permission, or raises his hand in blessing, and then returns to the rocking chair for another year of somnolence . . . "

I wonder if this picture is not overdrawn. The evidence upon which such remarks are based attests to the following: that immediately preceding the enactment of most laws, the agenda of Congress has been addressed to proposals brought to it by the executive branch. Further, the resources of the executive branch have been focused upon the enactment of these proposals. This focusing process rests discretionarily and principally in the hands of modern American presidents. Thus when the president adopts a proposal as part of his legislative program, when the president sends a bill to Capitol Hill, the president mobilizes resources behind a particular policy alternative, choosing one and excluding others. Through the power and the authority of his office he makes a strong and often a successful claim on the attention of Congress. Thus, more than any other single actor, he can harness political energy and focus the political process in a meaningful and consequential way. But is he initiating policy? The conventional view is that he is.

Yet no sophisticated student of contemporary American policy-making believes that policies normally spring fully formed from the overtaxed brow of the president or even from his immediate entourage. Nor does policy appear out of the sea like

Botticelli's Venus, dimpled, rosy and complete on a clam shell. Where, then, and how, are policies initiated in American politics?

A group of students are attempting with me to study the problem empirically, by looking through the literature on American national politics in a number of discrete policy areas, and in a few selected cases—Medicare, the Peace Corps, the Truman Doctrine, the Council of Economic Advisors, the National Science Foundation, the Nuclear Test Ban Treaty, Maximum Feasible Participation in Community Action Programs, and Civilian Control of Atomic Energy—we are attempting to look upstream and spell out the ways in which these policies were initiated.

It is not feasible (nor sufficiently entertaining) to discuss here all the details of what we have been finding. What I should prefer to do in any case is sketch in a first approximation of some of the more general conclusions that our detailed observations have begun to suggest. These come under three general headings.

Our first set of conclusions has to do with types of policy initiation. As we now see it, there are two general types: acute and chronic, inside and outside, short and long.

Policy innovations generally follow upon the identification of a "need". Needs are in one sense ubiquitous: everybody needs something. So, along with a simple state of tension somewhere in society there also must exist a doctrine, or theory, or idea, or notion, or attitude or custom which legitimizes governmental activity with respect to this need. And here is the first point at which the two general types of initiation diverge. For some innovations, the need is instantaneously recognized by all parties as palpable and more or less pressing. It is, for example, relatively easy to innovate with respect to needs created by organizational opportunities or custodial difficulties within public bureaucracies, since the innovation can be rationalized as necessary to the pursuit of goals already sanctioned by the existence of machinery.

Three cases of innovation in science policy may serve to illustrate the point. Scientists who began their work before World War II are, as a matter of course, incontinently nostalgic about the era before scientific activity became a major concern of the United States Government. The critical events that form the backdrop for governmental interest in science are well-known: the scientific discovery that certain very heavy atoms could be made to release enormous amounts of energy, the apprehension in the scientific community that this knowledge was, or would shortly become, available to scientists in the Third Reich, the maneuvers by prominent scientists in the United States to inform President Roosevelt, the decision by Roosevelt to mobilize American science through a science advisory committee, the formation of the Manhattan Project, and so on.

Once the war was well on the way to being won, a new set of problems naturally arose with respect to the continuing relations between science and government. To what extent would government continue to pay for the development of science? Who would set the priorities for scientific effort? How would the technologies that wartime science had created be managed and controlled? Questions such as these forced themselves upon the attention of scientists and political leaders as World War II drew to a close. In some respects the problems they posed were unprecedented. Other heavily mobilized parts of the economy could be demobilized and remobilized as needed: manpower, steel production, fabricating plants and the like. Factories—indeed, entire cities—constructed for the purpose of making components for atomic bombs seemed, on the face of it, less amenable to easy conversion to the private sector. The stake that government now had in the skills and activities of the scientific community was far different from the days before the war—and this difference did not apply to any other comparable group in the working population. Finally, there was the acute problem of the drastic change that science had wrought in the world balance of power.

Three postwar policy innovations (among others) addressed these problems: the proposal to establish civilian control of atomic energy, the establishment of a National Science Foundation, and the proposal of a nuclear test ban treaty. Because, at the time each of these innovations was proposed, science was almost totally an activity carried on under government auspices, the identification of the need and the proposal of alternative solutions took place almost exclusively within the government itself.

Furthermore, although there was disagreement on what to do about it, there was widespread agreement that each of these needs existed. No such agreement attended the birth of Medicare. The need for public medical insurance was identified in America as early as 1915, by a group of academics, lawyers, and other professionals, organized in the American Association for Labor

Legislation. In 1934 a New Deal economist, Edwin Witte, pressed a version of Medicare on President Roosevelt, who rejected it as politically too risky. During the 1940s, Senators Robert Wagner and James Murray and Representative John Dingell used to introduce a Medicare bill in every Congress. President Truman adopted the proposal in 1949, limiting the coverage of the bill to those on old age assistance, but even in this severely limited form, it failed to pass Congress. In the Eisenhower years the idea was nursed along in the Senate by Senator Hubert Humphrey, and by 1960 it was regarded as a standard part of the Democratic party national program. As a matter of course it was advocated by President Kennedy, and after the Goldwater landslide and the redistribution of party ratios on the House Ways and Means Committee, Medicare became law in the Johnson administration.

In general, then, there is a useful distinction to be made between acute, or emergency innovations, where recognition of the need to be fulfilled is widespread and swift, and slow innovations, where there is no immediate consensus about the presence of a need, and where, in consequence, a lengthy process of incubation has to take place before the need is recognized as legitimate by the government and policy is enacted to meet it.

Differences in the ways these two types of innovation arise also lead to other characteristic differences: crisis innovations are more likely to start within government. The production of alternative solutions is juxtaposed in time to the inclination of the organization to search for innovations. This leads to jerry-building, incrementalism and satisficing under severe time constraints. Bargaining between or among affected agencies and Congressional committees may be sharp, but it is relatively unideological, and capable of settlement by side-payments, compromises, log-rolls or other standard devices for antagonistic cooperation. Innovators are bureaucrats or government experts.

Long-haul innovations are much more likely to arise as the result of outside demands on government. Innovators are typically professors or interest group experts. In the process of identifying and dramatizing the need for governmental action, opposition is created. There is a higher probability that long-haul innovations will become enmeshed in party politics and hence in ideological— or at least what passes in the United States for ideological— struggle. Alternatives are the product of research, and elaborate—

and contested—justification. There is a separation between the production of alternatives and the activation of the propensity of the system to hunt for innovation. The process of incubation becomes crucial for the survival of alternatives over the long run.

These considerations lead to the second general set of problems currently occupying our research. We have become interested in stating in terms sufficiently general so as to facilitate cross-national or other comparisons, the conditions under which 1) systems provide for the expression of "needs" and the production of "alternatives", and 2) systems actively search for policy innovations. Among the conditions turned up by our research on the American political system to date under the second rubric we have found presidents needing programs, candidates needing issues, senators needing "specialties" and bureaucrats needing work.

The first two of these hardly need elaboration. Nor, really, does the last. Recall if you will the situation of the United States Navy in the heyday of the Strategic Air Command back in the 1950s. The inducements to the Navy to search for policy innovations were immense, and with the advent of rocket-bearing submarines, ultimately successful.

The condition of the senator needing a specialty may not be immediately clear, although it has played a role of increasing importance in policy initiation at the national level. I have argued at length elsewhere that the Senate has become an important locus for the incubation of ideas and careers. Thus, "passing bills", which is central to the life of the House, is peripheral to the Senate. In the Senate the three central activities are 1) the cultivation of national constituences (that is, beyond state lines) by political leaders; 2) the formulation of questions for debate and discussion on a national scale (especially in opposition to the president); and 3) the incubation of new policy proposals that may at some future time find their way into legislation. To succeed as a senator or to enhance his political future, a senator must develop a reputation for competence, a set of policy specializations, and ties to national constituencies beyond the bounds of a single state. Yet the division of labor in the Senate is not highly structured; while it rewards specialization, it provides few cues and fewer compulsions to specialization in any particular mode. So senators must search for ways to specialize on their own. Above all, from the standpoint of national policy-making, the Senate is a great forum. Occasionally this forum serves as the arena for the debate of grave national issues. But, more often by far, this forum is nothing more or less than a gigantic echo chamber, a publicity machine that publicizes things that individual senators want publicized. As nature abhors a vacuum, so do politicians abhor a silent echo chamber; thus the Senate has become a great incubator of policy innovation in the American system.

This is less true of the House, primarily because of its stricter division of labor, its restrictions on debate, and its greater mass of members who thus enjoy lesser notoriety. This makes the House structurally inhospitable to the hobbies and fancies of individual members, no matter how meaningful and constructive they are. Even so, from time to time, a member, or a subcommittee, finds a niche from which it can incubate policy innovation.

A characteristic pathology of this process is of course for policy incubation to degenerate into make-work, into careerism, into obsession. Some of this is, no doubt, unavoidable. It is in any case a small price to pay for the continued development of a national forum in the initiation of policy.

There is often a hiatus of years—sometimes decades—between the first proposal of a policy innovation and its appearance as a presidential "initiative"—much less a law. Commentators have greatly underestimated the role of the Senate in gestating these ideas, by providing a home for speeches, hearings and the introduction of bills going nowhere for the moment. This process of gestation accomplishes a number of things. It maintains a sense of community among far-flung interest groups that favor the innovation, by giving them occasional opportunities to come in and testify. It provides an incentive for persons favoring the innovation to keep up to date information on its prospective benefits and technical feasibility. And it accustoms the uncommitted to a new idea.

Thus the Senate is in some respects at a crucial nerve end of the polity. It articulates, formulates, shapes and publicizes demands, and can serve as a hothouse for significant policy innovation. So it has proven, at least, in a number of instances—and I think that as the Senate more and more takes on the aspect of a crowded on-deck circle for presidential election politics, policy innovations of all kinds will be nurtured and publicized and kept alive by senators seeking the favorable attention of the media.

It may be worthwhile to consider conditions under which systems are likely or unlikely to search and alternatives are likely or not to be kept floating in the air.

First, I should say, for systems to be likely to search for alternatives, they must embody a generalized cultural belief in the efficacy of rationality, a belief that there are such things as effects that are caused by causes, and capable of being altered by alterations in causes. Second, there has to be some method of explicit decision-making, or at least a method of choice among alternatives that is more explicit than the habitual repetition of inherited rituals. Finally, the existence of political competition seems essential: The piecemeal displacement of one generation's leaders by the next, the challenge of an encroaching neighbor, the need to make promises or engage the loyalties of constituents or voters. All these may impel a system to search.

Richard Scammon has recently described the process in American national politics:

> ... There really aren't any new solutions. There are modifications, adjustments. Most good ideas have already been thought of. You don't really come in ... with a totally new concept. You improve this, polish up that. You take a plan that was discarded four years ago, and you pull it out and look at it. And maybe you salvage Points One, Eleven, and Twenty-nine.

What puts these ideas in the air in the first place? Here it is pretty clear Lord Keynes was right: intellectuals. Or, more exactly, people who are specialized in society to the tasks of playing with ideas and putting them in the air: professors, interest group experts, government specialists. The Peace Corps idea was somebody's hobby in the United Auto Workers for years before President Kennedy happened upon it in a campaign speech he was reading out loud during the election of 1960. Brookings economist Lewis Lorwin, drawing upon analogies with similar bodies in European nations, proposed a Council of Economic Advisors years before it was slipped, almost by chance, into the House mark-up of the Full Employment Act of 1946.

The point is: Chancy as these events were, they became much

more probable by virtue of their having been explicitly invented and floated into the subculture of decision-makers.

I have no doubt that a similar fate awaits the Negative Income Tax. Already, under the guise of a "Family Assistance Program", the principle is being officially advocated by a president who needed a program. Only a short time ago a series of intensive interviews revealed that putting welfare on such a basis would command almost no support at all in Congress or among relevant interest groups. Yet the idea was taking on advocates. It was incubating in the writings of economists Milton Friedman, Robert Theobald, James Tobin and Joseph Pechman. Journals of opinion like *The New Republic* and *The Public Interest* carried articles in praise of it. Meanwhile, public and decision-maker consciousness of the "need" to do something about the administration of welfare grew apace.

The third general set of concerns being pursued by my students and myself has to do with the reevaluation of roles in the political system. "Effective" senators are for us no longer exclusively those who manage to introduce only bills that pass in the same session. Looking at the political system from the standpoint of policy initiation has induced us to rethink the role of the Senate, and, likewise, of senators. The same is true of ivory towers and their absent-minded inhabitants, who sometimes do no more than borrow creatively from a range of experience that is simply not available to ordinary politicians or bureaucrats with their own day-to-day concerns.

So far as we can judge, the American case does not present a picture of a system in perfect equilibrium, where alternatives are always ready when government decision-makers search for them. The very success, for example, of the 89th Congress in enacting programs for domestic welfare that had for the most part been in the air in one form or another since the days of the New Deal provoked a kind of crisis. By suddenly depleting the stock of ideas available for legislative enactment, the 89th Congress issued a challenge that was speedily repeated in a spate of newspaper and magazine articles bemoaning the exhaustion of ingenuity in the American political system.

President Johnson fought back by constituting anonymous task forces of experts—mostly from outside government—who were charged with coming up with new worlds to conquer. As it turned out, of course, there was still plenty of unconquered territory in the old world. The announcement of victory in the war on poverty turned out to be premature. For one thing: the Maximum Feasible Participation clause in the Community Action Program unexpectedly evened up the sides a little. But this doesn't change the main point, which is that the American political system at the national level, working at its normal rate, frequently provides opportunities for policy initiation, even when crises and emergencies of various kinds do not provoke the system to search for alternatives.

Finally, the existence of available alternatives, as I have said, seems to depend in great measure upon the ingenuity and the energy of men of ideas, who, if we look closely enough, and trace far enough back, can be observed creating the indispensable substance that the political process processes.

5

Applied Social
Science and Systems Analysis

YEHEZKEL DROR

The search for social science contributions to policy making is an intensive one which has been going on for quite a long time. It well antecedes modern social science, illustrated, for instance, by the work of Jeremy Bentham in England and by the Cameralists in Europe.[1] The founders of modern sociology were strongly interested in the policy implications of their knowledge, some of them trying to combine knowledge and power through personal political activity—such as Max Weber himself. In more recent periods, the question of "knowledge for what" has been asked continuously, and efforts to apply social science knowledge to social issues have been made for many years. Even when measured by quantitative criteria, the investments in social science research—including so-called applied studies—in the United States are considerable.[2]

Despite this interest in applied social science,[3] the output of social science in terms of knowledge relevant to policy is not easy to pin down. Certainly there is knowledge significant to some problems. But a social scientist who is asked to demonstrate the possible operational significance of his discipline for the main problems facing humanity and society is quite hard put to provide illustrations.[4] This is the case also when we adopt a broad concept of "problem significant knowledge," which looks for heuristic aids and not for answers. Even when we accept as relevant, knowledge that mainly serves to educate the frames-of-appreciation[5] of policy makers in clearly policy-relevant ways, few social science theories will pass this minimal threshold.[6]

Not only is contemporary social science knowledge disappointing in policy relevance,[7] but there seem to be few promising ways to change this state of affairs through incremental adjustments. Suggestions vary from doing more of what is being done now, to setting up additional problem-oriented social research organizations. Some of the proposals are highly interesting and promise to be useful.[8] But, as I will try to show later on, most of the suggestions do not face up to the quantum jumps in knowledge necessary for developing significant policy-relevant social science knowledge.

Applied social science constitutes one of the principal rational avenues to better social policy making. A second way is the analytical decision approach, operationalized best by systems analysis; that is by improving decision making through morphological analysis, logical structuring, explication of assumptions, examination of interrelations with interconnected variables and systematic use of a variety of decision sciences techniques.[9] Based on economics, systems engineering and operations research and reinforced by significant successes when applied to certain defense decision problems, systems analysis is widely regarded as a powerful instrument for better policy making.[10]

In fact, an increasing number of efforts to apply systems analysis to social problems is underway. But, again, any summary of the policy-relevant conclusions of these efforts is disappointing. Significant findings are available when the problem is susceptible to operations research techniques (for example, transportation networks) or when the problem can be treated with methods of economics and engineering economics (such as housing). But contemporary systems analysis is not really helpful in respect to the main problems facing present and emerging society. Neither does contemporary systems analysis demonstrate any inherent capacity for growth that will make them relevant for such problems in the foreseeable future.

The independent avenues of applied social sciences research and of systems analysis both being inadequate for significant policy-making improvements, I want to explore the idea that their fusion may provide much-needed help.

In doing so, I make no claim that this is the only worthwhile search for ways to improve the contributions of social science and analytic approaches to policy making. Other effective ways may include, for instance, building up the role of social science as a social critic—with close attention to value judgments, action programs, advocacy and issues usually repressed;[11] deductive construction of models of complex social systems.[12] The scarcity of knowledge and experience about how to deal with difficult issues may well require that a number of approaches be developed and utilized concurrently. But my impression is 1) that some fusion between analytical decision approaches and applied social sciences is itself a promising approach; 2) that despite lip service, this possibility is quite neglected; 3) that some fusion between analytical decision approaches and applied social sciences is essential if other approaches are to achieve desirable results;[13] and 4) that such a fusion will interact synergetically with other approaches. Hence, the idea of some fusion between applied social science and analytic decision approaches seems to justify exploration, but without any claim of exclusivity.

To explore the possibility of fusion between analytic and applied approaches as an avenue to better policy making, let us evaluate it from the points of view of systems analysis and applied social science respectively.

THE VIEW FROM SYSTEMS ANALYSIS[14]

If systems analysis in its present state were a useful way to deal with social problems or if a more promising analytic approach were available, there would be less need to search for innovations. But in its present incrementally advanced forms, systems analysis is helpless in the face of complex social issues. In particular, systems analysis is inadequate for treating complex social issues in eight main interdependent respects:

1) Systems analysis focuses on proposing preferable policies, neglecting the institutional contexts, both of the problems and of

the policy-making and policy-implementation processes. Thus, "institution-building" is not within its domain of applicability.

2) Systems analysis does not take into account political needs, such as maintaining consensus and building coalitions.

3) Systems analysis has difficulties in dealing with irrational phenomena, such as ideologies, charisma, high-risk commitments, martyr tendencies and unconventional life-styles.

4) Systems analysis is unable to deal with basic value issues and often inadequately explicates the value assumptions of analysis.

5) Systems analysis deals with identifying preferable alternatives among available or easily synthesized ones. Invention of radically new alternatives is beyond its scope, though it can perhaps help by showing the inadequacy of available alternatives.

6) Systems analysis requires some predictability in respect to alternatives. Situations of "primary uncertainty" (when not only the probabilities of various outcomes, but the dimensions of the possible outcomes are unknown) cannot be handled by systems analysis.

7) Systems analysis requires significant quantification of relevant variables.

8) Basic strategy choices—such as attitudes toward risk and time—are not explicitly faced by systems analysis. Rather, maximin or minimax and discount of the future ("positive interest rates") are usually assumed.

These eight characteristics are not equally shared by all systems analysis studies. Indeed, the best practitioners of systems analysis will clearly label such characteristics as inadequate and diligently search for ways to overcome them. But if we look at available systems analysis studies of real issues rather than at professions of faith, introductory statements or a few outstanding studies, then my list of inadequacies of present systems analysis may justly be criticized as too mild.

Let me try and illustrate the weaknesses of contemporary systems analysis by an enumeration of some typical (though not universal) omissions in three areas of studies:

Transportation studies: Preoccupation with "mix-of-modes" issues and with satisfaction of extrapolated consumer demands, within a cost-benefit framework. Some attention to pollution effects, especially when susceptible to translation into economic values. Ignorance of changes in the values to be served by future transportation, such as transportation tastes, aesthetic feelings, new patterns of leisure use. Neglect of transportation impacts on community life and social interaction. Ignorance of possible positive functions of inadequate transportation. Ignorance of political and power implications of transportation. Inadequate treatment of interfaces between transportation and communication, housing and various aspects of the patterning of human activities in space.

Defense studies: Preoccupation with low-level aspects of defense, including equipment and tactics. Just beginning to face issues of "nonrational" adversaries. Little explication of basic value assumptions and of scenarios based on radically different assumptions. Ignorance of internal political and cultural conditions and domestic implications of external defense policies. Very weak treatment of interfaces between socio-political-cultural issues and defense issues in other countries. Very weak treatment of relations between defense activities and other external activities, especially socioeconomic ones.[15]

Public safety: Tendency to define public safety in objective rather than phenomenological terms—number of crimes, rather than feeling of safety or propensity to deviate. Concentration on efficiency of law enforcement, rather than underlying causes of problems. Short-range approach, with very little attention to longer range interfaces between public safety and, for instance, youth culture.

Were we to try and examine applications of the systems analysis to broader problem areas, such as racial discrimation, we either would not find any illustrations at all or they would be even narrower and more limited. This does not imply that systems analysis does not make important contributions to such problems by illuminating some of their components. Thus, in respect to discrimination, the finding that unemployment is less of a problem in the black community than employment in low-paying jobs is highly significant. Similarly, findings that inequities sometimes result from rent control are highly significant for social policy, and reflect systems analysis at its best. But the pride of the analytical decision approach is in its claim to provide overall penetration and "systems solutions." I think there can be no doubt that contemporary systems analysis is unable to do so in respect to main areas of social problem.

To overcome these inabilities of present systems analysis, a new basic methodology is essential. This new analytical methodology, which I call policy analysis, accepts the fundamental tenets of systems analysis, namely:

☐ Looking at problems and alternatives in a broad way, which tries to take account of many of the relevant variables and of the probable results, that is, taking a systems view.

☐ Searching for an optimal, or at least clearly preferable, solution among available alternatives within a broad cost-benefit framework, without being limited to incremental changes.

☐ Explicit and rational identification of the preferable alternative (or alternatives) through comparison of expected results in terms of operational goals; this is done with the help of a large set of techniques, ranging from mathematical models to human gaming and from sensitivity testing to canvassing of experts' opinions.

But these tenets must be supplemented, with many of the needed changes being based on applied social sciences.

To this basic framework of systems analysis, policy analysis would add the following components:

1) Penetration into underlying values, assumptions, and strategies. These include, in particular a) exploration of the basic values at which policies should be directed; b) long-range goal research; and c) explicit analysis of alternative policy strategies (such as risk choices, incrementalism vs. innovation, and goal-oriented vs. resources development-oriented policies).

2) Consideration of political variables, including a) political feasibility analysis; b) evaluation of alternative political pathways for policy approval and implementation; c) examination of social power implications of alternative policies; and d) analysis of coalition needs and political consensus implications.

3) Treatment of broader and more complex systems, involving a) lower and new scales of quantification (for example, nominal and nonmetric); b) necessity to satisfy multidimensional and diverse goals; c) far-going primary uncertainty; d) institutional change as a main mode of policy change; and e) acceptance of min-avoidances (that is, avoidance of the worst of all bad alternatives) and sensitization and long-range impacts as important goals of policy analysis, in addition to "preferization."

4) Main emphasis on policy alternative innovation, involving a) intense attention to creativity encouragement; b) much reliance on

sequential decision making, learning feedback and social experimentation, instead of models, simulation and detailed policy
schemes (such as PERT); and c) much attention to new systems
design, in addition to redesign of systems.

5) Much sophistication in respect to social phenomena; for
instance: recognition of irrationality, ideologies, mass phenomena,
depth variables and similar nonrational phenomena as main
variables, both of social behavior and of legitimate goal formation,
and acceptance of apperception, intuition and experience as
valuable sources of knowledge and insight.

6) Institutional self-awareness, for instance in respect to a) the
necessity for multiplicity and redundance of analysis and analysis
units; b) early involvement of politicians, community leaders, and
so forth, in the analytical activities; and c) the limits of analysis as
a perceptive set for cognizing human reality and aspirations.

The social scientist will have little difficulty in recognizing
many items in this list of desiderata that can be supplied by social
science, either with available knowledge or by knowledge which
can in principle be obtained, if suitable research efforts are made.
Nevertheless, I doubt whether the social sciences, as they are
today, can supply all the requisites of policy analysis. This I think
becomes clear when we look at the situation from the point of
view of applied social science.

THE VIEW FROM APPLIED SOCIAL SCIENCE

The issues and problems of applied social science are more
difficult to discuss than those of systems analysis. This is the case
because of its much more heterogeneous composition, longer
history and higher state of development, and the complexity of
relations between "pure social science" and "applied social
science."

In fact, even the very use of the term "applied social science"
may be misleading if it is assumed that there is a single referent to
this verbal symbol. What we do have is a number of social sciences
which in different forms are applied to a large range of
heterogeneous social issues. These social sciences include, in
particular sociology, social psychology and political science.

A special case not usually included in the term "applied social
science" is economics, which has unique characteristics, including

a good deal of overlap of pure and applied elements. The well-recognized reasons for the special nature of economics include: the different intellectual history of economics, which has been more policy oriented; the susceptibility of large parts of its subject matter to quantitative treatment; the reductionability of many of its variables to a few aggregate categories which are operational and measurable; and the relatively simple characteristics of the interrelations among some main categories which permit simulation of important aspects of economic phenomena by compact and usable models (especially simultaneous equations and, nowadays, computer programs).

Another significant characteristic of economics which makes it especially useful as advanced policy-relevant knowledge, is that it links social science knowledge and analytical approaches. Economics covers two main types of concerns: knowledge about economic institutions and behavior, and knowledge how to "economize," in the sense of optimizing the use of scarce resources. It seems to me that this dual role in economics is a main source of its strength as policy-relevant knowledge, and in this respect it is a pioneer for social science as a whole.[16]

However one explains the special aspects of economics, it clearly is in a separate category. Therefore, I am excluding it from the term "applied social science," focusing my concerns on sociology, social psychology and political science.[17]

It is difficult to generalize from the heterogeneous bundle of attempts that sociology, social psychology and political science have made to become applied. Many of them still suffer from well-recognized weaknesses.[18] These weaknesses include in particular: oscillation between idiographic micro-studies and "grand theory"; a priori commitment to equilibrium and structural-function concepts, which result in do-nothing, or, at best, incremental change recommendations; timidity in facing acute social issues and in handling taboo subjects; perfectionism, which causes withdrawal from all problems with time constraints, that is, all significant social problems; and a deep feeling of guilt about getting involved in applications which go beyond "value-free," "pure," "factual" and "behavioral" research.

But, as just mentioned, these weaknesses are recognized by a growing number of social scientists who are committed to the improvement of the human and social condition. These social scientists are supported by the growing demands of government and the various publics for social science help in facing social issues, by student pressure for "relevance," and by a number of foundations and research centers. The first fruits of a new type of applied social sciences can be detected in ideas such as social reporting and social indicators;[19] policy-oriented methodologies, such as evaluative research and social experimentation;[20] attempts to face value issues;[21] orientations toward the future;[22] broader approaches to social policy issues,[23] and, most important of all, some contributions to a few important decisions and recommendations, such as the antisegregation Supreme Court decisions and the report of the Commission on Violence, as well as specific inputs into many current decision processes.[24] Also significant are the increasing amounts of work dealing with policy making as a subject for research and improvement[25] and with the role of scientists in policy making.[26]

This list of achievements looks, prima facie, impressive. And, indeed, it reflects significant progress in applied social science. But, in order to get a more balanced view, a number of additional points must be taken into account:

First, the advances in applied social sciences are not an integrated and mutually reinforcing set of activities. Instead, different items are developed in isolation. To illustrate: Most work on substantive issues ignores the implications of studies on policy making for the political feasibility and the institutional requisites of changing discrete policies. Similarly, most studies on substantive issues do not incorporate a future dimension and neglect to adjust recommendations to alternative future possibilities. At the same time, studies on policy making are seldom related to social issues and pay little attention to the future dimensions; and alternative-future studies tend to neglect the future dimensions both of policy making and of main social issues.

Second, the various modern applied social science activities are still marginal. Only a small (though increasing) amount of research time is allocated to them. More significant is their marginal position in respect to recognition; thus, it seems that applied subjects are not acceptable as doctorate thesis subjects at the large majority of graduate social science departments.

Third, "applied social science" is just now becoming self-conscious, in the sense of developing a self-identity and building up its own frames-of-appreciation, methodology and institutions. Instead, the different social sciences tend to have their own applied corners, with significant differences, for instance, between applied political science and applied sociology. As a result, the need to reorganize the social science system itself for application are nearly completely ignored.[27] This includes such obvious needs as adjusting graduate training in social sciences so as to prepare social science professionals for policy application roles. Also neglected are the problems of organizational location of social science advisors, required interaction arrangements between them and senior policy makers, problems of training of senior policy makers to enable them to utilize social science, the novel roles of policy research organizations, and so on.

Fourth, these weaknesses of self-perception are demonstrated, for instance, by the widespread tendency to compare applied social science and its relations with pure social science to engineering and its relations with physical sciences. This comparison ignores basic differences, such as:

1) The pragmatic base of much of engineering, which anteceded physical science knowledge and in some respects still operates on an experiential basis (e.g., acoustics and metallurgy), versus the impossibility of basing applied social science on similar pragmatic sources of invention and knowledge. (In this respect, politicians and executives are more in accord with the pragmatism of engineering.)

2) The existence of a clear chain from abstract knowledge to production, moving from pure research through development, engineering and pilot-testing to production, versus the completely different nature of applied social science outputs and therefore the need for other relationships to pure knowledge.

3) The differences between physical science knowledge and social science knowledge, and therefore again the presumption that different modes of application are necessary.

4) The differences between engineering a product in the sense of a tangible, material thing and dealing with social issues, which are in part intangible, immaterial, undefined, open, dynamic, contextually shaped and value-dominated.

5) The scarcity of pure social science knowledge on which application could be based and, therefore, the fallacy of comparison with the engineering phase, which takes pure knowledge and

its development more or less for granted, or at least as something
not to be planned for. The situation is different in applied social
sciences, where encouragement of relevant abstract research may
be a main component.[28]

Most serious of all is the absence of a methodology for
prescriptive and policy-oriented social science endeavors.

Let me emphasize that I am speaking only about a methodology
for prescriptive and policy-oriented research. Certainly, social
science does not lack an analytic basis for its traditional main areas
of concern—descriptions, analysis and understanding of behavior.[29] But the needs of prescriptive and policy-oriented
research are quite different and require methodologies of their
own. The absence of such methodologies is, in my opinion, among
the main reasons for some of the main substantive weaknesses of
much contemporary applied social sciences work, such as:

1) A tendency, when recommendations are put forth, to mix up
reliable factual knowledge, implicit axiomatic assumptions, provisional theories, conceptual taxonomies, doubtful hypotheses and
various types of hidden value judgments, such as on substantial
goals, on willingness to take risks and on evaluation of time.

2) A tendency to neglect important special characteristics and
requirements of policy-oriented. research, such as the scarcity of
time, the search for leverage points, the need for social invention,
and the necessity for experimentation.

3) A tendency to neglect interdependencies between what is
perceived as the problem and other social issues and facets, leading
sometimes to quite narrow and time-bound recommendation.

4) A tendency to proceed without serious efforts to understand
the relevant characteristics of politics and policy making (and, as
already mentioned, without integrating studies of substantive
issues with studies of policy making). As a result, there is
oscillation between naivity and cynicism, and therefore between
disregard for implementation and Machiavellian tactics. As a
result, little attention is devoted to improvements of the policy-
making system itself as a main avenue for better resolutions of
social problems (with some exceptions in political science, most of
them quite traditional).

5) A tendency to ignore the limitations of resources and therefore
to avoid the necessity to evaluate alternatives within a cost-benefit
framework.

The absence of prescriptive and policy-oriented methodology also serves to reinforce the previously mentioned weaknesses of applied social science. In the absence of such a methodology, or an awareness that such a methodology is needed, there is neither a condition of self-consciousness nor a focus for integration.

It is in the supply of a prescriptive and policy-oriented methodology that there lies the great promise of some fusion with systems analysis for applied social science.

TOWARDS A FUSION OF APPLIED SOCIAL SCIENCE AND SYSTEMS ANALYSIS

Our separate consideration of systems analysis and applied social science seem to support the conclusion that some fusion of these two may be useful, and even essential, for significantly increasing the contributions of either of them to better policy making.[30] This does not imply the disappearance of applied social science and of systems analysis in their present and emerging forms. Nor, as already stated, does it imply that such a fusion is the only effective way for improving the contributions of applied social science and of systems analysis to policy making. But it seems to me that there is a strong case for moving in the direction of some integration of applied social science and systems analysis.

The necessary integration can take different forms. As a minimum, the following specifications seem reasonable:

For systems analysis: changes in basic orientation, methodologies and concepts, so as to move from systems analysis to policy analysis, as explained above; understanding of basics of social sciences.

For applied social science: absorption of basic methodology of systems analysis, as a design for examining problems and proposing recommendations.

For both systems analysis and applied social science: a measure of shared concepts and frames-of-appreciation, sufficient to permit mutual communication, cross-stimulation and common work in interdisciplinary policy research teams.

Achievement of even such a minimum degree of fusion is hindered by many differences between the applied social sciences and systems analysis. These differences seem to include the following:

DIFFERENCES BETWEEN SYSTEMS ANALYSIS
AND APPLIED SOCIAL RESEARCH

	Systems Analysis	Applied Social Science
Differences in disciplinary bases	Economics, engineering, mathematics, operations research, decision sciences	Social sciences
Differences in main areas of application	Defense, water resources, hardware systems, transportation, some urban management	Social sub-problems related to welfare, communities, individuals
Differences in basic methodology	Prescriptive, rational, cost-benefit	Behavioral research methods
Differences in value orientations	"Efficiency," with increasing interest in "equity"	"Good Life," "social justice," "humanism," "social integration"
Differences in professional codes	Special relations with employer; often "the establishment"	Ideology of "free profession," though dependent on re-sources origin
Differences in reference groups	Mixed between peer-orientation and much outsider-orientation, mainly to policymaker	Much peer-orientation some orientation to action-groups
Success expectation	Low	Quite optimisitc
Differences in modes of work	Teamwork, moving from problem to problem	Individual and some teamwork; often specialization in particular problem area
Differences in organizational loci	Mainly special policy research organizations, many of them inde-pendent non-profit corporations	Mainly university departments and institutes
Career patterns	Continuous career and specific professional commitment; some exchange with teaching	Part of academic discipline; limited commitment to applied work, often auxiliary to teaching and academic research
Differences of culture	More clinical, detached, objectivizing, external-izing, "analytical"	More personally com-mitted, emotional, attached to subjects of study

Based, as it is, on personal observation and impressions rather than on a systematic survey, this list of differences is unreliable in its particulars. But I think it is valid in pointing out overall gestalt differences between systems analysis and applied social science. Moreover, I think that the differences are closely related to the present characteristics of systems analysis and applied social science as intellectual endeavors and social activities.[31]

Another aggravating factor is the scarcity of scholars and researchers who, individually, have crossed the barriers between applied social science and systems analysis and who have on their own achieved some fusion between the two. This, in part, is a testimony to the strength of the differences mentioned above, especially as there are many social scientists who have the quantitative knowledge and skills necessary for the analytical decision approaches, and certainly systems analysts can easily reach social science literature. Despite this availability of nominal access, it seems that even in the policy research organizations, where social scientists and systems analysts have many opportunities to interact and engage in mutual learning, they tend to keep apart. Indeed, quite a search is made by policy research organizations and by new university policy sciences programs for persons combining social sciences knowledge with knowledge in systems analysis, suitable candidates being very hard to find. At present, the best bet to meet urgent needs at policy research organizations for such people seems to be to develop in that direction before they become fully socialized in their respective disciplines. But this is an ad hoc emergency measure, which is more of a reflection of the urgent need than a way of meeting it.

Because of such difficulties, achievement of at least some fusion between systems analysis (and analytical decision approaches as a whole) and applied social science is not an easy matter. For some progress in this direction, the following activities seem essential:

☐ New courses in policy analysis and in social science to be offered at schools and departments of social sciences and at programs in system analysis respectively, so as to prepare at least the future professionals and scholars for the necessary fusion. These courses will have to be innovative in content and method, and their preparation is a difficult task. New texts and suitable active teaching materials (cases, games, projects and so forth) are required for them.

☐Teaching of applied social science and systems analysis must proceed to a significant extent through doing. This goes beyond active teaching methods in the basic courses, requiring work on real problems in workshops. For that purpose, again, new types of materials are required.

☐Indeed, more than classroom teaching is necessary to permit real learning by the students of the operational contents of systems analysis and applied social science respectively. Therefore, internship in applied social science institutes and in policy analysis organizations may well be necessary. During such internship, the students should work on mixed teams, so as to be exposed to approaches and orientations different from those they are familiar with.

☐In order to prepare the future applied social scientists and systems analysts for some fusion of their methods and knowledge, teachers are needed who have good experience in both areas. Such teachers are unavailable at present. Therefore, special programs must include both a period of intense study, for instance in the form of summer institutes, and a period of learning through exposure and participation—involving about a year in a social science department and research institute or in a policy analysis organization respectively. Special financing and arrangements are necessary to realize such a program.

☐University programs, and preparation of teachers and material for them, deal with the future. But immediate steps are essential to achieve significant retraining of the present generation of applied social scientists and analysts, to permit the fusion essential for enabling them to make significant contributions to better policy making. This requires a different set of workshops, special training activities and internships. I think that such retraining is highly important and should receive large resources, even if there is a short-term opportunity cost in terms of time and money.

The proposed steps constitute a minimum program for achieving absolutely essential degrees of integration between systems analysis and applied social science. Various levels of more ambitious proposals can be designed and are needed and useful. But even the minimum program as proposed, will be very difficult to implement. The intellectual, organizational and cultural barriers facing attempts to move in the direction of some fusion between applied social science and systems analysis are very formidable.

But even more forbidding are the psychological barriers facing any attempt to get mature and successful scholars and professionals to engage in quasi-formal learning and to accept explicitly the need to revise parts of their professional frames of appreciation, basic methodologies and work patterns. Nevertheless, the attempt must be made; but in the longer range, much more is needed.

THE NEXT PHASE: POLICY SCIENCES

Present social issues are very urgent, and more comprehensive larger range activities depend on present availability of suitable researchers and teachers. Therefore, a crash program to build up a group of scholars and professionals who link to some extent, applied social science and analysis (in its policy analysis form) is, in my opinion, most urgent. But, in the long run, it may be preferable to engage in design of new systems rather than redesign of systems and to build up a new supradiscipline profession oriented towards the application of systematic knowledge, organized creativity and structured rationality to the human condition. This is the case, also, because of the importance of continuing and accelerating the developments of social science and analytical decision approaches in their "normal" forms, to provide parts of the basic knowledge for policy sciences, and because of the importance of other possible alternatives for the advancement of applied social science and analytical decision approaches.

Therefore, I think we should move towards the establishment of policy sciences as a new supradiscipline and profession.[32] What policy sciences should provide is a new set of paradigms which can serve as a basis for novel research, teaching and application designs, methodologies and institutions. To be quite clear, I think we need a scientific revolution[33] in order really to get the kinds of knowledge necessary to make sciences fully relevant to human and social needs.

To be specific, let me tentatively indicate some of the required unique paradigms, some of which are based on a fusion between applied social sciences and system analysis and some of which are even more far-reaching.[34]

First, breakdown of traditional boundaries between disciplines and especially between the various social sciences and decision disciplines. Policy science must integrate knowledge from a variety of branches of knowledge into a supradiscipline focusing on public policy making. In particular, policy sciences are built upon a fusion between applied social sciences and analytical decision approaches. But they also absorb many elements from general systems theory, management sciences, conflict theory, strategic analysis, systems engineering and similar modern areas of study. Physical and life sciences are also relied upon, insofar as they are relevant.

Second, bridging of the usual dichotomy between "pure" and "applied" research. In policy sciences, integration between pure and applied research is achieved by acceptance of the improvement of public policy-making as their ultimate goal. As a result, the real world becomes a main laboratory of policy sciences, and the test of the most abstract theory is in its application (directly or indirectly) to problems of policy making.

Third, acceptance of tacit knowledge and experiences as important sources of knowledge, in addition to more conventional methods of research and study. Efforts to distill the tacit knowledge of policy practitioners and to involve high-quality policy makers as partners in the up-building of policy sciences are among the important characteristics distinguishing policy sciences from contemporary "normal" applied social science and analytic decision approaches.

Fourth, policy science shares with normal science a primary involvement with instrumental-normative knowledge, in the sense of being concerned with means and intermediate goals rather than absolute values. But policy sciences are sensitive to the difficulties of achieving "value-free" science and try to contribute to value choice by exploring value implications, value consistencies, value costs and the behavioral foundations of value commitments. Also, parts of policy sciences are involved in invention of different "alternative futures," including their value contents. Furthermore, organized creativity—including value invention—provides important inputs into parts of policy sciences (such as policy-making design and redesign of systems, policy design and policy analysis), and encouragement and stimulation of organized creativity. As a result, policy sciences should break a breach in the tight wall separating contemporary "social science" from ethics and philosophy and build up an operational theory of values (including value morphology, taxonomy, measurement, and so forth, but not the substantive absolute norms themselves) as a part of policy science.

Fifth, policy sciences should be very time-sensitive, regarding the present as a "bridge between the past and the future." Consequently, they should reject the ahistoric approach of much of contemporary social science and analytical decision approaches. Instead, it emphasizes historic developments on one hand and future dimensions on the other hand as central to improved policy making.

Sixth, policy sciences have a unique focus of interest, namely "metapolicies" (that is, policies on policies). These include, for instance, modes of policy making, policy analysis, policy-making systems, and policy strategies. While the main test of policy sciences is better achievement of considered goals through more effective and efficient policies, policy science as such is in the main not directly concerned with the substantive contents of discrete policy problems, (which should be dealt with by the relevant "normal" disciplines), but rather with improved methods, knowledge and systems for better policy-making.

Seventh, policy sciences do not accept the "take it or leave it" attitude of much of traditional social science, neither does it regard petition-signing and similar direct action involvements as a main form of policy sciences contribution (in distinction from scientists acting as citizens and from other concepts of applied social science to better policy making). Instead, they are committed to striving for increased utilization of policy science and to preparation of professionals to serve in policy science positions (without letting this sense of mission interfere with a clinical and rational orientation to policy issues).

Finally, policy sciences deal with the contribution of systematic knowledge and structured rationality to conscious human and social self-direction. But policy sciences clearly recognize the important roles both of extrarational processes (such as creativity, intuition, charisma and value judgment) and of irrational processes (such as depth motivation). The search for ways to improve these processes for better policy making is an integral part of policy sciences, including, for instance, even possible policy-making implications of altered states of consciousness. (In other words, policy sciences face the paradoxical problem of how to improve extrarational and irrational processes through rational means).

Clearly, the emergence of policy sciences as a separate inter-discipline has far-reaching implications. These implications involve the internal structure of policy sciences and its relationship to traditional disciplines (for example, special university programs in policy science[3][5] and new forms of policy research organizations), including important feedbacks to applied social science and analytic decision approaches in their various forms. More impor-tant, the emergence of policy sciences raises very difficult questions concerning the future forms of relationships between knowledge and power, such as changes required to enable politics to utilize policy sciences without being overwhelmed by them, and institutional arrangements necessary to prevent monopolization of policy sciences by the establishment and to assure utilization of policy sciences for improvement of broad democratic processes. Detailed discussion of such issues is outside the scope of this chapter.[3][6] But we should be aware that the establishment of policy sciences is a fundamental innovation, which may well result in quite novel forms of social guidance and changes in the roles of scientists and scientific knowledge.

NOTES

[1] There is an amazing scarcity of studies dealing with the history of applied knowledge and of social invention.

[2] See Gene M. Lyons, *The Uneasy Partnership: Social Science and the Federal Government in the Twentieth Century* (New York: Russell Sage Foundation, 1969).

[3] Some of the best work in applied social science is done in Europe. Thus, for instance, in the Netherlands, a special profession of "social geography" has been instrumental in applying social science knowledge to physical planning. The role of anthropologists in colonial administration provides a different set of illustrations of applied social sciences. The lack of literature in English on European experiences with applied social science is a grave omission, hindering learning and cross stimulation.

[4] As an exercise, I went through Bernard Berelson and Gary A. Steiner, *Human Behavior: An Inventory of Scientific Findings* (New York: Harcourt, Brace, 1966), trying to identify items which I would include in a "Handbook of Behavioral Sciences for Policy Making." The results are insufficient for a short article, not to speak of a "handbook." This same conclusion was reached by Alexander Syalair, who repeated my exercise. See Alexander Syalair "The United Nations and the Social and Behavioral Sciences," *The American Journal of International Law*, Vol. 64, No. 41, Sept. 1970, pp. 148-163, esp. pp. 156-157.

Similarly, an examination of the recent second edition of Gardner Lindsey and Elliott Aronson, eds., *The Handbook of Social Psychology* (Reading, Mass.: Addison-Wesley, 1968) provides very little findings which can serve as direct inputs into policy making. Volume Five is devoted to *Applied Social Psychology,* but despite the high standard of its contents, it has little direct policy implications for any major social issues.

[5] This very important concept is developed by Sir Geoffrey Vickers, *The Art of Judgment* (New York: Basic Books, 1965), Chapter 4. In contrast to the tendency in much of the United States problem-oriented literature—and especially in decision theory and systems analysis—to approach issues by decomposition and treatment of different decision components (such as goals, alternatives, and predictions), Sir Geoffrey Vickers emphasizes the need for a holistic Gestalt view of problems. See also his collection *Value Systems and Social Process* (New York: Basic Books, 1968).

[6] A good illustration is provided by the report of the Special Commission on the Social Sciences of the National Sciences Board, *Knowledge into Power: Improving the Nation's Use of the Social Sciences* (1969). The commission clearly tried hard to prove the importance of the social sciences for social problems and action. Nevertheless, the report is not at all convincing to someone who is not convinced in advance. This, I think, is a result of the real situation for which the commission is not at fault.

[7] A very good treatment of applied social science is provided in P. Lazarsfeld, W. Sewell, and H. Wilensky, eds., *The Uses of Sociology* (New York: Basic Books, 1967). Much relevant material is included in the four volumes on *The Use of Social Research in Federal Domestic Programs,* a Staff Study for the Research and Technical Programs Subcommittee of the Committee on Government Operations, House of Representatives, April 1967 (Washington, D.C.: U.S. Government Printing Office, 1967); and the three volumes of Hearings Before the Subcommittee on Government Research of the Committee on Government Operations, United States Senate, on S. 836, *A Bill to Provide for the Establishment of the National Foundation for the Social Sciences,* February and June 1967 (Washington, D.C.: U.S. Government Printing Office, 1967).

Problem-focused attempts in applied social science are illustrated, for instance, by Quincy Wright, William M. Evan, and Morton Deutsch, eds., *Preventing World War III: Some Proposals* (New York: Simon and Schuster, 1962) and by Elisabeth T. Crawford and Albert D. Biderman, eds., *Social Scientists and International Affairs: A Case for a Sociology of Social Science* (New York: John Wiley, 1969).

When we consider the growing number of books on social problems and sociology in action, the problem clearly is not one of knowledge being hidden. The severe limitations of most published material when viewed from the point of view of policy making (as distinguished from many other, not less important, criteria) must therefore be regarded as a valid and reliable reflection of the actual state of knowledge.

[8] Especially important are proposals of the Behavioral and Social Sciences Survey Committee of the United States National Academy of Sciences. See *Behavioral and Social Sciences: Outlook and Need* (Englewood Cliffs, New Jersey: Prentice-Hall, 1969).

[9] This characterization of analytical decision approaches is in no sense a definition or an exhaustive description. But it should help to clarify the meaning in which I use the terms "analytical decision approaches" and

"systems analysis." Such clarification is especially needed in this essay which is directed at a multiplicity of audiences, in the professional jargons of which these terms have different meanings.

In essence, I am using the term "systems analysis" in the sense in which it was first developed and used at The RAND Corporation. The best presentation of this view of systems analysis is provided in E. S. Quade and W. I. Bouchet, eds., *Systems Analysis and Policy Planning: Applications in Defense* (New York: American Elsevier, 1968).

This use of the term "systems analysis" must be kept clearly distinct from its uses as reference to: a) a general systems theory approach to description and analysis of behavior (e.g., as in the item "systems analysis" in the new *International Encyclopedia of Social Sciences),* and b) a computerized approach to social problem resolution and social management (as criticized, for instance, in Robert Boguslaw, *The New Utopians: A Study of System Design and Social Change,* Englewood Cliffs, New Jersey: Prentice-Hall, 1965).

The term "analytical decision approaches" covers the more general methodologies of which systems analysis is one operational expression. Other expressions of analytical decision approaches include, for instance, the classical works of Marquis de Condorcet; more modern Polish work in Praxeology (e.g., see Tadeasz Kotarbinski, *Praxeology: An Introduction to the Sciences of Efficient Action,* New York: Pergamon Press, 1965); recent work in decision analysis (e.g., see Howard Raiffa, *Decisions Analysis: Introductory Lectures on Choices under Uncertainty,* Reading, Massachusetts: Addison-Wesley, 1968); some efforts in various other areas, such as in architecture (e.g., see Christopher Alexander, *Notes on the Synthesis of Form,* Cambridge, Mass.: Harvard University Press, 1964); and the emerging, more comprehensive and inclusive "policy analysis" approach, which I will discuss later.

[10] The tendency to present systems analysis as a powerful tool for solving social problems is reflected, for instance, by Simon Ramo, *Cure for Chaos: Fresh Solutions to Social Problems Through the Systems Approach* (New York: David McKay Co., 1969).

More explicit about the limitations of system analysis in addition to Quade and Bouchet, *op. cit.,* are the works of C. West Churchman. See especially his books: *The Systems Approach* (New York: Delacorte Press, 1968) and *Challenge to Reason* (New York: McGraw-Hill, 1968).

[11] Such a conception of the characteristics and missions of useful applied social sciences is well represented, for instance, by *trans*action magazine.

[12] E.g., on the lines of the work of Jay W. Forrester, as illustrated in his book, *Urban Dynamics* (Cambridge, Mass.: MIT Press, 1969).

[13] Thus, improved governmental policy making, achieved in part through policy science based on fusion between analytical decision approaches and applied social science, is essential for effectively realizing new demands and ideas—which in turn may be developed and advanced as goals for governmental policy making with the help of other applied social science approaches.

[14] Parts of this section are based on my paper, "Policy Analysis: A Theoretic Framework and Some Basic Concepts," presented at the 65th Annual Meeting of the American Political Science Association, New York, September 2-6, 1969.

[15] The barriers to study of such issues in an appropriate way are brought

out in Irving L. Horowitz, ed., *The Rise and Fall of Project Camelot: Studies in the Relationship between Social Science and Practical Politics* (Cambridge, Massachusetts: MIT Press, 1967).

[16] At the same time, one should recognize that large parts of economics are weak in their behavioral contents. As a result, when actual behavior does not fit implicit behavioral assumptions, then contemporary economics theory provides wrong recommendations. This is the case both in respect to preindustrial countries and a growing number of situations in postindustrial societies.

[17] I include the general aspects of anthropology under sociology, and international relations under political science.

[18] See especially C. Wright Mills, *The Sociological Imagination* (New York: Oxford University Press, 1959).

[19] E.g., Raymond A. Bauer, ed., *Social Indicators* (Cambridge, Mass.: MIT Press, 1966); Eleanor Bernert Sheldon and Wilbert E. Moore, eds., *Indicators of Social Change: Concepts and Measurement* (New York: Russell Sage Foundation, 1968); and Otis D. Duncan, *Toward Social Reporting: Next Steps* (New York: Russell Sage Foundation, 1969).

[20] E.g., see Edward A. Suchman, *Evaluative Research: Principles and Practice in Public Service and Social Action Programs* (New York: Russell Sage Foundation, 1967); George W. Fairweather, *Methods for Experimental Social Innovation* (New York: John Wiley, 1967); and Elaine Cumming, *Systems of Social Regulation* (New York: Atherton Press, 1968).

[21] Recent approaches that are sensitive to the need of facing value issues but that do not adopt an extreme "advocacy" solution are well presented, for instance, by William E. Connolly, *Political Science and Ideology* (New York: Atherton Press, 1967) and by Rollo Handy, *Value Theory and the Behavioral Sciences* (Springfield, Ill.: Charles C. Thomas, 1969). See also Gideon Sjoberg, ed., *Ethics, Politics and Social Research* (Cambridge, Mass.: Schenkman, 1967).

[22] E.g., see Bertrand de Jouvenel, *The Art of Conjecture* (New York: Basic Books, 1967) and Daniel Bell, "Twelve Modes of Prediction" in Julius Gould, ed., *Penguin Survey of the Social Sciences, 1965* (Middlesex, Eng.: Penguin, 1965). Social scientists fulfilled important roles in the work of the American Academy of Arts and Sciences Commission on the Year 2000, as is reflected in the forthcoming six volumes of papers.

[23] E.g., see Howard V. Perlmutter, *Towards a Theory and Practice of Social Architecture* (London: Tavistock Pub., 1965); Leslie T. Wilkins, *Social Policy, Action, and Research: Studies in Social Deviance* (London: Associated Book Publishers, 1967); and Herbert P. Gans, *People and Plans: Essays on Urban Problems and Solutions* (New York: Basic Books, 1968).

Relevant illustrations of broad approaches to more general social issues are the contributions of social scientists to comprehensive efforts such as Bertram M. Gross, *A Great Society?* (New York: Basic Books, 1966) and Kermit Gordon, ed., *Agenda for the Nation* (Washington, D.C.: The Brookings Institution, 1968). More specific contributions are well illustrated by Daniel P. Moynihan, ed., *On Understanding Poverty* (New York: Basic Books, 1969).

[24] These inputs, which are of important aggregative impact, are well represented by the work of special social science research organizations, such as the Bureau of Social Science Research and the Center for Policy Research.

[25] E.g., see Thomas R. Dye, *Politics, Economics, and Its Public: Policy*

Outcomes in the American States (Chicago: Rand McNally, 1966); Austin Ranney, ed., *Political Science and Public Policy* (Chicago: Markham Pub., 1968); Raymond A. Bauer and Kenneth J. Gergen, *The Study of Policy Formation* (New York: The Free Press, 1968); Robert L. Crain, Elihu Katz, and Donald B. Rosenthal, *The Politics of Community Conflict: The Fluoridation Decision* (Indianapolis: Bobbs-Merrill, 1969); and Bertram M. Gross, ed., *Social Intelligence for America's Future: Explorations in Societal Problems* (Boston, Mass.: Allyn and Bacon, 1969).

[26] E.g., see Don K. Price, *The Scientific Estate* (Cambridge, Mass.: Harvard University Press, 1965); Robert Gilpin and Christopher Wright, ed., *Scientists and National Policymaking* (New York: Columbia University Press, 1964); Sanford A. Lakoff, ed., *Knowledge and Power: Essays on Science and Government* (New York: The Free Press, 1968); Donald A. Strickland, *Scientists in Politics: the Atomic Scientists Movement, 1945-46* (Purdue University Studies, 1968); and some chapters of Barnard Barber and Walter Hirsch, ed., *The Sociology of Sciences* (New York: The Free Press, 1962).

[27] But, again, there are some signs of a change. See, for instance, the proposal to set up special applied social science schools included in the report of the Behavioral and Social Sciences Survey Committee, *op. cit.*

[28] For instance, a strong argument can be made that theoretic study of macrosystems is essential for meaningful application, but is as yet neglected in sociology and handled badly in modern political science. See Amitai Etzioni, *The Active Society: A Theory of Societal and Political Processes* (New York: The Free Press, 1968).

[29] For recent work on the analytical foundations of "normal" social sciences, which builds on the strong foundations laid by persons such as Durkheim, Max Weber, Gunnar Myrdal and Merton, see, for instance, Richard S. Rudner, *Philosophy of Social Science* (Englewood Cliffs, New Jersey: Prentice Hall, 1966) and Robert Dubin, *Theory Building* (New York: The Free Press, 1969).

[30] It is important to note that such a fusion not only is one of several alternative essential conditions, but that sufficient conditions include also changes in the policy-making system (so as to permit it to better consider and absorb knowledge contributions) and in the transport channels between the knowledge system and the policymaking system. See Yehezkel Dror, "A General Systems Approach to Uses of Behavioral Sciences for Better Policymaking," in Ernest O. Attinger, ed., *Global Systems Dynamics* (New York: Karger, 1970), pp. 81-91.

[31] Systems analysis and applied social science are not the only decision-oriented disciplines and professional clusters. The legal profession, for instance, represents a quite different set of characteristics, as does also medicine and, to a lesser degree, management consultation.

[32] There are a number of precedents for emergence of new disciplines in the policy-related area, such as operations research, management sciences, administrative sciences, and, in a different way, urban studies and environmental studies. But, in my opinion, the most interesting case is that of strategic analysis, which clearly illustrates the development and significance of new policy-oriented academic and professional disciplines, with all the involved problems, potentials, and risks. This case should be carefully studied so as to permit learning for building up policy sciences. See, for instance, Bernard Brodie, "The Scientific Strategists," in Robert Gilpin and Chris-

topher Wright, *op. cit.,;* Irving L. Horowitz, *The War Game: Studies of the New Civilian Militarists* (New York: Ballantine, 1963); and Gene M. Lyons and Louis Merton, *School for Strategy* (New York: Praeger, 1965).

[33] My terminology follows Thomas S. Kuhn, *The Structure of Scientific Revolutions* (Chicago: University of Chicago Press, 1962). For a discussion of the applicability of this concept to sociology, see Robert W. Freidrichs, *A Sociology of Sociology* (New York: The Free Press, 1970) especially Chapters 1 and 2.

[34] On the characteristics of policy sciences, see my book *Design for Policy Sciences* (New York: American Elsevier, 1971). For a treatment of some of the substantive issues of policy sciences, see my book *Public Policymaking Reexamined* (San Francisco: Chandler Publishing Co., 1968).

[35] See Yehezkel Dror, "Teaching of Policy Sciences: Design for a University Doctoral Program," *Social Science Information,* Vol. 4, No. 2 (April, 1970), pp. 101-122.

[36] These issues are dealt with in the books mentioned in footnote 34.

6

The Misallocation of
Intellectual Resources in Economics

KENNETH E. BOULDING

The problem of the misallocation of intellectual resources has the unfortunate property of being clearly important and yet extremely intractable. We have an uneasy feeling that failures today, insofar as they are avoidable at all, are always the result of misapplied intellectual resources in the past. If we had thought about things differently or thought about different things or put our energies into the discovery of knowledge that would be relevant to present problems instead of knowledge that is not, we have a strong feeling that things would have been better. It is not easy to be wise after the event and to identify exactly what misallocation in the past prevented us from solving our problems in the present. To be wise before the event is much more difficult, for the judgment as to whether intellectual resources are being misapplied today must depend on our image of the future, and our image of the future itself is subject to serious and inevitable controversy.

Unfortunately, the general theory of allocation of resources as we find it in economics is not very helpful at this point. This theory states that if we are dividing a given quantity of resources among a number of different uses, an amount should be allocated to each use such that the marginal return per unit of resource is the same in all uses. The marginal return in any use is the additional return per additional small unit of resources employed. If the marginal returns are different in different uses, then it clearly pays to transfer resources from the uses in which marginal returns are low to the uses in which the marginal returns are high. Thus, if an extra unit of resources produces eight dollars in one use and ten dollars in another use, then if we transfer a unit of resources from the first to the second, we will lose eight dollars in the first and gain ten dollars in the second. If there is some law of diminishing returns to increasing use of resources, these transfers from uses of low marginal return to uses of high marginal return will raise the returns in the one and lower the returns in the other until they are finally equalized, at which point there is no further gain from shifting resources from among the uses and presumably the allocation is the best possible.

As a purely formal theory, this is fine, but it does not help us if we cannot measure the marginal returns; and in the case of intellectual resources this is extremely difficult, partly because of the uncertainty of the future in which these returns will be manifest and partly because of the extreme difficulty of allocating any specific future product, whatever it may be, to specific intellectual operations at the present. We simply do not know the production functions of most intellectual activity, and without this the calculation of marginal returns is virtually impossible. We have an additional problem of valuation in that many of the products of intellectual activity do not receive any obvious price in the market, so that even if we could define an aggregate of physical products of a specific intellectual activity, it might be quite difficult to calculate an overall valuation of this in terms of some numeraire, such as a dollar.

Attempts have been made to calculate the dollar value of education, for instance, at different levels and in different occupations, and this perhaps is the closest we can get to specific economic evaluations in the market of intellectual activity. There does seem to be a certain long-run tendency for the rates of return on investments in education to equalize themselves among the different occupations, if allowance is made for certain non-monetary advantages and disadvantages of the occupation itself, such as pleasantness or unpleasantness, the prestige it offers and so on. There may be considerable imperfections in this market. There is lack of knowledge and misinvestment, as for instance when people prepare themselves as obstetricians just before a sharp decline in the birth rate. While the information system in this market could certainly be improved, we do not have a feeling that it constitutes a major social problem. Somehow the educational market does allocate resources among the preparation of doctors, dentists, surveyors, pharmacists and so on, without running into extremely sharp or socially dangerous shortages or surpluses. There is, of course, a shortage of doctors among the poor, but this is because the poor are poor, and reflects the problem of distribution of income rather than the distribution of resources. There is at present a surplus of physicists, but this is because physics has become an unstable government enterprise.

It is when we get into what I have been calling the grants economy, that is, that part of the economic system in which resources are allocated by one-way transfers, that we begin to get into trouble, mainly because of the absence of feedback and the extraordinary difficulties of evaluation. The grants economy now comprises something between 15 and 20 percent of the American economy, and it organizes a much larger proportion of the distribution of intellectual resources, simply because the education and research industries are so dominated by it. Education, which is now 7 percent of the Gross National Product, is for the most part in what might be called the public grants sector, that is, it is financed by one-way transfers of funds from authorities which derive their revenues from the use of the tax power. Even private education is financed to a very large extent by grants from parents, from foundations and from endowments. The profit-making educational institution is so rare that it is regarded as positively disreputable and finds it has difficulties in becoming accredited. Research, especially pure research, likewise is heavily concentrated in the grants economy. Even in the case of industrial research the returns are so uncertain that the research budget has many aspects of a one-way transfer.

There is an allocation problem in the grants economy just as there is in the exchange economy, simply because the total of the grants is not indefinitely expandible, even though at any one time it may have a modest flexibility. If the total of grants is fixed, it is very clear that a grant to A means that there is going to be no grant to B. In this case, the allocation of grants, and therefore the allocation of the resources purchased by them, is very much in the control of the grantor. It is indeed a classic case of Kenneth Galbraith's "revised sequence," in which the initiative comes from the seller, and his decisions are very largely imposed on the buyers, in this case the recipients of the grants. In the exchange economy, there is more tendency to find the "accepted sequence" in which the buyer or consumer originates demands and the producer jumps to satisfy them. In the grants economy, the proposer proposes, but the Ford Foundation disposes.

There is something that begins to simulate the market in the grants economy, insofar as there are a large number of grantors and grantees, for then the grantee can shop around among the grantors and if he is turned down from one he may get accepted from another. Potentially this is a very important check on the arbitrary power of the grantors. How important it is, unfortunately, we do not know, for the one thing that does not get into the information system is failed proposals for grants. A study of these would be extremely illuminating indeed, and would not be impossible to do. It is not self-evident, of course, that the judgment of the grantees is necessarily any better than that of the grantors, and it may well be that a system of extensive interaction between grantors and grantees is most likely to give the best results, though in any system one would have to allow for a fairly large random factor.

In the absence of any accurate feedback or information about rates of return on the use of intellectual resources, one is forced back on considerations of structure; that is, is there anything in the machinery by which intellectual resources are allocated which might lead to serious biases? In the case of research we can look both on the side of the researcher himself, or the producer of knowledge, and on the side of the grantors who are in a sense the purveyors and the users of knowledge.

The main problem in pure research is the power structure within universities where most pure research goes on: old people usually have the power and young people the ideas. Of course the optimum age of creativity varies in different disciplines. It is apparently very low in mathematics and high in philosophy, and it is clearly the result of two factors operating in opposite directions. One is the sheer quantitative deterioration of the human nervous system with age: we lose about a hundred thousand neurons a day all our life. Counteracting this is the learning process which continually rearranges the declining stock of neurons into more and more elegant patterns. It is not surprising, therefore, to find that creativity in mathematics occurs at an early age, where a rich deposit of memory and experience is not so important as the ability to call on large resources in the nervous system. In philosophy and history, however, the accumulating quality of the structure is more important than the declining quantity for a longer period of time. These very physiological facts of aging make it important in all fields to avoid concentrating the granting power too much in the hands of the old and to organize the system so that there are checks and balances and that a young man with an idea who gets a rebuff at one place can find a sympathetic ear at another. It is curious how something like the simulation of the market is almost always the answer to the problem of undesirable concentrations of power.

Another structural problem that may cause misallocation is the phenomenon of fashion. This may be more important among the grantors than among the grantees. Even in the pure sciences there are fashions in research and a spectacular success in some field is likely to attract an unusually large amount of resources. Indeed it is one of the dilemmas of the dynamics of human learning, that whereas in the economics of the intellectual life nothing succeeds like success, in the total learning process what we are most likely to learn from is failure. Here again the only structural remedy for the vagaries of fashion would seem to be the atomization of the society, that is, the development of large numbers of subcultures in which different fashions may prevail in the intellectual life. Thus, the development of "competing schools" may have some effect in preventing the tyranny of fashion, for even though this tyranny may obtain in full force in one place, the person whose insights and information fall outside the rubrics of one school may find another school to go to somewhere else. The graduate student who cannot stand economics at the University of Chicago may find the University of Texas more congenial.

The danger of monopolistic power among the grantors is probably greater than that among the grantees. This is particularly true as national governments increase their importance in the grants economy and become the major sources of funds for research. Here, the accidents of political power or rhetoric have the potential at least of creating very serious misallocations of intellectual resources. If there is any one major source of this misallocation it is the setting up, perhaps for partly accidental reasons, of structures and organizations which then have a strong tendency to perpetuate themselves. We see this in the United States, for instance, in the great attention paid to agriculture, partly because of the structure of Congress, which in earlier days gave excessive weight to agricultural votes, and partly because of the establishment of the Department of Agriculture and of a remarkable tradition within it of the use of intellectual resources, which goes back to the establishment of land grant colleges in 1862. In the building industry, by contrast, there has been no such political pressure group, no such organization in the Executive Branch and no "university of the building trades" to correspond to the land grant colleges. It is not surprising under these circumstances that research in agriculture has been spectacularly successful and that we have had an increase in labor productivity in agriculture of almost 6 percent per year for almost 30 years, whereas the building trades have had a very low rate of development, practically none of which has come out of the building trades themselves. The deplorable condition of our cities is perhaps the main result of this particular misallocation.

One sees a similar distortion in the case of national defense. The fact that national defense is a prime expression of the national community gives it very high priority and so there has been a very serious brain drain into it which not only has very doubtful productivity but also has seriously impaired the quantity and quality of intellectual resources in civilian occupations. Perhaps the most dramatic expression of this misallocation of resources is in the fact that we have been spending yearly in preparations for chemical and bacteriological warfare almost as much as the whole budget of all the United Nations agencies. In the light of this fact, it is hard to believe that there are not strongly pathological processes at work in the structure of world society.

We may perhaps be able to take a small step towards analyzing this problem if we take a single discipline, such as economics, and try to analyze the distribution of intellectual effort within it, in the hope that this may reveal at least gross disparities between the proportion of intellectual effort devoted to a certain theme and its basic importance. In order to do this, we have to scan the *Index of Economic Journals* from 1886, classified according to subject matter; in order to get a total picture of the output of the profession, we should, of course, include books, but this task is beyond our present resources. Besides, articles give a good picture of the distribution of interests of the actively working members of the profession and tend to be more contemporaneous than books, which are often the product of work of previous years. It is reasonable to suppose, therefore, that articles give a good index of the interest of the economics profession in any one year. We have simply counted the number of articles rather than the number of pages, not only because articles tend to be approximately the same length, but also because the presence of an article may tend to be more significant than its length. By a rough check, about 10 percent of the articles are counted more than once, by being cross-classified. We assume, however, that a double or multiple classification increases the significance of the article.

The general growth of the economics profession is shown in Figure 1. The journal articles begin with the foundation of the *Quarterly Journal of Economics* in 1886. The total number of articles reached about 150 by 1892 and fluctuated around this level until about 1909, when growth began again and continued remarkably steadily at about an average of 6.8 percent per annum until the 1940s, doubling about every 11 years. It is curious that even if we take the number of articles, say, in 1886, and compound this at 6.8 percent per annum we arrive very much where we are in the sixties! This rate of growth, incidentally, is somewhat more than that of the Gross National Product, which suggests that economics is occupying a continually larger share of the product. This is not wholly surprising, as economics is, after all, what economists call a "superior good," that is, it is a luxury, the demand for which will tend to increase with increasing incomes. In the light of this consideration, the rate of growth does not seem to be excessive. A rather striking phenomenon is the quite substantial interruption of the growth of economics by the Second World War, from which the profession apparently never really recovered in the sense that, although the old rate of growth was continued, the gap made by the war was not made up. It may

Figure 1. The Total Number of Articles in the *Index of Economic Journals*, (1886-1965)

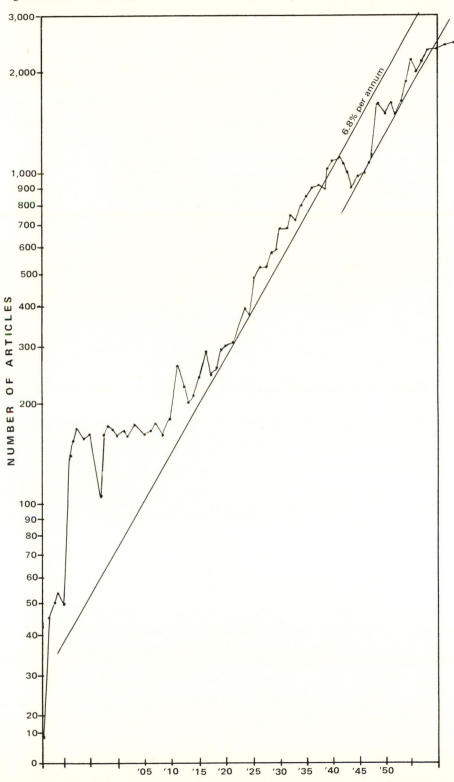

be, of course, that the rate of growth would have slackened anyhow, which would not have been surprising. But the interruption due to the war is surprisingly large and reflects the absorption of intellectuals in the war effort—and also the fact that meetings of the American Economic Association were not held during the war years.

The articles can be divided first into three categories. The first contains articles in which economists are writing to themselves, and about themselves, and about economics. This is a large category. I would put much of economic theory into it, the history of thought, and especially articles about economists, which is a large group. It is clear that economists have a fair amount of narcissism and that they like thinking about themselves and writing to each other about themselves, without a great deal of reference to the world outside. It would be interesting to know whether other scientists do as much of this. One suspects that it is particularly a habit of the social scientists and that physical and biological scientists are less given to it, but we would have to wait for a comparative analysis of other disciplines before we could confirm this hypothesis.

The second category consists of articles about the total economy, rather than about particular sectors of it. It is not always easy to distinguish these from that of the third sector, which consists of articles which refer to particular segments of the economy. The distinction, however, is necessary if we are to look at this third sector with a view to possible misallocation of intellectual resources. A very rough classification of categories gave 22 percent for the narcissistic articles, 33 percent for articles relating to the general economy, and 45 percent for articles relating to segments of the economy.

This breakdown does not seem unreasonable, though we clearly cannot impose any absolute rule on the distribution of the resources of economics among the above mentioned three sectors. We certainly expect to find all three and, while an individual may pass judgment that one of the sectors, especially the first, is excessive, it is hard to justify these judgments in any objective way. The great English economist, A.C. Pigou, is reported to have said, "We do economics because it is fun." Certainly no one would want to deprive economists or anybody else of their fun, and a great deal of the first section is fun of this kind; that is, it satisfies intellectual curiosity, it expresses the passion for order and consistency, and it produces at least some concepts and models that are relevant to the understanding of the economy.

Table 1 and Figure 2 show the breakdown of articles by the 23 categories of the *Index*, by ten-year periods, with the percentage of total articles in each period in each category. Considering what changes have taken place both in economics and in the world in these 80 years, the stability of these proportions is quite striking. There is a slight decline in the proportion in scope and method, a rise in theory, a decline in the history of thought, a rise (though less than might have been expected) in mathematics and statistics, a quite sharp decline in money, which is a little surprising, not much change in public finance, some rise in international economics. The proportion in economic fluctuations not surprisingly bulges in the Great Depression, although it is surprisingly high in the decade before. The proportion in war and defense economics likewise bulges in the period of the two world wars, but tails off very much in periods of peace. There is a rise in the proportion of the firm and a decline in industrial organization. The rise in the proportion in agriculture is quite striking, although it does peak in the thirties. The proportion in natural resources peaks about the same time and has been declining ever since. The proportion in labor economics has been declining and consumer economics has been fairly stationary with some ups and downs. The proportion in health, education and welfare has actually been declining until just recently, and regional planning has been increasing. The overall picture, however, is that of a very stable profession whose interests have not changed radically in 80 years. It is quite responsible to short-run changes in the economy, such as depressions and wars; it seems rather unresponsive to the long-run changes.

When we come to the distribution of effort of economists among segments of the economy, we do at least have something to compare this with in the proportion of the total economy which the particular segment occupies, as measured, for instance, by the proportion of the Gross National Product which each segment contributes. I am not suggesting, of course, that there should be a one-to-one correspondence here; some segments of the economy are intrinsically more interesting than others and have more difficult problems and one would certainly not expect to find the

Table 1

Percentage of Articles in the *Index of Economic Journals* (1886-1965), by Major Categories

	1886-1895	1896-1905	1906-1915	1916-1925	1926-1935	1936-1945	1946-1955	1956-1965	Totals	
Total no. of Articles	950	1,444	1,862	3,112	6,527	9,806	14,863	27,305	65,869	
1. Scope and Method	4.00	2.21	2.63	3.37	1.50	1.87	1.90	1.41	1.78	A
2. Economic Theory	12.21	7.76	8.81	8.26	10.39	12.56	14.45	17.49	14.40	A
3. Econ. Systems Planning	1.68	1.52	0.75	1.48	1.16	1.70	1.44	2.84	2.02	B
4. Hist. of Econ. Thought	7.26	6.03	4.56	3.18	4.19	4.36	3.66	2.99	3.64	A
5. Economic History	1.58	1.52	0.81	1.12	2.59	1.60	1.64	1.79	1.74	B
6. Contemporary Econ. Cond.	2.00	2.77	1.34	1.77	1.76	1.55	2.74	3.46	2.67	B
7. Mathematical Statistics	0.53	0.90	0.81	1.61	2.08	2.48	2.53	2.35	2.25	A
8. Social Accounting	3.26	1.04	1.61	2.60	2.38	2.03	2.78	2.99	2.64	B
9. Money, Credit & Banking	14.00	10.52	10.20	9.06	9.92	6.43	5.87	5.82	6.83	C
10. Public Finance	5.48	6.51	7.68	5.30	4.63	5.22	5.55	4.72	5.13	C
11. International Economics	7.15	8.73	6.45	8.23	8.20	6.14	9.35	9.02	8.44	C
12. Economic Fluctuations	0.21	0.21	0.32	3.21	3.27	1.88	2.20	1.92	2.06	B
13. War and Defense Econ.	0.42	1.18	2.31	7.17	0.25	9.78	2.21	0.51	2.63	C
14. Business Organizations	0.53	1.31	2.31	5.08	3.28	4.50	5.80	6.60	5.38	B
15. Industrial Organizations	13.58	20.85	21.80	14.65	17.42	13.54	11.45	11.61	13.10	B
16. Agriculture	3.37	5.67	5.64	9.54	12.73	9.54	9.91	8.72	9.32	C
17. Natural Resources	1.37	1.67	3.06	2.38	3.52	3.81	2.94	2.19	2.74	C
18. Population	1.89	1.73	1.72	1.06	1.52	0.95	0.95	0.89	1.04	B
19. Labor Economics	12.32	12.39	12.24	8.29	5.47	4.39	8.33	7.19	7.24	C
20. Consumer Economics	1.26	0.84	0.76	1.06	0.73	1.73	1.23	1.36	1.28	C
21. Health, Educ. & Welfare	4.63	2.56	2.90	0.80	1.29	1.66	1.13	1.17	1.36	C
22. Regional Planning	0.95	1.24	0.64	0.61	1.64	2.23	1.89	2.85	2.19	B
23. Unclassified	0.32	0.84	0.65	0.17	0.08	0.05	0.05	0.11	0.12	B

A = Narcissistic (22%), B = General Economics (33%), C = Segments of the Economy (45%).

distribution of intellectual resources among the segments of the economy to correspond exactly to the distribution of the Gross National Product or of National Income among the segments. Nevertheless, where there are large disproportions, questions can be raised as to why they exist. The distribution of intellectual effort, as we have seen, is a mixture of supply factors and demand factors, interest on the part of scientists constituting the demand and the interest on the part of the supporters of research constituting the supply. We can see both of these factors at work in explaining the major gaps between the proportion of resources devoted to study and the proportions of the economy.

Agriculture, as was noted earlier, is quite disproportionately studied, especially as we move towards the present. The very rapid decline in the proportion of the Gross National Product contributed by agriculture is not reflected in an equal decline in the amount of intellectual resources devoted to it. Interestingly, however, the fishing industry is much neglected (0.07 percent of total articles), especially as it presents some extremely interesting problems from the point of view of economists themselves.

At the other end of the scale from agriculture, we see things like education (0.025 percent), health (0.019 percent), and housing (0.051 percent) which have been quite scandalously neglected by economists. Education now represents more than 7 percent of the Gross National Product, by contrast with agriculture's 5 percent, and yet the output of works in the economics of education is still very small in spite of a recent upsurge. Part of the reason for this is again structural; for some reason, schools of education failed to develop departments of educational economics in the way that schools of agriculture developed departments of agricultural economics, perhaps because schools of education do not represent such an important political pressure group and also because educators themselves did not see the payoffs for latching on to the scientific revolution in the way that agriculturalists did. Whatever the reasons, the results are lamentable. One would not want to suggest, of course, that if the same intellectual resources had gone into education as have gone into agriculture in the last hundred years that education would also have developed the fantastic 6 percent per annum increase in labor productivity which we have seen in agriculture in the last 35 years. Still, it is hard to believe

Figure 2. Distribution of Articles in the *Index of Economic Journals*, (1881-1965)

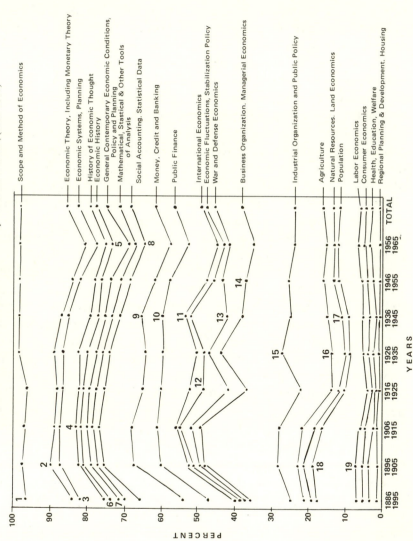

that a little more effort in the economics of education would not have had a high marginal productivity.

One sees a similar effect in medical economics. This is perhaps because these areas have been regarded as not quite worthy of the attention of economists, perhaps because they have been in the "grants sector" of the economy rather than in the market sector, and hence have been relegated to the dark underworld of doing good. Part of the difficulty here may also lie in the difficulties of measurement and the fact that the usual tools of the economists, which apply very well to the production functions of hogs, apply very poorly to the production functions of knowledge or of health.

Housing is an even more scandalous case. We might plead difficulties of measurement in the case of education and health, but housing, after all, is the production of perfectly straight-forward goods and services. Nevertheless, over 80 years there has been a mere 337 articles on housing (0.051 percent of the total) and what is worse, the interest in housing seems to have been declining ever since the 1920s. Economists were more interested in housing at the turn of the century than they are now. Here we see clear evidence of the enormous impact of demand on intellectual activity. The fact that the housing industry, by contrast with agriculture, has been anti-intellectual and anti-research, shows up dramatically in these figures.

Another much neglected area is that of war and defense economics, which rises as we might expect during the two world wars, fell to 0.51 percent of the total in the 1956-1965 decade, in spite of the fact that the war industry constitutes now about 9 percent of the GNP. The small amount of attention paid to consumer economics, only 1.36 percent of the total in 1956-65, in the light of the fact that personal consumption expenditure was 60 percent of the economy, again reflects a certain deficiency.

Table 2 shows the proportion of the total articles in a selected number of the second order classifications in which the time trend, or absence of it, is of particular interest. Thus, it is something of a shock to find that interest in the teaching of economics today is apparently less than it was in the first 50 years of the period, in spite of what seems like a good deal of current effort in the field. In economic theory, we notice the very marked increase in interest in aggregative economics and an equally

Table 2

Percentage of Articles in the *Index of Economic Journals* (1886-1965), by Selected Categories.

		1886-1895	1896-1905	1906-1915	1916-1925	1926-1935	1936-1945	1946-1955	1956-1965	Totals
1.3	Teaching of Economics	0.73	0.48	1.40	1.19	0.40	0.39	0.36	0.33	0.43
2.1	Value, Price, and Allocation Theory	2.73	2.56	3.44	3.12	4.15	4.82	5.28	5.58	4.98
2.2	Factors of Production & Distributive Shares	7.58	3.12	3.22	2.15	2.31	2.34	1.86	2.06	2.22
2.3	Aggregative & Monetary Theory, Cycles, Growth	0.85	1.25	1.13	2.09	3.68	4.85	6.32	8.93	6.38
3.2	Socialist & Communist Systems. Soviet Econ.	0.21	0.14	0.11	0.09	0.13	0.42	0.18	1.52	0.76
3.4	Cooperation. Cooperative Societies	1.26	1.04	0.27	0.77	0.14	0.18	0.17	0.19	0.24
4.8	Individuals (A-Z)	4.52	4.64	4.08	2.48	3.07	3.37	2.71	2.13	2.70
7.2	Statistical and Econometric Methods	0.21	0.90	0.75	1.55	1.88	2.18	1.78	1.55	1.67
9.2	Money. Currency. Monetary Standards	7.27	5.75	1.93	2.21	1.49	1.19	0.58	0.40	1.01
9.6	Prices. Inflation. Deflation	1.15	0.55	1.08	0.77	0.66	0.42	0.42	0.45	0.51
9.9	Monetary Policy. Central Banks	0.84	0.55	2.42	1.64	1.79	1.16	2.07	1.71	1.70
11.3	Balance of Payments. Mechanisms of Adjust.	2.10	0.97	1.18	3.79	3.82	2.95	5.71	4.17	4.09
12.2	Fluctuations. Forecasting	0.21	0.21	0.27	2.86	2.10	0.78	0.67	0.80	0.96
14.2	The Firm. The Businessman	0.43	0.55	1.18	1.45	1.06	0.72	1.21	1.12	1.07
14.5	Marketing	—	0.21	—	1.06	0.75	2.01	1.63	1.99	1.62
15.2	Market Structure and Behavior	0.84	2.14	1.34	1.09	1.10	1.38	1.20	1.66	1.42
15.6	Public Utilities. Electricity. Gas. Water	0.42	0.83	1.23	1.51	3.48	2.09	0.80	0.53	1.18
15.8	Transportation	5.37	5.96	8.54	3.79	3.69	2.13	1.73	1.76	2.43
17.2	Conservation	—	—	0.06	0.03	0.07	0.19	0.10	0.06	0.09
17.3	Land Economics	0.95	1.39	2.31	1.96	3.17	3.23	2.25	1.42	2.09
17.4	Forests	—	0.07	0.16	0.19	0.14	0.14	0.21	0.16	0.16
17.5	Fisheries	—	—	0.16	0.07	0.06	0.03	0.06	0.09	0.07
17.6	Water Resources	0.10	0.14	0.11	0.03	0.05	0.03	0.14	0.21	0.14
17.7	Minerals	0.32	0.07	0.05	0.03	0.01	0.07	0.07	0.11	0.08
20.2	Empirical Studies	1.05	0.70	0.70	1.00	0.62	1.50	1.16	1.21	1.14
21.4	Old Age Economics and Assistance	0.74	0.35	0.38	—	0.06	0.07	0.17	0.06	0.10
21.6	Unemployment Assistance	0.31	0.62	0.43	0.07	0.60	0.31	0.11	0.10	0.22
21.7	Medical Economics	0.21	0.14	0.53	0.06	0.12	0.09	0.24	0.19	0.18
21.8	Economics of Education	0.32	0.07	0.17	0.16	0.09	0.02	0.08	0.48	0.25
22.3	Urban-Metropolitan Studies	0.32	0.14	0.48	0.12	0.51	0.63	0.55	0.93	0.68
22.5	Housing	0.42	1.03	0.11	0.19	0.82	0.83	0.63	0.29	0.51

marked decline in interest in factors of production, with a slight increase, especially in recent years, in concern with socialist and communist systems and a not wholly surprising decline in concern with cooperation. The rise in studies of statistical and econometric methods is, of course, to be expected. Note, however, that these interests seem to have peaked some 30 years ago. The decline of studies of currency and monetary standards is very noticeable. The decline in interest in prices is perhaps more surprising. And it may come as a slight shock to members of the Chicago school to find that interest in monetary policy apparently peaked about 1910.

In international economics, the rise of concern with the balance of payments is rather surprising, and it is a little surprising also to find that interest in economic fluctuations peaked about 1920. We noted earlier the sharp fluctuations in interest in war and defense economics. It is curious that studies of the firm, indeed in business organization in general, which was rather low in the early years, rose sharply in the first decade of the century, and has remained fairly high ever since. It is a little sobering that the peak of interest in market structure was around 1900, long before the development of the theory of imperfect competition. The rise and decline of concern with public utilities is an odd phenomenon, reaching a sharp peak about 1930. Interest in transportation likewise has declined very sharply from its peak in the 1910 decade, which is a little surprising in the light of the fact that we feel such an acute crisis in this field at the moment.

In view of the current excitement about the environment, the very small interest in conservation, which peaked around 1940, and indeed in all the natural resource areas, is a striking comment on how ill-prepared we are to deal with the present environmental crisis. Even population studies were at their height in the first decade of this period and have declined fairly steadily ever since. It is sobering, too, to find that we were almost as much interested in empirical studies in consumer economics in the first decade as we were in the last of this whole period. We have already noted the shocking lack of interest in health, education and welfare, and what is even worse, the declining interest in this section. We were much more concerned with old age economics and unemployment insurance and even in medical economics around 1890 than we are now. The recent upsurge of studies in the economics of education has only brought it to double the minute proportion of the first decade. It is shocking to find that the interest in housing reached its peak about 1900, and that, in spite of the current to-do about urban metropolitan studies, interest has risen quite modestly since the early days.

There are many significant questions, of course, which cannot be answered by an analysis of this kind. It would require much more intricate and intensive analysis, for instance, to answer the question of the interrelation among these various parts of the structure. How far, for instance, did empirical studies modify the theories and the theories direct attention toward new empirical studies? This is perhaps one of the most interesting questions in the theory of epistemology, yet it is a question that is very hard to answer, especially with the rather superficial data of this paper.

One provocative conclusion, however tentative, is that the changes in the methodology of economics in this period did not very much affect its structure. The mathematical revolution in economics, of course, was underway even before the beginning of this period, with W.S. Jevons and Leon Walras coming in 1870, so that the period does not reflect the first transition from the more literary kind of economics and the use of mathematics grows very substantially during this whole period, something which this type of analysis underestimates. A count of the number of lines of mathematical symbols in these journals would, of course, be very interesting, but quite beyond the resources of this study. It would certainly reveal a very rapid increase, especially in the last 30 years. Refinement of mathematical techniques, however, does not seem to have changed very much the overall structure of the subject. It is perhaps too early to assess the impact of the computer, but up to now at any rate, the impact seems fairly small, again in terms of the actual structure of the subject. Up to now one would venture a guess that the impact of the computer has been in the direction of refinement rather than that of fundamental changes. This may not be true in the future.

Economics is one of the few sciences in which the structure of intellectual activity can be tested by any kind of structure in the outside world. However, an analysis of this kind could certainly be performed in the other social sciences and certainly would not be impossible in the field of medical research, where a comparison of the distribution of research effort against, say, the distribution of economic loss to disease, would be quite feasible and enormously interesting. There is room indeed for a large series of studies of this kind, but unfortunately there does not seem to be a great deal of motivation for such studies either on the side of supply or on the side of demand. Scientists, even social scientists, are somewhat averse to self-study, just as the universities are, perhaps because the results might be embarrassing, and these studies, at any rate up to now, have not become fashionable among the dispersers of research funds. An institute for the scientific study of science seems a long way off, yet perhaps there is hardly any other investment in which the granting agencies might indulge that would provide higher returns.

7

Conflict and Consensus
Between Social Scientists
and Policy-Makers

IRVING LOUIS HOROWITZ

How do politicians judge and assess social scientists, especially those in the academic community most intimately involved in the affairs of the political domain? The problem is to locate either the mutuality or incompatibility of interests involved between the two sectors.

PROBLEMS AND PROSPECTS IN THE INTERACTION BETWEEN SOCIAL SCIENTISTS AND FEDERAL ADMINISTRATORS

To construct a satisfactory framework we should focus on problem areas that are decisive for both groups: initially, how the interaction is perceived by the social scientists, to be followed by a presentation of problem areas perceived by political men. Apart from the interaction itself, there is the shadowy area of their consequences on the network of proposals and responses following from the relationship between the two contracting parties. Social scientists and politicians do not just interact with one another; the professional ideologies they arrive at and the norms they establish also guide present and future interactions.

One of the most serious and, at the same time, difficult to resolve aspects of the relationship of social scientists to politicians is
determining at what point normative behavior leaves off and conflictual behavior starts. Only with the latter sort of interaction does
a true problem-solving situation exist. For example, the norm of
secrecy that guides bureaucratic behavior contrasts markedly with
the norm of publicity governing most forms of academic behavior.
There is little question that this normative distinction leads to a
considerable amount of exacerbated sentiment. Yet, the differences between the two groups at this level are intrinsic to the nature of sovereignty and to the nature of science. Such differences
can hardly be "ironed out" or "smoothed over" simply because we
would have a nicer world if they were. Thus, at best, an explication
of the issues can permit an intellectual and ideological climate to
unfold in which differences may be appreciated and in this way
come to be lived with. This must be stated explicitly. Those who expect a set of recommendations for the governance of relations between social scientists and politicians should be dissuaded from the
advisability of such an approach, lest we find ourselves manufac-
turing perfect doctrinal formulas and juridical restraints that prove
far worse than the initial problem being considered.

PROBLEM AREAS PERCEIVED BY SOCIAL SCIENTISTS

The first and perhaps most immediate experience that social scientists have with politicians or their counterparts on various federal granting agencies relates to the financial structure of contracts
and grants. First, the difference between contracts and grants
should be explained. As an operational definition we can speak of
contracts as those agreements made with social scientists which
originate in a federal bureaucracy. Most research on Thailand and
Southeast Asia or on Pax Americana is contract work. Grants can
be considered as those projects which are initiated by the social scientists. Nonetheless, the distinction between contracts and grants
should not be drawn too sharply since, in fact if not in law, many
contracts do originate with social scientists. Such agreements may
be structured broadly to give the researcher a vast range of freedom or they may be narrowly conceived to get a project tailored to
an agency's "needs." The entrepreneurial spirit of social scientists,
particularly those working in nonacademic research centers,
makes them ingeniously adept at discovering what a government

administrator is ready to pay for. Thus, while a de jure distinction between contracts and grants is useful, it is limited on de facto grounds by the inability to track down who originates a proposal and also who really shapes the final project.

Perhaps more important than the formal distinction between contracts and grants is the disproportionate funds made available by various federal agencies for social scientific purposes. The Department of Defense in the fiscal year 1967 budgeted 21.7 percent of its research funds for the social sciences. The Department of State budgeted only 1.6 percent of its funds for the social sciences, and most of this was in the separately administered Agency for International Development. This disparity indicates that the "modern" Department of Defense (DOD) is far readier to make use of social science results than is the "traditional" Department of State. A related complaint is that most contracts issued, in contrast to grants awarded by agencies such as the U.S. Department of Health, Education and Welfare (HEW) or the National Institute of Health (NIH), allocate little money for free-floating research. Funds are targeted so directly and budgeted so carefully that, with the exception of the overhead portion which is controlled by administrators rather than scholars, little elasticity is permitted for work that may be allied to but not directly connected with the specific purpose of the contract itself. This contrasts markedly with contracts made with many physical scientists and even with researchers in the field of mental health, who are often able to set aside a portion of their funds for innovative purposes. Even so-called "kept" organizations such as the Institute for Defense Analysis (IDA), System Development Corporation (SDC), or RAND enjoy more latitude in developing their work programs than the usual "free" university researchers.

Related to this matter of financial reward for "hardware" and "high payoff" research is the funding available for social science research as a whole. Social scientists often claim that the funding structure is irrational. Government funds are available for individual scholarly efforts. The government reinforces big-team research by encouraging large-scale grants administered by agencies and institutes and by its stubborn unwillingness to contribute to individual scholarly enterprise. The assumption is made that large-scale ideas can be executed only by large-scale spending—a fallacy in logic, if not in plain fact. Large-scale grants are also made because they minimize bureaucratic opposition within the government and eliminate specific responsibility for research failures. At the same time, this approach contributes to the dilemma of the scholar who is concerned with research at modest "retail" levels, which may be far more limited than the grant proposal itself indicates. The present contract structure encourages a degree of entrepreneurial hypocrisy which is often alien to the spirit of the individual researcher and costly to the purchaser of ideas and plans. And while individual agency efforts, notably by the National Science Foundation, have moved counter to this bureaucratic trend, the bulk of funds continues to be made available without much regard for the persons actually engaged in the researches.

Social scientists have become increasingly critical of the government's established norms of secrecy. The professional orientation of social scientists has normally been directed toward publicity rather than secrecy. This fosters sharp differences in opinion and attitudes between the polity and the academy since their reward systems for career advancement are so clearly polarized. The question of secrecy is intimately connected with matters of policy because the standing rule of policy-makers (particularly in the field of foreign affairs) is not to reveal themselves entirely. No government in the game of international politics feels that its policies can be candidly revealed for full public review; therefore, operational research done in connection with policy considerations is customarily bound by the canons of government privacy. While social scientists have a fetish for publicizing their information, in part as a mechanism for professional advancement no less than as a definition of their essential role in the society, the political branches of society have as their fetish the protection of private documents and privileged information. Therefore, the polity places a premium not only on acquiring vital information but also on maintaining silence about such information precisely in the degree that the data might be of high decisional value. This norm leads to differing premiums between analysts and policy-makers and tensions between them.

Social scientists complain that the norm of secrecy often demands that they sacrifice their own essential work premises. A critical factor reinforcing the unwilling acceptance of the norm of secrecy by social scientists is that a great many government research funds are allocated for military or semimilitary purposes. U.S. Senate testimony has shown that approximately 50 percent of federal funds targeted for the social sciences are subject to some sort of federal review check. The real wonder turns out to be not the existence of restrictions on the use of social science findings but the relative availability of large chunks of information. Indeed, the classification of materials is so inept that documents (such as the Pax Americana research) designated as confidential or secret by one agency may often be made available as a "public service" by another agency. There are also occasions when documents that sponsoring government agencies place in a classified category can be secured without charge from the private research institute doing the work.

The main point is that relating the norm of secrecy to extreme patriotism makes it that much more difficult to question the research design itself. Social scientists often express the nagging doubt that accepting the first premise—the right of the government to maintain secrecy—often necessitates acceptance of a further premise, the necessity for silence on the part of social researchers who may disagree with the political uses of their efforts. The demand for secrecy has its most telling impact on social science methodology. Presumably, social scientists are employed because they, as a group, represent objectivity and honesty. Social scientists like to envision themselves as a wall of truth off which policy-makers may bounce their premises. They also like to think that they provide information that cannnot be derived from sheer public opinion. In some degree social scientists consider that they are hired or utilized by government agencies because they will say things that may be unpopular but nonetheless significant. Thus, the very agencies that contract out their "need to know" impose a norm of secrecy which strains the premises upon which most social scientists seek to work.

Terms of research and conditions of work tend to demand an initial compromise with methodology. The social scientist is placed in a cognitive bind. He is conditioned not to reveal maximum information lest he become victimized by the federal agencies who employ his services. Yet he is employed precisely because of his presumed thoroughness, impartiality and candor. The social scientist who survives in government service becomes "gingerly," or learns to play the game. His value to social science becomes seriously jeopardized. On the other hand, if he should raise these considerations his usefulness to the policy-making sector is likewise jeopardized. Social scientists believe that openness involves more than meeting formal requirements of scientific canons; it also requires that information be made universally available. The norm of secrecy encourages selective presentation of data. In this area the social scientist is opposed by the policy-maker because of conflicting notions of the significance of data and their general need to be replicated elsewhere and by others. The policy-maker who demands differential access to findings considers this a normal price extracted for the initial expenditure of risk capital. The academic social scientist has a general attitude that sponsorship of research does not entitle any one sector to benefit unduly from the findings; he believes that sponsorship by federal agencies ought not to place limits on the use of work done any more than when research is sponsored by private agencies or by universities.

The third major area which deeply concerns the social scientists is that of dual allegiance. The social scientist often expresses the charge that government work has such specific requirements and goal-oriented tasks that it intrudes upon his autonomy. He is compelled to choose between full participation in the world of the federal bureaucracy and his more familiar academic confines. He does not, however, want the former to create isolation in the latter. He thus often criticizes the federal bureaucracy's unwillingness to recognize his basic needs: (a) the need to teach and retain a full academic identity; (b) the need to publicize information; and, above all, (c) the need to place scientific responsibility above the call of patriotic obligation, when they may happen to clash. In short, he does not want to be plagued by dual or competing allegiances. The norm of secrecy exacerbates this problem. While many of the social scientists who become involved with federal research are intrigued by the opportunity to address important issues, they are confronted by bureaucracies that often do not share their passion for resolving social problems. For example, federal obligations commit the bureaucracy to assign high priority to items having military potential and effectiveness and low priorities to many idealistic themes in which social scientists are interested.

The social scientists connected to the government as employees or as consultants are hamstrung by federal agencies, which are, in turn, limited by political circumstances beyond their control. A federal bureaucracy must manage cumbersome, overgrown committees and data-gathering agencies. Federal agencies often protect a status quo merely for the sake of rational functioning. They must conceive of the academic in their midst as a standard bureaucratic type entitled to rise to certain federal ranks. Federal agencies limit innovating concepts simply to what is immediately useful, not out of choice and certainly not out of resentment to the social sciences, but from what is deemed as impersonal necessity. This has the effect of reducing the social scientist's role in the government to that of ally or advocate rather than that of innovator or designer. Social scientists, particularly those with strong academic allegiances, begin to feel that their enthusiasm for rapid change is unrealistic considering how little can be done by the government bureaucracy. And they come to resent the involvement in theory-less application to immediacy foisted on them by the "New Utopians," along with surrender of the value of confronting men with the wide range of possible choices of action. The schism between autonomy and involvement is, in its own way, as thorough as that between secrecy and publicity, for it cuts to the quick well-intentioned pretensions at human engineering.

The problem of competing allegiances is not made simpler by the fact that many high-ranking federal bureaucrats have strongly nationalistic and conservative political ideologies in marked contrast with the social scientist. The social scientist comes to the nation's capital not only believing in the primacy of science over nationalism but also defining what is patriotic in a more open-ended and consciously liberal manner than that of most appointed officials. Hence, he often perceives that the conflict involves more than research design and social applicability; it is a consequence of the incompatible ideologies held respectively by the social scientists and entrenched Washington bureaucrats. He comes to resent the "proprietary" attitude of the bureaucrat toward "his" government processes. He is likely to conclude that his social biases are a necessary buffer against the federal bureaucracy.

A question arising with greater frequency now that many social scientists are doing federally sponsored research concerns the relationship between heuristic and valuative aspects of work. Put plainly, should the social scientist not only supply an operational framework of information but also assist in the creation of a viable ideological framework? Does he have the right to discuss, examine and prescribe the goals of social research for social science? Whether social scientists in government service ever raise such issues is less important than the fact that some might refuse any connection with the federal bureaucracy for this reason. Many social scientists, especially those working on foreign area research, bitterly complain that government policy-makers envision social science to be limited to heuristics, to supplying operational code books and facts about our own and other societies, and that the social scientist is supposed to perform maintenance services for military missions. Social scientists, however, also consider their work in terms of its normative function, in terms of the principles and goals of foreign and domestic policy. Given their small tolerance for error, policy-makers cannot absorb mistaken evaluations. This inhibits the social scientist's long-range evaluations and renders empiricism the common denominator of investigation. Factual presentations become not only "value free" but "trouble free."

This is not so much indicative of a choice between pure and applied social science research as a consequence of differing perspectives on the character of application. Social scientists working for the political establishment realize that applied research is clearly here to stay. They are the first to announce that it is probably the most novel element in American—in contrast to European—social science. But federal bureaucrats operate with a concept of application that often removes theoretical considerations from research. Designing the future out of present-day hard facts, rather than analyzing types of action and interests and their relations in the present, comes to stand for a limited administrative Utopianism and creates the illusion that demands for theory and candid ideological commitment have been met.

The social world is constructed like a behavioral field, the dynamics and manipulation of which are reserved for policy-makers, upon which they design futures. But social scientists are aware that "interests" and their representative values are contending for influence on that field and that social planning is often a matter of choosing among these values for the sake of political goals. Thus, tension arises between social scientists, who consider their work set in highly political terms, and federal bureaucrats, who prefer to consider the work of the social scientists in nonpolitical terms. Indeed, federal administrators particularly go out of their way to depoliticize the results of potentially volatile social research so as to render it a better legitimizing device for their own bureaucratic activities. Social scientists come to suspect that their work is weighed for efficiency and applicability to an immediate and limited situation. The ability of the social system to confront large-scale and long-standing problems is left out of reckoning.

Federal bureaucrats measure the rewards of social science involvement in the government in terms of payoffs generated. These are conceived to be the result of "big-team" research involving heavy funding (like the Model Cities Program). Moreover, the high status of individuals is appreciated when they are at the center rather than the periphery of policy performance, having an opportunity to influence policy at high levels, to secure valuable information and to give prestige to projects in which they participate. And, it might be added, many social scientists who contract research from the government seek just such power rewards.

Even those social scientists most involved with the government—as employees rather than as marginal consultants—express profound reservations about the reward system. First, as we have noted, social scientists operate under various degrees of secrecy that stifle their urge toward publicity for the work they do. Recognition goes instead to the men they work for. Second, social scientists must share responsibility for policy mistakes. Thus, they may be targeted for public criticism under difficult conditions more frequently than praised when they perform their duties well. Finally, those social scientists closest to policy agencies are most subject to congressional inquiry and to forms of harassment and investigation unlike anything that may befall strictly academic men.

The government-employed social scientist runs risks to which his colleagues at universities are not subject. He often contends that these risks are not properly understood by academics or rewarded by policy-makers (salary scales, for example, are adequate in federal work but not noticeably higher than academic salaries). Marginal financial payoffs resulting from publication are often denied the federally sponsored social scientists. Publication is a sensitive area for other reasons. Social scientists' fears concerning their removal from channels of professional respectability and visibility seem to increase proportionately to their distance from the academy. Few of those in federal work receive recognition from their own professional societies and few gain influential positions within these professional establishments. The marginality produced by federal work means that scholars willing to be funded through government agencies, or even to accept consultantships, will reject primary association with a federal administration. For this reason the list of high-quality social scientists who choose to remain in the government as professional civil servants remains low.

While outsiders may accuse federally sponsored social scientists of "selling out," the latter defend themselves by pointing out that they make sacrifices for the sake of positively influencing social change. This self-defense, however, is often received skeptically by their colleagues in the academic arena (as well as by their would-be supporters in the federal bureaucracy), who regard such hypersensitive moralism with suspicion. The upshot of this matter of "rewards" is, then, that status derived from proximity to sources of power if offset by isolation from the actual wielders of power— academic no less than political.

PROBLEM AREAS PERCEIVED BY THE POLITICIANS

Social scientists' complaints about their difficulties with government-sponsored research have received more attention than administrative complaints against social scientists simply because social scientists tend to be more articulate in examining their feelings and in registering their complaints about the work they do. Also, the relationship of the social scientist to the bureaucrat has a greater import for the social scientist than for the bureaucrat. It is small wonder that government complaints about social scientists have been poorly understood.

Federal agencies and their bureaucratic leaderships remain skeptical about the necessity for employing basic social science data in their own formulations. Among traditionally appointed officials the local lawyer or party worker is the key means for transmitting information upward. For many sectors of the military, expertise comes mainly from military personnel performing military functions and does not require outside social science validation. As we witnessed in the military response to the Department of Defense "Whiz Kids," outside efforts may be considered intrusions. High military brass (as well as a number of politicians) "sounded off" hotly against the Defense Department and echoed in their critiques a traditional posture that pits military intuition and empirical proximity to the real world against mathematical techniques and "ivory tower" orientations.

When social scientists attempt to combat these doubts and suspicions by preparing memoranda and documents to prove the efficacy of social science for direct political and military use, they may do more to reinforce negative sentiments than to overcome them. When the academy responds that way to the polity (as it did in its recommendations to the Defense Science Board), then it underwrites its own lack of autonomy, if not its own ineptitude. It cannot prove its worth by moral declarations and public offerings to bureaucratic agencies. The total service orientation of social research, in contrast with the independent "feudal" academic orientation, is one that breeds contempt for the performer of such services and a lack of faith in his results. This helps to explain the resentment for social science research extending from the Joint Chiefs of Staff to the Senate Foreign Relations Committee. Suppliers of intellectual labor are well paid if they have a powerful union or guild—as many social sciences have—but they hardly command high status in a political atmosphere which strains toward quick and inexpensive solutions.

The first and perhaps most significant criticism made by administrators against the academy is that social scientists make excessive demands for funds and special treatment while working on projects that frequently have little tactical value. This is translated into a charge of impracticality. Typical is the critique made by the General Accounting Office against the Hudson Institute, headed by defense strategist Herman Kuhn. Underlining charges made by the Office of Civil Defense, the work of the Hudson Institute in the area of the behavioral sciences was scored for being "less useful than had been expected" and cited as unacceptable without "major revision." Various social science reports, particularly those prepared by semiprivate agencies, have been criticized for their superficiality, for their "tired" thinking, for their sensationalism and, above all, for their lack of immediate relevance. In response, social researchers claim that the purpose of a good report is imaginative effort rather than practical settlement of all outstanding issues. Government agencies should not expect a high rate of success on every research attempt, they argue. One reason for the persistence of this line of criticism is that demands for high-payoff utilitarian research are rarely contested. The questionable practicality of much social science research remains a sore point in the relationship which cannot be resolved until and unless social scientists themselves work out a comfortable formula governing the worth of relevance in contrast with the demand for relevance.

Another criticism leveled at academics by federal sponsors issues from the first: namely, that there are no systems for ensuring that results obtained in research are usable. A gap exists between the proposal and fulfillment stages of a research undertaking and there is an equally wide gap between the results obtained and the processes involved in grappling with problems. Proposals that are handsomely drawn up and attractively packaged often have disappointing results. And while many sophisticated agencies, such as NIH (National Institutes of Health), NSF (National Science Foundation) or OEO (Office of Economic Opportunity), are aware of the need for permissiveness in research design, those agencies more firmly rooted in hard science and engineering traditions are not so tolerant of such experimentations. Moreover, it is charged that academics engaged in government research "overconservatize" their responses to placate a federal bureaucracy. This may come, however, at the very point when the administrator is trying to establish some liberal policy departures. The chore of the federal agency becomes much more difficult since it must cope not only with bureaucratic sloth and the conservative bias of top officials but also with reinforcements for it in research reports by the social scientists from whom more liberal formulations might have been expected. Thus, not only is there a gap between proposal stage and fulfillment stage in the research enterprise, but also some reports may structure conservative biases into the programs assigned to the federal bureaucracy by congressional committees or by executive branch leadership.

The charge of inutility is often related to a differential intellectual style or culture. The government-versus-academy cleavage is largely a consequence of intellectual specialization of a kind that makes it difficult for the typical bureaucrat to talk meaningfully with the typical "modern" behavioral scientists. Most government officers in the Department of State, for example, are trained either in history or in a political science of a normative sort. International relations taught in the descriptive traditions of the twenties or, at the latest, in the style of a Morgenthau or a Schuman continue to prevail. Whatever difficulties may exist between the academy and the polity at the level of role performance, these can at least be overcome by those who share a common intellectual formation. But often communication cannot be achieved with those behaviorists whose vocabulary, methods and even concepts seem esoteric, irrelevant, occasionally trivial and not rarely fraudulent. Thus, at the root of the charge of inutility is a conflict of intellectual cultures that negatively affects the relations between the academics and the politicians.

Federal administrators point out that academic men often demand deferential treatment, contrary to the norms that govern other federal employees. They charge that social science personnel do not really accept their role as government employees but rather see themselves as transiently or marginally connected to the government. Particularly in areas of foreign affairs, the academic appears to want the advantages of being privy to all kinds of quasisecret information and of being involved in decision-making, yet avoiding normal responsibilities that are accepted by other government employees.

Such attitudes smack of elitism to federal officials, an elitism built into the structure of social scientific thinking. Trained to analyze problems rather than to convince constituencies, social scientists become impatient with the vagaries of politics, preferring the challenge of policy. One reason adduced by elected officials for preferring legal rather than scientific advisors is that the former have a far keener appreciation of mechanisms for governing people and being governed by them. The legal culture breeds a respect for the "popular will" rarely found among social scientists attached to government agencies. Indeed, the resentment expressed by many House and Senate committees against Defense Department and State Department social scientists is a direct response to the elitist streak that seems to characterize social scientists in government.

This is the reverse side of the "involvement-autonomy" debate. The government pushes for total involvement and participation while the social scientist presses for autonomy and limited responsibility in decisions directly affecting policy. Elitism rationalizes the performance of important service while enabling the social scientist to maintain the appearance of detachment. Although social scientists view their own federal involvement as marginal, at the same time they demand access to top elites so that they may be assured their recommendations will be implemented or at least seriously considered. But access at this level entails bypassing the standard bureaucratic channels through which other federal employees must go.

The social scientist's demand for elite accessibility, though said to be inspired by noble purpose, tends to set him apart from other employees of the federal government. He sees himself as an advising expert instead of an employee. The social scientist takes himself seriously as an appointed official playing a political role in a way that most other federal workers do not. The federal bureaucracy finds the social scientist has come to Washington to "set the world on fire" along with a presumptuous intention, one unmindful of the flame that also burns in the heart of the staff administrator.

The question of ready access to leadership rests on notions of the superior wisdom of the social scientist; however, it is precisely this claim that is most sharply contested by federal administrators. Reflecting popular biases, administrators claim that the easy admission of social scientists to the halls of power presumes a correctness in their policy judgments not supported by historical events and not warranted by mass support from popular sectors. The separation of science and citizen roles often justifies lack of citizen participation. The scientific ethos thus comes to serve as a basis for admission into a system of power by circumventing the civic culture. This precisely is why federal bureaucrats feel that they are defending their political constituencies (and not, incidentally, their own bailiwicks) by limiting social science participation in the decision-making process.

If social scientists chafe at being outside the mainstream of academic life during their period of involvement with the political system, the federal bureaucrats are themselves highly piqued by the degree of supplemental employment enjoyed and desired by the social scientists. Also, in clear contrast with other federal governmental personnel, social scientists are able to locate supplemental positions in the Washington, D.C., area. They work as teachers and professors; they do writing on the side for newspapers and magazines; they edit books and monographs; they offer themselves as specialist consultants capitalizing on their government involvement. They become active in self-promotion to a degree far beyond the reasons for their being hired.

In the more loosely structured world of the academy, such self-promotion not only goes uncriticized but is rewarded. Royalty payments for textbook writing, involvement with publishing firms in editorial capacities, honoraria connected with membership in granting agencies and payments for lectures on American campuses are all highly respected forms of supplemental "employment." But federal government employment involves 12 months a year and 24 hours a day. This condition and its demands are far different from the nine months a year and fluid scheduling endemic to most social scientist relations with academic institutions. Federal agencies disdain the marginal aspects of the academics' involvement in political life, and their awareness that men involved in government effort are often enough not representative of the most outstanding talent available in the social sciences also disturbs them, particularly because they traffic in the status spinoff of both the academy and the polity. The anomaly exists that men who may not have been especially successful in academic life make demands upon the federal bureaucracy as if in fact they were the most outstanding representatives of their fields. The same problems might well arise in connection with outstanding representatives from the social sciences, but the situation becomes exacerbated precisely because the federal bureaucrats know they are dealing with—at least in many instances—second- or even third-echelon federally employed social scientists.

IMPROVING INTERACTION

In this profile, the academics and federal administrators alike have been presented as more uniform in their responses to each other than is actually the case. It should not be imagined that the two groups spend all their time in bickering criticism of each other, for then certainly no stable relationship worth speaking of could exist. Still, the roles acted out by both parties make it clear that we are in a period of extensive redefinition. The criticisms that academics and politicos have of each other often have a mirror-image effect, each side sharply focusing on the least commendable features of the other. Significantly, the political context and content of this issue has in the main been unconsciously suppressed by both sides. The academics have preferred to emphasize their scientific activities in objective and neutral terminology while the politicos express their interests in organizational and bureaucratic terms. The strangest aspect of this interaction, then, is that in the world of politics it seems that nothing is more embarrassing than political analysis and synthesis. As if by common consent, social scientists and policy-makers have agreed to conduct their relations by a code of genteel disdain rather than open confrontation. The gulf between the two groups requires political distance as an operational equivalent to the social distance between competing tribal villagers.

There may be cause for concern that federal government sponsorship corrupts the character of social science output because it emphasizes big money, an overly practical orientation and limited dissemination of information, and because it fails to accept that any research may be potentially subversive. But, ironically, timid or opportunistic social scientific personnel are not recruited by the government. Most often the social scientist seeks the federal sponsor and becomes overly ambitious in the process of pressing exag-

gerated claims for unique research designs and high-payoff promises. The chief danger for the academic who has come to depend on
the federal bureaucracy for research funds and its variety of career
satisfactions is not more financial dependence; rather, it is that he
may begin to develop the loyalties and cautionary temperament of
the opportunistic civil servant per se.

Many interlocking appointments between the academy and the
polity have occurred at the organizational level without resolving
persistent questions as to what constitutes legitimate interaction
between social science and public policy. This indicates that the
line between the academy and the polity is blurred enough to
require precise determination of exactly who is stimulating what
kind of research and under what conditions. As it becomes increasingly clear that social scientists are the stimulants and administrators the respondents in a majority of instances, it becomes obvious
also that criticism must be leveled at social science participation
rather than at federal practice. To understand fully the sources of
tension in the interaction between academics and administrators, it
is necessary to illuminate the range of attitudes toward connection
between the government and the academy, which extends from advocating complete integration between administrators and academics to calling for complete rupture between the two groups. A
spectrum of positions is presented on this matter.

The quarter of a century from 1945 to 1970 represents a range of
attitudes from complete integration to complete rupture. From
World War II, and even prior to that during the era of the New
Deal, optimism prevailed about an integrated relationship between
academics and administrators. This was perhaps best expressed by
the "policy-science" approach frequently associated with the work
of Harold Lasswell.[1] In his view the relationship between social
science and the political networks would be an internal affair, with
political men involved in scientific affairs just as frequently and as
fully as scientific men would be involved in political affairs. The
policy-science approach was a noble effort to redefine familiar
departmental divisions of labor. Sociology, political science, economics and the other social sciences would be absorbed by a unified policy science that involved a common methodological core.
The problem with this exchange network, as Lasswell himself well
understood in later years, is that federal administrators spoke with
the presumed authority of the "garrison state," while academics
(even those temporarily in government service) spoke with the pre-

sumed impracticality of the "ivory tower."

The policy-science approach did in fact have direct policy consequences. The end of World War II and the fifties saw the rise of new forms of institutional arrangements for housing social science. But more than organization was involved. A new emphasis cut across disciplinary boundaries. Area studies emerged in every major university. Communism was studied as part of the more general problem of the role of ideology in social change. This was followed by centers for urban studies and the study of industrial and labor relations. But despite the rise of institutionalized methods for uniting specialities, university department structures had a strange way of persisting, not just as lingering fossils but as expanding spheres of influence. It soon became apparent that in the struggle to influence the graduate student world and to decide who shall or shall not be appointed and promoted in university positions the "department" held final authority. The separate departments of social sciences enabled the disciplines to retain their vitality. At the same time that the policy-science approach was confronting departmentalism, disciplinary specialization was increasing. During the postwar period, anthropology insisted on departmental arrangements distinguishing it from sociology and theology, while other areas such as political science and social work became more sharply delineated than ever before. The policy-science approach was able to institutionalize all sorts of aggressive and, at times, even progressive reorderings of available information, but failed to establish the existence of a policy-science organization. And this proved fatal to its claims for operational primacy.

The policy-science approach of the fifties was supplanted by the "handmaiden" approach of the early sixties in which social science was to supply the necessary ingredients to make the political world function smoothly. The reasoning was that the social sciences were uniquely qualified to instill styles in federal decision-making based on confirmed data. But this was not to entail complete integration of services and functions. This handmaiden approach was considered more suitable to the nature of both the sciences and the policy-making aspects of government, and was materially assisted by a rising emphasis on applied social research. The new emphasis on application and on large-scale research provided the theoretical rationale for janitorial "mop-up" services. Applied research was to make the search for the big news, for the vital thrust; participation in this intimate consensual arrangement would deprive the social sciences of their freedom but would guarantee relevance. The "theoryless" service approach was thus wedded to an action orientation.

Advocates of the handmaiden approach such as Ithiel de Sola Pool[2] vigorously defended social scientists' obligation to do meaningful research for government. It was noted that an organization like the Department of Defense has manifold needs for the tools of social science analysis as a means for better understanding its world. It was pointed out that the intelligence test had been an operational instrument in manpower management since World War I and that the Defense Department and other federal agencies had become major users of social psychology in military and sensitive areas. As the world's largest training and educational institution, the U.S. government had to acquire exact knowledge for the selection and training of an enormous number of human subjects. Equally significant was the federal government's needs for exact foreign area information. This thirst for knowledge of the particular cultural values and social and political structures of foreign countries increased as the world was carved up into potential enemies or potential allies of the United States.

The ironic aspect of this support for useful research is that although the handmaiden approach ostensibly left social science autonomy intact, it reduced that autonomy in fact by establishing criteria for federal rather than social science "payoff." High-yield research areas uniformly involved what the social sciences could do for the political structures and not necessarily the other way around. Thus, while the policy-science approach gave way to the service industry orientation of the handmaiden approach, the latter, too, was not based on any real parity between the academy and the polity.

A new approach, considerably removed from both the policy-science and handmaiden approaches, has been finely articulated by David B. Truman.[3] As theory, it expresses a renewed sense of equity and parity between social scientists and administrators. Under Truman's arrangement there would be frequent but largely unplanned interchanges between federal bureaucratic positions and university positions. This exchange of roles would prove valuable and could eventually be explored and encouraged on a systematic basis. Meanwhile, the selective participation approach advocates minimal formal structure in the system.

The most important aspect of the selective participation approach is that it is based upon a norm of reciprocity. A partial interchange of personnel could be accomplished primarily through regular seminars and conferences mutually attended by social scientists and government administrators, each cluster of men representing carefully designed combinations. Another method might be alternating presentations of scientific development and policy problems at these meetings. Unlike the normal consultant relationship of the handmaiden style, this would guarantee some kind of equity between the academy and the polity. Selective participation would include securing grants and promoting federal research for multidisciplinary teams of academics working on political problems, instead of the usual outright political employment of individual social scientists or academic talent. This, it was hoped, would provide a flexible arrangement of specialties that would fill the gap between scientific knowledge and public purpose without detriment either to social scientists or political policy-makers. Operationally, it meant a greater flow of funds from government agencies to research institutes housed on university campuses, a not inconsequential change over the policy-science approach, which projected a much more intimate ecological as well as ideological network.

The dilemma was that the selective participation approach implicitly assumed an exchange network with a parity of strength between political decision-makers and academics. The approach failed to demonstrate that the academic would be on a par with the administrator, for the latter had financial inputs while the former had the informational outputs. In point of fact the government agency still does the hiring, even in the selective participation approach; and the academics participate in a policy-making role without much expectancy of a payoff for social science theory or methodology.

This had given rise to what might be called the principle of "nonparticipation," which is increasingly being adopted. Social scientists continue to write and publish in areas of foreign research or in sectors vital to the national political arena but do not do so under government contract or as a direct response to a federal agency. It was felt that if the autonomy of the social sciences means anything at all, uses and findings legitimately arrived at will be incorporated into federal policy-making whether or not social scientists participate actively or critically. The principle of nonparticipation tended to be adopted by many conservative as well as radical social scientists who saw in the growth of federal social research a threat to the standard forms of status advancement in the professions and also a movement toward applied social planning which violated their own feeling for the generalizing nature of social science. On organizational and intellectual grounds, the principle of nonparticipation served as an effective response to the policy-science approach. The underlying assumption of the notion of nonparticipation is that the federal government has more to gain than does the social scientist by the interaction between them. Although interaction would be maintained, the order of priorities would be changed so that social scientists no longer would have the onerous task of providing high-payoff research for others with low yields to themselves.

In many ways the principle of nonparticipation suggested that the university department remain the primary agency in the organization of social science instead of the federal research bureau. The nonparticipant in federal programs often found himself to be the critic of bureaucratic research in general and of bureaucratic agencies attached to universities in particular. He did not want to have his research controlled by federal decision-making; more importantly, he did not want a federal agency to usurp what was properly a judgment in the domain of a university department. At the same time, the principle of nonparticipation spilled over into the principle of active opposition. This opposition was registered in the main by younger scholars in areas such as history and by graduate students in the social sciences, that is, among those often involved in student protest movements. From their point of view the matter could not be resolved on the essentially conservative grounds of selective use by the government of the best of social science. A conscious attempt must be made to utilize scholarship for partisan or revolutionary goals, which could under no circumstances be employed by the establishments linked to government agencies. As Hans Morgenthau indicated, this represented a movement away from the belief that the social scientist and the federal administrator inhabited mutually exclusive institutions to a belief in a more active opposition because they occupied mutually hostile positions with antithetical goals.

In one sense, the radical posture accepts the policy-science appraisal of a political world dominated by the "garrison state" but rejects its remedy of social science immersion to reorient government away from its predatory world missions. The policy-science view assumed the educability of military-minded rulers. The antiparticipation view assumes the reverse, namely, the ease with which social scientists become incorporated into the military and political goals of men of power.

Radical critics like John McDermott assert that in practice the goals of the academy and the polity have become antithetical. Furthermore, they say that, theoretically, they ought to be antithetical. A transformation of the dream of action into the nightmare of federal participation, in which the academy became in effect an adjunct of the federal establishment, has been brought about. Academic social scientists' dream of position and prestige has in some sense been realized by their transformation into men of action: academic men have become high priests of social change. The desire for social change has, in effect, overwhelmed the goals toward which such change was directed.

The move toward active opposition is a critique of the way in which the university, no less than the government, is structured. Those who moved away from federal participation simultaneously turned their energies on the university system. They hold that the academy itself, as beneficiary of federal funds, has become the political party of the academic man. The rash of student attacks against the university must be considered as, in part at least, symbolic attacks against the notion of integration of policy-making and academic performance. The most well-guarded nonsecret of the present era of university relationships to the government, at least insofar as these ties bear upon the notion of active opposition, concerns the general political and ideological climate that now prevails. Surrogate politics has now become a rooted pattern in American academic affairs, partly because academics come to politics by way of moral concern, while politicians come to moral concerns by way of political participation. Surrogate politics is also a reflex action of the expanding articulate but impotent social sectors against what have become the dominant political trends of the United States at this time.

Surrogate politics has its place in national affairs. Indeed, the question of the relationship between the academy and the polity is precisely a question of surrogate politics. A common undercurrent of moral revulsion for professional hucksterism and amateur gamesmanship has forced the present review of the status between social scientists and policy-makers. This same reexamination should have taken place a quarter of a century ago, despite the difficulties of the situation. But precisely because of the optimal consensus that existed in the past concerning the political climate, the issues now being discussed were considered improper topics for social scientists in pursuit of truth.

During the 1941-45 period, when the United States was engaged in a world conflict in which the overwhelming number of citizens felt involved in the very survival of civilization itself, there were no pained expressions about government recruiting on campuses. There was no resentment toward the retooling of universities to satisfy military research needs and psychological warfare, propaganda research or conventional bombing surveys. Nor were any scholarly panels held at professional meetings concerning the propriety of social scientists who accepted appointments under the Roosevelt administration in the Office of War Information or in the Office of Strategic Services, such as those panels which now discuss the propriety of relationships between social scientists and the Federal Bureau of Investigation or the Central Intelligence Agency.

Between 1946 and 1960, or the end of World War II and the beginning of the Kennedy era, the United States was involved in a cold war with the Soviet Union as its primary protaganist. We obviously are not here concerned either with the origins or sources of the cold war but with the fact of its existence. It was during this period that social science was perhaps most partisan in its commitment to the American foreign policy posture. This partisanship was manifested in many ways: the rise of think tanks with direct federal sponsorship for applied social science research, the emergence of specialized centers such as Russian centers, Southeast Asian centers, Latin American research councils, that once more were harnessed to the tasks of American foreign policy. Beyond that was the automatic assumption that social science did indeed have values, the values of the American century. The anciful illusion that this did not constitute an ideology was nothing more than a chimera behind which the values of social science meshed more perfectly, either before or since, with the tasks of American foreign policy.

This same era was not so much one of transition from wartime to peacetime, but rather a movement from an overt world struggle between democracy (then defined as both capitalist and Socialist in character) and fascism to capitalism and communism. As a result, this specific era witnessed in the West a growing resurgence of private enterprise. But in the United States, at least, this resurgence was more ideological than organizational. The bulk of funding for research and development continued to flow in ever-increasing amounts from public government sources. As a result, the real gap between state capitalism and state communism was far narrower in practice than in theory. It has been noted that this was also the period in which the real gap between scientific disciplines diminished to a commensurate degree.[4] This ambiguous line between disciplines reflected itself specifically in the emergence of task-oriented social research. The rise of "team" efforts, oriented toward predetermined "projects" had the result of making policy central. The scientific background of key personnel mattered far less than the social (or as it sometimes turned out antisocial) goals of the research design.

Between 1960 (the beginnings of the thaw) and 1972 (the end of the Vietnamese conflict) controversy over the relationship between social science and political performance increased in both intensity and quantity. The breakdown of the consensus was evident within the social scientific communities by a series of surrogate discussions over the legitimacy of the war in Vietnam, Latin American self-determination or civil strife in American ghettos. Unable to address such issues directly and unprepared to design structures for future alleviation of such world and national pressures, social scientists exaggerate the politics of inner organizational life. Professional societies engage in mimetic reproduction of central social concerns on a low-risk and probably a low-yield bases.

Organizational struggles also received, during this period, the encouragement and support of corresponding professional people and societies from the Third World and from minority groups. It is no accident that federal projects that had Latin American targets have come under particularly severe assault. The existence of a counter- social science establishment in countries such as Mexico, Chile, Argentina and Brazil provides vocal support for domestic United States academic opposition and for firming up such opposition by posing the threat of total isolation from foreign area research for a failure to heed the dangers of certain kinds of political research. Increasingly, black militants in this country have adopted a similar posture of nonparticipation in social science projects without clearly stating preconditons of protection of the "rights" of the subjects or sovereigns.

Since 1972 the fervor over heedless involvement in policy has eased considerably. However, the feeling that social science should still remain a respectable distance from policy has had a residual impact. The emergence of a détente between the United States and the Soviet Union and the reestablishment of diplomatic relationships between the United States and China, coupled internally with a growing conservatism with respect to the rights of the poor and the need for further welfare measures, has led to a situation in which social scientists have become increasingly aware of the commodity value of their researches and the mandarin effects of their findings. Thus, while the amount of social science activity has increased between 1941 and 1974 almost as a constant, the character of the association between the social scientists and the political establishment has been tremendously altered over time. The likelihood is that this pattern will continue into the foreseeable future. The very emergence of the game theory as a concept replacing organicism subjects the social sciences themselves to the very analysis they have placed the political actors under. As a result, the line between social science and political action may have blurred, while at the same time the worth of each to the other has never been more intensely felt.

On the other side of the river among the policy-making and evaluating sectors, the demand for social science research findings among government agencies continues unabated, despite reticence on the part of some sectors of the social science community to supply such information, and beyond that, the relatively desultory results thus far obtained in the areas of applied social research. In a recent report before the American Association for Public Opinion Research, Nathan Caplan noted the following: (1) There is a need felt among most federal officials to find better ways of plugging research into the decision-making process. (2) Top officials get most of their social science news from newspapers. (3) Policymakers see the need for more large-scale, community-based social experiments, such as the negative income tax study, along with a widening interest in developing noneconomic measures of social well being.[5] Social science research is used about as much as hard science data. Problems of utilization are generic and cut across the board, but top bureaucrats may be more suspicious about the validity and reliability of social science data. Even when policymakers cite physical science research, they are likely to notice social consequences first. For the money, the government probably gets its best utilization payoff from social science research. While there is a "motherhood" effect in support for getting information about noneconomic social indicators (94 percent of the respondents said it was needed) policy-makers make a distinction between survey research (valuable) and public opinion (not so reliable). Survey research was the third most frequently mentioned area of information needed from social science, following social experiments and quality of life. In terms of usefulness of science input, physics is at the top of the scale and psychiatry at the low end. Economics, psychology and sociology share the middle ground. When asked "Is it necessary to be familiar with the scientist in order to evaluate a set of findings?" almost half the users said "yes" for social science. The family is gaining importance as a research area as policy-makers become more concerned about family life alternatives, family arrangements, effects of family on child development. Despite this increased demand for policy-related social science, the teaching and learning of social science (both inside and outside of the university) and its relationship to public policy is still drastically underdeveloped and in need of further large-scale efforts among government and university structures alike.

One might say of social science what Walter Lippman long ago said of democracy: it is not a very good instrument for the making of public policy but it is about the best one available. Similarly, this does seen to be the case with the social sciences although on a less philosophical, more pragmatic basis than Lippmann initially had in mind. In the absence of a mass outpouring of democratic persuasion, and in the presence of political corruption in high office and political apathy among the ordinary citizens, the social sciences essentially perform the role of cementing American goals and presenting them in such a manner in which, at the very least, if it does not provide a rational solution to social problems it prevents an irrational solution from being adopted toward these same problems. This may not be saying much for the social sciences but it holds out considerably more promise than for any other method of political participation by the social science community under present conditions in American life.

NOTES

[1]Harold D. Lasswell, "The Policy Orientation," in *The Policy Sciences*, ed. H. D. Lasswell and D. Lerner (Stanford, Calif.: Stanford University Press, 1951).

[2]Ithiel de Sola Pool, "The Necessity for Social Scientists Doing Research for Governments," in *The Rise and Fall of Project Camelot: Studies in the Relationship Between Social Science and Practical Politics*, ed. I. L. Horowitz (Cam-

bridge, Mass.: MIT Press, 1967): 267-280.

[3]David B. Truman, "The Social Sciences and Public Policy," *Science* 160, 3827 (May 3, 1968): 508-512.

[4]Don K. Price, *The Scientific Estate* (Cambridge, Mass.: Harvard University Press, 1965): 5; Jean-Jacques Salomon, *Science and Politics* (Cambridge, Mass.: MIT Press, 1973): 46-48.

[5]Nathan Caplan, research cited in **Behavior Today** 5, 24 (June 17, 1974): 172-73.

8
On Being Useful:
The Nature and Consequences of
Psychological Research on Social Problems[1]

NATHAN CAPLAN and STEPHEN D. NELSON

There is considerable encouragement, support and pressure today for behavioral scientists to direct their attention away from the preoccupations of their vigorously irrelevant past and to engage in work with more obvious social utility. This move from peripheral functions at the edge of society to the more central activities of organized social planning enjoys the official sanction of two important study groups[3] and the promise of favorable financial support as exemplified by the National Science Foundation (RANN). Increased federal funding for "applied" research is already evident. Riecken[4] reported that from fiscal year 1968 to 1971, the total federal expenditures for basic research in the social sciences grew from $116 to $141 million, while federal expenditures for applied research during that same period grew from $134 to $257 million.

Those of us who have long felt that the social sciences have not met their social responsibility welcome this upsurge of interest in the problems of society. On the other hand, becoming useful is not as simple a matter as it might first appear. The application of psychological findings and thought to the improvement of societal functioning and human welfare is fraught with many potential problems. Our purpose here is to discuss some metaissues that raise doubts and uncertainties about the possible consequences of applying psychological thought and research—and the behavioral sciences in general—to the problems of society. We do this in hopes that both psychology as a profession and society as a whole may avoid potential pitfalls and unanticipated negative consequences that may ensue from injudiciously moving the orientation of psychology as a science into the public arena as a means for dealing with the problems that beset society.

To delimit the domain of "relevancy" with which this article is concerned we should emphasize three things: (a) in this article we deal with *social* policy and not other types of public policy issues; (b) our interest is in social policy at the national level, with nationwide implications; and (c) we are concerned with social problems and problem behavior, various kinds of so-called social pathology.

The discussion of these issues is organized into two parts. The first part deals with what may be called the "person-blame" causal attribution bias in psychological research on social problems. By this we mean the tendency to hold individuals responsible for their problems. Our concern is with (a) psychologically oriented research that focuses on "person-centered" characteristics (those that lie within the individual), while ignoring situationally relevant factors (those external to the individual); and (b) the tendency to attribute *causal* significance to person-centered variables found in statistical association with the social problem in question. Published research reports are used to illustrate this bias. In this section of the article we also discuss the social action implications of this person-blame bias and two major reasons for its prevalence among psychologists.

In the second part of the discussion we explore the utility and applicability of psychological thought and research to social problems within the framework of the issues raised in the first part of the discussion. Particular attention is given to the political implications and partisan advantages of person-blame interpretations and how unintended functions served by such a bias in causal attribution may become ends in themselves if well-meaning researchers continue to regard social research as if it were a neutral competency.

PROBLEM DEFINITIONS AND CAUSAL ATTRIBUTION BIAS IN PSYCHOLOGICAL RESEARCH

The Importance of Problem Definitions: Person Versus Situation

We have chosen to concentrate on problem-defining activities for three closely linked reasons.

1. First, what is done about a problem depends on how it is defined. The way a social problem is defined determines the attempts at remediation—or even whether such attempts will be made—by suggesting both the *foci* and the *techniques* of intervention and by ruling out alternative possibilities. More specifically, problem definition determines the change strategy, the selection of a social action delivery system and the criteria for evaluation.

Problem definitions are based on assumptions about the causes of the problem and where they lie.[5] If the causes of delinquency, for example, are defined in person-centered terms (e.g., inability to delay gratification, or incomplete sexual identity) then it would be logical to initiate person-change treatment techniques and intervention strategies to deal with the problem. Such treatment would take the form of counseling or other person-change efforts to "reach" the delinquent, thereby using his potential for self-control to make his behavior more conventional. Or if it seemed that person-centered impediments at the root of such "antisocial" behavior were too deeply ingrained or not amenable to routine help (e.g., causes such as birth order position or an extra Y chromosome), it would then follow that coercive external control techniques (e.g., confinement or possibly medical solutions) could be instituted. Under such circumstances, it could be argued with impunity that those officially defined as delinquent would have to relinquish autonomous control over their behavior and other rights in the service of the common good. Thus, where person-centered interpretations provide the foundation on which corrective intervention is based, little need be done about external factors since they would presumably be of lesser or no etiological significance in the determination of such behavior.

If, on the other hand, explanations are situation centered, for example, if delinquency were interpreted as the substitution of extra-legal paths for already preempted, conventionally approved pathways for achieving socially valued goals, then efforts toward corrective treatment would logically have a system-change orientation. Efforts would be launched to create suitable opportunities for success and achievement along conventional lines; thus, existing physical, social or economic arrangements, not individual psyches, would be the targets for change.

The way a problem is defined determines not only what is done about it but also what is *not* done, or what apparently need not be done. If matrifocal family structure is argued to be the basis for deviancy, nonachievement and high unemployment, then opportunity structure, discriminatory hiring practices and other system defects would appear less blameworthy as the causes of poverty. Likewise, if it can be shown that the use of nonstandard speech interferes with the ability to mediate thought and consequently is the cause of poor performance on formal academic tasks, then such a person-blame explanation would remove pressure for structural and institutional changes in the educational system to raise the educational levels of persons from "linguistically deficient" backgrounds. If leniency during child rearing could be shown to be characteristic of student activists, then their system-antagonistic actions could be discredited as the ravings of immature and spoiled children. If, on the other hand, we found that the dissidents are more likely to be cognitively correct about the issues in question than nondissidents or counterdissidents, then there would be reason to seriously consider their recommendations for change.

Whether the social problem to be attacked is delinquency, mental health, drug abuse, unemployment, ghetto riots or whatever, the significance of the defining process is the same: the action (or inaction) taken will depend largely on whether causes are seen as residing within individuals or in the environment. Thus, because the remedies proposed reflect the definition of the problem, it is crucial that the causal inferences made by problem identifiers, social policy planners and professional change agents—anyone who plans and guides large-scale action programs—be based on accurate and comprehensive information. Sartre, in *Saint Genet*, said it in a way that illustrates not only that how you define something determines what you do about it but also that what you do about a problem also defines it: "Action, whatever it be, modifies that which is in the name of that which is not yet."

2. Such definitions, once legitimated and acted upon, tend to define the problem indefinitely, irrespective of their validity. Once in effect, they resist replacement by other definitions. Program administrators and professional change agents develop a vested interest in maintaining established definitions since their very jobs, status, power and the employment of subordinates may depend on those definitions being accepted as correct. If intervention fails, the problem definition and the delivery system are seldom held responsible. Instead, the responsibility for failure may be avoided by

locating blame in the target group and by interpreting that failure as a further sign of the seriousness of the "pathology" being dealt with. As far as we know, no recent large-scale action program has been put out of business because research has shown its failure to fulfill its intended goals.

Also, to the extent that a problem definition conforms to and reinforces dominant cultural myths and clichés (e.g., Horatio Alger), as indeed most definitions must in order to become widely accepted, its change or replacement will be stubbornly resisted. Furthermore, people tend to conform to public definitions and expectations; even if there are doubts regarding their accuracy, they at least provide people with a publicly defined role and definite image of who they are and what is expected of them. Still further, of course, many groups have economic and political interests in seeing that certain definitions are accepted over others (e.g., the business community with regard to the causes of unemployment). In the context of such pressures, an invalid person-centered problem definition often has its most pernicious effect: it can convince the target population of its blame-worthiness as alleged.

Thus, problem definitions take on a life of their own; they set in motion a variety of social and psychological forces that give them important functional significance. Consequently, to question established definitions is to challenge important institutions and belief systems that have their origins in those definitions.

3. In view of the federal funds being invested in evaluations of social intervention efforts, it bears emphasizing that effective evaluation depends on linking program outcomes to the presumed causes of the problem behavior. Thus, a precise and explicit diagnosis of the problem is an indispensable preliminary to good program evaluation. Many different forces shape human behavior, and if remedial intervention fails to produce intended effects, it may be impossible to know the reasons for failure, that is, whether because of the limited changeability of the target population, whether the level of intensity of the treatment was inadequate to produce an effect, or whether the treatment program was inappropriate because it was premised on invalid problem definitions and incorrect assumptions about the causal factors involved.

In the foregoing we have described why problem definitions are crucial in determining what is done or not done about social problems and, more specifically, how person-blame definitions may deflect attention and energies away from important situational determinants, often to the detriment of those supposedly being helped. The significance of this discussion resides in the fact that regardless of the type of problem and the intent of the investigator, the findings of psychologically oriented research lend themselves more easily to person-blame than to system-blame interpretations of the problem. In consequence, such research frequently plays an integral role in a chain of events that results in blaming people in difficult situations for their own predicament. This article focuses on the processes by which this takes place and the implications for "problem" subgroups, the profession and society as a whole.

PERSON-CENTERED PREOCCUPATION AND CAUSAL ATTRIBUTION BIAS OF PSYCHOLOGICAL RESEARCH

It is often at the problem definition stage in the social policy formulation process that social scientists either volunteer, or are called on, to be helpful. It is expected that we will provide expert and unbiased information, but the meaning of "unbiased" is not identical for the consumers and the producers of social science information. To the knowledge user, it may mean (a) that the problem will be viewed from all vantage points and that the interpretation offered will depend on an assessment of a sufficient variety of competing hypotheses that reflect the complexity of the issues, and/or (b) that the new information does not challenge established definitions.

To the social science knowledge producer, on the other hand, "unbiased" is defined in terms of the canons of scientific methodology. However, there is a characteristic that distinguishes psychology from other disciplines, and while this distinction may or may not be a bias in a technical, methodological sense, the fact that the chief focus of interest for psychologists is on person-centered variables has a definite biasing effect on the inferential potential of the findings when used as a premise on which to base later action for "corrective" change. Psychologists study individuals and in particular their mental states: their thoughts, attitudes, motives, intrapsychic equilibrium, etc. Moreover, we prefer to view these factors as independent variables, that is, antecedent and causal in relation to other behavior; and while we may pay lip service to external factors influencing behavior and agree that man to a large degree is a simulator of his environment, when it comes to the actual study of that man and why he behaves as he does, we are more likely to limit our search for etiological evidence to what goes on between his ears and to ignore or exclude from consideration a multitude of external impingements that could justifiably be hypothesized as causal. Our assertion is not inconsistent with, nor should it be confused with, Carlson's recent claim of a "generalist" bias in person-. ality research (i.e., the tendency to concentrate on the effect of different experimental conditions on individuals, irrespective of individual differences). Her claim is relevant to a particular area of academic psychology, while we are concerned with the psychologist's research orientation to social problems. While the claim of her insightful and persuasive paper may be valid for the area to which she refers, we are convinced that quite another viewpoint is adopted when the psychologist turns toward the real world and its problems.

The Law of the Instrument. When psychologists turn their attention to social problems, we see something akin to what Archibald called the "clinical orientation" to the utilization of social scientific knowledge, which she characterizes as assuming that "if the shoe doesn't fit, there's something wrong with your foot."[7] The reasons for this parochial perspective are understandable. To begin with, it is an occupational expectancy that the psychologist would want to demonstrate the applicability of his skills and services. Kaplan called this widely observed tendency the Law of the Instrument: give a small boy a hammer, and suddenly he discovers that everything needs hammering. Train a person in psychological theory and research, and suddenly a world disastrously out of tune with human needs is explained as a state of mind. As we shall see presently, the probability of locating cause in variables outside one's area of familiarity or expertise is not great. "It comes as no particular surprise to discover that a scientist formulates problems in a way which requires for their solution just those techniques in which he himself is expecially skilled."[8] The difficulty is that, as Kaplan says, "The price of training is always a certain 'trained incapacity': the more we know how to do something, the harder it is to learn to do it differently."[9]

Evidence of the person-centered bias in psychology with regard to social problems. To illustrate the intrapersonal preoccupation of psychologists studying social problems, we examined the first six months' issues of the 1970 *Psychological Abstracts* (volume 44, numbers 1-6, plus the semiannual index). We took as an example the research dealing with black Americans, who represent the largest, most visible and most frequently studied group in a problematic relationship to the rest of society.

The following criteria were used for deciding whether a particular abstract should be included in the categorization:

1. We selected those items that either mentioned blacks specifically or were included under the index heading "Negro."

2. Abstracts from clearly nonpsychological journals (such as those for sociology, political science, etc.) were excluded, not because such journals are not of interest to psychologists but because psychologists are less likely to publish in them.

3. Because our interest is in American psychology, abstracts were included only if they appeared in a journal published in the United States or if the author was based in the United States.

4. Ph.D. dissertations were excluded.

5. Because we are concerned with psychological research, only data-based research studies were used. We excluded case reports, review articles and general discussions of the topic.

We sorted each abstract that met the above criteria into categories based on (a) the types of variables studied (i.e., person versus situation) and (b) the causal relationships between them as interpreted by the authors. We found a total of 69 items that could be meaningfully categorized. The categories, together with the percentage of the abstracts that fell into each of them, are presented in Table 1.

Authors of Category 1 studies, containing 15 percent of the research articles, reported an association between a problem characteristic and a personal characteristic and concluded that the personal characteristic is the cause of the problem. Thus, this category of studies lends itself most readily to person-blame interpretations. Category 2, containing 19 percent of the studies, also permits such interpretations, especially among those readers (whether social scientists or not) who do not concern themselves with the finer points of the logic of causal proof. While the authors of such studies make no explicit causal inferences regarding two correlated variables, the nature of the person-centered variables is such that a causal relation seems so plausible that the reader is easily led to conclude that the cause of the problem is psychological. Studies of the kind in Category 8, into which 48 percent of the studies fall, can also be pressed into service for person-blame interpretations of social problems, especially in view of the fact that a majority of such studies which could be compared cross-racially put blacks in an unfavorable light. Of the 33 abstracts that fell into this category, 14 reported unfavorable comparisons of blacks to whites, 2 showed blacks' performance as better than whites' and 6 reported no differences (11 could not be evaluated cross-racially).

Categories 4, 5 and 7 are amenable to system-blame interpretations of social problems. Of these, only Category 4, with 16 percent of the articles, contains any entries. It is noteworthy that no studies were found in Category 7, which is often held up as a model for social psychologists to follow. Despite our emphasis on the necessity of acknowledging the causal role played by environmental factors, we do not believe that this is enough, for even explanations that employ situational factors can be twisted into playing a person-blame role. Ryan eloquently described such interpretations:

> Victim-blaming is often cloaked in kindness and concern, and bears all the trappings and statistical furbelows of scientism; it is obscured by a perfumed haze of humanitarianism . . . and those who practice this art display a deep concern for the victims that is quite genuine. . . . Its adherents include sympathetic social scientists with social consciences in good working order, and liberal politicians with a genuine commitment to reform. . . . They indignantly condemn any notions of innate wickedness or genetic defect. "The Negro is *not born* inferior," they shout apoplectically. "Force of circumstance," they explain in reasonable tone, "has *made* him inferior."[10]

Whereas earlier, more conservative ideologies attributed the position of blacks in society to intrinsic or inherent defects, the new ones described by Ryan stress environmental causation.

> The new ideology attributes defect and inadequacy to the malignant nature of poverty, injustice, slum life, and racial difficulties. The stigma that marks the victim and accounts for his victimization is an acquired stigma, a stigma of social, rather than genetic, origin. But the stigma, the defect, the fatal difference— though derived in the past from environmental forces—is still located within the victim, inside his skin. With such an elegant formulation, the humanitarian can have it both ways. He can, all at the same time, concentrate his charitable interest in the defects of the victim, condemn the vague social and environmental stresses that produced the defect (some time ago), and ignore the continuing effect of victimizing social forces (right now). It is a brilliant ideology for justifying a perverse form of social action

designed to change, not society, as one might expect, but rather society's victim.[11]

Ryan argues persuasively that it is not personal defects produced by past environmental influences that account for blacks' social and economic position in society, but rather the present and continuing effects of situational forces acting upon individuals who, given the same opportunities as most of the rest of us, would do equally well or poorly. This is certainly a credible hypothesis and one as worthy of scientific testing as any other.

Another closely related question demonstrates the inadequacy of simply acknowledging that situational forces play determining roles in the emergence of social problems. This is the question of whether particular problems produced by the social structure are inherent in that structure and occur inevitably because of internal contradictions within the structure, or whether instead they are merely mistakes or unforeseen consequences, perhaps caused by significant but essentially random processes. The answer to this question will have profound implications for the policies proposed, for if the problems are seen as manifestations of the essential nature of the system as it normally operates, then policies that go farther to fundamentally restructure the system will be proposed.

Although our categories are admittedly a crude way of measuring fairly complex phenomena, the picture that emerges is one of psychologists investing disproportionate amounts of time, funds and energy in studies that lend themselves, directly or by implication, to interpreting the difficulties of black Americans in terms of personal shortcomings. Combining Categories 1, 2 and 8, we see that 82 percent of the classifiable psychological research dealing with black Americans reported in the six months of *Psychological Abstracts* under study are of this sort. It should be clearly understood that we do not condemn this preoccupation in and of itself, but rather because it overlooks the importance of other kinds of forces that operate on black Americans, and thereby reinforces the negative labeling of a group already politically and socially vulnerable.

As with telephone books, reading *Psychological Abstracts* can be instructive in ways not intended by those who compiled or organized it. Some peripherally relevant observations: (a) Although *Psychological Abstracts* abstracts articles from the journal *Social Problems* (roughly, sociology's counterpart to SPSSI's *Journal of Social Issues*), there is no category by that name or any variation of it in the subject index. (b) In the format outline used by *Psychological Abstracts*, the areas of crime, juvenile delinquency and drug addiction are among those grouped under the subheading of Behavior Disorder within the division of Clinical Psychology—again illustrating the bias of the field. (c) Perhaps reflecting their missionary zeal, Mental Health and Psychological Services listings can be found under the index heading Social Movements. (d) Even in the act of trying to select social problem areas with which to illustrate our thesis, our assertion was substantiated. Almost all "problems" listed are those of individuals or conventionally defined categories of persons. One searches in vain for serious treatment—whether as dependent, independent or merely correlated variables—of social system variables as they may relate to those psychological variables with which psychologists ordinarily concern themselves. Examples of social system variables that one might expect to play a role of some consequence are the following: the concentration of wealth and power, unequal educational or occupational opportunity, particularistic dispensation of justice at the hands of the police and the judicial system, national budgetary priorities for destructive as compared to social welfare purposes and the militarization of the economy. (Psychologists should not be singled out for criticism on this point, since until recently the standard sociological works on "social problems," "deviance" and the like, have also focused to a large extent on individuals, for example, crime, juvenile delinquency, alcoholism, suicide, etc.) Possible exceptions might include organizational (i.e., business and industrial) analysis and occasional use of variables that represent summaries of individual "problems" or problem behavior (e.g., crime rates, the magnitude of poverty in the United States, etc.). Another possible exception involves the uncharacteristic analysis of certain kinds of problem behavior (e.g., riots) in terms of a "system breakdown." For cogent critiques of this often misused concept, see L. Coser, *The Functions of Social Conflict* (Glencoe, Ill.: Free Press, 1956) and H. Buckley, *Sociology and Modern Systems Theory* (Englewood Cliffs, N.J.: Prentice-Hall, 1967).

Finally, we share with the reader a few items that came to our attention in our search of the abstracts. Admittedly, these are the more extreme examples of the tendencies to which this article refers, but it must be recognized that they differ only in degree and not in kind. The subject index description of a dissertation study (No. 564) concerned with attitudes toward "handicapped groups" reads as follows: "public vs. private attitudes toward stutterers & cerebral palsied & blind & Negroes." A study of conscientious objectors (No. 677) belonging to a fundamentalist religious sect showed "extraordinary inhibition of aggression" on their part, on the basis of MMPI scale scores which were "higher than *other* federal prisoners or *non*criminals" (authors' italics). A shallow understanding of the roots of urban disorders was evident in two other reports. One author investigating "use patterns & the effects of mass media" on black ghetto residents (No. 3570) stated that his results support the hypothesis that "open communication channels would lessen the tendency to riot." The second report (No. 2248), summarizing four studies of the Detroit riots, reported that results "revealed an obvious lack of communication between the black and the power structures. . . . It is suggested that psychiatry be used to further understand these matters." Showing that no bit of common wisdom is immune from the scrutiny of empirical investigation, another author (No. 2191) evaluated inner-city black youths' sense of rhythm, tonal memory and other musical talents, finding them "markedly deficient" by test standards (although he holds out the possibility that such "standardized testing programs" may be inappropriate for such populations). "Suicide, and white reformatory girls' preference for Negro men" was the subject of an article (No. 8798) which concluded that this preference results from both groups' rejection by society and feelings of worthlessness. The abstract of an article entitled "The Irrational in Economic Behavior" (No. 6825), although vague, suggested a focus on the individual consumer's irrationality and contained no hint of any recognition of such forces as ubiquitous advertising and a need-creating, redundant economy which may induce persons to act counter to their own best interests.

The occupational orientation of psychologists and its effects. A second major reason for this preoccupation with person-centered variables pertains to career gains. There is little chance for a career-conscious psychologist to become successful by helping people who are not. But it is possible to enhance one's own position among colleagues by conducting "relevant" research as a means for pursuing theoretical rather than applied interests, while at the same time contributing to the profession as a whole by offering explanations and solutions within the paradigms of a particular discipline.

It is the good will and approval of our colleagues in the scientific community, not that of the target population members affected by our work, that get us ahead. A social scientist's findings may provide or influence the underlying assumptions on which "corrective" programs affecting thousands or perhaps millions of persons will be predicated. It is ironic, then, that his career gains will depend more on his contribution to the advancement of his discipline from studying applied problems than on the success or failure of those programs.

This would not be a cause for such serious concern if, as tends to be the case in academic psychology, the only risk is that of bad or incorrect theory. But, what is good for science and the individual scientist may not be good for those on whom the research is based. As we have recently seen, to talk of hereditary and environmental effects on intelligence (long a concern of psychologists) means one thing when discussed in terms of its relevance to psychological theory but quite another when applied to those in a problematic relationship to the rest of society (cf. Jensen and his critics in *Environment, Heredity, and Intelligence*). Similarly, to focus on the role of different nuclear family units and their consequences on childhood development is one thing when discussed on theoretical grounds and another when applied to real groups living under extraordinarily difficult circumstances (cf. Moynihan's *The Negro Family* and the ensuing controversy).

The repercussions of our research findings—the views of the world they inspire or perpetuate—may seem like epiphenomena to us, but they are often painfully real for those affected by them. Thus, psychology as a profession has special reason to consider a more balanced approach in the selection of variables for the study of social problems. In addition to the usual reason for acknowledging the necessity of such an approach, namely, that any discipline-bound approach to any given social problem is at best only partially correct and at worst just plain wrong, psychologists have added reason to show caution: person-blame explanations of social problems, whether valid or not, hold the potential for reinforcing established stereotypes and thereby perpetuating the condition of the "problem" group.

A closely related set of incentives further contributes to the psychologist's bias toward person-centered research on social problems. It is based, in part, on Becker's notion of a "hierarchy of credibility":

In any system of ranked groups, participants take it as given that members of the highest group have the right to define the way

things really are. . . . From the point of view of the well socialized participant in the system, any tale told by those at the top
intrinsically deserves to be regarded as the most credible account
obtainable. . . . And since . . . matters of rank and status are
contained in the mores, this belief has a moral quality. We are, if
we are proper members of the group, morally bound to accept
the definition imposed on reality by a superordinate group in
preference to the definitions espoused by subordinates. . . . By
refusing to accept the hierarchy of credibility, we express disre-
spect for the entire established order.[12]

Thus, when authorities offer person-blame explanations for particular social problems and make research funds available, suddenly one's disciplinary outlook, career gains and socially acceptable
behavior all converge for the psychologist. By investigating a social
problem in terms given him, a mutually beneficial exchange relationship is established: the researcher is rewarded both materially
and in terms of prestige (in addition to remaining a "proper
member of the group") by using the tools of his trade; while on the
other side of the exchange, officialdom stands to have its preferred
interpretation buttressed by the respectability of "scientific data."

Little has been said in this section about the political and social
context of psychological research on social problems for the purpose of illustrating the implications of such research, independent
of other considerations. Even under the most ideal conditions of a
conscientious, well-meaning, responsive government and populace,
on the basis of psychological research, person-blame definitions of
social problems would be the likely outcome. Given the actual nature of government and the political process, however, this outcome is made even more certain, except that the consequences are
likely to be less benign for the "problem" group. In the next section we will consider these broader issues in order to understand (a)
why person-centered research findings lead so quickly to person-
blame public interpretations, and, in turn, (b) the social and political conditions favorable for the emergence of, and the uncritical
willingness among policy planners to embrace, person-blame interpretations.

UTILITY OF PERSON-BLAME PROBLEM DEFINITIONS

Problem Identification

Every society attempts to characterize its deviant segments as problematic, and therefore as candidates for change, sometimes because they represent a breach of norms and folkways, at other times for purely political or interest-based reasons. But the social scientist who becomes "relevant" seldom questions already established problem definitions, or the wisdom behind the process that lends to the identification of so-called social problems. Nor does he question whose ends are served by the entire definitional process and by his participation in that process. Instead he waits in the wings until the problems have been selected for attention. Only then does he become involved, as if accepting as given that (a) whatever becomes identified publicly as a social problem is a genuine problem, derived from universally recognized truths; and (b) the problem is of such priority that it deserves attention over other problems that go unattended or unrecognized.

Why does one kind of poverty concern us and another does not? Why do we constantly study the poor rather than the nonpoor in order to understand the origins of poverty? Why do we study nonachievement among minority group members as undesirable behavior but do not study exaggerated profit motive among "successful" businessmen as a form of deviance? Why do we study the use of marijuana as a "drug problem," but not federal government involvement in the drugging of "minimal brain dysfunction" (MBD) children in our grammar schools? Why is it illegal to be a "wetback" but not to hire one?[13]

These kinds of questions are rarely raised. Yet the social scientist should understand that by his involvement *qua* scientific authority in research, treatment and planning operations, he has—consciously or unconsciously, explicitly or implicitly—lent credibility and legitimation to a given problem as publicly defined and the treatment program launched to deal with that problem.

Certain groups within society become continually stigmatized as problem groups (e.g., migratory workers, mental patients, blacks, the poor) because they are visible and accessible, but, most especially, because they are vulnerable to the social scientist for research purposes. In this sense the criteria by which social scientists select "problem" groups for study are not unlike the criteria by which the wider culture selects certain groups as scapegoats. Indeed, the former process often follows the lead of the latter. Nonachieving lower income children are more identifiable and accessible as a research population than are greedy "entrepreneurially motivated" slum landlords, for example, and they command far less countervailing power and resources than do the landlords. Thus, there is much person-centered research data to justify initiating a program such as Head Start (all of the data suggesting, essentially, that it is the child who fails, rather than the school and the educational system). But, by contrast, there is a lack of data on landlords, bankers and city officials who permit building code violations that would justify using them as targets for person-change treatment efforts.

Moreover, just as we must concern ourselves with whose problem definition we are being asked to validate, we must constantly examine what is *not* being done. Social ills that are ignored through oversight, ignorance or deliberate non-issue-making may be as important as those "problems" that become issues. Dubos said:

> The greatest crime committed in American cities may not be murder, rape, or robbery, but rather the wholesale and constant exposure of children to noise, ugliness and garbage in the street, thereby conditioning them to accept public squalor as the normal state of affairs.[14]

These issues are of particular concern at this time because of the rise of interest in social indicators. It would be expected that those charged with the responsibility of conducting such research would use this opportunity to participate in identifying social problems and thereby make the study of social indicators something more than social seismology. But this seems unlikely, judging from Bauer, one of the movement's main advocates:

> The decision to observe a phenomenon implies a decision to be responsible for it, if such responsibility is within one's own power. . . . It is wisdom, not cynicism, to urge caution in extending diagnostic measures of social phenomena beyond the system's capacity to respond to the problems which are unveiled.[15]

Contrary to the Dubos position, Bauer implies that something becomes a social problem only if it is politically feasible to deal with it. As long as such attitudes prevail among the leaders of the social indicator movement, there should be no question as to whose welfare and interests—dominant political and economic interests, or the wider society—will be served by the selection and gathering of social indicators. If social scientists choose to be morally indifferent social bookkeepers and leave the selection of indicators and their use in the hands of others, then, to use Biderman's term, social "vindicators" would be a better name for such measures.[16] If our apprehensions are confirmed, these vindicators will take the form of person-blame data collected for the political management of guilt and culpability.

Blame Displacement and the Use of Social Scientists

Whether or not the problems we study are true social problems, or whether they deserve the attention that they receive vis-à-vis other social ills, is open to debate. However, a more serious and less obvious danger is the use of social science and social scientists to displace the blame for prior political and technological failures. Such failures are often the end result of a series of short-run political and technological accommodations for which there may no longer be either short- or long-term political, technological or social solutions. But because breakdowns in the political-economic system produce serious social *consequences*, social scientists are called on to deal with these so-called "social" problems. Their involvement carries with it the implication that socially undesirable behavior is the problem, rather than the inevitable by-product of political trade-offs and technological fixes, thereby distracting attention from the real causes. Kramer succinctly warned. "Never forget that your research may seem like an end in itself to you, but to rank outsiders with other agendas, it may be a means to other goals."[17]

To a substantial extent, transportation, public housing, education, environmental pollution, possibly even drugs and many other such problems associated with the management of urban life fall into this category. Public housing problems provide a good example. At the early planning stages the important decisions about such housing are often based solely on political and technological grounds, for example, the level and timing of appropriations, the selection of sites, the choice of building materials and design and production methods. It is only after the housing is completed and people do not want to live in it, or are afraid to live in it, or those who live in it do not behave in some desired way, that public housing becomes viewed as a problem requiring social science expertise, and thereafter becomes publicly defined as a "social" problem. The "problem" behavior may in fact be a straightforward reaction to external realities of causal inversion, the victims of poor planning become treated as if they were the cause of the situation in which they find themselves.

The Negotiation of Reality[18]

Perhaps one of the more important but subtle political advantages of person-blame research is that it can permit authorities to control troublesome segments of the population under the guise of being helpful, even indulgent. Normally one would expect that those who control power and resources would be unrelentingly noncooperative with system-antagonistic "problem" groups. "Cooperation" with such groups is possible, however, if a person-blame rather than system-blame action program can be negotiated. Thus, they can be "helpful" as long as the way in which the target group is helped serves the interests of those offering assistance. Under these circumstances the definitional process remains in the control of the would-be benefactor, and "help" will be forthcoming as long as the public definitions of the real problem behind the system-antagonistic acts are explained in person-centered terms.[19] The system-antagonistic poor become "deserving" of help only if they accept personal blame for their social and economic position in society; that is, because of personal impediments, they would be unable to effectuate personal and social goals even under the most ideal conditions. Otherwise, they remain "undeserving" of help and are ignored or controlled through the exercise of negative sanctions.

For example, in 1969, a group of Indians occupied and attempted to reclaim Alcatraz Island shortly after its use as a prison facility had been discontinued. They argued that it should rightfully be returned to them since it was in effect surplus federal land. The government refused to recognize the legitimacy of their claim and made it exceedingly difficult for the group to survive on the island. Finally, after two years, the Indians were forcibly removed.

These events in San Francisco Bay contrast with a similar incident on the opposite coast. In the summer of 1970, a small group of blacks landed on Ellis Island in New York Harbor and attempted to claim it because, like Alcatraz, it was federal land no longer being used. They were immediately threatened with expulsion, and the illegality of their actions was made public. After several days of negotiation, however, authorities agreed to provide a major drug rehabilitation center on the island, and the dispute was thus settled.

The outcomes on Alcatraz and Ellis Island might have been reversed, however, if the Indians had agreed to the establishment of a treatment center for alcoholism among Indians (thus adding credibility to a stereotyped person-blame explanation to account for their social and economic position in America), and if the blacks had denounced white repression and demanded to use Ellis Island as the base for establishing an independent black nation.

We do not mean to appear unduly alarmist by implying that every problem group, particularly those who are system antagonistic, has a rendezvous with a deviancy label, nor that the social sciences will inevitably become insidious political arms of the state, nor that the government will go to the extreme of hospitalizing its political opponents as mentally ill. We have not come to that, nor are we likely to, at least not in the near future. We should realize, however, that the potential for manipulation of problem definitions for purely political ends, while now only partially realized, could become a fully exploited reality.

SUMMARY AND CONCLUSIONS: TRUTH OR CONSEQUENCES

Causal Attribution Bias

We have demonstrated the existence of a person-centered preoccupation and causal attribution bias in psychological research which, when applied to social problems, favors explanations in terms of the personal characteristics of those experiencing the problem, while disregarding the possible influence of external forces. Because of the ominous prospects that can ensue from the narrowly circumscribed range of action possibilities derivable from person-centered data, there is reason to question whether such findings would be a suitable foundation for the development and promulgation of ameliorative programs.

Because these issues are complex and their implications are far reaching, we should caution the reader against possible misinterpretations. First, we are not concerned with which academic disciplines have a hegemony over truth. We are not saying that person-centered variables are less valid or etiologically less important than situational variables in accounting for social problems. Second, we do not object to psychologically oriented research on social problems because it offends our sense of egalitarianism by documenting individual or group differences. Such differences may or may not exist, but that alone is not our concern here. Third, the reader should not conclude that we are blindly enamored of an approach that stresses environmental factors to the exclusion of person-centered factors. That would be an error in the opposite direction. Instead, our concern is not with the truth of propositions about human behavior so much as with their social, political, economic and human consequences.

A dogmatic system-blame orientation has its own dangers, in addition to also being part of the truth. Just as such an orientation once liberated man from supernatural or biological conceptions of his destiny, it may now become increasingly repressive of man's initiative and spirit. Reifying environmental factors as causal agents may deny, and thus have the effect of dampening, the autonomy and dynamism of the individual.[20] This raises the serious question of people's attitudes toward their responsibility for their behavior. Unless counteracted in some way, an excessively system-blame perspective carries with it the potential for providing the individual with a ready explanation for avoiding responsibility for his own behavior.

One of the most serious philosophical and psychological problems of our age may be to provide a view of man and his surroundings that recognizes the validity of situational causality without leaving the individual feeling helpless and unable to shape his fate. Part of that view will have to contain a more complex and sophisticated view of causality than the implicit constant-sum model that most people seem to hold (i.e., the more my environment is responsible for my outcomes, the less responsible I am, and vice versa). But until that state is reached, social scientists, especially those concerned with environmental determinants of behavior and thought, have a responsibility: we must recognize that much of our work holds the potential for further eroding an already changing social order and crumbling value system; and, therefore, it may be argued that we have an obligation to put something better in the place of that which we help destroy. It is in this spirit that Miller suggested that perhaps the most radical activity that psychology can undertake is to build a new image of man, more valid and hopeful than those of the past, and to freely dispense that image to anyone who will listen.[21]

Functions of Person-Blame Research

Although the initial intent behind the use of psychological research and analysis on social problems may have been an effort of responsible government to be responsive to human needs, because the data psychologists provide stress person-centered impediments to account for societal problems, they serve other ends as well. We have distinguished at least five latent functions of person-blame interpretations of social problems.

1. They offer a convenient apology for freeing the government and primary cultural institutions from blame for the problem.

2. Since those institutions are apparently not the cause of the problem it may be legitimately contended that they cannot be held responsible for amelioration. If they do provide such help, they are credited with being exceedingly humane, while gaining control over those being helped, through the manipulation of problem definitions in exchange for treatment resources.

3. Such interpretations provide and legitimate the right to initiate person-change rather than system-change treatment programs. This in turn has the following functions: (a) it serves as a publicly acceptable device to control troublesome segments of the population, (b) it distracts attention from possible systemic causes, and (c) it discredits system-oriented criticism. Some of these functions were illustrated in a recent, much publicized address to correctional psychologists by Judge David Bazelon:

> Why should we even consider fundamental social changes or massive income redistribution if the entire problem can be solved by having scientists teach the criminal class—like a group of laboratory rats—to march successfully through the maze of our society? In short, before you respond with enthusiasm to our pleas for help, you must ask yourselves whether your help is really needed, or whether you are merely engaged as magicians to perform an intriguing side-show so that the spectators will not notice the crisis in the center ring. In considering our motives for offering you a role, I think you would do well to consider how much less expensive it is to hire a thousand psychologists than to make even a minuscule change in the social and economic structure.[22]

A few academics have pointed with undisguised glee at what they perceive to be an inherent contradiction in claims variously attributed to radicals, students and various other critics. On the one hand, they assert, the social sciences are accused of being "irrelevant" and inconsequential; yet, on the other hand, they are also accused of being power serving. How can these both be possible? The apparent inconsistency vanishes when one recognizes that the two charges pertain to different domains, the first to those academic and theoretical issues that occupy most of the space in journals and many texts, and the second to the realm of social problems and public issues, in the ways demonstrated by this article. We regard both charges as being more accurate than false.

4. The loyalty of large numbers of the well-educated, melioristic-minded nonneedy is cemented to the national structure by means of occupational involvement in "socially relevant" managerial, treatment and custodial roles required to deal with those persons designated as needing person-centered correction.

5. Person-blame interpretations reinforce social myths about one's degree of control over his own fate, thus rewarding the members of the great middle class by flattering their self-esteem for having "made it on their own." This in turn increases public complacency about the plight of those who have not "made it on their own."

The major conclusion that can be drawn from the above is that person-blame interpretations are in everyone's interests except those subjected to analysis.

Assuming that person-blame interpretations can produce the political benefits described above, the provocative question of function versus intent must be considered. Are these effects merely unforeseen consequences of decisions made for purely humanitarian reasons, or are they the products of decisions made deliberately with these political gains in mind? The more conspiratorial view would argue that such outcomes are intended, while the more benign view would hold that they are both unintended and unanticipated. Both views probably have elements of truth, but each misses the mark to some degree.

Unquestionably, conscious and deliberate use has been made of person-blame arguments, buttressed by psychologically oriented research, with a view toward protecting the established order against criticism. Although those who have relied on person-blame arguments in these ways have been associated with dominant economic, social, and political institutions, it must be emphasized that others in these same institutions have not been and would not be engaged in such activities.

Following Ryan, we suggest that for most persons (including psychologists and other social scientists) who subscribe to person-blame interpretations of social problems, the functions that such explanations serve are indeed unintended and probably even unsuspected as yet.[23] These interpretations derive largely from epistemological biases and "blinders" deeply embedded in cultural beliefs that favor person-centered interpretations of either success or failure. Citing Mannheim,[24] Ryan states that while such belief systems distort reality and serve specific functions (namely, maintaining the status quo in the interests of particular groups), the distortion is neither conscious nor intentional. Thus, in the main, person-blame interpretations have the function, but not necessarily the intent, of serving the interests of the relatively advantaged segments of the society.

In conclusion, we would like to turn our attention to the legitimacy and appropriateness of the volatile issues raised in this article, such as (a) what is the relative emphasis the social sciences should place on the truth of propositions about human behavior, on the one hand, and the action implications, often political, that flow from them, on the other; (b) to whom are social scientists responsible and to whom should they be responsible; and (c) more generally, what is the proper role of science and of individual scientists with regard to research on "relevant" social issues? Increasingly we will have to face such issues, both as individuals and as a profession, and the quality of our solutions will not be improved by postponing the discussion. The purpose of this article was to show why we must be wary of uncritically accepting the idea that the promotion and dissemination of social science knowledge are intrinsically good, moral, and wise. The sooner we recognize that such knowledge is not truth divorced from the realities of time, place or *use*, the better will be our chances of making a truly responsible contribution to societal improvement.

NOTES

[1]An earlier version of this article was presented at the annual meeting of the American Psychological Association, Washington, D.C., September 1971. The article is supported in part by Grant MH 19313 to the authors from the National Institute of Mental Health, United States Public Health Service. The final version of this article appeared in *American Psychologist* 28 (March 1973): 199-211.

[2]The authors wish to express their appreciation to Joyce Kornbluh for her help in preparing the manuscript.

[3]O. G. Brim, Jr. et al., *Knowledge into Action: Improving the Nation's Use of the Social Sciences*, (Report of the Special Commission on the Social Sciences of the National Science Board, Washington, D. C.: National Science Foundation, 1969), and National Academy of Sciences, Behavioral and Social Sciences Survey Committee, *The Behavioral and Social Sciences: Outlook and Needs* (Englewood Cliffs, N. J.: Prentice-Hall, 1969).

[4]H. W. Riecken, "Social Change and Social Science," (Address in the Science

and Public Policy Series, Rockefeller University, January 26, 1972, mimeo-graphed).

[5]The reader should be forewarned that in the discussion to follow, a constant-sum model of causality is used, which assumes in its weakest form that person-centered causes and situation-centered causes are inversely related (i.e., the more one type of causal factor is shown to operate, the less the other type is assumed to operate, in bringing about particular outcomes). In its most extreme form, this model would assume that person-centered and situation-centered causal factors are dichotomous and mutually exclusive (i.e., if one type of factor is shown to be causally operative, it is assumed that the other type does not operate at all). The authors labor under no such simplistic notions and are well aware of the complexi-ties of causal interpretation and multidetermined outcomes. The arguments in this article follow this simpler model, however, because of (a) the tendency of the public to think in such either-or terms with respect to causality and (b) the ea-gerness of political actors to take advantage of that tendency.

Further, because we are dealing with the public phenomenology of causality, the article necessarily blurs two concepts that would be carefully distinguished in a more rigorously analytical article. These are the concepts of (a) the *cause* of an event or condition, which according to the scientific ideal can be factually and em-pirically ascertained and then communicated in a purely descriptive, nonevalua-tive fashion; and (b) *responsibility* for an event or condition, which includes both credit and blame and, as these words suggest, is more evaluative and value laden, based on certain normative assumptions including an evaluation of the event and, in the case of personal or group agents, intentionality. There is an even sharper analytical and often empirical distinction between these two concepts and a third, that of responsibility for changing an undesirable event or condition.

[6]R. Carlson, "Where is the Person in Personality Research?" *Psychological Bulletin* 75 (1971): 203-19.

[7]K. Archibald, "Alternative Orientations to Social Science Utilization," *Social Science Information* 9, no. 2 (1970): 7-34.

[8]A. Kaplan, *The Conduct of Inquiry* (San Francisco: Chandler, 1964), p. 31.

[9]*Ibid.*

[10]W. Ryan, *Blaming the Victim* (New York: Pantheon, 1971), pp. 6-7.

[11]*Ibid.*

[12]H. S. Becker, "Whose Side Are We On?" in *Qualitative Methodology: First-hand Involvement with the Social World*, ed. W. J. Filstead (Chicago: Markham, 1970). p. 18. Originally published in *Social Problems* 14 (1967): 239-47.

[13]Cf. J. A. Bustamante, "The 'Wetback' as Deviant: An Application of Labell-ing Theory," *American Journal of Sociology* 77 (1972): 706-18.

[14]R. Dubos, "Life is an Endless Give-and-Take with Earth and all her Crea-tures," *Smithsonian* 1 (1970): 14.

[15]R. Bauer, "Societal Feedback," in *Social Intelligence for America's Future*, ed. B. Gross (Boston: Allyn & Bacon, 1969), p. 67.

[16]A. D. Biderman, "Social Indicators and Goals," in *Social Indicators*, ed. R. Bauer (Cambridge, Mass.: MIT Press, 1966).

[17]J. R. Kramer, "The Social Relevance of the Psychologist," in *Psychology and the Problems of Society*, ed. F. Korten, S. W. Cook and J. I. Lacey (Washington, D. C.: American Psychological Association, 1970), p. 32.

[18]The phrase is borrowed from T. J. Scheff, "Negotiating Reality: Notes on Power in the Assessment of Responsibility," *Social Problems* 16 (1968): 3-17.

[19]Scheff, "Negotiating Reality," pp. 3-17 discussed analogous relationships between psychotherapists and their patients, and between defense lawyers and their clients.

[20]A. Gouldner, "Toward the Radical Reconstruction of Sociology," *Social Policy*, May/June, 1970, pp. 18-25.

[21]G. A. Miller, "Psychology as a Means of Promoting Human Welfare," *American Psychologist* 24 (1969): 1063-75.

[22]D. L. Bazelon, Untitled, (Address to the American Association of Correctional Psychologists' Conferences on "Psychology's Roles and Contributions in Problems of Crime, Delinquency and Corrections," Lake Wales, Florida, January 20, 1972, p. 6, mimeographed).

[23]Ryan, *Blaming the Victim*.

[24]K. Mannheim, *Ideology and Utopia*, trans. L. Worth and E. Shils (New York: Harcourt, Brace & World, 1936).

Table 1

Distribution of Types of Causal Attribution in Research on Black Americans Found in *Psychological Abstracts*, 1970, 44, No. 1-6

Category	Variable type	Type and direction of association	Variable type	% of abstracts
1	Personal characteristic[a]	Casual	Problem Characteristic[b]	15
2	Personal characteristic	Correlation	Problem characteristic	19
3	Personal characteristic[b]	Causal	Problem characteristic[a]	0
4	Situational or environmental characteristic[a]	Causal	Problem characteristic[b]	16
5	Situational or environmental characteristic	Correlation	Problem characteristic	0
6	Situational or environmental characteristic[b]	Causal	Problem characterisitic[a]	3
7	Both personal and situational characteristics[a]	Causal	Problem characteristic[b]	0
8[c]	Group membership (e.g., black or white)	Correlation	Personal characteristics	48
9	Group membership (e.g., black or white)	Correlation	Situational characteristics	0

[a] Independent variable.
[b] Dependent variable.
[c] To illustrate the difference between Category 8 and Categories 1 and 2, let us take a hypothetical example. If a study merely documented the existence of an alleged "deficit" in blacks as compared to whites, it would fall into Category 8. If, however, the study tried to relate an alleged "deficit" among blacks (e.g., in standard English language skills) to another socially relevant "problem" of blacks (e.g., educational underachievement), then it fell into either Category 1 or 2 depending on whether a causal relation was specified or not.

Part II
THE PRACTICE OF SOCIAL POLICY

9

The Social Science Study Groups

GENE M. LYONS

During the past few years three major reports have been published on the role of the social sciences in American society: *The Behavioral Sciences and the Federal Government,* published in September 1968 by an Advisory Committee of the National Academy of Sciences–National Research Council; *Knowledge into Action,* a report of the Special Commission on the Social Sciences to the National Science Board, in May 1969; and, in November 1969, *The Behavioral and Social Sciences: Outlook and Needs,* the report of the Behavioral and Social Science Survey Committee (BASS), cosponsored by the National Academy of Sciences–National Research Council and the Social Science Research Council.[1]

These three reports came at the end of a decade that had marked a formidable increase in the use and support of the social sciences by government, particularly at the federal level. For 1960, the National Science Foundation reported a total of $73 million in federal obligations for basic and applied research in the social and psychological sciences; by 1970, this total was estimated at $345 million.[2] Whatever problems of definition and comparability might be involved in interpreting these figures, they nonetheless testify to the magnitude of the increase of social science enterprise in the federal government. This growth, moreover, was accompanied by an increasingly pervasive use of social science with the advent of new social programs during the decade, particularly the antipoverty, education and training, and public health programs.

The increase in federal spending for social science was more than a technical trend in financial support, however. Indeed, by the end of the 1960s, federal programs in science, including social science, tended to reach a plateau and, in some areas, began to cut back. The increase in social science research was nonetheless now built into the system. This is not to suggest that social science research was effectively used by government. But it does suggest that the programs of the federal government were caught up in a wide variety of social processes and, for better or for worse, there was a serious interest in what social science research could offer in understanding their complexities. For some 30 years or more, there had been a general tendency to seek almost totally economic solutions to national issues—at least, so far as the federal government was involved. Now economic measures were clearly not the whole story and social research, beyond economic analysis, was required.

In many respects, the reports of the social science study groups can be seen as an attempt to develop a rational pattern of government-social science relations after a decade of pragmatic growth. But by a stroke of irony the reports were published at the beginning of a more complex period of relations characterized not only by the need for social as well as economic approaches, but also by a deep suspicion of governmental authority on the part of many academic groups, sharp divisions among social scientists about their proper role in regard to public policy, and a widespread intellectual debate over the social role of knowledge. The debate took, as its immediate foci, the war in Southeast Asia, the condition of blacks and the poor in American society, and the effects of ecological disruption (beginning with the pollution of the natural environment but soon broadening out into the more total and complex issues involving the "quality of life"). However, the implications of the debate also extended beyond immediate questions of public policy to the same overall issue the social science study groups had dealt with: the relation of social science to public policy and government authority. And in the process, the debate went even further in being part of a restructuring of government-science relations as they had evolved since World War II.

Despite their coincidence, the reports of the three study groups and the debate over the social role of knowledge were not really joined, at least immediately. The reports took shape in Washington offices and in the councils of professional associations, while the debate grew on college campuses and among dissenting groups of intellectuals. But the future is likely to be shaped by both movements, which are forced to come together in the open conventions of the professional social science associations. This confrontation has led to the rise of dissident factions challenging the authority of the established social science power structure and, in the process, its view of the proper role of social science in relation to government. This chapter is an attempt to come to grips with both movements by examining the origins and recommendations of the study group reports and analyzing their implications against some of the more searching questions raised by the critics of the social science "establishment."

THE ORIGINS OF THE REPORTS

A first observation about the three study groups is that none of them was especially initiated by social scientists. In one respect, they all have roots in the continuing efforts to find a role for social science in the federal government, efforts that have evolved through the "social trends" study published in the early 1930s, the planning agencies of the New Deal and the bevy of social science research teams that operated through the Second World War.[3] More directly, however, all three study groups were formally established through the intervention of physical and biological scientists, operating within the government structure of scientific development and utilization that had developed since that war.

For example, the first group, the National Academy Advisory Committee on Government Programs in the Behavioral Sciences, grew out of the controversy over Project Camelot, that ill-fated, army-sponsored research project on social change and internal revolution in South America. The irony of Camelot was that it was designed as a highly ambitious operation to try to get at questions of considerable interest to social scientists; but it wound up, in the eyes of many, as a catastrophe in which social science was seen as an embarrassing waste of taxpayer's money and/or as an unwitting instrument of social engineering in the hands of the military establishment.[4]

The fact is that responsible officials of the Department of Defense (DOD) were as concerned (from their own point of view) about the implications of Project Camelot as were social scientists. By then (1965) the department had a certain investment in social science that it certainly wanted to protect. It was anxious that Camelot be judged, not as typical, but in terms of the very difficult problems the military establishment faced, not by itself or for its own parochial purposes, but as one of several instruments of American foreign policy. At the same time, the subservience to dubious purposes, which Camelot seemed to represent, had to be seen against the two decades of highly professional support that the military had given to social scientists through agencies like the Office of Naval Research.

It was against this background that the Defense Department, through its Directorate for Research and Engineering, approached the National Academy of Sciences, asking for assistance in exploring the problems involved in military-supported social science research. The fact that DOD approached the academy is interesting in itself. At that time, the academy was only beginning to broaden its capacity to deal with the social sciences. From the early part of the century, the academy—and its operating arm, the National Research Council—had included within its orbit only the disciplines of anthropology and psychology from the social sciences and, within these disciplines, had generally emphasized sub-fields of interest to the dominant membership of physical and biological scientists. Not until the early 1960s did the National Research Council expand its Division of Anthropology and Psychology into a Division of Behavioral Sciences and not until the late 1960s did the National Academy of Sciences elect a small number of social scientists to join its ranks.

Certainly, the Defense Department could not, in 1965, have come to the academy with its problem because the academy represented social science. If social science was *represented* (whatever represented may mean), it was not in the academy, but in the Social Science Research Council and the professional social science organizations. What the academy did represent was a key point of contact between the scientific and government communities, the kind of point of contact that, for all intents and purposes, was not available elsewhere in the social sciences. At the same time, the academy was part of an interconnected scientific establishment that had developed since World War II and that had grown in influence and in confidence by dealing with—and resolving—knotty problems in government-science relations (and Camelot was certainly knotty).

And so the academy took on the task of exploring the role of the social sciences in the federal government, but on its own broad terms and not on the more limited basis of either Project Camelot or the DOD program of social science research. It inaugurated an inquiry into the full range of federal programs involving the social sciences—their use and their support—and expanded the base of finance for the study by a grant from the Russell Sage Foundation, which supplemented the funds made available through defense agencies.

The origin of the National Science Board's Special Commission on the Social Sciences in many respects followed similar trends. Project Camelot spawned not only the National Academy Advisory Committee, but also a series of investigations in the Congress that led to the proposal for a National Social Science Foundation (NSSF). At one level, the proposal for a separate foundation was projected as a means of divorcing support for advanced research in the social sciences from the political missions of federal agencies, particularly the military departments. More broadly, it was seen as a means of expanding the total amount of federal support for social science in order to create a stronger framework and "infrastructure" of social science research that could be subsequently applied to a full range of public policy issues.[5]

It is important to remember that the idea of a separate foundation had never had great currency among social scientists. There was a curious absence of testimony about a separate social science foundation in the early debates over the National Science Foundation (NSF) and in the more recent discussions (until Project Camelot). The reason may lay in political realism—belief that the social sciences could never muster the political support that would be required to establish such an agency and then keep it funded. But at least in the early years after the Second World War, there also existed certain anxieties about government funding, a fear that the freedom of inquiry might be seriously impaired, especially in areas of political sensitivity. Then, later, as research appetites grew larger and many government agencies began to develop highly professional methods for supporting research, social scientists began to share in the increasing research budgets of agencies like the Department of Defense, the National Institutes of Health and the NSF. There really was little incentive to roil the waters.

Within NSF itself, support for the social sciences began to develop by the mid-1950s under the so-called "permissive but not mandatory" doctrine; that is, under its legislative mandate, the NSF was not required to support social science, but, as a result of its legislative history, was "permitted" to do so; By 1970, a Division of Social Science had been created under this rubric and in 1968, an amendment to the NSF Act made the whole business even more legitimate by giving the social sciences equal recognition in law. Recognition in law and recognition in fact, however, may be quite different. And so, proponents of a separate social science foundation—given its first significant political support in the post-Camelot debates—insisted that, while increased support for the social sciences from the NSF was encouraging and commendable, the Foundation would—by its nature, history and make-up—always be dominated by the priorities of the physical and biological sciences. The only way the social sciences could achieve full recognition of their problems, needs and role was therefore through a separate foundation.

The Special Commission on the Social Sciences was created by the National Science Board at the height of the debate over an NSSF in 1968. But the commission was not asked to address itself to the subject being debated, a separate foundation. Its mandate was framed in terms of the potential application of social science research to the problems of American society. The commission was in many respects the creation of a brilliant and skilled "statesman" of science, the chairman of the National Science Board, Philip Handler, who has since become the new president of the National Academy of Sciences. What the Special Commission was asked by the Board—in a period of increasing federal support for social science and in the midst of often-heated dispute over the organization of research agencies—was to provide an articulate and persuasive argument for increasing even further and strengthening even more the level of public support for social science developments. Certainly such a call—which could hardly be ignored— might also indicate that the priorities of social science could be established and championed within a broad-based scientific agency (the NSF) and did not require the creation of a separate and possibly competing agency (an NSSF).

Finally, the Behavioral and Social Science Survey (BASS) has its origins in a series of studies designed to provide guidance for federal support for science. Stimulated by physical and biological scientists, these studies, in turn, go back to the quest for new ways to formulate federal science policies in general. Under the Act of 1950 establishing the NSF, the foundation was supposed to assume responsibility for drawing up and recommending science policies to the President. In practice, the foundation has never been able to do this: the nature of "science policy" remains ill-defined; the foundation, during its early years, had to spend most of its energies surviving and developing its internal procedures, and, under these conditions, was in no position to recommend science policies that affected agencies that *competed* with it for research dollars in the federal budget.

By the early 1960s, the quest for science policy led to two movements, one inside government and the other outside. Inside government, the Office of the President's Special Assistant for Science and Technology was strengthened through the establishment of the Office of Science and Technology. But many scientists—among them, scientists who had served in top level posts in government—felt that efforts in government to develop science policies would forever be frustrated by the fragmenting tugs of competitive agencies and interests and by the demanding problems of short-range programs and budget cycles. What was required was a mechanism outside the government to examine and set out broad policy lines and alternatives on a time scale and against scientific objectives that could only gain short shrift in the overcharged environment of government bureaucracies.

In order to build such a mechanism, therefore, the National Academy of Sciences established its Committee on Science and

Public Policy (COSPUP). COSPUP, in turn, developed a work program that included a series of studies designed to set down the present state and future needs of all the sciences. Such a series of studies would then provide a blueprint for federal support of science, indicating those directions and fields that specialists within the disciplines considered to be the most important and the most ready for nurturing. Behind the venture was the assumption that, by now, federal support for science was a commitment that no longer needed debate; it now needed guidance. The BASS project is one of the latest products of this venture.

The origins of the three social science study groups show that the publication of three such reports within a short period was not entirely coincidental. By the mid 1960s, two trends had begun to take mature shape: one, the federal commitment to support science, not only as a by-product of political missions, but as an end in itself and as a concomitant to federal support for higher education. The growth of this commitment could not for long ignore the question of extension to the social sciences, whether or not Project Camelot had occurred. Camelot hastened the debate; it did not create it. For by then a second trend, of which Camelot was a symptom, had emerged: the increased role of social science research in federal programs—not just in defense, but in education, in mental health, in urban affairs, in the poverty projects—in a new period of social change in the United States.

These two trends, the federal commitment to support science and the policy demands of a new period of social change, brought to a head the need for some kind of a clarification of the social sciences in contemporary America. Whether the three study groups have provided that clarification is another matter. But the fact that they were all established through structures and procedures largely directed by physical and biological scientists is of some significance. For the substance and the style of the reports reflect the framework of analysis and a frame of reference of the "hard" sciences. The fact is that physical scientists have, since the Second World War, carried on a much more serious and systematic search for clarification of their role in government and politics than have social scientists. It is they who, like J. Robert Oppenheimer, felt they had come close, too close, to "sin" and "evil."

THE PROPOSALS OF THE REPORTS

The final report of the National Academy's Advisory Committee includes a range of recommendations: from measures to strengthen the internal structure of social science research programs in federal agencies to the establishment of a new National Institute for Advanced Research and Public Policy. Framed in a perspective that *accords politics its primary role in governmental decision-making* the report nonetheless emphasizes the social sciences as an important source of information, analysis and explanation about group and individual behavior and thus an important resource for policy formation.

From the experience of research in the fields of statistical services and economic analysis, the Advisory Committee draws lessons for using the knowledge and methods of the social sciences effectively in government. These lessons then lead to a series of practical suggestions, including staffing studies to identify positions for which social science training and experience should be required, in-service training programs in the scope and methods of the social sciences, and methods of organizing and reviewing social science research in any department or agency in terms of a set of strategic goals that relate agency missions to developments in the social sciences.

In the area of foreign affairs research—the area dramatized by Project Camelot—the report spells out two sets of proposals. The first was the establishment of an interagency research planning group in order to develop better balance than exists in the research effort among agencies with foreign operations and to begin to do something that has never been begun—to build cumulative bodies of knowledge on international problems. A second set of proposals, designed to contribute to international cooperation in social science research, places major responsibility on science and education agencies to support university programs for overseas research and student and faculty exchanges in the social sciences.

Beyond recommendations related to research programs in individual agencies and in special fields like foreign affairs, the report also tackles the problem of central organization for social science policies. Here, the committee opts, not for a separate social science structure, but for a serious integration of social scientists into the existing structure for formulating science policies, in the NSF, the Office of Science and Technology, and the President's Science Advisory Committee. The committee's conclusions in this regard are generally based on two broad assumptions: that major public policies in fields such as education, health and urban development, require concerted programs of research from all fields of science; at the same time, there is no less a need for coherent federal policies with respect to scientific and educational development. Two separate structures for scientific advice and programming would, in effect, weaken any effort at effective cohesion.

Finally, the Academy's Advisory Committee suggests a structural capstone to what is a kind of total "system" that it seeks to promote. The committee's recommendations are consciously interrelated, designed to produce a continual process of action and reaction through which the application of social science research would be strengthened at multiple levels of government and the financing of basic research would be sustained through pluralistic sources of support. The whole process is to be kept under surveillance by establishing central responsibility in the Office of Science and Technology. Finally, the Advisory Committee recommends the creation of a National Institute for Advanced Research and Public Policy in Washington, financed by Congress but independent in organization and operation, devoted to future-oriented studies and methodological problems that would, under the best of conditions, receive little attention in federal agencies plagued by the limits of time and jurisdictional interest.

In general, the NSB Special Commission on the Social Sciences concurs in the recommendations of the Academy's Advisory Committee. In one respect, the perspective of the commission's report is narrower; in another, it is broader. It does not deal with the field of foreign affairs; but it extends its recommendations far beyond the agencies of the federal government, into society at large. A series of proposals are thus devoted to strengthening social science research in the practicing professions, in private groups, like business and labor, in community organizations, as well as in every level of government.

A major issue in proposing so wide a program is the lack of means and organizations within the social sciences to enable the findings of social science to be effectively applied to social problems. Recognizing this, the Commission proposes the creation of new social problem research institutes through NSF grants, ultimately hoping for a network of some 25 such institutes throughout the country. Incorporating both research and action functions, the institutes are seen as organizations where social problems will be analyzed by teams of specialists and where contacts will be maintained with social action agencies so that the implication of research studies can be carried forward in terms of policy and program alternatives.

The NSB Special Commission sees as one of its major purposes, "the development of better channels for the flow of social science resources into American life." Its discussion is thus focused on existing institutions like the professions and on the creation of new institutions like the social problem research institutes. The Behavioral and Social Science Survey, however, had the task of assessing the status and future needs of the social sciences in terms of their future development as scientific disciplines. The survey has thus published a series of studies, each devoted to a separate discipline. A general report has also been published, exploring certain aspects of development that involve all the social sciences.

The recommendations of the BASS report fall into several categories. In terms of the development of the social sciences, the report recommends an annual increase of "between 12 and 18 percent" for both basic and applied research funded by the federal government in order "to sustain the normal growth of the research enterprise over the next decade." In a second category of recommendations, the report calls for substantial support for the development of "social indicators", both inside and outside the government, and for further development of the concept of a "national data center" to provide continuing and comparable information for the formulation of both theories and policies of large-scale social change. In connection with the national data center concept, as well as more generally, there is also provision for developing mechanisms to insure that social research, at all levels, protects the anonymity of individual respondents, especially as new technologies provide means of invading privacy.

One section of the general report, entitled "Institutes and University Organization for Research on Social Problems," is directly related to similar issues raised by the Academy's Advisory Committee and the National Science Board's Special Commission.

In both these latter groups' reports, there is a clear emphasis on the need for social scientists with the capacity and will to deal in applied problems. But as the Academy Committee pointed out: "The capacity for bringing knowledge to bear on practical problems has been given little attention in the education of [social] scientists. The emphasis has been on teaching and original research." This observation is reinforced in the BASS report that goes on to conclude that applied research will not be given warranted value in disciplinary departments and must be developed through a separate base in the university structure.

So far, as the BASS report shows, specialized research institutes have almost always had hard sledding in academe: they are usually orphans, do not control tenure positions, have to raise their own funds, cannot provide stability and long-term posts to young colleagues, and frequently take on doubtful assignments in order to survive. The BASS report therefore recommends a new form of organization: a graduate school of applied behavioral science. In presenting its proposal, the BASS suggests that there are several ways in which the model might be developed. In every case, however, the school should be multidisciplinary, should be engaged in continually testing the methods and findings of social science against actual social behavior, and in the process, contribute both to the development of theory and methods and to the solution of real social problems.

The BASS proposal is different from the social problem research institutes recommended by the NSB Special Commission, but it is complementary. The commission's institutes are designed as action agents to serve as transmission belts for the application of social science resources to social problems. The BASS graduate schools are research and educational programs in a university setting, organized on functional rather than disciplinary lines, but engaged in "real world" problems, both on their own terms and in terms of educational purposes.

Both the BASS report and the Special Commission—and the Academy's Advisory Committee emphasize the important connections between work in applied fields (which they all advocate) and advances in basic research. All three study groups would, I think, subscribe to these words in the BASS report in support of the graduate school notion:

... An academically sound and organizationally firm base is needed for the development of behavioral and social science applicable to the large problems of society. The attack on such problems should not wait for crises to call attention to social pathology, but should be on a continuing and long-range basis, with full attention also to the real theoretical contributions that can be made. Through research on genuine social problems, social scientists can improve the substance of their fields according to their own aspirations, while also serving society.[6]

THE IMPLICATIONS OF THE REPORTS

Within the proposals of the three study groups there persist several themes: that social science research, albeit with limitations, has a positive contribution to make to the formation of public policy and the execution of public programs; that, generally and with some exceptions, policy makers have failed to deal with social science as an important resource for policy-making; that social scientists themselves have neglected the policy implications of their work in their quest for specialized development of their individual disciplines; and that the model of government-science relations that had evolved since 1945 is appropriate for the social sciences. These themes provide the bases for general recommendations that run through all three reports: that the utility of the social sciences justifies public support for their development; that a series of interdisciplinary and policy or problem-oriented arrangements are required to bring home to both policy makers and social scientists the links between research and policies; and that the general federal system of grants, contracts and development provides a flexible framework within which social scientists can both serve society and protect their intellectual integrity.

The themes in the reports seek to consolidate and rationalize the system that had grown up during the 1960s. But they run counter to the criticism of those social scientists who are dissenting against the prevailing social science "establishment" and social science "ethos." There are, of course, varieties and contradictions among the dissenters and any generalized description bears the usual risks of being too simple and sweeping. But, by and large, the dissenters argue that social scientists may not have been too little, but too much involved in official policy-making; that too often social scientists have permitted research based on too little information and too little theory to be exploited without question by policy makers for the latter's own political purposes; that all of science, but most especially social science is inextricably wound up with social values and cannot be intellectually free under the terms of the "service" function which has priority in existing government-science relations; that the consequence of advocating a "value-disinterested" (if not "value-free") social science is to support the present political balance against pressures for change; and that, in a number of cases, social scientists share the ideological predilections reflected in the present structure of authority (which the dissenters consider biased) and deliberately use their professional capacity for its perpetuation.

The dissent, whatever its general themes, runs along a spectrum moving toward extreme radicalism. On the one hand, a member of the Caucus for a New Political Science writes that

The Caucus for a New Political Science is . . . a caucus of political scientists *within* the association of political scientists . . . Our major aim is the reformation of American political science, its revitalization and redirection . . . For too long the [American Political Science] Association sustained with little comment the values it had inherited and those of the social and political system in which it found itself. Research, together with the money which funded it, the panels which reported its results and the teaching and writing which was influenced by it, drifted away from critical areas where serious questioning would have exposed cherished views to doubt and controversy . . . The Caucus believes that the drift can be checked and that the Association, by self-conscious design can be turned from a passive, value-sustaining institution into a critical, value-examining and changing institution . . . [7]

While the attack here is on the professional association, its accusations of passivity and "value-sustaining" are flung more broadly against the academic architects of the profession, of this and several generations back. In another more radical statement of dissent there is no doubt who and what are the targets (this statement was delivered before a shocked meeting of the American Sociological Association in 1968):

... This assembly [of sociologists] here tonight ... is a conclave of high and low priests, scribes, intellectual valets, and their innocent victims, engaged in the mutual affirmation of a falsehood ... the profession is an outgrowth of nineteenth-century European traditionalism and conservatism, wedded to twentieth century American corporation liberalism ... the professional eyes of the sociologist are on the down people, and the professional palm of the sociologist is stretched toward the up people ... he is an Uncle Tom not only for this government and ruling class but for any.[8]

The reports of the social science study groups are a light year away from this kind of radicalism and, in many respects, seem, on first reading, to be operating on a completely different wave length than the dissenters, in general. But this is a superficial reading, even though none of the reports fully confronts the arguments of the dissenters. At the same time, all of the reports, while accepting the desirability and indeed the need for change, also accept the existing "system" as a mechanism for change. To this extent, they stand opposed to the most radical of the dissenters. But beyond this, the reports recognize, in a variety of ways, the risks of social science involvement in public policy-making, the requirements for maintaining an independent base for scientific growth, and the multiple roles that social scientists must (and will) play in a variety of institutional settings.

The National Academy's Advisory Committee, for example, was the most directly concerned with strengthening the internal research organization of federal agencies. Yet the Committee's report found "limits upon support for innovative research by operating departments and agencies ... ":

... However broadly conceived and imaginatively administered department and agency programs may be, important areas may still receive inadequate attention and fields of support may be too greatly influenced by existing department and agency commitments and by the operating assumptions of existing policies ...[9]

The immediate recommendation of the Committee was to set up a government-endowed but independently administered institute for research and public policy " ... free from the pressures of political preoccupations and constraints ... to examine the full range of problems the society faces, not only in the immediate future, but beyond, when new and only dimly perceived forces for change will begin to take effect."[10] The idea of such an institute was to bridge the gap between innovative research that emerged from scholarly investigation and the policy-making process. For the Committee recognized the need to develop institutional links between "free" innovative research that challenged "operating assumptions" and strategic points in the decision-making process. Thus, it placed the institute in Washington, D. C. where it could become part of a communications network involving policy makers and social scientists engaged in fundamental research.

Of the three reports, the BASS report pointed to the dual usage of social science research, to sustain or to change the existing order. In a concluding discussion, the report observed that

A good deal of attention is given, in social science, to how social order is generated and maintained, as well as to how it is changed. This emphasis on the study of normal social functions sometimes leads observers to consider the social sciences as inherently conservative and the handmaidens of establishments of various sorts . . . In fact, however, the . . . social sciences are potentially . . . revolutionary . . . This is true basically because their findings call into question traditional assumptions about the nature of human nature, about the structure of society and the unfolding of social processes . . .[11]

In all three reports, there is an underlying assertion that the social role of social knowledge is hardly a new problem. But admittedly it takes on a special intensity when government begins to employ social knowledge more deliberately than it had earlier and when, at the same time, critics of government policy call for a role for social knowledge no less political, but one that supports antigovernment movements. Between these two sets of demands any simple recourse to a "value-free" social science is meaningless. For that matter, social research is often directed as much by the subjective values of the research, in his choice of subject, methodology and conceptual framework, as by the policy interests of major patrons, government and other social agencies. The professional criteria for evaluating social research, moreover, remain limited under the fragmented and decentralized structure of the social science enterprise. By the same token, the results of social research can, through a process of popularization and even vulgarization, become a basis for political rhetoric and policy without any professional judgment on their objective validity (or, for that matter, the concurrence of the original researchers).

Both the study group reports and the criticism of the dissenters recognize the risks of being "co-opted," of being "used." At the same time, the reports all emphasize the need for developing links between research and government in order to contribute to intelligent public policy while the dissenters emphasize the need for dissociating research from public authority in order to contribute to social criticism. What both require, however, is an independent base which will permit social science, on the one hand, to contribute to public policies without being disorted and, on the other, to provide criticism of public policies without being censored. Professional ethics, rigorous methods of research, open publication, all contribute to this independence which both service and criticism demand. But research freedom also requires an institutional setting within which it is nourished for its own sake, and here the university has a vital role to play, a role that is essential to the vitality of social science as a source of both social policy and social criticism.

There is no point in trying to reconcile the themes of the study groups with the criticisms of the dissenters. For one thing, neither the themes nor the criticisms stand for single large opposing factions among social scientists. Indeed, social scientists are factionalized into many more political, methodological and ideological clusters than two broad divisions could possibly represent. For another thing, even if the functions of contributing to government policy and to social criticism were reconciled in some bland, theoretical way, those adopting one or the other route would soon fall apart when dealing with distinct policy issues or when seeking some kind of explanation for these functions. The need for the protection of free and independent universities is, however, vital for both. But is made more difficult and complex by the recommendations for a policy or problem-oriented approach to social science that runs through all three reports—and that is, for that matter, as necessary for the function of social criticism as it is for contributing to rational government.

All three reports underscore the multidisciplinary nature of social problems and the need for multidisciplinary instrumentalities to meet them. These things have to be said, but they are not new. They should awaken memories of the early urgings of

Charles Merriam and the later brilliant articulation of Harold Lasswell. Many social scientists have, at one time or another, been fascinated, instructed and stimulated by Lasswell's concept of the policy sciences. Everyone recognizes, at the same time, the obvious and inevitable multidisciplinary character of social problems. But most academic social scientists must have either experienced or witnessed continuing frustrations at launching multidisciplinary programs—especially teaching programs—in colleges and universities. Only in the "think-tanks", like the RAND Corporation, have real multidisciplinary enterprises been mounted.

There are, of course, reasons for this being so. Social scientists have, in a way, been seeking their own self-dignity and self-confidence for several decades. They have been seeking to strengthen the rigor of their methods, devising programs of quantitative analysis, exploring the possibilities of comparison, and trying to enlarge and test theoretical bases. In all these efforts, they have borrowed from colleagues in the other social sciences, so that, for example, political scientists speak of political psychology and political sociology as sub-fields and test political systems against economic models. Relations with other social sciences have largely been formed in terms of the development of one's own discipline. What the three study groups are confronting is the possibility of forming new sets of relations in terms of social problems.

Again this is not unlike the challenge raised earlier by Merriam, Lasswell and others. At earlier times, social scientists largely ignored the challenge, fearing, I would suggest, that a response would have diverted their attention and energies from the developments in their disciplines as sciences. Perhaps, a major question is to ask whether social scientists have as yet sufficient internal strength to devote more time and resources to the policy orientation—in substance as well as process—in collaboration with colleagues in other disciplines, and whether universities have the internal strength to support and protect this orientation. For the applications of social science to social problems discussed in all three reports are applications that take place in political environments or are highly related to political choices. And it is too easy to assume that the role of social science is simply to clarify the alternatives among which policy makers might choose. Clarifying political choices is, in itself, part of the political process.

In the final analysis, therefore, the reports of the three social science groups, no less than the urgings of the dissenters, move social science into the orbit of American politics. But to make this move without insuring the protection of a free university system would be a disaster. For only in the universities can the professional standards be sustained, against which the role of social scientists in politics can be rigorously evaluated. Without these standards, charlatans could flourish, partial knowledge could become frozen dogma, and sloppy research could lead to political myth. Nor, it goes without saying, would the social sciences develop in terms of adding to the store of fundamental knowledge.

The implications of the study group reports are thus two-fold: a more systematic orientation of the social sciences toward social problems and a continuing but more alert and sensitive protection of academic freedom. Both tasks have been emphasized in uncompromising terms by John Gardner:

I would not wish to see anything happen that would alter the character of the university as a haven for dissent and for creative, scholarly work. That must be preserved at all costs. But I believe that those parts of the university which are . . . involved in extensive interaction with the larger community are going to have to take that relationship more seriously than ever before . . . We need in the university community a focused, systematic, responsible, even aggressive concern for the manner in which the society is evolving—a concern for its values and the problems it faces, and the strategies appropriate to clarify those values and to solve those problems.[1][2]

NOTES

[1] *The Behavioral Sciences and the Federal Government,* NAS Publication 1680, Washington, D.C., National Academy of Sciences, 1968 ("The Academy Report"); *Knowledge into Action: Increasing the Nation's Use of the Social Sciences,* Report of the Special Commission on the Social Sciences, Washington, D.C., National Science Board—National Science Foundation, NSB 69-3, 1969 ("The National Science Board Report"); and *The Behavioral and Social Sciences: Outlook and Needs,* Washington, D.C., National Academy of Sciences, 1969 ("The BASS Report").

[2] Federal Funds for Research, Development and Other Scientific Activities, Fiscal Years 1968, 1969, and 1970, Vol. XVIII, NSF 69-31, Washington, D.C., National Science Foundation, 1969, p. 258.

[3] For earlier history, see Gene M. Lyons, *The Uneasy Partnership: Social Science and the Federal Government in the Twentieth Century,* New York, Russell Sage Foundation, 1969.

[4] For a full discussion of Project Camelot, see Irving L. Horowitz (ed.), *The Rise and Fall of Project Camelot,* Cambridge, Mass., M.I.T. Press, 1967.

[5] For the debate on the proposal to establish a National Social Science Foundation see *National Foundation for Social Sciences,* Subcommittee on Government Research, Committee on Government Operations, U.S. Senate, 90th Congress, First Session, Parts 1, 2 and 3, Washington, D.C., 1967.

[6] "The BASS Report," *op. cit.,* p. 201.

[7] H. Mark Roelofs, "Plebiscitory or Legislative Democracy," in *P.S., Newsletter of the American Political Science Association,* Vol. II, No. 3, pp. 273-273.

[8] Statement by Martin Nicolaus, quoted in Alvin Gouldner, *The Coming Crisis of Western Sociology,* New York, Basic Books, 1970, p. 10.

[9] "The Academy Report," *op. cit.,* p. 103.

[10] *Ibid,* pp. 105-107.

[11] "The BASS Report," pp. 271-272.

[12] Quoted in Thomas E. Cronin and Sanford D. Greenberg (eds.) *The Presidential Advisory System,* New York, Harper & Row, 1969, p. 329.

The Management
of Federal Expenditures
for Research on Social Problems

BENJAMIN CHINITZ

The Kennedy-Johnson years were boom times for social science researchers. Federal expenditures for such research more than quadrupled in the years between 1960 and 1966, rising from $73.1 million to $325.1 million.

This enormous expansion of research budgets accompanied the proliferation of federal programs designed to deal with a long list of domestic problems: poverty, unemployment, slums, crime, inferior education and medical care, urban decay, pollution and more. The typical new program was shot through with uncertainty and ambiguity as to what its goals and objectives were, how they should be evaluated, or even what the problem was that the program was supposed to help. Therefore, even a Congress generally skeptical of the value of social science research was persuaded of the need to appropriate the funds required to clarify and test the assumptions and performance of the new programs.

Research dollars were spent in a variety of ways: to augment the research staffs of federal agencies, to finance studies by university professors and their graduate students, to augment the support of graduate education in the social sciences, to develop new centers and institutes inside and outside universities, to finance studies undertaken by commercial research corporations and independent consultants, to finance new surveys and new tabulations of existing data in the Bureau of the Census and other data-oriented agencies within the government. A variety of techniques and approaches have been pursued but the implicit, if not explicit, fundamental objective has always been to improve policies and programs, that is, to achieve a more favorable ratio of output in the form of social progress to input of financial and intellectual resources.

The notion that expenditures for research would yield positive returns was itself a hypothesis in defiance of the Biblical proverb "he who increases knowledge increases pain." But even before the pain, there were many potential slips 'twixt the cup and the lip: Would the expenditures yield new knowledge? Would the new knowledge be relevant to policy? Would the new relevant knowledge be perceived as such by policy makers? Would they act on the new relevant knowledge?

Currently there is widespread uneasiness over the Kennedy-Johnson efforts to improve the welfare of our people and the quality of the environment. There is frustration, of course, over the diversion of resources for the war in Vietnam. But there is also the nagging suspicion that we really don't know how to use what resources we have effectively, and that most new programs have fallen far short of achieving even the most modest objectives. The incumbent administration is reacting to the latter feeling with new policies and programs that are generally designed to diminish direct federal intervention, relying instead on private and local government initiative and management with federal financial support.

At the same time, there is the suspicion that the money spent on improving policy making in the domestic fields has also not produced results that justify the investment. The presumed failure of policy could be viewed as prima facie evidence of the failure of research. But while this simple deduction might be true, it is not sufficient to support the indictment against research expenditures. More direct evidence, however, is available to fortify the suspicion that the average rate of return on such expenditures is distressingly low.

Let me hasten to define what I mean by low, and to indicate the nature of the evidence. By low I mean failure to contribute adequately to *any* of the following objectives:

☐ The development of new capacity to service the research needs of government.

☐ The development and communication of new techniques and methodologies that are potentially useful to policy.

☐ The development and communication of new knowledge about socioeconomic phenomena that are the objects of policy.

☐ The development and communication of reliable information and unequivocal conclusions with respect to specific issues, questions and policies.

Low rates of return therefore implies that the sum of all the positive contributions under each of these categories is too small to justify the cost, and/or that an equivalent output could be achieved at much lower cost. It makes due allowances for the uncertainties inherent in the production of research. In other words, if we think of research as a fishing expedition, we are making the judgment that the probability of success is too low in relation to the expenditure of resources.

The ideal evidence for this judgment does not exist. There has been no systematic and certainly no comprehensive attempt to evaluate the results of government expenditures for research. Nevertheless, there is a disconcertingly large number of individuals on both the supply and the demand side of the research market who do not hesitate to characterize the bulk of the effort as totally unproductive. Many question the scientific quality of the work. Others are skeptical of its relevance to the needs of policy. Still others doubt whether any findings, however sound and relevant, can ultimately have an impact on policy.

I hope eventually to provide a somewhat firmer foundation for these judgments. Here I need only assert that there is considerable doubt about the effectiveness of government sponsored research. My concern is with the *process of procurement*, a term I will use to mean the way government goes about the business of managing research. To revert to my fishing analogy, a good way of finding out whether a man will have a good catch is to look at his technique.

MY STUDY IN PERSPECTIVE

Following the framework suggested by Yehezkel Dror in a recent paper,[4] we can identify three "systems": research, public policy-making, and the target systems (for example, health, education, transportation, urban renewal and the like). Roughly speaking we are (collectively) involved in trying to fashion at least two productive links: we want to make research a more effective tool in the making of policy and we want to use public policy to achieve progress in the target systems. The latter aspiration is not strictly tied to the former. Government may well achieve a very high level of effectiveness in dealing with social problems without a significant research contribution. That may be an unlikely outcome, but given the level of frustration with research, we had better hold on to such slim possibilities or yield to those who are already convinced that government cannot achieve anything in social problems. In any case, the link between policy and progress is almost entirely outside the scope of my study.

My concern is with the contribution of research to policy. Here, too, there are many large issues which I will get into only as they impinge upon my concerns. How do we produce knowledge which is useful to policy? How do we recruit talent into the relevant fields? How do we structure the disciplines at the university? What kinds of relationships do we encourage between researchers in different fields and between researchers and policy makers? And on and on. Again I refer you to Dror's work in which he has attempted to deal with many of these questions and to the large literature which he has painstakingly annotated for us in his footnotes and bibliography[5]

My point of departure is the dollars that government spends largely with the explicit purpose of developing knowledge useful to policy. Naturally, such dollars do not account for or coincide with the total effort in our society to improve the policy yield of research. The aggregate value of other sources of support, including the implicit support offered by universities in their light teaching loads and the burning of midnight oil by energetic scholars may very well exceed governmental outlays and may in fact be more effective in generating knowledge useful to policy. Whatever the case, government outlays surely loom large in the total effort and are likely to influence the total effort. Moreover, the study of the management of such outlays provides another opportunity to analyze public policy-making which is in itself a major area for research in the social sciences.

Finally, I should say that which will be painfully evident in a few moments, namely, that this essay is an attempt on my part to

Table A

Federal obligations for research in the social and
psychological sciences, by agency, 1960 and 1966[1]
(In thousands of dollars)

	1960	1966
Health, Education and Welfare	$23,411	$169,421
Defense	18,436	24,938
Agriculture	16,760	29,109
National Science Foundation	4,420	24,188
Commerce	3,042	20,469
Small Business Administration	1,990	445
Labor	1,562	8,459
Interior	1,107	3,852
Veterans' Administration	1,005	2,961
National Aeronautics Space Administration	430	6,584
Smithsonian Institution	174	2,422
Civil Service Commission	159	195
Federal Trade Commission	143	303
Office of Civil and Defense Mobilization	135	(2)
State	122	1,663
Civil Aeronautics Board	108	81
Federal Aviation Agency	54	29
Advisory Commission on Intergovernmental Relations	10	130
Office of Economic Opportunity	(2)	26,000
Arms Control and Disarmament Agency	(2)	2,000
Tennessee Valley Authority		759
Peace Corps	(2)	500
Housing and Urban Development	(2)	330
Federal Home Loan Bank Board		205
Post Office		50
Total	$73,095	$325,093

Source: National Science Foundation
[1] Fiscal years: 1960 figures are actual, while those for 1966 are estimates; both intramural and extramural obligations are included.
[2] Independent agency not then in existence.

articulate some very preliminary ideas which may or may not survive further scrutiny as my study proceeds.

SOME PRELIMINARY HYPOTHESES

What I have to offer is a series of hypotheses which emerge from what I hope is a judicious blending of a priori reasoning, introspection, observation and experience (my own and others'). In developing these hypotheses, it will be helpful on balance to have a particular domain of federal policy in mind. I say "on balance" because while there is a clear advantage in dealing with specifics, there is also the risk that the specifics may undermine the generality of the observations.

I hope I will be forgiven if I choose a domain with which I am intimately familiar both as a researcher and a policy-maker, namely, area economic development. I think it provides a fair illustration of the gap between where we are and where we would like to be in our public policy-making, a gap that the government is trying to fill partly with research.

AREA ECONOMIC DEVELOPMENT: A PROFILE

The Phenomenon (The Scientific Perspective).

There is and has been substantial variation in overall economic growth, in levels of per capita income and rates of unemployment between different sections of the country.

The Problem (The Social Perspective)

When a substantial *proportion* of the population in a local area is relatively impoverished and/or unemployed for sustained periods, the individual's disability and distress is accompanied by cumulative anemia in both the public and private local sectors. Therefore, normal ameliorative and rehabilitative measures are not likely to be adequate. How do we help these people and their descendants?

Policy Alternatives

☐ Provide artificial inducements to out-migration to augment those offered in the market place.

☐ Enlarge the flow of transfer payments and services to individuals and provide greater than normal financial and technical support to local government.

☐ Provide artificial inducements to employers to augment the demand for labor and the wage level in the area.

The Policy Choice Reflected in Actual Legislation.

Principal reliance has been placed on the third alternative mentioned above, in the Area Redevelopment Act of 1961, the Appalachian Regional Development Act of 1965, and the Public Works and Economic Development Act of 1965, the three pieces of legislation specifically addressed to this problem. Some of the provisions in these Acts and in other federal legislation have the effect intended by the second alternative and a small pilot program not restricted to distressed areas follows the strategy suggested in alternative one.

The Procedure

☐ Designation of areas as eligible for assistance.

☐ Preparation of Economic Development Plans.

☐ Financing of specific projects.

The Tools of Policy

☐ The stimulation of an organized effort in the local area to accelerate economic development.

☐ The provision of technical and financial assistance to facilitate overall planning and the identification and design of feasible projects.

☐ Grants and/or loans to help finance components of the local infra-structure essential to industrial expansion.

☐ Long-term low interest rate loans to enterprises locating or expanding in the local area.

Here, then, is an example of a domain of federal policy and our question is, what research capabilities need to be developed to serve the needs of the decision-maker? At the risk of not being exhaustive, I offer the following classifications.

1. The capacity to develop reliable economic indicators (for example, rate of unemployment, per capita income) for small areas on at least an annual basis.

2. The capacity to identify the critical obstacles to more rapid development in specific areas.

3. The capacity to estimate and evaluate the impacts of specific projects, after the fact.

4. The capacity to estimate and evaluate the impacts of specific projects, before the fact.

5. The capacity to measure and evaluate the marginal contribution of each of the authorized tools of policy.

6. The capacity to measure the impact of "outside" events (inclusive of other federal policies) on the economic status of distressed areas.

7. The capacity to cooperate with decision makers in the articulation of objectives and the development of decision rules.

This classification is intermediate in detail between the statement that what is needed is data and analysis, on the one hand, and on the other, a list of more specific end-uses for research, such as:

1. The efficient allocation of the present budget among competing projects.

2. The preparation of the next year's budget.

3. The preparation of longer term budgets and recommendations to the president and the Congress for modifying the basic tactics and strategy of federal policy in this field.

The administrator who sees his needs in these terms will unquestionably find the state of the research art sorely lacking on almost every count. There is economic information on small areas in government and private publications but it is far from adequate for his purposes. There is survey and data gathering capability in the research community but it is severely limited in relation to the growing demands in and outside of government. There is a modest literature and a heritage of academic research on the whys and wherefores of industrial location, population shifts and regional development but it is largely sterile in terms of concrete guidance to policy. He finds the methodology of project evaluation in a very primitive state, notwithstanding the Corps of Engineers-inspired development of cost-benefit analysis. In short, he finds that he cannot pluck the answers to his questions from existing research reports and manuals and he finds a meagre supply of competent individuals and organizations oriented to his problems. But he does have authority to spend X millions for research. His problem then is to use these resources efficiently to begin to fill the gaping holes in his knowledge. What are the elements of a good strategy to achieve that objective?

Control

If the administrator views research as critical to his decision process he will want to manage his research budget in a way that maximizes his control over the allocation of resources. Quite simply, he will want to feel confident that the allocation is guided by his objectives and needs. Since he cannot be his own research director, he will want to hire one who will act on his behalf in securing that kind of control over the research program. The research director, in turn, will want to maximize his control over the program by the careful selection of competent staff similarly oriented.

This may suggest that all research should be done in-house, to maximize control. But even assuming that the administrator could spend all his funds on staff and that the right people could be found, this might not be the optimal strategy, for there are significant economies of scale in certain kinds of research. In other words, control comes at the expense of higher average costs or lower quality for a given cost. Specialized organizations with accumulated experience can presumably provide an increment of effort on behalf of the agency at lower cost than the same effort in-house. For example, the cost of a survey conducted by Michigan's Survey Research Center ought to be less than the cost of the same survey mounted by the agency staff.

In the real world the balance between control and quality is even more heavily tipped in favor of outside procurement because of severe constraints on in-house staffing. There is first of all the overriding imperative to hold down the size of the federal payroll. There is in addition a quality constraint because the authorized grade structure precludes the hiring of more than a few top flight experienced people. Finally, a given job does not necessarily attract and hold the best candidate because, while federal salaries and working conditions are often quite competitive, there are many features of federal employment that do not appeal to professional social scientists. The result is that research staffs are typically too small and/or inferior in average quality.

I offer this as my first hypothesis: *in most federal agencies the in-house capability is much too limited to secure an acceptable measure of control.* Lack of control manifests itself in many different ways: poorly articulated research objectives, poor selection of contractor or grantee, inadequate monitoring of progress, and an inability to review reports critically, to interpret results to decision makers, and to relate results of other relevant research. The conscientious contractor or grantee is often frustrated by an unresponsive, passive and incompetent client. The incompetent or irresponsible contractor or grantee can get by with shoddy performance. At best you get a product which is of some academic value to somebody; more typically you get a product which is of no value to anybody.

A particularly vicious and wasteful form of in-house failure is high turnover of research directors and staffs. Well conceived projects launched in an atmosphere of good relations between contractor and client often degenerate because along the way the client has changed his identity and his research interests and objectives. There is typically greater stability and continuity on the supply side than there is on the demand side.

Short and Long Run Research: A Bad Mix

I asserted above that my administrator confronts a world sorely lacking in the expertise most relevant to his needs. The NASA chief who was directed to land a man on the moon before 1970 also faced an inadequate technology and personnel. But he had no alternative to investing in the development of the requisite Technology and personnel. The Great Society administrator operated in a more complicated decision-making context. His mandate was considerably less precise in the large and much more detailed in the small. He had to begin to obligate funds for specific projects in specific areas shortly after his appointment. Neither the Secretary of Defense nor the Congress could tolerate an extended gestation period. He needed research assistance to guide the allocation of resources in the short run, while the ground was being prepared for improved policies and decisions in the long run. There are, however, many factors that work against the successful reconciliation of short and long run research needs.

My second hypothesis, therefore, is this: *it is inefficient for agencies administering programs on a day-to-day basis to sponsor basic research, that is, research designed to develop fundamental capacities of the kind enumerated above.*

Why can't there be a workable division of labor within the agency? The demand for instant wisdom where there is monumental ignorance is infinitely elastic. No matter how large the staff and how generous the budget, it is still painful to engage in roundabout methods of production, to invest in people, techniques, data and other basic needs. Despite, if not because of, the fact that current consumption of research is extremely costly—supply is extremely inelastic and quality is poor—there is increasingly less sympathy for research projects that do not even offer the promise of any yield in the short run. In the extreme case, the lack of sympathy is reflected in low or zero allocations for basic research. More often, however, the result is not such a happy one. The research program goes on but it is divorced from the central concerns of the agency and is not geared to be useful even in the long run. The overwhelming pressure to seek results of immediate relevance in the short-run project leads paradoxically to a total neglect of relevance in the long-run project. "If you can't help me today, go play ... "

Concentration versus Dispersion of Support

What is most desperately needed in research on social problems is a cumulative process of learning. As eager as we are to solve our problems in a great hurry, we are not likely to learn from a process of trial and error unless we can accumulate the experience. This argues for a reasonable concentration of effort because the communication of experience between organizations is itself a very time consuming process and one that is not generally effective in the early stages of scientific development. Yet many agencies are like the gambler who bets on many horses, fond of spreading their largesse far and wide because it increases the probability that they will win gross, if not net. There are also outside pressures that inhibit concentration such as the fear of inviting congressional investigation, the need to respond to special interests and the unrelenting pleas of contractors for a piece of the action.

My third hypothesis is therefore: *dispersion of awards inhibits the orderly development of capacity to respond effectively to the research needs of policy.* The creation of the Poverty Institute at the University of Wisconsin and the Urban Institute in Washington suggest an attempt by the federal government to achieve a greater degree of concentration of research expenditures. I shall have more to say about these institutions later.

Competitive Bidding vs. Sole Source

Research awards are made in the form of grants and contracts. In the case of a grant there is no compulsion on the part of the agency to defend the award in explicitly competitive terms. The reason for this is that a grant is explicitly not intended to yield specific outputs. Rather it is an expression of faith on the part of the agency in the research potential of a given investigator or group of investigators, a university center, or a nonprofit institute. Grants are, of course, tied to proposals that indicate specific research interests and methodologies but, after the fact, the government is in no position to withhold payment on performance criteria. Such criteria are only relevant to future decisions on new grants.

A contract, however, carries with it the implication that the government is procuring a product with specified characteristics, a concept that owes its origins to hardware procurement. The implication is reinforced by the issuance of a document by the agency known in the trade as a (RFP) Request for Proposal which describes the desired product and invites the submission of proposals. Such proposals are expected to detail how the potential contractor proposes to produce the desired product: the methodology, the resources, their costs, and the form of the output. The RFP generally provides certain guidelines as to duration and level of effort, and these, along with other aspects of the Agency's interests, are elaborated at a "bidders' conference" which is scheduled well in advance of the deadline for the submission of proposals.

This seemingly rational approach to procurement is fraught with inefficiency and is often frustrating to all parties on both sides. The inefficiency is suggested by the unfavorable relationship between the total costs of selecting a contractor in this manner and the value of the contract. These costs are borne initially in part by contractors in the preparation of proposals and in part by the agency in the review of proposals, but ultimately they are all borne by the government in the form of overhead charges against specific contracts.

I am not yet able to offer any precise statistics but I have no doubt that there are some instances in which the cost of selecting a contractor exceeds the dollar value of the contract and many instances in which the cost is a very high percentage of the value of the contract. Of course, the ratio itself is not prima facie evidence of cost-ineffectiveness. After all, if we had to spend a million dollars to discover a genius and he offered his services gratis, the ratio would be infinity, yet the process could not be deemed to be inefficient. Unfortunately, there is no genius to be discovered by competitive bidding and the process is both costly and unproductive, that is, it contributes little to the success of the project.

Where to begin? I suppose the logical starting point is the RFP itself. Very often an RFP boils down to a plea of this sort: "We're at the base of this mountain and we want to get to the top. Show us how you propose to get us up there in three (or six) months using roughly three man years of professional effort. Oh yes, and take no more than three weeks to prepare your proposal."

Examples: We wish to know how to measure and evaluate the impact of specific infrastructure investments on area development. Can you help us with that problem? How?

We have been financing a great variety of technical assistance projects. Do they serve a useful purpose? How can we tell a good project from a bad one? Can you suggest ways of solving that problem?

My point is that very often, if not in the majority of cases, an RFP is really a call for highly imaginative innovation and experimentation, but put forth as a call for a specific set of outputs. This pretense is costly for many reasons. First, it prompts the bidder to go along with it and to lay claim, via an elaborate statement with a lot of window dressing, to skills, data sources, techniques and experience which simply don't exist, and/or to greatly underestimate the difficulties of acquiring them. The resulting proposal further stimulates the expectations of the agency to the point where they begin to believe that what seems to be an impossible task can indeed be performed under severe time and resource constraints. Later, there will be the inevitable disillusion as both the contractor and the client find that it is indeed impossible to scale the peak without the proper equipment. Unfortunately, hope springs eternal, and the contractor, driven by the pressure to generate revenue, and the client, by the pressure to make or defend decisions, will repeat the same learning experience again and again.

The main point to be made here is that *when an agency is in fact looking for a contractor to explore unchartered areas of research, competitive bidding adds little to the capacity to make a rational choice among alternative bidders.* Information about the firm—its staff and track record—can be secured relatively cheaply without requiring formal proposals. The proposal, which is costly to prepare and to review, adds little to the evidence on which a choice should be made. The time of the in-house staff would better be spent reading and evaluating the firm's prior output and checking with their counterparts in other agencies who may have had prior experience with the same firm. The time of the contractor's staff would better be spent in improving the quality of their performance on existing contracts.

Sometimes, the RFP errs in the opposite direction. It describes in detail both the product and the process and leaves little or no scope to the initiative of the contractor. An honest response to such an invitation would be to describe the firm's credentials and then simply quote a price on a job which has been fully described in the RFP. But then there is the haunting suspicion that the agency will interpret this "cool" approach as indicative of a fundamental lack of interest in the project. This suspicion is fed by a teasing clause in many RFPs which invites the bidder to suggest "other" approaches to the problem. The contractor is then prompted to educate the agency in its proposal and sometimes this bold strategy pays off. More often the proposal goes over the ground covered by the RFP adding a point here and there. Again, the agency's review of the proposals adds little to its capacity to pick the right contractor.

Given the state of the art, there are very few cases in between, where the desired product has fairly well defined characteristics but there are alternative ways of producing the product. For such cases, the RFP begins to make sense, but even so it can be abused and mismanaged. There is no point in encouraging dozens of firms, as often happens, to bid for the same contract, regardless of the scope and value of the project. Preliminary screening of credentials will almost always narrow the field very considerably and when a small number of firms have been selected on this basis it *may* make sense to invite each to submit a proposal.

My fourth hypothesis is therefore: *Procurement on the basis of RFPs and proposals is generally a highly inefficient technique for selecting the appropriate organization to do research under contract. It. is a poor substitute for the judicious placement of grants and sole source contracts.*

As my work proceeds I will generate additional hypotheses regarding the efficient mobilization of resources for policy-oriented research. I hope eventually to be able to offer some informed judgments on the relative merits of alternative forms of organization on the supply side: university centers and institutes, independent non-profit, and commercial operations. I also intend to include in my purview the research expenditures of state and local governments. How far I can get in this effort will depend on how I go about verifying my hypotheses. This difficult problem is, however, fit subject for a whole other essay.

NOTES

[1] 90th Congress, 1st Session, House of Representatives, *The Use of Social Research in Federal Domestic Programs*, A Staff Study for The Research and Technical Programs Subcommittee of the Committee on Government Operations, April 1967.

[2] In addition to the earlier citation, there are the three volumes of hearings before the Subcommittee on Government Research of the Committee on Government Operations, U. S. Senate, on S-836, *A Bill To Provide For The Establishment Of The National Foundation For The Social Sciences*, February and June 1967 (Washington, D. C., U. S. Government Printing Office, 1967). Also, National Academy of Sciences, Advisory Committee on Government Programs in the Behavioral Sciences, National Research Council, *The Behavioral Sciences and The Federal Government* (Washington, D. C., National Academy of Sciences, 1968); and Special Commission on the Social Sciences of the National Sciences Board, National Science Foundation, *Knowledge Into Action*, 1969.

[3] Harold Orlans, *On the Quality of University Research Supported by the Government*, reprinted in The Use of Social Research in Federal Domestic Programs, Part II, Page 618.

[4] Yehezkel Dror, *A General Systems Approach to Uses of Behavioral Sciences for Better Policymaking*, RAND P-4091.

[5] Yehezkel Dror, *Public Policymaking Re-examined.* (San Francisco: Chandler, 1968).

[6] As simple as this concept may seem, I owe a debt to Worth Bateman of the Urban Institute in helping me to formulate it in these terms.

11

Public Policy and the White Working Class

JOHN HOWARD

The United States lacks many types of social welfare programs taken for granted in other industrial democracies.[1] And the consequences of this are borne by broad sections of the population. Much attention in this regard has been focused on the poor, but a far larger segment of the population, including most of the white working class, feels the consequences of this lack as well, for it is at best marginal economically. Both the poor and the economically marginal would benefit enormously from social welfare programs. Paradoxically, however, the white working class, unlike nonwhites and some segments of the white intelligentsia, scarcely conceives of the need for new and more adequate social welfare programs. Consequently, as such programs come into existence they are popularly viewed as being for blacks or other minorities. This reinforces white working class resistance to them and reinforces their identification as racially-oriented programs.

In simple Marxist terms the white working class manifests "false consciousness." The political scientist Robert Lane has indicated that they moralize downward rather than upward,[2] becoming indignant about the welfare mother who receives a few dollars a year over her alloted stipend but shrugging off the price-rigging businessman who might have bilked the public of millions. This chapter discusses the foundations of this perspective, and its consequences as regards the character of social welfare policy in the United States.

Social scientists, like other Americans, have traditionally been concerned with the powerful and with social outcasts. Consequently, as Peter Schrag observed of the white worker, "there is hardly a language to describe him, or even social statistics." Poverty and affluence are the subject of endless studies and books, yet white workers are neither poor, nor, in any meaningful sense, affluent. Their life style can be conveyed in literature but social scientists have no adequate conceptual category to define their existence. Schrag attempted a summation: "between slums and suburbs, between Scarsdale and Harlem, between Shaker Heights and Hough, there are some eighty million people (depending on how you count them)". It is the world of American Legion posts, neighborhood bars, the Ukrainian club and the Holy Name Society. They live in tract homes in Daly City and south San Francisco, Bay Ridge and Canarsie, "bunting on the porch rail with the inscription 'Welcome Home Pete'. The gold star in the window."[3] This population is culturally square and traditionalist. Rock music and movies as an art form are not within their cultural purview; what the hip regard as "camp", they take seriously; what the hip take seriously they regard as boring, annoying or disgusting. It is a measure of the partial validity of the term "forgotten American" that they cannot be as precisely defined as those at the bottom or those at the top.[4]

This essay is divided into three parts, the first two of which take up the question of whether the white working class has a set of interests which might reasonably be served by changes in social welfare policy. In the first, on "comparative social welfare policy" the United States and other industrial democracies are compared. This comparison suggests that the United States lacks a number of social welfare programs commonly found in other industrial countries. In the second, the economic characteristics of the white working class are discussed, and it is indicated that they are far from being affluent. These two sections lay the foundation for the third, which identifies and analyzes those factors which generate and sustain white working class perspectives on social welfare

policy and their seeming hostility despite being potential beneficiaries.

This essay rests on the assumption that public policy is formed
partially in response to the constellation of pressures to which
office holders are subjected. Here, the pressures to be focused on
are those of the white working class as an interest group. Their
attitudes and behavior cannot be accounted for in terms of any
simple Marxian model. The issue is one that has agitated American
radicals for decades; it is also an important question for political
sociology. And, of course, it is important in grasping the tone and
direction of American society.

COMPARATIVE SOCIAL WELFARE POLICY

The United States is conventionally thought of as the most
advanced nation in the world. It can be plausibly argued however
that in many ways the country is rather backward, for it lacks a
number of social welfare programs taken for granted in western
democracies. It is the thrust of my discussion that this has
important consequences as regards the quality of life in the society
and that it can be accounted for partially in terms of the absence
of any strong sense of class interest or political consciousness on
the part of white workers, those whom I have termed economically marginal.

The relative dearth of social welfare programs in this the most
advanced nation in the world has been noted by several commentators. For example, Alvin Schorr has observed with regard to
family allowances that "A majority of the countries of the world
and all of the industrial West, except the United States, now have
such programs." James Vadikan points out that family allowances
" . . . constitute a means of redistributing income in such a way as
to benefit the child-rearing portion of the population."[5] In most
countries it is a fairly modest sum. Under the Canadian system, for
example, the amount per child ranges from $6 a month to $10 a
month depending on the child's age. By contrast, the French
system is quite generous.[6] "The payment there varies according to
region, the number of children in the family, and their ages. In
Paris in 1964, for example, a family with four children received
between 380 and 450 francs ($77 to $111) a month, exceeding
the legal minimum wage at the time. In addition, various special

payments may be made during pregnancy, at birth, (and) for improved housing."[7]

Edgar Z. Friedenberg has suggested that the United States " . . . still provides less in the way of social services, especially to the ill and aged, than an Englishman or Scandinavian would expect as a matter of right." National health insurance plans are found in one form or another in all of the industrial democracies, although the extent of benefits varies from place to place. In Great Britain complete medical, surgical, pharmaceutical and dental services are offered. In Australia, one finds restricted pharmaceutical benefits, hospital benefits, and various other kinds of services. But there are basically three types of national health programs: The government may own facilities and hire the professionals, patients may pay fees and be reimbursed, or professionals may render services under contract to the government. Most West European countries have the latter type of program. There is a good deal of nonsense talked in the United States about the British system. No doctor is forced to join the national health service but 95 percent have chosen to do so. Their income is lower than that of doctors in the United States but higher than they were before Health Service came in and higher than that of other professionals in Great Britain.

Social welfare policy extends beyond the provision of certain kinds of services and income redistribution to embrace the creation of opportunities. All developed nations have specified policies with respect to manpower and employment. These policies vary in terms of the extent to which they sustain the worker during periods of unemployment and facilitate his re-employment. Sweden has a number of sophisticated manpower programs, leading Carl Uhr to observe that "We in the United States have not yet developed as comprehensive and coordinated a set of labor policies and institutions as have evolved in Sweden." In addition to a variety of training programs for older workers whose skills have become obsolete and younger people without marketable skills, there are mechanisms for matching up workers with jobs. "Workers living in labor-surplus areas," says Uhr, "are induced by a system of allowances to move to available jobs, known to the employment service, in labor shortage areas. Unemployed persons who need and want to move great distances to job opportunities in other locations may apply for and receive travel expenses to seek new work in these areas. If they locate jobs, they may immediately receive a 'starting allowance.' This is in substance a grant which becomes repayable in part only if they do not hold the new job for at least 90 days." Other problems associated with worker mobility are anticipated: "If housing for their families is not available in their new work location, they may receive 'family allowances' for the separate maintenance of wife and children for up to 9 months in their former location. These allowances pay the rent for the family up to a maximum figure, plus a cash allowance for the maintenance of wife and children."[8]

Few of these critics argue that the United States should simply mirror other industrial democracies with regard to social welfare policy and programs. These approaches are not ends in themselves but are designed to alleviate certain kinds of mass deprivation, deprivation that is readily visible and apparently persistent in this country, which has adopted few of these policies or programs. Some scholars have pointed to what they believe to be the tangible consequences of the paucity of comprehensive social welfare measures in the United States. Daniel Patrick Moynihan has stated that "The teeming disorganized life of impoverished slums has all but disappeared among North American democracies—save only the United States. It requires some intrepidness to declare this to be a fact, as no systematic inquiry has been made which would provide completely dependable comparisons, but it can be said with fair assurance that mass poverty and squalor, of the kind that may be encountered in almost any American city, simply cannot be found in comparable cities in Europe or Canada or Japan." Robert Heilbroner echos this, "I maintain that to match the squalor of the worst of the American habitat one must descend to the middle range of the underdeveloped lands."[9]

Infant mortality rates in the United States are considerably higher than those in other industrial democracies. In 1968 with a rate of 22.1 infant deaths per 1,000 live births the country ranked above most other western, industrial democracies. It is estimated that the nation ranks eighteenth in the world, just above Hong Kong. Some might argue that this is a consequence of the extraordinarily high rate among nonwhites, but even if we consider the rate among whites only (in Mississippi, for example, 23.1 among whites; in Pennsylvania 20.3; Maine, 22.8; New Hampshire, 20.1; Vermont, 21.0; Illinois, 20.3; West Virginia,

24.8), the national performance is inferior to that of other western countries.[10]

Vadikan has observed that "Almost 40,000 babies die in America each year who would be saved if our infant mortality rate was as low as that in Sweden. In 1967, one million babies, one in four, [were] born to mothers receiving little or no obstetric care."[11]

To reiterate, whether the United States is the most developed nation in the world or underdeveloped depends upon the dimension one examines. If one looks at the number of automobiles per 1,000 of the population the United States leads the field. If one looks at infant mortality rates, or number of hospital beds per 1,000, or number of doctors per 1,000, or average rates of unemployment over time, the country lags, and along some dimensions lags badly.

Some might counter that the United States has programs that other democracies lack ("New Careers", Headstart, Upward Bound and so forth). It is the case, however, that these programs are directed at the poor and are not intended to meet the needs and problems of those who are marginal. Secondly, although international comparisons are difficult to make, it does appear to be true that all things taken together (save education) the United States spends relatively less on social welfare than many other countries. Bert Seidman has observed that,

It generally surprises most Americans to find out that their country, the wealthiest in the world, uses less of its natural wealth for the social welfare of its citizens than other advanced industrial nations and frequently less than many poor and developing nations which make considerable sacrifices to do so.

For example, an International Labor Organization Report published in 1964 shows that West Germany, Luxemburg, Austria, and Italy used 17 percent, 16.8 percent, 14.8 percent and 14.7 percent respectively, of their gross national product for social welfare measures. None of the 15 nations in Western Europe, except Spain and Portugal, spent less than 8.9 percent. This contrasts with 7 percent of the gross national product spent by the United States for such programs.[12]

The United States spends more on education and has a much higher proportion of its college age population in college than

West European countries. This is partially a consequence of having different channels of access to employment. However, the lower proportion of the European college age population in college does not mean that there is mass unemployment or that jobs go begging, rather the system of matching up man and job is different. There is a school of thought however which suggests that European technological development and entreprenurial efficiency may be hurt in the long run by not having a work force with as much formal education as that in the United States. If that occurs and European countries move to spend more on education, the relative position of the United States in terms of social welfare spending would remain unchanged.

Mike Harrington has indicated that "the American percentage of the gross national product devoted to direct social benefits has yet to achieve even half the typical European contribution." It is not a matter of course that the white working class with greater political consciousness would be demanding precisely these programs, but rather that they would be demanding something.

Let us now look more closely at the economic status of white workers.

THE POOR AND THE MARGINAL

It is assumed by many observers that the white working class has become conservative because it has become affluent and therefore does not need amplified social welfare legislation. Actually about 12 percent of the white population is poor while another 55 to 60 percent is economically marginal.

Like poor nonwhites, poor whites have been clearly identified by demographers, economists and sociologists. In 1967 of the 26,146,000 people in the country defined as poor, 17,764,000 were white.[13] Among the 384,000 young men in 1964, who were 20 to 24 years of age and unemployed, 310,000 were white and 74,000 were nonwhite; 450,000 or 554,000 unemployed young men 14 to 19 in 1964 were white.[14] In December, 1969, 1,137,000 white males 16 years of age and over were unemployed and 266,000 blacks. The black rate was higher, of course—5.3 to 2.5 for whites. But the figures and the rates belied the notion that unemployment was solely or primarily a black problem.

The economically marginal white is much harder to identify. His existence defines the inadequacy of the simple dichotomy between the poor and the affluent. Below, five quantitative measures are employed to define the existence of this class: income distribution, standard of living, real income, credit status and liquid assets.

As regards income distribution, in 1966, 31 percent of white families made less than $5,000; 39 percent made $5,000 to $9,999, while another 30 percent made more than $10,000 a year.[15] Seven families of ten then were poor or marginal. But income figures per se mean little unless they are related to purchasing power and standard of living. An inference with regard to the meaning of the income of white workers can be made by an analysis of reports published by the Bureau of Labor Statistics, U.S. Department of Labor. The bureau regularly devises a "standard family budget" for a four person family consisting of working husband, nonworking wife, son, age 13, and daughter, age 8. This closely approximates actual family structure. The budget is derived from "scientific and technical judgment regarding health and social well-being" and is designed to indicate the cost of a "modest but adequate" standard of living in urban areas. In 1967 the required sum ranged down from $10,092 in Honolulu to $9,744 in the San Francisco-Oakland area, $9,079 in Philadelphia and $8,641 in Durham, with a low of $7,952 in Austin, Texas. The average for 39 cities and metropolitan areas was $9,243.[16]

In the same year, production and nonsupervisory workers on nonagricultural payrolls averaged just over $5,000 a year ranging from a high of $8,060 for construction workers to a low of $4,264 for those in wholesale and retail trade. All fell well below the government's own figure of the amount needed to enjoy a moderate level of living in urban areas.[17] The mean income of craftsmen and foremen was $9,310, otherwise no workers year to year even approach the average of the Standard Family Budget.

Further the effects of inflation eroded the money gains made by the blue collar class. Between 1965 and 1969 the average wage of 47 million production and nonsupervisory workers in private industry went up $14.74 from $96.21 to $110.95 per week; at the same time, the worker with three dependents saw his tax rise by $4.80 a week. The four year increase in prices from a base of 100 in 1965 was $11.18. Adding the price rise to the tax increase and subtracting from the 1969 wage, the worker had $1.24 per week less to spend in 1969 than in 1965.[18]

None of this proves, of course, that the American blue collar and working class lives in misery and desperation. Obviously, it does not. Nonetheless, it seems undeniable that they are far from affluent, that life is probably a worrisome thing, and that the opportunity to get very far ahead seems more and more distant.

Apart from the bureau's "modest but adequate" standard, we also have to look into consumer finance to find the meaning of dollar income. The Economic Behavior Program of the Survey Research Center of the University of Michigan yearly collects detailed information on "family income, financial assets and debt, automobiles, other durable goods, and housing." Multi-stage area probability sampling is used to select a sample of dwelling units representative of the nation.

The debt status of economically marginal whites can be summed up as follows. About 55 percent of the families in the income category $5,000 to $7,449 had installment debt and 61 percent in the income category $7,500 to $9,999. Being unmarried and having no children reduced the probability of being in debt. About 65 to 70 percent of households with children were in debt. In 1967 the mean amount of debt for all families was $1,260. Payments for automobiles were most common but were closely followed by payments on other durables and for personal loans.[19]

The meaning of debt is amplified if viewed in terms of financial assets at the command of workers. About 80 percent of wage earners making $5,000 to $10,000 a year in 1967 either had no checking account or had less than $500 in an account. Sixty three percent of families making $5,000 to $7,499 either had no savings account or had less than $500 in an account; 46 percent of those families making $7,500 to $9,999 had no account or had less than $500 in an account. The amount of liquid assets then is meager and most families are a paycheck or two away from public assistance.[20]

The life style of the marginal class is suggested by other data. Less than half take vacations and those who do rarely spend much money on it. It is not the case then that there is an affluent blue collar or working class white collar class. Most white families are either poor or economically marginal. If they are marginal they have not had a rise in real income since 1965 despite a rise in paper income. Federal data suggest that they may barely make a modest but adequate standard of living. They have acquired certain household goods and durables by going into debt and have the slenderest resources to sustain themselves in a crisis.

The American worker has to purchase out of his pocket services that are publicly provided in many other industrial democracies. He is taxed but there is no commensurate return as regards public services. For example, the American worker, except under highly restricted circumstances, bears out of his own pocket the cost of moving to a locale where he may find work, the cost of supporting his family while looking for work, and the cost of moving them. A whole complex of expenditures, which as we saw is a matter of public responsibility in Sweden, is paid for privately by the American worker.

Social scientists have devised a number of classificatory systems to describe the American population. To further delineate the position of economic marginals within the society I have formulated a rather gross system which does, nevertheless, make certain important distinctions.

I would, for purposes of this discussion, divide the American population into four categories.

At the bottom there are the poor (a disproportionate percentage of the black population and of Indians, Mexicans and Puerto Ricans, a disproportionate percentage of the elderly and of families headed by a female). The poor subsist on public monies, inadequate incomes or both. They are unable to make ends meet and thus may suffer from malnutrition or a wide variety of debilitating, untreated medical conditions. A segment of the black population and, increasingly, parts of the Indian, Mexican and Puerto Rican populations, show some degree of political consciousness and some conception of the need to develop national policy approaches to the problems of the deprived.

Then there are the marginals. Most of the white working class population falls into this category, and indeed most of the population. Their characteristics have already been described.[21]

Above them is a class that has substantial money income but does not own or control wealth (the distinction between income and wealth is important). They sell brain power and relatively uncommon skills and are handsomely rewarded. In this category are such persons as the upper echelon professors at the more prestigious universities, the new experts at information control, systems analysts, middle and upper echelon advertising and media men, most business management people, and the like. These people are affluent and some of them have influence with the powerful. Basically they are well-paid laborers however. The politics of this group spans the spectrum and it is difficult to tell what the factors are that account for value differences.

Last there are the true magnates, the corporate elites, the people who own or control the wealth of the country. The upper 5 percent of consumers in the country control 53 percent of the wealth. There is much greater inequality in the distribution of wealth than there is in the distribution of income, accounting for the class of income-affluent persons.

The marginals appear, for reasons we shall explore, to consider themselves closer to the top than to the bottom when in fact they are much closer to the bottom than to the top.

POLITICAL VALUES OF THE WHITE WORKING CLASS

It should be clear by now that the white working class is not affluent. Neither, of course are white workers poor. They make enough to meet daily living costs and are able to acquire appliances, durables and some other kinds of goods through installment buying. They have little in the way of liquid assets and are highly vulnerable in the event of loss of job, illness or any of a number of other kinds of misfortunes. They would benefit enormously from a wide variety of social welfare measures that are quite conventional in other industrial democracies. But they are not politically active in the pursuit of these or other social welfare measures and have left lobbying and agitation for more effective and broadly based programs up to blacks and to white liberals and radicals. They are the people whose sons get drafted and sent to Vietnam and whose children are less likely to get into college even when they are extremely capable. Inadequate opportunity for higher education is generally seen as a problem of nonwhites. The existence of inadequate educational opportunities is widespread. With regard to higher education, Project Talent, a survey funded by the United States Office of Education revealed a "marked relationship between reported family income and college entry." Data were gathered on 60,000 students. Basically, the findings were that males in the 98th to 100th percentile were likely to go to college irrespective of family income. Below that, social class became very important, with the mediocre male at the 50th percentile whose family made $12,000 a year or more being more likely to have entered college than the talented boy at the 89th percentile whose family made $3,000 a year or less. The reality behind these data are neither perceived nor translated into political reality by poor and marginal whites.

Why are economically marginal whites not further to the left politically? Why are they not active in promoting the kinds of policy approaches and programs that would appear to serve their own interests?

To be a supporter of movements to realize the kinds of social welfare policy discussed earlier in this chapter implies that one, a) recognizes the existence of certain kinds of problems, b) accounts for these problems in system terms, and therefore, c) calls for given policy approaches to cope with them. Obviously, if an individual either does not recognize the existence of particular problems, or accounts for them in personalistic terms then he does not seek system changes or new policy approaches.

Evidence on how the white worker defines his own situation is vague and inconclusive. The data provide no basis for anything other than hypothesis and speculation. Therefore let us hypothesize and speculate.[22]

The results of public opinion polls suggest that white workers have a sense of the inadequacy of their position but are at a loss to explain it. Something is wrong but they are not clear as to what. Lloyd A. Tree and Hadley Cantril, reporting on a representative national sample, indicate that personal economic conditions and employment status were cited by three out of four persons as their most pressing concerns.[23] This seems to have surprised the researchers. "Even in affluent America, the leading item mentioned under personal wishes and hopes was an 'improved or decent standard of living.' As one Arizona housewife pointed out, 'They say it's prosperous now, but I sure as heck don't notice it.' " This chapter suggests that the Arizona housewife was more nearly correct than Tree and Cantril.

Alongside an appreciation of a precarious material situation was complete confusion with regard to policy and meliorative approaches. On the one hand, the overwhelming majority of respondents making $10,000 a year or less favored government programs to accomplish social ends, but only one-third believed

the government should more readily use its power. Less than
one-third believed that corporate powers should be curbed while
almost half favored greater government control over labor unions.

The task then is to make sense of this, to understand it, to grasp
the underlying logic and rationale. If there is an underlying logic it
is probably something on the following order: "Yes," the worker
says, "I would benefit from various kinds of government programs; they would help me meet real and pressing material
problems. Those problems, however, are caused by other segments
of the population. Therefore, alternatively, the government might
force these people to stop doing the kinds of things which cause
problems for me."

Enlarging on this, contemporary workers who recall the
desperate and hungry souls populating "Hoovervilles" during the
depression, who use them as a kind of negative reference group,
are likely to feel comparatively well off. Those too young to have
experienced the depression undoubtedly have it recalled for them
by parents. Their dollar income is substantially greater, the
number of household possessions is greater, they have greater job
security. This relative satisfaction with having enjoyed a certain
amount of mobility probably decreases the workers' proclivity to
criticize the politico-economic system or view it as inequitable and
unjust. It decreases any sense of a need to agitate for new policy.
It is also the case, however, that the worker still has trouble
making ends meet. These difficulties, implicitly, pose a question
for him. "If I'm so much better off and make so much more
money than guys made before, how come I'm still having a rough
time?" His belief that the system has afforded him the opportunity for a better life decreases the likelihood that he will account
for his difficulties in terms of system defects. If the system were
not benign he would not now be in a position where he should be
enjoying a better life. In absolving the system he also absolves
those who, in some sense, run it.

There are a number of ready-made scapegoats the worker can
focus on in attempting to account for his difficulties (blacks,
communists, hippies, liberals, "peace creeps"); of these, blacks are
the most plausible and the most accessible. As blacks demand
programs to deal with poverty, as they demand a guaranteed
annual income, or an improved system of distribution of food to
the needy and the hungry, as they demand a whole complex of

social welfare legislation, they must seem to the white worker to be unwilling to take advantage of the opportunities he believes exist for any person willing to work. They seem to be making vigorous raids on his pocketbook. They appear to be cheaters, people unwilling to play by the rules, people who "want something for nothing." And he believes the something comes out of his pocket.

This kind of explanation posits genuine misperception on the part of the worker. An alternative (psychologically "deeper") approach might posit displacement of frustration and hostility onto scapegoats. Roughly, the position would be phrased as follows: the worker has some glimpse of the precariousness of his position and some sense of the reasons for it. However to consciously entertain notions of system defects of that sort, would be to admit harboring ideas that are "un-American" or "communist inspired." And for the man who pastes his American flag decal on the car windshield and puts an "Honor America" sticker on his bumper, this might be no small matter. It might in the political sphere be the equivalent of a man admitting to having fleeting sexual thoughts about other men. Rather than countenance thoughts he has come to view as subversive and immoral, it is psychologically easier to displace hostility onto outgroups—blacks, hippies, "bleeding hearts", "limousine liberals" and other freaks of nature.

Additionally, there are internal differentiations in the white working class which probably act to impede the expression of a common point of view or common sentiments with regard to problems and their solutions. The 80 million or so people who comprise the marginal class are differentiated by geography, ethnicity and occupation. A number of students have discussed the persistence of ethnic identity in American communities. Michael Parenti has observed that "in a single weekend in New York separate dances for persons of Hungarian, Irish, Italian, German and Polish extractions are advertised in the neighborhood newspapers and the foreign language press.[24] Herbert Gans[25] and Gerald Suttles[26] have discussed the persistence of a tightly knit network of relationships among Italians living in Boston and in Chicago. Occupationally, the $5,000 to $10,000 category embraces secretaries and assembly line workers, senior clerks and cab drivers. Geographically workers spread out over the south with its racially dominated politics, the midwest where fear of communism is a serious sentiment, and the northeast where problems of traffic congestion and state financial support for parochial schools excite political passions.

In other words, there are a number of cross-cutting loyalties and interests that reduce any sense of common identity.

The trade unions embrace a larger portion of the American working class than any other organization. The union movement itself however is internally fragmented. Additionally (not counting about two million blacks who are trade union members) only about 14 million whites in a work force of over 70 million are union members. The American union movement very early fell into the trap of racism, excluding blacks and thereby creating a pool of strike breakers for employers and depressing the wage level of whites by insuring low wage levels for blacks. The unions neither ideologically nor organizationally are prepared to define radically progressive policy alternatives.

The muted role of the trade unions has been crucial. The political interests of most citizens are mediated through organizations. This is particularly important for populations (white workers, for example) less likely to participate electorally in the political process. Thus, for example, the underrepresentations of blacks at the ballot box is counterbalanced somewhat by the existence of a variety of politically vigorous organizations (the NAACP and The Urban League are the oldest and most resilient). Traditionally, these organizations have been the vehicles of the black bourgoisie, probably in large part because lower class people in general are less likely to belong to voluntary organizations. Recently, however, a number of groups drawing their membership from street and ghetto blacks have become prominent (the Black Panthers, the Black Muslims and DRUM, an organization of black workers in automobile plants, are the most vigorous).

Many of those who have written on the white lower class suggest that they have "a deficient sociocultural milieu," that they possess undifferentiated and unsophisticated notions with regard to the nature of the socio-politico-economic system, and that they are bigoted and suspicious.[27] The lower middle class is seen as rigidly moralistic and concerned with propriety. The self-defeating definitions of the situation entertained by these two groups go unchallenged by major alternative formulations put forth by the trade unions who have not played the educational role vis-a-vis white workers that civil rights groups have played vis-a-vis blacks. The orientation of the unions has been to conserve and preserve rather than significantly expand or explore in terms of social welfare legislation.

The white worker is not wholly unmindful of his economic interests,[28] but he doesn't translate this knowledge into any consistent conception of major programatic and policy change. This is left to a segment of the black movement, thereby decreasing further the white workers' likelihood of subscribing to such views.

One consequence of this political orientation of the white working class we have already seen in the relatively poor showing of the United States with regard to social welfare programs. Another important consequence is that the pursuit of more adequate social welfare legislation becomes equated with the pursuit of racial justice.

The black movement has focused attention on the deprived status of blacks. There has been no equivalent movement among whites to sensitize policy makers to the marginal status of most whites. While there are a variety of ethnically-based organizations—Hibernian clubs, Sons of Italy, Polish American clubs, Greek American clubs—none has a clearly formulated program with regard to the class problems of its members.[29] Many non-white groups, however, are so oriented. The black movement is too well-known to need discussion. Among Mexicans *La Huelga* has mobilized many Mexican-American agricultural workers in California and the southwest, while Rijes Tijerina and "Corky" Gonzales have rallied Mexicans in New Mexico and Colorado. Recently Indians have demanded that attention be paid to their economic and social problems.[30]

Consequently, as meliorative policy is formulated, it is done so implicitly (and sometimes explicitly) in racial terms. Seligman has observed with regard to the poverty program that "Everyone [connected with its formulation] accepted the political view that the War on Poverty was mainly for Negroes." And in fact, blacks and other nonwhites do participate more extensively than poor whites in federal programs; for example, the percentages of black and other nonwhite in the following programs is: New Careers, 67 percent; Concentrated Employment Program, 72 percent; Neighborhood Youth Corp, Summer, 56 percent; in-school, 76 percent; out-of-school, 52 percent.[31]

Social welfare policy in the United States is discussed with the vocabulary of race rather than that of class. In addition to posing analytic problems, the excited hostilities and passions of poor and marginal whites make it difficult for even meagerly financed and minimally intrusive programs to function successfully. In the meantime they themselves do without.

NOTES

[1] It is a measure of American thinking that the very term "welfare" is equated with husbandless mothers receiving public assistance. In the broader sense of the term it refers to policies intended to redistribute national wealth in terms of need. Pekka Kuusi, the Finnish social scientist, Gunnar Myrdal, and other European scholars have written extensively on social welfare. See, for example, Richard Titmuss, *Commitment to Welfare*, Pantheon Books, New York 1968.

[2] Robert Lane, *Political Ideology: Why the American Common Man Believes What He Does*, Free Press of Glencoe, Glencoe, Illinois, 1962, pp. 330-331.

[3] Peter Schrag, "The Forgotten American," *Harper's*, August 1969, vol. 239, No. 1431, p. 27.

[4] Christopher Jencks and David Riesman, "On Class in America," *The Public Interest*, No. 10, Winter 1968, pp. 65-86.

[5] James Vadikan, *Children, Poverty, and Family Allowances*, Basic Books, Inc., New York and London, 1968, p. 6.

[6] Some people might object to the introduction of a program of this sort into the United States on the grounds that it would have the effect of raising the birth rate. Vadikan concludes however that "Based on world wide experience over a considerable period of time, it would appear safe to conclude that a program of family allowances of modest size such as exists in Canada or such as might be considered in the United States could have no significant effects in increasing the birth rate." *Children, Poverty, and Family Allowances*, p. 101. Not even in France where family allowance benefits average one-fifth of the family budget of low-income people has it accelerated the birth rate.

[7] Alvin Schorr, *Poor Children: A Report on Children in Poverty*, Basic Books, Inc., New York and London, 1966, p. 148.

[8] Carl Uhr, "Recent Swedish Labor Market Policies," *The Manpower Revolution*, ed. Garth Mangum, Anchor Books, Doubleday and Company, Inc., Garden City, New York, 1966, p. 376.

[9] Robert L. Heilbroner "Benign Neglect in the United States" *transaction*, vol. 7, 12 October, 1970, p. 16.

[10] The New York Times: Encyclopedic Almanac 1970, ed. Seymour Kurtz, The New York Times, Books and Educational Division, New York, 1969, pp. 245-299; and U.S. Bureau of the Census, *Statistical Abstracts of the United States (1955 edition), Washington, D.C., 1970*, p. 5.

[11] James Vadikan, *op. cit.*, p. 24.

[12] Bert Seidman, "The Case for Higher Social Security Benefits," *The American Federationist*, vol. 74, 1, January 1967, p. 5.

[13] *New York Times: Encyclopedic Almanac*, p. 301.

[14] Arthur Ross and Herbert Hill, editors, *Employment, Race, and Poverty,* Harcourt, Brace, and World, New York, 1967, pp. 30-32.

[15] George Katond, James N. Morgan, Joy Schmiedeskamp, and John A. Sundquist, *1967 Survey of Consumer Finances,* University of Michigan, Ann Arbor, Michigan 1967, p. 11.

[16] Department of Labor, Bureau of Labor Statistics, *Monthly Labor Review,* April, 1969.

[17] Department of Labor, Bureau of Labor Statistics, *Employment and Earnings,* vol. 16, 7, January 1970, p. 67.

[18] Nathan Spero, "Notes on the Current Inflation," *Monthly Review,* vol. 21, 2, June 1969, p. 30.

[19] Katona, *op. cit.,* pp. 15-43.

[20] *Ibid.*

[21] For an excellent discussion of this population, one roughly parallel to the discussion undertaken here see "'Middle Class' Workers and the New Politics", Brendan Sexton in *Beyond the New Left,* edited by Irving Howe, McCall, New York, 1970, pp. 192-204.

[22] Among the useful works on poor and marginal whites are: *Uptown: Poor Whites in Chicago,* Todd Gitlin and Nanci Hollander, Harper & Row, New York, 1970; Eli Chinoy, *Automobile Workers and the American Dream,* Doubleday, Garden City, New York, 1955; Lee Rainwater, Richard Coleman, and Gerald Handel, *Workingman's Wife,* Oceana Publications, New York, 1956; Lee Rainwater, *And the Poor Get Children,* Quadrangle Books, New York, 1960, and William F. Whyte, *Street Corner Society,* University of Chicago Press, Chicago, Illinois, 1943.

[23] Lloyd A. Tree and Hadley Cantril, *The Political Beliefs of Americans,* Simon & Schuster, New York, 1968, pp. 9-10, 96, 99, 190, 195-196, 218.

[24] Michael Parenti, "Ethnic Politics and the Persistence of Ethnic Identification," *American Political Science Review,* LXI (September, 1967), 719m.

[25] Herbert Gans, *The Urban Villagers,* Free Press of Glencoe, New York, 1962.

[26] Gerald Suttles, *The Social Order of the Slums,* University of Chicago Press, Chicago, Illinois 1968.

[27] See, for example, Albert R. Cohen and Harold Hodges, "Lower Blue Collar Class Characteristics," *Social Problems,* Spring 1963, vol. 10, 4, pp. 303-334. Jack L. Roach, "A Theory of Lower-Class Behavior," *Sociological Theory: Inquiries and Paradigms,* Llewellyn Gross, ed. Harper and Row, New York, Evanston and London, 1967, pp. 294-315.

[28] See, S. M. Lipset, *Political Man,* Garden City, Doubleday, 1960, pp. 97-130 and A. M. Lipset and Earl Raab, "The Wallace Whitelash," *trans action,* Vol. 7, 2, December 1969, pp. 23-36.

[29] This is no longer wholly true. In both Cleveland and New York ethnically based groups have begun to stir. The major impetus has probably been the surge of the black population, but these groups may conceivably turn out to have ends and objectives which are not simply anti-black.

[30] For a discussion of protest movements by these other minorities, see John Howard, *The Awakening Minorities: American Indians, Mexican Americans, and Puerto Ricans,* Chicago, Aldine, 1970.

[31] *Handbook of Labor Statistics 1970,* U.S. Department of Labor, Bureau of Labor Statistics, Washington, D.C., 1970, p. 123.

12

Race, Policy and Schooling

RAY C. RIST

There have been few debates in American society related to domestic social policy that have involved such a complex mix of law, social science and cultural values as those over school desegregation. In the two decades since the monumental *Brown* v. *Board of Education* Supreme Court decision of 1954, the United States as a society has been grappling judicially, philosophically and pedagogically with the situation of white and black children learning and participating together within public-school classrooms.

The thrust of the 1954 Supreme Court decision was to outlaw de jure segregation; the Court decisions of the 1960s and early 1970s have moved to do likewise to de facto segregation. The rationale is much the same: black children are denied equal academic opportunity and equal social justice by being isolated in all or predominantly black schools. It is assumed that the act of separation results unavoidably in the handicapping of achievement potential in black children. Thus the courts order the disestablishment of predominantly one-race schools and the physical mixing of black and white children within the same educational facility. The implication is that desegregation of student bodies relates directly to the opportunity for minority-group achievement.

ASSIMILATION VERSUS PLURALISM

Various researchers argue that color and class play a critical role in how the integrated situation is defined. Research evidence suggests either may become the dominant motif in an integrated setting. The findings suggest academic success and self-esteem are both directly linked to one's social class—the higher the class, the higher the probability of academic success or reward. If it is the view of teachers that class supersedes color, then assumptions by various participants in an integration program that the children are involved in a race issue are not borne out in the classroom.

As color and class represent the alternative definitions of the salient attributes of the children within integrated classrooms, so assimilation and pluralism represent the broadly sketched alternative responses to these same children. Pressure on minority groups to accept assimilation within the framework of White Anglo-Saxon Protestant conformity appears to be the most frequent response, due in large part to the power and authority of dominants to create conditions they perceive to be to their own advantage.

The notion of Anglo conformity has been the most prevailing and powerful perspective on majority-minority relations during the course of the nation's history. Schematically, one might interpret the call for Anglo conformity as follows: $A + B + C = A$, where A, B and C all represent racial or ethnic groups and A is the dominant group. Assimilation within this framework is ultimately a theory of majority conformity. The basic premise is that in order to succeed, one must take on the values, life-style and world view of the dominant group. Whereas early dominant-group concerns related to issues of religious, political, and cultural differences, the struggle of late has been that of color. At the time of WASP concern with the Irish, such groups as the Afro-Americans, Mexican-Americans and native Americans were in no position to present any challenge to the cultural and political hegemony of the dominant group. But that is, of course, no longer the case. Yet this change is of more than passing interest. What has emerged is a shift in the attention of WASPs from immigrant minorities to subordinate minorities.

In the attempt of the dominant group to impose on various minority groups the values and beliefs of Anglo conformity, there is held out to the minority groups the notion that there are benefits in accepting such a view. The dominant group implies others should take on their values and assimilate into their culture. It is yet an open question, if, in fact, dominants do want assimilation of all minority groups or merely display a pretense of such wanting so as to hold within current institutional arrangements the aspirations of minority groups to partake of the American Feast. Alternatively, from the view of the minority group, and a subordinate minority group in particular, there is the question of whether to accept Anglo values and hope for assimilation, or to reject them in favor of separatism, or to act as if one accepts them, and hope that will suffice for acceptance, or some mixture of the above, based on voluntarism.

The implications are immediately apparent for any school integration program where that school adheres to Anglo conformity in terms of its values and curriculum. The task of the school is to legitimize those parts of the American experience that reflect Anglo values and culture and delegitimize those parts that do not. Again, $A + B + C = A$. If the metatheory of reality for an individual teacher is one that is framed by an assumption of the validity of the dominance of Anglo values, the integration process within the classroom then becomes one of instilling one perspective in all students, regardless of their backgrounds. Those children who possess Anglo culture prior to their coming to school need only reassurance. Those who do not possess it need salvation.

The development of the concept of pluralism within the study of majority-minority group relations came as a reaction against the assimilationist assumptions that some cultures are inherently superior to others. The initial development of the perspective carried three central propositions. First, a person has no choice as to his ancestry. Therefore, it is undemocratic to penalize him for what he did not voluntarily consent to have as a part of his permanent identidy. Secondly, each minority and ethnic culture has within it valuable and positive attributes that could be a contribution to the fabric of American society. To deny these aspects of minority culture is ultimately to lessen the value of the dominant culture. The Constitution itself in its wording "All men being created equal" makes the implicit assumption of differences between men that all merit equal respect and treatment. If it were not presumed that men were different, it would be meaningless for writers of the Constitution to stress the need for equality. Taking these three points together suggests that the concept of pluralism as it was initially formulated represented an ideological struggle on the part of minority groups to maintain cultural and social traditions in the face of pressures for Anglo conformity.

More recently, the concept of pluralism has undergone a division. There is need to distinguish structural pluralism from cultural pluralism. Structural pluralism is seen as the development of institutions, organizations and even entire communities that are separate from others in the society along lines of religion, race, and ethnicity. Both majority and minority groups opt for certain forms of structural pluralism. This is evident in the media, religious organizations and educational institutions. Structural pluralism is not of direct concern, as any discussion of either segregation or integration in American public schools has a priori assumed the existence of a unified school system, independent of its internal differentiations.

Cultural pluralism is of more immediate concern as it raises a critical question: Can undimensional institutions (those that are structurally assimilated) retain cultural differentiations? Given the entrenched power of WASP culture to currently dominate public institutional arrangements and ideologies, the tentative answer in the American context appears to be negative. The question of whether to attempt to reverse that answer is at the crux of the current debate over the nature of the integrated-school experience. Minority groups in particular have argued for the necessity and the right to maintain cultural distinctions within a single institutional framework. Not to be able to do so is interpreted as a manifestation of white determination to maintain a cultural hegemony in all areas of interracial contact. Cultural pluralism implies that if several distinct groups come together within a single institutional setting, they are able to maintain their distinctions over time. Schematically, $A + B + C = A + B + C$. There is no guarantee that such coexistence over time will remain peaceful, or necessarily must. Quite the contrary. It may be conflict ridden, but the groups seek to find means to maintain themselves, as appears to be the present situation in such diverse institutional settings as the military, the university and the political arena.

For any school or individual teacher to provide an atmosphere of cultural pluralism, there must be either a willingness to affirm cultural traditions that are non-Anglo-Saxon, or else be afraid not to do so. The outcome in either case is a school program and curriculum that represent the diversity of heritages and life experiences of all the children involved. No cultural system is defined in pejorative terms as deficient or inferior to the dominant system. For most members of the dominant system, recognition of cultural pluralism necessarily implies the willingness to forsake Anglo conformity as the means by which to construct one's world view. For teachers from the dominant group in particular, the struggle against Anglo ethnocentrism has in most instances to be done in spite of the prevailing curriculums, entrenchments of school-board members, and lack of rewards from other teachers for doing so. The overwhelming pressures toward Anglo conformity make cultural pluralism a rare event in American education.

INTEGRATION AS RACIAL ASSIMILATION

This category of integration is one most frequently supported by the dominant white group as well as by portions of various minority groups. It essentially views integration as the means by which to socialize nonwhite students to act, speak and believe as much as possible like white students. The dominant group would support such a program for it leaves intact their own values, beliefs and cultural forms. It also may affirm whatever notions of racial superiority they may have, for one way in which to interpret this type of integration is to see the need for nonwhite peoples to learn the white ways to become fully human. Assumptions about the inferiority of nonwhite culture have been attacked as assuming a deficit model that is without empirical substance. The motivations that would prompt the support of this form of integration by minority groups are more difficult to ascertain. Several, only tentative, explanations come to mind. There may be the belief on the part of minority groups that as they come more and more to resemble the cultural styles of the dominant group, they will be accepted by the dominants and invited to the Feast. The inverse of this is the fear that if they fail to take on Anglo values, they continue to risk present or future persecution and oppression. Or minority-group members may possess a great deal of self-hate and manifest it by adopting the characteristics of the dominant group and rejecting those of their own culture.

To operationalize this alternative for school integration, it would suggest there be few numbers of nonwhite children among many whites. In this way, there would be no danger of sufficient numbers of black or other nonwhite students having the opportunity to reinforce within their peer group any traits that would be perceived as nonwhite. In short, one keeps the critical mass of nonwhite students low so as to ultimately render them invisible, or nearly so, particularly to the dominant group. Likewise, the curriculum retains its traditional orientation to WASP values and myths, with little or no attention to nonwhite contributions.

Many in the area of race relations and school integration would not consider racial assimilation as a form of integration. Some would conceptualize this alternative as token desegregation. The distinction, however, between token desegregation and racial assimilation is more than one of semantics. It relates to profoundly different social constructions of reality. For many whites, racial assimilation is integration and is the only kind they will voluntarily support. To imply that racial assimilation is not integration again suggests a different assumption as to what the integrated experience entails. Yet, the growing racial consciousness in nonwhite communities has emerged as a powerful counterforce to the socialization attempts by dominants to have nonwhite peoples think and act white. Thus for many nonwhites, such a program of education as that implied by a racially assimilationist approach is entirely unacceptable. They believe that a form of integration that pressures children to deny their background solves none of the educational problems of nonwhite children and may generate self-hate and even more problems instead.

INTEGRATION AS RACIAL PLURALISM

As the dominant group in American society would most likely support racial assimilation as the framework for school integration, so it appears significant numbers of minority-group members would favor racial pluralism. Such a perspective allows for the affirmation of other than Anglo culture. It places value on what Anglo conformity demands be hidden and denied. Further, it assumes nonwhite groups have developed cultures with an internal order and logic that by their very nature deserve respect for they serve as vehicles by which people pattern and order their world— no less than does Anglo-Saxon culture for most whites.

Each option for integrated education has many variations and alternatives. Within the context of racial pluralism, there would appear to be a continuum of integrated settings from very little stress on the culture of the minority group to those of very great stress, but short of complete separatism. It has been suggested that black people are essentially bicultural in that they possess cultural traits of the dominant group as well as those distinctive to themselves. This would imply the need to create integrated settings where those values and cultural forms valued by the minority group would be retained, but also where minority-group members would be equipped to partake of the dominant culture as they desire.

For a school to be truly racially pluralistic, it would be necessary to structure patterns of social interaction and organization so that children, teachers and parents of all racial groups receive equal status and are able to assume roles of equivalent power and prestige. Not to do so creates only a veneer of pluralism while the actual control remains with the dominant group. It is only to state the obvious that the creation of such a school or school system is a difficult process, for not only are there historical and cultural obstacles to overcome but seldom do members of the dominant group willingly give up control of an institution. Thus, in some instances, the struggle for racial pluralism in the school has been encompassed within the struggle for community control. In other instances, white and nonwhite participants in the life of the school have been able to work together toward achieving a system of shared power and responsibility. The infrequency with which one can locate truly racially pluralistic integrated schools attests to the fact that if they do occur, they are in spite of the prevailing institutional arrangements within American society, not because of them.

But not all problems related to the creation of multiethnic or racially plural schools are those of power; many are problems of pedagogy. The notion of the school responding to the diversity of the backgrounds of the children is an important one. The pedagogical problem becomes one of deciding how one creates the various categories of student backgrounds and further, how many such categories to create. When are the categories to be based on color, when on class and when on culture? As an extension of the creation of a diversity of programmatic responses, there is the issue of how intensely the members of one group would participate in the curriculum developed for another group. For example, if one has developed a language program that utilizes Spanish, the English of black Americans and the dominant standard American English, do all three groups get all three, or two of these, or one? The question is not only how multiethnic should the program of the school become but also how diverse should the children themselves become.

INTEGRATION AS CLASS ASSIMILATION

The classical notion of education in American society assumes the provision of equal educational opportunity to all children, regardless of the inequalities with which they may come to school. Joseph White voiced this view as long as 120 years ago in a report to the Massachusetts Board of Education. More recently, notions of class assimilation have found expression in much of the writing related to the education of what has been termed the culturally disadvantaged, the culturally deprived and the like. A close examination of this literature suggests a view of American society that is essentially open, mobile and nonascriptive. Thus for any person to remain poor or culturally disadvantaged is the result of personal cultural factors, not of systematic exclusion and discrimination. Such was a part of the prevailing rationale for the creation of Head Start programs. What poor children needed was an initial boost of socialization to acquaint them with the values, behaviors and ideas of nonpoor middle-class Anglo conformity so that they would have aspirations to do well in school and thus pull themselves out of poverty. The arms of the affluent were said to be open to all those who sought to climb the ladder of mobility and join them.

Class assimilation as a framework for school integration functions essentially as if it were color blind. The color-blind perspective defines racial and ethnic differences as irrelevant to education. Each child is to be treated, in terms of racial categories, like every other child. Thus all will have equal educational opportunity. To make special responses to the presence of nonwhite students would be interpreted as reverse discrimination.

By stressing class as against color, this alternative for school integration allows members of both white and nonwhite groups to support it. If one has middle-class status, one can argue that it was achieved by self-determination, hard work and perseverance. It may be particularly appealing to those of recent upward mobility for it allows a self-congratulation upon arrival and the assumption of having gained a secure middle-class status for one's children. Further, for those who think too much emphasis is placed on issues of race in American society, a stress on class assimilation is appealing. Such a perspective is highly congruent with the notion of America as an open and economically mobile system with rewards for those who want to work. It allows for the celebration of the economic and political system when mobility does occur and the opportunity to blame the poor for remaining poor.

INTEGRATION AS CLASS PLURALISM

This is the least likely of any of the alternatives to find proponents and thus is least likely to be inferred as a meaning of integration. For in recognizing class-based differences, one must deal not only with the middle- and upper-class value systems, but with those of the poor as well. Thus such a perspective necessitates a legitimation of the values and attitudes and culture of the poor—and in a society bent on economic mobility, poverty is a sign of failure, not of simply being different. Furthermore, there are few parents or teachers who would push for class pluralism as it would suggest that lower-class children should grow with pride in their poverty and lack of resources. Such a view is so completely antithetical to the commonsense notions of reality held by most Americans, white and nonwhite, so that to opt for class pluralism as a model for school integration would be to invite first disbelief and then outright hostility.

To grant that the poor possess a distinctive lower-class culture is not enough to achieve class pluralism in an integration program. There would have to be an affirmation of that culture and the desire to transmit it to one's children through the formal socialization process of schooling. That will not happen. The desires, if not for one's self, then for one's children, to get ahead and to make it supersede any notion in American society of the legitimacy of lower-class culture. Further, it would be interpreted by many poor persons as an attempt by the affluent to hold the children of the poor black from full opportunity; this is, that the affluent would be content for the poor to be contented.

INTEGRATION AND PUBLIC POLICY

The implications are several as to the interrelations of theory and policy with respect to American school integration. First, there can be no taken-for-granted notions that a commonality of meanings exists for the terms most frequently used in a discussion of integration. It would appear more prudent to assume the opposite— that there are a variety of meanings imputed to the concepts by the various participants. Second, the differential assumptions of participants as the natural pattern of interaction between white and nonwhite children will be linked to the position one has in the social system. How closely any particular integration program fits with a perception of appropriate cross-racial interaction would influence whether one thought it to be a good program. Third, though definitions of the integrated experience may vary, not all groups are equally able to have their views adopted as the official guidelines for the program. The absence of disagreement does not necessarily imply consent: it may be the consequence of powerlessness and an inability to find means to have alternative views expressed. Thus the tendency on the part of school officials to move an integration program in any one of the directions outlined may appear as simply an apolitical administrative decision. Yet what assumes the contour of an apolitical decision is actually deeply political, but occurs in a context without articulate and organized opposition. It is political for the decision to opt for one or another of the alternatives, which ultimately implies a single construction of reality will become the official reality for all.

For those concerned with the policy implications of school integration, the desire to reach some end condition as the optimal experience for children necessarily implies the use of knowledge about the causal relations among variables to achieve the goal. If policy analysts seem to share any one attribute in common, it is a metatheory that causal relations do exist in the social world and they can not only be discovered, but manipulated.

To opt for one model of school integration as opposed to another suggests how one attributes causality to the critical variables involved. Further, it also suggests what one believes in, and what ought to be. Policy analysts will have to bring their background assumptions into the foreground where they can be examined and interpreted for what they hold as to the nature of white and nonwhite interaction, the rights of children, and, most basically, the nature of social justice. For in a society where options and power are grossly disparate, it is imperative the powerful and the powerless alike know the answer to the question, "Where do we stand?"

13

The Violence Commission:
Internal Politics and Public Policy

JEROME H. SKOLNICK

The 1960s are already infamous for assassinations, crime in the streets, student rebellion, black militancy, wars of liberation, law and order—and national commissions. We had the Warren Commission, the Crime Commission, the Riot Commission and the Violence Commission; and the point about them was that they were among the major responses of government to the social dislocations of the decade. Millions of people followed the work of these commissions with interest and gave at least summary attention to their reports. Social scientists were also interested in commissions, though skeptical about their value. Most would probably agree with Sidney and Beatrice Webb's description of Royal Commissions, "These bodies are seldom designed for scientific research; they are primarily political organs, with political objects."

I share this view, yet I have worked with three commissions, albeit under very special arrangements guaranteeing freedom of publication. The discussion that follows is partly analytical and partly autobiographical, especially where I discuss my work as director of the task force on "Violent Aspects of Protest and Confrontation" for the Violence Commission. If the autobiography stands out, that is because I did not participate in commissions to observe them. I studied the phenomena at issue—crime, police, protest and confrontation—not commissions. Still, my experience may be helpful in understanding commission structures, processes and dilemmas.

CONSTITUENCIES

Commissions have three functioning groups: commissioners, the executive staff, the research staff, with overlapping but distinctive interests.

Andrew Kopkind has recently written that President Lyndon B. Johnson chose the 11 commissioners for his National Advisory Commission on Civil Disorders because of their remarkable qualities of predictable moderation. The Violence Commission, chaired by Dr. Milton Eisenhower, was perhaps even more predictably "moderate" than the Riot Commission. It included a member of the southern and congressional establishment, Congressman Hale Boggs; Archbishop, now Cardinal, Terence J. Cooke, Francis Cardinal Spellman's successor; Ambassador Patricia Harris, standing for both the political woman and the Negro establishment; Senator Philip A. Hart, Democrat of Michigan, associated with the liberal establishment in the Senate; Judge A. Leon Higginbotham, a Negro and a federal judge from Philadelphia; Eric Hoffer, the president's favorite philosopher, presenting the backlash voice of the American workingman; Senator Roman Hruska, Republican of Nebraska, a leading right-wing Republican; and Albert E. Jenner, Jr., prominent in the American Bar Association and in Chicago legal affairs. In addition, there was Republican Congressman William M. McCulloch of Ohio, who had served on the Kerner Commission and was the only overlapping member of both commissions. In response to criticisms that the Riot Commission contained no social scientists, Dr. W. Walter Menninger was appointed, although he is a practicing psychiatrist and not a social scientist. Finally, there were Judge Ernest W. McFarland, the man whom Lyndon Baines Johnson had replaced in the House of Representatives, and another Texan, Leon Jaworski, a close personal adviser to the president and a prominent and conservative lawyer.

Obviously, the commissioners themselves cannot perform the investigative and analytical work of the commission. Commissioners are chosen because apparently they represent various economic and political interests, not because they have distinguished themselves as scholars or experts. In fact, they do not "represent" anyone. What they best mirror is a chief executive's conception of pluralist America.

Moreover, even if a commissioner should have the ability to do the research, he or she usually has other demands on their time. Inevitably, then, the staff of the commission does the work—all of the leg work and the research and most of the writing of the final report, with, of course, the commission's approval.

The staffs of both the Riot Commission and the Violence Commission were similar. The executive staff, working out of Washington, was charged with getting the research and writing job done and with organizing the time of the commission. In each case, the director of the executive staff was a leading Washington attorney who had ties with the Johnson administration, David Ginsburg for the Riot Commission, Lloyd Cutler for the Violence Commission. Moreover, younger attorneys were named as their closest associates.

There had been considerable friction in the Riot Commission between the research staff and the executive staff, as well as between both and the commissioners. According to Andrew Kopkind, the social scientists under Research Director Robert Shellow drafted a document called "The Harvest of American Racism" which went further than most top staff officials thought prudent in charging that racism permeated American institutions. "Harvest" characterized the riots as the first step in a developing black revolution in which Negroes will feel, as the draft put it, that "it is legitimate and necessary to use violence against the social order. A truly revolutionary spirit has begun to take hold . . . and unwillingness to compromise or wait any longer, to risk death rather than have their people continue in a subordinate status." According to Kopkind, both Ginsburg and Victor Palmieri, his deputy director, admitted that they were appalled when they read "Harvest." Shortly after its submission many of the 120 investigators and social scientists were "released" from the commission staff in December 1967 (on public grounds that money was needed to pursue the war in Vietnam). But Kopkind says that there is every reason to believe that the "releasing" was done by Palmieri (with Ginsburg's concurrence) because of the failure of

Shellow's group to produce an "acceptable" analytical section. The commissioners themselves are reported to have known little of the firing or of the controversy surrounding it but were persuaded by Ginsburg to go along with it.

I tell this story only because it bears on the central question of what effects, if any, informed researchers and writers can have on the final reports of commissions, the public face they turn to the world. Kopkind, for example, argues that the "Harvest" incident proves that the Kerner Report would have been "liberal" regardless of events preceding its final writing. He concludes, "The structure of the Commission and the context in which it operated suggest that its tone could have hardly been other than 'liberal.' The finished product almost exactly reproduced the ideological sense given it by President Johnson more than half a year earlier. The choice of Commissioners, staff, consultants and contractors led in the same direction." Yet that outcome is not at all evident from the rest of Kopkind's analysis, which argues, for example, that the commissioners were selected for their predictable moderation, that one commissioner, Charles Thornton, attempted to torpedo the report just before its launching and that the findings of the report were patently offensive to President Johnson. It is at least arguable that the "liberalism" of the final report was not inevitable, that it might have been far more on the conservative side of "moderate" and that the "Harvest" document had something to do with moving it to the Left.

THE EISENHOWER VIOLENCE COMMISSION

When Senator Robert F. Kennedy was assassinated and the president appointed yet another commission, many observers were suspicious. Was this the only response that Washington could give to domestic tragedy? Even the press gave the Violence Commission unfavorable publicity. The commissioners seemed even more conservative than the riot commissioners. Some considered the commission a devious plot by President Johnson to reverse or smudge the interpretation of civil disorders offered by the Riot Commission.

Furthermore, what could the Violence Commission say that hadn't already been said by the Riot Commission? The distinction between civil disorder and violence was not, and still isn't, self-evident. Moreover, because of the flap over the firing of the social scientists on the Kerner Commission, many of that community were deeply and understandably dubious about the possibility of doing an intellectually respectable job under commission auspices.

The executive staff saw this problem and coped with it, first, by establishing the position of research director, so that social scientists (James F. Short, Jr., jointly with Marvin Wolfgang, as it turned out) occupied a place in the hierarchy of the executive staff, a club usually limited to corporation lawyers. Authority still rested with the executive director, but the research directors performed four important functions; they initiated the commission policy of independent task forces with freedom of publication; they helped select the social science staff; they served as liaison between the social scientists, the executive staff and the commissioners; and they served as good critics and colleagues.

Furthermore, they promoted another departure from Kerner Commission practice, namely that social scientists and lawyers are the co-directors of task forces.

Some additional comments are warranted here because organizational structures and rules may seriously influence intellectual autonomy. University social scientists with little legal or governmental experience may assume that freedom to write and publish follows from well-intentioned assurances of future support. Yet as one experienced man with whom I shared a panel recently put it: "He who glitters may one day be hung."

The social scientist must understand the ways he can be hung and protect himself accordingly. First, his materials can be used and distorted. Second, his name can be used, but his material and advice ignored. This is particularly possible when social scientists hold highranking but relatively powerless titles on the commission. Ultimately, they are placed in the dilemma of seeming to endorse the final product. (In the Violence Commission, for example, the names of James F. Short, Jr., and Marvin Wolfgang seemingly "endorse" the scholarly merit of the final report. In addition, the presence of a recognized social science staff does the same. To this extent, we were all "co-opted," since none of us, including Short and Wolfgang, were responsible for the final report.) Third, he may experience subtle (sometimes not so subtle) pressures to shape or present his findings in favored directions. Finally, his work may be suppressed.

In general, one receives maximum protection with a *written* contract guaranteeing freedom of publication. Beyond that, however, experienced Washington hands can be quite charming—which holds its own dangers for one's intellectual independence.

From the very beginning, the executive staff expressed some doubts about the ultimate impact the commission's own report would have on public policy, or even the shape it would take. Recall that this was the summer of 1968, following the assassination of Senator Kennedy and before the national conventions of both parties. Who could foretell what future event would have what future impact on national politics? Who could, with confidence, predict the nominees for the presidency, the victor and his attitude toward the commission?

TASK FORCE REPORTS

Like the able corporation lawyers they are, the executive staff came up with a prudent primary goal, a set of books called *Task Force Reports*, which they hoped could be a solid contribution to understanding the causes and prevention of violence in America. I call this goal prudent because it set a standard that was at least possible in theory. From these studies, it was felt, the commission would write its own report; the initial idea was to have each task force report provide the materials for a summary chapter for the commission report.

Modest as this plan was, it soon ran into difficulty. Commissions are usually run at a gallop. With all the best intentions and resources in the world, it is virtually impossible to complete eight books of high quality in five months, particularly when no central vision controls the research and writing. Our own report, *The Politics of Protest*, was completed on time, but we worked under enormous pressure. Still, we had several advantages.

First, a shared perspective among key staff members contributed to a fairly consistent analysis. We shared a deep skepticism about counterinsurgency views of civil disorder as a form of "deviant" pathology that needed to be stamped out as quickly as possible. On the contrary, we assumed that insurgents might conceivably be as rational as public servants. Our approach was influenced, first, by subjectivist and naturalistic perspectives in sociology, which lead one, for instance, to take into account both the point of view of the black rioter and to assume his sanity, and to assume as well the sanity of the policeman and the white militant. Second, we were influenced by revisionist histories of America, which see her as a more tumultuous and violent nation than conventional histories have taught us to believe. Finally, we were influenced by social historical critiques of the theory of collective behavior, which interpret seemingly irrational acts on the part of rioters as forms of primitive political activity, and by an emphasis upon social history in understanding such collective behavior as student protest, rather than upon analysis of "variables."

Another advantage in favor of our task force was that our headquarters was at the Center for the Study of Law and Society at Berkeley. This kept us away from the time-consuming crises of Washington, although the tie-line kept us in daily touch with events there. In addition, the center and the Berkeley campus offered a critical mass of resources that probably could not be duplicated anywhere else. Our location, then, combined with my status as independent contractor with the commission, offered a degree of independence unavailable to the other task force directors. For example, the staff members of our task force were not required to have a White House security clearance.

Finally, the staff was far from unhappy about working for a national commission. Those involved, regardless of expressions of skepticism, were not opposed to making a contribution to a national understanding of the issues involved. My contract with the government, and its contract with me, assured the staff that its best understanding of the issues would be made public.

Given time limitations, it was impossible to undertake the original research one would need for a large-scale social science project. My inclination, shared by the research directors and the executive staff, was to recruit a staff experienced in research on the areas under study. We saw the five-month period as an opportunity to summarize findings rather than to undertake original investigation.

We did, however, conduct original interviews with black militants and with police. As can be imagined, these interviews were not easily obtained. For black militants our interviewer was a man with extensive connections, but who stipulated that he would interview only if we agreed to listen to and not transcribe the tapes and make no notations of who was being interviewed. The interviews substantiated much that we suspected and served to sharpen our analytical outlook. Similarly, the interviews we held with policemen—conducted, incidentally, by a former policeman —served to fill gaps in our thesis that the police were becoming an increasingly politicized force in the United States.

I should also add that our emphasis on social history and political analysis seemed to violate some of the expectations of some portions of our audience.

AUDIENCES AND HEARINGS

The Politics of Protest staff worked with three audiences in mind. First, we were concerned with trying to persuade the commissioners of the validity of our findings and the validity of our analysis. They were our primary audience. Our second was the general public, an audience we had little confidence in being able to influence except, perhaps, through persuading the commissioners. Most reports have a limited readership—and *The Politics of Protest* isn't exactly *The Love Machine*. So our third audience was the academic community and the media representatives. In the long run, the university had to be our major audience, since the report is scholarly and the media treated its publication as news, quickly displaced by other stories.

The audience for the hearings was both the commissioners and the general public. Several members of the executive staff believed that one reason the Kerner Commission failed to gain public acceptance was its failure to educate the public along the way. The "predictably moderate" commissioners had been emotionally moved in the hearings, especially by representatives of the black communities of America, but the public had never been allowed to hear this testimony. Consequently, the Violence Commission hearings were made public and each task force was given three days for hearings.

Hearings are a form of theater. Conclusions must be presented to evoke an emotional response in both the commissioners and the wider television audience. In this respect, the planners of the hearings can be likened to the author and director of a play with strategy substituting for plot. Yet strategies can and do go awry, and so the outcome of the play is not determined, nor can one guarantee whether the effect on the audience will be tragedic or comedic.

A staff tries to get across a point of view on the subject matter. At the same time, however, it is also expected to be "objective," that is, lacking a point of view. The expectation is that staff and commissioners will walk along fresh roads together, reaching similar conclusions. This expectation derives from the image of a trial. Such an adjudicatory model must, however, be largely fictional. The "judges," the commissioners, already have strong views and political interests, though they are supposed to be neutral. The staff, too, is supposed to lack opinions, even though it was selected because of prior knowledge.

Since strategy substitutes for plot, there really are only three possible outcomes. The play may be a flop, that is, the staff perspective is not communicated; or the perspective is communicated, but unemotionally so as to merely make a record; or emotional engagement is achieved. Here social science as theater reaches its ultimate art.

Commissioners are used to hearings, are used to testimony and probably cannot be moved in any new direction unless emotionally engaged. Commissioners are culturally deprived by the privatized life of the man of power. Whatever may have been their former backgrounds, commissioners are now the establishment. They may be driven to and from work, belong to private clubs and remain out of touch with the realities of the urban and political worlds they are assumed to understand. They are both protected and deprived by social privilege.

Moreover, their usual mode of analysis is legalistic and rationalistic. Not intellectuals, they are decision makers interested in protecting the record. Furthermore, they are committed to the prevailing social, economic and political structures, although they will consider reforms of these structures and may well be brought to see contradictions within them. In addition, they are affiliated with certain political and social interests. Consequently, there are practical limits to the possibilities of persuading any of them to a novel position.

The public is another audience for the hearings, but there are also constraints on teaching the public. All that "public hearings" means is that the media are present, not the mass of the public, and the media reports only the most dramatic messages. Also, commissioners themselves become part of the cast. The TV will register an exchange between a witness and a commissioner. So a strategist (director) must anticipate what that exchange might be.

Finally, the presence of the press alters the atmosphere of the hearing room. We held mostly public hearings and some hearings in executive session. With the television cameras and the radio people and the newspaper people present, the commissioners were stiff and formal. When the press left, the commissioners visibly relaxed.

Given these conditions, how does one go about casting? First, we tried to present witnesses who represented a variety of points of view. That was elementary. But within that framework we had to decide: what kinds of witnesses representing what kinds of points of view will bring the most enlightened position with the greatest effect both on the commissioners and on the general public?

There are practical limitations in hearings. Obviously, it may not be possible to get the witness you want, or to get him for a particular day. Ira Heyman, general counsel, and I were given three days for hearings to discuss the antiwar and student movements, black militancy and the responses of the social order. This was not enough time for any of these topics to be adequately discussed. The one day of hearings on black militancy was especially inadequate, although undoubtedly the most exciting. It was also the most difficult to arrange, the most trying and the most rewarding.

HOFFER VS. THE BLACKS

First, there was some question as to whether any well-known black militant would have anything to do with the Violence Commission. Even if he should want to, anybody who stepped forward to represent the militant black community could be charged with playing a "personality" game and disavowed as representing even a segment of the black community. After much thought, we decided on Huey P. Newton, minister of defense of the Black Panther party, as a widely acceptable representative of black militancy. He was willing to cooperate, politically minded and seeking an opportunity to present his point of view.

Herman Blake, an assistant professor of sociology at the University of California at Santa Cruz, joined me in interviewing Newton and was to present the interview to the commissioners. Although Blake would not officially be representing the Panthers, Newton knew him, knew of his work and trusted him to make an accurate analysis of the tape of the interview that was to be played to the commission.

As it turned out, there was no problem at all. Both Blake and I, in Charles Garry's presence, interviewed Newton in the Alameda County Courthouse Jail where he was being held while standing trial for the alleged murder of an Oakland policeman.

The Newton tape, and Blake's testimony, produced an emotionally charged confrontation between Blake and Eric Hoffer and a dignified censure of Hoffer by Judge Higginbotham, vice-chairman of the commission.

Mr. Hoffer: I tell you there is rage among the Negroes on the waterfront. It is at the meetings when they get together. Suddenly they are repeating a ritual. A text. You are repeating it. Now I have . . . I don't know of these people, where they were brought up. All my life I was poor and I didn't live better than any Negro ever lived, I can tell you. When I was out picking cotton in the valley the Negroes were eating better than I did, lived in better houses, they had more schooling than I did . . .

Mr. Blake: Have you ever been called a nigger?

Mr. Hoffer: Let me finish it. By the way, the first man in the U.S. I think who wrote about the need to create a Negro community was in 1964 when I . . .

Mr. Blake: Why do you stop calling it a community then?

Mr. Hoffer: I say that you have to build a community. You have to build a community and you are not . . .

Mr. Blake: We can't build a community with white people like you around telling us we can't be what we are.

Mr. Hoffer: You are not going to build it by rage. You are going to build it by working together.

Mr. Blake: You are defining it.

Mr. Hoffer: They haven't raised one blade of grass. They haven't raised one brick.

Mr. Blake: We have been throwing them, baby, because you been out there stopping them from laying bricks and raising grass.

Judge Higginbotham: Mr. Chairman . . .

Dr. Eisenhower: Mr. Blake . . .

Mr. Jenner: Would you do me a personal favor and stay for a moment, Mr. Blake?

Judge Higginbotham: Mr. Chairman, if I may, I feel compelled because I trust that this Commission will not let statements go in the record which are such blatant demonstrations of factual ignorance that I am obliged to note on the record how totally in error Mr. Hoffer is on the most elementary data.

The McCone Commission, headed by the former director of Central Intelligence, who I assume while he may not be the philosopher which Mr. Hoffer is, that he is at least as perceptive and more factually accurate. The McCone Commission pointed out that in Watts, California, you had unemployment which ran as high as 30 and 40 percent. Sometimes 50 percent among youth. It pointed out in great detail [that] in the Watts area you had the highest percent of substandard housing any place in L.A.

If my colleague, Mr. Hoffer, who I would like to be able to call distinguished, would take time out to read the data of the McCone Report, which is not challenged by anyone, based on government statistics, at least the first portion of his analysis would be demonstrated to be totally inaccurate, and I am willing, as a black man, to state that what I am amazed at is—that with the total bigotry, patent, extensive among men who can reach fame in this country—[not] that there has been as little unity as there has been. It is surprising that there has been as much.

I think that Mr. Hoffer's statements are indicative of the great racist pathology in our country and that his views are those which represent the mass of people in this country. I think that what Toynbee said that civilizations are destroyed from within, that his comments are classic examples of proving that.

Dr. Eisenhower: Mr. Blake, only because we have two other distinguished persons to testify this afternoon, I am going to conclude this part of our testimony. I want you to know that I personally had some questions to ask you but my good friend

Judge Higginbotham asked precisely the questions in his part that I had intended to do. So on behalf of the Commission I thank you for your willingness to come, for your candor, for being with us and I accept the sincerity and truth of what you said to us.

Mr. Blake: Thank you.

That day, I think it is fair to say, was the most emotional day of the hearings for the Violence Commission. Eric Hoffer was an exemplary witness for the depth of racism existing in this country. No wealth of statistics could have conveyed as well to the other commissioners and to the public in general what racism meant to the black man.

Yet Hoffer is also a popular public figure. Moreover, only a minute or so of the hearings was shown on national television. There, Hoffer was seen shouting at a bearded black man in a dashiki. It is doubtful that much enlightenment was achieved by the televising of that exchange. I believe that in the long run the reports themselves will have a far greater impact than the TV time allocated to the hearings.

A first draft of *The Politics of Protest* was sent off to the executive staff of the commission on December 27, 1968, approximately five months after the initial phone call from Washington. They received the report with mixed feelings. They were, I know, impressed with the magnitude and quality of the report, but it violated the kinds of expectations they had about commission reports. We were clearly less concerned about "balance" and "tempered" language than we were about analytical soundness, consistency and clarity. Some of the commissioners were described to me as "climbing the walls as they read it." And this did not make an easy situation for the executive staff. They suggested in January that it be toned down, and I did *not* tell them to go to hell. I listened carefully to their suggestions and accepted most of them concerning language and tone. But I did not alter the analysis in any of the chapters. I. F. Stone was later to call our analysis "brilliant and indispensable," and a *Chicago Tribune* editorial ranked it alongside the Walker Report as "garbage."

THE IMPACT OF COMMISSION REPORTS

Since the report was published, I have often been asked the question: Of what use is all this? Does it actually contribute to public policy? My answer is, I don't know. *The Politics of Protest* apparently made little impact on the commission itself. It was cited only once in the final report of the commission, and then out of context. But the book has been given considerable publicity, has been widely and favorably reviewed and has been widely adopted for classroom use. The major audience for *The Politics of Protest* will probably be the sociology and political science class, although more than most books on this subject it will find its way into the hands of decision makers.

The Politics of Protest will also provide an alternative analysis to the main report of the Violence Commission. Naturally, we think our analysis is more pointed, more consistent, more scholarly and more directed to the historical causes of American violence than the commission's own report, which adopts a managerial, counterinsurgency perspective that looks to symptoms rather than causes. But history will tell. Reports sponsored by commissions are ultimately intellectual documents subject to the criticism that any book or investigation might receive.

Yet they are something more as well. Despite the increasing tendency among radicals and intellectuals to challenge the usefulness and integrity of commission reports, they do tend to create an interest over and above that of similar work by individual scholars. One can even point to a series of commission reports that have had an enormous impact—those used by Karl Marx in developing his critique of capitalist production. Without the narrative provided by these commissions, Marx's *Capital* would have been a much more abstract and predictably obscure document and simply would not have attracted the readership it did. Marx himself, in his preface to *Capital*, offers an accolade to these investigative commissions.

Commission reports, whatever their analytical strictures, defects or omissions, come to have a special standing within the *political* community. If a social scientist or a journalist gathers "facts" concerning a particular institution, and these facts are presented in such a way as to offer a harshly critical appraisal of that social institution, the fathering and the analysis of such facts may be called "muckraking." But if the same or a similar set of facts is found by a commission, it may be seen as a series of startling and respectable social findings.

And herein lies the essential dilemma posed by the commission form of inquiry. On the one hand, we find a set of high-status commissioners whose name on a document will tend to legitimize the descriptions found therein; and on the other hand, precisely because of the political character of the commissioners, the report will be "balanced" or "inconsistent" depending on who is making the judgment. A commission, upon hearing one expert testify (correctly) that there is darkness outside and another testify (incorrectly) that the sun is shining will typically conclude that it is cloudy.

Nevertheless, whatever facts are gathered and are presented to the public, they are in the public domain. No set of facts is subject only to one interpretation and analysis. Surely it was not in the minds of the commissioners of inquiry in nineteenth-century England to provide the factual underpinning for a Marxist critique of capitalist production. Yet, there was no way to stop it. So my point is simply this: to the extent that a commission of inquiry develops facts, it necessarily has done something of social value. Its interpretations can be challenged. How those facts and how those interpretations will be met and used depends upon the integrity and ability of the intellectual community.

14

Pitfalls and Politics
in Commissioned Policy Research

KURT LANG

Subjects that arouse the curiosity of social scientists usually have to do with conditions whose remedy lies within the realm of public policy. There is a widespread belief that social science and its methods can be a source of new ideas and serve as a policy guide. Yet, up to now research efforts have not been organized along lines that encourage broad and concerted attacks on major social issues. Instead research proceeds piecemeal, taking one small problem at a time. This leads to loss not only of perspective but of data; valuable information disappears into archives.[1] Other research that is clearly crisis-oriented tends to be hurried; methods are often slipshod and reports polemical. Despite such shortcomings, the documents that result usually gain attention not only from social scientists but also from policymakers, legislators and the attentive public.

Many persons perturbed over the current state of society see one answer in allocating more resources toward the search for solutions. Surely any increased investment in the tertiary sector, of which the knowledge industry is rightly considered a part, could do no harm and would probably do good. But it does not follow that the marginal returns in terms of useful policy input would automatically justify marginal costs. Certainly those resources now available are not being put to optimum use. On the plausible assumption that anything can be had for money, there is a good deal of talk today about the prospects of solving social problems by organizational devices along the model of the Manhattan Project which developed nuclear explosives, or of the Apollo Project which put men on the moon.

But projects directed towards solving social problems would have to reflect the different nature of social science research. The Manhattan and Apollo Projects were directed toward a single clearly defined objective. The social costs hardly received consideration—at least, not as part of the programs. Such considerations are basic to the endeavors of social scientists. Their research must take account of values and priorities. That is to say, the knowledge they seek concerns not only technical feasibility but also the acceptability of programs based on their findings to those who frame policy and to those whose lives will be affected. Neither social scientists nor their sponsors can easily ignore the political implications of what they report.

With this assumption, I want to look at the ways in which research efforts of some federal advisory and policy-making bodies have been shaped by the situations and structures within which they have been conducted. I shall use illustrative examples drawn from an area broadly defined as "equal opportunity"—an area that has been central to the interests of sociologists. Sociology, after all, arose from the recognition that the incapacities of many people were not really a consequence of physical hazards or incapabilities but were caused by socially imposed risks and obstacles determined by their position within the social structure.

Three case histories—necessarily abbreviated—are used to draw some simple and tentative conclusions about issues social scientists will have to resolve if they want to assure the objectivity of their input into policy decisions. The potential effectiveness of their efforts, after all, rests ultimately on the public's belief in the objectivity of their conclusions. The case studies deal with research on civil disorder, communication gaps and educational achievement.

CIVIL DISORDER

The National Advisory Commission on Civil Disorders, generally known as the Kerner Commission, was clearly a crisis response to the long hot summer of 1967 when violence of some severity exploded in the racial ghettoes of over 200 cities. Governments typically respond to such crises by calling for investigation, but President Johnson gave this Commission a broad mandate, indeed. That is to say, the charge to the commission was not simply to investigate and recommend "methods and techniques" for averting and controlling such disorders and to define the appropriate role to be played in such efforts by local, state and federal authorities; the inquiry was clearly intended to go beyond these technical and legal requirements, as the presidential directive states, to consider the "basic causes and factors leading to [the recent] . . . disorders and the influence, if any, of organizations or individuals dedicated to the incitement or encouragement of violence."[2]

The task of the commission, as defined by this presidential charge, would seem to have provided a unique opportunity for and challenge to basic social science research. While previous governmental commissions had looked into cases of civil disorder, almost all had confined their attention to specific outbreaks. At no time since the challenge by the Confederate states to federal authority had domestic tranquility been threatened as directly as it appeared to be, given the scale of the existing disorder. It was nevertheless clear that the report the commission was expected to produce would be a political rather than a social science document. In this respect, advisory commissions dealing with broad social issues usually have had much less autonomy than such standing bodies as the Council of Economic Advisers, where economists are in firm control.

The importance of political considerations is evidenced by the persons appointed as commissioners. As is customary for such commissions, the membership was carefully balanced politically with each of certain major interest groups represented. Thus, the commission was chaired by the Republican mayor of New York City. Besides several members of Congress, equally divided among the parties, the commission included a moderate civil rights leader, a liberal police chief, an appointed state official, a businessman, a trade union leader—but not a single social scientist.

Of course, given their part-time involvement in the actual work of any commission, one would expect the commissioners to exercise less control over the final report than their formal status might allow. The Kerner Commission was no exception: the contents of its report are largely the work of a full-time paid professional staff. Direction of the commission's staff work rested almost exclusively in the hands of politically experienced lawyers, who knew their way in and out of government. Lawyers do indeed bring special qualifications to this kind of job. They are usually experienced brokers capable of soliciting cooperation needed from various groups if the task is to be completed within the prescribed time. Most important, they are habituated to working up a case under pressure, using to the fullest whatever evidence may be available. Although the commission was eager to obtain the services of a prestigious social scientist, partly to lend credibility to its report, his was not to be, so it appears, a position of major responsibility. Several who were approached turned down the offer.[3]

The final report included a good deal of historical and statistical information on Negroes and on conditions in the ghettoes, very little of which was new. The chance for the commission to use its resources to break new ground lay elsewhere, namely in the work of its field staff, but here the lack of influence of social scientists at the higher staff levels had adverse effects. The investigations headed by lawyers were apt to emphasize riot chronology, eyewitness accounts, official responses to the rioting, and an assessment of damages. Notwithstanding the importance of such information and the overall quality of many reports, they often bypassed the very questions most critical for the kind of interpretation that the social science staff was to deliver.

The potential contribution of social scientists is not only as technical analysts. Their perspectives are needed to help frame the questions and to define the terms in which these can best be answered. The nature of their expertise has sometimes been obscured by the mushrooming of social science research organizations called into existence by the growth of federally sponsored social research. Commercial enterprises seeking to profit from this demand have often been poorly staffed, with some ready to bend in any direction when there is an opportunity to reach contract. Lawyers, who lack the esoteric knowledge to judge the soundness and feasibility of various proposals, are thus dependent on social science advice. When it received several unsolicited proposals for a computerized analysis of vast masses of data, the commission rejected these on the advice of its own social scientists. It also heeded their counsel to publish—in a companion volume to its own report—three supplementary studies, conducted within an academic setting, two with the financial support of the Ford Foundation.

Not quite so sanguine was the commission's response to one specific question, included in its original charge, "What effects do the mass media have on the riots?" This is a basic sociological question, but as every experienced researcher knows, the complexity is such that hard data to answer the question are almost impossible to obtain. Yet the commission, on the hunch that a highly sensational coverage of the riots contributed to an atmosphere of tension and helped keep violence going once it had erupted, decided to sponsor a content analysis of news output of television stations and newspapers in 15 of the cities to which it had sent field teams.

I have less than full knowledge about which social scientists were consulted, but I do know that the decision, made at a higher level, to undertake this task caused dismay among the commission's own social scientists. At least one university-based institute with a staff experienced in content analysis—at least of print media—turned down the study. The commission finally turned to a commercial firm, which agreed to do the job, despite the failure of its own advisory group, hastily assembled, to validate this undertaking. The group's judgment was that the study, even if conducted in a technically impeccable fashion, would shed little light on the question it was supposed to answer.

The study, as conducted, was vulnerable from the outset. The firm to which the contract had been let lacked a sufficiently experienced staff. It assured the commission that its work would be overseen by a four-man committee, but the group never met. The chairman of that committee could not exercise effective supervision, being only a part-time consultant without authority or any clear knowledge of the terms of the contract or of the resources and time available to complete the study. Apparently lawyers on the commission staff, themselves under great pressure to deliver, did not become aware until the deadline was upon them that such an arrangement was unlikely to yield the kind of research findings needed.

The pressure of the deadline was obviously a major factor in the work of the commission. The decision by the Commissioners to skip the interim report due on March 1, 1968, and to issue, instead, a final report by that date was an accommodation to certain political facts. They had become concerned over the appearance of an increasing number of interpretations in the press that attributed the persistence of rioting to a conspiracy. Early issuance of the report, it was felt, would help counter these interpretations, especially since information so far collected permitted the conclusion that "the urban disorders of the summer of 1967 were not caused by, nor were they the consequences of, any organized plan or 'conspiracy.' "[4] It was unlikely that the report would satisfy all those ready to see a conspiracy, but given the diffuseness of the rioting, it was also unlikely that a counter-case could be easily built by fastening on to certain unexplained events (as a counter-case had been built in response to the findings of the Warren Commission). Meanwhile, the report could try to focus attention on conditions in the cities where violence had occurred.

Where research is aimed at the acquisition of knowledge, it is far more difficult to accommodate it to such stringent deadlines. The advancement of the deadline and the resultant cutbacks in staff occasioned much dismay among social scientists. Already at work under great pressure, they knew that their own efforts would be further hampered. They also resented the priority given to other investigative activities. Within this climate, as far as I have been able to gather from available accounts,[5] the cleavage based on professional orientations became superimposed on a split that had its basis in politics. The field staff of the commission included a significant proportion of young lawyers and returned Peace Corps volunteers with strong sympathies for the cause of the Negro. These people responded politically to developments within the commission. Their suspicion that more conservative staff directors might counter the younger staff's push toward reform by screening material for its political acceptability linked up with the concern of social scientists that their professional contribution would not receive due weight. Accordingly, a rough and early draft of the social science analysis, a document entitled *The*

Harvest of American Racism, began to acquire considerable importance both as a statement of faith and as a potential political weapon.

This document, which was internally circulated, apparently had some impact on the conclusions of the commission. Distrust was so great that some members deliberately spread rumors of an impending whitewash, hoping to forestall what they evidently feared; they also played with the idea of subsequently publishing the *Harvest* on their own in the event the commission ignored its basic import. Yet what impact the *Harvest* document did have on the commission's conclusions—for example, the single reference to "white racism," which appears in the summary statement—came not so much from these pressure tactics as from the use of its contents as the basis for considerable discussion *within* the commission. Very little of its original content appeared in the final report.

There is little point in reviewing here the various "findings" of the commission. They include a good bit of rhetoric. Its "basic conclusion: Our Nation is moving toward two societies, one black, one white—separate and unequal"[6] runs counter to what every student of American history has long known, namely that things have always been this way. The social scientist is normally assigned the task of producing hard facts, while the drafting of the rhetoric is left to other professionals. The point is that the social scientists working on the *Harvest,* by using riot profiles supplemented with other information, sought to formulate the latent rhetoric behind the violence the commission was appointed to investigate. This kind of analysis by present standards would be considered "soft" and likely to be ignored to the extent that it is nonstatistical. All three studies published as supplements to the report were essentially quantitative summaries: responses to survey questions and characteristics of riot arrestees. The documentation contained in the *Harvest* was not as vigorous or systematic as that in the supplementary studies. The final report did retain many of the statistics in the *Harvest* but without accompanying interpretations.

In its evaluation of the media coverage, the commission apparently felt bound by the statistics its researchers had produced but free to ignore their import. The quantitative analysis was said to indicate a media policy of deliberate caution and restraint in riot coverage, though the commission gave full play to certain errors in fact brought to its attention by local officials and media personnel. The media do not fully deserve the clean bill they received from the media study.[7] Some puzzling statistical findings have simple explanations. For example, the low proportion (4.8 percent) of TV sequences that showed people participating in "riot activity" is accounted for by the fact that, whenever police were shown, the scene was coded as "containment." I also have reservations about the significance of coding the "aftermath"—showing broken windows, burnt out buildings, and boarded stores—as "calm" and/or "normal." As regards the newspaper analysis, the work was not, as far as I know, pushed beyond the treatment of racial issues to the actual coverage of riots. Since as a rule national racial issues tend to receive more front-page space than strictly local incidents, the finding that local newspapers tended to print more stories dealing with racial disorders or troubles—read, "racial issues"—outside the strictly local context becomes plausible but not relevant to the riot coverage. It does seem clear that in the period after the Kerner Report the press gave undue prominence to unverified reports of sniping, suggesting that there had been a basic change in the nature of the violence.[8] This underlines a suspicion that interpretations drawn from the content analysis are highly questionable. No conclusions can be drawn from them, positively or negatively, about the impact on the rioting of the way the media handled their coverage.

If the use made by the Kerner Commission of its social science input is any guide at all, we may conclude that members of such commissions are likely to be bound by and to present quantitative data that, used in a report, give it the aura of objectivity. But when issues arise over how to interpret such data, the social scientist becomes involved in delicate negotiations in which he finds it hard to separate his professional role from his role as a member of the commission, involved in its internal politics.

MASS COMMUNICATION

The media of mass communication in the United States, as everyone knows, are operated as private businesses rather than as public utilities. Media performance is judged by its acceptability to an audience, most of whose members are content to choose among the available offering. Because the American mass communication system (as in most industrially advanced nations) represents a sector separate from public education and is rarely used to promote social goals, the industry has almost always been able to shield itself against even legitimate pressure by invoking the First Amendment, while most of the initiative and much of the financing for educational television has come from foundations whose officials, critical of the media performance, were eager to provide alternative services. Government carries no clear responsibility for mass communication, as it does for education. The activities of communication agencies are subject to regulation only insofar as limitation of the spectrum makes it necessary to license competitors who would otherwise crowd one another off the air. Basically federal control is confined to transmission facilities.

The Federal Communications Commission (FCC) is the agency entrusted with this regulation. Yet understaffed as it usually is and caught between competing pressures—from applicants, from the executive and legislators—the FCC is hardly the source from which to expect basic policy-oriented research. This helps explain why—at a time when all of North America was not yet within range of a clear TV-signal—no one seized the opportunity for a systematic and experimental study of the impact of a new medium. Most research then was clearly dominated by commercial interest, while government was by no means prepared to fill the gap.

The researcher, often preoccupied with suspected negative effects of the mass media, has designed much of his work to fit a quasi-medical framework with the media viewed as a possible source of contamination and some types of content as a virus responsible for certain social ills. The communication industry has used these studies to defend itself. It can cite the failure to show beyond doubt and outside the laboratory that the media are the direct cause of serious behavior or psychological problems or can persuade people to accept as true or right viewpoints or opinions they are strongly inclined to resist. There are parallels in the health field—indeed with regard to drugs and food additives, legislation calls for the producer to provide evidence of positive benefits before he can market his products. Even a far less stringent test would be unacceptable to broadcasters—they would view it as a violation of their freedom of speech.

In March 1969, under pressure from Senator Pastore, chairman of the subcommittee on communications, who appears willing to grant broadcasters a permanent franchise provided they agree to conform to his own preferred standards for program content, the Department of Health, Education and Welfare prepared to launch under its own auspices a broadly based inquiry into the subject of television and violence. It was billed as a definitive study, comparable to the major project on cigarettes and health previously conducted through the Surgeon General's office: There had been no prior investigation of program content as sweeping as this and since the findings would, presumably, be a guide for setting programming standards, it was to be supervised by an impartial advisory body made up of representatives of the various health professions.

That the broadcasting industry should exhibit concern over the outcome is only natural. Networks immediately moved to invest some of their own resources in studies of this very problem. The power of the industry is furthermore evident in some of the procedures by which the Scientific Advisory Committee on Television and Social Behavior, the name given to the advisory body, was chosen. Members of the staff of the National Institute of Mental Health drew up a comprehensive list of potential members from names solicited through a variety of sources. The list included persons from several disciplines, many of them well known for their contributions to mass communication research, not excluding some in the employ of the networks. What is significant is that, to ensure in advance the active collaboration of the television industry in the studies to be sponsored, the entire list of nominees was submitted to the networks and [according to *Science*][9] to the National Association of Educational Broadcasters, whose representatives were asked to indicate any individuals who they believed "would not be appropriate for an impartial scientific investigation of this nature." It was made clear at the same time that it would not be necessary to state the reasons for such a negative judgment.[10]

To scrutinize the credentials and objectivity of persons serving on this kind of advisory panel is an obvious and sound practice, but blackballing those who for some undetermined reason may be unpalatable to the industry most directly concerned is not, unless the other side is given the same opportunity. It should be noted that at least one network (CBS) declined to express its preferences among the names contained in the list of some 40 nominees. Nevertheless, a total of seven were rejected—undoubtedly because of views they had published or publicly expressed since they obviously did not lack scientific credentials. The scientific credentials of the individuals on the committee, as finally constituted, were similarly impeccable, but in view of the solicitous concern for the sensitivities of the networks the selection of several with close ties to the industry, by virtue of present or past employment or through their consultant capacity, while some viewpoints remained underrepresented, can hardly be taken as coincidental.

It is of course possible to argue that the degree of balance within the committee is a trivial matter. The scope of the research had been defined in advance with review by the committee largely a formality, greatly influenced by preparatory work of the NIMH staff, and confined pretty much to technical advice. True as this may be, it stands to reason nevertheless that the committee members would pass on any final report. And here one must recognize that the various attempts to establish conclusively the effects of cumulative exposure to television fare will inevitably founder on the near-impossibility of disentangling the role played by the mass media from the numerous other influences that also impinge on children's lives, including the influence of the general social climate, which the media are said to merely reflect rather than to disseminate. Any case made against television is likely to remain unproven, and extreme skepticism about anything less than an unambiguous test is generally viewed as a commendable scientific attitude.

Still another facet of the scientific attitude is a highly fragmented approach to social problems. For example, the decision to exclude from this research the violence so prominent in news reports means passing up a great opportunity to follow up some of the concerns of the Kerner Commission.[11] In this case, the framework of the study was largely defined by the Congressional Committee and, following the assumptions of that committee, was limited to an evaluation of existing commercial program content. There was no intent to chart out what the media could potentially accomplish. Most of the initiative and pressure in this direction has come from outside the industry.

The problems created by advances in communications technology do, on the other hand, force an occasional review of some of the assumptions guiding communications policy. Formulated along fairly narrow lines after radio was well established as a mass medium, this initial policy—except for reserving certain TV channel frequencies for exclusive educational use—has hardly been changed. The appointment by President Johnson on August 14, 1967, of a Task Force on Communications Policy was a response to developments in satellite technology and to the growth of cable TV. Decisions had to be made since huge investments and financial interests were involved.

Since the membership of the task force consisted of "distinguished government officials," it is not surprising that the report stresses, among other things, the positive interest of various government agencies in the use of communication facilities.[1][2] The director of research for the group was a RAND Corporation economist with prior experience on the project on communications satellites systems, sponsored by the Ford Foundation. Although the task force did not interpret its mandate to require a study of TV content, their report does note the lack of diversity and variety in existing programming. They also find, in several contexts, that the main obstacle to the full use of broadcasting in the public interest lies not primarily in the lack of hardware but in the difficulties encountered in the search for talent and incentives to produce the proper software. That the report was controversial is evidenced in the delay of its release and the release of the supporting research. Completed in December 1968, it was kept under wraps for a full five months. Only after its contents had been leaked to the press was it finally forwarded, without endorsement, to the House Committee and officially released.

Much of the research that went into the report sought answers to questions of technical feasibility and costs. But the work of the task force is distinguished in two respects: It represents a comprehensive approach to the dissection of a major social problem, drawing on the expertise of both engineers and social scientists. Further, in commissioning a pilot project, it departed from the usual practice of policy studies emanating at the federal level. The usual procedure has been to launch extensive surveys, the prime purpose of which is to give an "accounting" of what exists rather than to indicate the as yet nonexisting potential. The pilot project[13] specifically explores ways in which new communication facilities could make a vital contribution to various programs designed to compensate some minority groups for disabilities they face.

This pilot study was, to be sure, of modest proportions. The RAND team that conducted it interviewed only 253 Negroes in two communities. Yet in queries about where these residents learned about jobs, schools, health and welfare services, housing and so forth, the researchers were able to document the inadequacy of information sources and to indicate how the lack of communication services contributed to the isolation of the ghetto residents. A fair test of the policy implication, namely that telecommunications techniques "when properly and creatively used can be an effective means for improving urban life," they concluded, would still require a well-designed research, test and evaluation program. The task force report incorporated a proposal for an experimental program and research designed to change the quality of ghetto life.

What they are suggesting is not just an action program with evaluation built into it, as a look at the stated objectives makes clear. The research is to determine benefits and costs, test the hypotheses set forth in the pilot study, determine how long it would take to alter old viewing habits and to create credibility, and finally to identify the kinds of institutions and organizational support needed in order to make the program work. As in new nations, where talent is so precious, the idea is not to acquire new knowledge but to create experiences that will aid in putting knowledge to use. Involvement of social scientists in such programs would create new roles, both for the participating individuals and for their disciplines. Both the reward structure of a career in the social sciences and the relation of social science to administration would no doubt be affected.

EDUCATION

Most attempts to guarantee equality of opportunity have focused not on communication agencies but on the schools. The school is still perceived as the major avenue for the entry of minority group members both into jobs and into the mainstream of American life. To provide the requisite education for all has traditionally been a concern of government, but since there are disparities among the resources that different regions and communities can devote to this purpose, pressure has built to increase the federal contribution, part of this in the form of research and development that local systems cannot provide.

To be specific, the United States Office of Education, beginning in 1963, financed a network of research and development organizations and educational laboratories. In addition, Section 402 of the Civil Rights Act of 1964 specifically instructed the commissioner of education to conduct a survey "concerning the lack of availability of equal educational opportunities for individuals by reason of race, color, religion, or national origin in public educational institutions . . . " By this legislation Congress extended the techniques of social accounting to a new area. The study resulting, now called the Coleman Report,[14] was initially designed to document the existence of segregation and discrimination in American education and to trace, on the basis of nationwide information, some of their effects.

Some findings could hardly have been surprising: The great majority of American children attend schools where most of their fellow students are of the same racial background; this segregation by race is more complete in the South; achievement levels of minority group children, most of whose educational experiences are in schools largely segregated by race, are lower than those of other children; and this gap between the minority and majority groups tends to grow, rather than diminish, as children progress through the grades. Somewhat disconcerting to the liberal mentality however, was the finding that the differences in the schools attended by children of different groups with regard to such matters as plant and facilities, curriculum offerings, and quality of teaching staff was far less than the disparity of achievement might suggest. In these respects the minority groups turned out, at least on a national basis, to suffer no disadvantage at all.

Through an elaborate statistical analysis, the Coleman team attempted to account for the sources of variability in school achievement. This effort has led many people to consider the Coleman Report one of the most important social science documents of our time. Illustrative of its findings: first, that within-school variation accounted for over 70 percent of all variation in achievement and that between 30 and 50 percent of the variance (between as well as within schools) is a function of individual background and attitudes; second, that school factors accounted for only about 10 to 20 percent of the variance in achievement but that their influence was somewhat greater for minorities; and, third, that the most influential school factors contributing to student achievement were certain characteristics and attitudes of the student body, which were themselves closely related to the social environment from which students came.

These findings were hard for some people to accept—particularly the conclusion: in cases where Negroes appeared to benefit—as judged by achievement levels—from attending schools with a majority of white students, the apparent benefit was attributable less to the racial mix than to the relatively privileged educational background and higher educational aspirations of the average student in these schools.[15] Such a finding ran counter to the premise that justified pressing for immediate integration: totally segregated black schools, even with equal facilities, are ipso facto, inferior schools.

The reaction of the Civil Rights Commission to these findings is therefore of particular interest for it obviously could not ignore them. When in the following year the commission released its own report,[16] it took issue not only with the conclusions of the Coleman study but also with those of another study it directly commissioned. This second study from the University of California was, if anything, even more unequivocal in stating that the racial composition of the school has no effect on the achievement of its pupils once social class composition has been controlled.[17] This conclusion is supported by new tabulations derived from the data of the Coleman Report, data that were designed to show that the breakdown of racial segregation would have desirable consequences.

The staff of the Civil Rights Commission in its report reasoned that the potentially positive effects of desegregation were often neutralized through practices that led to at least a partial resegregation within the class room. According to its analysis the achievement of Negro children with prolonged experience in integrated class rooms was found to be slightly higher than that of others only integrated at the highest grades or with no experience in an integrated setting. This apparent effect was found to persist regardless of the racial composition of the school.

Yet the statistical controls were clearly inadequate. A careful reading of the tables selected to support the case for integration reveals that the level of parental education in the majority white classes was higher than that in the classes where all or the majority of children were Negro. What counts, given the current social class differences between Negroes and whites, is the increased opportunity for contact with classmates from a higher average social and economic background.[18] Also, Negroes in schools where they are likely to attend a majority white classroom tend to come from families that are economically better off, while those attending heavily Negro schools but classes where the majority of classmates are white are likely to have been selected because, whatever their background, they exhibited unusual ability. Sociologists have long believed that the track system tends to discriminate against Negroes; authorities are often reluctant to place middle-class white children in classes made up of "low achievers" if it puts them in a predominantly Negro class. Only recently a study of Plainfield, New Jersey, demonstrated that the average achievement of Negroes within a track was higher than that of whites in the same track.[19]

One can, of course, press for integration as a value in itself: by providing an opportunity for interracial contact and removing the stigma that so often has been attached to the segregated school, it can foster positive attitudes. The Civil Rights Commission report[20] offers evidence that an interracial school setting promotes desirable attitudes. Still by the mid-sixties the thrust of the civil rights movement in Northern cities was shifting away from integration towards other measures—community involvement and community control among others. There is little evidence in the Coleman Report to justify this shift which was mainly the product of frustration as, despite all efforts, school segregation increased rather than decreased. It was also part and parcel of the newly emerging orientation towards black power and black pride. The vast array of findings within the Coleman Report has been selectively interpreted to sustain the advocates of different conceptions and solutions.[21] The kind of multivariate analysis applied to highly variable cross-sectional data that the Coleman Report represents lends itself to this use inasmuch as statistical relationships do not suffice to establish causal responsibility.

Most important, a study meant to assess the degree of equality of opportunity differs in design and use from a study meant to set priorities for remedial intervention. Though a particular factor may account for only a small proportion of the variance (in achievement levels, for example) it may be simple to manipulate and the change can have cumulative effects. Thus, even if the racial composition of the student body has no relationship to school achievement other than that attributable to its social class composition, the shortest route to full equality of educational opportunity may still be to change the racial composition of the segregated Negro school in order to expose the students to fellow students of a different social class. One should also note that the concept of equal opportunity guiding the Coleman study was a condition in which a similar input results in similar outcomes. Yet the school cannot compensate for every inequality and, as Coleman himself has put the case since, to achieve parity the Negro needs more than equal opportunity.[22] Racial integration would raise the achievement of some black students but not without some adverse effects on others, whose social background assigns them a position of permanent inferiority vis-a-vis classmates with whom they cannot compete.

Concern over the self-concepts of Negro children—their sense of personal worth—and the feeling of many of them that they have no control over their environment has, of course, supplied some of the thrust behind the drive for community control, because it could be shown that these had a strong relationship to achievement. "As the proportion of whites in the school increases, the sense of control of environment increases, and his self-concept decreases," states the Coleman Report.[23] This apparent paradox arises from the fact that the self-concept of the Negro child is strongly related to his belief that he has or hasn't some control over his environment, whereas that of the white child reflects primarily his actual achievement in school relative to that of his peers. Thus, the black child, when placed in an integrated school, may come to recognize better than before that his own plans and efforts have consequences, but at the same time, his self-concept may come to depend less on this sense of control than on his actual performance. Those Negro children from relatively favored backgrounds, such as most of those now attending integrated schools, may be better able to handle the strain of the keener competition encountered there. To place others in a competitive situation for which their background does not prepare them can damage their self-esteem.

No matter how we look at all these various findings, they point to the overriding importance for achievement of social class background and, secondarily, of social class climates. All this should not have occasioned any surprise. Only the unwillingness of many reformers to take with sufficient seriousness the reality of social class leads them to view certain social problems primarily in terms of their attitudinal and interpersonal components. In Israel, for example, where race is not a major factor, but cultural differences are, the children of fathers from industrially advanced countries acquired the basic skills far more rapidly than other children within the community attending the same grade-school classes. The difference was markedly evident by the end of their second year in school.[24] The UNESCO world mathematics survey has yielded essentially similar results. Moreover, when the leaders of the Soviet Union in the 1920s made a deliberate effort to proletarianize the universities and technical colleges by encouraging the children of the poor to enroll in secondary schools, they could not succeed. By the end of their first academic year, the majority of those from poor backgrounds had left—presumably because they lacked sufficient support from their families. The schools, in the phrase of Bukharin, became sieves retaining only the children of the better-off elements.[25]

The problem of redressing social inequalities is quite different from documenting their existence. As a first step toward remedial action, the United States Office of Education, beginning in 1963, financed a network of educational research and development organizations. The network came, ultimately, to include some 20 regional educational laboratories, whose mission unfortunately never became clearly defined. They were to conduct basic research, to create and demonstrate a rich array of tested alternatives to existing educational practices, to encourage and speed the dissemination and utilization of their research. This last mission was the real challenge.

The proposals submitted by these federally funded labs to justify their funding were full of promises bolstered by an eloquent phraseology. Each organization tried to carve out for itself an area not duplicated by any other. The point is that far from innovating, either in the area of research or imaginative new programs, many followed the political currents of the period. In 1965 and 1966, some were heavily involved in school desegregation, but three years later their emphasis had shifted. They were playing it safe. Almost all were concerned with developing curricula and teaching aids that required limited or no structural changes to implement.

It was highly dubious from the beginning that these organizations, tied as they were to the educational establishment in Washington and required, by the terms of the legislation, to serve the region in which they were located, could ever have become the agencies for more than the most minor innovation. By and large, they came to duplicate the work routinely undertaken by many ongoing agencies or tried to serve a need that commercial enterprises, eager for a share of the rapidly expanding educational market, were already prepared to serve for profit. New products, often poorly tested but incorporating new technologies, seem abundantly available but the problem of getting a school system to modify its basic practices seems nearly insurmountable and has certainly not been solved by research.

The investment in existing practices is tremendous: the share of public monies routed to the educational complex and the activities it supports is exceeded only by the proportion siphoned off to the military-industrial complex. The investment extends to research activities, many of which are dominated by professional educators for whom they provide avenues of career mobility. No matter how politically liberal the announced goals of the educational establishment, most of its members tend to be highly conservative with regard to most matters, including research, that are included within its professional sphere.

POLICY-ORIENTED RESEARCH: THE NEED FOR INDEPENDENT SYNTHESIS

The examples I have used only illustrate the range of settings in which social research is geared to policy making. In each of the three settings discussed, social research operates against a background of vested interests. Governmental commissions, such as the riot commission, are primarily political responses. The diverse interests existing within society usually receive representation on the commission itself, but the time pressure under which they must discharge their task gives the staff a not inconsiderable leeway. In the framing of policy on mass communication, private economic interests constitute the main pressure group which is forever pitted against governmental encroachment, but engineering problems force compromises that only the government can effectively enforce. Finally, in education we are witnessing the growth of a national establishment, intimately tied to research activity yet intent on keeping innovation confined to the marginal areas.

The bureaus and institutes of social research, inside and outside of universities, are another element in the newly emerging pattern. These organizations often pursue their own economic interests. Where the overhead is large, a continuing flow of government contracts and grants becomes a prerequisite for survival. Therefore, tooling up for many different types of research tends to devalue substantive expertise in favor of routines for processing data. Such research, while perhaps increasingly sophisticated in its methods, is not likely to become a source of new ideas.

It is a well-established principle that innovations typically arise from activities conducted at the periphery of organizations. Research too closely tied into existing structure is unlikely to produce major inventions even in the technical area; instead these often emanate from mavericks working independently—provided the maverick can find a sponsor to act as a broker and take over the job of promoting the new idea. In this respect, the lack of close links between academic social scientists and policy-making bodies in their area of concern may be a distinct advantage. Too close an involvement in the practical affairs of interagency rivalry can cause the social scientist to lose the detachment from which the value of advice derives. Governmental bodies eager to avail themselves of social science expertise are not always as keen in their search for fresh points of view. They may be more intent on harnessing the prestige carried in the name and title of their social science consultants.

Whatever the parochialism inherent in the agency perspective, it is sometimes surpassed by the sterile scholasticism of the academic. There is a real need for synthetic research, for working over, from a fresh perspective, materials that are routinely gathered with ever greater efficiency, though not necessarily sophistication, by the agencies themselves. Such activity basically constitutes a form of social criticism, and while some of the special studies by ad hoc advisory bodies and federally supported laboratories and institutes are supposed to perform this function, they have not always, as I have tried to show in this paper, performed in any way that even approached optimum. Hence, there is a place for the independent or university-based researcher, provided he can free himself from the hustle for support that he increasingly needs to compete in the intellectual marketplace. To perform effectively, however, such people must have access to certain information and be given the opportunity to familiarize themselves with the issues that confront the policy maker. If these academic faculty could spend their sabbaticals without other obligation in independently funded centers for policy studies and devote part of their time to examining the problems of particular agencies, a bridge might be built between two worlds without creating new pressures on the academic researcher or making it inevitable that he be so coopted as to lose his ability to play the role of critic.

NOTES

[1] It is clear, for example, that many of the social problems that reached crisis proportions in the 1960s were already on the horizon in 1933 and taken up in the President's Committee on Recent Social Trends. Yet, "the massive distortions of the depression called for crisis remedies, so that the long-term significance of 'trends' was overlooked." See *The Behavioral and Social Sciences: Outlook and Needs.* Washington, D.C.: National Academy of Science and Social Science Research Council, 1969, p. 108.

[2] *Report of the National Advisory Commission on Civil Disorders,* March 1, 1968. U.S. Government Printing Office, 1968 0-281-729.

[3] Robert Shellow, "Social Scientists and Social Action from Within the Establishment." Paper read before the 24th Conference on Public Opinion Research, May 16-19, 1969.

[4] *Report,* p. 4.

[5] See, in addition to Shellow, *op. cit.,* Michael Lipsky and David J. Olson, Riot-Commission Politics, *transa*ction, 1969, V. 6 (9), 8-21.

[6] *Report,* p. 1.

[7] See *Report,* ch. 15.

[8] Terry Ann Knopf, "Sniping-A New Pattern of Violence?" *transa*ction, 1969, V. 6 (9), 22-29.

[9] May 22, 1970.

[10] Correspondence on this matter was made available through the courtesy of Dr. Frank Stanton.

[11] That task has since been undertaken by the National Commission on the Causes and Prevention of Violence.

[12] President's Task Force on Communications Policy. *Final Report,* December 7, 1968. U.S. Government Printing Office: 1969 0-351-436.

[13] H.S. Dordick, L.G. Chesler, S.I. Firstman, and R. Bretz, *Telecommunications and Urban Development.* RAND Corporation Memorandum RM-6069-RC, July 1969.

[14] James S. Coleman *et al., Equality of Educational Opportunity.* U.S. Government Printing Office, 1966, FS 5-238:38001.

[15] *Ibid.,* p. 307.

[16] *Racial Isolation in the Public Schools.* A Report of the U.S. Commissions on Civil Rights, 2 vols. U.S. Government Printing Office: 1967 0-243-637.

[17] A.B. Wilson, *The Consequence of Segregation: Academic Achievement in a Northern Community.* Univ. of California, Berkeley, Survey Research Center, 1969.

[18] See *The Segregated Student in Desegregated Schools,* Johns Hopkins University, Center for the Study of Social Organization of Schools, Report No. 21.

[19] See *Grouping Students for Instruction in the Plainfield, New Jersey, School System,* Teachers College, Columbia University, Institute of Field Studies, July, 1969.

[20] *Op. cit*

[21] See, for example, the symposium on Race and Equal Educational Opportunity, *Harvard Educational Review,* 1968. V. 38 (1).

[22] See the contribution of Coleman to symposium, *Ibid.*

[23] *Op. cit.,* p. 323f.

[24] Sarah Smilansky, Evaluation of Early Education, in M. Smilansky and L. Adar (Eds.), *Evaluating Educational Achievement.* UNESCO Educational Studies and Documents, No. 42. Paris, 1961.

[25] Cited in Fedotoff-White, *The Growth of the Red Army.* Princeton, N.J.: Princeton University Press, 1941, p. 293.

15

Science, Social Science and Presidentialism: Policy During the Nixon Administration[1]

JAMES EVERETT KATZ

Does presidential power directly affect science and social science policy? Or are the scientific needs of the national society so inherently stable that whoever occupies the executive office of the president can only affect science policy to a relatively miniscule degree? A central feature of this examination of science policy is the area of policy for social science. For the purposes of this analysis, social science is viewed as operating within the larger dynamics of science policy *per se*. At the same time, social science has unique features that shall be analyzed later in the chapter. The influence and impact of the presidency on policy for social science is a major issue.

The American system of science policy construction and execution can be characterized in highly pluralistic terms. Earlier formulations of the sociology of science policy tended to emphasize multiple centers of power, interest and funding.[2] In contrast, there is a great deal of evidence to indicate that the president and his executive officers have been able to expand their power incrementally over time.[3] Has the historical process of the expansion of presidential power been carried into the arena of science policy? Along with the incremental growth of presidential power, has there been established a capacity for the president and his officers to establish priorities, principles and policies in the federal support (or lack thereof) for science? If this presidential intervention takes place, how is it accomplished?

In order to solve these general queries, two points must be pinned down: (1) Has the presidency been able to affect science and social science policy? (2) Through what mechanisms has the effect been put into action?

The answers to these questions are sought by examining the functioning of three mechanisms of presidential power over science policy during the Nixon administration. These three mechanisms are the Office of Management and Budget (OMB), the structure of executive organization over science policy responsibility and the nature of presidential appointments in science policy positions. Following this discussion an analysis of unique features of policy for social science during the Nixon administration is undertaken.

The OMB is the "lengthened shadow" of the president across the entire spectrum of federal government operations.[4] As such, it defends the interests of the president against the pressures of the departmental bureaucracies. The OMB also serves the president as a watchdog, insuring that the policy priorities of the president are carried out within the agency and department bureaucracies.

The OMB was formerly called the Bureau of the Budget and was reorganized by the Nixon White House in 1970. The new organization was undertaken in order to "provide the President with a significantly strengthened capability to manage the vast resources of the executive branch and to streamline Federal operations."[5]

Nixon stated that:

Improvement of Government organization, information and management systems will be a major function of the Office of Management and Budget. . . . Resistance to organizational change is one of the chief obstacles to effective government; the new Office will seek to ensure that organization keeps abreast of program needs [message transmitting Reorganization Plan Number Two to Congress, 1970].

Thus the OMB was designed to be a major means of implementing presidential policy priorities into the policy conduct and formulation network within the government. Rather than being relatively passive, the OMB was intended to take active initiative to oversee the execution of presidential priorities.

It is clear that the OMB does not and could not review science policy and programming in its entirety. It is doubtful that any federal agency could keep track of all the diverse projects, equipment, manpower and facilities involved in federal research and development (and thus science). The OMB singles out policies and programs that appear to have significance to the president's priorities instead. Significance to the president in this context means having potentially negative or positive pay-offs for presidential power, influence or prestige. "The Budget Bureau has an enormous influence on R&D budgeting—an influence both positive and negative. . . . [Its potential for] discouraging projects before they can reach the President is extremely large."[6] The interest of the OMB goes beyond simple budget questions. "The breadth of the Bureau's involvement is awesome."[7]

The Office of Management and Budget is concerned with questions of science legislation. In dealings with Congress, OMB officials have presented the administration's position on matters such as the measure to create the National Social Science Foundation and a bill to establish a department of science. The executive branch position of questions raised by Congress regarding science is established by OMB. For example, congressional inquiry into the sufficiency of executive planning and coordination efforts for science was answered under the direction of the OMB. OMB assisted in the decision as to whether grants for academic science should be made consistent to a predictable cluster of highly rated universities or be dispersed geographically.[8]

The organization and management of science enterprises within the federal bureaucracy are also subject to OMB scrutiny. It has also dealt with questions such as how to structure a new agency for aeronautics and space research or what the criteria should be for dividing research and development funds between federal intramural and industrial contracting.

Research-grant management is within the realm of OMB authority. Areas upon which the OMB has had a decided influence are: guidelines for allocating indirect costs to research grants, guidelines for principles of cost-sharing grants to universities, common systems of auditing grants received from various federal departments.

Problems of interdepartmental coordination have received the OMB's attention. The OMB divided responsibilities between the Atomic Energy Commission and the National Science Foundation for the support of the construction of university physical research facilities.

Yet the most significant impact the OMB has over science policy is at the level of setting budget priorities. In relation to the science budget of the various agencies, OMB used its review power to ensure the agencies' response to presidential priorities. As stated earlier, this power over the budget is exerted mainly in its reduction.

Elmer Staats, formerly deputy director in charge of research and development with OMB states that research and development review is "a necessarily selective process which tries to identify and resolve critical question."[9] He says of basic research: "We do not in the Bureau deal with basic research through a project-by-project review and decision procedure. . . . [Instead we prefer a more general approach examining] a slice of basic science on a government-wide basis. . . ."[10]

The social sciences are unique in that it is more difficult to measure in any precise terms the achievement of research goals. Former Budget Bureau director Charles Schultze has documented the tremendous upward surge in funds allocated to research on domestic programs.[11] Even so, the administration evinces a qualified belief in the utility of the social sciences. This conviction was echoed by an OMB staff member: "We support social science at a higher level than we can actually justify. It just seems that it will be one investment that will eventually pay off."

The OMB itself is "the most effective control mechanism" over social science policy.[12] It monitors the progress of the evaluation of social programs and terminates those that do not seem to yield the desired results.

It focuses on policies and occasionally programs that appear to have a realizable payoff for the president's goals and assigned missions. William D. Carey has had more responsibility for a longer time for science policy on a broad basis within the OMB than any other person. He observes that, to the extent it is possible to take charge of the diffuse network of science, this responsibility has become OMB's. "I do feel to the extent that anyone's in charge (of science policy), it's the Office of Management and Budget."[13]

Impoundment is an effective weapon in the OMB's arsenal. By withholding funds, the OMB can actually eliminate unwanted programs, authorized by Congress, which are not in line with presidential priorities. Table 1 demonstrates the growing magnitude of the use of impoundment in the budget of the National Science Foundation.

Cost/benefit analysis is one of the most significant innovations in OMB intervention in science and social science research. By weighing the criteria for choice within a framework of presidential priorities, the goals and strategies of achieving those goals are made explicit in any cost/benefit analysis. This makes it possible for the OMB to easily scrutinize such programs. The bureaucracy must defend its own programs in terms of the president's priorities, in contrast with earlier methods of budget examination in which the examiner was forced to question the decisions of the bureaucracy. Examples of effective utilization of cost/benefit analysis include: (1) an analysis of the summer Head Start program which showed insignificant measurable gains resulting in a shift of resources to the full-year program; (2) a study of alternative research programs in law enforcement that helped to identify areas of highest priority for social research.[14]

An overview of the top-level science advisory organization shows the development of an executive advisory structure and its subsequent demise. The science advisory organization in the White House was initiated by the establishment of the Science Advisory Committee early in 1951. This was formed to fill a need for high-level scientific advice that would be free from the influence of the Defense Department and the Atomic Energy Commission.[15] After the 1957 launching of the Russian sputnik, Eisenhower established the President's Science Advisory Committee (PSAC). Eisenhower stated that the foundation of PSAC, and the appointment of James Killian of the Massachusetts Institute of Technology as science advisor to the president, was an attempt to "relieve the current wave of near hysteria" after the Russian space spectacular.[16] Kennedy institutionalized the science advisor post on a subcabinet level in all appropriate federal departments. In addition, he established the Office of Science and Technology in the executive office of the president to oversee federal science and technology activities.

Social scientists began participating in the White House advisory network in the late 1960s. Three social scientists were invited to join PSAC, but this only occurred when the committee's influence was waning. The Office of Science and Technology used social scientists to evaluate the social impact of technological change.

The Nixon administration dramatically reversed this trend toward centralized high-level scientific organization and has followed a pattern of growing neglect for science-advisory structures. In January 1974, the presidential science advisory organization that had been in the executive office of the president since the Korean War was disbanded. The president's science advisor's resignation was accepted, the Office of Science and Technology was abolished and the President's Science Advisory Committee became moribund. During Congressional hearings on the dismantling of the entire White House Science Advisory structure, it was stated that this action was based on "a not very profound perception of science and technology as mere ways and means of executing a variety of Government programs, rather than factors in the Nation's potential which rate a seat at the policy table."[17]

Table 1
Dollars Impounded from the National
Science Foundation by Fiscal Year

Fiscal Year	Amount (in Millions)
1971	9.5
1972	31.0
1973	62.0

Source: National Science Foundation

Responsibility for science advice fell to Guyford Stever, director of the National Science Foundation. It is Stever's responsibility to coordinate federal science policies, much as the Office of Science and Technology did before, and report to the White House. However, Stever has received no increase in funds or power to accomplish his new responsibility, although his office did receive some of the former staff members of the Office of Science and Technology. The Science and Technology Policy Office has been established in the National Science Foundation to formalize this arrangement.[18] "The federal science policy will no longer be made by top-ranking elite scientists. Instead, policy is in the hands of bright young Republican lawyers in the White House."[19] This new arrangement permited immediate access to and control over particular scientific and technical issues that are identified by the White House as being significant to its power.

Inside the White House, Kenneth Dam, a lawyer trained in economics at the University of Chicago, has broad responsibility for science and technology. James Cavanaugh, another White House staff lawyer, has a portfolio in this area with special emphasis on biomedical research. Both Dam and Cavanaugh report to the Domestic Countil.[20]

The major point here is the bifurcation of the organization. Responsibility and power over policy are shifted upwards into the White House and the OMB. Administration of coordination and advice "on tap" are moved downwards into the National Science Foundation.

During the Nixon years, an important shift in emphasis within social science budgets occurred in terms of the ideological perspective of the institutions receiving funds. Recently a clear-cut preference for conservative "think tanks" and nonprofit organizations has been shown by the Nixon administration. Overall, the picture does not vary between Republican and Democratic administrations. By this is meant that there has been no bias on the part of previous administrations as to which institutions, viz. private industry, nonprofit organizations or government research groups, would receive social science or physical science funds. It is noteworthy that there is little evidence to support a *pro* social science bias on the part of the Democrats and an *anti* social science stance on the part of the Republicans; yet, within individual administrations a definite policy bias can be discerned.

A prime example of this ideological shift is the ascendancy of the Hoover Institution at Stanford University and the attenuation of the Brookings Institution as centers for government research and the recruitment of advisory personnel. Hoover Institution, with a reputation for staunch anticommunism and having the largest private archives in the world, has added a strong domestic policy studies program to its internationally focused scholarly investigations.[21]

The two million dollars to finance this new domestic program were raised largely through private donations among which are: $1.2 million in the form of Hewlett-Packard stock, a gift of Mr. and Mrs. David Packard (who was undersecretary of Defense in the early years of the Nixon administration); $750,000 from the Scaife Family Foundation (Richard Scaife contributed one millions dollars to the 1972 Nixon campaign); and $600,000 from the Lilly Endowment, which traditionally funds anti-Communist, conservative organizations.[22]

Martin Anderson, former special assistant to President Nixon

(1969-71), is responsible for the task of developing Hoover Institution's domestic studies program. He would like to produce studies that would aid government policy-makers in evaluating social programs. His experience in the White House has demonstrated that there is a need for this type of conservatively oriented evaluative criteria.

Along with Anderson, Hoover Institution will rely on aid from scholars at the American Enterprise Institute for Public Policy in Washington, D.C., who also had close ties to the Nixon administration. Geoffrey H. Moore, former commissioner of the Bureau of Labor Statistics (1969-1972), G. Warren Nutter, former assistant secretary of defense, Robert H. Bork, former acting attorney general, Paul W. McCracken, former chairman of the Council of Economic Advisors and many others now serve the American Enterprise Institute. The AEI Policy Studies Program, conducted jointly with Hoover Institution, will be able to draw on the experience of these men.[23]

It is also of interest to note that the president of the American Enterprise Institute, William J. Baroody, serves on the Board of Overseers of Hoover Institution along with Justice William H. Rehnquist,[24] which shows an interlocking directorate with a largely conservative bent. The financial support of both Hoover Institution and the American Enterprise Institute shows striking similarities too. Baroody has stated that the Lilly Endowment and the Scaife Family Foundation are heavy contributors to AEI as well.[25] What this indicates is a high degree of interest and involvement on the part of the Nixon administration with conservative research organizations having policy studies programs.

While there is a tilt toward conservative "think tanks," there is a concomitant animosity toward liberal centers of research. The Brookings Institution, which has been in the forefront of liberal policy analysis, has been "seeking to improve its political balance by attracting some Nixon Administration officials to its staff."[26] While Leslie Gelb, a Brookings Institute staffer, has stated that there is a decided "standoffishness on the part of the Administration,"[27] this attitude has become outright hostility in view of the Colson plan to firebomb Brookings.

Political bias has also affected the broad range of research and development funding. Massachusetts Institute of Technology, a leader in scientific research, became a target of the Nixon White House. This hostility to institutions having a reputation for liberalism is confirmed by two White House memos recommending cuts in Department of Defense contracts and the elimination of federal funding of nondefense research programs at MIT. MIT President Jerome B. Weisner's public opposition to the ABM is the reason cited in the memos for the cutback of funds to the university.[28] Hence, the political ideology of the White House sensitizes the policy-maker to sources of social science research and policy analysis that have a similar political affinity at the executive level.

The third mechanism of White House control over science and social science policy is the appointment process. This section demonstrates the increasing politicization of an area which had been traditionally free of political interference. Killian, Eisenhower's science advisor, has stressed that Eisenhower did not make political party distinctions among his science advisors. Describing the President's Science Advisory Committee he said, "In giving advice, they sought to be nonpartisan, whatever their private political beliefs might have been."[29] In 1960, Wiesner was an active campaign assistant for Kennedy. He offered Eisenhower his resignation from PSAC, but Eisenhower refused to accept it, stating that he felt that political affiliation had no effect on the quality of scientific advice.[30]

Kennedy filled many of his top posts with Republicans. In the area of scientific advice, he invited most of the Eisenhower appointees to stay in their posts.[31]

The Vietnam War exacerbated the split between the world of the pure politician and the pure scientist. Political support or at least silence on the war became a prerequisite for government science advisors. For example, a storm of controversy broke out when Hornig withdrew an appointment of history professor William R. Taylor of the University of Wisconsin after he learned that the advisor had been active in antiwar teach-ins.

Originally, the levying of political requirements to those holding scientific advisory posts was limited to sentiments on broad national questions such as the Vietnam conflict. Then criteria for such posts were narrowed down to particular issues such as the ABM program. Most recently the criteria mandate the personal loyalty of the advisor to the person of the president.

The Nixon administration applied unprecedented political tests for appointive offices. This has been true throughout the government, but is especially prominent in the scientific posts. Most of these positions, although nominally presidential appointments, were considered apolitical. They were distributed largely on personal achievement and peer evaluation during the Eisenhower, Kennedy and Johnson administrations. During the Nixon years, however, this is not the case; the prime requirement became loyalty to the president and his policies.

One of Nixon's first appointments was that of Lee DuBridge as science advisor. DuBridge announced that he hoped that science funding would grow 10-12 percent per annum for several years and then level off with the GNP.[32] A few months later DuBridge said that, despite other problems, Nixon wanted to maintain or even increase spending for basic science. However, the funding for basic science was cut that year.[33]

When DuBridge was appointed he saw as his major task the healing of the breach that had developed between the scientific community and the government. DuBridge wanted to draw scientific leaders much further into the presidential decision-making machinery.[34] Yet in his years of office he succeeded in doing the opposite of his avowed intentions. DuBridge was not even admitted to the OMB meetings discussing the science budgets; when they were announced, he was taken completely by surprise. He offended the scientific community when he bucked the advice of his own President's Science Advisory Committee panel on ABM and publicly supported Nixon's Safeguard.

Suddenly, in February 1970, DuBridge announced his resignation from the Nixon team. The White House announced immediately that a replacement, Edward E. David, Jr., had been selected as science advisor. DuBridge was, in effect, fired because he was seen as "a lobbier for science rather than a wholly committed member of the Nixon team."[35] DuBridge was viewed by the Nixon public relations men as generating the image (albeit unintentionally) that Nixon was ruining science.[36]

Edward E. David, DuBridge's replacement, was the first science advisor to come into office without university affiliation. He had spent 20 years at Bell Labs and was noted for being an excellent administrator. His selection was strongly influenced by Republican industrialists close to the White House, and especially W.O. Baker of Bell Labs.[37]

The first action David took was to reorganize the Office of Science and Technology in order to establish closer rapport with the OMB and to insist that an OST representative be present at all science budget decisions.[38] He sees his role as a manager to carry out policy decisions smoothly and efficiently and to forward options up to the White House. In this he was highly efficient in the openly antagonistic atmosphere of that administration. For example, he said, "when money is tight is the best time to try to improve the quality of work going on in the (scientific) community."[39] David has warned the National Academy of Sciences not to "speak loudly,"[40] and has otherwise responded to attacks on administration policy.[41] In this way, and through his support of the supersonic transport and the antiballistic missile, David has shown himself to be a very competent manager of administration decisions and a good team player.[42] When the Office of Science and Technology and the presidential science advisor posts were disbanded, David was offered the chairmanship of the Atomic Energy Commission.

Loyalty to presidential priorities was a benchmark in the Nixon science policy manager, not only during the manager's tenure of office but also as a criterion for appointment in the first place. For instance, Nixon, personally blocked the nomination of John Knowles as assistant secretary of health and scientific affairs of the Department of Health, Education and Welfare in order to win the support of the American Medical Association and southern congressmen. Senator Edward Kennedy stated that, "Men in high places in public life and organized medicine have conspired to prevent the nomination."[43] Senator Walter Mondale saw it as an attempt to curry the favor of conservatives. This political interference is even more striking since the Department of Health, Education and Welfare provides approximately one-third of all federal obligations for social scientific research.

Political intervention has taken place in many appointments in the National Science Foundation. The Foundation provides about 12 percent of federal social science research monies. As one example, Raymond Bisplinghoff had his appointment as deputy director at the National Science Foundation held up for several months because of his antiwar activities. Indeed, George Hammond who had been tapped for the position, had his nomination withdrawn because of a public address he made against the Cambodian incursion. In his speech he urged responsible dissent against the Nixon administration on this issue.[44]

The administration tendency to pick its own men for scientific posts reached ominous proportions according to Harvey Brooks. This past year, as required by law, the National Science Board submitted its list of recommended appointees for vacancies on the board. The president, however, is not bound by these recommendations and for the first time none of the individuals on the list was selected. Instead a "pretty conservative group politically"[45] of Nixon adherents was substituted. Although this political interpolation began during the Johnson administration it has just reached significant dimensions. Brooks maintains that gradually political reliability will be the major criterion for appointment. The ultimate impact will be the deterioration of professional standards. Eventually such bodies as the National Science Board will consist of "ax men to bring the scientists into line."[46]

SOCIAL SCIENCE POLICY

In addition to the strictures operating in science policy in general, what features are unique to social science policy? Two features are apparent:

1. With the growth of social and human resource programs, a convergence between empirical research and the construction of social programs has been demonstrated.
2. The political importance of the social-scientific evaluation of social programs has been emphasized.

The Nixon administration emphasized and institutionalized social sciences to evaluate social programs. It had nothing but "suspicion for non-targeted (social) research." The new trend was away from outright grants for social science research toward specific contracts.[47]

Biderman and Sharp[48] have emphasized the isomorphic quality of social science research and social policy analysis. The convergence of these areas led to the rise of the social program evaluation research industry, (which Biderman has labeled SPER). Evaluation methodologies were originated in the defense sector, especially in the RAND Corporation. Human resource spending by the federal government has been burgeoning, as can be seen by Table 2. Some of these human resource programs have been oriented toward altering the structure of power and hence have politically volatile aspects.[49] The result is the "increasing acceptance of the principle that these (sensitive social) programs should be subject to explicit, systematic, independent, professional evaluation."[50]

This means that policy for social science is deflected toward an emphasis on evaluation rather than innovation. When the Nixon

Table 2A
Percent of Budget Representing Outlays
for Human Resources

Year	Outlays for Human Resources
1955	21%
1958	26
1961	30
1964	29
1967	32
1970	37
1973	45

administration took office, Undersecretary of Labor L. H. Silberman warned that the policy stress would be on relevance in social scientific research. Only small, sound steps would be undertaken in social science rather than ambitious programs as had been done in the past. He further observed that the personal policy bias on the part of the researcher would no longer be tolerated.[51]

"Evaluation, together with management improvement generally, has become a keynote of the Nixon Administration."[52] In 1967 and 1968, Congress altered some of the central pieces of Johnson's Great Society legislation so that mandatory evaluation would be included in all programs. The Economic Opportunity Act, for example, was altered in such a manner. The Nixon administration capitalized on this nascent trend. In August 1969, Nixon proposed the Manpower Bill to Congress, which would have reorganized the Department of Labor. This bill, had it passed, would have effectively turned the Department of Labor into "an agency for program evaluation and curtail its allocation activities."[53]

The administration pursued this course. On August 11, 1969, Nixon sent a message to Congress on the reorganization of the Office of Economic Opportunity. In this message, Nixon stressed the need for tough "managerial discipline" and recommended the establishment of an Office of Planning, Research and Evaluation with the OEO. Nixon described the functions:

The Office of Planning, Research and Evaluation. . . will have responsibility for reviewing existing programs, for comparing the results of projects with the objectives which have been set for them, for commenting on the adequacy with which both programs and objectives are formulated and for recommending alterations in existing programs as well as new experiments. . . . [This office] will provide a regular source for that independent appraisal of Federal social programs which often is not available

Table 2B
Outlays for Human Resources by Type of Program[b]
(In Millions of Dollars)

Year	Education and Manpower	Health	Income Security	Veterans Benefits & Services	Total
1971	8,654	14,463	55,712	9,776	88,606
1972	10,140	17,024	65,225	11,127	103,516
1973	11,281	18,117	69,658	11,745	110,801

Source: Biderman and Sharp, *The Competitive Evaluation Research Industry* (Washington, D.C.: Bureau of Social Science Research, 1972), p. 6.

at present.[54]

The Nixon administration interest in OEO went beyond the emphasis on evaluation; the office became a special target of the Nixon White House. H. J. Phillips was appointed director of the OEO with a direct mandate from the president to dismantle the OEO.[55]

Beyond a symbol of social reform, OEO provided $59.7 million for research in the field of sociology in fiscal year 1973. This figure represented 52 percent of all federal obligations for research in sociology and 19 percent of all federal obligations in the social sciences.

On March 3, 1970, Nixon advanced several new proposals in his education message to Congress. A salient point that emerged was that accountability as well as demonstrated performance[56] would be important considerations in the direction and level of future federal support in this area:

Until we know why education works when it is successful, we can know little about what makes it fail when it is unsuccessful. This is knowledge that must precede any rational attempt to provide our every student with the best possible education. . . . There comes a time in any learning process that calls for reassessment and reinforcement.[57]

With these three messages, Nixon made it clear that evaluation was a major emphasis in the Department of Labor, the Office of Economic Opportunity and the Office of Education. Together, these three agencies provide a full one-third of all federal funds for research in the social sciences. The Nixon White House was directly concerned with the ability of the social sciences to provide significant payoff in terms of the evaluation of social programs.

There is a direct political benefit to be obtained by emphasizing evaluation. Low-cost experiments on social problems can be used to subvert attempts to solve social problems through direct social change. In addition, the experiments are inexpensive when compared with broader-gauged social action programs. This discrimination in the application of social experimentation and social evaluation requirements emerges when such redistributive programs are contrasted with more traditional social programs. This is plain in such "welfare" programs as urban renewal, agribusiness subsidies and merchant marine subsidies. "None of the older, well-established, and 'safe' domestic programs have evaluation requirements. . . . Program evaluation requirements were an important by-product of a general policy of bringing controversial programs under control."[58]

The Nixon policy for social sciences has been summed up by former assistant to the president for urban affairs Daniel P. Moynihan: "The role of social science lies not in the formation of social policy, but in the measurement of its results."[59] Yet the role of social sciences in the evaluation of social programs has also been criticized. A 1969 National Science Foundation report condemned both the frequency and quality of evaluations as being much too low.[60] One of the most penetrating examinations of evaluation research has been performed by the Urban Institute. The analysis complained that there was almost no uniformity between evaluation studies and that such studies generally lacked policy meaning.[61] At the same time, social scientists have criticized the federal government's approach to using social science as a form of sociotechnics and social engineering.[62]

Nowhere is the coupling of engineering and social science clearer than in the Department of Justice's Law Enforcement Assistance Administration (LEAA). The LEAA emphasizes tactical hardware, rather than social science "software" in its efforts to combat crime. This can be seen by the linkage of computer technology to the sociology of crime and criminology. One system undergoing research by LEAA is a project to reduce recidivism among released convicts and bailees. It is called the "crime deterrence transponder system" and is being developed in conjunction with the

Table 3
Research Obligations of the Law Enforcement
Assistance Administration by Field of Science,
Fiscal Years 1969-1974
(in percentages)

Field of Science	Fiscal Year					
	1969	1970	1971	1972	1973	1974
Social Science	60.0	72.6	59.9	61.7	61.7	57.5
Engineering	20.0	8.1	8.1	31.9	31.9	32.5
All Other Sciences	20.0	19.3	9.8	6.4	6.4	10.0
Total	100.0	100.0	100.0	100.0	100.0	100.0
Total Funds (Thousands of dollars)	870	4,495	11,200	11,200	17,098	25,200

Source: National Science Foundation, 1970; 1974

National Security Agency. The project involve "tagging" or implanting each "subscriber" with a radio transponder. Through a surveillance network, each subscriber would be tracked and his whereabouts monitored at all times. This is especially useful in an instance of a violation whereupon computer-commanded policemen would "hunt" and "apprehend" the violator. Particular value is foreseen in controlling high-crime areas in black neighborhoods, juvenile delinquency and civil disobedience.[63]

The rise in the proportion of the LEAA's research budget devoted to engineering during the Nixon administration is shown in Table 3. The percentage of funds for engineering research has risen from about 8 percent in 1970 to more than 30 percent in the fiscal year of 1974. (Twenty percent of the research budget for LEAA's first year of operation was allocated to engineering. This first budget is quite small when compared to later years.)

It is apparent that the executive office of the president is able to exert a concerted and direct influence over certain specific areas of science and social science policy, despite the vast and decentralized structure of scientific research in the United States. The president or his office can exert a high degree of influence on the direction of science policy that has a payoff for the political priorities of the president. The exercise of presidential priorities in policy choices are manifested primarily through the mechanisms of the OMB, the executive organization and appointments.

Presidential intervention involves only a part of the total scientific and social scientific enterprise, and generalizations and principles about presidential power must be drawn in this regard. Yet it is crystal clear that previous studies in the sociology of science policy have overlooked the crucial role of presidentialism in influncing specific areas of science and social science research policy. The president is also an important influence in establishing the larger principles that modify the contours of scientific and social scientific research in the United States. There are some features of social science policy which make it unique in terms of the imposition of political priorities. These features are the isomorphism between the growth of social scientific research and social programs, and the political utility of evaluation. Thus, political intervention at the highest levels poses a significant threat to the automony of empirical research and particularly to the thrust of social scientific research.

NOTES

[1]The author wishes to thank Professor Irving L. Horowitz for his insightful criticism of the manuscript and Karen T. Keller for her editorial assistance.

[2]Sanford Lakoff, ed., *Knowledge and Power* (New York: Free Press, 1966); Don Krasher Price, *The Scientific Estate* (Cambridge, Mass.: Harvard University Press, 1965); Price, "Purists and Politicians," *Science* 163 (1969): 25-31; Richard Barber, *The Politics of Research* (Washington: Public Affairs Press, 1966); Harvey Brooks, *The Government of Science* (Cambridge, Mass.: Massachusetts Institute of Technology Press, 1968).

[3]Irving Louis Horowitz, *Foundations of Political Sociology* (New York: Harper and Row, 1972), p. 478; Dennis W. Brogan, *An Introduction to American Politics* (London: Hamish Hamilton, 1954); Brogan, *American Aspects* (London: Hamish Hamilton, 1964); Brogan and Douglas Verney, *Political Patterns in Today's World*, second edition (New York: Harcourt, Brace and World, 1968); Raoul Berger, *Executive Privilege: A Constitutional Myth* (Cambridge, Mass.: Harvard University Press, 1974).

[4]Henry Jackson, ed., *The National Security Council* (New York: Praeger, 1965), p. 56.

[5]House of Representatives, House Committee on Government Operations, "Reorganization Plan Number Two of 1970" (Washington, D.C., 1970), p. 70.

[6]*Scientific Research*, July 1967, p. 20.

[7]*Ibid.*

[8]William D. Carey, "Science policy making in the United States," in *Decision Making in National Science Policy*, ed. A. De Reuk and J. Knight (Boston: Little, Brown, 1968), pp. 149-50.

[9]Elmer B. Staats, "The Federal research and development process: The decision making process," statement before the House Committee on Government operations (Washington, D.C., 1966).

[10]*Ibid.*

[11]Charles L. Schultze et al., *Setting National Priorities: The Budget* (Washington, D.C.: The Brookings Institution, 1971).

[12]Henry Riecken, "The Federal Government and Social Science Policy," *Annals of the American Academy of Political and Social Science* 394 (1971): 104.

[13]William D. Carey, Personal interview with former OMB Science officer in Washington, D.C., September 12, 1973.

[14]House Committee on Government Operations, 1970, pp. 329-30.

[15]H. L. Nieburg, *In the Name of Science* (Chicago: Quadrangle Books, 1966), 142-43.

[16]Dwight D. Eisenhower, *Waging Peace* (New York: Random House, 1965), p. 211.

[17]House of Representatives, House Committee on Science and Astronautics, "Federal policy, plans, and organization for science and technology," (Washington, D.C., 1973), p. 159.

[18]*Ibid.*

[19]*Science* 167: 112.

[20]*Science* 179: 455.

[21]Daniel J. Balz, "Washington Pressures/AEI, Hoover Institution Voices Grow in Policy Debates During Nixon Years," *National Journal Reports* 5, no. 51 (December 1973): 1893.

[22]*Ibid.*, p. 1900.

[23]*Ibid.*, p. 1901.

[24]Hoover Institution on War, Revolution and Peace, Report 1969-1972 (Stanford, Calif.: Standord University Press): xi-xii.

[25]Balz, p. 1897.

[26]Andrew Glass, "Brookings Seeks Balanced Image by Hiring Nixon Cadre as Staff Scholars,: *National Journal Reports* 4, no. 7 (1972): 252.

[27]*Ibid.*, p. 254.

[28]Deborah Shapley, "White House Foes; Weisner Target of Proposal to Cut M.I.T. Funds," *Science* 181 (July 1973): 243-46.

[29]James R. Killian, Jr., "Science advice for the White House," *Technology Review* 76 (January 1974): 12.

[30]Killian, "Toward a research-reliant society: Some observations on government and science," in *Science as a Cultural Force*, ed. H. Woolf (Baltimore: Johns Hopkins University Press, 1964).

[31]Herbert York, *Race to Oblivion* (New York: Simon and Schuster, 1970): 147-148.

[32]*Science* 166: 350.

[33]*Science* 167: 360.

[34]*New York Times*, December 17, 1969, p. 1.

[35]Science and Government Report 1.

[36]*Science* (1970): 417.

[37]William O. Baker, personal interview with president of Bell Laboratories in Murray Hill, N.J., April 8, 1974; Phillip H. Abelson, personal interview with editor of *Science* magazine in Washington, D.C. September 11, 1973.

[38]*Science and Government Review* 6.

[39]*New York Times*, August 21, 1970, p. 11.

[40]Daniel S. Greenberg, "David and Indifference," *Saturday Review* 55 (September 30, 1972): 41-43.

[41]*New York Times*, December 16, 1970, p. 46.

[42]Edward E. David, "Lecture at Rockefeller University: (New York: speech on April 19, 1972); David, "Science Advice for the White House," *Technology Review* 76 (January 1974): 9-19.

[43]*New York Times*, June 28, 1969, p. 16.

[44]*Science* 168: 1189.

[45]Harvey Brooks, personal interview with Harvard dean of science and engineering in Cambridge, Mass., October 18, 1973.

[46]*Ibid.*

[47]Elliot Liebow, personal interview with HEW grant supervisor in Washington, D.C., September 11, 1973.

[48]Albert Biderman and Laure Sharp, *The Competitive Evaluation Research Industry* (Washington: Bureau of Social Science Research, 1972).

[49]Peter Marris and Martin Rein, *Dilemmas of Social Reform*, revised edition (New York: Atherton Press, 1972).

[50]Biderman and Sharp, p. 5.

[51]*Washington Science Trends*, July 3, 1972, p. 75.

[52]Allan Schick, "From analysis to evaluation," *Annals of the American Academy of Political and Social Science* 394 (1971): 58.

[53]*Ibid.,* p. 59.

[54]Public Papers of Richard M. Nixon, 1969, p. 328.

[55]*New York Times*, March 3, 1973, p. 13; June 14, 1973, p. 46.

[56]See Creta Sabine, ed. *Accountability: Systems Planning in Education* (Homewood, Illinois: ETC Publications, 1973).

[57]Public Papers of Richard M. Nixon, 1970, pp. 236-37.

[58]Thomas Morehouse, "Program Evaluation: Social Research versus Public Policy," *Public Administration Review* 32 (1972): 873.

[59]Daniel P. Moynihan, *Maximum Feasible Misunderstading* (New York: Macmillan, 1969): 193.

[60]National Science Foundation, *The Nation's Use of the Social Sciences* (Washington, 1969).

[61]Joseph Wholey et al, *Federal Evaluation Policy* (Washington: The Urban Institute, 1970).

[62]See Amitai Etzioni, "Faulty engineers or neglected experts," *Science* 181 (1973): 32.

[63]Joseph A. Meyer, "Crime deterrence transponder systems," *IEEE Transactions* AES-7 (January 1971): 1

Part III
THE THEORY OF FOREIGN POLICY

16

Government Sponsored Research on International and Foreign Affairs

PIO D. ULIASSI

These are opportune times to reflect on the relationship of social science to the federal government and to public policy. Social scientists have been favored by official patronage on a scale unimagined only a generation ago, urged to come to grips with public problems and encouraged—although little encouragement is needed in most cases—to minister to the needs of officials in Washington who, as the collective modern prince, obviously require all the enlightenment that reason, in its modern dress, can offer.

One of the consequences of this unaccustomed affluence, honor, and (on occasion) even palpable influence has been to provoke controversy among those who hold differing and sometimes conflicting views of the social sciences and of their actual or potential relationship to the polity. There are, as there always have been, social scientists cultivating their fields, with or without governmental help, who remain indifferent to the demands of politics and public affairs and who, indeed, even scorn too conspicuous a concern with immediate relevance as itself unbecomingly worldly—although most of them, I suspect, believe or hope that in the long run what they do will prove of some practical good. But many others are more passionately engaged. At one end of the spectrum, for example, Ithiel Pool, confident of the beneficent utility of social research and of the virtues of its practitioners, argues boldly for close communion with men of power as the best way of taming them into a semblance of civility: "The only hope for humane government in the future," he writes, "is through the extensive use of the social sciences by government."[1] At the opposite extreme, others see federal support for research—or at least the way in which this support has been institutionalized—as at best a mixed blessing, a golden flow of temptation; they suspect that even social scientific flesh may discover, with Oscar Wilde, that the easiest way to deal with temptation is to succumb to it, and fear that the new mandarins may be transformed into corrupt servants of power.[2]

A good deal of the debate (which often sounds like a dialogue of the deaf) has centered on the government's financial support of studies that deal more or less directly with international and foreign affairs, and much of it has been prompted by a few spectacular *causes celebres:* Camelot, after all, still serves as a classic though somewhat tiresome cautionary tale. There are several reasons for this—essentially no different from those that affect any kind of sponsored research, but "national security" and foreign affairs studies seem, somehow, to place scholar and policy-maker in particularly sharp conflictual relationships.

We must start, I think, with the fact that the "project" system is firmly entrenched as the basic device used by the government to finance social research. It is commonplace to observe that the world of scholarship and the world of politics follow different rules and that some tension is inevitable between the pursuit of "truth" which ideally inspires the social scientist and the pursuit of "power" and practical ends that presumably animates the bureaucrat and the politician and even the statesman. What is less often remarked is that the system of federal support for social research is almost deliberately designed to bring these two worlds together. We have nothing in this country resembling the British University Grants Committee, for example, which might provide federal funds for research while minimizing federal influence over their use. Instead, the American system is characterized by contracts and grants administered by government agencies for rather specific projects, which inevitably gives some voice in—and often virtual control over—the direction of research to federal officials and bureaucracies, mostly "operating" bureaucracies in the case of research on foreign affairs.[3] The arrangement undoubtedly has its merits: For one thing, it harmonizes with an activist strain in the American academic tradition which considers the university as an institution providing "services" to the community, or at least to whatever part of the community is willing and able to pay for them. But it also tends to clash with other traditions now especially emphasized by younger social scientists—the independence of the intellectual and his critical stance toward the dominant forces and ways of his day.

Of course there is more to the matter than this. The very nature of the executive agencies that have provided most of the financial support for research on foreign affairs until recently—those with intelligence, military, diplomatic and other "missions" traditionally associated with a state's high policy—makes their relations with social scientists more strained in some ways than those of departments with primarily domestic responsibilities (scientific or other) are likely to be in the normal course of things. Agencies dealing with high policy have to function in two political systems at once, the domestic and the international,[4] and it is a fact, perhaps unpleasant but very real, that the two systems impose different and sometimes conflicting standards of conduct. Research projects that are intimately linked to such agencies through contracts and grants therefore tend to get caught up in some of the problems and dilemmas of foreign and military policy in a democratic society: the requirements of confidentiality in many of the processes of international politics, the occasional imperatives for responsible statesmen to practice the venerable diplomatic art of speaking the truth without actually revealing it, their constant and sometimes agonizing efforts to reconcile the national interest and the interest of some other or larger community come to mind immediately as examples. Thus, despite the intellectual and financial liberality that frequently has inspired the research programs of such operating agencies, there are, I think, structural tensions between their purposes and practices and the presumably more open and universal norms of the scholarly and scientific professions.

Nevertheless, social scientists and their clients and patrons in Washington for many years had a remarkably untroubled relationship, grounded on a substantial consensus regarding the main lines of American foreign policy that was created during and after the Second World War. This is not to say that all social scientists who collaborate with military and civilian operating agencies do so from the purest of motives; as a group they probably share with their now numerous critics a normal human incidence of opportunism. (Einstein once observed that if an angel of the Lord were to drive from the temple of science all those who inhabit it for reasons other than the love of truth, "it would become embarrassingly empty.") But I think most are moved by nobler sentiments, by a sincere agreement with broad national purposes that enables them to avoid ultimate value questions in justifying their conception of social research as the handmaiden of state policy. What has changed in recent years is the political climate.[5] Those who no longer are content with the fundamentals of high policy as they understand it naturally demand a more critical role for the social sciences and a stronger guarantee of professional autonomy than they perceive in existing arrangements.[6] In short, some relationships between the federal government and the social sciences that were largely taken for granted in an era of ideological good feeling are now judged as problematic.

These preliminary observations suggest what I suppose is the theme of this chapter: the difficulties of developing, with federal encouragement, a social science that is at the same time relevant to public concerns, responsive to the needs—as they seem them—of public officials, and autonomous. The argument—if an argument can be traced in such wide-ranging and frequently superficial observations—runs something like this: The net effect of federal interest in research on foreign affairs has been to create a vast and varied complex of programs, most of them at least symbolically linked to operating agencies. The linkage has created some ambiguity of purpose—it is not always clear whether a government sponsor is buying services in the academic marketplace or sustaining a socially desirable scientific activity without instrumental motives, or even doing the latter in the guise of the former—and this creates some problems for social scientists (and occasionally for their government patrons). One of the ironies in the situation, it seems to me, is that despite the considerable "politicization" of research resulting from the circumstances of sponsorship, it is not used as effectively as some advocates wish and some critics fear. In reviewing these matters, I am led, finally, to conclude that many discussions of social research for policy purposes, especially in the area of foreign affairs, reveal a somewhat technocratic perspective which, among other things, takes a rather narrow view of what the social sciences may have to offer and, moreover, frequently ignores the fact that the use, misuse or nonuse of social research is itself part of a broader political process.

I will deal with a few of these topics empirically, drawing on whatever reliable information is available; others will necessarily call for impressionistic judgments and speculation. It goes almost without saying that as someone closely, if modestly, involved in federal research, I must cope with the bureaucrat's dilemma when he writes for a public beyond the circles of his official colleagues—either to utter platitudes or to commit indiscretions—which social scientists will quickly recognize as a clear case of role conflict.

FEDERAL SUPPORT FOR SOCIAL RESEARCH

A simple fact provides the starting point: federal programs of support for research on foreign affairs are small but important tributaries swelling the river of research gold that flows from Washington. The government has spent about $30 to $40 million annually on such studies in recent years. This is not, perhaps, an impressive amount when compared to all government outlays for the social sciences, which have grown spectacularly in the last decade, but it is still substantial enough to have considerable influence on the work of private scholars who study international politics, foreign and security policy, and the variety of topics conventionally assigned to the category of "foreign areas."[7]

However, money for such research has become much scarcer lately. Congressional and other pressures have forced a measured retrenchment in federal agencies whose bounty once seemed almost unlimited; and the International Education Act of 1966, which seemed to promise much, remains unfunded. According to preliminary estimates, federal allocations for foreign affairs research plunged to some $21 million in the 1970 fiscal year. To make matters worse, private foundations, which once supported international studies generously, increasingly have channelled their resources into domestic programs.[8] The situation has prompted a prestigious political scientist (Karl Deutsch) to warn of a "partial one-sided intellectual disarmament" in tones somewhat reminiscent of similar pronouncements that were common in the more financially austere 1950s, when respected academic leaders divined disastrous consequences if American behavioral and social researchers were overtaken by their Soviet counterparts.[9] Social scientists are perhaps as prone as other mortals to confuse their corporate misfortunes with public calamity, but there is no denying that the funding crisis is all too real and constitutes a serious depression for academic and other organizations that have experienced a revolution of rising expectations and now find themselves the victims of fluctuations in the project marketplace.

I will not try to trace here the many consequences that may follow from such erratic funding. One could assume, for example, that a reduction of about one-third in the budget from one year to the next might have some effect on the quality and direction of research on foreign affairs, on the kinds as well as number of people and institutions that may be attracted to it or repelled from it as financially or professionally unrewarding, and so on. But overall budget levels do not seem to alter drastically some basic patterns that perhaps have a more significant bearing on the present uneasy relationship between the government and the social sciences, and I want to note a few of these—covering sponsors, performers, and programs—drawing on sketchy but still useful information.[10]

Sponsors

In foreign affairs research, as in other fields of science, federal programs are the result of a great number of historical decisions, each carrying its weight of tradition and vested interest, rather than of a deliberately conceived overall policy. What we have is a polycentric system which so far, for better or worse, has defied serious coordination[11] and which few perhaps would pretend represents the most "reasonable" allocation of funds from the public purse that scholars, bureaucrats or politicians might devise. Table 1 gives an overview of sponsorship patterns through a breakdown of "obligations" for the four fiscal years for which such information is now available. The sponsors are grouped into four main categories—three which include operating agencies of various kinds and the fourth, agencies that have a more central or exclusive responsibility for research.[12] The most obvious and elementary fact to emerge from the table is that social research on international and foreign affairs is supported by many agencies and departments.[13]

The material summarized in Table 1 reveals a number of things about the role of operating agencies in the research programs of the federal government. It shows, first of all, that half of the funds dispensed from the federal treasury now come from action units of the executive—that is, from departments and independent agencies that sponsor research as an ancillary or staff function in support of their primary mission. The table reveals a second interesting although hardly startling fact: not all operating agencies have the same enthusiasm or capacity for financing research. With the exception of 1966, the Department of Defense has had a much larger budget for "external" research (studies not carried out within the government itself by regular employees) than the combined budgets of all the civilian agencies dealing mainly with foreign affairs.[14] Finally, it is also clear from the table that the budgets of these civilian agencies taken as a group are more flexible, perhaps more vulnerable, than those of the Department of Defense. Their share of the total budget dropped from a high of 39 percent in 1966 to a low of 14 percent in 1969—a precipitous decline due mainly to the shrunken coffers of the Department of State's Bureau of Educational and Cultural Affairs and of the Agency for International Development. In contrast, the Department of Defense budget has remained stable at about one-third of the federal total—indeed, it has risen a bit from 29 percent in 1966 to 33 percent in 1969. These patterns and trends account for the worries now frequently expressed in Congress and among academics about the "critical imbalance" in the research efforts of the executive units dealing with national security and foreign affairs.

There is more to the tale, however, even if one limits observations to gross trends. It is worth emphasizing that half of all government-financed research on foreign affairs is now administered by civilian agencies with educational, scientific and cultural responsibilities—the Department of Health, Education and Welfare, the National Science Foundation, the Smithsonian Institution and the National Endowment for the Humanities. Indeed, even in the short period covered by the table, such institutions have steadily increased their share of the research budget from about 30 percent in 1966 to 50 percent in 1969; and, despite

Table 1
U.S. Government Agency Obligations – Social Research
on International Affairs and Foreign Areas
Fiscal Years 1966-1969*

Agencies and Departments	FY 1966 Amount	FY 1966 % of Total	FY 1967 Amount	FY 1967 % of Total	FY 1968 Amount	FY 1968 % of Total	FY 1969 Amount	FY 1969 % of Total
Educational-Cultural-Scientific								
Department of Health Education & Welfare	$6,627,554	18.55	$10,104,370	24.88	$8,952,303	26.20	$9,498,489	28.49
National Endowment for the Humanities	—		892,440	2.20	702,960	2.06	842,637	2.53
National Science Foundation	3,337,300	9.34	5,686,850	14.00	5,219,230	15.27	5,282,800	15.85
Smithsonian Institution	803,649	2.25	920,231	2.27	1,118,335	3.27	1,175,535	3.53
Total	$10,768,503	30.14	$17,603,891	43.35	$15,992,828	46.80	$16,799,461	50.40
Civilian Foreign Affairs								
Department of State	$6,450,947	18.05	$1,351,679	3.33	$992,688	2.90	$421,844	1.26
Agency for International Development	5,932,708	16.60	5,568,922	13.22	3,510,347	10.27	2,457,682	7.37
Arms Control & Disarmament Agency	828,520	2.32	985,286	2.43	558,238	1.63	678,675	2.04
Peace Corps	265,597	.74	292,829	.72	284,626	.83	639,491	1.92
U.S. Information Agency	427,621	1.20	537,887	1.32	550,268	1.61	589,226	1.77
Total	$13,905,393	38.91	$8,536,603	21.01	$5,896,167	17.24	$4,786,918	14.36
Military								
Army	$4,818,000	13.48	$4,853,005	11.95	$4,412,170	12.91	$4,992,462	14.98
Navy	405,000	1.13	331,762	.82	432,000	1.26	821,000	2.46
Air Force	1,556,000	4.35	1,946,289	4.79	1,702,713	4.98	2,236,578	6.71
Advanced Research Projects Agency	1,227,000	3.43	3,937,000	9.69	2,876,500	8.42	1,358,000	4.07
International Security Affairs	2,000,000	5.60	1,947,632	4.79	1,875,000	5.49	1,752,727	5.26
Miscellaneous	225,000	.63	90,337	.22	132,000	.39	—	
Total	$10,231,000	28.62	$13,106,025	32.26	$11,430,383	33.45	$11,160,767	33.48
Other								
Dept. of Agriculture	$305,592	.86	$525,062	1.29	$419,868	1.23	$204,687	.61
Dept. of Commerce	—		—		—		16,450	.05
Dept. of Labor	—		—		—		162,700	.49
Exec. Office of the President	—		461,477	1.38	78,756	.23	126,300	.38
National Aeronautics and Space Administration	—		—		355,000	1.04	—	
Miscellaneous	522,326	1.46	280,892	.69	—		78,734	.24
Total	$827,918	2.32	$1,367,431	3.36	$853,624	2.50	$588,871	1.77
GRAND TOTAL	$35,732,814	99.99	$40,613,950	99.99	$34,173,002	99.99	$33,336,017	100.11

*Adapted from *FAR Horizons*, Vol. III, No. 1 January 1970. This is a bimonthly newsletter published by the Department of State's Office of External Research for the inter-agency Foreign Area Research Coordination Group (FAR), a government committee headed by the Department.

overall cuts in federal expenditures in fiscal 1970, preliminary information indicates that the proportions among the major *types* of agencies included in Table 1 remain substantially the same.

There are complex historical reasons for the picture that emerges, but I can only touch on them here. After World War II (the conventional starting point in such matters) many government administrators turned to the social sciences with hope, if not always with confidence, for help in coping with their enlarged bureaucracies and their vastly expanded and varied activities in world affairs; and they found, among academic intellectuals, many social scientists whose wartime experiences in Washington had given them a taste for close collaboration with federal officials interested in policy-relevant studies. Sponsorship by operating agencies had several advantages in the circumstances of the early postwar years: it gave a pragmatic justification for research at a time when the government was not disposed to finance quests for ·pure truth; by linking the social sciences to national symbols—military power, national security, Cold War goals—it gave a measure of ideological respectability to intellectual enterprises that were suspected, in some quarters, of subversive tendencies; and it provided a modest niche for the social sciences in the federal system at a time when doubts about their scientific status (especially among natural scientists) made it impracticable to support them in any significant way through such institutions as the National Science Foundation. Since then, the dominant mood has changed considerably in Washington: in and out of Congress, people are more willing to accept a federal responsibility for the social sciences; somewhat suspicious, if anything, of too close and exclusive an affinity between social research and political authorities and interests; and more anxious to find a place for social research in institutions with presumably impeccable credentials as disinterested patrons of science and even the humanities.

A significant progression is evident: Federal support for social research begins, it seems, with narrowly instrumental objectives closely linked to governmental interests and, once legitimated, gradually is modified to serve broader intellectual and social purposes.

Research Performers

After this glance at those in the government who give, let me turn briefly to those in private life who receive—the research "performers," as federal jargon has it. Table 2 summarizes information on over 600 projects in progress or completed during one year only, but it well describes, I think, some of the overall patterns of any recent period.

It shows, for example, that a surprisingly high proportion of all projects (21 percent—141 of the 664 total) are carried out by foreign contractors or grantees, although this, as I will try to show later, probably exaggerates the actual "internationalization" of

TABLE 2

Distribution of Active Projects
(By Types of Sponsors and Researchers)
June 1968 – July 1969

Types of
Agencies and Departments   Types of Contractors or Grantees

	US Academic	US Non-academic	Foreign	Other	Total
Education Cultural Scientific	178	11	84	3	276
Civilian Foreign Affairs	96	38	28	12	174
Military	53	100	3	—	156
Other	23	9	26	—	58
Totals	350	158	141	15	664

(Compiled from various sources.)

government-fostered studies. It also reveals that among the domestic recipients of grants or (more commonly) contracts, commercial and nonprofit organizations equipped to conduct social
research now compete effectively with universities—a point worth
elaborating.

On the basis of the common assumption that, as a rule, the
social sciences flourish best in campus soil, it is significant to find
that slightly over half of all the projects included in the calculation
were carried out by Americans working in universities, an indication that research on foreign affairs is still, by and large, a predominantly academic enterprise. The system, however, is not
overly generous to those who toil in academia: they do, probably,
a smaller proportion of all studies financed by federal agencies
than their relative numbers along among all active professionals
would lead one to expect.[15] This is not entirely the result of
conscious design but is related to and in a sense caused by the
continuing financial weight of operating agencies: Although the
educational-cultural-scientific agencies included in Table 2 placed
94 percent of the domestically-based projects (178 of 189) with
social scientists attached to universities, the civilian foreign affairs
agencies placed 72 percent (96 of 134) and the military agencies
only 35 percent (53 of 153).

Which leads to the other side of the story. Nonacademic research organizations now exist in numbers and varieties unknown
in the early post-World War II years, when government sponsors of
mission-oriented work relied heavily on universities, partly because

institutional alternatives were not readily available. Such organizations have become extremely important performers of research directly related to federal policies and programs in national security and foreign affairs. But it is difficult to generalize about them. They include affiliates of industrial firms; free lance operations with conspicuously developed entrepreneurial skills; and nonprofit institutes in bewildering diversity—some tenuously linked to universities and others completely autonomous, some emulating academic styles of work and others scorning them, some virtually bound to a single governmental client and others more catholic in the institutions and publics they consider themselves qualified and committed to serve.

"No generalization is worth a damn," Justice Holmes once said—but he urged men to try to form "general propositions" anyway. The academic—nonacademic categories used here imply a familiar general proposition of sorts: that there are meaningful variations in the kinds of professionals typically found in such different institutional settings, in the kinds of work they prefer to do, and in the way that they characteristically define their relationships to patrons or clients. My impression—the evidence is hardly conclusive for some points—is that nonacademic researchers working in the field of foreign affairs do tend to differ from their academic colleagues in certain respects that are especially pertinent in defining the impact of the social sciences on public policy. A few tentative generalizations must serve as examples. First, they probably span a narrower ideological range than their academic peers[16] and in their particular environments they are for the most part well insulated from the winds of campus political passions. Second, they are on the whole more favorably disposed toward applied research, which after all has a certain cachet for practical administrators who are one of their primary reference groups; indeed, nonacademic social scientists can become highly sensitized to the "needs" of their clients, undistracted by ancillary functions such as teaching and unencumbered by pressures to do academically more prestigious types of research.[17] Finally, nonacademic social scientists are more prone than their university colleagues to accept contractual relationships involving considerable deference to their clients' formulations of research problems and a measure of tolerance for the proprietary demands of sponsors.[18]

PIO D. ULIASSI

Nonacademic research organizations have, in any event, established themselves as a new institution displaying some of the characteristics associated with its middle position between the intramural intelligence and research organizations of the government and the completely autonomous academy.[19]

Characteristics of Programs

Even the most cursory survey of government-sponsored work would not be complete without some discussion of the kinds of work that federal agencies support. Although there is no single listing of studies, the available information provides ample evidence of the scope and variety of programs. An inventory of research on foreign affairs recently published by the Department of State, for example, while incomplete, includes more than 500 projects carried out under the auspices of 13 major agencies during a single year.[20] Yet not too long ago, Herbert Kelman, a friendly critic, could say that there was a distressing dearth of federal support for basic research on foreign policy and foreign areas that could meet the "criteria of true independence and international conception."[21] How accurate is Kelman's observation?

In truth, basic research has not been a dominant feature of federal programs, most of which have been inspired by more immediately practical objectives than the advancement of social science. Most of the international and foreign area studies financed by the government have been justified by being linked to the missions of operating units of the executive branch and any program that has strayed too conspicuously from applied studies of almost self-evidence short-run utility the possible accusation of "irrelevance" from within the bureaucracy and the always present danger of political suspicion or attack from without. All of which has not prevented some operating agencies, particularly the Department of Defense, from nourishing, over the years, a considerable body of research in psychology and the social sciences of more than transient intellectual interest. But even now, despite the soundly established position of programs not linked to executive units engaged in foreign policy and operations, only about one-third of the federal budget is allocated for what the sponsors themselves will publicly describe as "basic" research.[22]

To take one of Kelman's other points, it is difficult to say how "independent" research funded by Washington—basic or other—is or should be. Ideally, one could hope for some balance between commissioned research responding to the practical concerns of administrators—and reflecting their views and policies to some extent—and more autonomous research uncolored by official interests and unfettered by political considerations. A tendency toward this ideal can be sensed in two characteristics of the present situation. One is pluralism: The federal government provides many alternative sources of support for research on foreign affairs within and among agencies and even among different kinds of agencies and thus provides some protection from complete dependence on a single client or patron. But pluralism is more limited than it seems. Most studies in agricultural economics, for example, are naturally financed by the Department of Agriculture and it is no revelation that most studies of education abroad are financed by the Office of Education; but even in a broader subject area such as "political processes" most studies are financed by a relatively small number of agencies. The other characteristic is the growing role of grant-giving educational, scientific and cultural institutions with programs that are more responsive to academic interests than those of operating agencies often can be. But here again there are limits: Such institutions do not administer, as a rule, major programs dealing with the more central problems and issues of contemporary foreign policy. In short, the more specific a research topic, the more likely it is to depend for financial support on a single or on a few potential sponsors; and the more central a project is to contemporary political issues the more likely it is to be financed by operating agencies which themselves are prominent actors in foreign affairs. But on balance, the conclusions reached by a committee of sociologists are, I believe, no more than just: "Government research support is now more often given for purposes and through mechanisms that are consistent with scholarly autonomy than ever before . . . "[23]

Kelman points to another aspect of government-financed research—the extent and nature of participation by foreign scholars. Two-thirds or more of all projects carried out with federal money involve some travel or research abroad, although the proportions vary among agencies. Most of these projects require only informal

or casual encounters with foreign scholars. But a far from negligible number call for international collaboration of some sort, with
foreign specialists providing technical services, engaging in their
own locally conceived studies, or even occasionally joining American colleagues in genuinely collaborative cross-cultural research.
Nevertheless, despite the good intentions of many federal administrators, relatively few projects financed by the federal government provide for a degree of foreign participation that constitutes,
as one official document puts it, a "truly symmetrical relationship
between American and foreign specialists." [24] Whatever the intellectual consequences of this exclusion may be (presumably foreign
scholars might occasionally have significantly different perspectives on research problems), it helps to fire the suspicions of
"scientific colonialism" that have been aired so frequently in recent years.

Obviously commissioned research still dominates federal programs. But it would be rash to conclude that commissioned research is always narrowly subservient to the interests of its puta-
tive sponsors. The research needs of operating agencies seldom
emerge spontaneously within bureaucracies but are often articulated for or with them by private consultants and therefore reflect
the intellectual and political outlooks of some sectors, at least, of
the highly diverse communities of social scientists. Moreover,
mission-related government requirements occasionally have served
as a rationale to support basic work under contractual conditions
that respected the favored researchers' freedom of inquiry. Under
the circumstances, it is understandable that many social scientists
have considered the "impurity" of funds from operating agencies
of only slight importance and in any case a minor price to pay—so
long as private or governmental alternatives were not readily available—for the public benefits (and no doubt the private pleasures)
of scientific affluence. One could make the best of an imperfect
world and prudently echo St. Augustine's cry: "Make me chaste,
O Lord—but not yet."

The aforementioned facts about government-sponsored studies
on foreign affairs are easy to establish and, I think, beyond serious
controversy. Government help has made possible a vast amount of
work that probably would not have been done, or not done so
thoroughly, without federal aid and the help has been channeled
through an increasing variety of agencies, mechanisms and pro-

grams. Moreover, government support has prompted or strengthened a number of institutional developments of considerable significance. For example, it has enshrined the project system as the normal research arrangement and of course has encouraged the evolution and proliferation of nonacademic organizations, the "think tanks" and their commercial imitators and competitors. Even social scientists themselves have been affected. Once virtual strangers to the inner ways of government, they are now--as someone once said of RAND men—almost as thick in Washington as Jesuits were in the seventeenth century courts of Vienna and Madrid.

What such facts may imply for the social sciences and, for that matter, the government is something else again, and is far more difficult a matter to deal with objectively.

SOME CONSEQUENCES OF SPONSORSHIP

Even such a rapid survey of the patterns of international and foreign area studies favored by governmental agencies suggests a number of problems and issues. As Albert Biderman among others has remarked, the dominant note of public debate changed in the sixties "from concern with achieving greater acceptance and support for social science to apprehensions regarding the corrupting influence of dependence on government financing."[25] But "corruption" is far too strong a word and hardly does justice to the range of opinions, which cover a wide spectrum from those of "establishment" social scientists who look upon the government experience and find it at least passingly good to those of radical critics who indiscriminately condemn all who accept federal monies as a "willing stable of intellectual mercenaries convinced that their work is independently conceived and in the national interest."[26] I know of no fully satisfactory way of categorizing the types of concerns that are expressed in this debate, but it seems to me that for international studies, at least, arguments tend to cluster around three topics—the intellectual, political and ethical consequences or implications of government sponsorship. All three kinds of arguments are closely linked to the uses, or alleged uses, of research by government bureaucracies and perhaps this will excuse my venturing into observations that normally are reserved to those close to the academic scene.

Selection and Formulation of Problems

Social arrangements, fortunately, are for the most part too messy to encourage us to reduce all intellectual work to the presumed interests of its patrons, but it is only common sense to assume that the problems that are selected for study and the ways they are formulated are influenced if not mechanically determined by government interest and support. Let me try to identify some of these influences.

The selection of topics, which is affected both by negative and by positive factors, poses the easiest problem. On the negative side there are, at any given time, powerful conventions regarding what it is inappropriate for *any* organ of the government to sponsor in the social sciences. The most conspicuous and significant case is the treatment of American society itself. Except as incidental inputs into planning and evaluation studies, it is difficult to find, among the thousands of government financed projects of the last two decades, any significant body of work on intrasocietal topics: the characteristics of American elites, bureaucratic and political processes, the underlying attitudes, interests and institutions that may affect United States foreign relations. The operating agencies are "other" rather than "self" oriented when it comes to foreign affairs as an area of research, more inclined to think in terms of the international environments in which they must act than in terms of the domestic system in which they are imbedded. And both they and the federal agencies with more purely scientific responsibilities are wary of probing into contemporary national affairs that have not, as yet, been sanctioned as proper subjects for government-financed studies.[27] Cynics may consider this only a case of political discretion as the better part of scientific valor, but there is more to it than that.[28]

On the positive side, agency budgets loom as the controlling factor. Apart from areas that are politically taboo, the focus of research reflects the relative distribution of funds among units of the executive branch. No agencies are completely free to act as patrons for all kinds of research—certainly not the operating ones, although some have enjoyed a remarkable latitude in developing their programs. The Department of State, United States Information Agency (USIA), Arms Control and Disarmament Agency (ACDA), Agency for International Development (AID), the Peace

Corps and the many units of the Department of Defense—all have their particular interests as well as their common concerns in research and their particular interests naturally tend to dominate their programs. What and how much is done, then, on economic or political development, social change, insurgency or counterinsurgency, "psychological warfare," arms control and so on depends largely not on whether such topics titillate scientific curiosity, or respond to some abstract notion of the public good, but on the financial resources of particular bureaucracies committed, by the nature of their functions, to pay some attention to them: an elementary but hardly a trivial observation.[29] Funding variations among the executive departments have an especially marked impact on research patterns because of the already noted absence of any effective mechanism for establishing government-wide goals and priorities in foreign affairs research even for the operating agencies.

It is more difficult to demonstrate that sponsorship seriously affects the way in which research problems, once selected, are formulated. This is not an overresearched subject and the evidence I can muster is, for the most part, anecdotal and impressionistic. However, operating agencies do often claim a share in the shaping of research, at least to the extent of insisting on "relevance" to their perceived needs, with some interesting consequences.[30] It is also clear that occasionally even "undirected" research may be subtly affected by sponsorship: Camelot, to take an overworked but usefully familiar case, bore the intellectual marks of its gestation in an environment sensitive to the counterinsurgency interests of its remarkably tolerant Army sponsors, according to some commentators.[31] But what is probably as important as the flow of influence in individual cases is the apparent statistical tendency for government sponsors to seek out or to attract social scientists whose general outlook is congenial to them: "A hundred flowers have no doubt bloomed," a reviewer of American political-military literature once observed, "but they have almost without exception been tactical flowers on a single strategic stem."[32]

This is not the occasion to pursue this subject. My objective is simply to note what should be obvious, that government sponsorship is not indiscriminate or "neutral" and that it affects what is done and how. This is a matter of some importance both to those who have an academic interest in the advancement of knowledge and to those who are concerned about the distinctive strengths and weaknesses of sponsored research as an input into the policy process.

Politicization of Research

But for the moment, I want to discuss a second aspect of the linkage that has been established between many social scientists interested in foreign affairs and the government: the "politicization" of research, or what may be described as the transformation of scholarly activities into political acts. All social research admittedly is political in some sense: the most cloistered scholars, comfortable in their once-secure retreats, act politically as they probe into the nature of society, help to define social problems and issues, and influence, however indirectly, public decisions on the allocation of values. But social science financed by operating agencies is political in a special way: it is connected to the nonscientific purposes of its sponsors, governmental organizations which themselves have, as a rule, jurisdictional responsibilities in the area of inquiry and known or suspected policy preferences in it. The association affects both the way in which research is administered and the way in which it is perceived by attentive publics here and abroad. Let me be a bit more specific.

Whatever social scientists may think, most government administrators have no doubt that when they finance mission-related research in foreign affairs they are doing something "for which the government must bear a degree of political or diplomatic responsibility that is not usually associated with federal research support motivated largely or exclusively by an interest in the advancement of science," as one official put it candidly.[33] In plain language, this means that the government claims in principle, if not always in practice: first, a considerable share in defining the scope and objectives of research; second, some control over research activities, especially over field work abroad that may prove politically or diplomatically sensitive; and finally, some control over the dissemination of research information and results—all of this justified by policy considerations which "sometimes require a degree of confidentiality even in the posing of research questions closely related to foreign policy and operations" and by respect for foreign publics who may not always be edified by the candor of science in the service of policy:[34] "The good ambassador," goes an ancient diplomatic injunction, "will watch over his words, never deride the country he is in, nor disparage the prince to whom he is accredited." The point here is not the legitimacy of such claims—although I think them reasonable—but the fact that politicization prompts political authorities (including those strongly committed to freedom of inquiry) to demand a voice in research decisions that traditionally have been reserved to social scientists and their professional peers.

There is another aspect to politicization that has been made familiar by the difficulties of many American social scientists attempting to work in developing countries. The association of research with actors in controversial areas of public affairs also inevitably colors the way in which people here and abroad perceive it. It is difficult in practice, however admirable in theory, to compartmentalize attitudes toward social scientific work—even basic work—from its sponsors and what they may symbolize at a particular time and place. Thus the financial nexus between social research and operating agencies makes it, to some extent, hostage to political fortune. There is something ironic, for example, in the fact that much of the social scientific work financed by the federal government was once legitimized by being related to the practical concerns of operating agencies and is now sometimes stigmatized for the same reason.[35] And I need hardly elaborate the fact that the linking of research to operating sponsors has sometimes proved detrimental both to United States foreign relations and to the interests of private scholars in maintaing a favorable climate for research abroad. Foreign publics, intellectuals, and leaders are understandably inclined to see such research as serving political rather than disinterested scientific purposes and to react to it on the basis of their own calculations and ideological dispositions— sometimes favorably and sometimes not.[36]

Robert Nisbet once put it tartly: "When a major Federal department—be it Defense, State, or Commerce—sponsors a scientific project, even one composed of dues-paying psychologists and sociologists, it is elementary that not even the elixir of scientific method is sufficient—to wipe away the fact of sponsorship."[37]

The Moral Dimension

It is impossible to discuss the politics of research without at some point drifting into a discussion of professional ethics. One other consequence of the federal government's heavy investment in national security and foreign area research has been an increased concern for the moral dimensions of the social sciences. Not so long ago, Edward Shils put his hope for protection against the potential abuses of research in the academic community itself: "The social sciences," he wrote, "are conducted within and under the auspices of the great universities, which nearly everywhere in the West are the Gibraltars of genuine humanism."[38] Whether or not the universities were or remain such bastions of humane learning, individual scholars, professional associations, and the government itself have, in the last half dozen years especially, argued the need for more explicit and perhaps more formal standards of professional conduct.

The fundamental reason for this, I suppose, is to be found in the increasing involvement of social scientists with the rest of society. Part of the new involvement is of course due to changes in the social sciences themselves--their quantitative expansion, their greater precision, their "intrusiveness" into once confidential spheres of private or public life, their greater relevance for detailed application and their potentially greater effectiveness as instruments of manipulation or control. Part of it is also due to the shift in the institutional setting of social scientific work; the proliferation of nonacademic centers of applied research raises such questions, for example, as whether the people working in such institutions are or should be bound by precisely the same codes as those that may apply to the academy.[39] And, finally, part of the involvement results from the enormously expanded influence of exogenous forces, mainly governmental, on the work being done in many fields of social research. It is this last development that has provided the occasion for a great deal of personal and professional soul searching among social scientists.

At the personal level, the problem usually comes down to the question of what political or moral responsibilities the social scientist incurs in the choice or acceptance of financial patrons, especially when his sponsors or clients are public agencies with operational missions. If his research is "applied" he is linked unambiguously with the uses to which his professional skills and knowledge may be put. If his work is "basic" there is frequently a reasonable presumption that, given a sponsor's interests, some applications of his findings (among many conceivably possible ones) are more likely than others.[40] But even if his work bears no relationship to the political actions of a sponsor, the social scientist who accepts funds gives his benefactor, in return, a measure of legitimation—to the institution if not to a particular policy or set of policies. Under such circumstances, a social scientist can hardly be morally indifferent as citizen if not as scientist, to the source of funds, even if he retains full freedom to pursue his intellectual interests.

At a more clearly professional level, the problem has been to identify significant problems of ethics, to clarify what are complex issues in which the "facts" themselves are sometimes elusive, and to prescribe normative rules that are, it seems, extremely difficult to operationalize. It is impressive to see how many professional associations, other private groups, and components of the federal government itself have launched studies, issued reports and sketched guidelines dealing with standards of professional conduct—and how many of these deal with the troublesome issues associated with international and foreign area studies financed by operating agencies—especially such matters as the acknowledgement or nonacknowledgement of financial support, classification or open publication, and the obligations of social scientists and their patrons or clients to foreign publics, colleagues and authorities. [41]

In short, the more extensive and intimate involvement of social scientists with other institutions, especially governmental ones in the field of foreign affairs, has created difficult and sometimes novel problems of personal moral choice and honorable professional conduct for which the inherited canons of academic scholarship provide neither clear guidelines nor firmly institutionalized rules.

Almost 20 years ago, Robert Merton and Daniel Lerner pointed to what they considered "a central problem confronting the policy-oriented social scientist today, as he faces the choice of affiliations with the academic, business or government communities. If he is to play an effective role in putting his knowledge to work, it is increasingly necessary that he affiliate with a bureaucratic power-structure in business or government. This, however, often requires him to abdicate the academic privilege of exploring policy possibilities which he regards as significant. If, on the other hand, he remains unaffiliated to a power structure in order to preserve fuller freedom of choice, he usually loses the resources to carry through his investigations on an appropriate scale and the opportunities of getting his findings accepted by policy makers as a basis for actions."[42] Since then, social scientists have indeed affiliated with the government on a scale that Merton and Lerner probably did not anticipate and the problems for social scientists resulting from the affiliation have been considerable, as I have tried to suggest here. But has the linkage really led to more and better use of social scientific knowledge in public policy? This is a difficult and perhaps an impossible question to answer with any assurance.

THE USES, OR NONUSES, OF SOCIAL SCIENCE

In theory, all the social research financed by the operating agencies of the federal government is supposed to be useful to them. In practice, the situation is quite different and many people in Washington, as well as many social scientists, are all too well aware of the discrepancy between the government's investment in research and its actual use of the product.

This, of course, is an impressionistic observation and one, more-over, that has to be qualified. In the first place, private social scientists routinely provide officials with a vast amount of descriptive information which the government, like any sophisticated bureaucracy, absorbs in vast amounts, however selectively, and probably applies in some way. There are also areas in which the more direct and specific impact of research on policy is fairly evident. Perhaps the most conspicuous example is provided by the work of RAND and similar organizations, which has had a significant influence on strategic doctrine and defense management techniques. And of course there is always the climate of opinion in which official policy is made and which social scientists perhaps help to mold more than most intellectuals.

Nevertheless, there are limits, however vaguely defined, to what can be claimed. It would be hard to say, for example, that the Department of Defense, which has fostered so much social science, has really applied all its studies. The Agency for International Development has for years struggled with the problem of communicating research findings convincingly to those charged with policy and operations. The Department of State has had, on the whole, mixed results even with its modest contract program. On balance, it is hardly an exaggeration to say that the utilization of extramural research leaves a great deal to be desired from the point of view of those who do not share the extreme skeptic's opinion that the relevance of social science to public policy, at least to foreign policy, is largely a figment of the academic imagination.

There is, no doubt, "an irreducible gap between research and action which, no matter how much we may narrow it, and how frequently we may bridge it, will never be closed," as a high federal research administrator has observed.[43] There are any number of useful ways of trying to understand the reasons for this gap; I find it convenient, in a brief survey such as this, to see it in terms of relevance, communication and bureaucratic processes.

What Is Relevant?

One of the more common complaints voiced by people in Washington is that a great deal of work in the social sciences seems meaningless to those who have to get on with the practical business of governing. For example, E. Raymond Platig of the State Department, though a firm advocate for the social sciences, has some harsh words on the subject: "The policy and program implications of much private research are either so irrelevant to the world view of the policy-action officer or so implicit that a major and often unrewarding intellectual effort is required to extract them."[44]

It should hardly be necessary to insist that behavioral and social scientists do some things that are quite unrelated to public policy in any immediately practical sense, but it *is* necessary because it has become fashionable, in some quarters, to justify practically every scientific activity in utilitarian terms. Some of this, I suspect, is probably no more than the expression of a mild form of anti-intellectualism which is uncomfortable with science for its own sake as an intrinsically satisfying play of human curiosity. But I also suspect that the sometimes heavy dependence of social scientists on operating agencies has encouraged them to make, more or less consciously, premature or extravagant claims for the utility of their wares, with the result that they frequently sound, to government officials, like the deaf men of literature muttering answers to questions that no one has asked.

The search for relevance sometimes can be frustrating to the social scientist and disillusioning to his client. Most people in policy or operational positions are inclined to look to research (as they do to its intramural version, "intelligence") for "facts"—only to find, all too often, that the facts of the social scientist may not be any fuller or better than those provided by common sense and their own resources. They look for studies with definite "findings"—and discover that there are rarely definitive answers to complex policy problems. They are encouraged, especially by more scientifically-oriented researchers, to expect predictions—only to discover that the predictive powers of social scientists are usually little more than an aspiration when applied to the concrete and often unique cases with which they have to cope.

I am exaggerating, of course, but one essential condition for winning acceptance for the social sciences in the policy process is to do work that is both meaningful to the man of action *and* distinctively "social scientific"—that is, that appears to him as something different from and superior to, folk knowledge, high journalism, or the wisdom of any politically seasoned sage. This is seldom easy.

Problems of Communication

However we define relevance, the application of social research to policy matters involves communication. The social scientist is not usually himself the policy-maker (although a growing number of people in Washington have some training in the social sciences) and ways must be found to bring the two together. Social scientists, accustomed to the conventions of the academy, tend to ignore this problem, or at least to assume that the communications model that serves to bind a community of professional intellectuals, with its formal emphasis on scholarly publication in a common technical language, is roughly transferable to the political realm. This is questionable.

The first difficulty in communication is, as everyone knows, getting attention. Most bureaucrats and higher officials simply do not have the time, even if they have the inclination and preparation, to peruse the scholarly literature that may have some bearing on their work. Something probably could be done to improve communications through the use of "middlemen" and "translations." But the value of such devices is limited by the nature of social science itself. If, except in the most narrowly technical fields, what the social sciences have to offer are new perspectives, new interpretations, rather than conclusive findings and firm policy recommendations, then the communication that is required must be something more than a condensed and mechanical transmission of "findings." What is called for is something akin to a dialogue—a difficult and time-consuming process.

Even this may imply an overly rational model of communication. As we move from more technical areas to more complex problems of social and political analysis, prediction and prescription, research itself becomes more difficult, more infused with values, more tentative in its results. At the same time, the policymakers to whom it is addressed are themselves men and women of flesh and blood who cannot be expected to respond to research, in all cases, with dispassionate intellectuality. It is remarkable, I think, how little attention has been paid to this aspect of the communication process. We would never expect to change attitudes, for example, without understanding something about the functions they serve in the psychic economy of an individual; and we rarely assume that they can be changed by the gentle persuasiveness of reason alone. Yet this is precisely what we do assume most of the time and almost casually when we talk about the communicating research that is relevant to policy matters.

The Bureaucratic Context

This rather pessimistic observation leads me to a final point on research utilization. Policy-making, we all too easily forget, is a social process—as Raymond Bauer put it, "a social process with intellectual elements contained within it rather than an intellectual process" alone.[45] To illustrate, let me show how one senior RAND analyst, James Schlesinger, once described this social process in a bureaucratic organization: "Whatever their disciplinary background," he notes, analysts tend to treat policymaking "as if it were governed by a rational and unified deciding unit." But

The reality is quite different. Decisions are nominally made by senior political figures who are harried, have insufficient time to study problems in detail, who are gripped by emotions of their youth or by prior experiences, and who are susceptible to claims made by subordinate groups which are couched in a way to appeal to their prejudices. Below them are a set of mutually jealous and warring bureaucratic groups, clamoring for resources and anxious to protect established preserves. To the extent that they are not closely watched, the subordinate bureaucratic groups will attempt to achieve their objectives quietly or even surreptitiously. Moreover, their capacity for resistance to high-level objectives enunciated from above, but to which they take exception, is breathtaking. Actual programs and allocative decisions will consequently diverge quite sharply from those that would be predicted on the assumption of a national intelligence. Instead they will be strongly influenced by prejudice, incompetency, and by infighting, deviousness, and bootlegging within the bureaucracies. Changes which appeal rational and desirable will be compromised half to death, and the compromises themselves will be slow in coming. [46]

Those who have worked in bureaucratic organizations or have studied them can judge for themselves whether Schlesinger exaggerates, but I doubt that anyone would consider him completely off the mark. But very little serious research has been done on the bureaucratic aspects of decision-making, or for that matter on the way in which bureaucratic conflicts and choices themselves are constrained by the larger political system. And, consequently, very little is known about the role of knowledge in such a process.

CONCLUDING OBSERVATIONS

Let me round out this essay by recapitulating some themes.

The social sciences and the federal government need each other and whatever the strains in their relationship, the relationship itself is now firmly established. Social research has become, in considerable measure, "big" science, dependent for its continued vigor on the kind of financial assistance that only the federal government can provide, even if private sponsors help to ensure pluralism and to encourage innovation. In international and foreign area studies, the federal government itself now provides support in forms that are more consonant with traditional images of what the scholar-scientist ought to be than was the case in the years immediately following World War II, even with the continued predominance in many sectors, of operating agencies and their interest in policy-relevant studies tailored to their largely self-defined requirements.

Yet, despite the utilitarian emphasis in government sponsorship, we know very little about how the social sciences are used by public agencies. We can see that much research is simply ignored even by its sponsors, that some may be used for special pleading before the political act and for legitimation after, and that some of it may actually have some independent effect on policy decisions. But there is little empirical evidence of a systematic kind about such things. And there is no really satisfactory model of the uses of social sciences in public policy. The expert-client (or patient) relationship established in such areas as law, applied psychology and medicine, for example, does not seem to fit the realities of bureaucratic and political processes.

Which brings me to the final and most tentative observations. To the extent that there is a model implicit in current practices, it seems to be a rather technocratic one. One manifestation of this technocratic orientation is, I believe, the striking emphasis that is placed on sponsored research as the most direct and reliable way of influencing public policy—when sponsored work can be, in most instances, only a small and partial selection of scientific material that is in some way relevant to public debate and choice. To the extent that sponsored work must be roughly consonant with the basic values and outlooks of its sponsors, it seems most likely to be used for the implementation rather than the formulation of policy and thus the social scientist who commits himself largely to sponsored work tends toward an "engineering" conception of his role. Another aspect of the technocratic orientation is the almost exclusive commitment of policy-oriented social scientists to the executive branch of the government. The interest of many operating agencies in research is, I am convinced, an excellent thing in its own terms, whatever the problems it leads to. Few, I think, could seriously argue that modern government would be more efficient, more responsive to public need, more humane even, if it were cut off even more than it is from social research and social scientists. Nevertheless, it is curious that so little thought has been given to the implications, for a democratic polity, of the cult of social science expertise and the conspicuously uneven distribution of intellectual resources among the various components of the political system.

The views expressed in this paper are strictly those of the author and do not in any sense reflect the official position of, or even the informal consensus within, the Department of State.

NOTES

[1] Ithiel de Sola Pool, "The Necessity for Social Scientists Doing Research for Governments," in Irving Louis Horowitz (ed.). *The Rise and Fall of Project Camelot* (Cambridge and London: M.I.T. Press, 1967), p. 268. At his pugnacious best, Pool is well worth reading as one of the most informed and candid academic paladins of social research sponsored by operating agencies of all kinds.

[2] The recent literature reflecting such views or anxieties is so vast that I can only mention a few examples that I have found particularly helpful or provocative, in addition to some of the papers in the just-cited Horowitz volume. Among the more polemical works are two that deal with sponsored research incidentally as part of a broader critique of liberal scholarship: Theodore Roszak (ed.), *The Dissenting Academy* (New York: Vintage, 1968) and Noam Chomsky, *American Power and the New Mandarins* (New York: Pantheon, 1969). A review article by Philip Green, "Science, Government, and the Case of RAND—A Singular Pluralism" *World Politics*, Vol. XX, No. 2, January 1968, pp. 301-26) is a rare and controversial example of a thoughtful examination of government-sponsored work in a nonprofit setting seen as part of a larger bureaucratic-political process. Perhaps the single most useful collection is Elizabeth T. Crawford and Albert D. Biderman (eds.), *Social Scientists and International Affairs* (New York: John Wiley, 1969). The value of the reprinted articles, which themselves cover a number of issues from a variety of perspectives, is augmented by the editors' commentaries and by their conscious effort to deal with the subject in terms of a "sociology of social science." I should add that concern about the impact of government funding on research is not limited to radical criticis. For example, a pillar of the academic and Washington Establishment, while an Under Secretary of State, told members of the International Studies Association: " . . . I am not one who views the development of large programs of Government research financing happily, especially in the social sciences. I rejoice that so many people still do their research alone, with relatively small budgets obtained from their universities or from a scattering or private foundations, and write their books without the benefit of expensive apparatus which in the end can only be provided by Government." Eugene V. Rostow, "Safeguarding Academic Freedom," reprinted in *Far Horizons,* Vol. 1, No. 3, May 1968, p. 2.

[3] Here I am glossing over important differences in the mechanisms devised by various Washington agencies to administer research. The role of central bureaucracies is modified, in many instances, by the use of professional advisory groups even in operating agencies and, in the more scientifically-oriented institutions, by panels of private behavioral and social scientists with virtual decision-making power over grants.

[4] Of course almost all government departments are now involved in foreign affairs and it is difficult to make a clear distinction between domestic and foreign policy. Still, when the primary object of official attention and operations are political entities outside the state's jurisdiction we may reasonably

talk about "foreign" policy, with "high policy" defined as those elements of policy that are, in the eyes of political authorities, most closely related to national welfare, prestige and security.

[5] Anyone familiar with the content of government-sponsored programs over the past two decades would question, I believe, the assumption that there has been a change in these programs sufficient to explain recent hostility toward them. If anything, I would say on the basis of very rough impressions, most government projects are now more congruent with dominant academic values than those of ten or twenty years ago. It is interesting to note, for example, that hardly anyone seems to have questioned the propriety of Air Force funding, in the early 1950s, of work on a World Urban Resources Index by a university-affiliated institute, with the expectation that the project would "enable analysts to make comparative studies of urban and regional complexes and develop more dependable methods for the selection of air targets," according to an account of the military applications of sociology. See Raymond V. Bowers, "The Military Establishment," in Paul F. Lazarsfeld, William H. Sewell and Harold L. Wilensky (eds.), *The Uses of Sociology* (New York: Basic Books, 1967), pp. 241-42.

[6] This is not to say that ideological peace reigned supreme in the forties and fifties. But radical dissidents—and even not-so-radical ones—were evidently fewer, quieter and in any case less concerned about the impact of government funding on the social sciences since government programs did not loom very large.

[7] Funds for research on foreign affairs have ranged from about 15 percent of total federal expenditures on the behavioral and social sciences in the mid-sixties to about 10 percent in more recent years. Apart from publications of the National Science Foundation, the most convenient sources of information on funding are: *Far Horizons,* a bimonthly newsletter issued by the Office of External Research of the Department of State, which covers programs in foreign affairs; and *The Behavioral and Social Sciences: Outlook and Needs*, a report by The Behavioral and Social Sciences Survey Committee created under the auspices of the Social Science Research Council and the National Academy of Sciences (Englewood Cliffs, New Jersey: Prentice Hall, 1969), which includes a chapter on federal financing of the behavioral and social sciences.

[8] See Education and World Affairs, *A Crisis of Dollars: The Funding Threat to International Affairs in U.S. Higher Education.* (New York: Education and World Affairs, 1968).

[9] Deutsch's statement appeared in what I believe was a fugitive memorandum several years ago that I have not been able to retrace. The earlier prophets were a committee formed at the initiative of then Vice President Richard Nixon and their views may be found in a phamphlet, *National Support for Behavioral Sciences* (Washington, D. C., February 1958). According to Harold Orlans, a master at deflating scientific pretensions, although Mr. Nixon's "subsequent recollection of the group was courteous, rumor has it that officials were so appalled at the sums requested that the group's final report . . . had even less influence than its contents merited." See Orlans, "Social Science Research in U.S. National Science Policies," unpublished remarks prepared for the UNESCO Round Table on Social Research Policy and Organization, Copenhagen, 1969, pp. 17-17.

[10] For two other analyses based on the records of the Department of State and covering substantially the subjects of this section, see: Department of State, Foreign Affairs Research Council, *A Report on the First Three Years,* August 1968 (Xeroxed; available from the Department's Office of External Research); and Cyril E. Black, "Government-Sponsored Research in International Studies" *World Politics,* Vol. XXII, No. 4, July 1970, pp. 582-96). In 1964, the Department of State took the initiative in creating a voluntary interagency Foreign Area Research Coordination Group (known as FAR) as a means of encouraging consultation among federal organizations financing research on foreign affairs and as a medium for discussing common interests and problems. FAR serves as a useful function, but its most ardent defenders would, I believe, make modest claims about its effectiveness in "coordinating" the research satrapies of Washington.

[11] In 1964, the Department of State took the initiative in creating a voluntary interagency Foreign Area Research Coordination Group (known as FAR) as a means of encouraging consultation among federal organizations financing research on foreign affairs and as a medium for discussing common interests and problems. FAR serves a useful function, but its most ardent defenders would, I believe, make modest claims about its effectiveness in "coordinating" the research satrapies of Washington.

[12] Nothing in life is simple. The Department of Health, Education and Welfare is an "operating" agency too, but I still think it appropriate to link it with Washington's culturally and scientifically oriented institution.

[13] If administratively distinct programs, rather than departments and agencies, are counted, there are more than 30 sponsors of foreign affairs research in the executive branch of government.

[14] But we must be wary of statistics. The 1966 figures for the Department of State included more than $5,000,000 allocated by the Bureau of Educational and Cultural Affairs for institutional grants which the Department decided, upon reflection, did not strictly qualify for inclusion in a survey of research financing. They were not included in later years.

[15] This is an informed guess based on crude comparisons of professional employment. For patterns of employment of economists, psychologists, sociologists and political scientists in the National Scientific Register, see talbe in Neil J. Smelser and James A. Davis, *Sociology* (Englewood Cliffs, N.J.: Prentice-Hall, 1969), p. 130. Without pursuing the complications of this problem here, there is presumptive evidence for the statement in the text.

[16] This appears to conflict with Roy Licklider's finding that among specialists on nuclear weapons policy the locus of employment is not correlated with significant intellectual or political differences. See pp. 000-000. There are other ways of looking at the problem, however, even if limited to weapons policy matters. For example, in Robert Levine's *The Arms Debate* (Cambridge: Harvard University Press, 1963), *passim* those social scientists he classifies as "anti-Communist marginalists" and "middle marginalists"—the two categories that I know contain the largest number of people who have worked with government funds-are found in *both* academic and non-academic settings. The "antiwar marginalists" and the "antiwar systemists,"

however, include numerous academics but practically no social scientists identified with a nonprofit or commercial research institute actively engaged in doing contract work for clients. See also below, f.n. 32.

17 It is interesting to note, for example, in view of the pattern of government funding, that every one of 18 "most influential" scholars in the field of international relations named in a recent study works on campus. See Bruce M. Russett, "Methodological and Theoretical Schools in International Relations" in Norman D. Palmer (ed.), *A Design for International Relations Research: Scope, Theory, Methods, and Relevance* (Monograph 10, The American Academy of Political and Social Science, Philadelphia, October 1970) p. 101. Most of the 18 have worked with government support at some time. Presumably the far more numerous nonacademic social scientists who work with government support must, by necessity or choice, get their satisfactions elsewhere, probably through a stronger commitment to client acceptance rather than to broader peer recognition.

18 See Harold Orlans' remarks in the introduction to a Congressional report on the administration of federal social research: the reduction or elimination of "government control over the release of information gathered in the course of research *on campus* . . . has led to a lack of information (or even of that vital precursor to information, questions) about controls on the release of research information. For the problem has now, in large measure, been moved to a new institutional sector—that of the independent nonprofit or profit-making organization which subsists in good part by *doing* proprietary work for private and governmental clients. With a few notable exceptions . . . [such organizations] are accustomed to offering proprietary services, and are unlikely to complain about them." U.S. Congress, House of Representatives, Research and Technical Programs Subcommittee of the Committee on Government Operations, "The Use of Social Research in Federal Domestic Programs— Part IV, Current Issues in the Administration of Federal Social Research," p. 18. The same volume includes responses from numerous federal officials to a committee request for information on the kinds of controls maintained over the dissmeination of research products and the rationales for them.

19 A study of the best-known member of the species is Bruce L. R. Smith, *The Rand Corporation: Case Study of a Nonprofit Advisory Corporation* (Cambridge: Harvard University Press, 1966). The Green article cited earlier is a review of this book.

20 *Government-Supported Research—International Affairs, Research Completed and In Progress, July 1968-June 1969,* a report prepared for the Foreign Area Research Coordination Group by the Office of External Research, Department of State, November 1969. The next few pages draw largely on this document and the two reports cited in f.n. 10.

21 Herbert C. Kelman, "The Use of University Resources in Foreign Policy Research," *International Studis Quarterly,* Vol. 12, No. 1, March 1968, p. 24).

22 This is an estimate based on preliminary unpublished figures, prepared by executive agencies, for fiscal year 1970. Definitions of "basic" and "applied" research are of course notoriously variable.

23 Report of the Committee on Government Sponsorship and Freedom of

Research, American Sociological Association, published in *The American Sociologist*, Vol. 3, November 1968, pp. 39-41.

[24] Department of State, Foreign Affairs Research Council, *Report,* p. 17.

[25] Albert D. Biderman and Elisabeth T. Crawford, "Paper Money: Trends of Research Sponsorship in American Sociology Journals," in *Social Science Information,* Paris, Vol. 9, No. 1, February 1970, p. 51.

[26] Africa Research Group, "African Studies in America: The Extended Family," (Cambridge, Mass., 1969), p. 2. (Pamphlet).

[27] In the late 1950s, for example, a congressional committee criticized the Department of State for commissioning domestic opinion polls. But the polling was stopped, mainly for economy reasons, even before the congressional action.

[28] The reluctance of the National Science Foundation, for example, to incorporate political science in its programs may have been due, according to some commentators, as much to political as to scientific reasons—unless political science is, indeed, less "scientific" than (say) anthropology.

[29] Paul F. Lazarsfeld once put it succinctly: "The main danger of commissioned research arises from the fact that for some practical problems there is more money available than for others." Lazarsfeld (in collaboration with Sydney S. Spivack), "Observations on Organized Social Research in the United States," A Report to the International Social Science Council (New York, August 1961), p. 37. Xeroxed.

[30] One consequence is of course to push research toward the "applied" end of the "basic-applied" spectrum. Applied research may, also, take on a somewhat conservative cast if the terms of reference discourage innovative work that may be too risky or too far removed from the short-term concerns of its sponsors.

[31] See, for example, Horowitz, "The Rise and Fall of Project Camelot," in Horowitz (ed.), *op. cit.,* especially pp. 30-34.

[32] The quotation is from T. V. Sathyamurthy, "From Containment to Interdependence," *World Politics,* Vol. XX, No. 1, October 1967, p. 147. The author seems to refer to "establishment" authors in general, not all of them necessarily financially linked to government patrons. But of the five "schools" identified by Levine in *The Arms Debate,* the three "marginalist" ones dominate "the councils of government, particularly of the executive branch," he says (p. 280). It seems likely that two of the three—the "anticommunist marginalists" and the "middle marginalists"—dominate among government counselors. On a somewhat different subject, Donald L. M. Blackmer deals with some aspects of the "unusually" close communication and rapport between academic specialists on the Soviet Union and their government counterparts in "Scholars and Policymakers: Perceptions of Soviet Policy" (a paper prepared for the 1968 Annual Meeting of the American Political Science Association). Crawford and Biderman (*op. cit.,* pp. 156-58) deal more generally and impressionistically with "political affinity and disaffection" in the relations of social scientists and the government and emphasize the great variety of considerations that have colored the attitudes of social scientists toward contractual arrangements.

[33] Letter from ·Thomas L. Hughes, Chairman of the State Department's

Foreign Affairs Research Council, published in the *American Anthropological Association Fellow Newsletter*, June 1968, p. 9.

[34] *Ibid.*

[35] Domestic political concern about the role of *operating* agencies in foreign affairs research is perhaps best reflected in the Senate's efforts to restrict the activities of the Department of Defense. Section 203 of the Military Procurement Authorization Act for Fiscal Year 1970 establishes that "none of the funds authorized to be appropriated by this Act may be used to carry out any research project or study, unless the project or study has a direct and apparent relationship to a specific military function or operation." In practice it is very difficult, however, to establish firm boundaries to the research interests of *any* agency.

[36] Many observers have rightly pointed out that government sponsorship is only one aspect of foreign sensitivity in research matters. See, for example: Klaus and Knorr, "Social Science Research Abroad, Problems and Remedies," *World Politics,* April 1967, Vol. XIX, No. 3, pp. 465-85.

[37] Robert A. Nisbet, "Project Camelot: an Autopsy," in *The Public Interest,* No. 5, Fall 1966, p. 59.

[38] Edward A. Shils, "Social Inquiry and the Autonomy of the Individual," in Daniel Lerner (ed.) *The Human Meaning of the Social Sciences* (New York: Meridian Books, 1959), p. 153.

[39] Gunnar Myrdal dealt with this problem almost 20 years ago: "The employment to an ever-increasing extent of social scientists in all sorts of practical tasks and, particularly, the coming into existence of a commercialized branch of social science raise, as I see it, the demand for a code of professional ethics for the guidance of social science practitioners." "The Relation Between Social Theory and Social Policy," in *The British Journal of Sociology,* Vol. IV, September 1953, p. 230. Many government agencies distinguish between nonacademic and academic contractors in their research programs, on the principle that the latter should be exempt from certain restrictions that may properly be imposed on the former.

[40] See Kelman, "The Use of University Resources," *loc. cit.,* p. 25: "When the sponsor has a visible interest in the outcome and a significant likelihood of acting on the findings, any one of us takes on a measure of responsibility by accepting his support."

[41] From the government side, two important recent statements are: "Privacy and Behavioral Research," issued by the Executive Office of the President, Office of Science and Technology, Washington, February 1967; and "Government Guidelines for Foreign Area Research," issued by the member agencies of the Foreign Area Research Coordination Group and published in *Far Horizons,* Vol. I, No. 1, January 1968. Among the more comprehensive documents issued by professional associations are: "Background Information on Problems of Anthropological Research and Ethics," prepared by Ralph L. Beals and the Executive Board of the American Anthropological Association, published in the *American Anthropological Association Newsletter,* Vol. 8, No. 1, January 1967; and "Ethical Problems of Academic Political Scientists," Final Report of the American Political Science Association Committee on Professional Standards and Responsibilities, published in

P.S., Newsletter of the American Political Science Association, Summer 1968, Vol. I, No. 3.

[42] Robert K. Merton and Daniel Lerner, "Social Scientists and Research Policy," in Lerner, Harold D. Lasswell and others, *The Policy Sciences, Recent Developments in Scope and Methods* (Stanford: Stanford University Press, 1951), pp. 29293.

[43] Raymond Platig, "Research and Analysis," in *Annals of the American Academy of Political and Social Science,* Vol. 380, November 1968, p. 53.

[44] *Ibid.*

[45] Raymond A. Bauer, "Social Psychology and the Study of Policy Formation," in *American Psychologist,* Vol. 21, No. 10, October 1966, p. 935.

[46] James R. Schlesinger, "The 'Soft' Factors in Systems Studies," in *Bulletin of the Atomic Scientists,* November 1968, pp. 14-15.

17

Individual Values, National Interests and Political Development in the International System

J. DAVID SINGER

A widely shared notion among social historians is that almost every reformation or revolution is likely to be followed by a counterrevolution or counterreformation. Those who will examine the development of Western political science in the mid-twentieth century seem destined to have yet another case in support of that contention. Even as many scholars remain untouched by the behavioral revolution and several disciplines remain largely unmoved by its central themes, a counterrevolution of sorts is under way. Two dominant strands characterize this nascent counterrevolution. One is a renewed emphasis on normative and policy concerns, as opposed to the alleged detachedness of the behavioral approach.[1] The other is a renewed interest in explanation, as opposed to the focus on "mere" description, which allegedly characterized the behaviorist school.

At the risk of being identified with a doctrinaire behavioral position, and unsympathetic to any criticisms of that orientation, let me state my reservations vis-à-vis these two trends. While recognizing that some of the behavioral research looks suspiciously like mindless empiricism, I would nevertheless caution against the drive for premature explanation. Put bluntly, we cannot explain and account for phenomena until the regularities of such phenomena have been observed and described, and while admitting that a good many behaviorists have indeed embraced a "value-free" position, we would not only note that this point of view was with us in the social sciences long before the post-World War II developments, but also that many of the behaviorists have explicitly rejected it all along.[2] In this paper, while working from the description-before-explanation viewpoint, my main concern will be that of the delicate and refractory relationship between science and the ethics of public policy.

We will limit ourselves to a single (but very broad) set of policy questions: How might we ascertain the level of political development in the international system and identify the instrumentalities which enhance or inhibit that development?[3] We begin from two assumptions: (a) the concept of political development is as applicable to this larger system as to any national social system; and (b) science is not only compatible with deep ethical concerns, but also absolutely essential to serious involvement with those concerns. The article will propose what seem to be some critical refinements in the concept of political development and suggest and evaluate a number of indicators.

All of this, in turn, will be in the context of an explicit and self-conscious rejection of the doctrine (still widely held by economists) that the selection of ends is a purely political matter and that the scholar only enters the picture to recommend the means and policies designed to realize the assigned objectives. In addition to the fact that today's ends are tomorrow's means, and that means and ends impinge continuously on one another, I would argue that even the most fundamental ends can in principle be evaluated and compared by scientific criteria. Moreover, I urge that every man must be held accountable for the direct and indirect consequences of his public actions (and inactions), and that the extent to which he can predict those consequences will be a function of: (a) the state of social science knowledge, and (b) his grasp and application of that knowledge. Put another way, many of humanity's tragedies might have been avoided had the social sciences been further along and had the relevant knowledge been available to (and credible to) those whose acts contributed to such tragedies.[4]

MEASURING POLITICAL DEVELOPMENT

The concept of political development is as applicable to the global system or to a single urban region as it is to the national society. But regardless of the social-territorial unit to which it is applied, four important modifications would seem to be in order; two are essentially methodological, two raise serious normative issues. The first is that the criteria must be converted from highly intuitive and subjective form into more operational language. To some extent, those who study national political development are beginning to recognize this need and the issue need not be further belabored here. Second, development is meaningful only in a comparative context and that comparison may be not only across different social systems at a single point in time but also for the same social system across several points in time. By and large, most students of national political development are responsive to the need for comparison in the first sense of the word but remain relatively indifferent to the need for longitudinal comparisons.[5] These two modifications should require little discussion and will be incorporated in the approach used here.

The next two modifications are, however, more fundamental and require some extended discussion. One concerns the need to differentiate between development in terms of the physical, structural and cultural attributes of the social system at hand, and development in terms of the quality of life of those human beings who comprise the sytem. The other, intimately related, is the need to distinguish between indicators of development that are best thought of an instrumental and those that are more intrinsic in nature.

Most research on national political development remains ethically insensitive to the distinctions between national (or other group) interests and individual interests, and between indicators that reflect the growth or change in instrumentalities of development, and those which reflect the extent to which these instrumentalities have indeed led to the satisfaction or maximization of those intrinsic values by which the quality of life might be ascertained.

As to the first point, it hardly seems necessary to emphasize that what is "good" for a given social system, qua system, may not necessarily be "good" for most of the individuals who live within (or under) that system. The literature of political philosophy and classical sociology fairly brims over with logical argument (and some empirical evidénce) that the needs and interests of the rulers are not only different from but also often incompatible with those of the ruled. Whether the focus be on order versus freedom, authority versus representation, coercion versus consent, stability versus change or privilege versus equality, the picture is much the same: the preferences of elites and of masses can seldom be fully (or even adequately) reconciled. To put it another way, events and conditions which may be highly functional for a given system—or those who either exercise a high degree of control over it or benefit most from its current state—are often considerably less functional (or even dysfunctional) for that much larger number whose influence and benefits are relatively low. In sum, one must be—as the expression goes—either a fool or a knave to equate the national interest with the individual interest.

Having taken this strong position, I do not mean to suggest that it is always a *very* few whose interests (psychic and material, short-run and long-run) are synonymous with that of the system, and that the overwhelming majority are necessarily the exploited and the betrayed. In many systems (and the United States during the past two decades may be a prime example), the short-run benefits of the status quo extend to an appreciable fraction and, perhaps, even half of the total population. The extent to which certain valued objects or conditions are equally distributed throughout any social system is indeed one important measure of political development.[6]

These comments lead to the other critical distinction suggested above. My view is that a valid measure of such development must not only differentiate between the systemic and the individual but between the instrumental and the intrinsic. That is, Western students may believe that a high level of industrialization, a two-party political structure or a complex communication network constitute evidence of political development, but I would contend that if there is no appreciable improvement in the quality of life of most of the system's members, it is invalid to speak of increased development. Put differently, it is essential to distinguish between development and such phenomena as modernization, mobilization, urbanization and industrialization. As I define it, these latter are best viewed as potentially instrumental to the realization of certain intrinsically valuable conditions, but no more. To the extent that such changes *do* lead to improvements in the general quality of life, they may be treated as instrumental indicators of development, but rather than assume that they do we must demonstrate that they do. At this writing, the evidence across time and across social systems is far from conclusive. With these considerations in mind, let us turn to the problem of intrinsic measures of political development, that we may later return to the association between them and those of an instrumental nature.

IDENTIFYING THE INTRINSIC VALUES

So far, our references to the quality of life enjoyed by any population have been rather vague and general; the need now is to become more specific. Yet until we have identified the key dimensions, and defended that choice, operational measures would be premature. How, then, do we establish the criteria of the "good life"?

There are four basic routes. First, we can merely operationalize the revealed wisdom, as handed down by the tribal deities and their elite disciples. Second, we might conduct one version or another of an opinion survey, asking people what they desire in life. Or we can try to ascertain the particular or universal needs of people. Finally, we can select our own, reflecting the biases of Western, modern, liberal scholars. Let us consider each of these, briefly, in turn.

While sharing the view that the definitions of the good life handed down by the bureaucratic elites of church and state over the centuries have been essentially self-serving, the criteria they enunciated cannot all be dismissed out of hand. While some had only the effect of persuading people that servitude is righteousness, that pain is virtue and that deprivation is the road to worldly or otherworldly salvation, others of these criteria may be worth preserving. This is especially true of those articulated (or re-articulated) by systematic philosophers who served no institutional masters; we will return to these shortly.

The alternative of asking people—the living and the dead, the rich and the poor, the educated and the ignorant—has the virtue of being democratic, but suffers from certain fatal inadequacies. First of all, neither the opinion survey nor the inference from historical traces (following, for example, the methods of McClelland's *Achieving Society*)[7] gives us valid distinctions between the transitory and the persistent, or between the superficial and the fundamental.[8] Second, and more important, the preferences of too many humans in too many epochs have been artificially induced or "neurotically based" to use Bay's language.[9] Third, and perhaps most important, this approach requires an acceptance of the utilitarians' view that what people desire is indeed desirable, and what is desirable is therefore valuable. John Stuart Mill, for example, ended up defining virtuous behavior as that which leads to the "multiplication of happiness." Finally, how do we handle the distribution of incompatible preferences? Does a simple or special majority define the criteria for all who occupy a given time-space domain?[10] And, of course, how are the boundaries of those domains to be drawn?

The third option—that of trying to identify the basic and eternal needs of people—is ethically most attractive since it requires little or no elite intervention. But it not only assumes that such needs can indeed be empirically ascertained, via the biological and psychological sciences, but it also assumes continuity in such needs across time and space. I suspect, despite the confidence of some biologists (for example, Gerard)[11] that such needs may turn out to be quite elusive, and that even if identifiable in a given empirical domain, they are just transitory enough to defy scientific generalization.

Does this suggest that the only defensible route is to recognize the inadequacies of the first three alternatives and go ahead with an explicitly subjective delineation of the criteria by which the quality of men's life may be evaluated? Not quite. Rather, let me fall back on a synthesis in which each of the four components' contributions is admittedly quite uncertain.[12] The strategy is unsatisfactory, but given the number of philosopher-years that have been invested in the search for a solution so far—without success, in my judgment— one need not feel too sheepish about such an intellectual compromise. I argue, then, that there *are* certain basic needs typical of most humans across space and time and that these can be partly (and increasingly) inferred from behavior and verbal expression as well as from the sort of institutions men have built. Finally, I proceed from the assumption that, despite their basic inability to pin these needs down, the major Western philosophers have nevertheless given tentative expression to them.

The Intrinsic Indicators Specified

Despite this somewhat unsatisfactory search for a legitimate basis, let me go on to a specification of the five intrinsic values by which we might measure the political development of the international, or any other, social system. Lest there appear to be any conceptual or definitional slippage in our argument, I repeat the basic theme here. Until we know the extent to which certain individual values have been realized in a given social system, one cannot evaluate its political development. Certain structural conditions or behavioral regularities may indeed be conducive to the realization of such values, but that is an empirical question; and even if these instrumental factors do turn out to enhance the intrinsic individual values in certain empirical domains, this is no basis for reifying them or treating them as eternal verities. Our ultimate task, then, is to: (a) develop valid and reliable indices of the intrinsic values; (b) ascertain the extent to which they have obtained over the past several centuries in the separate nations and in the world as a whole; and (c) identify the instrumentalities that best account for the presence and absence of these intrinsic conditions. Here, we can do no more than propose a set of criteria, discuss some possible measures and present a few scattered observations. The value dimensions proposed are: (a) bodily survival, (b) material well-being, (c) liberty, (d) self-fulfillment and (e) justice. The dominant preoccupations of Hobbes, Marx, Locke, Maslow and Tawney, respectively, will be quite evident.

Bodily Survival

Despite our sympathy with the view that there are things worse than death, and that there are indeed principles worth dying for, it is obvious that bodily survival is a precondition for enjoying any other values. Hence, any social system which is functional for its members is one which offers them a high probability of dying a natural death and a low probability of dying violently and/or unexpectedly. In other words, in any particular social system with certain levels of medical care, public health measures, food and shelter, there is a normal life expectancy. That expectancy figure may be pathetically low in contrast to other societies or more recent decades, but it is nevertheless a useful benchmark. However, not everyone lives that long, owing not only to the inevitable statistical distribution around the mean expectancy figure but also the less inevitable but ever-present incidence of violent and sudden death.

Among the philosophers who most concerned themselves with survival and physical security as a major purpose of political organization, Hobbes is perhaps best known. In Part Two of *Leviathan* he argued that the "final cause, end, or design of men who naturally love liberty and dominion over others, in the introduction of that restraint upon themselves in which we see them live in commonwealths, is the foresight of their own preservation...."

The most valid and reliable measure of the ability of man's political institutions to assure him a "natural" death would be one that reflected its successes and failures in terms of deaths due to such events as war, revolution, massacre, execution, homicide, suicide and occupational or transportation accidents. We choose, however, to eliminate two of these on validity grounds. Thus, even though there is a fair amount of data (however unreliable they may be) on the incidence of suicide, and that incidence is partially a function of societal inadequacies (and occasionally the only alternative to other forms of violent death), it is, in the end, a decision taken by the individual human being. Second, accidents of farm, factory or road, in addition to being recorded for only the more recent years in many parts of the globe, are also to a large extent the result of the individual's own behavior. Like suicide, such deaths usually occur under specific societal conditons, but they fall outside our category of "violent death inflicted by others and unexpected at birth." In a later report, we will present some statistical estimates of the extent to which the political instrumentalities of the global system and its national subsystems have succeeded, failed, or actually produced death due to war, revolution, massacre, execution and homicide.[13]

Material Welfare

Once man's bodily survival is assured, it would seem that the next function of his political institutions is to permit him to live a life relatively free of disease, starvation and punishment by the elements. To these ends, he may reasonably expect his institutions to provide, permit or encourage an adequate amount of food, shelter, public health facilities and medical care. This has indeed been a concern not only of men themselves but of those who have theorized about the relationship of men and their social organization.

Traditionally, we think of the material needs of life as composed of food, clothing and housing. The latter two may legitimately be combined under the rubric of shelter not only on logical grounds but also since there should be a high correlation between them in terms of both need (due to climate, etc.) and availability. One finds in the literature several possible measures of shelter, ranging from a crude dwelling unit per capita index to those reflecting number and quality of rooms per capita, and often including scales of modern plumbing, telephones and so forth. Given the great variety of shelter requirements depending on climate, occupation, education, etc., the validity of any shelter availability index across regions, nations or cities, as well as across so long a stretch of time is likely to be quite dubious, and an alternative approach is required. As to food, there are usually two basic indicators used; one is that of estimated caloric intake per capita per day (ranging from about 1,500 to 3,000) and the other is somewhat more refined in that it focuses on proteins only (with a range from about 45 to 95 per day). These ranges tend to confirm the impression that food requirements, like those of shelter, vary too much to permit a compelling comparison of availabilities. That is, in both the shelter and food cases, one should first develop a baseline by which we can control for physical need before going on to comparing availability.

There may, however, be a fairly simple alternative by which we can get at the general variable of material well-being. If such well-being, in the form of food and shelter, as well as preventive and curative medicine, is important because of its contribution to the sort of physical environment within which humans can be born and then continue to thrive, it may well be that a very adequate indicator of the quality of that environment is the infant mortality rate. In other words, rather than try to get at this particular quality of life directly, the suggestion is that we look at those figures which seem most likely to reveal the consequences of material well-being. Some evidence that infant mortality rates do indeed offer a valid measure is the fact that we find a high (and of course, negative) correlation between these conditions on the one hand and such mortality on the other.[14]

Liberty

Compared to bodily survival and material wellbeing, this third intrinsic indicator of political development is certainly more elusive and quite subject to disagreement over the validity of almost any measure we might devise. One may think of liberty in individual or collective terms, and may differentiate among those several sectors of activity which characterize most social systems: political, economic, artistic and so forth. We mean to embrace all public and private sectors of life, from the bedroom to the marketplace and from the artist's garret to the political forum, and to include not only those who conform to the norms of the moment but also those who do not. The idea may best be conveyed by the current expression "feel free," and has to do with freedom from constraint and the absence of anxiety over the political and economic consequences (but not that of mere social ridicule or disapproval) of one's thoughts, behavior and associations.

Several possible ways of measuring this dimension come to mind, but none seem quite satisfactory. First, one might look at the statutory and administrative provisions that exist in the towns, provinces and nations of the world, but this would be exactly the approach that is opposed here. That is, it would reflect the often unwarranted assumption that political rules almost always produce the consequences which are alleged to inhere in them, rather than treat the matter as one requiring empirical investigation. Closer to the intrinsic end of the continuum might be indicators that reflect— if the information for so many nations and years could be found— the frequency of political imprisonment, political trials, secret arrests, books banned or plays censored, correspondence intercepted, telephones tapped, houses searched and so forth. Another approach might be to content-analyze representative samples of the literature, press or correspondence, in order to estimate not only the extent of interference with expression and association but also to infer it even more indirectly on the basis of how much uniformity or diversity of views and styles is found.[15]

Self-Fulfillment

Just as freedom and liberty represent the absence of constraints, the idea of self-actualization represents the presence of positive opportunities. While some may quarrel with its inclusion as a basic consideration by which to ascertain political development, it at least poses fewer measurement problems than that of liberty.

Dividing the dimension into its vocational and avocational sectors, the obvious measure for getting at the former (at least in its elementary sense) is that of employment. Using the standards of each period, we might first establish the extent to which all of the world's employable people are indeed so occupied; such a measure would have to take into account not only self-employment in agriculture, husbandry, retailing and the crafts, but also the extent to which self- or other-employed people are underemployed due to seasonal or commercial conditions. But that is only part of the story. Equally critical—and here is where the values of the individuals concerned become most important—is the degree of satisfaction which is derived from such employment. It is difficult, at least for me, to imagine that Africans or Europeans or Americans who are often fully employed in the mines (for example) are really getting much satisfaction from such work, regardless of education, aspiration level or cultural deprivation.

Then there is the matter of avocational opportunity. Even though it is only recently that social scientists in the industrial nations have begun to pay attention to the problem of leisure time, it is a phenomenon that anthropologists have noted regularly in their descriptions of preindustrial societies. Depending on the technological level of the society, one might be able to get at this factor by ascertaining the opportunity for, frequency of and participation in, all sorts of ludic activity, ranging from dancing and lacrosse to concerts and cinema.

Equality as Justice

As broad and sweeping a concept as either liberty or self-fulfillment, the idea of justice is, in essence, a comparative one. That is, we tend to ask whether certain basic values are equally realized by all the people in a given social system or whether there is a discernible maldistribution in them. Alternately, instead of comparing one person's conditions with those of others, we might compare them to some desirable, but abstract, state of affairs. In this article, we employ both approaches. The four intrinsic indicators are meant to reflect the extent to which those basic values have been fully realized by the people who constitute the international system; they reveal the discrepancy between some ideal condition and a given empirical reality. In this section, however, the first meaning is used: How equal is the distribution of the other four values, or in contemporary language, to what extent has "distributive justice" been achieved?[16]

As most data-oriented scholars are well aware, almost all of the figures proposed here (along with many alternative indicators) are usually built around the nation as the unit of analysis. Thus, they not only offer little evidence as to the intranational distributions and inequalities thereof, but also even less as to worldwide interpersonal inequalities. Quite clearly, any measures that do not reflect such inequalities at either the national or global levels can be quite misleading and thus fail to offer valid indicators of political development.

In certain cases, however, there is an approximate solution. When the national data are broken down by region, social class or ethnic groupings, for example, such frequency distributions permit us to go on to compute a measure of the intranational inequality. Furthermore, there will sometimes be Lorenz curves or numerical indices accompanying the data.[17] For those nations, years and variables that meet either of these conditions, one strategy might be to calculate each nation's inequality score, multiply it by that nation's population, add up the total and divide it by the number of people constituting the international system. This procedure has, however, a number of serious inadequacies. First, it assumes that intranational breakdowns will be fairly similar, permitting the calculation of comparable indices. Second, it assumes that most of the maldistributions will run in the same direction. And, third, because of these and other difficulties it will tend to underestimate the irregularities when converted from the national to the international level. While any competent statistician could add to this catalog, we are not at all certain how they would propose to handle those cases in which there are no within-nation breakdowns.

Confronted with gross national data, or even national per capita data, there seem to be two possible strategies, neither of which is fully satisfactory. One is to try to estimate intranational inequalities by looking at a variable whose inequalities are known and which are likely to correlate highly with those of the variable under consideration (such as land ownership or education) and then proceed as above. The other is even more approximate and requires that we ignore intranational inequalities and go on to plot those of an international nature, weighting for each nation's population. Quite clearly, these are only stop-gap solutions, and while the quality of some of the data available may not justify anything more refined, any improvement in the reliability and validity of the proposed indicators requires us to either "clean up" existing figures or search out better ones, and at the same time try to solve the problem of inequality indices.

So much, then, for the proposed intrinsic indicators of political development in the global system. Recognizing that they reflect an unspecified mix of traditional doctrine, classical concern, scientific generalization and personal preference, they should nevertheless provide a point of departure and an interesting challenge to scholars of both an empirical and a normative bent, as well as those from a variety of disciplines. Let us turn now to the political development indicators of a more instrumental nature.

IDENTIFYING THE EFFECTIVE INSTRUMENTALITIES

In the opening section, I suggested that one must not only differentiate between intrinsic and instrumental indicators of the political development of any social system, but that those of the latter class which are generally used in comparative politics need to be examined with considerable skepticism. Even if the intrinsic indicators proposed here are largely normative in origin, the validity of the instrumental ones can only be evaluated on the basis of empirical evidence. What is needed, then, is a systematic search of the literature in comparative politics, political philosophy, political development and international law and organization, as a first step toward identifying those structural, cultural and behavioral conditions which allegedly contribute to the quality of life. Many of the potential indicators turned up in such a survey could, of course, be quickly dismissed on the grounds that they are obviously self-serving for the political elites, have since been shown to have no appreciable link, direct or otherwise, to the lives of the general publics, or have been shown to have an overall negative correlation which the intrinsic values.

Another problem which crops up often in this connection is the fact that few of the researchers from whom we might be borrowing make (or even recognize) a distinction between *indicators* of, and *predictors* of, political development. While some of the literature seems preoccupied with the matter of ascertaining how politically developed a given national social system *is*, some of it—often in the same work, but not explicitly differentiated—seems concerned with identifying those factors which lead that system to become developed. Rather than dwell on that particular sort of confusion each time it arises, let us note here that while our preoccupation is strictly with indicators and not with predictors, we will be considering a number of variables which their users might be using in either or both roles.[18]

Types of Instrumental Indicators

There are, of course, many ways in which to categorize those aspects of a social system which affect (for better or worse) the quality of life of those who comprise the system. The taxonomy used here is that used in a number of earlier papers[19] and seems to be relatively straightforward and operational. Very simply, it differentiates among the attributes of any given system and the relationships, interactions and behaviors that occur within it.

Every social system may be described, and compared to others, in terms of three sets of attributes: physical, structural and cultural. The physical ones embrace geographic, demographic and technological properties; the structural embrace organizational and institutional (but not necessarily static) phenomena, and the cultural (somewhat as in much of the recent literature on comparative politics) embrace the distribution of personalities, attitudes and opinions found among those who comprise the particular social entity. Entities may not only be compared to one another at the same time and at the same level of analysis, but also across different levels of analysis and with themselves at different points in time.

These entities behave and interact and experience relationships with one another. Their relationships—or bonds or interdependencies—may well emerge out of prior interactions, but relationships should not be confused with interactions; the former tend to be stable and slow-changing, while the latter are more instantaneous. Furthermore, we may infer and describe the structural attributes of a system by observing the relationships amongst the people or subsystems which are its component units, describe its cultural attributes by observing the psychological attributes of the individuals who comprise it[20] and describe many of its physical attributes by observing the distribution of such attributes among its component units.

Needless to say, there is an intimate set of causal connections among these phenomena. Behavior (and therefore interaction) is certainly a function of the immediate social structure and culture within which it occurs, and to the extent that his personality, attitudes and opinions affect each individual's behavior, there too we see the indirect influence of structure and culture on behavior. Moreover, any regularity of behavior manifested by some fraction of a population inevitably has some effect (reinforcing or modifying) on the structural and cultural attributes of the system. Finally, structure is often a consequence of the cultural patterns and, conversely, it is difficult to see how culture could fail to be at least partially shaped by the formal and informal structure of the system under examination.

We make the above digression not only to define certain key terms but also to illuminate the ways in which the political phenomena of an instrumental nature which are associated with any social system can impinge on, positively or negatively, the intrinsic values outlined earlier. Let us now look at several possible instrumental indicators for the international system, via a brief glance at some of the representative ones which are found in the comparative national political literature.[21]

Some Indicators from National Politics

One of the most widely used paradigms of the politically developed social system comes to us from Weber, via Parsons, and embraces structural, cultural and behavioral variables. Reference is to the bureaucratic society, manifesting the following general characteristics. First, there is a high degree of functional specialization and differentiation in the political structure, with a fairly large number of independent organizations and agencies, which are, in some versions, well coordinated through strong leadership. Second, associated with this structural condition are cultural norms which emphasize rationality over superstition in the rise to power and impersonal universality over a personalized particularism in the application of rules. Usually associated with these attributes are such cultural phenomena as loyalty to the regime, widely shared social values, a sense of collective identity and mutual trust, belief in the democratic process, a conviction of the importance of mass participation in the political process[22] and often an acceptance of broad political mobilization.[23] Among the structural attributes generally connected with the idea of a politically developed society are interest aggregation and interest articulation,[24] a high degree of pluralism in the sense of many cross-cutting associations and an accompanying degree of cross-pressure on many of the citizens.

This is but a sampling of the possible indicators which turn up most frequently in the comparative political literature. It could be expanded not only by a more sustained perusal of that literature but by converting many of these rather broad verbal concepts into more specific operational measures of an ordinal or interval nature.

The Relevance of National Indicators for the International System

As the earlier discussion on inequalities in the distribution of intrinsic values suggested, there are some difficult empirical questions involved in the application of nationally based information to the larger system. But the conversion of our measures is only part of the problem; of equal importance and greater concern for the moment is the matter of theoretical applicability.

In recent years we have seen a number of excellent articles trying to formalize some of the critical similarities and differences between national and international politics.[25] Needless to say, attention has been directed more to the differences than to the similarities, and even though our impression is that the differences tend to be overdrawn—partially because of the short time orientation of most political scientists—they are far from negligible.

In any event, if we use the traditional definition of government as it is understood in the national context, it is clear that many of the attributes of government by which we appraise political development just cannot be utilized at the global level. But if we think of it in a more literal sense and note the great range in types and efficacy of those institutions by which men try to govern their public relationships, the comparisons become more feasible.[26] Following that orientation, let us look at the applicability and relevance of those indicators summarized in the prior subsection, especially those emerging from the bureaucratization outlook.

In a very rough way, we might be able to approximate a measure of functional differentiation and specialization by identifying the number of social groups that play a high, medium or low (but some) direct role in international politics. Those organizations which interact across national boundaries, or which impinge directly (rather than in a mediated fashion) on national governments other than that of the territory in which they are located, could be classified as to their size or wealth, activity type and intensity or frequency of such direct involvement. The point here is that this particular political development indicator would be very low when almost all international political activity is in the hands of national governments, but would rise as IGOs (international intergovernmental organizations), their specialized agencies, transnational corporations, professional associations and the like, increased in number, size, and direct involvement. Likewise, as such functional differentiation rose, we might expect that the loyalties and interests of individuals and smaller groups would become more complex and multidirectional, leading to upward changes in any sort of pluralism index.[27]

But the other side of the coin also deserves attention. That is, to what extent would increases in the functional specialization and pluralism of the system be accompanied by the conditions which present the appearance of near anarchy? Thus, indices of effective centralized control as well as of shifts toward or away from a global loyalty would have to receive equal attention, as would the extent of shared norms regarding resource allocation, conflict resolution and the like.[28] We might get at this by some such rough indicator as the ratio between expenditures of supranational political organizations and those of national governments[29] or perhaps by staff size. But a more valid, if less reliable, index might emerge from some effort to identify the range of activities of the many overlapping and partially contending political aggregations in the system, and to measure the frequency with which each prevails in early bargaining or in a showdown.[30]

One of the ways in which social systems can often handle the sort of change outlined here, and the appearance of new and somewhat countervailing tendencies, is through interest articulation and aggregation. One would expect the former to correlate in a positive and fairly strong fashion with the growth in the number of direct actors, ranging from professional pressure groups to specialized IGOs. Interest aggregation would not, on the other hand, be an almost inevitable consequence of the growth in the number of direct actors. One might more reasonably expect a considerable time lag before the middle and upper elites of the world began to discern the erosion of power which national states and other territorially based entities were suffering as the more functionally specific entities moved into positions of influence. Once that trend was, however, both established and recognized, the formation of political parties could be expected to follow at a rapid rate. Based on a mix of considerations including region, race, language, income, education, profession, personality and so forth, as such parties grew in domain, scope and power[31] interest aggregation would appear as a political reality at the global level. But some scholars have pointed out that important variations in party organization, role and strength can occur, and some of these might well suggest additional indicators. Cutright, for example, uses the strength of minority party representation in legislative bodies, plus the degree of interparty competition in the selection of executive officials as measures

of political development at the national level,[32] and many would
also look at the mere number of parties in the system.[33]

A closely associated structural condition in developed national
societies is vertical social mobility, and this might well be measured in two ways when applied to the larger system. One would be
the standard sociological way in which we ascertain individual
changes in social status, education, employment, income, etc. The
other would take nations or other social entities as the unit of analysis and try to ascertain their changing positions in hierarchies
based on power[34], diplomatic importance,[35] wealth, standard of living[36] and the like. Also of interest in this context is the structural
notion of lateral mobility in which we measure the rate at which
nations or other entities move into or out of alliances,[37] trade networks, voting blocs,[38] diplomatic networks,[39] etc. Finally, one
thinks of the idea of subsystem autonomy as an indicator,[40] but we
must then go on to ask which of the international system's subsystems are the ones whose autonomy might be more conducive to a
maximization of the intrinsic values.

In addition to the above indicators, there are those less exotic
ones which have enjoyed a traditional place in the literature of international politics and law, or which flow from the more recent
literature on political integration and international organization.[41]
Even a straightforward count of the number of IGOs weighted by
the number and importance of their memberships could offer a
useful guide.[42] Beyond that, we might examine the content, scope
and applicability of the international and transnational law[43] of the
past, as well as the yet unknown types of formalized norms that
can be expected to spring up in the future. In this regard, a content
analysis of elite and public attitudes toward such norms, combined
with an analysis of the extent to which these norms are actually
adhered to, would offer further and critical evidence as to the
governance of the global system. Similarly, it would be a mistake
to overlook the substance, depth and reconcilability of divisions as
revealed in debate, negotiation and voting in many extranational
and supranational organizations.[44]

One could, of course, go on cataloguing the possible ways in
which development of the international (or global) system might be
measured, but this survey will have to suffice for the moment. In
closing this section it is necessary to emphasize that we have at
hand a good many contenders among our alternative instrumental
indicators, and that the measurement and data problems have

barely been touched to date. For the international system, as for its national and other subsystems, we have yet to develop adequate descriptions by which each can be compared with itself over time and with others at the same point in time.[45] As we urged in the introductory paragraphs, until we have described a set of phenomena we can say very little about either the antecedents or the consequences of those phemonena, no less enter into ambitious explanatory enterprises.

CONCLUSION

The social sciences in general and political science in particular are at a critical stage in their development. As the quality and quantity of the knowledge we acquire have shown a promising increase, too many of us have been remiss in designing our research and in teaching our students. While these sins are not nearly as extensive as the intellectuals of the New Left might have us believe, the charges are far from unfounded. The literature in comparative politics and its subfield of political development, as we see it, is particularly inadequate in the senses noted in our introduction, and particularly on ethical matters, neglecting as it does the crucial distinction between national or elite group interests on the one hand and individual values on the other. Our purpose here is not only to make that distinction and apply it to the international system but also to prod those whose empirical focus remains at the national level of analysis.

As to any findings, it is perfectly clear that we have little evidence for believing that we know very much about the conditions or consequences of political development as defined here. First of all, it is difficult to know whether, on balance, we have made much progress toward improving the quality of life for most of the world's citizens. Second, whatever trends toward or away from the maximization of the intrinsic values have occurred, we have almost no data on the kinds of instrumentalities which predict or account for such trends. Even if we shift our level of analysis from the system to the nations themselves, we find little in the way of longitudinal data which might permit us to say whether certain political structures, sets of social beliefs or patterns of behavior are conducive to the realization of these values or not. At the international level, we have found, for example, that the establishment of structural arrangements such as IGOs shows almost no correlation with fluctuations and trends in the incidence of war,[46] and that alliances, while helpful in this regard during the nineteenth century, have actually been associated with an increase in war during the current century.[47] But even these modest investigations seem to have not yet been paralleled at the national level. Thus, let me conclude with a plea for considerable tentativeness in establishing and proposing instrumental indices of political development. Until we have not only agreed on the ends, but demonstrated which structural, cultural and behavioral patterns are most conducive to the realization of these ends, it is premature to equate modernization or Westernization with political development any place in the world.

Finally, my conviction is that we must, in one fashion or another, break away from the normative assumptions that seem to be implicit in so many of the formulations found in contemporary social science. Whether the orientation is toward national interests, social order, political stability, economic growth or one or another of the many structural-functional paradigms, we seem to be in increasing danger of forgetting that the basic unit of any social system is the individual human being and that any scientific formulation must take cognizance of that fact. In my judgment, no theory that ignores the single person is scientifically adequate or morally defensible. In sum, what is proposed here is that we begin some systematic research that can simultaneously "think big" and "think small," and which embraces in a rigorous synthesis both the lone individual and all of mankind. One of the more valuable byproducts of such research might be the demise of the invidious distinction between empirical and normative theory in the social sciences.

NOTES

[1]One critic accuses most modern social scientists as failing to see that politics is, at least in potential, "an instrument of reason, legitimately dedicated to the improvement of social conditions." See C. Bay, "Politics and Pseudopolitics: A Critical Evaluation of Some Behavioral Literature," *American Political Science Review* 59 (March 1965): 14.

[2]D. Easton, *The Political System* (New York: Knopf, 1953), p. 220, for example, he urges that one effect of more rigorous methodology is to impose upon political science "an obligation to re-examine and revise the way moral theory has been studied." As a matter of fact, two members of the original panel had already published important books representing a conscious effort to evaluate social science in terms of fundamental ethical criteria and to apply such knowledge to an improvement in the human condition; see A. Etzioni, *The Active Society* (New York: The Free Press, 1968) and H. C. Kelman, *A Time to Speak* (San Francisco, Calif.: Jossey-Bass, 1968). A useful anthology on the relationship between contemporary social needs and the *physical* and *biological* sciences is N. Kaplan, ed., *Science and Society* (Chicago: Rand McNally, 1965).

[3]While we would prefer to refer here to the global, rather than the international system, the relevant data sets are almost inevitably restricted to, and arranged in terms of, national states and their citizens only. See J.D. Singer, "The Global System and its Sub-Systems: A Developmental View," in *Linkage Politics: Essays in National and International Systems*, ed. James N. Rosenau (New York: Free Press, 1969).

[4]Lest there be any misunderstanding, these statements are to be read in the most probabilistic sense. I see social events as a mix of the deterministic, the stochastic and the voluntaristic, with several or many factors normally necessary to account for their incidence. This view recognizes that even the most regular and recurrent patterns have their exceptions, and that we are always playing, to some extent, the "numbers game." See J. D. Singer, "Knowledge, Practice, and the Social Sciences in International Politics," *A Design for International Relations Research* (Philadelphia: American Academy of Political and Social Science, 1970), pp. 137-49.

[5]One frequently heard reason is that the data are seldom available, but I would disagree; a combination of diligent research in the archives and monographs, plus some ingenuity in the construction of measures—even if only ordinal or nominal, rather than interval in nature—should remove many of these difficulties. A second is that these systems allegedly change radically over time and are so different across time as to be virtually incomparable. My only response to that allegation is that the nature and magnitude of those differences is an empirical question, and one to be examined, rather than assumed away.

[6]Closely related, but often overlooked, is the fact that what may enhance the values of an overwhelming majority in *one* system may be quite detrimental to a few or many in a neighboring or distant system. Only if we believe that "morality stops at the water's edge" can we take group or national interest arguments seriously.

[7]D. McClelland, *The Achieving Society* (Princeton, N.J.: Van Nostrand, 1961).

[8]Some of the possibilities and pitfalls of the survey approach are evident in the careful and suggestive *Reports on Happiness* by N. Bradburn and D. Caplovitz (Chicago, Ill.: Aldine, 1965). Also relevant are: W. A. Scott, "Empirical Assessment of Values and Ideologies," *American Sociological Review* 24 (1959): 299-310; E. Albert, "The Classification of Values: A Method and an Illustration," *American Anthropologist* 58 (April 1956): 221-24; F. R. Kluckhohn, "A Method for Eliciting Value Orientations," *Anthropological Linguistics* 2 (February 1960): 1-23.

[9]Bay, "Politics and Pseudopolitics."

[10]One fundamental issue, which has long engaged our best economists, but which we side-step here in the need for brevity, is that of the transitivity and dominance of preferences for the individual, and within the group. Among the treatments of this class of problems are: K. Arrow, *Social Choice and Individual Values* (New York: John Wiley, 1951); R. Dahl and C. Lindblom, *Politics, Economics, and Welfare* (New York: Harper and Row, 1953); D. Black, *The Theory of Committees and Elections* (Cambridge, U. K.: Cambridge University Press, 1958); J. Buchanan and G. Tullock, *The Calculus of Consent* (Ann Arbor, Mich.: University of Michigan Press, 1965).

[11]R. W. Gerard, "The Scope of Science," *The Scientific Monthly* 44, no. 6 (1947): 496-515.

[12]Among those who have explicitly dealt with this question are: H. D. Lasswell and A. Kaplan, *Power and Society* (New Haven, Conn.: Yale University Press, 1950); R. C. Angell, "The Moral Integration of American Cities," *American Journal of Sociology* 57, pt. 2 (1951); C. Bay, *The Structure of Freedom* (Standord, Calif.: Stanford University Press, 1958); B. M. Russett et al., *World Handbook of Political and Social Indicators* (New Haven, Conn.: Yale University Press, 1964); D. Braybrooke, *Three Tests for Democracy* (New York: Random House, 1968).

[13]By way of an interim report, if we control for the population of the nations in the system, there is a very modest increase in the incidence of battle-connected deaths over the past century and a half. See. J. D. Singer and M. Small, *The Wages of War, 1815-1965: A Statistical Handbook* (New York: John Wiley, in press, 1972). Some sources of data on domestic violent deaths are: L. F. Richardson, *Statistics of Deadly Quarrels* (Pittsburgh, Pa.: Boxwood Press, 1960); R. J. Rummell, "Dimensions of Conflict Behavior Within and Between Nations," *General Systems Yearbook* 8 (1963): 1-50; I. K. and R. L. Feierabend, "Aggressive Behaviors Within Politics, 1948-1962," *Journal of Conflict Resolution* 10 (September 1966): 249-71; R. Tanter, "Dimensions of Conflict Behavior Within and Between Nations, 1958-60," *Journal of Conflict Resolution* 10 (1966): 41-64; T. Gurr, *The Conditions of Civil Violence: First Tests of a Causal Model* (Princeton, N.J.: Princeton University Press, Center for International Studies, 1967).

[14]A very tentative reading of the infant mortality data shows a less consistent downward trend than might have been expected, with upswings in certain nations appearing in the wake of rapid urbanization.

[15]While verbal speculation on the meaning of liberty and freedom is almost endless, there has been little effort to operationalize the concept; a suggestive exception is F. E. Oppenheim, "Degrees of Power and Freedom," *American Political Science Review* 54 (June 1960): 437-46.

[16]R. Brandt, *Ethical Theory* (Englewood Cliffs, N. J.: Prentice-Hall, 1959), chap. 2.

[17]The Lorenz curve shows graphically the actual distribution in terms of cumulative percentages; for example, that 5 percent of the population suffer 20 percent of the infant mortalities, 10 percent account for 35 percent of them, and so on, and that perhaps the most privileged 40 percent only experience 3 percent of them. The area represented by the difference between this curve and the perfect equality line (running at 45 degrees out from the origin of the vertical and horizontal axes) gives the index of inequality, and is usually computed by the Gini or Schutz equations. See H. R. Alker and B. M. Russett, "On Measuring Inequality," *Behavioral Science* 9 (July 1964): 207-18; and J. D. Singer and J. L. Ray, *Measuring Distributions in Macro-Social Systems* (Ann Arbor, Mich.: Mental Health Research Institute, 1971).

[18]In a longitudinal analysis, of course, this distinction often becomes blurred, since the statistical associations between *predictor* variables and the intrinsic development indicators are often based on varying time lags, while the same instrumental variables used as an *indicator* would be correlated against the intrinsic value without any such lag.

[19]Singer, "The Global System and its Sub-Systems."

[20]J. D. Singer, "Man and World Politics: The Psycho-Cultural Interface," *Journal of Social Issues* 24 (July 1968): 127-56.

[21]Two summaries of a wide variety of indicators (with data) are A. Banks and R. Textor, *A Cross-Polity Survey* (Cambridge, Mass.: MIT Press, 1963) and K. W. Deutsch, "Toward an Inventory of Basic Trends and Patterns in Comparative and International Politics," *American Political Science Review* 54 (March 1960): 34-57; suggestive treatments of the problem in general are: G. H. Almond and J. S. Coleman, *The Politics of Developing Areas* (Princeton, N.J.: Princeton University 1960); L. W. Pye, *Aspects of Political Development* (Boston, Mass.: Little, Brown, 1966); S. P. Huntington, "Political Development and Political Decay," *World Politics* 17 (April 1965): 386-430; R. T. Holt and J. E. Turner, *The Political Basis of Economic Development* (Princeton, N.J.: Van Nostrand, 1966); P. Cutright, "National Political Development: Measurement and Analysis," *American Sociological Review* 28 (April 1963): 253-64. The papers presented at the August 1971 Workshop on Indicators of National Development at Lausanne under the direction of Stein Rokkan promise a real improvement in the subtlety and solidity of such measures in the near future.

[22]G. A. Almond and S. Verba, *The Civic Culture* (Princeton, N.J.: Princeton University Press, 1963).

[23]K. W. Deutsch, "Social Mobilization and Political Development," *American Political Science Review* 55 (September 1961): 493-514.

[24]Almond and Coleman, *The Politics of Developing Areas.*

[25]C. Alger, "Comparison of Intranational and International Politics," *American Political Science Review* 57 (June 1963): 406-19; R. D. Masters, "World Politics as a Primitive Political System," *World Politics* 16 (July 1964): 595-619; T. Parsons, "Order and Community in the International Social System," in *International Politics and Foreign Policy*, ed. Rosenan (New York: Free Press, 1961).

[26]Particularly revelant here is the view that all social systems are essentially coalitions of greater or lesser cohesiveness and integration, and that there probably never has been the sort of unity—voluntary or coerced—which is assumed by the textbook writers and practitioners, especially the unity they attribute to societies other than their own.

[27]A recent article on social and cultural pluralism in the *American Journal of Sociology* turned out to have indicators (with one exception) which are measures of ethnic, religious and linguistic heterogeneity, rather than pluralism, at least as it is understood in sociology and political science. See M. R. Haug, "Social and Cultural Pluralism as a Concept in Social System Analysis," *American Journal of Sociology* 73 (November 1967): 294-304.

[28]The loyalty problem is particularly intriguing in the bureaucratization context, since if rationality is to replace superstition we will have to find some alternative to the superstitious belief in the moral infallibility of tribal (i.e., national) saints and deities.

[29]N. Neunreither, *Budget Expenditures as Indices of Political Integration* (Brussells: International Political Science Association Meeting, September 1967).

[30]Closely associated with decisional effectiveness and control is the point made by some of the "conservative" economists that a politically developed system is one in which the number of "political" decisions is minimized and the number of

"economic" ones is maximized. In their view of political decisions, the will of the majority is imposed on the minority, but in economic ones, each individual allegedly is free to decide for himself. The principle strikes us as a sound one, but there always remains the extent to which unequal distributions of power make a mockery of individual choice.

[31] Lasswell and Kaplan, *Power and Society.*

[32] Cutright, "National Political Development."

[33] A. Lijphart, "Typologies of Democratic Systems," *Comparative Political Studies* 1 (April 1968): 3-44.

[34] C. German, "A Tentative Evaluation of World Power," *Journal of Conflict Resolution* 4 (March 1960): 138-44.

[35] J. D. Singer and M. Small, "The Composition and Status Ordering of the International System, 1815-1940," *World Politics* 18 (January 1966): 236-82.

[36] Russett et al., *World Handbook of Political and Social Indicators.*

[37] J. D. Singer and M. Small, "Formal Alliances, 1815-1939: A Quantitative Description," *Journal of Peace Research* 3 (January 1966): 1-32.

[38] Alker and Russett, "On Measuring Inequality."

[39] C. Alger and S. Brams, "Patterns of Representation in National Capitals and Intergovernmental Organizations," *World Politics* 19 (July 1967): 646-63.

[40] M. A. Kaplan, *System and Process in International Politics* (New York: John Wiley, 1957).

[41] E. Haas, *Beyond the Nation State* (Stanford, Calif.: Stanford University Press, 1964); A. Etzioni, *Political Unification* (New York: Holt, Rinehart & Winston, 1965); J. P. Sewell, *Functionalism and World Politics* (Princeton, N.J.: Princeton University Press, 1965).

[*½] J. D. Singer and M. Wallace, "Intergovernmental Organization and the Preservation of Peace, 1816-1964: Some Bivariate Relationships," *International Organization* 24 (Summer 1970): 520-47.

[43] P. C. Jessup, *Transnational Law* (New Haven, Conn.: Yale University Press, 1956).

[44] H. R. Alker and B. M. Russett, *World Politics in the General Assembly* (New Haven, Conn.: Yale University Press, 1965); T. Hovet Jr., *Africa in the United Nations* (Evanston, Ill.: Northwestern University Press, 1963); R. E. Riggs, *Politics in the United Nations: A Study of the United States's Influence in the General Assembly* (Urbana, Ill.: University of Illinois Press, 1958).

[45] In a volume by J. D. Singer et al., *A Structural History of the International System, 1816-1965*, a good many of them will be presented along with the data by which they are measured.

[46] Singer and Wallace, "Intergovernmental Organization."

[47] J. D. Singer and M. Small, "Alliance Aggregation and the Onset of War, 1815-1945," in *Quantitative International Politics*, ed. J. D. Singer (New York: Free Press, 1968).

18

The Underdeveloped Political
Science of Development

RAYMOND B. PRATT

In the decade of the 1960s a great deal was written by U.S. political scientists about modernization and development. After examining the high points of this literature, such as works of or sponsored by the Committee on Comparative Politics of the Social Science Research Council,[1] it is easy to conclude that much of it is of distinctly limited utility for two purposes of overwhelming significance for that majority of the world's population who live in the underdeveloped or Third World (and who are purportedly the subject of this literature):

1. Understanding, at the level of the international economy, the extremely uneven distribution[2] of wealth and income between nations and peoples of the contemporary world—a well-documented and increasing situation of inequality.

2. Providing some guidance for formulation of national policies designed to close this income gap and overcome economic dependency on and domination by the nations of the North Atlantic (the United States in particular) and achieve the necessary high rates of capital accumulation and investment required to overcome the severe social problems confronting them. That these are both political *and* economic problems seems obvious; it suggests political scientists working in the development area should speak of the *political economy* of development.

There is a certain irony in the fact that in spite of the conceptual infatuation among political scientists with topics of development, we have neither had nor seen any significant body of studies by political scientists which shed any light on this international maldistribution of wealth. Indeed, with few exceptions political scientists have said nothing about the origins and persistence of world economic inequality. Yet, this is an issue which, directly or in terms of its consequences, could be considered central to the politics of the contemporary period. How do we explain the political irrelevance of most of these political science development studies?

On the basis of my survey of existing literature, studies of underdeveloped areas by those within the discipline of political science have shown little concern with the human dimension of development, with the costs and benefits to different social groups entailed in divergent developmental and allocative strategies. It should be understood the use of the term "development" does not refer to political development in the sense of political institutions and structures. There is no intent to imply by the term the degree to which United States-style political institutions exist or are being approached. Far from it. The concern is with *outputs*—outputs of political goods, those goods "that satisfy 'needs'—not just the needs of the state as such, matters that will enable it to persist, but *human* needs whose fulfillment makes the polity valuable to man and gives it its justification. . . ."[3] These are not merely material goods but also more intangible symbolic goods, as well as feelings of dignity and competence and self-fulfillment. That the lack of concern for these dimensions of development is not confined to political science is demonstrated by John G. Gurley[4] in his discussion of economists' views of Chinese development policies.

Within the field of public policy analysis in political science one finds some of these perspectives operating, though there is little of the fundamental criticism of existing sociieties that is required. Yet they have not been extended to the international sphere and to questions of development and underdevelopment and the examination of policies and programs designed to achieve high rates of economic growth. A recent major work in public policy analysis[5] directs the attention of political scientists to really fundamental political questions of the allocation of resources or "who gets what" at the expense of which social groups. This approach should be extended to analysis of the political-economic relations of developed and underdeveloped nations, focusing particularly on the political and economic role of the giant multinational corporations, the analysis of the political and social effects of international policies and programs such as those of the Agency for International Development (AID), multinational leading agencies and development banks and United Nations programs, *all* ostensibly directed at helping the underdeveloped nation out of its underdevelopment.

Yet, as significant as this area of inquiry may seem, there are few solid scholarly studies by social scientists in these areas. If we look at the list of what might be termed "intersystem"[6] or international political-economic studies, the field, though beginning to grow, is practically barren when it comes to contributions by political scientists. For example, in spite of the gigantic proportions of multinational oligopolies like Standard Oil of New Jersey, which in terms of gross assets dwarf the budgets and the GNPs of the majority of members of the United Nations, not a single, independent academic monograph exists on the political impact of Jersey Standard in a particular national context, as David Horowitz has pointed out.[7] Nor are there many studies of U.S. AID programs or multinational leading agencies and development banks.

What are the real effects of these programs in terms of political, social and economic outcomes in host countries? What social sectors are the prime beneficiaries of these programs? What social patterns are perpetuated by them at what costs to other social groups? In spite of a new wave of interest in such topics stimulated by the Vietnam War, these questions remain virtually unexplored in scholarly social science literature.

Certainly this area contains phenomena central to "politics": the processes of appropriation, allocation and distribution of valued goods and services, the distribution of wealth, the meeting of human needs and wants with political goods and all the related political conflicts. As far as the fields of comparative and international politics are concerned, it has not, until quite recently, constituted a significant field of inquiry, illustrating what some[8] have referred to as political scientists' substantively empty vision of which phenomena should constitute the central core of the discipline.

While there may be no general agreement on what constitutes political acts, there is an element of commonality in some of the difinitions of recent decades such as those of Harold Lasswell, David Easton's "authoritative allocation of values" or Christian Bay's concern with activity directed at meeting human needs in accord with some conception of the public good.[9] That common element seems to be the concern with outputs—what people in a society get out of a system of relationships and why they get what they do. It seems increasingly important that this notion should be central to our concerns internationally as we examine the political-economic relations of dominant or metropolis states with the dependent or satellite nations loosely defined as the Third World.[10]

We should not assume that among scholars in social science disciplines other than political science the topics that concern us here have somewhat higher stature. As Charles Moskos and Wendell Bell have pointed out in an article on the ideologies of U.S. social scientists and studies of underdeveloped areas, such concerns are by no means central to activities of disciplines like sociology or even economics.[11] In their view, "one of the most outstanding features in the writings of American social scientists [is] . . . the failure to explore the contingencies on political and social development resulting from the growing gap between the rich and the poor nations." Further, while there is a literature on the gap, "it is authored by persons who are outside or on the periphery of American social science. Books on the inequalities of the world order are generally written by Europeans, or by men removed from the mainstream of professional social science, or by social scientists from underdeveloped countries. . . ."[12] Why should this be so?

Conventional political science approaches to development of the past decade have suffered from several misplaced emphases. The first of these lies in the failure to recognize that the politics of development at base involves power and wealth—who controls it and how it is used. Politics is *about* something, and that is usually related to economics. Economic development in the broad sense of attaining high rates of growth and achieving control over national resources (questions of accumulation of savings, or capital, and its allocation) and national independence from colonial or neocolonial economic relations, was *never* the "uncontroversial and presumably narrowly technical problem" that some have suggested it is.[13] Beyond that, the political issues mentioned in most political science development literature are really only *internal* to the underdeveloped nation and say nothing of *international* political considerations involving the penetration of underdeveloped nations by developed nations' military and economic aid programs, international financial organizations like the World Bank and multinational corporations centered in the United States and Western

Europe. The political and "the purely economic" as well as the national and international are inextricably intertwined. Indeed, in such programs as the AID Specific Risk Investment Guarantee Program and, more recently, the Overseas Private Investment Corporation (OPIC), the government of the United States assures U.S. investors against the inability to convert into dollars other currencies or credits in such currencies received as earnings or profits, or loss of investment in "approved" projects due to expropriation or confiscation by foreign government and loss due to war, revolution and insurrection.

Here are examples of misdirected emphasis in political science development literature:

1. Some stress the alleged radically new position in which underdeveloped societies are supposed to find themselves at the termination of *formal* foreign colonial political domination. Thus one could point to Lucian Pye's work[14] as a model of mystification and studied ambiguity in ignoring the more important continuities that persist in the social and economic structure of new nations. Indeed, independence has often existed merely in terms of political forms. These nations remain enmeshed in an international system of raw materials production and export for markets over which they have little control. One has only to look at the suggestive little study by Fitch and Oppenheimer to get an excellent sense of how this relationship operates and implications of the Nkruma government's failure to deal with it in Ghana. Yet, Pye asks, "how can the student regain the inherent advantages of historical perspective when he is dealing with societies that do not seem to be responding to conventional concepts of historical growth and evolution?"[16] Such vacuities have not advanced our understanding or problems of underdeveloped nations. The conventional concepts and paradigms Pye mentions are obviously no good!

2. Some stress the significance of the low level of institutionalization of political organization and procedures and its importance for economic development. In the best recent example, [16] the "degree" of government is put forward as the most important quality differentiating the nations of the world. Undoubtedly, well-organized institutionalized political movements have produced profound economic changes, but these have come about in nations such as the Soviet Union or China, and perhaps Mexico, which experienced profound social revolutions in which the political apparatus for governing the new society was forged. In addition, these

nations have sufficient size, population and internal markets so as not to be dependent on a single or few export commodities and to occupy a position of dependence vis-à-vis a tightly organized and controlled world production and marketing system. In the case of many nations of Latin America, as Merle Kling pointed out, the contradiction between "the realities of a colonial economy and the political requirements of legal sovereignty" has produced a chronic political instability.[17] And this is to leave aside the question of the profound effects on political stability of covert internal manipulation or outright acts of armed intervention to achieve its ends on the part of the United States in that area (the massive suppression of the 1965 revolt in the Dominican Republic and current counterinsurgency and "internal security" aid and training are good examples).

3. Some point to the importance of a supposed scarcity of crucial entrepreneurial skills.[18] But one wouldn't doubt entrepreneurs are certain to be scarce in areas laboring under a colonial heritage of 400 years. Where *real* economic opportunities arise, entrepreneurs appear.

4. Characteristics peculiar to the people of underdeveloped nations are often seen as having great importance for understanding underdevelopment. Some point to the non-Western, nonindustrial time perspective. Others stress the importance of achievement motivation implying sequential relation between its presence in developed economies and their development that has never been adequately demonstrated.[19] Still others[20] place great emphasis on cultural factors that supposedly inhibit cooperative behavior which, by implication, has great importance for understanding the underdevelopment of southern Italy. Weiner's notion of integrative behavior states much the same thing.[21]

The stressing of individual attitudes or behavior allegedly important to, or associated with, developed nations (with implications that such factors somehow cause development, or will lead to it) is to emphasize what, while it may be, or may have been, significant in the United States, seems likely to be trivial compared to the role of structural and institutional factors with much greater importance for producing and maintaining underdevelopment.

5. Certainly significant, but also of secondary importance, is the emphasis on the efficiency and smooth functioning of public bureaucracies[22] and the level of government capabilities.[23]

These approaches all share a common characteristic: without

reference to the international context of present patterns or their historical origins, certain specific social traits discovered to be associated with contemporary economic underdevelopment are implicitly or explicitly put forward as its causes. This sort of approach neglects the totality of the international context and relations of underdevelopment. This is really circular reasoning; these factors are really properties of the phenomenon developmentalists are seeking to explain. It amounts, as Paul Baran pointedly remarked,[24] to identifying poverty as being associated with squalor, and then thinking one has explained its existence!

Ignoring the question of the empirical adequacy of these studies, i.e., whether these investigators were really warranted in reporting what they *said* they found, the subnational level of analysis and the variables in terms of which these developmentalists ply their explanatory trade would seem to make it difficult not to reach similar conclusions. A more fundamental question to be asked is what these results mean interpreted in a context wider than that of the single underdeveloped nation—that is, in terms of an international system of economic and political relations.

There has been a serious failure in political science development literature to appreciate the crucial importance of the *international* context of underdevelopment and its historical dimensions. Roots of contemporary underdevelopment often lie in colonial relations established nearly 500 years ago. Latin America provides a prime example[25] but an examination of the history of other areas in Asia and Africa is revealing. To classify these countries as traditional societies as many political scientists have begs the issue and implies either that the underdeveloped countries have no history or that it is unimportant. Yet,

> evidence is gradually being accumulated that the expansion of Europe, commencing in the fifteenth century, had a profound impact on the societies and economies of the rest of the world. In other words, the history of the underdeveloped countries in the last five centuries is, in large part, the history of the consequences of European expansion. . . .[26]

It seems clear that comparative politics of development could benefit from a strong infusion of ideas reasserting the primacy of political economy—a "turning on its head" of the corpus of theoretical approaches emphasizing subnational, noneconomic factors characteristic of the political science of development of the last decade. To understand the nature of economic dependency and underdevelopment, political scientists must break out of the limitations of conventional approaches, emphasizing subnational and national levels of analysis to seek out *intersystemic linkages* through which underdevelopment is perpetuated.

The Problem of Contrasting Approaches to the Study of Underdevelopment

My examination of existing literature suggests that how one approaches and seeks to explain underdevelopment relates not only to one's purposes, ideology and identification with the fortunes of center or periphery nations but also to one's socialization into certain professional paradigms. Thus, one body of explanations arising in the United States has tended to neglect international economic relationships and focus on the underdeveloped nations and their characteristics.[27] Explanations of their status of current economic stagnation and growing internal inequalities (even where progress is evident in terms of GNP and industrial production growth) are cast in terms of scarcities and gaps in certain *internal* factors and forces. These gaps are usually seen as necessitating the strengthening of a particular type of international economic relation involving increased investment of foreign capital and expansion of exports. Programs put forward, or implied, in these works involve maintaining and even strengthening ties which to date have *not* produced the kind of growth that has brought any significant improvements in the level of existence of the mass of their citizens: increased direct foreign investment, various forms of loans (which have involved ever-greater proportions of national budgets being allocated to servicing debts) and economic integration of particular regions (which would be of the greatest benefit to those economic entities with the greatest amounts of ready capital—the multinational corporations centered in the United States, Western Europe and Japan).

From analysts in the underdeveloped world and from a limited but growing sector of U.S. social scientists that might be termed radical, critical or even Marxist realists come formulations with quite different emphasis, stressing international system relationships involving the outflow of internally generated surplus, or capital, through profit remissions, dividends, license fees and internal costs between branches of multinational enterprise; the terms of trade favoring the industrial nations; foreign domination of crucial sectors of underdeveloped nations' economies; national specialized dependence on one or a few raw material or agricultural exports; and the increasing burden placed on national budgets merely to service the external debt. In the application of these critical perspectives among American and British writers, one should note the work of Harry Magdoff,[28] the most succinct and dramatically stated exposition of the systems and mechanisms of economic power and influence through which, it is persuasively argued, advanced industrial powers, often in the guise of aiding underdeveloped nations, maintain their position of dominance in the world economy, the United States in this case being the most powerful of these nations. This relatively brief, though powerful statement provides more in terms of insights and examples of the mechanisms of contemporary economic domination and dependency between the United States, Europe and the Third World than any, and perhaps all, works published by political scientists during the 1960s. Yet, for all that, it requires a great amount of elaboration, specification and testing through studies of the operation of particular mechanisms Magdoff sees functioning to maintain dependency and underdevelopment in particular national contexts. Simply proceeding with Magdoff's framework and seeking to detail the operation of particular mechanisms through monographic studies in national or area contexts opens the way for literally hundreds of studies.[29]

Among Latin Americans, a group that might be termed the dependency theorists includes, among others, Celso Furtado, Fernando Henrique Cardoso, Enzo Faleto, Aníbal Quijano, Aníbal Pinto, Osvaldo Sunkel and Teotonio Dos Santos. Dependency, as these writers put it, is

> a situation in which the economy of a certain group of countries is conditioned by the development and expansion of another economy, to which their own [economy] is subjected . . . it is an historical condition which shapes a certain structure of the world economy such that it favors some countries to the detriment of others, and limits the development possibilities of the [subordinate] economies . . . .[30]

Dependency means, essentially, "that the alternatives open to the dependent nation are defined and limited by its integration into and functions within the world market."[31]

In terms of concrete policy proposals, these analysts have suggested a variety of national policies for achieving economic independence, closing off outflows of surplus and attaining rapid growth, all stressing internal structural reforms, particularly in the agricultural sector, and the reduction of imports through increasing agricultural productivity, industrial development and various strategies for regaining national control of different sectors of economies dominated by foreign interests.[32] Most recognize but perhaps fail to place enough emphasis on the crucial importance of mobilizing national populations to support or bring to power governments committed to development stretegies embodying such proposals such as exist in different ways in contemporary Peru, Chile and Cuba.

These contrasting approaches to the problem of underdevelopment present us with an interesting problem in the sociology of knowledge. While they deserve close attention in a substantive sense, they also raise some questions about the operation of political science as a scientific enterprise. It seems clear that political science developmentalists, with some exceptions, failed to adequately consider the fundamental international and complementary internal structural relations which have produced and maintained an international system of stratification of rich and impoverished nations. Why should this be the case?

The failure of U.S. political science in this area stems from the hegemony of a conception of the kind of inquiry that ought to be pursued, a conception that denies the legitimacy of the critical perspective on the study of politics and societies one finds in Marx or the architectonic impulse of classical theorists. In spite of the inadequacies of many of Marx's specific findings and predictions for understanding our contemporary situation, the method and strategy of analysis pursued by Marx remain particularly valuable. As Barrington Moore points out, even granting concessions to most critics of Marx, what remains is

> still very impressive. The conception of social class as arising out of an historically specific set of economic relationships and of the class struggle as the basic stuff of politics, constitute some of the most important ideas that students of history and political behavior carry around in their heads, whether they are Marxists or not.[33]

One of the most crucial aspects of Marx's strategy of analysis as a social scientist is that he started with "the conviction the social institutions of his day were evil." Yet, as Moore indicates, Marx

> believed that this evil was both transitory and unnecessary. At the same time he thought of himself as a scientist—a savage one to be sure, constantly using hard facts to strip away the veil of

hypocrisy and unconscious self-deception that concealed the ugly realities underneath. For Marx there was no conflict between his position as a moralist and a scientist. The whole enterprise of science made sense for him *only* in terms of moral convictions.[34]

In this Marx differs profoundly from the dominant spirit in contemporary political science. Much of the irrelevance of the work in the comparative politics of development stems from the absence of this kind of critical perspective. Essentially, in these works we see a failure to think theoretically as Sheldon Wolin uses the term.[35] The great epic political theorists, Wolin[36] argues, have been concerned with what they regarded as political systems that are systematically mistaken or deranged. As he puts it, when particular problems are seen as "the *necessary* result of a more extensive set of evils which can confidently be expected to continue producing similar results. Such a system would be *systematically* deranged."

The real issue here from the point of view contemporary political science is, Wolin says,

> not between theories which are normative and those which are not; nor is it between those political scientists who are theoretical and those who are not. Rather it is between those who would restrict the "reach" of theory by dwelling on facts, which are selected by what are assumed to be the functional requisites of the existing paradigm, and those who believe that because facts are richer than theories, it is the task of the theoretical imagination to restate new possibilities.[37]

In the broadest sense, the difficulties and weaknesses in the literature under discussion are those of contemporary social science and the mainstream of political science, and lie in the failure to envision new political possibilities and a progressive political purpose for political science knowledge. In effect, to direct our inquiry toward the overcoming of the central problems of the age and fulfillment of human needs. But there are other factors as well. We can only suggest what some of them might involve.

Problems of Strategy and Pretheory

By "pretheory" I am referring to what Ralf Dahrendorf[38] has called "metatheoretical" approaches: those views, even feelings, we all have about the phenomena we study before we begin theorizing or empirical inquiry. The components of such approaches include one's own sense of how order is possible, of what problems are significant and of what the direction of change ought to be. What I am implying is that one kind of pretheoretical position may lead to more fruitful hypotheses than another, to a strategy that opens up new possibilities rather than limits the questions one can consider. As Francesca Cancian[39] pointed out some years ago concerning Talcott Parson's definition of the social system in terms of normative integration or shared values, and how it limits the questions one can consider (in the sense of failing to provide a theoretical basis for deriving explanatory hypotheses about particular types of phenomena): "If shared values define the system, it is difficult to treat major conflict and deviance in the area of values as part of the system. And if one assumes stability of values, major structural change of the system is excluded by definition." In terms of our concerns here, if one adopts the strategy of understanding and explaining underdevelopment mainly in terms of factors and forces internal to the underdeveloped nations, one will be hard-pressed to explain (and, even more so, to provide useful policy guidance in regard to) problems linked to external forces in terms of mechanisms we have already mentioned.

Political Ideologies and Political Context

What are the effects of political ideological context and the ideologies of political science developmentalists on the kinds of studies carried out and the results obtained in the field? It is common for students of the subject to admit privately to the pervasiveness of cold war scholarship. But few will do so in print. Political science lacks and certainly needs extensive study of the role of ideological elements in comparative political literature of the cold war period in spite of this recognition.

Most of the U.S. political scientists I have mentioned have been or are, in the U.S. context, essentially liberals, not at all opposed to some vague conception of progress and development, provided it is not carried out under Communist or revolutionary Socialist auspices. The major impetus to the study of underdevelopment arose out of the cold war competition between capitalism and communism for the Third World. The real question remains: How does (or did) the cold war influence work in this area? What are the mechanisms involved? All ritualistic statements about facts, values, neutrality and objectivity notwithstanding, the political context in which political science is practiced does condition its activity and results and the meaning attached to those results. How does this come about? Why hasn't anyone studied it? Is it a collective failure of nerve? To what degree is it imposed from above by those who decide where to allocate research funds?

The Data-Gathering Enterprise: Distortions and Finances

Certain common units of analysis, especially the individual and his opinions and voting behavior, call for certain research instruments, the attitude survey in particular, which can lead to a most distorted and partial view of the political process and are expensive to utilize, requiring large foundation grants. Beyond this, certain kinds of questions, approaches and techniques are supported by foundation funds, others not. What do we know about the basis for granting or refusing foundation support? What analyses have been done of the influence of foundation decisions on the direction of research in political science?

> The effect of large grants is to give to those in control of the allocation of research funds a highly strategic position for determining *which* problems will be investigated and which ones will not. . . . [It] is difficult to conceive of the foundation director who will readily allocate several hundred thousand dollars for a research project that is likely to come up with conclusions that reflect very seriously on important interest groups in the United States. . . .*?

All these factors impose serious constraints on the study of the comparative politics of development and quite likely have produced severe inadequacies in the literature both in terms of the theoretical formulations arising from it and the utility of those formulations for generating and guiding national development policies in the Third World.

Limitations of the Behavioral Paradigm

The complex of factors discussed seems peculiar to the behavioral approach to political science. It should be understood that this approach is not coextensive with, nor does it exhaust the range of, scientific approaches to the study of politics.

Central among the characteristics of the behavioral approach have been, as Robert Dahl pointed out in a classic statement, its concern with "the study of *individuals* rather than larger political units, and an emphasis on understanding the *psychological* characteristics of homo politicus: attitudes, beliefs, predispositions, personality factors."[41] In addition, Dahl said, "in his concern for analyzing what *is,* the behavioral political scientist has found it difficult to make systematic use of what *has been*: i.e., with history ... despite disclaimers and intentions to the contrary, there seems to me little room for doubt that the actual content of almost all the studies that reflect the behavioral mood is *ahistorical* in character."[42]

Three aspects, in Dahl's view—the particular units (individuals and groups) and levels of analysis (subnational), the types of variables examined (largely psychological) and an essentially ahistorical perspective—have usually characterized behavioral inquiry. A fundamental weakness of this approach lies in its isolation and segmentation of political things resulting in a failure to comprehend the totality of the political process, a common failure of non-Marxian inquiry discussed by Lukacs.[43]

Focusing on individuals rather than structures or on the total system and its linkages with other systems introduces a psychological reductionism that obscures even more important relations than an approach characterized by the most dogmatic economic determinism. To the extent there is dependence on certain kinds of psychological data (particularly attitude survey data), the overriding importance of institutionalized political-economic relations and the exercise of power over the appropriations, allocation and distribution of resources is overlooked.

Achieving a historical perspective on underdevelopment is one very important way of understanding its nature. Through achieving an understanding of the roots of past dependency relations and their variation over time, the development policy analyst may be provided with significant insights into ways current conditions of dependency might be overcome.

As the authors of *The American Voter* pointed out with respect to voting studies (and the same could be said with even *greater* relevance for political science approaches to development):

It is evident that *variables of great importance in human affairs may exhibit little or no change in a given historical period.* As a result, the investigator whose work falls in this period *may not see the significance of these variables* and may fail to incorporate them in his theoretical statements. And even if he does perceive their importance, the *absence of variation will prevent a proper test of hypotheses* that state the relation of these factors to other variables of his theory.[44]

One cannot gain an adequate understanding of, for instance, the underdevelopment of India and the relative priority of various variables in terms of which it could be explained by examining only twentieth-century India without making reference to its economic status before the onset of British colonization the significance of the destruction of native industry.[45]

TOWARD AN INTERNATIONAL POLITICAL ECONOMY OF DEVELOPMENT

In seeking to understand the origins of underdevelopment, its maintenance and, most important, what to do about it in terms of formulating effective and productive national policies of development, there are far more useful ways of conceptualizing it than analysis at the level of single nations.

Central to any discussion that attempts to do this must, first, be some recognition of the *international* context of underdevelopment. Second, we must be clear about what it is that political systems and governments oriented to development must do and what they must do it with. Extremely useful for this purpose is the concept of the social or economic surplus:

> The social surplus may be viewed as a residual factor—that which remains from total output after necessary consumption has been substracted. In every organization or society, past or present, the total annual production of goods and services may be either consumed or saved in the form of additions to the country's stock of capital. . . . The main features of economic development have to do with the size and distribution of the social surplus. Thus it is that a model of development must be examined in terms of its impact on the size and distribution of the social *surplus.*[46]

The concept of surplus is central to the analysis of underdevelopment put forward by Paul Baran, Celso Furtado and a recent analysis of Soviet development and its relevance to underdeveloped nations by Charles Wilber.[47] Its heuristic utility is undeniable. Yet political scientists have failed to face up to the fact that the politics of development involves economic considerations which are also undeniably political insofar as they involve questions of who shall appropriate the surplus and how it shall be allocated.

Beyond this, a crucial utilization of this concept lies in the notion of a "*potential* economic surplus." As Baran defines it, *potential* economic surplus is the difference between the output that *could* be produced in a given natural and technological environment with the help of employable productive resources, and what might be regarded as essential consumption. Its realization presupposes a more or less drastic *reorganization* of the production and distribution of social output, and *implies far-reaching changes in the* structure of society.[48]

The existing social order is no longer to be taken as a given. The very use of the concept carries implications of the necessity of profound, even revolutionary change.

While it is clear that vast outflows of potentially investable surplus from the Third World to the developed economies have already taken place (and continue), simply closing off such sources of loss of surplus as Magdoff outlines[49] is not a sufficient strategy to begin development. Many nations have been so drained and have fallen so far behind that closing the immense gap that exists would take decades even with maximally efficient utilization of available resources. The development that is attained with the surplus that might now remain or be generated, assuming outflows are stopped, depends on how that surplus is allocated, by whom and according to what system of priorities. The assessment of developmental prospects requires something of a refined class analysis and leads, as well, to some strictly political questions of internal strategies for mobilizing social groups behind certain programs. As Celso Furtado pointed out in a recent essay:

> Economic development in the problematical conditions Latin America is called upon to face at the moment requires . . . the cooperation of large masses of the population and active participation by important sectors of this population. . . . The most difficult tasks are of a political rather than a technical nature.[50]

Given aims of high rates of economic growth and a desire to make expenditures for social welfare, certain directions for surplus utilization seem imperative: a carefully planned and high level of investment in the domestic economy being the major one. That is why the programs of aid backed by the United States involving investment of private capital (not really aid for anyone but U.S. businessmen and bankers and a narrow stratum of the recipient country, as a number of studies suggests[51] and some members of the U.S. Senate recently began to recognize) have been failures in terms of stimulating per capita GNP or industrial or agricultural growth much beyond that required to keep up with population increases. There is evidence from some countries that internal disparities have actually *increased* and significant social sectors have experienced actual *declines* in real income over the post-World War II period.[52]

From the point of view of the development-oriented Third World nation private investment, particularly foreign private investment, has a number of inherent limitations, the major ones lying in its high costs—in the fact that a portion of the surplus produced flows out of the country in the form of dividends, internal fees and payments between divisions of multinational corporations, license fees and royalties. The growth of the giant multinational corporation has made things particularly difficult because of the ability of such organizations to conceal costs and profits by artificial internal charges between branches and the shifting of profits from branches in high-tax to low-tax countries. Michael Tanzer's[53] work on the world petroleum industry provides an excellent description and analysis of the process. Frank[54] cites a number of other distinctive consequences of foreign private capital for underdeveloped countries, all adding up to its incompatibility with a planned, maximally productive development program that works in the interest of the mass of the population.

Given the limitations of approaches relying on direct foreign investment or national private capital, the real hope for underdeveloped nations lies in successful execution of socialist development policies. In spite of periods of chaos in Chinese experience and a recent slowdown in Soviet growth rates, Charles Wilber[55] persuasively argues in his study of the Soviet economy and the relevance of its history to underdeveloped nations that the best hope for maximal economic growth lies in Socialist solutions—in efficient, realistic and humane central planning with maximal utilization of the available surplus. This is also a major point in Gurley's[56] analysis of Chinese development doctrine, though his purposes are to highlight Soviet-Chinese differences.

The fundamentally nation-centered character of U.S. political science studies of underdevelopment has contributed to ignorance of the relevance of the intersystemic factors that have for decades drained surplus from Third World nations and that can only be effectively dealt with through socialization of significant sectors of their economies and effective central planning. In the case of Latin America recent works we have already mentioned by Frank, the historians Stein and Stein and the British economist Keith Griffin,[57] who also emphasizes the similar experience of many nations of Africa and Asia, underscore the contemporary relevance of the colonial heritage of these nations to their current economic mis-development, stagnation and their dependency, illustrating the irrelevance of the nation-centered analysis.

SUMMARY AND CONCLUSIONS

Proceeding from the conventional national level of analysis of underdevelopment that characterized the work of political science developmentalists of the 1950s and 1960s leads to the examination of outward manifestations of underdevelopment without recognition of the fundamental influencing role of the international system of relations of colonial dominance and dependency rooted in the colonial relations of 400 years ago.

The failure to adopt a pretheoretical stance that looks at the totality of underdevelopment and seeks the relations of underdeveloped nations to developed ones, instead of the common micro-system or subsystem analysis only at the level of the dependent nation, many blind the analyst to crucial underlying intersystem relationships which structure and limit the options for action of both national entrepreneurs and governmental policy-makers. These relationships impose severe constraints on the policy alternatives before national, political and economic leadership.

Policies such as those advocated by the United States directed toward aiding the underdeveloped nations which do not attack the fundamental international structural relations of underdevelopment, and which result in or allow the continuation of a net drain of surplus from the Third World, aim largely at applying palliatives on the symptoms of underdevelopment. The overcoming of underdevelopment involves a revolutionary transformation of the internal social structure and external relations of Third World nations which can only be achieved through a variant of a revolutionary Socialist development policy.

Political science developmentalists must move in the direction of a new political economy of development which, while recognizing the costs and benefits of different allocative strategies and policies and the importance of a calculus of choice, does not rest within the limits of what is. It must be a critical theory. It is imperative that political scientists in the development field begin to exercise an architecture political vision, putting forward visions of what might be, directing their work toward ways of making those visions attainable—to tell us, as Lenin did, "what is to be done." There is, indeed, a "political economy of change."[58] but the greatest contributions to it to date have been made not by political scientists but revolutionaries.

NOTES

[1]The SSRC-sponsored works include Gabriel Almond and James Coleman, *The Politics of the Developing Areas* (Princeton, N.J.: Princeton University Press, 1960); Lucien Pye, "Introduction," in *Communications and Political Development*, ed. L. Pye (Princeton, N.J.: Princeton University Press, 1963); Joseph Lapalombara, ed. *Bureaucracy and Political Development* (Princeton, N.J.: Princeton University Press, 1963); James S. Coleman, ed., *Education and Political Development* (Princeton, N.J.: Princeton University Press, 1965); Lucien Pye and Sidney Verba, eds., *Political Culture and Political Development* (Princeton, N.J.: Princeton University Press, 1965); Lapalombara and Weiner (1966). My judgments about the irrelevance of these works for any significant policy guidance in the development area tend to be confirmed by John D. Montgomery, "The Quest for Political Development", *Comparative Politics* 1 (January 1969): 285-295 and Robert Packenham, "Utilities of Political Development Theory for Policy and Policy-Makers" Honolulu: presented at Annual Meetings of Western Political Science Association (April 3-5, 1969).

[2]For documentation of the widening gap in the 1860-1960 period see L.T. Zimmerman, *Poorlands Richlands: The Widening Gap* (New York: Random House, 1965), pp. 240-44; Irving Louis Horowitz, *Three Worlds of Development* (New York: Oxford University Press, 1966), pp. 164-92; Pierre Jalee, *The Third World in World Economy* (New York: Monthly Review Press, 1969); P. Jalee, *The Pillage of the Third World* (New York: Monthly Review Press, 1968).

[3]J. Roland Pennock, "Political Development, Political Systems, and Political Goods," *World Politics* 18 (April 1966): 415.

[4]John G. Gurley, "Capitalist vs. Maoist Economic Development," in *America's Asia*, ed. Edward Friedman and Mark Selden (New York: Vintage Books, 1971).

[5]William C. Mitchell and Joyce Mitchell, *Political Analysis and Public Policy* (Chicago: Rand McNally, 1969).

[6]For one example of the notion of intersystem relations, taking the position that the structure of political-economic relations between the United States and Latin America should be considered an independent variable and purely national features of social structure and politics a merely intervening role, see James Petras, "U.S.-Latin American Studies: A Critical Assessment," *Science and Society* 32 (Spring 1968): 148-68.

[7]David Horowitz, "Social Science of Ideology," *Social Policy*, September,October 1970, pp. 30-37.

[8]John G. Gunnell, "Reason and Commitment: Political Values and the Problem of Justification," New York: paper presented at the annual meetings of the American Political Science Association, September 2-6, 1969, pp. 17-20.

[9]Harold Lasswell, *Politics: Who Gets What, When and How?* (New York:

Meridian Books, 1958); David Easton, *The Political System* (New York: Knopf, 1953); Christian Bay, "Politics and Pseudo-Politics: A Critical Evaluation of Some Behavioral Literature," *American Political Science Review* 59 (March 1965): 39-51.

[10]A number of scholars stress the importance of examining the linkage of underdevelopment in the Third World with development in the nations of the North Atlantic, none of them political scientists. See particularly André Gunder Frank, *Capitalism and Underdevelopment in Latin America*, rev. ed. (New York: Monthly Review Press, 1969); Gabriel Kolko, "The United States and World Economic Power," in *The Roots of American Foreign Policy* (Boston: Beacon Press, 1969), pp. 48-87; Stanley J. Stein and Barbara H. Stein, *The Colonial Heritage* of Latin America: *Essays on Economic Dependence in Perspective* (New York: Oxford University Press, 1970); Paul Baran, *The Political Economy of Growth*, rev. ed. (New York: Monthly Review Press, 1962); André Gunder Frank, "Sociology of Development and Underdevelopment of Sociology," in *Latin America: Underdevelopment or Revolution* (New York: Monthly Review Press 1969), pp. 21-94 reviews. Several studies demonstrating "the crucial role played by the underdeveloped countries in financing the capitalization of the new developed ones" in past centuries. The same process Frank argues persuasively is at work today.

[11]Charles Moskos and Wendell Bell, "Emerging Nations and Ideologies of American Social Scientists," *American Sociologist*, May 1967, pp. 67-72.

[12]Among works by U.S. social scientists the authors could at the time find only Baran, *The Political Economy of Growth*; Robert Theobald, *The Rich and the Poor* (New York: Mentor Books, 1960); I.L. Horowitz, *Three Worlds of Development* (New York: Oxford University Press, 1966). Baran's work is perhaps the single most important analysis of the nature of underdevelopment and developmental strategies. Horowitz's book is important for a number of reasons, particularly for its attention to the fundamental questions and dilemmas confronting any nation seeking rapid development—such as raising the possibilities of positive payoffs from revolution, something one will not find in such prudential works by political scientists such as Charles Anderson, *Politics and Economic Change in Latin America* (Princeton, N.J.: Van Nostrand, 1967).

[13]Pye, "Introduction," in *Communications and Political Development.*

[14]Lucien Pye, "The Developing Areas: Problems for Research," in *Studying Politcs Abroad*, ed. Robert Ward (Boston, Mass.: Little, Brown, 1964).

[15]*Ibid.*, p. 7.

[16]Samuel P. Huntington, *Political Order in Changing Societies* (New Haven, Conn.: Yale University Press, 1968).

[17]Merle Kling; "Toward a Theory of Power and Political Instability in Latin America," *Western Political Quarterly* 9 (March 1956): 21-35.

[18]Seymour Martin Lipset, "Values, Education and Entrepreneurship" in *Elites in Latin America, ed. S. M. Lipset and Aldo Solari (New York: Oxford University Press, 1967).*

[19]David McClelland, *The Achieving Society* (Princeton, N.J.: Van Nostrand, 1961).

[20]Edward Banfield, *The Moral Basis of a Backward Society* (New York: Free Press, 1958).

[21]Myron Weiner, "Political Integration and Political Development," *Annals*, March 1965, pp. 52-64.

[22]LaPalombara, *Bureaucracy and Political Development*.

[23]Gabriel Almond and G. Brighman Powell, *Comparative Politics: A Developmental Approach* (Boston, Mass.: Little, Brown, 1966).

[24]Baran, *The Political Economy of Growth*, p. 326.

[25]See Stein and Stein, *The Colonial Heritage of Latin America: Essays on Economic Dependence in Perspective* (New York: Oxford University Press, 1970).

[26]Keith Griffin, *Underdevelopment in Spanish America* (London: Allen and Unwin, 1969), p. 33.

[27]Dean Rusk, "Trade Investment and United States Foreign Policy," Department of State Bulletin, November 5, 1962, pp. 638-88; W. W. Rostow, *The Stages of Economic Growth: A Non-Communist Manifesto* (Cambridge, Mass: MIT Press, 1962); Marvin Bernstein, ed., *Foreign Investment in Latin America* (New York: Knopf, 1966), pp. 175-238; Anderson, *Politics and Economic Change in Latin America* (Princeton, N.J.: Van Nostrand, 1967).

[28]Harry Magdoff, *The Age of Imperialism: The Economics of U.S. Foreign Policy* (New York: Monthly Review Press, 1969).

[29]We should note, in addition, the work of economist Michael Tanzer, *The Political Economy of International Oil and the Underdeveloped Countries* (Boston: Beacon Press, 1968); Michael Tanzer and Arthur Cordell, "Multinational Corporations: Price to the Host Country," *Nation*, July 6, 1970, pp. 17-20, among the best of the small body of very good published studies; Keith Griffin (*Underdevelopment in Spanish America*, 1969), who has written the single best work on Latin America: André Gunder Frank, author of a slashing critique of dominant sociological approaches to underdevelopment ("Sociology of Development and Underdevelopment of Sociology," 1969, pp. 24-94) and a powerfully suggestive, though not very precise, formulation on Latin America, the political scientists James Petras ("U.S.-Latin American Studies," 1968; Petras and Zeitlin, 1968) and Susanne Bodenheimer ("Dependency and Imperialism," 1970); and sociologists such as James Cockroft and Dale Johnson (Cockroft, Frank and Johnson, *Dependence and Underdevelopment*, Garden City, N.J.: Anchor Books, 1972). Some very interesting work comes, as well, from study groups such as North American Congress on Latin America (NACLA), whose excellent studies of U.S. military are clearly in debt to the work of Baran (*The Political Economy of Growth*, 1962).

[30]Susanne Bodenheimer, "Dependency and Imperialism: The Roots of Latin-American Underdevelopment," NACLA Newsletter, May/June, 1970, p. 18. This is the best summary and synthesis of the position of these theorists.

[31]Bodenheimer, "Dependency and Imperialism," p. 19.

[32]One of the best discussions in English of these factors and their relation to problems of underdevelopment and the development of national strategies for overcoming economic dependence is Osvaldo Sunkel, "National Development Policy and External Dependence in Latin America,: *Journal of Development Studies 6* (October 1969): 23-48.

[33]Barrington Moore, Jr., "Strategy in Social Science," in *Political Power and Social Theory* (New York: Harper Torchbooks, 1965), p. 116.

[34]*Ibid.*, p. 117.

[35]Sheldon Wolin, "Political Theory as a Vocation," *American Political Science Review* 63 (December 1969): 1062-82.

[36]*Ibid.*, p. 1080.

[37]*Ibid.*, p. 1082.

[38]Ralf Dahrendorf, *Class and Class Conflict in Industrial Society*, (Stanford, Calif.: Stanford University Press, 1959); "In Praise of Throsymachos" (Eugene, Ore.: University of Oregon, Henry Failing Distinguished Lecture, April 1966).

[39]Francesca Cancian, "Functional Analysis of Change," *American Sociological Review* 25 (1960): 6.

[40]Moore, "Strategy in Social Science," p. 140.

[41]Robert Dahl, "The Behavioral Approach in Political Science: Epitaph for a Monument to a Successful Protest," in *Behavioralism in Political Science*, ed. Heinz Eulau (New York: Atherton Press, 1969), p. 77.

[42]*Ibid.*, p. 87.

[43]Georg Lukacs, *History and Class Consciousness* (Cambridge, Mass.: MIT Press, 1970).

[44]Dahl, "The Behavioral Approach to Political Science," p. 88, emphasis added.

[45]Moore, "Strategy in Social Science," pp. 314-410; Baran, *The Political Economy of Growth*, pp. 144-150; Daniel Thorner, "De-Industrialization in India," Proceedings of the International Conference on Economic History, 1960.

[46]Charles Wilbur, *The Soviet Model and Developing Countries* (Chapel Hill, North Carolina: University of North Carolina Press, 1969), p. 12.

[47]Baran, *The Political Economy of Growth;*Celso Furtado, *Development and Underdevelopment* (Berkeley, Calif.: University of California Press, 1964), p. 79; Wilbur, *The Soviet Model and Developing Countries* (Chapel Hill, N.C.: University of North Carolina Press, 1969).

[48]Baran, *The Political Economy of Growth*, pp. 22-24.

[49]Harry Magdoff, *The Age of Imperialism: The Economics of U.S. Foreign Policy* (New York: Monthly Review Press, 1969).

[50]Celso Furtado, "U.S. Hegemony and the Future of Latin America," in *Latin American Radicalism*, ed. Irving Louis Horowitz *et al.* (New York: Random House, 1968), p. 73.

[51]For a meticulously documented and incisive criticism of U.S. policies of foreign aid and their relation to the maintenance of underdevelopment see Magdoff, *The Age of Imperialism*, pp. 115-72. Very important for what it says about the nature of the Alliance for Progress in Latin America is Heliodoro González (pseud.), "The Failure of the Alliance for Progress in Colombia," *Inter-American Economic Affairs* 23 (Summer 1969) and the U.S. Senate Foreign Relations Committee study (*Survey of the Alliance for Progress: Colombia—A Case History of U.S. Aid*, Washington, D.C.: U.S. Government Printing Office, 1969) on which it is based. One can conclude from these two studies dealing with Alliance Programs in Colombia that aid was a major factor in the failure of Colombia to meet even extremely minimal Alliance goals.

[52]Griffin, *Underdevelopment in Spanish America*, 1969; Anibal Quijano, "Tendencies in Peruvian Development and Class Structure," in *Latin America: Reform or Revolution?* ed. James Petras and Maurice Zeitlin (New York: Fawcett Publications, 1968).

[53]Tanzer, *The Political Economy of International Oil*, M. Tanzer and Arthur Cordell, "Multinational Corporations: Price to the Host Country," *Nation*, July 6, 1970, pp. 17-20.

[54]Frank, *Capitalism and Underdevelopemnt*.

[55]Wilbur, *The Soviet Model*.

[56]Gurley, "Capitalist vs. Maoist Economic Development."

[57]Frank, *Capitalism and Underdevelopment*, 1969; Stein and Stein, *The Colonial Heritage of Latin America*, 1970; Griffin, *Underdevelopment in Spanish America*, 1969.

[58]The reference is to the title of the work by Warren F. Ilchman and Norman T. Uphoff (The Political Economy of Change, Berkeley, Calif.: University of California Press, 1969). This is useful and insightful work by standards of what W. C. Mitchel would call the "New political economy." Its major weakness arises from the authors' explicit exclusion of critical theory and revolutionary models. As they say. "A model of politics should not impose a logic external to the system and its participants, *it must operate within the assumptions of the polity it is analyzing*" (p. 17, emphasis added). This is precisely the point at issue. As Griffin (Underdevelopment in Spanish America, p. 49) said in his excellent work on Latin America: ". . . the object of development policy is to turn historical constants into variables. . . . Policy in underdeveloped countries cannot be concerned exclusively with allocating resources in the usual sense: it must also be concerned with creating new institutions and reforming existing ones." This is what Baran meant when he said, "economic development has historically *always* meant a far-reaching transformation of society's economic, social, and political structure." A successful development policy *cannot* operate within the assumptions of a given polity, but must postulate new assumptions.

19
The Political Center
and Foreign Policy

AMOS PERLMUTTER

A fundamental fact of modern politics is that the politics of security and diplomacy are central to society. Historically, foreign and
security politics have been main priorities of the political center
and have been conducted primarily at the level of the center. Great
political theorists from Aristotle to Hobbes identified the purpose
of the political center, the state and the regime with security. The
centrality of the center in modern times (and in the historical bureaucratic empires) is caused by the fact that the administrative
staff in the Weberian sense—persons, structures, institutions and
machines—which handles the functions of security and diplomacy
is exclusively administered by the political center. In the absence of
a well-integrated political elite, a highly centralized political party
(or parties) and a powerful corporate and permanent bureaucracy
and civil service (especially administrative staff at the highest
level), the political center in the United States is located geographically in Washington, physically in the White House and personally
in the president.

The function of the center that is not shared by any other source
of authority in society is the defense of the realm. Both classic and
modern political and social theorists define a ruling organization

as political insofar as it is charged with the safeguarding of territorial area.[2] In the United States, there is no one center of values, beliefs and symbols that govern society. But geographically and politically the focus of government—the executive, the legislative and the judiciary—is located at the political center in Washington. Washington is the center of the American political system even if it is not its social, economic and intellectual center.

Political power is diffuse in America. So is the political order. The governmental system in Washington is not the only source of authority, but it is the highest and final authority system. In that sense the federal government is a surrogate agent of the political center—but authoritative nonetheless. There is little need to turn back to early and nineteenth-century American history to discover that in the United States, at least through most of its history, there was no single center of values and symbols; therefore, the federal system has developed into the central authority system. Parsons[3] contends that American society is characterized by the "non-political stress in American social structure." He convincingly argues that for historical reasons the American political system (i.e., the government) lagged behind that of the economy. According to Parsons this is a function of "the economic emphasis inherent in our system of values, and the relative lack of urgency of certain political problems because of our especially protected and favoured national position."[4]

The political center and above all the foreign affairs and defense departments are "occupied" once in every four years by a president and his bureaucratic, appointed entourage—his court—composed of experts, counselors, cronies and advisors. The constitutional as well as the political practice of the president is to maintain a reservoir of talent at the political center, for which he continuously recruits from outside the center. Those who become his security and diplomacy administrative staff are, by the definition of presidential powers, his subordinates.

America is blessed with political talent, has abundant political skill and potential, if not experience. Yet the diffusion of political power in America deprives the center of an efficient way to successfully recruit the reservoir of political talent, located in 50 states, hundreds of cities and thousands of local political focus areas. The significance of the political center, however, lies in the fact that it draws from the major reservoirs of values, symbols and beliefs, and recruits into the center from a variety of elites throughout the land.

A political center is dominated by elective politicians, party politicians, bureaucrats (civil service, military, scientists) and intellectuals. The American political system is notorious for the absence of a central cohesive and sustaining political party system. The bureaucracy is isolated, especially when the higher and key civil service positions are not permanent. Neither American political parties nor governmental bureaucracy are in a position to exclusively dominate the central functions of the political center, i.e., foreign and security affairs. This is not to say that the party bureaucracy is in a better position to dominate the socioeconomic functions of the political center, but that the political parties and the bureaucracies are not well integrated, cohesive or dominant. Part of the explanation why the political center was so notoriously absent in American politics is the absence of cohesion in these major political structures and between the wide variety of elites. In the absence of a central party and a cohesive bureaucracy the political center remains vulnerable and at times could be fragmented.

The political center has been and still is dominated by a small group that has been known by derogatory titles: "the elite," "the establishment," "the 200 families," "the power elite," "the political directorate," "the rulers," "the power structure," "the military-industrial complex," "bureaucratic politicians," and others. Not all of the above mean the same. "The 200 families," for example, could also mean only the "military-industrial complex"; "the bureaucratic politicians" are certainly not Mosca's rulers; and the "power structure" is the broadest coalition of social, economic, intellectual and political power, while "the political directorate" is a coalition of the "real" rulers (i.e., the corporate, political and military-industrial elites). Nonetheless, from Mosca, Pareto and Michels to C. Wright Mills, when one speaks of the "power elite" this means the elite that dominates the political center, and since the centrality of the center in modern time and in the United States since 1941 is represented in the politics of security and diplomacy, the power elite is easily identified (or confused) with foreign defense elites.

Talcott Parsons shrewdly observed that "American society has not developed a well-integrated political-governmental elite, in the sense that it has developed a relatively well-integrated business-executive group."[5] This picture has now been reversed. The federal system has finally become the political center primarily due to economic and external challenges. The Great Depression called for a revolution of priorities and of values. This meant governmental expansion and intervention. The wild growth of corporate industrial powers also called for the development of what Parsons calls the political system, by which he means the federal government.[6] American involvement in World War II and the cold war enhanced the growth of the federal system in size, level of influence and scope to an extent American society had never known before. If before 1914 one could still distinguish the political center from the federal government, gradually since 1945 the two have become convergent, and in the minds of many are today a single monolith. If between 1933 and 1941 the federal system — the government — wrested increasing influence away from the diffuse economic centers, since 1941 the major indicator for growth in the federal government's scope of political influence (if not acutally in size) has been security and diplomacy. Certainly the defense budget is the highest spending item of the federal government and a considerable size of the GNP. What was clearly not dominant previously— the defense budget and military spending—has now become the dominant item in the agenda of the political center, enhancing central authority.

THE DYNAMICS OF THE POLITICAL CENTER

On the dynamics of the political center, the following is examined: (a) the constitutional, institutional arrangements of the political center in its foreign-security functions; (b) the types of elites attracted and recruited to the various elements of the center; and (c) the structure of their competition/cooperation (consensus/dissensus). The Constitution as interpreted since Lincoln arrogated to the federal executive via his power as commander-in-chief a most awesome political power: the inherent power of the defense of the territory, the maintenance of peace and, above all, command over the armed forces. "Despite their strong fear of standing armies the authors of *The Federalist* tried to convince their readers of the necessity for such an army."[7] Hoping that the functions of the Republic would depend on peace and trade, the Federalists nontheless delegated to the chief executive, along with the central political power, the security system of the United States. The necessity for political domination of standing (i.e., professional) armies was one of the Federalists' strongest reasons for supporting the Union, "for they maintained that peace among the several states depended upon having a central government which alone had the authority to maintain a professional army. Indeed, without this provision a federal state would dissolve into component elements, each finding it necessary to support a standing army. A continuous condition of military rivalry would make it impossible to sustain republican governments."[8]

Since 1914 this power has reached staggering proportions. The concentration of political power at the center, especially in the office of the chief executive, along with the nature of modern warfare and diplomacy, lifted the office of the president into the single dominant power over security and diplomacy. Of the functions of the federal system—executive, legislative and judicial—it was to the executive that the primary responsibility over the executive-legislative coalition and the so-called bipartisan foreign policy enhanced the political power of the president in foreign affairs. It certainly buttressed the political center's consensus over foreign policy. However, the power of the president over foreign affairs was enhanced by the constitutional interpretation of his inherent power and of the centrality of foreign policy. The towering power of the president over the Senate in foreign affairs—constitutionally, institutionally and behaviorally—is not just a matter of elite domination and bureaucratic politics. Constitutionally and institutionally Congress is the president's chief partner and rival over the central functions of the political center. Congress has not met the challenge.

Even if these powers were "given" to the president on the stipulation that they be used with "the advice and consent of the Senate," it is the diffusion of the powers of the Senate that has deprived (and still does) the latter from exercising control in the realm of foreign affairs. This again is mainly due to the absence of central political parties at the center. The fact that Congress, especially the Senate, is an element of the political center—one of the structures of the federal government—must have escaped several analysts who sometimes write and speak of the Senate as if it were not. The reason why it has been less dominant than the president in the deliberations of foreign affairs has lain in the fundamentals not so much of the federal system, but of the development of the American political system. The Senate was given derivative constitutional—not inherent—powers: those of advice and consent. Institutionally, the powers of the Senate are diffuse. Behaviorally, the Senate's political elite is not as well integrated as that of the president.

The origin of the political impotence of the Senate is not only constitutional but also institutional. Senators are powerful elective officers and some are brilliant politicians, but they are not a cohesive and well-integrated group—certainly not when confronting the president. The powers of the president stem not only from the unique constitutional blessings of his office but also from the institutional arrangements which place his office supreme to the Senate in diplomacy-security, from the nature of the political center and from the absence of party centrality and bureaucratic cohesion. But this is also true of the Senate; it could also take advantage of the weaknesses of the political center, since the Senate has been since Truman's time the major recruitment area for presidential candidates and presidents. The latter could neither constitutionally nor institutionally establish a court even if the staff of the most influential Senate committees on security and diplomacy desperately emulated the president's court through unsuccessful attempts to challenge it. This could be done by recruiting the bureaucratic strategic counterelite to staff the key Senate Appropriations Committee. What strengthens the president's office considerably is that, by virtue of the singularity of his constitutional power and his almost complete freedom in the choice of his court advisors and appointees, it becomes a basis and the center for a well-integrated elite cluster. The presidential arrangement and the absence of elective officials' challenge makes the strategic elite effective only in the sense of the three Cs—cohesive, continuous and conspiratorial (in the sense of "common will to action") institutional arrangements of the American political system (on the three Cs, see Meisel and Parry).[9] The dynamics of security and diplomatic politics must be explained not only in terms of executive-legislative competition and rivalry, or in terms of rivalries within the well-integrated strategic elite of the president's office, but also in terms of (a) the president's handling of the security-diplomacy consensus; (b) the president's manipulation of the strategic elites; and (c) the absence of restraining power over the president's function as commander in chief.

The Senate was constitutionally deprived of equal powers with the executive, and the interpretation of the role of the president as commander in chief has considerably reduced the power of Congress over foreign affairs. The absence of a central political party reduced senatorial power and left its elite disparate. The Senate's key structure for domination of security-diplomacy, the committees on foreign relations, armed services and appropriations, is also diffuse. The three heads of the committees are not only elected politicians but also independent, powerful senators who come from different parties and orientations and who often checkmate one another. They possess diffuse, autonomous and equal power, as do the committee members.

By contrast, the president as chief administrator does not act as primus inter pares with his cabinet but as the singular and authoritative officer he is—the individual elected by all Americans and commander-in-chief over security and diplomacy. His partners in fulfilling these functions are not elective equals, but bureaucratic subordinates. Even the departments which have asserted some independent power are in no position to seriously challenge their supreme commander. In this matter George Reedy is most perceptive.[10] The president, he claims, is a monarch. The office of the president can be compared with the monarch-emperor-caliph of the historical bureaucratic empires.[11] Although the president, unlike the rulers of the historical centralized empires, is not a patrician or usurper but a democratically elected official, he is the master of an administrative staff and of an organization under his total domination, hardly challenged by the other elements of the political center. (Very seldom does the Senate fail to confirm a cabinet member or an ambassador. And in the case of his private advisors, the Senate to its chagrin is impotent to challenge his appointments.) He is never seriously threatened by counterelites in the realms of security and diplomacy. The office of the president in the Weberian[12] sense is a ruling organization where members are subjected to rational domination by virtue of the established and legitimate national political order. The president, like the ruler of the centralized historical bureaucratic states, has almost unlimited autonomy in security and diplomacy functions. He is free and has exercised his powers since 1941 to develop autonomous political security goals.

The Presidential Court

The elite that the president recruits is a nonelective, private set of bureaucrats, advisors, counsellors, public relations men, scribes, intellectuals and cronies. (The office of the president functionally resembles the court of the historical centralized empires.) The president is seldom challenged by the court even if some of its members possess high status, excellent social background, education and achievement. Former dignitaries, ex-politicians, learned men, supermanagers, technicians and Nobel Prize-winning scientists all are equal, subject to the whims of his idiosyncrasies and under the shadow of his total power—provided they are in the court.[13]

The president's court has emerged in the absence of a cohesive political center, a central political party and a centralized and continuous bureaucracy, compounded by the bureaucratic malpractices of modern complex organizations perpetuated in the state and defense departments. These were summarized by Henry Kissinger[14] as being rigid and noninnovative, having a tendency to encourage average performances where the "machine becomes a more absorbing occupation than defining its purpose," where decisions avoid innovation and where studying the problem can turn into an escape from coming to grips with it." The president's court is a bureaucratic structure erected to overcome the professional military and diplomatic corps and the systems of merit and tenure. The surrogate political center's most important institution, the office of the president, is a project-like system of action which unfolds once in four or eight years.

The policy of recruitment depends on the president's style, experience and weltanschauung. A preponderance of conservative businessmen, bond lawyers, military officers and small-city bankers are found in an Eisenhower administration. The Kennedy court was composed of technicians, foreign-policy professionals, scribes, diplomacy professionals, intellectuals, belletrists and nonconservative military professionals. The Johnson court was saturated with Texans and what Eric Goldman calls "pragmatic liberals." Nixon's court, with the exception of Kissinger and Moynihan, was packed with public relations and advertising executives.

What is most significant about the recruitment of the strategic elites is that they are recruited not, as the power elite theorists[15] would have us believe, because of their class, status and power in American society or because of their institutional proximity. They are chosen by both conservative and liberal presidents because they are thought to represent the central values, symbols and beliefs of American society.[16]

This buttresses my thesis on the nature of the political center in the United States: that, since the political center is surrogate and constitutionally divided, the nonpolitical centers—the disparate pluralistic centers of values, symbols and beliefs—are the reservoirs for the political center and that, in the case of the president, the chief recruitment strategy for ideas and men is to turn the political center into a temporary (thus surrogate) center of symbols, values and beliefs. I further argue that it is only in the realm of

AMOS PERLMUTTER

security-diplomacy that the court represents an almost full spectrum of the continuum of opinion and ideas in the United States (minus the extreme poles of radical left and right), which again is behaviorally in the context of the American political system. In this area the president's office and court represent the American consensus on security and diplomacy. The court is recruited on the basis of foreign-policy consensus represented by the advanced (I continuously avoid "progressive") men of society.

The president functionally represents the advanced ideas of the nation even if he does not represent the most up-to-date ideas and practices. He does not represent the extreme poles of opinion or those which are filled with moral indignation. If I take only the intellectual-educational foreign-policy elite and armchair strategists as an example, the list of Harvard's Center for International Affairsexecutive committee will demonstrate the fact that recruitment of persons to the court is from the center of the intellectual universe,[17] which would also be true of the procedures for recruitment from business, industrial and technocratic universes. Class, status, social and educational background of the courts' strategic elites may be relevant factors for their recruitment, but they fail to distinguish one administration from another or to underline the specificity of recruitment among carefully selected elites.

Background factors of strategic elites are relevant only in an analysis of how the centers are being formed. Despite the fact that the advisors come from diffuse nonpolitical centers, they are nonetheless the representatives of society's progressive centers of values, symbols and beliefs. Any analysis of the president's court since 1960 will demonstrate that even if some presidents are less interested in recruiting persons most representative of contemporary American values, the latter infiltrate into the court. Even Johnson's pragmatic liberals and Nixon's public relations experts do in the end depend on the central ideas of representative American men and women.

The Structure of Consensus and the Court

A valid argument can be made that there are considerable differences in ideological orientation, emphasis of values and manipulation of symbols between one court and another, within a single court and the noncenters and between the president and the Senate. Since 1965 we have witnessed a marked change in ideologies and placement of values, a shift in priorities between and within the political center. To those who are morally indignant or those who believe in a total revolution, this may well seem irrelevant. To those, however, who believe in reform and incremental but cumulative change it is most relevant. Thus, when we speak of consensus we speak of several factors.

Consensus is the broadest and most generalized acceptance of specific but universal orientations, beliefs, practices and procedures. Consensus is a basis for actions; a pillar for successful policymaking. Consensus is not a program or a policy; it is a collective perception and identification of friends and foes and of issues. In foreign affairs, consensus is also an aspect of a community of support for regimes and authorities.[18] It is, however, an analytical and nonempirical concept. We know of no good definition of consensus or even an acceptable procedure for its measurement. Of one thing there is little doubt: consensus is a property of the political community that is articulated, if not invented, mainly by the elites outside the political center. It becomes a pillar of policy when executed by the president and the court. When we speak of consensus as policy, we speak of those who identify consensus with a specific political orientation or action. Hence it ceases to be a property of voters and consumers and becomes a property of authority. When the foreign affairs elites speak of consensus there is little doubt whose consensus they speak of. So when we speak of the location of consensus security and diplomacy we speak of the little-challenged property of the elites for center. When we speak of the court we speak of well-integrated elites which are integrated by virtue of institutional factors and consensus. Counterelites in the noncenters speak of a different consensus, and the political center speaks of the latter's consensus as dissensus. What makes the strategic elites of the court well integrated are the three Cs, which include their common will to action—conspiracy. Here consensus is the most influential integrating variable of the elite of the court.

Consensus is the security and diplomatic ideology (Pareto's derivative) of the presidential court. The elites of the noncenter who are not oriented toward the consensus, i.e., the ideology of the center, will not join the court. They are the counterelites, always hopeful to influence the center but only on the condition that its dissensus becomes the new court's consensus. They conspire against the center. In Mannheim's sense, the ideology of the elite becomes the utopia of the counterelite. Consensus is not only an element for elite recruitment but, once in the center, consensus is an instrument of their political integration. Next it becomes the court's function to inculcate the consensus into the political community. The relationship between the maintenance of consensus and its support are crucial for the maintenance of the presidential function in diplomacy-security.

The elite of consensus diffuses the ideas of the cold war, peaceful competition, polycentrism, and so on. The president and the court are in this sense custodians of the consensus. Consensus becomes the structure of the system of support. Consensus, however, is broad and diffuse. It can, for example, handle support for lifting the Berlin blockade, helping the Greek regime in 1947, supporting anti-Communist praetorian "progressives" in Asia and Africa and maintaining the balance of terror. These are the outputs of a policy supported by consensus. Paradigmatically, in Thomas Kuhn's sense,[19] the cold war was the "normal science" of the 1950s (when theory and fact were in closer agreement and were affirmative). The cold war was the assent of the relevant community—the foreign policy elite which integrated around this consensus in the court. Again, as with Kuhn's analysis of the scientific revolution, the revolution is not in nature but in mind. Consensus is in Kuhn's sense response to crisis—an anomaly. A new paradigm, a new consensus, is tantamount to a change in perception or a change in vision. It was the nature of the vicissitudes of the cold war that formed the cold war consensus. The consensus not only identifies the properties of a new paradigm but also denies the basis for the old consensus—that the cold war only exists in the minds of the power elite at the center, and that the new consensus is not a change in nature but in man's mind. Yet the function of the court is to insist on "normal science," the accepted paradigm, and to refine, extend and articulate it. Thus one should not expect authority to perceive and act against its accepted cognitions. This is the function of the court, especially in the absence of serious antagonists in the realm of security and diplomacy in the political center.

Analysis of diplomacy and security in the context of two American traumas (Cuba and, especially, Vietnam) and of those who really dominate the security and the diplomacy of the United States, stands a better chance when we analyze the locus and the degrees of power in each case. To explain the dynamics of foreign policy and ascertain why "things" went wrong, one must go into but also go beyond the politics of the presidential court, his scribes and technocrats, and certainly beyond a conspiratorial theory of arrogant power elites exclusively engaged in conspiracy, secrecy and deception, dominating the politics of diplomacy and security in the United States.

NOTES

[1]Max Weber, *Economy and Society*, vol. 1, ed. C. Witich and G. Roth (To-towa, N.J.: Bedminster Press, 1968), pp. 212-15.

[2]*Ibid.*, p. 215.

[3]Talcott Parsons, "The Distribution of Power in American Society," *Structure and Process in Modern Societies* (New York: Free Press), p. 216.

[4]*Ibid.*, p. 213.

[5]*Ibid.*, p. 216.

[6]I reject Parsons's narrow definition of the political system, i.e., the government. But for our purposes his definition of the political system is what I prefer to call the "surrogate political system." Government is certainly not the American political system.

[7]I am most grateful to David Rapoport's *Praetorianism: Government without Consensus* (Berkeley, Calif.: University of California, unpublished Ph.D. dissertation, 1958), p. 174 for his perceptive analysis of the Federalists and executive power in its civil and military contexts.

[8]*Ibid.*, p. 175.

[9]J. Meisel, *The Myth of the Ruling Class* (Ann Arbor, Mich.: University of Michigan Press, 1962); Geraint Parry, *Political Elites* (London: Allen and Unwin, 1969), pp. 31-32.

[10]George E. Reedy, *The Twilight of the Presidency* (New York: World, 1970).

[11]S. N. Eisenstadt, *The Political Systems of Empires* (New York: Free Press, 1963).

[12]Weber, *Economy and Society*, pp. 212-54.

[13]George E. Reedy and Harry McPherson, *A Political Education* (New York: Littlle, Brown, 1972); Eric Goldman, *The Tragedy of Lyndon Johnson* (New York: Knopf, 1969).

[14]Henry A. Kissinger, "Domestic Structure and Foreign Policy," *Daedalus*, Spring 1966, p. 344; see also Kissinger, *The Necessity for Choice* (New York: Harper & Row, 1969), pp. 340-58.

[15]See Richard Barnet, *Roots of War* (New York: Atheneum, 1972) for an adequate, even if opinionated, review of the types of court recruitees. Here C. Wright Mills, *The Power Elite* (New York: Oxford University Press, 1956) was a major source of inspiration.

[16]By "advanced" I mean that a conservative president will choose the most liberal of conservatives and vice versa.

[17]The Harvard Center for International Affairs is a case in point. R. Bowie was a high official in the Eisenhower administration. S. Huntington was a Humphrey advisor in 1968. Both were members of the Policy Planning Staff of the State Department. Henry Kissinger was President Nixon's national security advisor and was advisor to presidents Kennedy and Johnsonadvisor to the president of the World Bank. Stanley Hoffmann was advising Senator McGovern. Thomas C. Schelling was advisor to Secretary McNamara.

[18]On the conceptual and analytical aspects of support, see David Easton, *A System Analysis of Political Life* (New York: Wiley, 1965), 170-89. I do not accept the conceptual usefulness of this functional analysis. However, I know of no author other than Easton who has posed the problem analythically.

[19]Thomas Kuhn, *The Structure of the Scientific Revolutions 2*, no. 2, 2nd. ed. (Chicago: International Encyclopedia of Unified Science).

Part IV

THE PRACTICE OF FOREIGN POLICY

20

Policy Scientists and Nuclear Weapons

ROY E. LICKLIDER

In studying the relationships between social science and public policy, nuclear weapons policy provides a useful and informative case study for several reasons. The first is simply that it has been around for some time, at least since Hiroshima. Certainly the postwar years witnessed the mobilization of physical scientists concerned about the use of nuclear weapons.[1] Another landmark date was 1951, when the Wohlstetter bases study at RAND was initiated; this study marked the development of strategic thinking under government contract.[2] The ideas percolating among the insiders entered the public realm in the middle fifties, with the publication of pioneering books by William W. Kaufmann and Henry Kissinger in 1956 and 1957 and the subsequent concern over Sputnik and the missile gap.[3]

Second, the field has produced major intellectual developments, involving the whole complex of related concepts of deterrence, credible threats, first and second strike forces, counterforce and countervalue targeting, stable and unstable deterrents and arms control. Moreover, these ideas came from sources outside government, although many were closely connected with it. They included the private research institutes (exemplified by the RAND Corporation), university research centers, and groups of concerned intellectuals, especially the atomic scientists. Generally speaking, the research institutes started from physical science and operations research, the university research centers started from diplomatic history and traditional foreign policy (and later from social science theory), and the concerned intellectuals from particular policy and moral concerns about nuclear weapons. They came together in the area of nuclear weapons policy.[4]

The variety of institutions in the field was matched by that of the individuals within the institutions. The study of military policy by a significant group of civilians was a new phenomenon in the United States;[5] there were no accepted channels of recruitment or credentials for entrance. Moreover, the nature of the field was such that almost any substantive interest provided sufficient "handle" to justify involvement, from the geologist's work in detecting underground nuclear tests to the theologian's concern over the morality of nuclear war. Thus many people could be peripherally involved through their normal work, but for anyone to specialize in the area involved something of a break with his own profession or discipline. It therefore seems typical of many policy areas related to social science, enhancing its utility as a case study.

Moreover this body of ideas had significant effects on the policy of the United States government. In this respect, whatever one's attitude toward the results, the success of those working in nuclear weapons policy in influencing important government policy may seem a desirable model to follow. Important aspects of this included the research institute and the government research contract as links with government. In fact several of the people whom I surveyed specifically said that nuclear weapons policy had adventitiously been the first substantive area of postwar social science policy work and that other areas were developing in a similar manner.

The major data source for this paper was the material gathered in a larger study of civilians outside government who had done work in nuclear weapons policy, whom I called the "private nuclear strategists."[6] The population was composed of 491 individuals who had written one book or three articles or papers on nuclear weapons policy between 1946 and 1964 inclusively, while not directly employed full-time by the government. Employees of organizations under government contract were included. Probably the major difficulty with this criterion was lack of access to bibliographies of classified documents; therefore anyone who did only classified work in the area would not have been included. Despite some connotations of the word "strategist," publication, not policy preference, was the criterion used, and the full range of policy and methodological variety was represented.

All members of the population were sent an 11-page mail questionnaire in the middle of 1966; 191, 39 percent, eventually returned it and became our sample. Nonrespondents were studied by using standard biographical publications such as *Who's Who*. The sample seems to be representative of the population. It is somewhat slanted toward those who have written more about nuclear weapons policy and over represents political scientists. However, differences were not statistically significant[7] on the following attributes: highest academic degree, school of highest degree, sex, and ex-military status and service.[8]

This essay focuses on three particular aspects of general concern in social science policy issue-areas: distribution of ability to influence government within the field, which in turn involves its internal power structure; the importance of different types of employing institutions, particularly universities and research institutes, as barriers within the field; and the academic-policy tension inherent in any such area. In each area it is suggested that the conditions that seem to hold within nuclear weapons policy may indicate the direction in which other, more recent social science policy fields will develop.

EXTERNAL INFLUENCE AND INTERNAL POWER

The ability to influence policy, especially government policy, is a vital issue, as can be seen by monitoring the shop talk of workers in any such field. In the field of nuclear weapons policy the issue has been raised explicitly in public discussion and continues to generate a good deal of emotional heat.[9]

The issue of influence cannot be definitively settled. This study furnished no objective evidence of the influence of the private nuclear strategists upon government policy or who exercised this influence, if any. Such a study would involve studying the consumers of strategic expertise as well as its producers. However, there are several indicators of how much influence respondents *think* they have on policy. Two such questions concerned the influence of the group as a whole and of the particular respondent as an individual.

The sample had a high opinion of its influence, both individually and collectively. In response to Question 28, "How much would you say civilians not employed by the government have influenced American defense policy since World War II?" 14 percent said "not at all" or "not very much," 26 percent said "somewhat," and 57 percent said "a good deal" or "very much" (N was 177). A remarkable 41 percent of the sample said that they "as an individual [had] significantly influenced a policy of the United States government in the field of strategy and disarmament" (Question 27), while 35 percent disagreed (N was 183).

As in any social group, influence was not distributed equally. Another criterion of influence utilized the traditional academic approach, the judgment of an individual's colleagues, in Question 34:

> In your opinion, what individuals have made the most significant contribution to the study of strategy and disarmament since World War II?[10]

The first five responses were coded; less than 5 percent of the sample named more than this number. Forty members of the sample were named by one or more members of the sample (self-choices were excluded); this group was called the "perceived influentials." Again there is no way of determining objectively whether these individuals have indeed had this influence.

Given that influence is distributed unequally, just how unbalanced is its distribution? Have the perceived influentials arrogated all the power to themselves, leaving the remainder of the population in frustrated impotence? Perhaps, but it does not appear so on this admittedly rather limited indicator of influence. While it is true that 50 percent of the perceived influentials claim to have significantly influenced a government policy themselves, as compared with only 39 percent of the rest of the sample, the difference is significant only at the .15 level (N's are 38 and 145). Moreover, of the respondents who said they had significantly influenced a government policy, 70 percent were *not* perceived influentials. While this does not guarantee satisfaction by the "noninfluentials" (perhaps they want to influence more than one policy), it suggests that influence is perceived to be widely distributed throughout the population. This position is buttressed by the fact that, with the exception of an academic trend (which we will discuss later) and age, the differences between the perceived influentials and the rest of the sample are unimportant; this included a battery of policy questions.

How is influence gained? Unfortunately there were no direct questions on this subject, but among the possible answers that come to mind are publications, political action, personal influence of decision-makers and government research contracts. There is evidence on the first and last possibilities.

Since the selection of our population was based upon publication criteria, data on this point was readily available. Each respondent was scored for publication points, on the basis of one article or paper (widely interpreted) as one point and a book as three points. Three points, of course, was the minimum, since it defined our population. Relating publication point scores to status as a perceived influential confirms a strong relationship between them. While 37 percent of the perceived influentials had publication point scores above 15, only 8 percent of the others did (N's were 40 and 140, and the difference was significant at the .001 level). In fact, of the 27 individuals who had scores over 15, 56 percent were perceived influentials, suggesting that if you publish a lot you have an even chance of being regarded as influential.

Similarly it was expected that perceived influentials would be more likely to have done government research. Question 21 asked "Have you ever worked on a government research contract in the area of nuclear strategy and disarmament?" 67 percent of the perceived influentials said that they had, as opposed to 41 percent of the rest of the sample (N's were 39 and 150, and the difference was significant at the .05 level).

As usual in survey research the causal implications of correlations are unclear. It may be that perceived influentials find it much easier to publish articles and receive government contracts because of their status. Alternatively their success in these areas may create their status. The former position is supported by some fragmentary data discussed later which suggests that status may come from status in the parent academic discipline. However, in a new field of study the question of where the status comes from in the first place remains a problem, especially since many of the

Table 1
Consequences of Publishing Material Disapproved by
the "Establishment"
All percentages are totaled across. N is 144.

	% YES	% CONDITIONAL
Not listened to by the government	33	7
Difficulty in obtaining research funds	15	9
Loss of general respect among colleagues	13	8
Difficulty in obtaining good university appointments	8	10
No effect; there is no "establishment"	17	10
No effect; the "establishment" has no real power	14	9
OTHERS:		
The "establishment" exists but judges work on its merits	10	4
The "establishment" exists but has no power over this particular respondent	9	1
Difficulty in getting published	7	2
Respondent specifically mentioned having had trouble with the "establishment" himself	3	5
There is more than one "establishment"	3	2
Other answer implying existence of the "establishment"	21	5

respondents are fairly young and have not done much work outside the field. Since there seem to be no other significant differences between the perceived influentials and the rest of the sample, it seems likely that their status is largely a product of their work rather than vice-versa.

A related indicator concerning perceived influence within the field was Question 37:

> It has been suggested that there is an "establishment" in the field of strategy and disarmament, a group which sets the limits (perhaps unconsciously) within which strategic debate and discussion is carried on. If you published material of which the "establishment" disapproved, what effects do you think this would have on you? (Check as many as you feel are appropriate.)

Aside from the six alternatives listed on the questionnaire, the five mentioned most frequently as "other" were also coded. Table 1 shows the results. There was general agreement that an "establishment" exists; 117 respondents, 81 percent of those who replied to

Table 2
Full-time employment in strategy and disarmament
"Have you ever been employed full-time *for* over four months *by any of the following types of institutions, doing work that was* directly related to nuclear strategy and disarmament? *(Check as many as are applicable.)" (emphasis in questionnaire)*

	N	%
College or university (teaching full or part time)	44	19
College or university (no teaching responsibility)	19	8
Research institute affiliated with a college or university	29	13
Private, non-profit research and/or educational institute	64	27
Private corporation (not non-profit)	16	7
Periodical (privately owned)	18	8
Federal government	36	15
Other (please specify)	7	3
	233	100

the question, checked at least one consequence. However, there was no consensus on the consequence of opposition to the "establishment," suggesting that this perception is hazy at best. None of the alternatives received the support of half of the sample; the highest was "not listened to by the government" with 33 percent agreeing and another 7 percent uncertain. Sanctions that remain this vague seem unlikely to be particularly effective, confirming the impression of a relatively loose internal power structure.

EMPLOYING INSTITUTIONS

One of the major divisions among people working on nuclear weapons policy is that different types of institutions employ them. This in turn seems likely to serve as a precedent for other policy areas. The assumption that a man's employer shapes his opinions is widely held and is often used to judge his work. In particular the distinction between the university and the research institute, especially those dependent upon government support for their funds (as most of them are), is thought to be important. It was therefore expected that there would be significant differences between respondents employed in different types of institutions, especially research institutes. Specifically I hypothesized that respondents who had been employed by research institutes would have been significantly more motivated by intellectual than policy considerations, would be more anti-communist in policy attitudes, and would read different periodicals than the rest of the sample. These hypotheses generally were not supported by the data.

The customary duality of universities and research institutes does not do justice to the proliferation of institutions in the area. Many universities, for instance, have established research institutes of their own, some of which have done work in strategy and disarmament.[10] The relationship between their personnel and the regular departments varies, but joint appointments tend to be rare and limited to senior members.[11] Faculty positions without teaching responsibilities are similarly difficult to categorize easily.

Outside the universities there have been other institutional developments. The well-known, nonprofit research institutes such as RAND have been supplemented by other corporations which are not nonprofit. These include research corporations such as Arthur D. Littie, Inc., United Research Inc., and Abt Associates as well as several major corporations in aerospace and electronics which have either established research branches or done work within existing administrative structures, such as Bendix, Boeing and General Electric (which has published a journal in the area, the *General Electric Defense Quarterly*). RAND, after all, was originally a branch of Douglas Aircraft. Political action groups have also been involved, and our stress on publication criteria brought in individuals employed by periodicals, of whom the military correspondents are perhaps the most prominent.[12] Question 7 asked:

> Have you ever been employed *full-time* for *over four months* by any of the following types of institutions, doing work that was *directly related to nuclear strategy and disarmament?* (Check as many as are applicable.) [Emphasis in questionnaire.]

Table 2 lists the results on the seven types of institutional employment: college or university (teaching full or part time); college or university (no teaching responsibility); research institute affiliated with a college or university; private, nonprofit research and/or educational institute; private corporation (not nonprofit); periodical (privately owned); and federal government. A surprisingly large number had done such work; 126, 66 percent of the sample, named at least one institution. Conveniently, the sample divided almost equally between universities with and without teaching responsibilities and nonprofit research institutes.

I expected that respondents who had worked for different institutions would have had different motives for entering the

Table 3
Reasons for working in strategy and disarmament
"Opposite each of the following possible reasons for doing work in the area of strategy and disarmament, please indicate whether it had not much influence, some influence, or very much influence in your decision to enter the field."

Reason	N	% VERY MUCH	% VERY MUCH OR SOME
Concern about the threat of modern weapons to the human race	159	65	87
Intellectual interest in international security affairs	150	64	88
Desire to significantly alter American foreign policy	159	40	75
Desire to encourage world disarmament	155	34	66
Desire to teach and disseminate knowledge in this area	150	34	71
Concern about the moral problems of current American military policy	148	32	63
Desire to influence young minds	143	20	52
Experiences during World War II	142	20	41
Specific job opportunity	133	20	49
Related problem in another field	128	19	46
Desire to combat world communism	145	16	37
Influence of an individual working in the field	132	14	45
Desire to promote democracy throughout the world	137	12	44
Influence of a book or publication in the field	130	9	28
Casual exposure to the area	122	7	38
Availability of research funds in this field	128	2	23
Influence of an individual not working in the field	118	3	9
College course in the field	124	2	11
College course in another field that included a section on this area	128	2	13
Other	28	89	100

field. Kathleen Archibald, in a study using a smaller sample and more intensive interviews, found that those employed in universities said they had originally become involved because of policy interests, while those working for nonprofit research institutes had been more influenced by intellectual motives; over time the two groups became more similar in their motives.[13]

Question 32 stated:
Opposite each of the following possible reasons for doing work in the area of strategy and disarmament, please indicate whether it had not much influence, some influence, or very much influence on *your* decision to *enter* the field. [Emphasis in questionnaire]

Table 3 gives the responses of the sample to this question. The nineteen alternatives were divided into motives (internal factors) and influences (external factors). Motives in turn were divided into policy and intellectual. This gave three categories: policy motives (threat of modern weapons to the human race, altering American foreign policy, desire for world disarmament, concern about moral problems of American policy, threat of world communism and desire to promote democracy), intellectual motives (intellectual interest, teaching and disseminating knowledge and influencing young minds), and influences (World War II, a specific job opportunity, related problem in another field, a publication in the field, availability of research funds, a person or college course in or out of the field, and casual exposure to the area). Table 3 suggests that motives have been much more important than influences (implying policy and intellectual motives) and that policy motives seem equally important. The direction of the policy motives is also interesting; with the threat of modern weapons as one of the most important motives (65 percent said it had had "very much" influence) and concern about world communism second lowest of nine motives (16 percent), the sample appears to be unpromising material for an anti-communist nuclear crusade, although this as sumes a link between motives and policy positions that may be incorrect.

In line with my initial hypothesis, I expected those who had worked for universities to have been more influenced by policy motives and those in nonprofit research institutes to have been influenced by intellectual motives. Table 4 does not confirm this hypothesis. The motivations of the two groups seem to be very similar. Indeed, of the six policy motives, the research institute respondents had higher percentages on two, on three there was no difference, and only on the general motive of altering American foreign policy did the expected greater policy interest of the academics appear. There was also no significant difference on the intellectual interest motive, although the academic motives of teaching and influencing young minds were more prevalent among college teachers.

I had not expected the motives of those who had been employed by the federal government to differ significantly from the rest of the sample; while this was generally true, they had been significantly more motivated by the threat of world communism

Table 4
Factor loadings of periodicals and journals
In the first five factors, periodicals with factor scores equal to or larger than .5 are included; in the last three the cutting point is shifted to .3.

	FACTOR LOADINGS
MILITARY (17% of the variance)	
Army	.87
Journal Of The Armed Forces	.80
Air Force/Space Digest	.79
Air University Review	.79
United States Naval Institute Proceedings	.79
Aviation Week	.77
Missiles and Rockets	.76
Military Review	.75
Marine Corps Gazette	.74
Military Affairs	.66
Navy	.62
SOCIAL SCIENCE (13% of the variance)	
International Organization	.83
International Conciliation	.81
American Journal of International Law	.74
American Political Science Review	.73
World Politics	.70
Journal Of Conflict Resolution	.66
Annals Of The American Academy of Political And Social Science	.53
Daedalus	.51
Foreign Affairs	.50
Orbis	.50
ATTENTIVE PUBLIC (11% of the variance)	
Atlantic Monthly	.72
Scientific American	.71
Harper's	.70
Bulletin Of The Atomic Scientists	.67
New Republic	.62
Saturday Review	.60
Daedalus	.58
War/Peace Report	.53
PROTESTANT (7% of the variance)	
Fellowship (Fellowship of Reconciliation)	.79
Christian Century	.71
Worldview (Council on Religion and International Affairs)	.59
Intercom (Foreign Policy Association)	.56

CATHOLIC-JEWISH (6% of the variance)

America	.76
Commonweal	.64
Commentary	.57

HISTORY (5% of the variance)

American Historical Review	.69
Annals of the American Academy of Political and Social Science	.47
Military Affairs	.46
Virginia Quarterly Review	.43
American Political Science Review	.41
Current History	.39
Atlantic Monthly	.34

OPERATIONS RESEARCH (4% of the variance)

Operations Research	.63
Stanford Research Institute Journal	.39
Military Affairs	.31
Journal Of Conflict Resolution	.30

SURVIVAL (4% of the variance)

Survival (Institute for Strategic Studies, London)	.84
World Politics	.35
Orbis	.32
Reporter	.31

(30 percent said it had "very much" influenced them, while others ranged from 13 percent to 18 percent). This suggested the hypothesis that those who worked for the federal government would be more anti-communist on the questions of policy that we studied. This hypothesis was in addition to the one which predicted the employees of nonprofit research institutes to be more anti-communist than those from university positions.

Eleven policy attitude questions were included in the questionnaire. Nine of these were statements, with responses requested on a seven-point, agree-disagree scale (collapsed for analysis to three-point scales); they are listed here:

American foreign policy since World War II has not faced up to the fundamental problem of a hostile Communist foe dedicated to its destruction.

American foreign policy since World War II has placed too much emphasis on the threat of world communism and the Soviet bloc.

The aggressive tendencies of the Soviet Union have been greatly reduced since World War II.

In ten years China will be a greater threat to the United States than the Soviet Union will be.

It seems likely that, within this century, the Soviet Union and the United States will be allied against China.

The present system of deterrence seems unlikely to last until the end of the century without breaking down into a central nuclear war.

The American policy of containment of the Soviet Union has been a success.

In the nuclear age, the American government must regard itself as being responsible, not only to the American people, but also to the people of the world.

Some form of world government is the only long-term solution to the problem of destructiveness of modern weapons and opposing nationalisms.

In addition, Question 62 asked:

The major threat to American national interests abroad since World War II has been: (choose one)
Communist ideology
Russian and Chinese national power

And Question 42 asked:

Within the past five years, have you publicly disagreed with a position of the United States government in the area of strategy and disarmament?

Combining these eleven policy questions with the seven types of institutions generated 77 different relationships. Only one was significant at the .05 level; employees of private corporations are more likely to see the major threat to American interests abroad as being communist ideology rather than Russian and Chinese national power. Since a .05 significance level means one chance in 20 of happening at random, I dismissed this finding and concluded that no significant policy differences appeared in the sample. The hypothesis that employees of the nonprofit research institutes and the federal government tended to be more anti-communist in foreign policy attitudes than the rest of the sample was therefore rejected; once again the university-research institute barrier proved to be more fragile than expected.

The role of periodicals as agents of communication is obviously significant; indeed a persuasive classification of schools of thought in the field has been made in terms of "communication networks" and stressed the role of certain journals.[16] Question 30 read:

Opposite each periodical listed below, please indicate about how often you usually read its articles on the subject of strategy and disarmament.

Forty-three periodicals were listed in alphabetical order. They were chosen because they had carried significant articles in the area, and some effort was made to include as many different types of journals as possible. Newspapers were excluded. Opposite each title was a five point scale: "not familiar with periodical," "read only occasional articles," "read less than half the articles on this topic," "read more than half the articles on this topic," and "read nearly all the articles on this topic," as well as "don't know." All other journals listed by more than one individual were also coded; of the 25, only one was listed by more than ten respondents, *Survival* (the journal of the Institute for Strategic Studies, London), which had been excluded from the original list because it was British; it was added.

A factor analysis was performed on the results for the 44 periodicals.[17] Eight factors were rotated; together they accounted for 66 percent of the variance. Table 4 shows the periodicals that related closely to each of the eight factors. The names of the factors have been invented by the author on the basis of the journals loading highly on each; they have no other significance or validity.

Factor scores of respondents were used as an index of periodicals read. Of the 56 relationships generated by eight factors on seven types of institutions, only three were significant above the .05 level.[18] However, since they were all on the same factor and all well above .05, they are worth examining in more detail. Analysis was based on the percentage of respondents who had factor scores of 1.0 or above on each of the factors. This percentage varied from 0 percent in a couple of cases to 19 percent, except for the "social science" factor. Although the nonprofits actually had a slightly higher percentage here than on any other factor (16 percent), they were significantly lower than the university research institutes (38 percent), university teachers (41 percent), and university non-teachers (47 percent) (N's and significance levels were 29 and .01, 44 and .001, and 19 and .01 respectively). This may reflect the general preeminence of physical scientists at research institutes;[19] however, considering the pride of the nonprofits in their success in interdisciplinary work, it is rather surprising to see their low percentages on the factor which includes the major professional journals in political science, international relations, international law and general social science.

This is an important difference, but it should not obscure the fact that differences on the other seven factors between different types of institutions are negligible. The pattern is a single deviation from homogeneity rather than the systematic differences we had expected. With the single exception of social science periodicals, there are no important differences among employees of different types of institutions working on nuclear weapons policy in motives for entering the field, policy attitudes and periodicals read. It seems clear that a common subject matter has overcome the potentially divisive effects of different sorts of institutions. There are certainly major differences within the sample, but they do not seem to coincide with different types of institutions. Nor is there any obvious reason to suppose that this pattern will not be repeated in other policy fields of social science.

ACADEMIC-POLICY TENSIONS

This is not to say that employment is entirely unrelated to questions relating to policy. Part of the reason for the lack of difference between universities and research institutes is undoubtedly the fact that many individuals within the universities have also worked for the government on research contracts, and people who have never done such work have very different attitudes about its morality than those who have.[20]

The dichotomy between academic and policy goals is a prominent feature of every social science policy field. The rather abstract and seemingly consistent goals of knowledge for theory development and for policy guidance in practice develop into major differences in orientation, style, credentials, media, audiences and institutions. Nuclear weapons policy is an interesting example of this precisely because the tension has been so apparent. We have seen that intellectual and policy motives seem to have stimulated the sample to work in the area about equally. Indeed the division has been institutionalized with the development of the research institutes and corporations, as previously discussed, and these seem likely to remain a permanent part of the policy process in the United States. In fact, several of them have been consciously attempting to shift into other policy fields recently.

One would expect to find a strong division between respondents on various indicators relating to this distinction, and indeed upon first inspection the data seemed to support this conclusion. However, a somewhat more complex analysis indicated a different pattern. If the sample is divided by two dichotomized factors (age and status as perceived influentials) into four groups, the older noninfluentials are significantly less academically oriented than the rest of the sample in terms of the highest earned academic degree and affiliation with an academic discipline. Moreover the younger respondents seem to have been motivated by intellectual rather than policy motives. Assuming that the influentials and the younger members of the sample indicate the future development of the area, I concluded that the field of nuclear weapons policy is becoming more academic over time. Moreover it seems likely to be an indicator of future developments in other fields.

The criterion used to establish status as a perceived influential has already been discussed. The second question on the questionnaire asked for the respondent's date of birth. The answers were divided rather arbitrarily into those born before and during 1919 and after that date; this divided the sample almost equally (92 older members and 90 younger members).

Since there are no Ph.D.'s being offered in national security studies at an American university,[2][1] it is not intuitively obvious that possession of a doctoral degree is a useful indicator of the quality of an individual's work in nuclear weapons policy. Nevertheless among the older respondents 70 percent of the perceived influentials have this degree as compared to 35 percent of the older noninfluentials (N's were 23 and 69; the significance level was .006). At the same time, 71 percent of the younger influentials and 48 percent of the younger noninfluentials had the Ph.D.; N's were 14 and 76, and the difference was not significant. The American academic community, of course, has traditionally stressed the importance of the Ph.D.[2][2]

Question 16 asked: "Do you consider yourself affiliated with an academic discipline?" On the surface such identification would seem to make it more difficult to achieve eminence in an area outside the discipline (unless national security policy itself is regarded as a discipline, but it was not by our respondents). After all, identification with a discipline usually involves some consideration of one's disciplinary colleagues as a potential audience, and this may well conflict with either a client such as the government or with the audience or others working in nuclear weapons policy with different disciplinary identifications.[23] However, among older respondents 100 percent of the perceived influentials said that they were affiliated with a discipline, as compared to 50 percent of the older noninfluentials (N's were 22 and 68; the difference was significant at the .001 level). Comparable figures for younger respondents were 91 percent and 71 percent (N's of 13 and 74, with the difference not significant). The weakening of this distinction between influentials and noninfluentials among the younger group is due to the much larger percentage of younger noninfluentials who identify with a discipline as compared to their older counterparts.

The pattern on these variables is the same. Among the older age group, the perceived influentials are more "academically" oriented than the remainder of the group. Among the younger respondents, the differences are not significant. The differences between the two age groups are due to the younger noninfluentials having become more academically oriented than their older counterparts. A causal relationship should not be inferred here, although it is tempting to view this as an example of the role of the perceived influentials as a "leading group" for the rest of the sample. But this assumption is not necessary to the basic conclusion that, barring large-scale recruitment, individuals working in nuclear weapons policy are likely as a group to become more academically oriented, even though they presumably retain their interest in policy research.

If academic criteria are so important, one would expect that, despite immersion in this special area, qualifications for being perceived as influentials would continue to reflect criteria used in the parent discipline. This could be checked by seeing if perceived influentials were named on a similar list of their own disciplines, but only one such list was discovered. In a survey of political scientists, the top 19 perceived influentials were listed;[24] the only two who were in my population were also on the list of perceived influentials, suggesting that influence in one's discipline may transfer directly into a policy field.

Another supportive finding concerns motivation for doing work in the field. In this area the distinction between perceived

Table 5
Age and motives for working on nuclear weapons policy
Percentage Influenced "very much" by motive

MOTIVE	BIRTH DATE				SIGNIFICANCE
	1880-1919		1920-1939		LEVEL
	%	N	%	N	
Desire to significantly alter American foreign policy	53	72	28	81	.008
Concern about the threat of modern weapons to the human race	73	73	58	81	.14
Desire to encourage world disarmament	47	71	24	79	.007
Concern about the moral problems of current American military policy	45	67	22	78	.009
Desire to combat world communism	20	61	13	79	N.S.
Desire to promote democracy throughout the world	15	55	10	77	N.S.
Intellectual interest in international security affairs	54	63	73	82	.01
Desire to teach and disseminate knowledge in this area	41	64	30	81	N.S.
Desire to influence young minds	27	64	15	75	.03

influentials and others drops out, but the difference between the age groups remains strong. Table 5 shows the results of combining the nine motives with an age differential. On five of the nine the difference is significant, and on a sixth it is notable. Older respondents were significantly more motivated by the policy motives of altering American policy, encouraging world disarmament, and concern about the moral problems of current American military power. They were notably more motivated by a concern about the threat of modern weapons to the human race, and they were significantly less motivated by intellectual interests. Table 5 also indicates that a significantly larger percentage of older respondents than younger were very much influenced by a desire to influence young minds, which was classified by us as an academic motive. At the risk of torturing the data, the wording of this motive, with its stress on young minds, means that it is probably inherently more attractive to older respondents. Even if taken under the original classification it weakens, but does not seriously undermine, my basic conclusion that the private nuclear strategists seem to be developing in an academic direction.

CONCLUSION

The field of nuclear weapons policy is seen by its participants as having been influential upon government policy and the sources of such influence seem fairly widely dispersed within the community. The divisions between employees of research institutes and universities do not seem to be particularly important, although the population as a whole seems to be moving toward an academic outlook as far as motivation and status qualifications are concerned. What is it that links these diverse findings together?

All three seem to indicate that the field of nuclear weapons policy has stabilized. Taking them in reverse order, the development of academic status qualifications is probably the normal process that any new field or area goes through in the process of becoming legitimate. Moreover, it allows the institutionalization of the field within the universities, freeing at least a cadre of members from the uncertainties of working for research institutes that depend upon the mood and purse of the federal government. Similarly, the fact that the divisions between research institute and university seem relatively unimportant suggests that the field has acquired legitimacy of its own, that it is relatively independent of the institutions to which its practitioners are attached.

By the same token, the fact that respondents seem to perceive influence and power as being widely dispersed within the field should reduce frustrations and help keep people within the area; indeed when respondents were asked a series of questions about how much of their professional time they spent in the field five years ago, today, and how much they expected to spend five years in the future, the results indicated relatively little decline in participation over time.[25] The fact that the sample seems little concerned about internal power problems, however, does not satisfy the frustrations that may arise from an unwillingness within the government to listen to their advice. This essay has suggested that the private nuclear strategists had significant influence upon American military policy, but it should be noted that this reached its high point in the early sixties, under the rather unusual political conditions attendant upon a new Democratic administration in office which was both sympathetic to new ideas and concerned with defense problems. The ease with which they were able to translate theory into policy may have given some of the private nuclear strategists an exaggerated view of their political prowess, which may lead to frustration in the future if this success is not repeated.

None of this, of course, answers the more basic question of why the field of study of nuclear weapons policy has become accepted, an important question when attempting to draw lessons from the experience for other fields. There seem to be two main reasons, however: the problems that gave rise to work in the field continue to demand attention, and civilians outside government seem to have found an accepted position within a division of labor among those concerned with these problems.

The first is perhaps the more obvious point. Although the field is in something of a hiatus at the moment, with the feeling that its "golden age" of the early sixties has come and gone, major problems remain in the area. Recently, even though Vietnam has continued to have a strong claim on intellectual resources, the questions of the antiballistic missile system, MIRV, the nonproliferation treaty, and the SALT talks have again brought the field into prominence. Nor is there much realistic hope that the problems of nuclear weapons will soon be solved and forgotten.

The idea of an accepted role for civilians outside government may be less obvious, but it is no less crucial for the long-term stability of the field. The strategic community, those who are concerned with nuclear weapons policy inside and outside government, can be conveniently divided into the private nuclear strategists, the professional military and civilian government employees and officials. The community seems to be developing a pattern of division of labor on issues, although whether this pattern will survive the Democratic administrations which spawned it is less clear at the moment. The private civilian strategists, who have developed practically all of the strategic concepts since World War II, carry on a continuing debate over the major issues in nuclear strategy and disarmament. This debate, which may be called the strategic debate, is carried on partly in public (increasingly so in recent years) and partly within and between government agencies. In the latter area, the government research contract is the key that brings the private strategist temporarily inside of government, although less direct means such as publication may accomplish the same ends.

From this debate, certain concepts tend to emerge as prominent solutions, to use Schelling's term. This, in turn, gives rise to a second level of debate, over the translation of these concepts into policy. In this policy debate, the other two groups within the strategic community hold dominant positions. The professional military man speaks as the practitioner who must put the ideas into operation. As such, he rightly demands and receives a major voice in the debate. The government official's role may vary with the individual personality. However, he normally represents the rest of the government within the debate; thus he is often responsible for introducing factors such as the budget or public opinion. One of the drawbacks of the system is that he often also tends, by default, to be responsible for bringing in political, as opposed to military, questions; if he does not do so, they may never be raised.

It is unlikely that this system will change radically in the forseeable future. The private strategist continues to possess both expertise and available time, making him a valuable ally in the policy debate. Nor is there any sign that other groups within the strategic community are prepared to take over the strategic debate, despite occasional exhortations for them to do so.[26] Within the policy debate, to do in-house the work now contracted out would require an immense increase in the government bureaucracy, of a kind that few are likely to advocate, at least not as long as the quality of the contract work remains reasonably high.[27]

What, then, has been the impact of the development of the private nuclear strategists upon the more general question of social science policy work? The area has developed the key institutions of the research institutes and the government research contract and has given them legitimacy. Moreover, it has established a pattern in which intellectual work has been successfully translated into government policy. Finally, it has furnished a cadre of experienced personnel who seem prepared to move from the area into other policy fields. It thus has served as an entering wedge for what may become one of the major intellectual phenomena of our time.

This paper is in part a product of my doctoral dissertation, and my debts are immense. I acknowledge with gratitude the major contributions to the larger study made by Robert Axelrod, Karl W. Deutsch, Harold D. Lasswell, J. David Singer, and H. Bradford Westerfield. It was financed by a grant from the Council on International Relations, Yale University, and by supplementary computer funds from the National Science Foundation. Stephen A. Salmore smoothed the potentially traumatic change from one computer center to another. Computations for this particular paper were supported by a grant from the Center for Computation and Information Services, Rutgers University. But my primary debts are two, one individual and one collective, to Bruce M. Russett who was a model dissertation director and to the 191 individuals who took time to answer my importunities and complete my questionnaire.

NOTES

[1] For extensive discussion of this movement, see Robert G. Gilpin, *American Scientists and Nuclear Weapons Policy* (Princeton: Princeton University Press, 1962) and Alice Kimball Smith, *A Peril And A Hope: The Scientists' Movement in America,* 1945-1974 (Chicago: University of Chicago Press, 1965).

[2] A. J. Wohlstetter, F. S. Hoffman, R. J. Lutz, and H. S. Rowan, "Selection and Use of Strategic Air Bases," R-266, RAND Corporation, Santa Monica, California, April 1, 1954 (declassified 1962), 383 pp. For discussion of this study see Bruce L. R. Smith, "Strategic Expertise and National Security Policy: A Case Study, *"Public Policy* XIII (1964), pp. 76-87, revised as Chapter VI, Smith, *The RAND Corporation: Case Study Of A Non-Profit Research Institute* (Cambridge: Harvard University Press, 1966), pp. 195-240; E. S. Quade, "The Selection and Use of Strategic Air Bases: A Case History" and Albert Wohlstetter, "Analysis and Design of Conflict Systems" in E. S. Quade (ed), *Analysis for Military Decisions* (Chicago: Rand McNally & Company, 1964), pp. 24-63 and 122-127.

[3] W. W. Kaufmann (ed), *Military Policy and National Security* (Princeton: Princeton University Press, 1956) and Henry A. Kissinger, *Nuclear Weapons And Foreign Policy* (New York: Harper & Brothers, 1957). For the missile gap, see my "The Missile Gap Controversy," *Political Science Quarterly,* LXXXV (December, 1970), pp. 600-615.

[4] The best single history of this process is Gene M. Lyons and Louis Morton, *Schools for Strategy: Education and Research in National Security Affairs* (New York: Frederick A. Praeger, 1965).

[5] For discussions of American traditions in military expertise, see *inter alia* Samuel P. Huntington, *The Soldier And The State: The Theory and Politics of Civil-Military Relations* (Cambridge: Belknap Press of Harvard University Press, 1959), pp. 143-312; Paul Y. Hammond, *Organizing For Defense: The American Military Establishment In the Twentieth Century* (Princeton: Princeton University Press, 1964), pp. 1-106; Louis Smith, *American Democracy And Military Power* (Chicago: University of Chicago Press, 1951), pp. 102-151. For an attempt to integrate the phenomenon of the private

nuclear strategists into a more general discussion of the changes in American civil-military relations since World War II, see my *The Strategic Community: Contemporary American Civil-Military Relations* (forthcoming, 1971).

[6] Roy E. Licklider, "The Private Nuclear Strategists," Ph.D. dissertation, Department of Political Science, Yale University, New Haven, Connecticut (April 1968); to be published by Ohio State University Press, 1971.

[7] "Significance level" is the probability that the relationship in question would occur by chance if there were no differences between the groups under consideration. By convention the .05, .01, and .001 levels are considered thresholds of statistical significance; however, although they are useful, they are only conventions and have no particular intrinsic significance. For the purposes of this study, significance levels over .05 were considered *significant*, those between .05 and .20 *notable*, and those under .20 *not significant*. All significance level figures in this study are based on the chi square statistic. Strictly speaking, this measure is not appropriate, since we do not have a random sample. However, the sample does appear to be fairly representative of the population, and we felt that the value of having a measure of the strength of statistical relationships justified the risks, as long as it was not interpreted too strictly.

[8] Licklider, "The Private Nuclear Strategists," pp. 15-24.

[9] Two excellent summaries of opposing points of view on this issue are Wesley W. Posvar, "The Impact Of Strategy Expertise On The National Security Policy Of The United States," *Public Policy*, XIII (1964), pp. 36-68 and Philip Green, "Science, Government, and the Case of RAND: A Singular Pluralism," *World Politics*, XX (January, 1968), pp. 301-326.

[10] Lyons and Morton, pp. 127-199; Kathleen Archibald, "The Role of Social Scientists As Outside Experts In Policy Formulation," Ph.D. dissertation, Department of Sociology and Anthropology, Washington University, St. Louis, Missouri, to be published by Basic Books, Inc., Chapter III, pp. 29-33, 51-52; Charles V. Kidd, *American Universities and Federal Research* (Cambridge: Belknap Press of Harvard University Press, 1959), pp. 175-188, cited in Archibald.

[11] Lyons and Morton, pp. 127-199; Archibald, Chapter III, pp. 30-31.

[12] For a rather inconclusive study of this group, see George V. Underwood, Jr., "The Washington Military Correspondents," unpublished M. A. thesis, School of Journalism, University of Wisconsin, Madison, Wisconsin, 1960.

[13] Archibald, Chapter III, pp. 33-34.

[14] This distinction is one of several that I owe to observations by respondents on the questionnaire.

[15] The data is given in Licklider, "The Private Nuclear Strategists," pp. 102-105.

[16] Archibald, Chapter III, pp. 43-44.

[17] Strictly speaking, factor analysis was not an appropriate statistical technique, since the data was ordinal rather than interval. However, it was felt that the benefits of reducing 44 variables to 8 factors justified the risks. The program used was Yale Computer Center's No. 6S, using the principle axis method and varimax rotation of factors with eigenvalues equal to or greater than one.

[18] The data is presented in Licklider, "The Private Nuclear Strategists," pp. 111-112.

[19] Smith, *The RAND Corporation*, pp. 60-65.

[20] Licklider, "The Private Nuclear Strategists," pp. 187-195.

[21] Such a program was considered by M.I.T. some years ago but was not adopted.

[22] Theodore Caplow and Reece J. McGee, *The Academic Marketplace* (New York: Science Editions, Inc., 1961), p. 162.

[23] For valuable further discussion of the problem of audiences, see Archibald, Chapter V, pp. 12-31 and Chapter VI, pp. 8-9, 12-13, 17-19, and 39.

[24] Albert Somit and Joseph Tannenhaus, *American Political Science: A Profile Of A Discipline* (New York: Atherton Press, 1964), p. 66.

[25] Licklider, "The Private Nuclear Strategists," pp. 156-157.

[26] An example is Colonel Robert N. Ginsburgh, "The Challenge To Military Professionalism," *Foreign Affairs*, XLII (January, 1964), pp. 255-268.

[27] For a more detailed discussion of these points, see my *The Strategic Community* (forthcoming, 1971).

21

The Politics of Territorial Waters

ARTHUR D. MARTINEZ

If one carefully observes maps of Peru being sold on the various streets of downtown Lima, one will notice that the cartographers have subtly but clearly indicated Peru's ownership of the 200-mile strip of Pacific Ocean which bathes its nearly 1,000 miles of shoreline. This representation is in keeping with a presidential decree issued by former President José Luis Bustamante y Rivero in August 1947, as well as with the overwhelming sentiments of Peruvian citizenry. Following more than three months of investigation among various sectors of the Peruvian population, only scant opposition to the 200-mile limit has been evidenced.

Following President Harry S. Truman's proclamation in September 1945 regarding the right of the U.S. government to complete jurisdiction and control of the continental shelf and its resources, as well as a fisheries conservation zone, the Bustamante y Rivero administration quickly used this precedent to proclaim its exclusive jurisdiction and sovereignty over the coastal sea to a limit not less than 200 nautical miles.

In an interview, Enrique García Sayan, the minister of foreign affairs who formulated and also countersigned the Peruvian proclamation, told me that his country had not been arrogant or arbitrary in setting the limit at a distance of 200 miles: "On the contrary, we researched the matter very thoroughly with the assistance of some of the best experts in Peru. For instance, I had several meetings with Irwin Schweigger, the prominent Peruvian geographer, who made clear to us that the Peruvian current varied in its distance from the coast, but that it generally averaged about 200 miles. Thus, the 200-mile limit is based on extensive scientific data."

Neither country purported to interfere with the traditional rights of free and inoffensive passage and freedom of communications and overflight. Both were primarily concerned with the national prerogative and right of exploiting the vast riches of the ocean. The United States was especially interested in sinking more oil wells on the ocean floor off the coasts of Texas and Louisiana; Peru was barely awakening to the possibilities of exploiting the huge and rich fishery resources off its Pacific coast.

Over the years, the two nations have had diplomatic squabbles over the question and interpretation of national sovereignty over the ocean. The U.S. government has steadfastly maintained from the beginning that it had not proclaimed its sovereignty over the epicontinental waters, but only over the continental shelf and its resources. The United States, along with Great Britain, the Soviet Union and others, has adamantly refused to recognize Peru's extension of jurisdiction and sovereignty over the continental shelf, and especially over the epicontinental waters, out to a distance of 200 nautical miles.

Why has the United States government resisted the Peruvian proclamation? Essentially, as is the case with most of the great maritime and fishing nations of the world, because of the fear that such an extension of sovereignty might someday result in the interference of world commerce or the obstruction of free and unfettered passage for ships, aircraft and submarines necessary for maintaining the military or strategic position of these countries. Less important, but significant, is the fact that these nations also harbor public and/or private fishing fleets that have the technological capability and capital required to fish thousands of miles from their own shores, primarily in large intensive fishing operations. Their fishing industries would suffer if they were forced to retreat behind a 200-mile barrier such as already exists along the coasts of nine Latin American countries (Peru, Nicaragua, Panama, Ecuador, Chile, Brazil, Argentina, Uruguay and El Salvador).

A common reply to the case of the major maritime powers is

that given by Peru: free and open access to the fishery resources of the world up to the traditional 3- or even 12-mile limit would invite, in the words of Ambassador Alfonso Arias Schrieber, director of sovereignty and frontiers at the Peruvian foreign ministry, "savage exploitation" by those who have the technological capability. Ambassador Arias Schrieber stated that the licentiousness Ambassador Arias Schrieber stated that the licenciousness advocated by the developed nations would be tantamount to acceptance of the law of the jungle, wherein the richest and most powerful peoples survive and prosper and the rest would continue to suffer. Going a step further, he pointed out that a just and humane world could not allow this to come to pass. Peruvian representatives have emphasized at numerous regional and international forums that the issue of national sovereignty over the sea is fast developing into a struggle between the developed northern half of the globe and the underdeveloped southern portion.

Peru has benefited greatly from its virtually exclusive exploitation of the 200 miles of ocean off its coast. In about 1955, as reported to me by Nicholas Asheshov, editor of the *Peruvian Times* (Lima), Peruvian industrialists began to invest extensively in fishing fleets and fishmeal and fishoil plants along the length of the coast, completely transforming sleepy fishing villages such as Chimbote, Chicama and Ilo into relatively large and, by Peruvian standards, prosperous communities of fishermen and factory workers. Chimbote is reported to have grown from a small fishing village of 15,000 people into an industrial city of more than 200,000 in the space of 20 years, largely under the impulse of the fishmeal boom. The fleets and factories of this new big-money industry attracted droves of immigrants, both from the rural interior and from other coastal cities, not all of whom could be absorbed by the fishmeal operations. Significant also is that approximately half the population of Chimbote is directly or indirectly dependent on the 22 local fishmeal plants, which produced at least 25 percent of Peru's total output in 1970.

In June 1972 I visited Chimbote to interview public and private persons connected with the fishing industry. Franco Baca Bazán, secretary general of the Fishermen's Union of Chimbote (Peru's largest fishermen's union), expressed that his more than 6,000 members were not at that time engaged in fishing operations because the closed season (*veda*) was in effect; however, many of his officers and members were busily preparing for the festivities associated with Fishermen's Day. Most of the city's population was caught up in the holiday spirit, which provided an outlet for the temporarily unemployed citizenry.

A visit to Pesquera Trujillo, a local fishmeal plant, verified what the union leader had said. Carlos Colona Reta, director of production at the plant, provided me with an extensive and educational tour of the facility. In the course of the tour, it was plain that there had not been any processing of anchovy for a considerable period of time. According to the company official, the anchovy had migrated south toward Pisco to escape the warm waters of the Niño current. In his own words, "It just isn't worth the expenses to send our fishermen out to sea. We will wait until the anchovy reappear." Germán Mackay Zelada, one of the company's engineers, told me that since the migration of the anchovy, the average catch in the area was 5-10 tons per day. "This is to be compared to our usual catch of 185-200 tons per day. Actually, our company has not been sending out its fishing vessels for serious fishing since early April."

Articles in Peruvian magazines and newspapers have revealed that some Peruvians, though they are intensely proud of their fishing accomplishments and progress, at the same time are beginning to react to the uneven development and apparent lack of civic concern for clean and beautiful cities along the coast. In a recent example of criticism, one Peruvian writer strongly chastised the gradual deterioration of one coastal city, explaining that he had found barely one green, watered park there.

In figures released in April 1972 by the UN Food and Agricultural Organization (FAO), Peru was listed once again as the first fishing nation in the world regarding volume of catch, but it also, for the first time, replaced Japan as first in dollar value of fishery exports. Peru's first-place position results from intensive anchovy fishing operations, which bring in 10 to 12 million tons of this species a year. The small fish is boiled and ground into fishmeal and fishoil for the world market, primarily as a protein supplement for livestock and poultry.

Catalina Tomatis Chiappe, a member of the Legal Section of the Ministry of Energy and Mines, characterized the world market for Peruvian fishmeal as good and expanding. She further explained that Peru had in the past been too closely dependent upon U.S. and West German markets, and that since 1970 her country had successfully diversified its commercial affairs. Peruvian officials of the state-controlled Ministry of Fisheries travel far and wide seeking new customers for their products. Local newspapers continually report commercial dealings not only with Western countries but also with Africa, Asia and countries from the Socialist bloc. Rumania, Bulgaria, Yugoslavia, China, the U.S.S.R., East Germany, etc., have either established or strengthened trading relationships with the military government of General Juan Velasco Alvarado.

The Revolutionary Military government seized power from former President Fernando Belaúnde Terry in October 1968; it was soon thereafter—about 1970—that the Velasco government began to establish formal diplomatic relations with various Socialist bloc countries. This was done for various reasons, two of which are, first, that the military government was riding a popular wave of nationalism following the expropriation and subsequent wrangles with the United States over the IPC affair and saw the advantages of continuing to assert its independence and self-determination; and second, that international relations between the United States and Peru were soured over the IPC expropriation and the takeover of U.S. business interests such as some properties of the W.R. Grace Company. The military junta sensed this estrangement and also the possibility of economic reprisals, and immediately took steps to establish or strengthen diplomatic and commercial relations with countries from the Socialist bloc.[1] In the words of Catalina Tomatis Chiappe: "The Socialists are good trading partners. They ask for our products (primarily fishmeal and fishoil), we deliver, and they pay. So far as we are concerned 'he who pays shall receive.' That is good business, is it not?"

As a consequence of this expansion and diversification, the present market for Peruvian fishmeal is genuinely worldwide. The U.S. market still looms large, but it is not paramount. It would be incorrect, however, to underestimate the overall importance of the U.S. market to the expanding Peruvian economy. There was widespread clamor from official as well as private sectors in Peru when members of the U.S. House of Representatives sought to cut back Peru's sugar quota in 1969-70; moreover, the recent discovery of oil in the Amazon jungle near Iquitos (Pavayacu) and the projected construction of a pipeline over the Andes to the port of Paita will make the United States a logical market for oil products. U.S. mining companies such as Marcona, willing to abide by the present nationalistic and intricate Peruvian investment and production regulations, are either expanding or investing in new operations.

A brief note on the port of Paita is in order. The Peruvian government has long coveted a projected fishing port complex on the northern coast in order to expand and rationalize its fishing industry. Since at least 1970, almost all discussion was centered on the tiny port of Bayovar, located on a bay in the northern district of Piura. When the present Peruvian government began negotiating with the Soviet Union for the loans and credits necessary for the construction of the port complex, the discussion was somehow switched from Bayovar to Paita, a larger fishing port which is farther north, but still in the district of Piura. The Soviets believed that it would be more rational to expand the facilities at Paita than to begin from scratch at Bayovar.

Commander Luis Rivero Valdeavellano, captain of the port of Paita, told me that preliminary work was expected to begin at Paita very soon. The mayor of the port, César Ginocchio, told me that officials from the Ministry of Fisheries had consulted with him and that one of the first construction goals would be to level a few surrounding hills and use the dirt and gravel for filling in a flat tabletop extension out into the waters of the bay. He stated that "Paita will realize considerable progress and growth if and when the port is expanded. For example, the electrical, water and transport systems will undoubtedly be modernized and enlarged. With the introduction of these changes in infrastructure, we will finally be able to invite large industry to Paita." It is also certain that increased employment opportunities will be made available to the local citizens. These and other interviews have revealed that the major aim of the Peruvian government is to develop a table-fish industry in this northern region. I visited various fishing companies in the Paita area and was a witness to the presence of several dynamic fishing operations. Large refrigerated (or iced) trucks were in line waiting to be loaded with tons of fish for the markets of Lima, Arequipa, Piura, Cuzco, Trujillo, etc.

Although the military government officially declared in May 1972 that the port would be financed by the U.S.S.R., it was at the same time emphasized that the port would be built by Peruvians. Yet, one former senator in the Peruvian legislature (abolished by the Velasco administration) told me that the Soviets would undoubtedly build the port "to their own specifications, because they harbor the desire to use it." It was the former senator's opinion that the Soviets were intensely interested in fishing in Peruvian waters, that is to say within 200 miles of the Peruvian coast. However, the senator and others were quick to express their feeling that only joint Peruvian-Soviet fishing operations were likely to materialize. The danger in their view was that the Soviets would come in with their huge fishing and processing factories and destroy the biological balance of the Peruvian current.[2]

Fernando Noriega Calmet, chairman of the Department of Social Projections at the National University of Engineering in Lima, expressed that the presidential decree of August 1947 sought to bring the Peruvian current under national control and jurisdiction. He stated that many years ago he had participated in government tests and surveys to determine the width of the current, and while following Norwegian whaling vessels he and his colleagues had discovered that the whales would stay a short distance from the outer limits of the Peruvian current in the warmer water yet near enough to the seafood and fish that abound in the cold current. They were eventually able to determine that the outer limits of the varied according to the time of year, but that it seldom extended farther out than 200 miles. Thus, in his opinion, the Peruvian government had sought to nationalize control over the current. My own subsequent research has substantiated the fact that the major fishery resources are indeed located within the Peruvian current.

My travels along the Peruvian coast confirmed what many Peruvians have claimed: the entire length of the Peruvian coast is a barren and arid desert, with only few exceptions along the swift-flowing river valleys. This inhospitable environment has developed primarily as a consequence of the cold winds from the Peruvian current and the presence of the high Andes barrier. These and other factors combine resulting in almost no rainfall for the coastal region. Consequently agriculture is a difficult and unproductive venture, except for intensive farming along some river valleys. Since it is impossible for Peruvians to satisfy their nutritional requirements from this dry region, from time immemorial they have turned to the sea for their sustenance and survival. As Ambassador Arias Schrieber told me, "We believe our right to the foundation of riches off our coast is based in the just and humane right of people to survive the best way they are able in the prevalent conditions. In our case the answer is obvious—the sea."

A very large percentage of the Peruvian population is undernourished. An engineer at the Ministry of Fisheries, Raúl Erazo Tipacti, said that the general population of Peru was suffering from a lack of sufficient protein; fish could fill the protein gap that presently exists. He showed me an experimental study being carried out by the Scientific and Technical Section of the Ministry of Fisheries, with which these researchers hope to develop a method whereby anchovy can be placed on the domestic market for human consumption. This would be "a major accomplishment, because to date anchovy has been used primarily for fishmeal and not for human consumption; also, this particular species is found in great abundance along the entire Peruvian coast."

Peruvians are dependent upon the fishery resources off their coast—which exist primarily within the Peruvian current, or roughly out to 200 miles or so. This present dependency is real and meaningful, not because they are earning valuable foreign exchange (at least 35 percent of the total) from their fishmeal and fishoil exports. But the Peruvian Ministry of Fisheries has created two new state-controlled fishing agencies and hopes to change matters considerably: EPCHAP has been set up to finance the fishing industry and centralize the marketing of its products; EPSEP is charged with developing a table-fish (as opposed to fishmeal) industry and encouraging the consumption of fishery products in lieu of Argentine and Bolivian beef, which costs so dearly in foreign exchange. The government's *veda* system of 15 meatless (beef) days a month attests to the degree of national effort to preserve foreign exchange and develop new consumption habits.

It is difficult to ascertain whether the consumption habits of Peruvians are changing, but it is certain that critical foreign exchange is being saved and utilized for other socioeconomic and political purposes. Citizens do buy more fishery products at the markets which have been set up all over the country, including the high sierra and the jungle.[3]

In short, Peruvians critically need the economic resources of the sea. They exploit these resources vigorously, yet they apply closed seasons on fishing whenever a set quota is reached. Peruvians want, in the words of Felipe Chávez Blacker, director of public relations at the National University of Engineering, to "prevent the overfishing and pollution which already exists in many maritime regions of the world."

Yet, what about the stated concerns of the maritime powers? They too have a vital interest in the oceans. Of paramount concern are military and defensive (strategic) considerations; next is their commercial or economic concern with the fishery resources. These nations seek to preserve the unfettered freedom of movement for their fleets, submarines and aircraft. To realize this aim, the United States, Great Britain and the Soviet Union, to name a few, are advocating a 12-mile universal maximum territorial waters limit. Nations such as Peru are condemning this 12-mile proposal as yet another scheme by the technologically developed nations against the poor, underdeveloped nations of the world.

Can there be a solution? There can be a compromise solution which would recognize both the primordial military or strategic rights of the major maritime powers and the fundamental economic rights of the underdeveloped nations. This aim can be accomplished if two-thirds of the nations of the world at the Geneva Conference next year (1973) vote in favor of the so-called patrimonial sea concept.[4]

Mexico has been perhaps the leading world advocate for the emergence of a patrimonial sea, in addition to the classic territorial sea. Mexico proposes a universally accepted accord that would provide each coastal nation with total jurisdiction (sovereignty) to a maximum distance of 12 miles and an extension—to a maximum of 200 miles—of patrimonial sea, wherein the coastal state would enjoy limited jurisdiction. It is expected that this limited jurisdiction would provide the coastal states with control over the exploration, exploitation and conservation of economic resources both in the epicontinental waters and on the continental shelf. Under this arrangement, the underdeveloped states and the major maritime powers would realize their major aims.

In an interview with Ambassador Arias Schrieber of the Peruvian Foreign Ministry, I was told that more than 50 countries were in favor of such a compromise solution. He stated that although Peru would prefer total jurisdiction out to the 200-mile limit, there would be intense international diplomatic pressure to accede to the territorial sea plus patrimonial sea arrangement if two-thirds of the nations at Geneva voted for such an accord. However—and this theme was repeated by many—the ambassador was also quick to state that those nations willing to back the territorial sea plus patrimonial sea proposal had made it clear that there would be no 12-mile territorial sea limit if there was not also an extension for a patrimonial sea out to a maximum of 200 miles.[5]

NOTES

[1]Former President Belaúnde Terry had made it clear during his administration that Peru had no objection to establishing trade relations with Communist coun-

tries. Previously, ever since the question of relations with Communist countries became an issue in world affairs, Peru had maintained a firm anti-Communist line.

[2]Peruvians are quick to mention that the explorer Alexander von Humboldt himself felt that the ocean current along the western coast of South American ought to be named for Peru.

[3]In June 1972 General Tantalean Vanini, minister of fisheries, inaugurated the opening of new and expanded refrigeration facilities in Cuzco, a large city in the southern mountains of Peru. The government is intensifying its present efforts to make fishery products available to the entire nation. The aim is to get a quality product to the consumer at a fair price.

[4]Enrique García Sayan told me that he prefers the concept "national economic zones," rather than "patrimonial sea."

[5]Representatives of 13 Caribbean nations met at Santo Domingo, capital of the Dominican Republic, and ratified the Declaration of Santo Domingo, wherein they proposed the territorial sea plus patrimonial sea solution. Furthermore, the participants passed a resolution calling for a convocation of all Latin American countries for the purpose of arriving at a single unified position which they can all support at the upcoming Geneva conference.

22

Policy Guidelines for Collective Bargaining and Family Planning

OLIVER D. FINNIGAN III and DIONISIO PARULAN

In some developing countries where collective bargaining is a well-established tool for instituting change in the agroindustrial setting, the potential of deriving satisfactory family planning services through negotiation is being overlooked. Additionally, the fact that savings accrue to management when workers have fewer children is being overlooked as a potent area for income redistribution and profit sharing. This article attempts to explore the issues with the hope that the ideas generated may be of help to labor in securing necessary services and in obtaining increased economic security.

WHY FAMILY PLANNING?

There is little doubt that family planning is of benefit to mankind. The reduction in the world death rate due to better medical care has not been accompanied by a similar reduction in the birthrate. This fact has caused competent scientists in every sphere to question the very ability of this planet to continue to support human life at any level of existence, as long as this growth rate continues unchecked.[1]

This explosive growth of world population is felt most strongly in the undeveloped four-fifths of the world where excessive numbers of new dependents have led to unemployment, underemployment, urban glut and decay, increasing seasonal labor gluts in the agricultural sector and the pervasive ills of overcrowding, environmental deterioration and a decrease in the quality of life.[2] In some cases, the cart is put before the horse when it is contended that the only problem is one of redistribution of existing wealth and creation of new jobs by a concerned society. In reality, even if the financial resources of most undeveloped countries were shared equally among all citizens, the average per capita income of the laborer would probably not increase by more than half, and this would be quickly negated by the steady increase in population size. Viewed from another financial perspective, it has been estimated that the provision of U.S. $40,000,000 for family planning in the Philippines will prevent over 4,000,000 births, yet the same amount of money would produce less than 5,000 new jobs if used as investment capital.[3] In other words, it is not an either/or situation; in order for development to take place, birthrates must fall at the same time that new jobs are created.

This situation is difficult to bring home to the ordinary working person who has no reason to care for demographic figures. Yet reducing the number of children from national averages of seven or more to four or fewer per family can have far-reaching effects at the personal level. Maternal health is generally accepted as being inversely related to number of children, as are the intelligence and nutritional status of children.[4] Family welfare, the capability to save money, to educate children, to provide adequate parental supervision and to guarantee successful employment or marriage all depend to some extent on family size decisions made by parents.

In countries or situations where laborers must depend on the productivity of their children to provide old age support, the advantages of reducing family size are minimized when the family dips below a certain number of children. It is sensible from all points of view to reduce family size from six children to four; however, it is not sensible from the insecure position of laborers without pension plans to reduce their family size to three or two children, since this number is too small to insure that at least one of them will be successful, remain filial and support his or her parents. The establishment of a family planning program for workers has also the objective of elevating the standards of family life in general. Until workers can be convinced that their children will receive health care, education and employment, and that they will be economically secure in old age, it is difficult to convince them of the many benefits of child spacing and small family size. These include improved health, better nutrition, less emotional stress, stronger family solidarity and a larger share of parental love for each child. When this is achieved its aggregate effect will also be beneficial to the productive capability of management.

The View of Management

When asked to give their views on family planning or on any other program for the benefit of workers, management quite logically asks three questions: (1) How much will it cost me to promote this program? (2) How much will it save for my company? (3) How can I minimize cost and maximize profits? One manager in the Philippines puts the case this way:

> We provide P2,000,000[5] every year for housing, electricity, water, recreational and educational facilities for 25,000 workers. We must add two or three new classrooms and teachers each year. We are certain that by investing in family planning for our workers we can save money in the area of delivery of these social services. At the same time, we will be supporting our nation's efforts to reduce the population growth rate; and we will be enhancing the quality of life of our workers. Our directors are willing to wholeheartedly support this program, if we can adequately document his savings.[6]

The View of Labor

The task of defining labor's viewpoint in this area is best undertaken from the perspective of behavioral science. Certain contingencies impinge on workers to influence their decision-making regarding family size. These vary from culture to culture but generally include among others: the economic value of children either as sources of labor or for old age security; the costs associated with child raising; the societies' concept of "good" family size; desire to prove masculinity or maternalness; the pleasures associated with raising children; awareness of the fact that safe means exist for preventing pregnancy; the health of the mother; desire for privacy; influence of in-laws or other relatives; desire to perpetuate the family name or to pass on property; awareness of a population problem.

Any situation which either decreases or enhances the value of any of the factors listed above can have profound effects on family size. Thus it could be argued that if education is provided for free, and income tax deductions favor additional children, the balance is tipped in a worker's mind toward having additional children. On the other hand, if workers are separated from in-laws, or if property laws are changed to discourage dividing land, these contingencies would favor a smaller family.

With regard to family planning, therefore, labor quite logically asks, in the vernacular: "What's in it for me?" More precisely, the onus falls on management and on labor leaders to inform workers of the advantages of family planning, and to help enhance the contingencies which favor small families. In the end two questions persist: "If I accept the concept of family planning, what will I get in the way of benefits, especially economic security?" and "If I have fewer children than I previously planned, what benefits can I obtain to replace the potential labor of those children who were not born?" The proper answers to these questions can best be gained through negotiation. Examples of cases where "benevolent" management foresaw that these questions were amenable to logical reply come from Japan and India.

THE CASE OF JAPAN

The Japanese experience of introducing family planning into the industrial setting began during postwar reconstruction. In a pioneer project begun in 1953 at the NipponKokan Steel Company in Kawasaki City, the employer's decision to begin the program.was inspired by the correlation between industrial safety (loss of labor and man hours) and a stable family life. In this factory, management calculated that about 70 percent of all accidents might be attributable to difficulties in the private lives of employees.

In 1957 the Nippon Express Company, the biggest road haulage company in Japan, began to provide family planning services for workers as a result of a collective agreement initiated by management. Union endorsement, however, imposed several restrictions: that the family planning project should be considered as only one of several measures to promote welfare; that it should not serve as a pretext for refusing a wage increase, cutting back on family allowances, or interfering illegally in the internal affairs of the union; and that the scheme should be operated by the employer in a democratic manner based on principles of free consent and noninterference in employees' private lives.

According to estimates made by the Japanese National Railways, costs of implementing full-scale family planning programs for their employees were fully offset by the decrease in expenditure on family allowances, confinement, nursing and so on.

In general, trade unions endorsed family planning projects initiated by employers, although their enthusiasm varied from implicit consent to financial participation. Where these programs were treated with reserve it was generally because the following apprehensions were felt by employees: (1) they suspected that employers were trying to interfere in their private lives (especially where workers lived in company-owned housing estates); (2) they suspected the program was part of profit-maximizing rationalization efforts that employers in Japan made in order to survive in conditions of cutthroat postwar competition; (3) they suspected that the employer's true motivation in initiating such projects was to reduce the expenditures on family allowances. Most trade unions sought assurance from the employers that a family planning project would not adversely affect the system of family allowances.

In almost every case where employers wished to introduce a family planning scheme, they had to engage in lengthy consultation and negotiation with trade unions. Doubts and suspicions were only dispelled when labor participation in policy-making and application was built into the program. In the preparatory stages the question was often raised whether the introduction of a family planning project would most benefit employers or employees, especially in relation to the possible effect of reductions in births on payment of family allowances. The fact that in Japan "all the employers undertook to channel savings on family allowances into the various workers' welfare services" may have little bearing on similar programs in other countries where management is not as benevolent or is acting primarily on the profit motive.[7] The experience in Japan serves both as an example and as a warning. The fact that the benefits from adoption of family planning were shared with labor must be attributed in part to labor's suspicious attitude and their insistence on sharing in the economic rewards which came from participation.

THE TEA ESTATES PROGRAM

The best example of a program using savings from social welfare to reward families for remaining small comes from India. India has had a nationwide family planning program since 1952. It has only been fully operational since 1965 when the government greatly increased the budget and enlisted the assistance of all private and public bodies in promotion of the small family norm.

Some of the largest agricultural employers in India are the tea estates. The social welfare system employed by these estates includes payment for maternity benefits, hospital care and child allowances which amount to Rs. 160[8] for the first year, Rs. 100 for each year thereafter until the child reaches 12 and approximately Rs. 15 for medical care for each year until the child reaches 18. The estate loses the productivity of the woman during predelivery confinement and during maternity leave. Her productivity and that of her husband is lessened if the children are sick or need extra attention. The health of the woman may suffer due to repeated pregnancies. Also, the estate may find itself saddled with additional problems due to the presence of idle young people on the property.

The estates calculated that they could afford to set aside an amount of money approximately equal to Rs. 5 per month for each month that a woman averted a birth. This money comes directly from the funds that would normally have to be set aside to provide for maternity and child support programs outlined above. Operation of this plan and financial implications for the couples who enroll are as follows: for each female worker capable of having children the estates set up a joint savings account in the name of the company and the woman. The estate pays into this account a certain amount for every month that the woman is not pregnant. The account cannot be drawn upon until the woman completes her childbearing years, but it accumulates interest in the interim. If the woman becomes pregnant she forfeits a substantial amount of the funds that have been paid into the account, although she is eligible to continue in the program starting sometime after the birth of the child. The funds that she forfeits revert back to the company and help defray some of the company's costs due to the birth. The accounts draw interest at the normal rate for long-term bank deposits which in India is 6.5 percent.

If a woman stays in the program from age 35 to age 50 without any forteiture she will accumulate Rs. 1,500; if she joins at age 25 (by which time the typical woman has had her third child) and has no children thereafter, the family will accumulate Rs. 3,500.

The discounted cost to the tea estates of a birth is approximately Rs. 1,000. The discounted cost of paying Rs. 5 per month for 13 years in only about Rs. 500. In other words, if the company paid Rs. 5 per month to a woman for 13 years and as a result she had one less child than she otherwise would have had, the company would have saved Rs. 500.

When the normal pattern of childbirth and child spacing among tea plantation employees was reviewed it was found to be more likely that two, three or even four births would be prevented. Since each birth prevented saves the company Rs. 1,000 the plan pays for itself several times over.[9]

A FORMAT FOR NEGOTIATION

In seeking an equitable distribution of whatever profits may accrue through reduction in employee birthrates, the establishment of high-quality family planning services should not be overlooked as one of the objectives of the collective bargaining process. At the same time that profit sharing is discussed, negotiation should include the contraceptive delivery network, the motivational system, training of personnel and provision of funds, facilities and materials. Time off for recovery from operations and other procedures could be written into contracts and should not detract from sick leave provisions. Where employees are receiving no family welfare payments it may be wise in negotiation to concentrate on setting up high-quality contraceptive delivery systems. In this situation, management has less to gain by providing family welfare payments. Labor has the upper hand if they can convince management that substantial savings will accrue as a result of this program. Where previous negotiations have resulted in some or all of the following services and benefits to workers the advantage of labor over management in renewed negotiation is obvious: maternity benefits for unlimited numbers of dependents; child allowances for unlimited numbers of children; educational benefits; medical care for dependents, company housing and/or services such as electricity and water supply.

Where more of these benefits have been granted, the fact that absenteeism, sick leave, marital problems and emotional instability may tend to increase with increasing family size can be used to gain bargaining leverage. Collective bargaining should give workers some advantage in case management wishes to reduce or cut off benefits above a certain number of children in order to save money or, as more altruistically stated, "to help our country reduce its population growth rate." In negotiation, labor can say that it intends to wholeheartedly support management family planning efforts for the purposes of saving money, or for the general national welfare, as long as a share of this savings or welfare is put back into the hands of the workers. For example, labor could say that it is willing to share in the establishment of family planning services and in the recruitment of clients, as long as 60 percent of the savings accrued by management from families with three or fewer children are returned to those families in the form of education or pension benefits.

SPECIFIC AREAS OF RESPONSIBILITY

The traditional inputs of management and labor into contractual arrangements consist of capital and facilities on the part of management, energy and organization on the part of labor. This logical division persists when one thinks of joint responsibility with regard to the establishment of family planning motivation, facilities and services. When a group of labor and management representatives sat down recently in Cebu, Philippines, to map out the areas of responsibility of labor and management in the provision of family planning services, they arrived at the following set of guidelines. These are offered only as a pattern for others to review in formulating their own approach to this problem

Management could: (1) Provide training of existing or new personnel to insure that they are competent and well motivated to promote family planning. (2) Provide quality clinical services including follow-up and treatment of normal minor side effects. (3) Where clinical services are not available, are inadequate or are not well administered, provide paid referral to competent, nearby private or public facilities. (4) Integrate family planning into existing service and education programs including applied nutrition, community development, extension classes and education. (5) Attempt to influence surrounding communities which are adjacent to the industrial establishment. (6) Provide time off for workers to attend lectures and clinics. (7) Provide company transport, if available, to get workers to the clinic. (8) Provide lecture halls, projectors, visual aids and printed materials for motivational meetings. (9) Schedule information sessions and clinical services to insure that all workers get the opportunity to be exposed to the program. (10) Develop or procure from government channels, materials that can be understood by laborers and focus on their normal fears and needs. (11) Insure that government forms and reporting procedures are followed so that the involvement of the organization in the national program is secured.

Labor could: (1) Provide moral support for the program including support for information programs. (2) Insure that employees attend information sessions that are set up by management; attend clinics as scheduled, report complications as discovered and follow medical instructions. (3) Train shop stewards and/or their wives to act as motivators and communicators to enhance the image of family planning. (4) Help organize employees into groups to reinforce continuation such as wives' clubs or worker family planning groups. (5) Identify dissatisfied acceptors and employees or their wives who are speaking against the program and help persuade them to stop speaking against the program, if possible. (6) Integrate family planning education into normal activities of community development, social action and education undertaken by unions.

Both labor and management could: (1) Explore the possibility of plowing back a portion of whatever savings are accrued by management into a pension scheme to compensate workers for the loss of labor caused by having fewer children than were previously anticipated; and to promote pilot projects and studies in this area. (2) Commission a competent body to undertake a study to define the categories of side effects and to make recommendations regarding the legal responsibility of medical authorities in the area of treatment and care. (3) Continually reassess the status of the program to determine the awareness, acceptance and continued practice of family planning and to renegotiate provision of informational and motivational activities. (4) Negotiate with competent government authorities the coverage of workers who are not represented in unions or by management.[10] These guidelines should be presented not as inflexible demands but as a means of arriving at a consensus between labor and management in the hope of finding mutually satisfactory solutions to the problems of establishing and operating effective services.

NOTES

[1]National Academy of Sciences, *Resources and Man* (San Francisco, Calif.: National Research Council, Committees on Resources and Man, 1969); Donella Meadows et al., *The Limits to Growth* (New York: Universal Books, 1972).

[2]Paul Ehrlich and Anne Ehrlich, *Population, Resources and Environment* (San Francisco, Calif.: W. H. Freeman, 1970).

[3]Information derived from a lecture by Onofre D. Corpuz, Chairman, Fund for Assistance to Private Education, at Cebu City, Philippines, January 29, 1972.

[4]Joe D. Wray, "Population Pressure on Families: Family Size and Child Spacing," *Reports on Population/Family Planning* 2, no. 7 (New York: Population Council, August, 1971).

[5]P1.00 equals U.S. $0.16.

[6]Francisco Paraan, assistant vice-president, Benguet Consolidated Mines, Inc., Cebu City, Philippines, January 29, 1972.

[7]Toshinobu Kato and Takeshi Takahashi, "Family Planning in Industry: The Japanese Experience," International Labor Review 104 (September, 1971): 161-79.

[8]One rupee equals U.S. $0.13.

[9]Ronald Ridker, "Savings Account for Family Planning: An Illustration from the Tea Estates of India," *Studies in Family Planning* 2, no. 7 (New York: Population Council, July, 1971) as updated through correspondence with United Plantation Association of South India.

[10]Second Managers, Trade Union Leaders Conference, *Report* (Cebu City, Philippines, January, 28-30 to April, 1972).

23

United States Policy and Political Development in Latin America

YALE H. FERGUSON

We must deal realistically with governments in the inter-American system as they are," stated former President Nixon in his address of October 31, 1969, outlining the major aspects of his administration's policies toward Latin America. With these words he ratified the fact that the official attitudes which prevailed during the Johnson years regarding the domestic political environment in Latin America were something more than a temporary aberration. Gone were the ringing phrases of the Kennedy period about the dawning of a new era of democracy and development in the hemisphere. No less than 17 military coups d'etat, the staggering gap between aspirations and accomplishments in the balance sheet of the Alliance for Progress and the apparent decline of the guerrilla offensive that was anticipated in the wake of the Cuban Revolution all had taken their toll.

The posture of overt pragmatism reaffirmed by the Nixon administration reflects both grave doubts that the United States can have a substantial constructive influence upon the political dimension of the modernization process in Latin America and also—aside from any lingering threat of radical revolution—an acceptance of the status quo as generally consistent with U.S. interests.

While congressional critics of the Nixon policies urge abandonment of anticommunism—partly to avoid another incident like the 1965 Dominican crisis—and complain that U.S. aid bolsters unprogressive military and civilian governments, the alternatives they advance involve less (rather than more) attempted interference with indigenous patterns of Latin American political change. They would have the United States largely "disengage" from Latin America and come to terms with what they envisage as increasing diversity and nationalism in the region.

The most striking thing about U.S. policies relating to domestic politics in Latin America has been their cyclic character: What has usually been termed the "promotion of democracy" in the area alternately has—or has not—been high on Washington's list of priorities. Although, as we shall see, there have been significant variations in comparable parts of the recurrent cycle and a concern for the best interests of the United States (read differently at different times) has undergirded them all, the cyclic pattern has been dominant. In the sense that policies on the democracy question came full circle between 1959 and 1964, this tumultuous period constituted one complete cycle. However, in the perspective of history, it is only one of several.

U.S. PRO-DEMOCRACY POLICIES

From the outset of inter-American relations in the early nineteenth century, the United States has periodically adopted unilateral policies designed to further contemporary standards of democracy in (at least) various parts of the hemisphere. The fact that most of the newly independent states of Latin America framed republican constitutions initially helped them to secure recognition from the United States. As the Latin American independence movement progressed, the conviction grew that it would lead to the establishment of "regimes whose political orientation . . . was of the same general revolutionary and liberal type as that represented by the United States and combatted by the 'allied despots of Europe' [the Holy Alliance]."[2] Monroe himself explained his recognition decision as in part motivated by a desire to promote "the establishment of free republican governments." In his famous doctrine, Monroe spoke of a dramatic contrast between the republican governments of the Western Hemisphere and the absolute monarchies of Europe. Dexter Perkins observes: "Against [the] Old World order, based on the doctrines of absolutism, Monroe opposed a new one, based on the right of the peoples of the world to determine their own destiny and to govern themselves."[4] Nearly a century later, the United States underwrote the Central American (Tobar) treaties of 1907 and 1923, which (among other things) denied recognition to regimes emanating from coups d'etat. The 1907 treaty provided for the withholding of recognition until free elections had been held after a coup. The 1923 treaty went further, to deny recognition even to governments elected following a coup when an individual serving as president, vice-president or chief of state was: (a) one of the leaders of the coup or a relative of same; (b) a member of the military command or secretary of state within the six months prior to the coup, during the coup or while the election was in progress; (c) anyone disqualified by the constitution from holding these offices.[5] Wilson began an essentially separate campaign for constitutional government when he assumed office in 1913.[6] Hoover's secretary of state, Henry A. Stimson, tried to lay the foundations for democracy during the latter stages of the U.S. intervention in Nicaragua.[7] In 1933 Undersecretary Sumner Welles journeyed to Cuba with instructions from President Roosevelt to see to the liberalization of the Machado dictatorship or to help bring it down.[8] At the close of World War II, U.S. ambassador to Argentina and then assistant secretary for inter-American affairs, Spruille Braden made Perón the principal target of a short-lived democratic crusade.[9] In 1948 the Truman administration contemplated a more modest pro-democracy effort in reaction to several coups thought possibly to be Peronist-inspired.[10] A decade later, the Eisenhower government went beyond mere compliance with OAS resolutions in levying diplomatic and economic sanctions against the Trujillo regime.[11] Finally, support for democracy was again a prominent feature of U.S. policies during the Kennedy years.[12]

POLICY GOALS

U.S. attempts to foster democracy in Latin America have stemmed from the interplay of two central motives: (1) a desire to bring the blessings of liberty to benighted countries south of the border, implying the goal of democratic government; and (2) a concern for the security interests of the United States, including the objective of political stability in Latin America. Emphasis upon one or the other goal has shifted from one period to the next, but (both altruists and cynics beware) in only one instance does it appear that U.S. policy-makers proceeded on the basis of a single motive alone: this in the Tobar era when Secretary of State Hughes privately acknowledged that the Central American formula substituted no guarantee of free elections for the resort to revolution which the treaties supposedly abolished. Hughes wrote: "The question whether . . . the policy . . . is a good one is very debatable. In these . . . countries revolutions and *coups d'état* are often about the only reform measures available to the people . . . to dislodge corruption. Elections there frequently don't mean much . . . [therefore] these people are entitled to their revolutions. . . . But . . . it would have been impossible . . . to take the position that they must not take this step to make revolutions less likely; that we wouldn't agree to it; and that we insisted that they have revolutions [because] revolutions in Central America . . . are not advantageous to us. We cannot tolerate much disturbance in the Caribbean region, because of the vital importance to our self-defense of the Panama Canal. . . . If the disturbances are of such a character in injuring life and property that foreign governments would take control if we were supine, then it is absolutely essential that we intervene."[13]

Wilson's and Braden's policies rate highest on the scale of unabashed idealism; however, these men too regarded a pro-democracy posture as serving U.S. security interests. To Wilson's mind, the only way to achieve lasting stability was to allow the people to elect their own leaders and to teach them the benefits of the rule of law.[14] Braden was convinced that the hemisphere would never be completely secure as long as what he labeled "Nazi-Fascist" regimes remained in power.[15]

In other periods, the security goal has been even closer to the surface of U.S. policy. Monroe sympathized with Latin America's espousal of republicanism, but he was principally concerned about the dangers of European intervention inherent in monarchical plots. This was the implication of his warning to the Holy Alliance that the United States "should consider any attempt on their part to extend their political system to any portion of this hemisphere as dangerous to our peace and safety."[16] The Tobar treaties were part of a U.S. design to curb civil strife in the Central American vicinity of the Panama Canal. The Truman administration bestirred itself about postwar coups primarily out of fear that Peronism was beginning to spread.[17] After years of indifference, the Eisenhower government joined a vigorous assault against Trujillo not only because the United States needed Latin American votes to isolate

Castro, but also because it had belatedly come to believe that the very presence of the Dominican tryanny encouraged radicalism in the Caribbean. Slater comments: "Herter's Dominican policy was based on a simple relation: 'Batista is to Castro as Trujillo is to—,' and the United States wanted to insure that it could help fill in the blank."[18] Kennedy and several of his closest advisers were ideologically committed to democracy; yet they too—in a much wider sense than their Eisenhower counterparts—thought democracy was the only acceptable alternative to communism in Latin America.

Policy-makers have assumed that most of the international and domestic preconditions for the kind of democracy they envisaged in Latin America already existed. However unrealistic some policies appear in retrospect, the fact remains that many self-styled "practical" men did not consider them to be unrealistic at the time: the dictates of idealism and realism thus have often seemed to coincide. Following the American and French revolutions and colonial victories in the wars of independence against Spain, it is understandable that Monroe might have been optimistic about the republican course of the Western Hemisphere. Wilson interpreted the increasing pressures for liberalization and self-determination experienced by various European monarchies as an indication that democracy would soon sweep the world. Braden expected that the defeat of the Axis totalitarian powers in World War II would lead to the downfall of other authoritarian regimes in Latin America, particularly those which had admired Fascist models and harbored Axis agents. When Kennedy became president, long-standing dictatorships were crumbling throughout the hemisphere. Odría, Rojas Pinilla, Pérez Jiménez and Batista had fallen; and Trujillo was obviously in trouble. After a century and a half, the age of the classical caudillo was clearly drawing to a close.[19]

The Kennedy administration added a major new dimension to the policies of earlier periods. Previously pro-democracy policies had focused solely on obeisance to essential constitutional norms and carried no specific connotations of economic and social change. Washington had generally regarded the latter with suspicion, as possibly posing a threat to the investments of U.S. nationals. In contrast, New Frontier decision-makers posited a mutually reinforcing relationship between democracy, security (political stability) and economic and social development in Latin America. Another remarkable aspect of the Kennedy administration was the

sheer intensity of its concern with Latin America. Theodore C.
Sorensen has written that "no continent was more constantly in the
President's mind . . . than Latin America."[20] Richard N. Good-
win told the author that a day hardly passed without Kennedy's in-
quiring personally about current developments in the hemisphere.
He took a keen interest in the minutest details: for example, in the
composition—down to the last man—of U.S. delegations to inter-
American conferences.

In the Kennedy view: If the "twilight of the tyrants" had come at
last to Latin America, the "revolution of rising expectations"
meant that it was also "one minute to midnight." Because of the
rapidly escalating desires of Latin America's masses for a better
life, the region was in the throes of a fundamental economic and
social revolution that was as inevitable as it was explosive. The
question was not whether dramatic structural change would soon
take place, rather whether it would assume the character of peaceful reform (evolution) or violent revolution (chaos), manipulated
by Communists and indigenous radicals hostile to the United
States. If other Castroite revolutions were to occur in Latin America, the traditional U.S. sphere of influence, it might well have a
drastic impact on U.S. prestige and positions of strength the world
over.

Kennedy policy-makers reasoned that they could forestall violent revolution under the aegis of Communism and native radicalism only by offering a *viable* alternative: It had to be clear to the
humble citizens of Latin America that their lot could be improved
some other way. Reliance upon caudillos or even ostensibly democratic, oligarchical regimes to suppress domestic discontent would
pave the way for the very elements that the United States was striving to defeat. Schlesinger remarks. "Kennedy fully understood—
this was, indeed, the mainspring of all his thinking about Latin
America—that, with all its pretensions to realism, the militant an-
tirevolutionary line represented the policy most likely to strengthen
the communists and lose the hemisphere."[21] The Alliance for
Progress could provide desperately needed capital for development; however, it would not succeed unless there also existed responsible Latin American governments dedicated to—and capable
of engineering—fundamental reforms.

Reviewing the contemporary political scene in Latin America,
the groups most likely to organize such governments appeared to
be the Latin American democratic Left.[22] In the judgment of Ken-

nedy and his staff, all other political groups were either too oriented toward the status quo or too radical. The Latin American military might fall into either category, depending upon whether the
sample selected was a typical set of *golpista* officers or a Perón.
According to Schlesinger, the Kennedy administration's assessment was that when the military were not entirely unprogressive,
they tended to be "revolutionaries of a sort themselves, like
Nasser, and hardly more agreeable to the capital-commanding
class than a Castro."[23] Military leadership which would be more
progressive than the former and less inclined to xenophobic nationalism and a demagogic domestic ideology than the latter was initially considered an intellectual possibility, but was ultimately dismissed as little more than that for the foreseeable future.

Prospects looked bright for the democratic Left. They alone
seemed to have effective party organizations, drawing support
from a supposedly dynamic middle sector in Latin American society, and ideologies stressing evolutionary reform. Moreover, their
recent political successes in Venezuela, Colombia, Costa Rica,
Honduras, Peru, Bolivia, Brazil and Argentina gave them claim to
being the dominant political force in Latin America. It was presumed that they would win elections, if elections were held, and
would subsequently prove willing and able to carry out the reforms
they preached.

New Frontier decision-makers concluded that the United States
should lend its enthusiastic moral and material backing to the
Latin American democratic Left. This support, they believed, accorded nicely with the United States's own democratic tradition
and offered the best hope that the Latin American revolution
would take a moderate course instead of embracing a radicalism
inimical to U.S. security.

THE SOURCES AND LIMITS OF U.S. PRO-DEMOCRACY INFLUENCE

The geographical scope of U.S. pro-democracy policies has
broadened over the years. With the exception of the Monroe Doctrine (which was little more than rhetoric when it was first declared), the United States has applied its policies to the entire
hemisphere only since World War II. The range of the Tobar and
Wilson policies never extended beyond the Caribbean, while Stimson and Welles each focused on a single Caribbean country. Wil-

son indeed believed that—in terms of political and economic progress—the ABC countries and Uruguay in South America belonged in a completely different category than the banana republics of the Caribbean area.[24] Once the United States had emerged from World War II as a superpower with global operations and responsibilities, South America—even Argentina—no longer seemed so far away. Braden was as (mistakenly) confident of his ability to defeat Perón as Wilson, Huerta. Kennedy paid no less heed to coups in Argentina and Peru than to those in the Dominican Republic and Honduras.

Contributing to the pro-democracy influence of the United States has been its capacity and willingness to institute sanctions against those who dared to challenge its policies: verbal castigation, nonrecognition, severance of diplomatic relations, economic pressures and the threat and use of force. Most Latin American governments have coveted recognition from the United States since the era of independence. The economic weapon was forged by World War II—and earlier in the Caribbean—as the United States became a leading market for Latin American commodities and supplier of arms and other industrial goods. Control over the distribution of steadily increasing amounts of economic and military assistance, culminating in the Alliance, gave Washington further leverage. The ultimate sanction—force—has continued to play an important role. Wilson precipitated the Veracruz incident in a fit of pique with Huerta. Stimson's efforts to educate Nicaraguans in the ways of democracy proceeded under U.S. military occupation. Kennedy dispatched warships to Dominican waters in November 1961, when it appeared that the "wicked uncles" of the Trujillo family were plotting a return to power. Had the warship maneuver failed and, in another case, had Duvalier bowed to U.S. pressures to abandon the Haitian presidency upon the expiration of his constitutional term in May, 1963,[25] it is very possible that Kennedy would have ordered the landing of marines.

As the Kennedy administration partially realized from the outset and other administrations have discovered to their dismay, the utility of sanctions is extremely limited. In the judgment of Kennedy policy-makers the actual use of force was feasible only with respect to a few small Caribbean countries and then could prove prohibitively costly in terms of human lives and its implications for inter-American solidarity. Until 1965, Latin Americans regarded marine occupations as strictly a thing of the past. Moreover, the record of previous occupations offered no evidence that democratic practices would persist much longer than the physical presence of the United States. U.S. Ambassador John Bartlow Martin wrote of the situation at the time of the 1963 Dominican coup: "How could we restore a Dominican President to the Palace whose own voters did not protest his overthrow? We could do it, of course, with armed force. But ought we? What kind of democracy is it that can be kept in the Palace only by a foreign fleet in the harbor? By so using force to 'support democracy,' you destroy the thing you try to create. We had the force. But we could not use it. Force alone is not power. Force may be unlimited. But power is always narrowly limited. And the greater the power the narrower the limits. . . ."[26]

The practical effect of other sanctions was equally problematical. Compared with being ousted from office, U.S. nonrecognition and economic pressures presented relatively low-level threats to unconstitutional regimes. Recalcitrant governments could always tighten their belts and, up to a point, compensate by leaning more heavily upon extracontinental markets and sources of supply.[27] Finally, there was the chance that, by triggering latent anti-Americanism, coercive measures might have the counter-productive effect of strengthening target regimes. Both Huerta and Perón had skillfully manipulated nationalist resentment against *gringo* (foreign) interference. Cline describes the atmosphere in Mexico at the end of 1913: "After all Wilson's threats, bombast, scurryings and alarms, a rupture of relations and war between Mexico and the United States seemed imminent. Mexicans rallied around Huerta, who now became (to his own surprise) a symbol of political independence in the face of Wilsonian pressures. Probably he was never so strong. He seemed impregnable."[28]

With armed intervention customarily ruled out of the question, sanctions have not offered the possibility of crushing offending regimes. Their availability thus has not constituted an infallible deterrent, nor has their application guaranteed a particular outcome. However, as serious inconveniences to be avoided or removed, they have given the United States additional bargaining power before and after specific challenges have arisen.

U.S. policy-makers have envisaged their direct exercise of pro-democracy influence as merely supplementing the efforts of Latin American democrats who presumably enjoyed wide popular followings. They have relied upon the people of Latin America and

democratic leaders to provide vigorous support at the domestic
level for U.S. pro-democracy policies. Washington has generally
been disappointed in this respect. Wilson was deeply disturbed
when fighting continued after the collapse of Huerta's government
and the leading contender for power, Carranza, carefully disassoci-
ated himself from the United States. The U.S. negotiators at the
Niagara meeting reported to Washington on a conversation with
unofficial representatives of the Constitutionalists as follows:
"They insisted that they might be willing to take up the question of
surrender with someone outside the mediation with which the
United States had nothing to do, but that as far as mediation was
concerned they would absolutely decline to receive anything from
the Mediators or through the mediation; that they would not accept as a gift anything which the Mediators could give them, even
though it was what they were otherwise seeking; that they would
not take it 'on a silver platter.' They declined to discuss names or
propose names for provisional president, saying that no one would
be satisfactory that was appointed by the Mediators, even if it was
Carranza himself, because anything that came from the Mediators
would not be accepted by their party or by the Mexican people."[29]
Braden's plans went awry when the standardbearers of a coalition
of Argentine democratic parties proved no match for Perón in the
1946 election. Kennedy was distressed that few ordinary citizens
appeared willing to fight for democracy when coups swept Latin
America in 1962-63. The complete failure of the general strike
called by APRA in Peru was pivotal in convincing him that the
United States would have to battle the military almost alone. In
many Latin American countries, the middle sector was itself divided, and the rest of the populace was either unmobilized politically
or so accustomed to the rapid rise and fall of governments that
they despaired of any dramatic shift for the better.

Yet target military regimes themselves were unable to rally substantial popular support, and the anti-American bugaboo did not
materialize. The most encouraging case was an early and exceptional one: the "wicked uncles" episode in the Dominican Republic. Kennedy decision-makers were pleasantly surprised when the
sight of U.S. ships on the horizon brought—not cries of gunboat
diplomacy—but cheers from residents of the capital who celebrat-
ed in the streets.

Still another limited source of support for U.S. policies has been
other hemisphere governments. Even before the nonintervention

principle became the so-called cornerstone of the inter-American system in the mid-1930s, the Colossus of the North occasionally felt the need for some collective underwriting of its policies; and to this extent its pro-democracy campaigns spilled over into the multilateral sphere. Although the Tobar treaties were fostered by the United States and depended for success upon U.S. influence, they did involve a formal international agreement. Wilson imperiously "consulted" with the ABC powers on two separate occasions during the Mexican crisis, once immediately following the incident at Veracruz and again when it was necessary to decide between rival claimants after Huerta's defeat.[31] In 1945 Braden unhesitatingly endorsed an abortive proposal advanced by Uruguayan Foreign Minister Rodríguez Larreta which called for inter-American sanctions against hemisphere dictatorships.[32] The timing of the proposal and the prompt approval it received in Washington gave rise to the impression (still unsubstantiated) that it had been instigated by the United States.[33] Three years later, Secretary of State Acheson received a cool response when he asked Latin American governments to consider whether the newly established OAS might take some action to discourage further coups. The Eisenhower and Kennedy administrations made effective use of the multilateral umbrella provided by OAS sanctions in negotiations leading to the post-Trujillo democratic experiment in the Dominican Republic. Both administrations also gave strong support to the ad hoc OAS electoral assistance and observation program which grew out of the early Dominican experience. Finally, Kennedy tried to no avail to interest the OAS in planning to exercise a form of trusteeship over Haiti should the need arise.

The legitimacy of the use of nonrecognition and additional coercive measures as instruments of pro-democracy (and other) policies has long been a controversial issue in the Americas.[34] In 1930 Mexican Foreign Minister Genero Estrada announced that his government regarded the institution of recognition as an affront to state sovereignty and would henceforth follow the practice of merely maintaining or withdrawing its diplomatic representatives as circumstances required. Many Latin American governments initially seized upon the "Estrada Doctrine" or a variant, the virtually automatic recognition of new governments, as one means of countering U.S. interventions in the days of "Dollar Diplomacy." In later years, this position has continued to attract governments which have opposed in principle external meddling in domestic politics and/or those which have had something to fear from pro-democracy offensives.

The principal challenges to the noninterference posture emerged during periods of democratic successes in Latin America (1944-48 and 1958-63) when a number of governments were charged with a spirit of democratic evangelism and an even more compelling desire for international protection. Several of these governments adopted unilateral policies denying recognition to unconstitutional regimes, explicitly or implicitly in accordance with the "Betancourt Doctrine."

Militant Latin American democratic governments also urged a similar course of action upon the OAS after World War II. Indeed, it has been they—rather than the United States—which have originated most of the pro-democracy proposals which have been considered at the international level. They maintained that the inter-American organization should support democracy not only as an ideal but also because there existed a relationship between the promotion of democracy and the primary function of the OAS, the maintenance of hemispheric peace and security. The precise nature of the threat to security that they posited changed with the times. At the close of the war, with Axis examples fresh in mind, it was fashionable to assert that dictatorships were inherently expansive. The 1942 meeting of Ministers of Foreign Affairs at Rio created a seven-man Emergency Advisory Committee for Political Defense (EACPD). The following year the EACPD promulgated the so-called "Guani Doctrine," recommending consultation between the American states before recognition of new governments instituted by force, to discourage the establishment of regimes inimical to hemispheric security. With the support of the EACPD, the United States proceeded to apply economic pressures against the Villarroel government in Bolivia and successive military regimes in Argentina. Several Latin American governments were uneasy about the Guani Doctrine and were distressed by the coercive policies of the United States, which—coupled with the Braden vs. Perón episode—undoubtedly made them less receptive to proposals for multilateral pro-democracy programs after the war.

At the Mexico City Conference in 1945, the Arévalo government in Guatemala presented a draft resolution calling for abstention from recognition of and diplomatic relations with antidemocratic regimes, including those emanating from coups against existing democratic governments. The conference passed the proposal on for study by the Inter-American Juridical Committee (IAJC), which expressed its disapproval in an opinion that even today stands as one of the most profound analyses of democracy.[37]

When Rodríguez Larreta made his proposal several months after the Mexico City gathering, less than half of the American states indicated interest and only a few offered their unequivocal support. More recently, pro-democracy spokesmen argued that dictatorships lead to civil strife and related international frictions (exile invasions emanating from neighboring countries), and that they are breeding grounds for communism (oppressed masses turn to radicalism).

The inter-American controversy over the democracy issue has produced far more debate than practical prodemocracy action. Latin American democrats failed in their effort to frame the Rio Treaty so as the place deviations from democracy on a par with other "threats to the peace" occasioning inter-American consultation and possible collective sanctions.[38] Upon their insistence, the Bogota Conference accepted Article 5(d) of the OAS Charter, making the maintenance of governmental systems of representative democracy a binding obligation of member states. However, the conference neither clarified the exact nature of the Charter democratic norm nor provided enforcement procedures.[39] Subsequently, the OAS has applied sanctions against only two dictatorships, the Trujillo and Castro regimes. Both of these cases were obviously exceptional, not the least in that Trujillo and Castro left themselves open to Rio Treaty penalties by advocating and materially assisting the violent overthrow of fellow Latin American governments.[40] After Trujillo's assassination, the OAS became more deeply involved in Dominican politics than many governments had originally intended; but a clear majority felt an obligation to insure a democratic outcome of the transitional situation which the organization was partially responsible for creating.[41]

Otherwise: OAS member governments gave their approval in 1959 to a rough definition of democracy incorporated into the "Declaration of Santiago"[42] and have continued to support OAS observation and technical assistance in electoral matters, extended by the Secretariat only upon the request of the governments concerned. The Fifth Meeting of Foreign Ministers also directed the OAS Council to prepare a draft convention on the "effective exercise of representative democracy"; asked the Inter-American Council of Jurists (IACJ) to study "the possible juridical relationship between respect for human rights and the effective exercise of representative democracy, and the right to set in motion the machinery of international law in force"; and entrusted the Inter-American Peace Committee (IAPC) with the task of examining the "relationship between violations of human rights or the non-exercise of representative democracy . . . and the political tensions that affect the peace of the hemisphere." Finally, the conference established the Inter-American Commission on Human Rights and resolved to have the IACJ draft a convention on human rights.

Of all the steps outlined above, only the initiatives related to human rights produced much in the way of concrete results. Through its investigation of complaints and publication of reports, the Inter-American Commission on Human Rights has made a modest contribution to the welfare of particular individuals suffering political repression under undemocratic regimes. The human rights convention has gone through several revisions to date and is still under formal consideration by the OAS.

Regarding the other measures envisaged in 1959: The OAS Council produced a Draft Convention on the Effective Exercise of Representative Democracy, but the treaty failed to gain any appreciable support and is now, for all practical purposes, dead. The proposed text is Appendix A in *Acta ordinaria*, December 15, 1959, OEA/Ser.G/II/C-a-353. The IAJC found a clear relationship between human rights and democracy; however, its study strongly recommended that the American states concentrate on establishing procedures furthering human rights rather than democracy per se. The IAPC asserted in its report that there existed a relationship between democracy, human rights and peace; yet it was unable to suggest a formula for action that would not violate the nonintervention principle. The report is in OAS, Pan American Union, Inter-American Peace Committee (1960, Appendix E). Urgent appeals from Latin American democratic governments menaced by the military in 1962-63 finally resulted in an OAS call for a meeting of foreign ministers.[43] The meeting was never convened, largely because pro-democracy ranks were by then decimated. In 1965 the Second Special Inter-American Conference reinforced what has usually been standard diplomatic practice by recommending informal consultation before the recognition of governments arising from coups.[44]

The Kennedy administration gave only cautious encouragement to proposals for multilateral action advanced by militant democratic governments. The U.S. representative on the OAS Council supported the request for a foreign ministers meeting in 1962, but he suggested that the OAS delay indefinitely setting a date for the meeting. At the same time, he forcefully maintained that the non-intervention principle did not constitute a barrier to OAS action in the democracy field. He said: "In the view of my government, aside from the grave peril of Communist subversion, the great danger facing the countries of America today is *not* a threat to our *in*dependence through intervention but our possible failure to realize and act fully and jointly upon the challenging truth of our *inter*dependence." (See *Acta extraordinaria*, August 22, 1962, OEA/Ser.G/II/C-a-460:2-7.) Assistant Secretary of State Edwin M. Martin made essentially the same points in his Pan American Day address of April 16, 1963.[45] Aware of the likely deadlock in the OAS on anything much beyond the voluntary election observation program, Kennedy policy-makers wanted to avoid U.S. identification with initiatives that were doomed to fail. Moreover, even had it been possible to agree on collective action, they were generally reluctant to trade the flexibility of unilateralism for the constraints inherent in genuine multilateralism. They far preferred meshing unilateral policies with other Latin American governments informally to channeling pro-democracy activities through the OAS, which would have institutionalized Latin American influence and committed the United States to specific measures embodied in an operative resolution or treaty.[46]

On the other hand, the Kennedy administration recognized the usefulness of a multilateral umbrella in the post-Trujillo Dominican and 1963 Haitian episodes, when nothing less than a plan for national political reconstruction was involved. But a strong thread of unilateralism ran through both of these cases as well. The naval show of force that frightened the Trujillos was not cleared in advance with the OAS. Kennedy showed every intention of carrying out the marine occupation of Haiti if necessary, in spite of OAS unwillingness before the fact to authorize a possible inter-American trusteeship. Indeed, the Haitian case was not so much an instance of Washington's miscalculating on its rule to avoid advancing proposals that had slim chance of approval, as it was an attempt to lay the groundwork for the subsequent multilateralization of an operation if the United States had to present the OAS with a *fait accompli*.

Although the OAS was stalemated on the democracy question

and only a handful of Latin American governments adhering to the Betancourt Doctrine joined the United States in unilaterally ostracizing unconstitutional regimes, there was strikingly little overt hostility in Latin America to the Kennedy posture. The Chilean foreign minister cautioned the United States against the possibility of being "more royalist than the king."[47] We have already noted that the anti-American bugaboo did not materialize among domestic constituencies: the same might be said for the international reaction. Lack of public criticism—even by governments traditionally hypersensitive about intervention like Mexico—was evidence of the continued strength of the regional democratic ideal and of widespread support for the development objectives of the Alliance, which depended for their realization upon the Latin American democratic Left. It was also silent testimony to Latin Americans' faith in the motives of the Kennedy administration.

THE FAILURE OF WILL: SELF-IMPOSED LIMITS ON U.S. PRO-DEMOCRACY INFLUENCE DERIVING FROM COMPETING POLICY GOALS

The United States itself has been responsible for some of the most significant limits on its influence in pro-democracy periods. Those administering U.S. pro-democracy policies have applied them with such apparent inconsistency as to raise the question of whether a true dedication to democracy existed. They have done so largely because they were simultaneously pursuing other objectives, originally deemed consistent with democracy, which in important respects proved incompatible. We may examine these problems under the category of U.S. failures of will, reflecting tensions between the goals that pro-democracy policies have been designed to serve.

By far the most serious clash has been between the goals of democracy and security. Political stability has been a continuing security objective of U.S. policy-makers, and they have often supported democracy because they regarded it as the most stable form of government. Nevertheless, furthering democracy has regularly involved condoning a considerable amount of immediate instability. Toppling an old dictatorship or even a new unconstitutional regime is by definition a destablilizing act—at least in the short run. The Central American Tobar treaties actually encouraged revolutions in the sense of making it more difficult for the leaders of a coup to consolidate their control. During the same period, Washington more than once found it impossible to tolerate the opposition elements (seen as scoundrels)—for example, the Liberals in Nicaragua—who might have come to power through the democratic process. Although the Grau San Martín government in Cuba clearly enjoyed wider popular support than its predecessor, Welles never forgave it for arising out of the overthrow of a provisional regime which he had hand picked to follow Machado. Kennedy faced difficult choices when coups occurred in Guatemala and Ecuador in 1963: one of these was support democracy and accept the probable victories in upcoming elections of former presidents with demagogic proclivities (Arévalo and Velasco Ibarra respectively) or rely upon the "stabilizing" intervention of the military.

The threat of communism has further complicated judgment. In an earlier era, immediate instability raised the prospect of another dictatorship and, at worst, the increasingly hypothetical danger of European meddling. However, by 1933 Welles's successor as U.S. ambassador to Cuba, Jefferson Caffrey, was expressing himself as "disturbed at seemingly communistic tendencies in the [Grau] regime."[48] Of course, the later Guatemalan (Arbenz) and Cuban experiences have placed virtually any political vacuum in a new context. Primarily because of the short-run instability problem, the Eisenhower government initially urged that the OAS press for the steady liberalization of the Trujillo regime, rather than apply sanctions which might bring about its sudden collapse.[49] Moreover, both the Eisenhower and Kennedy administrations recognized that the task of building democracy in the Dominican Republic extended far beyond the downfall of the tyrant and therefore attempted to shape a program for the political reconstruction and socioeconomic development of that country. Kennedy had a similar program in mind for Haiti.

New Frontier decision-makers saw no contradiction between support for democracy and efforts to isolate the Castro regime and to strengthen the counterinsurgency and civic action capabilities of the Latin American military. From their perspective, defense against subversion was essential if Latin American democracies were to survive and proceed with evolutionary reforms. However, administration policies may have had at least a marginal effect in encouraging Latin American coups. The United States appeared to be inviting the military to judge a given government by its attitudes towards anti-Castro measures in the OAS and towards leftists at home, as well as (or even instead of) its degree of commitment to democracy and progress. The military accepted the invitation and in case after case cited "softness on communism" as one of the principal reasons for their intervention. In addition, U.S. training and civic action programs helped build the military's "modern" image of itself as the prime mover in national development.[50]

The Kennedy administration's security policies may have done a disservice to the cause of Latin American democracy in still more profound ways. The Alliance proclaimed that the democratic evolutionary road was the best route to modernization. But in the event that democratic governments could or would not move rapidly enough to meet the rising demands of their citizens, U.S.-trained and equipped counterinsurgency teams would insure that as little as possible (nonmilitary) violence shattered the calm of political impotence and indecision. One might argue that even more than some democratic governments needed a moratorium on violence to survive, they needed the specter of revolution to remind them constantly of the consequences of failure. Meanwhile, U.S. opposition and OAS sanctions presented Castro with an underdog image that was of great use to him domestically and abroad, none the least in that it served as a ready excuse for the less-than-spectacular performance of his own model for development.

To a lesser extent than democracy and security, the goals of democracy and economic and social change also proved incompatible. Curiously, Wilson started in Mexico with constitutional government as his main goal and little awareness of the socioeconomic dimension of the revolution in progress—and ended by giving priority to the latter over the former. At one point in the struggle against Huerta, Carranza's emissary succeeded in convincing Wilson that the constitutionalist's agrarian reform program was the precondition for political peace in Mexico.[51] Later, when the constitutionalists were themselves divided and Carranza at last appeared to be in firm control of the capital, Wilson no longer displayed his old enthusiams for free elections. On August 8, 1915, he wrote to Secretary of State Lansing: "The first and most essential step in settling the affairs of Mexico is not to call general elections. It seems to me necessary that a provisional government essentially revolutionary in character should take action to institute reforms by decree before the full forms of the constitution are resumed."[52] Another important consideration affecting the Kennedy responses to coups in Guatemala and Ecuador was the fact that the deposed governments had been singularly corrupt and slow to action on the economic and social front. For somewhat different reasons, the Kennedy administration was disillusioned with Juan Bosch in the Dominican Republic, whose government succumbed to the military after only eight months. In Washington's judgment, only a conciliatory leader could achieve reform in a situation so threatened with assaults from both the Right and the Left—and Bosch, though well intentioned, had a personal political style which polarized competing factions. Finally, Kennedy decision-makers painfully realized that denying recognition and aid to an unconstitutional regime involved the dilemma of suspending the Alliance to save the Alliance. It was particularly difficult to justify this course of action when—as in Guatemala and Ecuador—the military regimes that resulted from coups were less corrupt and no more unprogressive than the governments they replaced.[54]

THE BALANCE SHEET ON THE KENNEDY POLICIES

Rhetoric and performance are equally relevant to an understanding of Kennedy pro-democracy policies. Those principally responsible for administering the Kennedy policies genuinely believed in the democratic evolution vs. violent revolution rhetoric of the Alliance and took their public commitment of the United States to a pro-democracy posture very seriously. Indeed, the Kennedy administration's formal position on the democracy issue contrasts sharply with the unabashed espousal of pragmatism by succeeding administrations. Kennedy policies were policies of *purpose*, not an open admission of aimless drifting or perhaps (more insidious) of purposes which had to be concealed. Within the framework of their blanket commitment to democracy, Kennedy decision-makers adhered to the largely unarticulated guideline of flexibility. This approach derived mainly from the president's own political instincts, reinforced by the similar attitudes of White House Special Assistant Ralph Dungan and Assistant Secretary of State Edwin M. Martin, who had replaced the more ideologically inclined Richard N. Goodwin and Arthur M. Schlesinger, Jr. as Kennedy's key Latin American advisers by the time that the most serious threats to administration policies arose. Keenly aware of the limits of U.S. influence and, to some extent, of the problem of competing goals, the president determined almost from the outset to opt for minimum democratic progress if this were necessary to limit cost to the United States. Later, the sheer number and variety of coups and the disappointing lack of active Latin American support for a hard antimilitary line only increased his caution.

With the exception of pressures brought to bear for post-Trujillo democratization in the Dominican Republic and against the notorious Haitian dictatorship, the Kennedy administration did not elect to challenge existing regimes. Whenever a military coup appeared likely to occur, the strategy was to launch a vigorous diplomatic offensive to head it off. The administration went so far as to have the Pentagon detach U.S. military officers from service elsewhere around the world for emergency mission in Latin America. They were asked to counsel Latin American officers whom they knew personally from previous tours of duty or training sessions against involvement in political plots. Administration sources told the author that they felt the U.S. military had performed creditably in these assignments. If deterrence failed, Kennedy decisionmakers attempted to tailor U.S. response to the particular requirements of each situation as it developed. Schlesinger has commented upon Kennedy's "realist's concern not to place himself in positions from which he could neither advance nor retreat."[55] Washington did *not* insist that the military return to the barracks by sundown. If there was a ready "out" for the United States, the administration seized it:[56] against Martin's advice,[57] Kennedy decided to recognize Guido's military-intimidated regime in Argentina as the constitutional successor to the Frondizi government. When Frondizi was placed under arrest, Senate President Guido hurried to the Supreme Court and had himself sworn in—reportedly to the chagrin of the three military service heads, who were already forming a junta.[58] Otherwise, in the cases of coups in Peru, the Dominican Republic (1963), and Honduras,[59] Kennedy immediately withheld recognition and aid and searched for a way to resolve the crisis as soon as possible. Schlesinger's report of a conversation with the president during the Peruvian episode is indicative of Kennedy's thinking. He expressed his concern, in Schlesinger's words, that "we might have staked our prestige on reversing a situation which could not be reversed—and that, when we accepted the situation, as eventually we must, we might seem to be suffering a defeat." As he saw the problem, it was "to demonstrate that our condemnation had caused the junta to make enough changes in its policy to render the resumption of relations possible."[60] The eventual formula was an end to U.S. sanctions in exchange for the military's promise to hold free elections within a reasonable length of time and not to conduct any "bloodbaths" or "witch-hunts" in the interim. Technically, it was the Johnson administration that ultimately recognized the military governments in the Dominican Republic and Honduras. However, Kennedy was prepared to extend recognition by the middle of October and only refrained from doing so in order not to aggravate criticism from liberal senators. As a further measure in Peru, after recognition and a resumption of Alliance aid, Kennedy for some months left the U.S. embassy in the hands of a chargé d'affaires and withheld military aid.

The Kennedy administration's effort to eschew dogmatism in dealing with varying domestic conditions is undoubtedly praiseworthy. However, flexibility also proved to be that Achilles heel of the Kennedy posture, because the administration too often allowed it to degenerate into simple expediency. This was the self-defeating "old politics" showing through the "pre-new politics" of the Kennedy years, the muddling-through that sidetracked the "grand design" for Latin America, the shortsightedness that dimmed the administration's at least partially authentic long-range vision.

First, had Kennedy been less eager to resume normal relationships and continued U.S. sanctions until the military had actually kept their promise to return power to civilians, he might have achieved more in both symbolic and practical terms. As it was, the military soon discerned that the maximum price they would have to pay for coups was far from prohibitive and really not much more than a temporary inconvenience. With each crisis surmounted, the credibility of the deterrent presented by Washington diminished, and Kennedy pro-democracy policies thus steadily lost momentum.

Second, although there is an admittedly thin line separating the prudent decision from the gutless and/or unprincipled decision, it is a crucial one, and the Kennedy administration was on the wrong side of it in responding to coups in Guatemala and Ecuador. What happened to democracy in Latin America was clearly more important than any immediate political considerations in either country. Nevertheless, frazzled by successive crises, Washington in each instance barely protested the overthrow, and aid programs continued unabated. Following these object lessons, if not from earlier U.S. responses, the military in the Dominican Republic and Honduras can hardly be blamed for concluding that they could proceed to un-seat civilian governments with little to fear from the United States.

There has been some speculation as to whether Kennedy ad-ministration policies were substantially changing in the last dis-couraging months before Dallas.[62] This interpretation rests, in part, upon the obvious inconsistencies in Washington's reactions to the four coups of 1963. However, our analysis suggests that it is more accurate to view these experiences as merely the ultimate result of a tendency to carry flexibility too far.

A statement published by Assistant Secretary Martin[63] in the *Herald Tribune* on October 6, 1963—several days after coups in the Dominican Republic and Honduras—also helped generate the misleading impression that Kennedy policy-makers were reassess-ing their commitment to democracy. Approved by the White House, this statement represented neither a strictly personal initia-tive by Martin nor an administration "trial balloon" designed to prepare public opinion for a major shift in policy. Its timing and content were governed by the fact that the annual appropriations for the Alliance for Progress were scheduled for consideration in the Senate. Conservative senators were insisting that the Alliance had failed; while liberals were clamoring for drastic measures, ranging to the landing of marines to reverse recent military take-overs. The Kennedy administration was anxious to avoid both a reduction in the funds available for the Alliance and amendments to aid legislation which might tie its hands in negotiating with the Latin American military.

Martin's statement was a remarkably frank exposition of the fundamental formal and informal tenets of the Kennedy policies and a brief summary of the experiences of the previous two years. Among other things, it revealed that the administration by late 1963 was less confident than at the outset about the prospects for democracy in Latin America and, in addition, was inclined to be-lieve that its initial classification of the military as either dedicated to the maintenance of the status quo or too revolutionary had been overly simplistic. But there was no indication that the Kennedy government remained the only possible non-Communist road to development in the hemisphere.

Martin criticized both "impatient idealists" and "defeatist cynics" for a tendency "to measure current events not against his-torical reality and substantive progress, but against somewhat theoretical notions of the manner in which men should and do operate in a complex world."

He conceded—indeed stressed—that current conditions in Latin America made democracy a difficult goal to achieve:

Genuine concern with an overturn of the established order, fears of left-wing extremism, frustration with incompetence in an era of great and rising expectations, and a sheer desire for power are all formidable obstacles to stable, constitutional government—especially in countries where the traditional method of transferring political power has been by revolution or coup d'etat. In most of Latin America there is so little experience with the benefits of political legitimacy that there is an insufficient body of opinion, civil or military, which has any reason to know its value and hence defend it.

The assistant secretary also argued that the military was not "universal supporters of those who oppose change and the programs of the Alliance." Regarding the military governments that were the products of recent coups: those in Argentina and Peru had led to "two of the most progressive regimes either country has ever had" (the Illía and Belaúnde governments respectively), and those still in control in Ecuador and Guatemala had announced "reform programs of substantial importance."

Nevertheless, Martin firmly maintained that it was not in the interest of the United States to allow the military full rein: "Military coups thwart the will of the people, destroy political stability and the growth of the tradition of respect for democratic constitutions, and nurture communist opposition to their tyranny." Furthermore, "the military often show little capacity for effective government, which is a political rather than a military job."

How then should Washington respond to coups? Martin observed that "unless there is intervention from outside the hemisphere by the international Communist conspiracy, the use of military force involving the probability of U.S. soldiers killing the citizens of another country is not to be ordered lightly. "Moreover, past military occupations, "even when carried out with the best of intentions" had been "politically unproductive." Neither could the United States "as a practical matter, create effective democracy by keeping a man in office through use of economic pressure or even military force when his own people are not willing to fight to defend him." In the assistant secretary's opinion, the United States really had only one choice:

> We must use our leverage to keep these new regimes as liberal and considerate of the welfare of the people as possible. In addition, we must support and strengthen the civilian components against military influences and press for new elections as soon as possible so that these countries once again may experience the benefits of democratic legitimacy. Depending upon the circumstances, our leverage is sometimes great, sometimes small.

Martin closed his statement with the following remarks:

> I fear there are some who will accuse me of having written an apologia for coups. I have not. They are to be fought with all the means we have available. Rather I would protest that I am urging the rejection of the thesis of the French philosophers that democracy can be legislated—established by constitutional fiat.

> I am insisting on the Anglo-Saxon notion that democracy is a living thing which must have time and soil and sunlight in which to grow. We must do all we can to create these favorable conditions, and we can do and have done much.

> But we cannot simply create the plant and give it to them; it must spring from seeds planted in indigenous soil.

In spite of Martin's denial that he was presenting an apologia for coups, his statement did spark the rumor that the Kennedy administration was abandoning resistance to the Latin American military. Kennedy himself dampened the rumor in his press conference of October 9. He said that there was no change in policy, that Martin had been "merely attempting to explain some of the problems in Latin America, why coups take place, and what problems they present us with" (*New York Times*, October 10, 1963, p. 18).

The president cleared the air still further with a speech in Miami Beach on November 18. This was no casual address: in the words of one of his advisers, Kennedy recognized that "there had been some slippage" in U.S. policies in the previous year, and he was concerned lest he seem to be giving a tacit go-ahead to "all those guys down there" to seize power. Delivered only four days before his death, the Miami speech was Kennedy's[64] last testament on Latin American affairs. Among the foremost objectives of his administration, he unequivocally reaffirmed, was the promotion of democracy in the hemisphere:

> Political democracy and stability . . . is at the core of our hopes for the future. There can be no progress and stability if people do not have hope for a better life tomorrow. That faith is

undermined when men seek the reins of power and ignore the restraints of constitutional procedures. They may even do so out of a sincere desire to benefit their own country, but democratic governments demand that those in opposition accept the defects of today and work toward remedying them within the machinery of peaceful change. Otherwise, in return for momentary satisfaction we tear apart the fabric and the hope of lasting democracy.

The Charter of the Organization of American States calls for "the consolidation on this continent, within the framework of democratic institutions, of a system of individual liberty and social justice based on respect for the essential rights of man." The United States is committed to that proposition. Whatever may be the case in other parts of the world, this is a hemisphere of free men, capable of self-government. It is in accordance with this belief that the United States will continue to support the efforts of those seeking to establish and maintain constitutional democracy.

Most of the evidence indicates that Kennedy was far from ready to phase out his pro-democracy campaign in the fall of 1963. Whether he would *eventually* have done so is, of course, open to speculation.

Towards the end of his presidency, Kennedy had virtually decided to create the post of undersecretary of state for inter-american affairs. Even more important as a measure of his continued commitment to Latin America, he was very seriously considering giving the job to Robert Kennedy. He mentioned the RFK idea to Goodwin two days before his assassination; and RFK later told Goodwin that he thought he would have accepted the appointment, at least in the second term. He wanted to move into foreign policy and needed an independent area to avoid undercutting the secretary of state. In any event, it is difficult to conceive of the president assigning his brother—or, for that matter, any other leading administration figure—to oversee an area that he was likely to leave to the tender mercies of the military.

A balanced view dictates conjecturing where the flexibility guideline might have led the administration over the long haul. Given the president's high regard for U.S. Ambassador Lincoln Gordon and Goulart's erratic behavior, it is probable that Kennedy would have acquiesced in the 1964 Brazilian coup—though surely with less public rejoicing than Johnson and his assistant secretary, Thomas C. Mann. Thereafter, if the hemisphere trend towards militarism had appeared irreversible and the guerrilla threat had subsided to the level of recent years, who knows?

Whatever the future might have been, the record of Kennedy efforts to further democracy in Latin American is one of a few successes and numerous frustrations and failures. On the positive side: U.S. policies may have helped to avert some coups and to ameliorate the effects of others. Certainly, the Kennedy administration was largely responsible for ushering in the Bosch government in the Dominican Republic and for the elections of 1963 in Peru. But the administration was neither able to prevent a devastating series of military coups in Latin America nor to budge Duvalier from the Haitian presidency.

Yet we should not measure the success or failure of the Kennedy policies solely on the basis of the extent to which they actually fostered democracy. They also had an important impact upon the U.S. image in the hemisphere. From the Latin American standpoint, as significant as the Kennedy administration's support for democracy was its strong identification with the democratic Left. Along with the Alliance, Kennedy's pro-democracy policies represented a sincere attempt to place the United States in the vanguard of what then appeared to be the political forces most dedicated to constructive economic and social progress. In this respect, the policies were eminently successful, and they contributed mightily to making the Kennedy years a brief era of good feeling between the United States and Latin America.

U.S. Not—So—Pro-Democracy Policies

The other side of the cyclic pattern of U.S. policies has been relative disinterest in promoting—and, occasionally, suspicion of and outright hostility to—democracy in Latin America.[69]

Under the influence of Latin American domestic developments and the failures of U.S. pro-democracy campaigns over the years, optimism has often yielded to pessimism in Washington on the question of Latin American preparedness for democracy. Starting with the premise that, except for a very few countries, democracy is at best a long-range goal,[68] U.S. policy-makers have proceeded to rationalize an emphasis on other goals as follows:

The United States must deal in a pragmatic fashion with civilian and military unconstitutional governments simply because they are going to be part of the Latin American political milieu for the foreseeable future. It is possible to make a case for a lukewarm posture toward some regimes and even for direct opposition to a rare dictatorship that "outrage[s] the conscience of America." However, as a general rule, the United States can most effectively encourage democracy in Latin America by exercising subtle pressures in a "quiet, unpublicized way" on a "day-to-day basis" through the normal channels of diplomacy.[69] Public posturing on the democracy issue is not only futile but counterproductive: It makes a moral question ("good guys" vs. "bad guys")[70] out of what is basically a practical problem, diminishes the prestige of the United States in the hemisphere by committing it to overly ambitious political development goals, and engenders a negative reaction from undemocratic regimes which might otherwise be responsive to friendly persuasion. Finally, overt U.S. pro-democracy action is "patronizing" and "degrading" to Latin Americans and, from a legal standpoint, violates the inter-American principle of nonintervention.[71]

Lip service to democracy and the nonintervention norm aside, the fact remains that policy-makers in the periods under discussion have viewed the promotion of democracy as largely contrary to the security interests of the United States.

First, caudillos and military regimes have traditionally been strong supporters of U.S. security policies at the international level. FDR did not discriminate among various types of Latin American governments, in part so as not to interfere with the organization of security against the Axis.[72] The social calendar of the White House reflected his attitude when Somoza and Trujillo both paid state visits on the eve of World War II. Similarly, the Truman and Eisenhower administrations found conservative dictatorships among their most dependable allies in the postwar struggle against communism. Eisenhower symbolically bestowed the Legion of Merit on Peruvian dictator Manuel Odría in 1953. The Braxilian military publicly praised Johnson administration policies in Vietnam and made the largest Latin American troop contribution to the 1965 Dominican operation.

Second, Washington has often regarded undemocratic regimes as bulwarks of political stability and economic orthodoxy on the domestic front. During the Truman and Eisenhower years, many Latin American democrats (José Figueres of Costa Rica, for example) were believed to subscribe to "socialistic" development ideologies which were both repugnant in themselves and unfavorable to U.S. business. But the abiding preoccupation of U.S. policy-makers—reaching almost paranoid proportions during Mann's tenure in the Department of State and in the Rockefeller Report—has been with the danger that Communists or native radicals will exploit the stresses and strains inherent in the modernization process in Latin America. With the threat of another Cuba looming large in their thinking, they have been skeptical as to whether development can safely proceed in many cases without regimentation and repression. To policy-makers so oriented, the notion of the modernizing military in Latin America has seemed a godsend.[73]

Washington's identification with the Latin American military has not been entirely without reservations; one of which applies as well to old-style dictatorships like those of Duvalier and Stroessner. Paralleling the Eisenhower administration's final assessment of the Trujillo regime, Johnson and Nixon policy-makers have expressed some concern that excessive political repression and socioeconomic stagnation might eventually breed widespread popular opposition and violence. Unlike Eisenhower (with respect to Trujillo) they have not been sufficiently concerned to explore alternatives to support of the status quo. Nevertheless, there was one brief revival of apparently genuine pro-democracy sentiment under the Johnson administration, beginning in 1966, after Lincoln Gordon assumed the post of assistant secretary and Mann left the Department of State. In that year, Gordon gave full backing to U.S. Ambassador Edwin M. Martin's vigorous efforts to head off a coup against the Illía government in Argentina. Although the decision was made not to revert to the Kennedy practice of applying sanctions, Washington subsequently expressed its distress at the Onganía takeover (*New York Times*, June 29, 1966: pp. 1, 14). Gordon indicated to the press that he did not feel that the situation in Argentina was analogous to the Brazilian case two years before. Specifically, he said he did not believe that there was any real danger of economic collapse or Communist influence (*New York Times*, August 2, 1966:10). Shortly thereafter, the assistant secretary publicly criticized the Argentine military regime for raiding and then closing the state universities (*New York Times*, August 5, 1966: 1, 9).

Somewhat less openly, the United States also opposed the coup against the new Arias government in Panama in 1968. Washington was concerned both about the threat of violence by Arias supporters and about the effect of the revolt—coming soon after the Velas-

co coup in Peru and launched by a military establishment so closely associated wit the United States—in further eroding
Congressional support for the U.S. Alliance for Progress and military aid (*New York Times*, October 13, 1968: pp. 1-2). They have
also been a little uneasy about the possibility that the military
might itself develop into a radical nationalist political force. This
factor helped shape U.S. unenthusiastic attitudes toward coups in
Bolivia (1964), [74] Argentina (1966), Peru (1968) and Bolivia (1969
and 1970).

Mann[75] insisted that his pragmatic stance was no real departure
from the practice of the Kennedy administration. However, one
need only cite the 1965 Dominican case and the United States's
continued embrace of the Brazilian military regime long after its
extreme reactionary course was established[76] to demonstrate that
Mann's assertion was just another manifestation of the Johnson
administration's "credibility gap." By renouncing the blanket
commitment to democracy, the administration clearly implied that
it henceforth would not be answerable to criticism from the Latin
American democratic Left. Moreover, its analysis of Latin American political and socioeconomic realities betrayed an exceedingly
conservative ideological bias. Indeed, Mann represented precisely
that sector of governmental opinion, including the "old Latin
American hands" in the State Department and the Pentagon,
which Kennedy decision-makers had regularly overruled.[77]

Much the same outlook characterized the Nixon administration,
although Nixon officials appeared sincere in their announced goal
to achieve a "lower profile" for the United States in Latin America. In this regard, they largely ignored the Rockefeller Report's
dire warnings of increasing Communist terrorism, and late in 1970
officially adopted a "wait-and-see" position towards new leftist
governments in Chile and Bolivia. With Latin American nationalism on the rise and many hemisphere governments under rightist
control, the administration undoubtedly believed the less said
about politics the better. Its philosophy seemed to be that U.S.-La-
tin American relations may profit from what Goodwin has termed
"malign neglect"—under the guise of "partnership" and a "nuts-
and-bolts" approach to issues of aid and trade.

The emphasis on a lower profile has merely submerged, rather
than irrevocably revised the cold war attitudes traditionally prevalent in various parts of the executive branch. In March 1970, coin-
ciding with the Frei government's unilateral decision to break its

embargo on trade with Cuba, the Nixon administration began a quiet diplomatic campaign throughout Latin America to muster support for continued OAS diplomatic and economic sanctions against Castro (*New York Times*, July 13, 1970: p. 13). Later, shortly after Salvador Allende won a plurality in the Chilean elections, Nixon's closest foreign policy adviser, Henry A. Kissinger, ventured the prediction at an off-the-record press briefing that congressional confirmation of Allende's victory would lead to the establishment of a Communist government in Chile which would, in turn, threaten the neighboring countries of Argentina, Bolivia and Peru (*New York Times*, September 23, 1970: p. 13). Conditioned responses like these raise the question whether the administration will be able to resist more direct and conspicuous involvement in Latin American political struggles should the situation become still further polarized between the Left and the Right.

Meanwhile, rather ironically, U.S. policies currently downgrading problems of Latin American political development draw support from the Nixon administration's leading critics in Congress. Responding to disillusionment over Vietnam and the performance of the Latin American democratic Left, what began as an attack on the Johsnon administration's de-emphasis of the political goals of the Alliance soon developed into a call for U.S. disengagement from Latin America. Senators Frank Church and J. William Fulbright and other congressmen of similar views are now hypersensitive about U.S. interventionism and paternalism and are also gloomy about the prospects for reform under almost all existing Latin American governments. In their judgment, the Kennedy policies were naive, both because they posited a Latin American commitment to fundamental reform that rarely materialized and because they assumed that an essentially nonrevolutionary country like the United States could act as the agent of change in the hemisphere. Even were the United States dedicated to revolutionary goals, Church-Fulbright argue, its efforts to promote radical change would inevitably deliver the "kiss of death" to progressive Latin American politicians.

This reasoning leads Church-Fulbright to the conclusion that the way for the United States to improve its image is to stop its direct support of Latin American governments. According to their prescription[78] Washington should limit its assistance to aid for development channeled through multilateral institutions and remove barriers to Latin American trade. Church-Fulbright concede that such policies would indirectly help bolster conservative regimes along with the few progressive ones, but they point out that the responsibility for doing so would then rest primarily with the Latin Americans themselves. Moreover, they expect that the masses will everywhere benefit to some extent from development and ultimately, through an awareness born of improved living standards, come to demand more of their governments.

NOTES

[1]Richard M. Nixon, "Action for Progress for the Americas," *Department of State Bulletin* 61, no. 1586 (November 17, 1969), p. 413.

[2]Arthur P. Whitaker, *The Western Hemisphere Idea: Its Rise and Decline* (Ithaca, N.Y.: Cornell University Press, 1954), p. 54.

[3]Quoted in Whitaker, *The United States and the Independence of Latin America, 1800-1830* (Baltimore, Md.: Johns Hopkins University Press, 1941), p. 375.

[4]Dexter Perkins, *A History of the Monroe Doctrine* (Boston: Little, Brown, 1963), p. 63.

[5]For texts of the treaties and related documents, see U.S. Department of State, *Foreign Relations of the United States (FRUS)* 2 (1907): 665-727 and U.S. Department of State, *Conference on Central American Affairs*, (December 4, 1922-February 7, 1923). On the Tobar period see also D. G. Munro, *Intervention and Dollar Diplomacy in the Caribbean, 1900-1921* (Princeton, N.J.: Princeton University Press, 1964), ch. 10; T. P. Wright, Jr., *American Support of Free Elections Abroad* (Washington, D. C.: Public Affairs Press, 1964), chs. 3, 6-8; R. L. Buell, "The United States and Central American Stability," *Foreign Policy Reports* 7 (July 8, 1931): 161-86; Buell, "The United States and Central American Revolutions," *Foreign Policy Reports* 7 (July 22, 1931): 187-204); T. L. Karnes, *The Failure of Union: Central America, 1824-1960* (Chapel Hill, N.C.: University of North Carolina Press, 1961), pp. 585-601.

[6]See his famous statement in U.S. Department of State, *FRUS* (1913): 7. On the key Mexican case see especially R.S. Baker, *Woodrow Wilson: Life and Letters* (Garden City, N.Y.: Doubleday, Page, 1931), chs. 5-6; S. M. Bemis, *The Latin American Policy of the United States* (New York: Harcourt, Brace & World, 1943), ch. 10; Howard F. Cline, *The United States and Mexico* (New York: Atheneum, 1963), chs. 8-9; A. S. Link, *Woodrow Wilson and the Progressive Era* (New York: Harper and Row, 1954), ch. 5; Wright, *American Support of Free Elections* (1964), ch. 4; R. E. Quirk, *An Affair of Honor: Woodrow Wilson and the Occupation of Veracruz* (Lexington, Ky.: University of Kentucky Press, 1962); U.S. Department of State, *FRUS* (1913-1917).

[7]B. Wood, *The Making of the Good Neighbor Policy* (New York: Columbia University Press, 1961), ch. 1.

[8]*Ibid.*, chs. 2-3

[9]On the Braden vs. Perón episode, see especially H. F. Peterson, *Argentina and the United States, 1810-1960* (New York: State University of New York Publishers, 1964), pp. 443-57; O. E. Smith, Jr., *Yankee Diplomacy: U.S. Interventon in Argentina* (Dallas, Texas: Southern Methodist University Press, 1953),

ch. 7; A. P. Whitaker, *The United States and Argentina* (Cambridge, Mass.: Harvard University Press, 1954), pp. 131-34, 145-50; Robert J. Alexander, *The Perón Era* (New York: Columbia University Press, 1951), pp. 198-217. While Braden was assistant secretary, U.S. Ambassador to Brazil Adolf A. Berle, Jr. pressured Vargas to honor his pledge to hold free elections by making a speech on September 29, 1945, which hailed the move as an important step in the consolidation of hemispheric democracy. See mention of this incident in Thomas E. Skidmore, *Politics in Brazil, 1930-1964* (New York: Oxford University Press, 1967), p. 51, and R. J. Alexander, *Prophets of the Revolution* (New York: Macmillan, 1962), p. 234.

[10]U.S. Deaprtment of State, Inter-American Conference for the Maintenance of Continental Peace and Security: Report of the Delegation of U.S.A. International Organization and Conference Series 2, *American Republics*, no. 1.

[11]J. Slater, "The United States, the Organization of American States, and the Dominican Republic, 1961-63," *International Organization* 17 (Spring): ch. 5.

[12]On the Kennedy policies, see Arthur M. Schlesinger, Jr., *A Thousand Days: John F. Kennedy in the White House* (Boston: Houghton-Mifflin, 1965), chs. 7-11, 29-31; Edwin Lieuwen, *Generals vs. Presidents: Neo-Militarism in Latin America* (New York: Praeger, 1964), ch. 7; J. Slater, "Democracy vs. Stability: The Recent Latin American Policy of the United States," *Yale Review* 55 (December 1965): 169-81; T. J. Maher, "The Kennedy and Johnson Responses to Latin American Coups d'Etat," *World Affairs* 131 (October-December 1968): 184-97.

[13]Wright, *American Support of Free Elections*, p. 56.

[14]H. Notter, *The Origins of the Foreign Policy of Woodrow Wilson* (Baltimore: Johns Hopkins Press, 1937), pp. 268,307-8.

[15]Braden expressed his views perhaps most clearly and concisely in a radio interview late in 1945. See U.S. Department of State, *Report of the Delegation of the U.S.A. to the Inter-American Conference on Problems of War and Peace*, Conference Series no. 85, pp. 27-29.

[16]Quoted in Perkins, *A History of the Monroe Doctrine*, p. 28.

[17]Smith, *Yankee Diplomacy*, pp. 173-74.

[18]Slater, *The OAS and the United States Foreign Policy* (Columbus, Ohio: Ohio State University Press, 1967), p. 191.

[19]*New York Times* correspondent Tad Szuk captured the optimism of the period in his book *The Twilight of the Tyrants* (New York: Holt, 1959). The author recalls hearing Kennedy's campaign speech at the Alamo in September 1960, before an enthusiastic crowd composed largely of Mexican-Americans. Kennedy commented upon the declining number of Latin American dictatorships and fervently promised that—with him as president—there would soon be no more tyrannies in the hemisphere.

[20]Theodore C. Sorensen, *Kennedy* (New York: Harper & Row, 1965), p. 533.

[21]Schlesinger, *A Thousand Days*, p. 201.

[22]The administration applied this term generally to all political groups in Latin America which espoused political and socioeconomic development goals compatible with the Alliance. However, in the minds of Kennedy policy-makers, the core of the democratic Left was the popular parties, which recognized a vague ideological bond with Haya de la Torre's APRA party in Peru and whose leaders—ou-

twardly referred to as the "Caribbean Mafia"—shared acquaintances born of years in exile: Betancourt of Venezuela, Muñoz Marín of Puerto Rico (a personal friend of Kennedy's), Figueres of Costa Rica, Villeda Morales of Honduras, Bosch of the Dominican Republic.

²³Schlesinger, *A Thousand Days*, p. 198.

²⁴Bemis, *The Latin American Policy of the United States*, p. 194.

²⁵Slater, *The OAS*, ch. 6; R. D. Tomasek, "The Haitian-Dominican Republic Controversy of 1963 and the Organization of American States," *Orbis* 12 (Spring 1968): 294-313.

²⁶John B. Martin, *Overtaken by Events: The Dominican Crisis—from the Fall of Trujillo to the Civil War* (Garden City, N.Y.: Doubleday, 1966), p. 594.

²⁷Even the allies of the United States did not give full support to wartime sanctions against Argentina or to those later directed against the Trujillo and Castro regimes.

²⁸Cline, *The United States and Mexico*, p. 150.

²⁹U.S. Department of State, *FRUS*, 1914: 543.

³⁰Schlesinger, *A Thousand Days*, p. 787.

³¹Representatives from Guatemala and Uruguay also attended the second conference.

³²See Pan American Union, *Consulta del Gobierno del Uruguay y contestaciones de los Gobiernos sobre paralelisno entre la democracia y la paz, proteción internacional de los derechos del hombre, y acción colectiva en defensa de esos principios*, 1946.

³³On this point see L. Duggan, *The Americas* (New York: Holt, 1949), pp. 205-6. For Braden's denial of the charge see *U. S. Department of State Bulletin*, 1946, p. 28.

³⁴For full details and bibliographical information, see Yale H. Ferguson, *The Inter-American System, the United States and the Promotion of Hemispheric Democracy: Perspective on Intervention and Collective Responsibility in the Americas* (New York: Columbia University, unpublished doctoral thesis, 1967). See also C. N. Ronning. *Law and Politics in Inter-American Diplomacy* (New York: Wiley, 1963), ch. 2; Slater, *The OAS and United States Foreign Policy*, ch. 7; M. M. Ball, *The OAS in Transition* (Durham, N.C.: Duke University Press, 1969), pp. 485-502; D. M. Dozer, "Recognition in Contemporary Inter-American Relations," *Journal of Inter-American Studies* 8 (April 1966): 318-35.

³⁵For an early statement of this theme, see V. R. Haya de la Torre, *La Defensa Continental* (Buenos Aires: Editorial Americalee, 1942).

³⁶For texts of the Guani resolution and the replies of governments, see Emergency Advisory Committee for Political Defense, *Second Annual Report*, 1944. For a discussion of the Bolivian case, see W. L. Neumann, *Recognition of Governments in the Americas* (Washington: Foundation for Foreign Affairs, 1947), pp. 34-38. On United States-Argentina relations, 1939-45, see Peterson, *Argentina and the United States*, pp. 398-443; Smith, *Yankee Diplomacy*, chs. 3-6; D.M. Dozer, *Are We Good Neighbors? Three Decades of Inter-American Relations* (Gainesville, Fla.: University of Florida Press, 1959), pp. 136-46; H. M. Blackmer, *United States Policy and the Inter-American Peace System, 1889-1952* (Paris: n.p., 1952), pp. 109-30.

³⁷The English text of the Guatemalan proposal is reprinted in U.S. Department

of State, 1946, pp. 354-55. For the IAJC opinion see Pan-American Union, Inter-American Juridical Committee, *Defense and Preservation of Democracy in America Against the Possible Establishment of Anti-Democratic Regimens* [*sic*] *in the Continent*, 1946.

[38]See the text of the project of Uruguay in Pan American Union, *Inter-American Conference for the Maintenance of Continental Peace and Security* (Rio de Janeiro, 1946). Also the project of Guatemala, reprinted in *U. S. Department of State*, 1948, p. 96. The minutes of the debates on these proposals are in OAS, Pan American Union, *Conferencia Interamericana para a Manutenão da Paz e da Segurança no Continente: Diario*. OEA/Ser. N/2. N/2., pp. 157-58. It is interesting to note that while a majority of hemisphere governments gave little encouragement to pro-democracy proposals during this period, they were sufficiently irked by Somoza's unseating of the very government he had picked to succeed him in 1947 that they voted to exclude the Nicaraguan regime from participation in the Rio Conference. Nicaragua received invitation to the Bogota Conference in 1948 only after Somoza had partially legitimized his rule by holding "elections" and installing his elderly uncle in the presidency. See Pan American Union Governing Board, *Minutes of the Meetings*, July 21 and 28, 1947, and March 8, 1948.

[39]The Article 5(d) statement is: "The solidarity of the American States and the high aims which are sought through it require the political organization of those States on the basis of the effective exercise of representative democracy." The binding obligation aspect was quite clear in the debates at the conference. Indeed, Mexico offered the principal opposition to any mention of democracy in this, the 'Principles' section of the Charter, presicely on the grounds that the internal organization of a state should not be the object of a 'contractual obligation.' " See Novena Conferencia Internacional Americana, *Actas y Documentos*, Bogota, 1953-54, pp. 298ff. This apparently minor legal victory for pro-democracy forces held considerable significance for the future: It made it possible for them to argue that the promotion of democracy is not intervention, in spite of the fact that potential measures to this end did not receive a specific exemption from the nonintervention principle, like that accorded to peace and security measures in Article 19. (See also references to democracy and human rights in the Preamble to the Charter, which was not of sufficient legal significance to be controversial at Bogota.)

The conference rejected a definition of democracy proposed by Uruguay and postponed a decision on that country's suggestion that the EACPD should remain in existance for possible service as an advisory body in the democracy field (the OAS Council abolished the EACPD in October 1948). A majority of governments also proved unwilling to bar nondemocratic states and governments from membership and/or representation in the OAS and to establish a formal consultative procedure for the recognition of new governments.

[40]The technical basis for sanctions levied against the Dominican dictator by the Sixth Meeting of Foreign Ministers in 1960 was his personal involvement in a plot to assassinate President Betancourt of Venezuela.

[41]Even earlier, in January 1961, Argentina and Brazil led the opposition to an expansion of economic sanctions voted by the OAS Council, with the Argentine representative complaining that "the proposed measures can only invoke as jus-

tification the continuance of the governmental institutions or the internal political situation of the Dominican Republic." See OAS, Pan American Union, Council, *Acta de la sesión ordinaria celebrada el 4 de enero de 1961*, OEA/Ser. G/11/C-a-397. (Minutes of the Council sessions hereafter cited as *Acta ordinaria* or *Acta extraordinaria* as appropriate.)

[42]Resolution 1 in the Final Act of the Fifth Meeting of Foreign Ministers. For documents ,073relating to this conference, see OAS, Pan American Union, Reunión de Consulta de Ministros de Relaciones Exteriores, *Quinta Reunión: Actas y Documentos*, OEA/Ser. F/111. 5, 1961 and U.S. Department of State, *Efforts to Relieve International Tensions in the Western Hemisphere, 1959-60*, Consulta de Ministros de Relaciones Exteriores, *Quinta Reunion: Actas Y Documentos*, OEA/Ser. F/111. 5, 1961 and U.S. Department of State, Inter-America. *Efforts to Relieve International Tensions in the Western Hemisphere, 1959-60*, Inter-American Series no. 79, 1962.

[43]Under Articles 39-40 of the OAS Charter, providing for consideration of "problems of an urgent nature and of common interest to the American States." For the debates, see OAS, Council, *Actas de las sesiones* for the following dates: July 30, 1962; August 8, 1962; August 10, 1962; August 22, 1962; October 3, 1963; November 4, 1963; and November 12, 1963.

[44]Resolution 26 in the Final Act. The text of the Final Act is in OAS, Pan American Union, 1965, vol. 1, 489-563. Compare this resolution with the original proposals of Costa Rica and Venexuela, in *ibid.*, vol. 4, pp. 545-50, 565-57.

[45]Edwin M. Martin, "Interdependence and the Principles of Self-Determination and Nonintervention." *Department of State Bulletin* 48, no. 1245 (May 6, 1963): 710-15.

[46]According to one Kennedy aide, the administration had a low regard for the OAS as an instrument of multilateral diplomacy. Theoretically, negotiations in the OAS might have served as a useful substitute for the cumbersome procedure of consultations with foreign ministries situated in remote Latin American capitals. In fact, the latter procedure was unavoidable, since many Latin American governments persisted in assigning to the OAS diplomats of questionable competence or political persuasion whom they themselves distrusted.

[47]Schlesinger, *A Thousand Days*, p. 787.

[48]Wood, *The Making of the Good Neighbor Policy*, p. 99.

[49]See Herter's address to the Sixth Meeting of Foreign Ministers, reprinted in *U.S. Department of State*, 1962, pp. 285-87.

[50]D. Bronheim, "U.S. Military Policies and Programs in Latin America," in *Contemporary Inter-American Relations: A Reader in Theory and Issues* (Englewood Cliffs, N.J.: Prentice-Hall, 1972).

[51]S. G. Blythe, "Mexico: The Record of a Conversation with President Wilson," *Saturday Evening Post* 186 (May 23, 1914): 3-4

[52]U.S. Department of State, *Foreign Relations of the U.S., 1914-1920: The Lansing Papers* 2:547.

[53]The only likely reason why Arévalo would not have won the upcoming election in Guatemala was the fact that President Ydígoras was determined to impose as his successor an arch-conservative landowner whose estate had been a training ground for the Bay of Pigs.

Someone in the Kennedy administration did a semiserious calculation and concluded that President Arosemena of Ecuador was inebriated about 65 percent of the time.

[54]Although the Kennedy administration framed its response to the Peruvian coup under the assumption that the military intervention represented merely a reactionary attempt to bar APRA from power, the resulting junta subsequently proved to have some reformist tendencies which foreshadowed the later Velasco government.

[55]Schlesinger, *A Thousand Days*, p. 785.

[56]The first coup of the Kennedy period occurred in El Salvador in January 1961. Since it confronted the administration in Washington only a few days after the inauguration and represented merely an internal struggle among the military— the replacement of one unconstitutional government with another—it did not offer much of a test of the new pro-democracy policy. The United States soon recognized the junta, noting its pledge to hold free elections and to seek solutions to economic and social problems. For documents relating to this case, see M. M. Whiteman, *Digest of International Law* 2 (Washington: U.S. Department of State, 1963): 281-283.

[57]Schlesinger, *A Thousand Days*, p. 785.

[58]Lieuwen, *Generals vs. Presidents*, pp. 17-18.

[59]For documents on the Peruvian Case, *Inter-American Economic Affairs* 16:72. On the Dominican Republic and Honduras, see Whiteman, p. 73.

[60]Schlesinger, *A Thousand Days*, p. 787.

[61]See Department of State Bulletin, "The United States Extends Recognition to New Government of Guatemala," 48, no. 1245 (May 6, 1963): 703. Washington's lack of resistance to the coup in Ecuador looked particularly bad because the military seized power immediately following a dinner at which obviously inebriated Arosemena had bluntly criticized the U.S. in front of the U.S. ambassador and the president of the Grace Line. On the coup generally see M. C. Needler, Anatomy of a Coup d'Etat: Ecuador 1963 (Washington: Institute for the Comparative Study of Political Systems, 1964).

[62]Slater, "Democracy vs. Stability," pp. 176-77 and Slater, *The OAS and United States Foreign Policy*, p. 13.

[63]Martin, "U.S. Policy Regarding Military Governments in Latin America," *Department of State Bulletin* 49, no. 1271 (November 4, 1963): 698-700.

[64]John F. Kennedy, "Battle for Progress with Freedom in the Western Hemisphere," *Department of State Bulletin* 49, no. 1276 (December 9, 1963): 902.

[65]Schlesinger, *A Thousand Days*, p. 1002, mentions Sargent Shriver or Averell Harriman as possible choices for the post.

[66]Skidmore, *Politics in Brazil*, Appendix.

[67]On the Johnson policies, see Slater, "Democracy vs. Stability" in *The OAS and United States Foreign Policy*, pp. 14-17; Lieuwen, *Generals vs. Presidents*, ch. 9.

[68]U.S. Senate Committee on Foreign Relations, Subcommittee on Western Hemisphere Affairs, *Rockefeller Report on Latin America, Hearings* (November 20, 1969), 91st Congress, 1st Session, Committee Print, pp. 109, 113-15.

[69]Thomas C. Mann, "The Western Hemisphere's Fight for Freedom," *Department of State Bulletin* 51, no. 1321 (October 19, 1964): 999. The quotations in the preceding two sentences are from Mann. However, we might have gleaned similar

ones from other sources, for instance, Truman's letter to deposed President Rómulo Gallegos of Venezuela, explaining why the United States had not imposed sanctions following the 1948 coup: "This Government. . . is of the opinion that nonrecognition is seldom, if ever, effective in bringing about the broader aim of strengthening democratic governments. I feel that the United States can make its influence in favor of democratic relations maintained with all the governments of the hemisphere. The American governments probably can work together most effectively for hemisphere solidarity if they utilize, among other work together most effectively for hemisphere solidarity if they utilize, among other means, the continuing interchange made possible through normal diplomatic channels."

Or Rusk's statement at a press conference after the 1964 Brazilian coup: "If unhappily in a particular. . . country, there is. . . a military takeover—this does not present us with a situation which we can simply walk away from because we and other members of this hemisphere necessarily have an interest in what happens in that situation. Therefore we have to continue to live with it, work with it, try to assist a particular country in coming back to constitutional process" (*Department of State Bulletin*, "Secretary Rusk's News Conference of April 3," 50, no. 1295 [April 20, 1964]: 610)

Again, see Rockefeller's position in U.S. Senate, Committee on Foreign Relations, Subcommittee on Western Hemisphere Affairs (1970: 109, 115-33).

[70]The reference is to remarks reportedly made by John O. Bell, U.S. ambassador to Guatemala, interpreting Mann's exposition of his policy in a closed-door session at the State Department (*New York Times*, March 19, 1964, pp. 1-2).

[71]Thomas C. Mann, "The Democratic Ideal in Our Policy Toward Latin America," *Department of State Bulletin*, 50, no. 1305 (June 29, 1964): 998-1000. As has been the practice of other U.S. decision-makers, Mann coupled his homage to the nonintervention principle with mention of Resolution 35 in the Final Act of the Bogotá Conference: "That the establishment or maintenance of diplomatic relations with a government does not imply any judgment upon the domestic policy of that government." For Mann's dig at those who insist on nonintervention and yet argue for U.S. "support" of the non-Communist Left, see Mann, "The Dominican Crisis: Correcting Some Misconceptions," *Department of State Bulletin* 53, no. 1376 (November 8, 1965): 730-31.

[72]The Roosevelt administration also drew the conclusion from Welles's experiences in Cuba that "interference was capable of creating situations where intervention (defined as the landing of marines) might become unavoidable" (Wood, *The Making of the Good Neighbor Policy*, p. 137).

[73]U.S. Senate, Committee on Foreign Relations, *Rockefeller Report*, pp. 10-19, 85-87.

[74]Other considerations in the 1964 Bolivan case were the Paz government's pro-United States and anti-Communist orientation, as well as its related determination to resist pressures from the Left (spearheaded by Juan Lechín's tin miners) while revamping the Bolivian economy along the lines urged by Washington (*New York Times*, November 10, 1964, p. 2, November 11, 1974, p. 17).

[75]Mann, "The Democratic Ideal," p. 999.

[76]For example, Castelo Branco's letter of August 11, 1964, expressing approval of U.S. actions in the Gulf of Tonkin incident, elicited an effusive reply from President Johnson. Johnson wrote that "the struggle for freedom in Vietnam is closely

related to the struggle for freedom everywhere" and that the Western Hemisphere had "joined in that struggle in the Alliance for Progress." He added: "We in the United States have been heartened—and I believe the whole Hemisphere looks to the future with greater optimism—because of the vigorous manner in which your government has accepted this challenge." Finally, Johnson pledged his administration's "sincere support through the Alliance for Progress" (*Department of State Bulletin*, "U.S. and Brazil Reaffirm Commitment to Peace" 51, no. 1318 (September 28, 1964): 436.

[77]Schlesinger, *A Thousand Days*, p. 202, recalls that Mann "had an old Latin American hand's skepticism about the grandiose schemes of the New Frontiersmen and, on occasion, even responded a little to the crochets of Admiral Burke."

In some respects, Mann's attitude seemed to pass beyond conservation to a personal contempt for Latin Americans. He was "famed" in the State Department as the man who said: "I know my Latinos. They understand only two things—a buck in the pocket and a kick in the ass" (quoted in Schlesinger, "The Lowering Hemisphere," *The Atlantic* 2251 (January 1970): 81.

[78]Frank Church, "United States and Latin America: Call for a New Policy," *The Center Magazine* 2 (November 1969): 51-55. Also see, "Toward a New Policy for Latin America, in Congressonal Record 116, *Proceedings and Debates of the 91st Congress, 2nd Session*, no. 57 (April 10, 1970): S5538-5544; U.S. Senate Committee on Foreign Relations, U.S. Military Policies and Programs in Latin America, *Hearings*, 91st Congress, 1st Session (June 24, and July 8, 1969, Committee Print), pp. 31-52; *Rockefeller Report*, 1970, pp. 10-19.

24

The Administration of Economic Development Planning: Principles and Fallacies

BERTRAM M. GROSS

INTERDEPENDENCE OF PLANNING AND ADMINISTRATION

Progress in economic development requires a realistic awareness of the close interdependence between planning and administration. Lack of awareness may lead to a dangerous separation between plan formulation and plan implementation and to serious misunderstandings between planning technicians and administrators.

Planning As an Integral Part of the Administrative Process

In almost all countries, administration is regarded as the process through which administrators (or managers, executives, administrative assistance, etc.) help achieve certain purposes through the activities of people in an organization. The organization may be public, private or mixed. The administrators may operate at varying levels of authority, responsibility and prestige. They must deal not only with subordinates and immediate associates but also with the external environment of their organization (or unit). At the higher levels of administration, the administrators need many highly specialized administrative services. At the highest levels, they face environmental challenges of enormous breadth and must call upon specialist services of increasing complexity.

Planning is part of the administrative process. Henri Fayol identified five elements of administration, and the first was "to forecast and plan." The others: to organize, command, coordinate and control. Planning was one of the major preoccupations of Frederick Taylor. It was the first of the seven administrative processes in Luther Gulick's famous POSDCORB. It was a major concern of both Mary Parker Follett and Chester Barnard. It is a major orientation of the mathematically inclined technicians engaged in "management science." Even the most modern thinkers and teachers follow Fayol's lead by subdividing administration into planning and control or, with the term "control" split into its two components, planning, activating and evaluating.[1] Decision-making and communicating are often regarded as processes that enter into planning as well as into activating and evaluating.

Terminological difficulties develop with the expansion of specialized staff agencies to help administrators plan. Members of these agencies are often called "planners" and may even be thought of as "*the* planners." This terminology leads to the planners vs. doers illusion that the specialized technicians have some monopoly on planning and the administrators are involved only in doing. In fact, the most effective government planners are those involved in certain day-to-day activities of government.

Administrators are also more than mere doers. They are heavily involved in making critical decisions on programs and policies and in developing the network of commitments that make a plan feasible. They have the kind of contact with current decision-making without which people are scarcely qualified to understand the peculiar problems in each country, the uniqueness of every situation, the specific obstacles that must be overcome and the capacities of key institutions, groups and individuals. This contact may be obtained by participating in such critical current matters as the annual budget, handling foreign currency controls, reorganizing a major project, breaking critical bottlenecks or evaluating certain successes or failures. The major contribution of middle-range and long-range planning is to serve as a guide to such current action.[2] Conversely, planners for the middle-range and long-range future, both administrators and specialists, need contact with the immediate present.

Plan Administration As Social System Guidance

National economic planning deals with efforts to change the

structure and performance of an economy. This is why good economists and high quality economic analysis are essential for success in planned economic development. But it is not far from this truism to the dangerous fallacy of economic planning as merely economics. This fallacy has resulted in an underestimation of the critical roles that administrators and political leaders play in both the formulation and the implementation of economic goals. It has led to a tight monopoly by economists on positions of professional advice-giving. It has diverted the attention of many young economists from the tasks of institution-building and social reconstruction and contributed to their estrangement from administrators and national leaders. And it has helped the supersalesman of sophisticated econometrics present mathematical economics as the major conceptual tool for economic development. The result has been to waste good brains on refined technicalities with little or no basis in empirical data and to neglect the task of collecting more reliable data than can be put together through the less spectacular process of definition, addition and subtraction.

"Many of the conscious objectives and unintended consequences, as well as many of the means required for goal formulation, implementation and evaluation, are usually political, cultural, social or biophysical rather than merely economic."[3] In other words, all planners should recongize that economic considerations are intimately tied up with a large variety of noneconomic variables. Any real-life economic problem is usually also a problem in administrative and organizational change, in the political balancing of divergent interests, in changing cultural values, and in the technologies dealing with physical, biological or ecological processes.

But to jump around from one discipline to another is to risk a dilettantish loss of all perspective. The remedy for the narrowness of economic models may well be not the juggling of a large number of noneconomic models but rather the development of a general model of society that includes both economic and noneconomic concepts. Systems theory may provide such a model. Directions for future work are suggested by the following general systems model of a social system at the level of the nation-state.[4]

The model incorporates the major concepts traditionally used in national economic accounting, but broadens them from a set of economic indicators alone to a set of social indicators. According to this model, the State of any nation at any period of time . . . can be analyzed in terms of two interrelated multidimensional elements: system structure and system performance. The elements of system structure deal with the internal relations among the system's parts, the elements of system performance with the acquiring of inputs and their transformation into outputs. Both involve relations with the external environment. This mode, or any part thereof, may be flexibly applied to describe the unique characteristics of any country whatsoever, no matter what the level of industrial development or the type of political regime . . . The value of a general systems approach to all possible variables is that it provides a background for selecting those variables most appropriate to specific situations and for changing one's focus as the occasion warrants. It can prevent *ceteris paribus* from becoming *ceteris incognitis*.[5]

Administrators As Integrating Generalists

The concept of the administrator as generalist has been undermined from two directions. The tradition of the "gentleman generalist" has in some countries produced administrators with a narrow, parochial attitude toward specialized expertise in economics, engineering and other technical fields.[6] The fondness for specialization in certain other countries has led to an overemphasis on narrow techniques. This has been particularly apparent in the field of public administration, where such specialized techniques in work study, personnel matters and budgeting have often been regarded as the essence of administration, rather than simply as aids to administration.

With administrative theorists and "experts" deserting the generalist area, the fallacy of administration as technical gadgetry has become rather widespread. This has been most dangerous in the field of civil service reform. Attempts have been made to take job classification techniques and so-called merit systems originally developed for large, stable organizations in industrial societies and apply them to small, rapidly changing organizations in preindustrial societies. These reform efforts sometimes have the unintended effect of curtailing initiative and enterprise in development agencies, enlarging the heavy burden of regulations and paper work, and contributing to the evasion of civil service controls.

To cope with such problems, it is essential to build upon the concept of the administrator as generalist. The day of the "gentleman generalist" is over. Nor is it enough that development plans be administered by "middlemen generalists" who concentrate on making deals and compromises among the growing number of specialists. Effective development requires "integrating generalists."

Integrating generalists subordinate the use of administrative gadgets to the higher goals of social and economic progress. They are looked to for skills not only in communication and compromise but also in the constructive integration of divergent interests. They are expected to understand the organization's broad environment as well as, or even more than, its internal workings. They are expected to know enough about relevant techniques to enable them to understand, evaluate and coordinate the activities of many specialists and professionals.[7]

This means that the true generalist must learn enough about economics and other specialized fields to understand their limitations and their distinctive contributions. Rather than feeling uneasy when confronted by experts, the integrating generalist must always be aware of the benefits of conflicting expert judgments and the desirability of encouraging new and promising fields of expertise and specialization. He must never underestimate the tremendous contributions that can be made by the high-class, narrow expert who is concerned primarily with his own expertise. The administrator must be able to relate the work of such an expert to the society as a whole.

The integrating function extends not only to individual specialists but also to special groups and interests in the society. The integrating generalist knows how to build an "activation base" (or "support network") for development programs by organizing various coalitions and alliances among public and private groups and individuals. The role of the administrator has become "one of mobilization rather than supervision . . . (with) development based on activity, impetus and cooperation and not on hierarchy and authority.[8]

IMPLEMENTATION: STRATEGIC GUIDELINES

The generalist administrator tries to understand the broad environment within which he operates. If he fails, he may become thoroughly bogged down in the technicalities of complex issues and in the perverse intricacies of group conflicts and maneuvering. Certain general guidelines may help national planners achieve and maintain a balanced perspective.

The Emerging World Society

In the first flush of campaigns to win independence from colonial rule, leaders must appeal to nationalistic aspirations. They must stress the glories of self-rule and self-determination. After political independence is won, they often find themselves in control of a State, but not a nation. Nation-building efforts may also create a widespread illusion of national autonomy.

The environment of all national planners is the emergence of a world society of increasingly interdependent nations. As Bruce Russett has pointed out, " 'one world' has a meaning beyong the understanding even of those who lived just a generation ago."[9]

Unheralded and uncelebrated, a world society is slowly and painfully coming into being. It is characterized by the growth of increasingly interdependent nations, both industrializing and post-industrializing, of world-spanning organizations, of urban world centers, and of world-oriented elites. This growing interdependence is facilitated by communication-transportation systems that, for some activities, are continuously decreasing the space-time distance between Washington and Moscow more rapidly than that between Washington and Wichita or Moscow and Mintz.

The emerging "one world" hardly conforms to the visions of the utopians—any more than does the giant organization of "classical" ideas of administration, the megalopolis to the models of city planners, or the "great societies" to Keynesian theory. The world society includes a bewildering variety of subsystems increasingly locked together in conflict-cooperation relationships. The world polity is characterized by polycentric conflict, intersecting coalitions, continuing outbreaks of localized violence, many possibilities of "escalation," and spreading capacities for nuclear destruction. The political instrumentalities of conflict resolution and regional and world integration operate—as in nations, states, and cities—in an atmosphere of pressure and power politics, behind-the-scene lobbying, rotten borough representation, moralistic double-talk, deception, and self-deception. The world economy tends to be disorderly—neither free nor planned. The world culture tends to submerge national characteristics and values in a homogenizing flood of material goods and international styles. On the other hand, it includes vast value differences and sharp value conflicts. Like the megalopolis, the world society is a territorial entity without a government. It is an all-inclusive complex macrosystem with remarkably complicated and unpredictable—although increasingly structured—mechanisms of mutual adjustment.[10]

These confusing facts have at least three important implications. In their nation-building efforts, the leaders and administrators of industrializing societies must clearly see that they are building *interdependent* nations. They should not confuse political independence with dreams of perfect autonomy, autarchy or self-sufficiency. They must recognize the necessity of developing the capacity to engage in an ever-growing array of transnational operations, including trade, finance, tourism and politics.

The national planners in these nations must give even greater attention to strengthening the United Nations, its specialized agencies, its regional organizations and, above all, its central organs. The United Nations can perform functions in the promotion of economic and social progress that cannot possibly be handled in any other way. It can harmonize the national planning of individual countries—a vital function in an interdependent world. Overly nationalistic planning could easily lead to cut-throat international competition, "beggar thy neighbor" policies and international economic warfare. Only through greatly expanded and improved activities by the United Nations, on a worldwide as well as a regional basis, can the framework be developed for the kind of national planning that will contribute to both progress and peace.

The New Science-Technology Revolution

One of the most obvious factors in creating the new world society has been the remarkable growth of world-spanning communication and transportation systems. These systems, which will be much more spectacular in another five years, are merely a dramatic aspect of more far-reaching scientific and technological change.

In the United States this social transformation is already characterized by

1. An "information explosion" that, by creating great new areas of knowledge that few people can keep up with, has produced an "ignorance explosion";
2. Declining employment in the production of goods;
3. A vast expansion in services;
4. The growth of the "learning force" (the total number of people engaged in formal educational programs) to the point where it

will soon exceed the employed labor force;

5. Totally new relations between work, education, leisure and recreation;
6. New values and interests based upon abundance rather than scarcity; and
7. New social conflicts as people and institutions find difficulty in adjusting to new conditions.[11]

In the industrializing countries, the implications of the science-technology revolution are not yet clear. Lacking the scientific institutions and personnel capable of innovating or even of keeping up, the development planners in these countries must depend upon "pipelines" from those countries on the front lines of scientific progress. It may be possible in many areas to "leapfrog" obsolescent technology and, without being embarrassed by heavy investments in older methods, start out on a higher plane. To do this successfully, the industrializing countries must guard against being used as dumping grounds for obsolescent machinery and experts.

Development planners in these societies must never take for granted that technology that has proved itself elsewhere is the most appropriate for their own development. They must recognize that in a world of revolutionary scientific and technological changes, the planners of accelerated economic development must always be alert to the potentialities of new technology.

Planning for the Improbable

Like politics, administration has often been called the "art of the possible." If a major development project such as a new dam is to be feasible, planners need not only technical blueprints but also money; not only money but also the materials, machinery and trained labor to be obtained with the money; not only resources but also the administrators capable of using such resources and maintaining their supply; not only administrative capacity, but the political backing and coalition of supporting agencies necessary to overcome all sorts of inertia and resistance.

Once the first flush of enthusiasm for development planning has passed—once the planners begin to face up to the almost unbelievable difficulties in getting anything done—there is danger that they will swing so far toward emphasizing the possible that they will think mainly of short-run feasibility. They will be encouraged by economists accustomed to fighting utopia with myopia, that is, with "hard-nosed" calculations of small benefits that might be obtained quickly. The result can easily be that the planners will come to focus on the most possible and feasible outcome of all, namely, the inevitable. This is the fallacy of epiphenomenal planning.[12] The main advantage is that the planners can take credit for any minor progress that might have occurred anyway. If no progress takes place, they can justify their action by appealing to concepts such as "incremental meliorism," or the science of "muddling through."[13]

The possible covers a broad spectrum. It includes everything from the inevitable and the most feasible up to the somewhat and the highly improbable. In its highest forms, development planning is the art of the improbable.

"The danger of futile utopianism does not lie in the grandeur of a vision or the beauty of a dream. It lies rather in the failure to concentrate on the myriad details of today and tomorrow (for this is where the future is made) and the failure to learn today from yesterday's past errors."[14] Incremental meliorism is a major weapon of those who are masters of the improbable. No revolutionary change has ever occurred except through a sequence of small steps. The vision is lost only when the planners fail to deal with long, flexible sequences of small steps leading toward distant goals. "Muddling through," in the sense of making necessary compromises and shifting from one immediate goal to another, does not necessarily shatter the great dream, so long as the compromisers and goal shifters keep their eyes on the long-run strategic objectives that justify their daily tactics.

The Interest of Human Beings

One of the charges against industrialization is that people have been forgotten in the industrialized world. They have been treated, the social critics tell us, as cogs in a machine, commodities to be bought and sold, things to be manipulated and instruments of achieving power and building wealth—but not as human beings.[15]

The only justification of national planning is to help serve the interests of people. In response to this, many planners will point out that the long-run objective of their planning is to increase the material well-being of the people—and will then return to their projections, projects and budgets. But it is a terrible oversimplification to think of material well-being as the only interest that can be served through national planning. The interests of people in overcoming poverty, disease and ignorance are inextricably tied up with their equally deep human interests in justice, dignity, self-respect and the ability to participate in decisions affecting their lives.

This is not merely a matter of long-range objectives. The very viability of any national planning system depends upon what interests and whose interests it is seen as serving. Every important planning decision involves some calculation concerning the interests that will be served or frustrated. Any price index is merely a convenient way of reporting on the behavior of certain people in their roles as buyers and sellers of certain goods or services. Indeed, a plan itself usually describes how some people want many other people to behave. With every step in development, interests are apt to change. They are apt to change radically from one generation to another. It is thus extremely hard to appraise the extent to which the interests of any specific group have been satisfied or frustrated. The ubiquity of interest conflicts, as evidenced in pressure-group activity and civil unrest, may even lead some administrators and planners to the cynical conclusion that they cannot find any "public interest" or "common interest."

Some top administrators, when confronted with complex technical issues, are in the habit of asking, "What could this (or the other) course of action mean in the daily lives of people? Which people? When?" These are the kinds of questions that should be asked more frequently by development administrators. There is no place in national planning for administrators and planners who are uninterested in, or cynical and scornful of, public interest orientations.

IMPLEMENTATION: OBSTACLES

Plan administrators must also take a realistic view of the many obstacles standing in the way of progress. They must be capable of diagnosing the specific obstacles that impede action in the unique circumstances of time and place. But "like any other problem, the problem of getting desirable results through economic development planning is often responded to in an irrational manner. The existence of an implementation problem may at first be denied. When admitted, it may be handled in terms of a habitual reaction without any effort at diagnosis."[17] The attempted treatment may be irrelevant to the difficulties or may even accentuate them.

Resource Scarcities: Physical, Human and Organizational

Since expertise is an essential element in all forms of modern planning, there is a natural tendency to think that any obstacles to successful planning may be overcome by a greater application of expert knowledge. This "knowledge is all" illusion is, indeed, often fostered by "experts" themselves and by the administrators of technical assistance programs. But in industrializing countries, the first obstacles to economic growth are scarcities of physical, human and institutional resources.

The most obvious scarcities are physical. There is only a limited supply, very unevenly distributed, of housing, household equipment, food, clothing and medical supplies. There is only a limited supply of the resources needed to expand consumer goods: plant, equipment and machinery; a suitable infrastructure of communication, transportation, electric power and irrigation facilities; and a well-rounded natural resource base.

The Western world, including North America as well as Europe, has been more conspicuously endowed with resources than the rest of the globe.[17] Most of the poor countries suffer from serious resource deficiencies. Agricultural and forest lands suffer from erosion, soil depletion and recurrent droughts and floods. "The peoples of the present underdeveloped areas do not have the opportunity of moving to virgin land that is richer than the land now occupied. In most underdeveloped countries, the present distribution of population reflects very accurately the distribution of known resources, including soil fertility."[18] The situation with respect to mineral resources is very uneven. Where high quality resources have been discovered during previous periods of exploitation, this has usually led to lopsided economic development—as in Mexico, Venezuela and the oil-rich countries of the Middle East. Other known mineral reserves are often composed of low quality ores requiring expensive processes of extraction or refining. In many cases, the extent of mineral resources is not known; exploration and development are expensive and long, drawn-out processes.

People are the most important resource in any country. Natural and man-made wealth are "resources" only because people find them useful and develop them. The industrializing countries, particularly those with the largest and the most rapidly growing populations, are "people rich." Their people represent great untrapped reservoirs of productive power and undeveloped sources of purchasing power. But unlike other resources, a large population often constitutes a serious burden. An oversupply of people in relation to physical resources is usually accompanied by a serious undersupply of people with an adequate level of health and physical energy, literacy, education and training. Every "developing" country in Asia, the Middle East, Africa and Latin America is seriously handicapped by the lack of people with high level technical and managerial skills.

To the shortage of knowledge and skills must be added the lack of widespread, realistic motivation. After centuries of poverty and oppression, apathy and hopelessness tend to become a way of life. Recurrent failures to obtain small material improvements, together with the broken promises of politicians, support tendencies toward fatalism in the traditional culture. Kusum Nair, after visiting scores of Indian villages, reports upon the widespread phenomenon of "limited aspirations":

> A great majority of the rural communities do not share in this concept of an ever-rising standard of living. The upper level they are prepared to strive for is limited and it is the floor generally that is bottomless. . . . In a situation of limited and static aspirations, if a man should feel that his requirements are just two bags of paddy per year, he works for two bags, but not for more. If he looks to the stars, it is only to worship them, not to pluck them.[19]

Similar reports come from those who have visited among the peasants of Pakistan, Burma, Thailand, Indonesia and Malaysia. The "revolution of rising expectations," so widely hailed as the driving force behind economic development in the poor nations, certainly exists, but as a revolution of *uneven* expectations. It expresses the great aspirations of rising elites, particularly a minority of national leaders, intellectuals and entrepreneurs. When development motivations are aroused more broadly, many people tend to expect immediate miracles. This may lead to a "revolution of rising frustrations."

Realities of Social Conflict

Many planning technicians see national development planning as a "blackboard" exercise far removed from the real world of clashing values, competing interests and changing social systems. As Gunnar Myrdal has pointed out with reference to non-Marxist thought, "there has always been a tendency in economics to gloss over interest conflicts."[20]

Development planning is inevitably involved in various forms of open and hidden social conflict. The mildest conflicts take the form of simple inertia. Weighted down by habit and custom, people and organizations are not easily moved. As with physical objects, any effort to move or change them creates friction. An effort to move them far or quickly is apt to create active resistance and produce counterplans.

The most active form of resistance is based upon a felt conflict of interests.[21] In the case of "cross-sectoral" plans,[22] a certain kind of resistance can reasonably be anticipated from the very nature of the plans themselves. Thus plans for higher taxes will be opposed by taxpayers, price ceilings by merchants and so on.

The nature and intensity of the opposition will depend upon the specific circumstances and upon the degree to which the "injured" interests are organized. Sector and area plans emerge out of a competition for scarce resources by organizations in different sectors and areas. This process of resource allocation creates dissatisfactions, which inevitably give rise to efforts to change official plans or impede their implementation.

Action based upon new technology *always* produces serious interest conflicts. "Technological change of any significance whatsoever is a threat, real or imagined, to the power or security of someone. . . . In its more obvious aspects, any technological change which enables the production of similar output with less labor threatens to reduce employment. But even where such an effect can be counterbalanced by expanded production or by transfers to other work, the change itself threatens established positions and expertise. It renders obsolete the accrued capital of knowledge in the hands and minds of those who operated in accordance with the previous processes. It may even suggest that the people responsible for the previous processes are inferior individuals, as compared with the wiser souls who promote the new processes. Furthermore, it may turn upside down the old world of established relationships and lead to a complete reorganization of work groups, tasks, responsibilities, and individual status."[23]

Plans for changes in social structure, whether explicit objectives or merely corollaries of explicit objectives, lead the planners into the heart of deeply felt social conflicts. The limitation of caste or class distinctions, the control of monopolies, the regulation of any personal interests, the reorganization of industry or agriculture, the promotion of new cooperatives, trade unions or trade associations, the "leveling down" of privileged groups, the "leveling up" of the underprivileged—all such objectives pit planners against plan opponents. It is rare if the social conflicts inherent in (or provoked by) certain plans for changes in social structure are not reflected in internal competition among the central planners themselves. "The more ambitious and dynamic the planning, the sharper this competitive process tends to be, and the more far-reaching are the implications for broader conflicts throughout the entire social structure."[24]

Errors by Planners

One of the implicit premises underlying the behavior of many national planners is the myth of planners' rationality. Since national planning represents concerted effort at the rational allocation of resources in the service of the general welfare, it is often taken for granted that any major decisions or proposals by national planners are ipso facto rational. This point of view is supported by political leaders who must build up their reputations for wisdom, administrators who are unwilling to take blame on their own shoulders and technicians eager to sell their services.

A more mature approach is to recognize that, like everyone else, planners make errors in both substance and methods. The effort to behave rationally, like all processes of human learning, involves trial and error. Some national planners seem to have learned from their own and others' mistakes, breaking with past polities and developing many new approaches, such as the rural public works programs and the use of private enterprises in distributing fertilizer and sinking tube wells in Pakistan. Another case of adaptability was the giant "villagization" program through which the government of Tanzania in 1964 committed itself to a plan for relocating hundreds of thousands of people into compact agricultural villages. For a while the government adhered to this plan, merely complaining about the difficulty of getting coordination among the many agencies dealing with housing, health, agriculture and other specialized aspects of village life. Within a year, however, the government leaders recognized that the plan itself was undesirable. By the end of 1965, the entire program was quickly converted to a small series of pilot projects.

It is likely that substantive planning errors are being made continuously on a large scale. Lauchlin Currie suggests that many economic advisers have been guilty of major errors in economic analysis, including the following:

1. Ignoring the role of improved income distribution in economic growth;

2. Identifying well-being with national income;
3. Exaggerating the role of capital investment and capital output ratios, thereby contributing to capital waste and underutilization of plant capacity;
4. Underestimating the importance of putting unemployed labor to work; and
5. Seriously underestimating the benefits to be obtained (including the expansion of demand for locally produced goods and the training of the labor force) from investing in housing and urban development.[25]

Currie believes it very important that certain national development plans—or certain parts of them—*not* be implemented.[26] In Eastern Europe there have been major efforts to uncover and correct previous planning failures by making new provisions for more decentralized decision-making. Some doctrinaire analysts in Asia and Latin America still have a long way to go in matching up with the "new-style socialism" that aims at utilizing market and price mechanisms and lightening the burden on the central government's planning officials.

There are certain methodological errors that enter into what might be called the administrative pathology of national development planning. Among them are the following.[27]

1. Document orientation: the tendency of planning technicians to hold that "the script's the thing," and not the play, concentrating their attention exclusively on memoranda and reports rather than the real-life behavior toward which the documents are supposed to contribute;
2. Paper planning: constructing plans without much critical analysis and then assuming the plans to be an accomplished fact, without much attention to details or intermediate steps;
3. Underevaluation: not getting information on the details of implementation and unexpected side effects or indirect results;
4. Overevaluation: developing evaluating mechanisms that distort the fact-gathering process, overload the administrative machinery, and provide substitutes for action or justification of inaction or bad plans.

Slow Growth of Useful Theory

There have been three major currents in the development of serious theory and research concerning national planning: ideological debate, econometric technique and empirical analysis.

Ideological debate, sparked by the initiation of the Soviet Union's five-year plans in the late 1920s, has consisted of many heated controversies on the relation of national planning to "freedom" or "serfdom."

The development of econometric technique has led to significant advances in national economic accounting, input-output analysis, linear programming and computerized models of various economic transactions. It has also helped bring into being the fiction of scientific planning. In the effort to attract attention and support, the econometricians—like the proponents of "scientific management," "administrative science" and "management science"—have often capitalized on their use of scientific methods to exaggerate the extent of their scientific achievements.

The empirical analysis current has started since 1960. In its earliest stages, the emphasis was on economic trends and the evolution of economic plans and policies in individual countries. More recent work has broadened to include social, political and cultural variables and to produce comparative international studies. There has been little pretense of firm scientific findings and a marked caution against indulgence in "premature prescription."

The scientific basis of national planning is still extremely weak, lagging behind both the achievement of natural science and the intuitive wisdom of the best planners. The weakness is most evident in the industrializing countries and the administrative aspects of planning. "Few Latin American economies," notes Currie, "have received prolonged analysis by outstanding economists who also understand something of the Art of Getting Things Done."[28] A similar comment—in still stronger terms—might be applicable to most countries in Asia, the Middle East and Africa.

Economic analysis of planning problems is far ahead of the work done in other branches of social science. Public-administration approaches to the subject have often been based upon static, formalistic concepts developed in the West and not attuned to the realities of dynamic social change. Very little has been done to apply the new advances in business management, organizational theory and planned social change in formal organizations and industrial communities. While there have been significant academic advances in the field of comparative government (sometimes mislabeled "comparative administration") and political development, outstanding thinkers in these areas have made little direct contact with the concrete problems of administering plans for national economic development.

One of the reasons for this slow growth has been the dogmatism toward national planning in predominantly private-enterprise countries. Another reason is the complexity of the elements involved. There are a vast number of variables, great problems of quantification and data reliability and almost no opportunities for even partially controlled experiments. The varieties of cultural conditions and political regimes, combined with serious linguistic barriers, make it extremely difficult to identify the unique permutations in which basic variables combine in any one country at any one period of time. The process of industrialization, "involving changes in nearly every important interpersonal and intergroup relationship within a society, is probably the most complicated subject man has attempted to study and understand."[29]

The dominant tendencies in modern science—specialization and emphasis on the natural sciences—both militate against progress in this field. With increasing specialization, an interdisciplinary approach becomes more necessary and more difficult. Because of their achievements, the natural sciences receive an increasing share of the world's resources devoted to science and technology, and the social sciences receive a declining share. A disproportionate amount of scientific activity is devoted to military and paramilitary purposes. In the industrializing societies, the total volume of scientific investment is remarkable small, and the amount devoted to the social sciences—upon which progress toward any "science" of national development planning must be based—is pathetically small.

IMPLEMENTATION: OPERATING PRINCIPLES

The major means for overcoming obstacles to plan implementation are mobilization and the use of influence.

Reference has been made to the process of mobilizing various interests (inside and outside of government) into an "activation" or "support" base. Attention must also be given to the following strategies and tactics:

1. Combining various types of persuasion and pressure into an "activation mix" appropriate to a given situation;
2. Managing conflict in such a way as to achieve acceptable compromises and integration of conficting interests, with little avoidance, deadlock, or defeat; and

3. Conducting action campaigns under conditions of considerable risk and uncertainty.

These involve concrete administrative operations which, while they all touch upon the processes of mobilizing support, using influence, managing conflict and conducting campaigns, are somewhat more technical and conventional in nature.

Budgeting: The New "Systems Analysis"

"Since annual budgets are the principal means by which governments authorize and control most of their expenditures, most outlays provided for in the public sector portion of a development plan must be incorporated into these budgets if the plan is to be carried out. . . . A government's budget is therefore a key element in converting a development plan into a program for action."[30]

The difficulty with budgeting for economic development is that the government budgeting techniques inherited from colonial days have been defective. Budgetary reform has often been inspired by people with the very formalistic ideas of *both* development and administration. Reform has been hindered by superficial considerations of comprehensiveness and classification, or dictated by budgetary faddism. One popular budgetary fad has been performance or program budgeting—the idea that a meaningful government budget should not be limited to listing the "inputs" (or resources) to be used, but should also list the "outputs," the services or facilities to be provided through the use of such resources. Yet, in the United States, where this new approach originated, insufficient attention was given to the complex problems involved in providing useful information on either input or output. "Program" or "performance" budgeting became a catchword, with budget "experts" who had not done very well at home attempting to install it in industrializing countries.

It was not until the recent "budgeting revolution" in the United States Department of Defense (1961-65) that the ideas were operationally refined. Success in efficient procurement and delivery of military goods[31] led the president to instruct the Bureau of the Budget to install the same "planning-programming-budgeting system"[32] throughout the federal establishment. This plan depends on adapting techniques developed for Defense Department purposes to the more intangible services of other federal agencies, and to aid programs to local, state or foreign governments. It also depends upon converting "old line" budgetary personnel into experts in program planning and administration—a long and difficult process. The planning-programming-budgeting system will not be in serious operation in half the agencies of the United States government before 1970.

Some of the most progressive industrializing nations will try to apply the new "systems analysis" to their own problems of budgeting for planned economic development. Efforts will be made to introduce planning-programming-budgeting. system concepts in the very form in which they have emanated from the United States Department of Defense, without recognition of the many fundamental changes being made in them by civilian administrators or the still more fundamental changes needed to adapt them to the needs of developing nations.

The budgeting of government plans should be based upon an appraisal of (a) the direct and indirect benefits likely to be obtained from (b) identifiable outputs (or services) to be provided by the use of realistically estimated inputs (costs). The compelling logic of the planning-programming-budgeting system is that it is a "benefit-output-cost" system. This is very close to what was previously called "cost-benefit" analysis, but with two important changes. It is now realized that costs (or the use of inputs) do not directly lead to benefits. The costs reflect the inputs used in producing certain outputs (such as health services, educational services, dams, etc.). The justification of these outputs is that they provide certain benefits, such as malaria eradication, literacy and water for irrigation. The word "output" must be inserted between "cost" and "benefit," but the major emphasis must be on the benefits. To neglect them is to take a narrow "cost-accounting" viewpoint, whereby attention may be directed to doing economically things that should not be done at all. Costs are merely foregone benefits. Hence the desirability of formulating the new approach in terms of "benefit-output-cost" analysis.[33] This places more emphasis on the comparison of alternative benefits through alternative output patterns.

Projects: Promotion and Review

There is a serious shortage of well-prepared projects relative to the funds available for financing them. "Foreign and international lending and donor agencies, which generally are unwilling to commit funds for projects which are not based on sound preinvestment and other studies, are frequently hard put to find enough well-prepared projects to help finance in less developed countries."[34]

Moreover, projects for which financing is obtained often turn out to be disappointing. A technician with considerable experience at the project level finds the following:

> Buildings left unfinished for lack of funds; new factories operating at only a fraction of capacity and at substantial losses; costly machinery and equipment idle for want of spare parts; water-storage dams washed out because of poor engineering or inadequate design data; farm lands excessively salinated because of too liberal water use from new irrigation facilities and inadequate drainage; new schools without desks or teachers; delicate communications equipment spoiling in poorly protected warehouses for want of buildings in which to install it; crop improvement projects spoiled because of inadequate protection against cross-pollination or through misuse of distributed seeds; hospitals without drugs, equipment, or nurses—such examples are perhaps more typical than uncommon. Many, perhaps most of them are due to poor project planning.[35]

Such situations are the result of the widespread fallacy of projections without projects. The macrofallacy is that "aggregate" macroeconomic quantities may serve as useful development targets apart from the specific enterprise, sectoral and cross-sectoral plans that may be aggregated.[36] The microfallacy is that specific ecnomic and engineering "feasibility studies" on paper will provide a project plan.

One of the key principles of development administration is that central planners should promote the formulation and review of large numbers of specific development projects in terms of the relevant technical, financial, administrative, political and cultural considerations. Development planners should "build up and maintain a 'stock' of well-prepared projects from which a suitable variety and number can be selected to provide a steady flow of new projects to be added to those already in process of execution."[37] Sectoral studies can help identify, as early as possible, promising projects in each sector.[38]

in Pakistan, over 100 project and program feasibility studies, beside a number of important sector surveys, were carried through at the same time in a specially organized "crash program." The program was inaugurated early in the Second Plan period to build up a stock of projects for the latter part of the Second, and especially for the Third Plan period. The availability of a large number of projects "ready to go" not only has

made it possible for Pakistan to obtain increased foreign aid, but also helps account for its success in fulfilling and exceeding its plan targets.[39]
But central planners cannot sit back and merely review projects developed by ministries and government corporations. It is much more important to take specific steps to promote the formulation of projects worth reviewing, and this applies to private sector projects as well. "Providing suitable incentives to private investors and eliminating administrative, legal, and other regulations and procedures which tend to dampen the interest of domestic and foreign investors"[40] is not enough. Private firms have often proved remarkably adept at devising attractive projects that have resulted in little social benefit or even in large, indirect losses of scarce foreign currency.

Market Administration

Experience has proved that there are serious limits on the quantity and type of decisions that can be made by government planners. Implementation, as well as the formulation of desirable plans, requires decentralization of decision-making. Markets and price systems may be useful in bringing about such decentralization.[41]
Some proponents of a larger public sector mistakenly equate the use of market and price systems with the laissez-faire views of Adam Smith and opposition to government intervention in market operations. The old-fashioned doctrinaire Socialists have not yet caught up with Eastern Europe's new wave of experimentation in the manipulation of markets and price systems by governments with centrally planned economies. Overenthusiastic proponents of market and price systems have sometimes gone to the other extreme of suggesting—or seeming to suggest—that these systems be allowed to operate on their own.
Despite both versions of the laissez-faire illusion, the effective decentralization of decision-making through markets and price systems requires highly developed skills in market administration. These skills involve:

1. Fiscal, monetary and credit policies (both general and selective) that promote the growth of private and mixed organizations;
2. The promotion and control of foreign investing and lending;
3. The imposition and/or liberalization or removal of foreign cur-

rency controls, import controls and excises;

4. Government buying and selling to promote or stabilize markets;
5. The imposition of various kinds of miminum, maximum or fixed prices;
6. Other forms of direct and indirect market and price regulation; and
7. The provision of market information and other kinds of data needed by buyers, sellers and investors.

All these activities are forms of intervention. They comprise a sphere of government decision-making which, if successfully handled, may result in a broadening volume of private decision-making that serves public interests.

Information Collection and Distribution

Information is the lifeblood of all planning. In the two countries with the most elaborate statistical machinery in the world, the USSR and the United States, there is increasing dissatisfaction with available data and the way they are used. Soviet planners are involved in a general reorganization of statistical collection, geared into a nationwide system of computerized collection, processing, retrieval and distribution.[42] In the United States the new budgeting system is oriented toward obtaining information not merely on inputs and outputs, but also on the benefits enjoyed by various groups in society as a result of government programs. This moves the federal government to contemplate revolutionary steps in obtaining noneconomic data on American society—a new orientation evidenced in the planning now under way for a social report of the president (to complement the president's economic report and budget message) or for a comprehensive State of the Union message or set of messages. An indication of the statistical work needed to do this is provided by Raymond A. Bauer's *Social Indicators*,[43] prepared under the auspices of the American Academy of Arts and Sciences.

All industrializing countries suffer from a serious shortage of statistical data. Ad hoc surveys and fact-finding inquiries by expert groups are costly and time-comsuming. Valuable information is jealously guarded by people and agencies anxious to enhance their power. Publicly available information tends to be embodied in documents that few people know about or that are "lost in the files." Some of the "facts" and estimates most widely in use suffer from appallingly large margins of error.[44] "Scarce professional talent can also be misused in the collection of data for, and the preparation of, input-output matrices, a favourable instrument of planning experts from the more advanced countries. . . . Quite a few less developed countries have constructed input-output tables of their economies, although it would be hard to find one which has made effective use of them for planning purposes."[45] This ritualistic elaboration of econometric projections stems from a dangerous faith in the number magic of figures without facts.[46]

"It would be useful to include in each national development plan a program or blueprint for expanding and improving the statistical and other data needed only to formulate and implement the next plan. The statistician or other fact-finder must always be ahead of the planner if he is to provide the planner with information when it is required. . . . A blueprint for statistical betterment related specifically to the next plan would be much more modest than most proposals to overhaul the statistical apparatus and practices prevailing in less developed countries."[47]

Development administrators cannot afford to allow statistical needs to be formulated by any one set of technicians. Economists tend to overemphasize national accounting estimates. Statisticians tend to overemphasize the improvement of data in separate sectors. Both usually neglect social and sociological data. The only way to make a strategic selection of priorities is to use some general model of all the different kinds of information relevant to accelerated change. This requires some form of social systems accounting. Although it will take at least another decade before social systems accounting can become operational in many countries, one practical step can be taken without much delay: the preparation of annual reports in which the chief executive (whether prime minister or president) gives the legislature and the nation a comprehensive picture of problems, progress and retrogression on all important fronts.[48]

Administrators should build and promote multiple channels for the flow of information, particularly "feedback" information. Too much may be channeled to central government offices and top administrators, with too little moving to the places where people can have the time to absorb it, the familiarity to understand it and the opportunity to act directly on it. Official government channels never suffice. As development progresses and the volume and complexity of information flow become greater, the channels provided by a competitive press, parliamentary discussions, professional journals, international media and face-to-face conferences and meetings become increasingly important.

Administrative Research and Development

The fallacy of hard-science research seems to pervade the offices of planning administrators and technicians. Agricultural, engineering, transportation research is more essential to these administrators than research on planning itself and the administration of planning, which might not provide immediate results. If it did, it might call for embarrassing changes in organizational structure or administration. One result is training programs existing without the training materials that only serious research can provide.

More effective development planning requires an increase in research and theory on planning problems and processes. A number of important steps must be taken. There should be a substantial increase in the funds made available for such research. The United Nations and other agencies have been expected to produce too much expert advice and training in proportion to the unsatisfactory research-theory basis for such activity.

Much greater use should be made of universities, research institutions and full-time research staffs in conducting international research on planning and planning administration. There is a definite limit to what can be accomplished by ad hoc meetings of experts and by detailed questionnaires mailed to government agencies in various countries.

Closer cooperation is needed between objective researchers and planning administrators. More national planning agencies should be willing to provide "access" and other assistance to serious researchers. A good example is the extensive assistance now being provided by the planning authorities in India, Pakistan, Venezuela and Kenya to a group of researchers engaged in a comparative study of building national planning systems.[49] National planners themselves should be given more opportunities to escape the "planning struggle" and engage in research and theory on the basis of their experiences.

Training for Top Administrators

National development planners generally recognize the tremendous importance of education and training programs in providing thorough social reconstruction. They have made provisions for training in business and public administration. They have recognized the need for training economists and other technicians. But they have been acting on the comfortable doctrine of education for other people. Planners too must learn.

Even an abundant supply of economic technicians—senior as well as junior—will not provide the range of skills and knowledge needed to formulate sound plans, implement them, and adjust them to meet new conditions. This point is increasingly recognized at the level of the individual enterprise, where general management training is rapidly expanding. This point should also be recognized by the central agencies of government. . . .[50]

Courses, seminars and workshops can meet the needs not only of specialists but also of leaders of interdisciplinary teams, top executives, political leaders and interest group leaders. Proposals for such educational programs are now being reviewed and revised on the basis of critiques by planning officials in many countries and of discussion at the INTERPLAN conference held in November 1966.[51]

"Transboundary" Dialogue

At international conferences, serious barriers to meaningful discussion are created whenever the participants are supposed to "represent" their countries. This puts them in the position of defending established positions rather than joining in the exploration of mutual problems and the frank discussion of common failures. Moreover, there are few conferences that bring together specialists from different disciplines. There are still fewer in which political leaders, administrators and specialists all meet and discuss problems together.

Planners need more opportunities for informal and continuing dialogue across national, disciplinary and "position" or "rank" boundaries. Various United Nations agencies have already made tremendous progress in this area. Much still remains to be done in developing more effective dialogues between national leaders, administrators and technicians—dialogues that likely are possible only in the informal atmosphere of nonofficial conferences and workshops.

MACHINERY FOR PLANNING

Any hopes for getting results through economic development

planning are apt to be frustrated without appropriate administrative machinery. The development of the complex array of organizations and institutions involved in plan formulation and implementation requires certain sensitive adaptations in the central machinery of national government; demands a pragmatic flexibility based more upon an interest in results and an abstract commitment to structural forms; and calls for continuing reorganization to meet new conditions and promote new and more creative policies and activities.

Central Guidance Clusters

Modern administrative theory has clearly recognized that in single organizations, whether public or private, the administrative processes of planning, activating (or in older terminology "directing"), and evaluating are interwoven at all hierarchical levels. In particular, all the higher organs of managment play vital roles in planning. . . . At the level of a nation also the specialized planning units account for only a very small part of the national economic planning that actually takes place. They tend to concentrate upon certain research functions involving the analysis of general economic trends and the formulation of proposals to be decided upon by others. . . . Nor are they even the coordinators of national economic policy and programs. In fact, their specific functions are extremely varied, and it is impossible to determine what these functions really are—or should be— without seeing them as an integral part of the complex network of *many* organs at the center of national government.[52]

Any single central planning agency serves such important symbolic and ceremonial purposes that it may be mistakenly regarded as *the* planning agency. This illusion is embedded in the widespread myth of central omnipotence. According to it, any organization or social system is run by a small group who issues commands that are binding on others.[53] The myth of central omnipotence is particularly powerful at the national level. National leaders seeking greater power may use specialized planning agencies as lightning rods to attract opposition and resentments. They may even exaggerate the power of a central planning agency in order to make it a scapegoat that can be publicly liquidated or reorganized whenever a new economic crisis develops.

Effective development planning requires a cluster of central government agencies performing various roles not only in the provision of specialized and general staff services but also in national leadership, financial management and the handling of critical problems. The special staff roles include (a) trend analysis; (b) goal analysis; (c) policy analysis; and (d) major project analysis. Most economic staffs provide the first two. The more effective ones concentrate on the last two. The general staff roles include (a) providing communication links among vital centers of power and expertise; (b) bargaining and negotiating among diverse groups; (c) evaluating performance; and (d) helping break bottlenecks and perform other functions necessary for expediting action. Many economists have developed impressive capacities for performing these noneconomic functions.

Both special and general staff services are particularly important in helping strengthen and support general leadership roles. These are the indispensable roles played by chief executives, prime ministers, formal cabinets and interdepartmental cabinet committees, formal councils representing major power groups in a country, informal control groups and personal advisers to top national leaders.

No matter what their formal relation to specialized planning agencies,

> central financial institutions *always* play a tremendous role in the formulation and implementation of national economic plans. This role is rooted in the tremendous significance of money as a claim against resources, in the political as well as the economic significance of accounting and auditing operations. It is strengthened by the fact that financial agencies are often the oldest and most redoubtable of government bureaucracies, with an influential network of local offices scattered across a country. Where these agencies are not well-developed, there is an institutional gap that cannot be filled.[54]

These financial management roles may be divided not only between a finance ministry (or treasury) and a central bank but also among the separate units of those agencies dealing with expenditures, current budgets, development of capital budgets and foreign currency budgets. In addition, there are often one or more separate national development banks or corporations handling government loans and investments in various sectors. And there are the strategically important and, at times, decisive roles played by defense ministries, national water boards, or other agencies with special responsibilities for handling critical problems affecting the entire country.

No single agency could ever handle all the many roles involved in the guidance of national economic change. They are too numerous, specialized, and different to be embodied in any single organization. Any effort to incorporate them all in a single organization would inevitably lead to such a large amount of subdivision as to convert the boundaries of the total organization into a formal facade. The subdivisions would become de facto formal organizations.[55]

Building Innovating Action Organizations.

One of the dangers of taking old-fashioned economic analysis too seriously is its concentration upon the so-called factors of production—land, labor and capital—as the source of economic growth. Its most extreme form is the proposition that there could or should be a stable relation between incremental investment and production.[56] This oversimplification has been partially counteracted by the recent discovery of "human capital" and "investment in people" through expenditures on such things as education and health.[57]

Both the "hard goods" concept of investment and "investment in people" are illustrations of the *atomistic illusion*. The former looks at machinery abstracted from the people who use it, the latter at people in their capacity as single individuals. Each overlooks the fundamental fact that the goods and services needed for human progress cannot be produced by machinery alone or by educated, healthy people acting individually. Capital and people can be effectively used only by building organizations or institutions with the capacity to use them.

The need for building greater organizational capacity at the very center of government, that is, in the central guidance cluster, has been discussed. The key agencies in this cluster can never be very effective unless they can rely on a large array of government ministries, public corporations and other action agencies to carry on specific programs, policies and projects. Another role may be added to those mentioned—the role of building action agencies. They should see this role as some of the most effective planners already see it—as that of creating organization-building ministries and corporations.

The process of building an organization always requires setting up totally new agencies. No change from an administration designed mainly to maintain law and order to one designed to accelerate economic growth has ever been achieved totally within the framework of traditional institutions. But to build an organization effectively also requires the adaptation and reinvigoration of old-line agencies. There is tremendous value in harnessing the capacities and unleashing the often-repressed energy and imagination of certain people in the traditional bureaucracy.

Another task of national planners is to build up private enterprise capable of both genuine initiative and public responsibility. At the same time, public corporations and mixed enterprises may also show great initiative and enterprise. Successful organization-building means finding individuals and groups with initiative and ability and providing them with the resources and encouragement needed for growth. "Islands of initiative" may be few and far between. It is more important in the early stages of development to promote innovative agencies, even those that resist central coordination, than to waste time coordinating agencies with little capacity to get anything done.

Private and Community Participation

Human relations researchers have found that greater participation in decision-making seems to result in improved output. At the national level, participative planning has been popularized by the achievements of French national planning in the 1950s and early 1960s. Although the French also made vigorous use of governmental measures to promote expansion by specific enterprises, they operated on the widely advertised principle of "the participation in policy-making of those who will have to bear the brunt of the implementation of measures decided upon."[58] Such participation is properly regarded as a step toward greater democracy. The representative democracy of parliamentary institutions is no longer sufficient to give people enough participation in the complex decisions affecting their lives and futures.

The new attention to participation has also given rise to "facade democracy." Participative techniques "are often used to provide ritualistic rather than genuine participation. Planners may merely want to give private groups the sense of participation in order to manipulate them into accepting as their own predetermined decisions and plans. Similarly, many representatives on consultative committees, both intra- and interorganizational, are mainly interested in the prestige accruing to themselves or their constituents through symbolic rather than actual participation."[59]

Effective formulation and implementation of development plans require genuine participation by major groups and communities. The application of this principle enables national planners to build an "activation base" (or "support base") composed of people with the power to get action. But genuine participation means that the planners must be willing to pay a certain price, namely, that the plans and actions emerging from the consultative process may never be fully known in advance. This sharing in decision-making unquestionably means certain differences in the nature of the decisions made.

"Genuine" does not mean "haphazard." In any industrializing society there are many people and groups who are not yet ready for a high degree of participation. Among these are trade unions, city governments, local community groups and business associations. The task of the development planners is to prepare the ground by moving from simple issues to more complex ones. The best way to prepare these groups is not to postpone consultation but to use consultative arrangements as a way of educating the groups in the complexities of developmental processes and programs.

CENTRAL-REGIONAL-LOCAL RELATIONS

National planning is a major contribution to nation-building. "A national plan serves as a unifying agent of an otherwise loose and fragile society. . . . Even if the economic and social goals are not realized, a plan is successful to the extent to which it serves to mobilize the people's energies, bring about national planning machinery and a measure of political consensus."[60]

Centralization Veins and Decentralization Arteries

In a country threatened or torn apart by sectionalism (often reinforced by linguistic, ethnic or religious ties), building a nation obviously implies centralization of power, responsibility and authority. The national plan is itself a symbol of centralization, and the machinery of planning creates a system of centralized decision-making.

But every practical administrator knows that in order to centralize some things, other things must be decentralized. "Neither centralization nor decentralization are absolutes. An extreme of either one would destroy any organization. Not only do the two always appear together; they complement each other. The arteries of decentralization bring the lifeblood of responsibility and authority to the various members, while the veins bring it back to the center."[61] The power to achieve significant progress can be obtained only through some combination of centralization and decentralization.

Within any organization there are three dimensions on which centralization-decentralization combinations may be measured: (a) the horizontal dispersion or concentration among the various head office units; (b) the vertical dispersion or concentration among the hierarchical levels of each; and (c) the geographical dispersion or concentration between field offices and other units in the organization.

Beyond the apparatus of national government, there are other basic elements that may enter into centralization-decentralization combinations: (a) subnational state governments, an important part of any federal system; (b) local governments below the state level; and (c) provincial governments or regional instrumentalities intervening between the central government and the subnational states. An increase in decentralization in, for instance, the delegation of additional authority to state or provincial agencies may mean greater centralization of the local governments. Similarly, more power by either state or local governments to do things on their own may mean an enlargement of the central government's power to get things done. One cannot help but be struck by the fact that effective central planning requires a vast amount of decentralization.[62]

Governments at Regional and Local Levels

One of the heritages of colonialism in many industrializing countries has been a network of the subnational officials of central government. These officials, who are called district commissioners, officers or collectors, usually had comprehensive formal authority in their respective geographical areas. The effort to preserve these roles—either through civil service officers or their replacement by political leaders—has been closely associated with the illusion of the single subnational coordinator.

There are two simple reasons why this is an illusion. In an industrializing society, the operations of national agencies become too complicated to be coordinated by the hierarchical authority of any official in a single region. Regional offices must operate in the light of many national considerations outside the legitimate scope of a regional officer. In the interest of welding a nation together and overcoming separatist influences, many countries need to follow the Mexican example of setting up semiautonomous national agencies located regionally or locally to carry on specialized regional or local programs. Such agencies can promote regional and local government by providing both a constructive example and healthy competition, which would hardly be feasible if they were under the authority of local leaders.

The existence and growth of local, provincial or subnational state governments cannot—and should not—be fully subordinated to the authority of a central government official. While such governments cannot develop to the point of being self-sufficient or completely autonomous, their growth is both inevitable and desirable. Even in "unitary" (nonfederal) nations whose central governments have complete formal authority over lower levels of government, central officials must often bargain gingerly with—and concede considerably to—local political forces.

A widely neglected principle of government at the subnational level is that regional and local coordination depends on the interaction of many subnational and national forces. This does not preclude efforts by subnational officers of central government to contribute to the coordination process. It does not preclude hierarchical coordinating efforts by those in positions of higher formal authority. It recognizes that many disputes among government and private agencies in a given region may be settled only by decision on the part of those with formal hierarchical authority in the central government. Difficult problems in a given region may be settled at times only by the active participation of a foreign government, a foreign corporation or an international lending agency. The possibilities of hierarchical coordination are extremely limited. They are greater only when there are continuing efforts at mutual adjustment coordination[63] among all the many organizations and groups involved in local matters.

Regional and local problems of government cannot be discussed appropriately under the simplistic heading of "regional and local government," if this term is used to exclude the agencies at higher government levels. The more appropriate term is "government at the regional or local level."[64]

The Content of Subnational Area Planning

One might think that a comprehensive framework for coordination in urban and regional local areas is provided by subnational area planning. Unfortunately, "planning activities at the urban level are concentrated on the physical (as opposed to the economic and social) aspects of planning."[65] At the regional level, planning usually becomes still less comprehensive, with special attention often given to certain large-scale development projects and even less attention to social considerations and the broad range of government promotional activities and operations. The professional city planner's fallacy of the master plan has led to comprehensive land-use maps. They are not designed to have much connection with the ongoing activities of people and organizations or with the purposes of the various structures and facilities to be built on the land.[66]

Subnational area planning should provide a comprehensive, continuing accounting of the state of the area as the framework for strategically selected development measures. There must be a new synthesis at the urban level of three previously separate specialities: physical planning, economic planning and social planning. This can be achieved only through the integrating power of a social systems approach. It requires a model of an urban (or regional) area as a loose, open man-resource system composed on a great variety of individuals, families, associations and private and public organizations. Such a model can help planners get away from the overreliance on the old-fashioned "hard goods" techniques of building regulation and land-use maps and the equally limited number magic of linear programming and systems analysis in mechanical terms. It can provide the basis for a growing body of increasingly reliable information on the changing population, resource and institutional structure of an area.[67]

The truth in the idea of "comprehensive planning" is that only by comprehensive economic, social and physical indicators is it possible to come to grips with specific projects. Otherwise, second-order consequences and third-party effects cannot be anticipated. The error in the concept of comprehensive planning is the thought that any government is capable of marching ahead with regional and local development programs on all fronts at the same time and with equal speed. The essence of strategy is selective measures at specific points. The value of a broad informational framework is that it allows such strategic selection to be discriminating.[68]

Urban Areas as "Development Dynamos"

Lauchlin Currie has suggested that most development economists have underestimated the benefits to be obtained from planned investments in housing and other urban facilities. Currie points out that "all the horribly expensive and dreary phenomena of American urban development—towering congested centers, blighted areas, sprawling suburbs, individual commuting to the center, and a tremendous investment in throughways, underpasses, overpasses, cloverleafs, etc.—are beginning to appear in countries that have not yet attained even a decent minimum standard of living."[69] One reason for such urban conditions in the industrializing nations is the fallacy of nonproductive urban investment.

This fallacy represents one of the major premises of many development economists. It is expressed in innumerable calculations concerning the great benefits flowing from investments in industry and agriculture, as compared with the extremely low benefits stemming from housing and urban facilities. In most cases the calculations are made entirely in terms of the more readily measurable *direct* income and output (or profits) resulting from industrial and agricultural investment. The calculations usually ignore the vast indirect benefits of urban investment in terms of (a) more and quicker employment; (b) the development of a modern labor force through work on construction; (c) the promotion of the local market for the products of the consumer goods industries and for local building materials; and (d) the development of an urban culture that provides hope of advancement for the masses and freedom from the confining traditions of peasant agriculture. Most important, sustained economic and social progress require urban areas that are dynamic centers of culture, education, science and technology.

This does not mean that there should be less attention to agriculture or rural community development. It *does* emphasize the need for a break with the romantic idealization of the small village as the source of all good, and the view of the big city as the source of all evil. While the modern urban area has great potentialities for both good and evil, without it there is little hope of developing either industry or agriculture, the city or the country. As centers of government, business, finance, education, science and technology, urban areas are the essential dynamos for progress in *all parts* of an industrializing country.[70]

NOTES

[1]These various concepts of planning are summarized in B. Gross, *The Managing of Organizations*, 2 vols. (New York: Free Press, 1964). A detailed analysis of

the administrative process of planning, activating and evaluating, linked with decision-making and communicating, is provided in chapter 29, "Rationality: Administrative Processes."

²This point is developed in B. Gross, "National Planning: Findings and Fallacies," *Public Administration Review*, December 1965.

³R. J. Shafer et al., "What Is National Planning?," in *Action Under Planning: Essays in Guided Economic Development*, ed. B. Gross (New York: McGraw-Hill, 1966).

⁴B. Gross, "The State of the Nation: Social Systems Accounting," in *Social Indicators*, ed. R. A. Bauer (Cambridge, Mass.: MIT Press, 1966).

⁵*Ibid.*, part I.

⁶B. Gross, *The Managing of Organizations*, P. 242.

⁷B. Gross, *The Managing of Organizations*.

⁸*Administration of National Development Planning*, report of a meeting of experts held at Paris, France, June 8-19, 1964 (United Nations document, ST/TAO/M/27), p. 5.

⁹B. Russett, *Trends in World Politics* (New York: Macmillan, 1965), p. 121.

¹⁰B. Gross, *Space-Time and Post-Industrialism*, CAG Occasional Paper, 1966, p. 45-46.

¹¹B. Gross, *Space-Time and Post-Industrialism*. See also the sections on "From Pre- to Post-Industrialism" and "Industrializing and Post-Industrializing Performance Patterns" in B. Gross, "The State of the Nation."

¹²"Epiphenomenal planning" is a term first used by Peter Wiles in *The Political Economy of Communism* (Cambridge, Mass.: Harvard University Press, 1962), pp. 72-75. Wiles uses the term broadly, including not only planning for what will happen anyway, but also planning backed up by persuasive efforts only. The term should preferably be confined to the first of these usages.

¹³C. E. Lindblom, "The Gamesmanship of National Planning," prefatory comment to Fred G. Burke, *Tanganyika: Preplanning* (Syracuse: Syracuse University Press, 1965), pp. xxviii-xxix.

¹⁵This criticism has been made by many authors, including Marx, Schweitzer, Orwell, Mumford, Huxley, Kafka, William H. Whyte, Fromm, Argyris and Marcuse. Their views have been briefly summarized in "Threats to Mankind," chapter 4, in *The Managing of Organizations*.

¹⁶B. Gross, "Activating National Plans," in *Action Under Planning*, ed. B. Gross.

¹⁷The percentage distribution of the world's supply of potential energy from all sources other than manpower (that is, from coal oil and natural gas, water, wood, manure and work animals) has been estimated as follows for 1948: the energy-rich areas—North America, Europe and the Soviet Union—had 83.2 percent, while the entire rest of the world had a scant 16.8 percent. W.S. Woytinsky and E.S. Woytinsky, *World Population and Productions* (New York: Twentieth Century Fund, 1956), p. 931.

¹⁸B. Higgins, *Economic Development* (New York: Norton, 1959), p. 244.

¹⁹K. Nair, *Blossoms in the Dust* (New York: Praeger, 1962), p. 193.

²⁰G. Myrdal, *The Political Element in the Development of Economic Theory* (Cambridge, Mass.: Harvard University Press, 1954).

²¹The rest of this section is based upon "Activating National Plans," in *Action Under Planning*, ed. B. Gross.

[22]The term "cross-sectoral" is based upon the proposition that national economic planning usually consists of some combination of five kinds of planning: aggregate, cross-sectoral, sectoral or subsectoral, enterprise and spatial. See "What is National Planning?" *Action Under Planning*, ed. B. Gross.

[23]B. Gross, *The Managing of Organizations*, p.355.

[24]B. Gross, "National Planning: Findings and Fallacies," *Public Administration Review*, December 1965, p. 267.

[25]L. Currie, *Accelerating Development: The Necessity and the Means* (New York: McGraw-Hill, 1966). Dr. Currie is director of the Department of Economics in the National University of Colombia and of its new Institute for Investigations in Development.

[26]"It is much more important to revise many national plans than to implement them, since I feel that many of them are defective in their statement of the problem of underdevelopment and the diagnosis of the cause of underdevelopment, in their adoption of a growth rate in the G.N.P. per capita as the objective of planning and as the criterion of success in development, and hence in their choice of strategies and tactics. . . therefore, if I am to be logical, I must probably say that they should not be implemented!" From a letter of May 9, 1966, by L. Currie to the author.

[27]"Activating National Plans," in *Action Under Planning*, ed. B. Gross.

[28]J. Currie, *Accelerating Development*, p. 7.

[29]I. Swerdlow, "Economics as Part of Development Administration," in *Development Administration: Concepts and Problems*, ed. I. Swerdlow (Syracuse: Syracuse University Press, 1963), p. 103.

[30]A. Waterston, *Development Planning: Lessons of Experience* (Baltimore, Md.: Johns Hopkins Press, 1965), p. 201.

[31]The success of these managerial methods in broader areas—such as the actual use of military goods in military operations—is open to serious question. With publicly available information bearing almost entirely on their use with respect to procurement and delivery, one may speculate whether they have been attempted at all by the United States defense establishment in the more important areas of performance.

[32]Quoted by Charles L. Schultze, director, Bureau of the Budget, in his foreword to D. Novick (ed.), *Program Budgeting* (Washington: United States Government Printing Office, 1965). This book (an abridgment of a larger volume prepared by the Rand Corporation and published by the Harvard University Press) emphasizes "the structural and information portrayal aspect of the total system envisioned by the President." It has become the standard reference of advocates of the planning-programming-budgeting system.

[33]See B. Gross, *The Managing of Organizations:*(a) on benefits in "Satisfaction of Interests" (chapter 20); (b) on output in "Output: Services and Goods," "Output: Quality and Quantity," and "Output: Operations and Functions" (chapters 21, 22, and 23); and (c) on costs in "Efficiency and Profitability" (chapter 24).

[34]A. Waterston, *Development Planning*, p. 325.

[35]L. J. Walinsky, *The Planning and Execution of Economic Development* (New York: McGraw-Hill, 1963), p. 73.

[36]An estimate of national output arrived at by appllying some assumed ratio between incremental investment and total output has not been aggregated by adding

up outputs in each sector of production. There is therefore something misleading in calling it an "aggregate" that may then be "disaggregated." The term "artificial aggregate" would be more appropriate.

[37]A. Waterston, *Development Planning*, p. 354.

[38]*Ibid.*

[39]*Ibid.*

[40]A. Waterston, *Development Planning*, p. 353.

[41]C. E. Lindblom, "Economics and the Administration of National Planning," *Public Administration Review*, December 1965.

[42]N. I. Kovalev, "The Problems in Introducing Mathematics and Electronic Computers in Planning," *Problems of Economics* 5, no. 4 (August 1962).

[43]R. A. Bauer (ed.), *Social Indicators* (Cambridge, Mass.: M.I.T. Press, 1966).

[44]O. Morgenstern, *The Accuracy of Economic Observations* (Princeton: Princeton University Press, 1963).

[45]A. Waterston, *Development Planning*, pp. 191-92.

[46]Econometricians are often much more interested in the abstract relations among variables than in the specific data necessary to describe these variables or in the painstaking nonmathematical tasks of definition and collection necessary to obtain such data. In this sense, they often have little appreciation of, or respect for, the problems of handling quantitative data.

[47]A. Waterston, *Development Planning*, pp. 194-95.

[48]The nature of such planning reports by a chief executive is touch upon in B. Gross, "The State of the Nation," and developed in greater detail, with special reference to one country only, in B. Gross, "Let's Have a *Real* State of the Union Message," *Challenge*, May/June 1966.

[49]This project is part of the Inter-University Program on Institution Building, conducted with the help of the Ford Foundation by the University of Pittsburgh, Indiana University, Michigan State University and Syracuse University.

[50]International Group for Studies in National Planning (INTERPLAN), *The Development of National Planning Personnel*: a preliminary report based on the April 1965 conference of INTERPLAN in Warsaw, Poland.

[51]INTERPLAN conference on the implementation of national planning held in Caracas, Venezuela, November 1966, at the invitation of Venezuela's Central Office of Co-ordination and Planning (CORDIPLAN).

[52]B. Gross, "The Managers of National Economic Change," in *Public Administration and Democracy: Essays in Honor of Paul H. Appleby*, ed. R. C. Martin (Syracuse: Syracuse University Press, 1965), pp. 115-16.

[53]See Victor Thompson, *Modern Organization* (New York: Knopf, 1966), pp. 10, 95, for a discussion of the "primitive monistic ideal" that allows adults in organizations to duplicate childhood experiences—subordination to, and dependence on, an all-powerful parent. This subject is also discussed in B. Gross, *The Managing of Organizations*, "The Dispersion of Power in Organizations, chapter 3, pp. 49-72.

[54]B. Gross, "The Managers of National Economic Change," p. 109.

[55]*Ibid.*, p. 114.

[56]For the fallacies in the capital-output approach to development, which is still the "conventional wisdom" among economists, see L. Currie in "The Capital Formation Approach," chapter 9, *Accelerating Development*.

[57]See particularly Theodore Schultz, "Investment in Human Capital," *American Economical Review* 68 (1961): 1-17. This approach has also been applied to industrializing countries in a number of books by Frederick Harbison.

[58]B. Gross, "Activating National Plans," in *Action Under Planning*, ed. B. Gross.

[59]*Ibid.*

[60]A. H. Rweyemamu, *Nation-Building and the Planning Processes in Tanzania*, unpublished doctoral dissertation, Syracuse University, 1965, pp. 95, 241.

[61]B. Gross, The Managing of Organizations, "People-in-Organizations: Formal Aspects," chapter 15, p. 385.

[62]This is one of the great lessons of Soviet-style planning and of the widespread experimentation by the central authorities of Eastern Europe with many forms of administrative and market decentralization.

[63]The importance of coordination through mutual adjustment in many forms has been analyzed by C. E. Lindblom in his recent book—of tremendous interest to national planners—*The Intelligence of Democracy* (New York: Free Press, 1965).

[64]The importance of dealing with intergovernmental relations at the local level is illustrated by L. C. Fitch, "Planning and Administration in Urban Areas," in the United Nations publication *Administration of National Development Planning*, part II, chapter II.

β‡*Ibid.*, para. 35.

[66]The limitations of the old-fashioned style of so-called master planning at the local level are dealt with in greater detail in B. Gross, "The City of Man: A Social Systems Approach," given at the annual conference of the American Institute of Planners, Portland, Oregon, August 16, 1966.

[67]More specific suggestions concerning the contents of annual "state of the area reports" are provided in both B. Gross, "The City of Man: A Social Systems Approach," and B. Gross, "The State of the Nation."

[68]For a detailed rebuttal of the idea that a comprehensive approach can be strategic and a convincing presentation of the selective nature of stretegy, see R. A. Anthony, *Planning and Control Systems* (Boston: Harvard Business School, 1965).

[69]L. Currie, *Accelerating Development*, p. 53.

[70]For a humanistic analysis of the potentialities of urban areas, see Harvey Cox, *The Secular City* (New York: Macmillan, 1965).

Name and Title Index

2